PREACHING THE PASSION
EPIPHANY (RCL)

PREACHING THE PASSION

EPIPHANY (RCL)

by

Roy Schroeder, ThD

*Cover Design and Illustrations
by Joy Helge Schroeder*

FOREWORD

This is the third book in the series <u>Preaching the Passion</u>. The first two volumes deal with the texts for Advent and Christmas. A fourth book is planned to take up the Lessons for Lent. A web site, preachingthepassion.com, provides information for securing copies of all volumes.

The premises of this study are stated in the Advent volume and repeated in the Foreward of the one for Christmas. These premises were derived primarily from a study of 1 Cor. 1:18-31 which is the Epistle Lesson for the 4th Sunday after the Epiphany – Year A. A study of this Lesson is contained in this volume, on pp. 222-235. Because the premises are stated there in expanded form, they will not be reviewed here.

Many preachers do not make Christ crucified the focus of their preaching. This is not always accidental. Some say that they cannot find Christ crucified in every text assigned by the lectionary. The purpose of this study is to suggest clues for preaching Christ crucified in all the Lessons assigned by the Revised Common Lectionary for all three years.

The presentation of each Lesson is not intended to be an exhaustive commentary of the text but more like an introduction. The preacher will want to dig deeper into the text and develop applications that meet the needs of the hearers. The goal of this study is not to be original and creative but to offer help in preaching Christ crucified.

The Lessons covered are listed in the <u>Handbook for the Revised Common Lectionary</u>, edited by Peter C. Bower (Louisville: Westminster John Knox Press, 1996). That book was recommended by one of the chief motivators and advisors of this study, the Rev. Benjamin Baldus.

The basic Biblical text used is the NRSV.

INDEX

Epiphany

The Greek word epiphaneia means appearance. The nativity of Jesus is the manifestation of God to mankind. The theological emphases of the Epiphany season include also the baptism of Jesus and the revelation of Jesus as the Christ, the Son of God, and the light of the world.

The Day of the Epiphany of Our Lord, January 6, is traditionally the feast of the manifestation of Christ to the gentiles and celebrates the visit of the Magi who are assumed to be the first gentile believers. The 1st Sunday after the Epiphany celebrates the Baptism of Jesus which marks the beginning of His public ministry. The last Sunday after the Epiphany is observed as The Transfiguration of Our Lord. The remembrance of this epiphany brings the Old Testament into Jesus' time. The Transfiguration offers a preview of Jesus' glory that is to come.

The Epiphany season has often been considered a time for emphasizing world missions.

It is a bridge between the seasons of Christmas and Lent. When Easter comes early, there are few Sundays after the Epiphany. More are observed when Easter comes late.

Green is the color used for all the Sundays of the season except January 6 and the 1st Sunday after the Epiphany. Their color is white. The green of Epiphany is frequently explained as the color of living, growing plants, suggestive of spiritual growth.

Day of Epiphany
The Epiphany of Our Lord
January 6

Years ABC

Isaiah 60:1-6

"A multitude of camels . . . shall bring gold and frankincense" – that sounds like the story of the wise men in Matt. 2:1-12, the Gospel for this day. It justifies the use of this Old Testament text on The Epiphany of Our Lord.

But a second look suggests another phrase even more fitting, "your light has come." The evangelist John uses that kind of language to talk about the birth of Jesus: "The true light, which enlightens everyone, was coming into the world," cf. John 1:9. He calls Jesus "the light of all people" in John 1:4. He says, "The light shines in the darkness, and the darkness did not overcome it" in John 1:5. John the Baptist "came as a witness to testify to the light, so that all might believe through him. He himself was not the light, but he came to testify to the light," cf. John 1:7-8.

Using Is. 60:1-6 as the first Lesson in the season of Epiphany reminds us that Christmas is not over. The message that Jesus was born to save all people continues.

The Lessons for January 6 serve as the transition from the season of Christmas to the season of Epiphany by emphasizing that Christmas is not a private birthday party. It is a revelation that transcends the city limits of Bethlehem. It is "joy to the world."

The Old Testament Lesson is a prophetic oracle intended to inspire the hope of salvation and of a glorious future in penitent people who have been exiled in Babylon for some time. The Lord was "displeased" with the people of Judah-Jerusalem because of their sins. Their lies, injustice, violence, and slaughter of the innocent "have been barriers between (them) and (their) God." The full range of their sins are recounted in Is. 59. The people are waiting for "light" and "brightness" as they experience "darkness" and "gloom," cf. Is.59:9-10.

God has not given up on His people. Is. 59:20-21 announces that the Lord "will come to Zion as Redeemer" of a penitent people. He will save them. God's "Spirit" and "words" will remain with them. The songs and poems of Is. 60-62 announce Jahweh's resolve to do good to Jerusalem. "Darkness (may) cover the earth, and thick darkness the people; but the Lord will arise upon you, and his glory will appear over you."

Isaiah calls out to the people, "Arise, shine; for your light has come." Things are changing. There will be security, well-being, prosperity, abundance, and a preeminent position among the nations. Jerusalem's material well-being will be highly visible in the world.

The confusion of tenses in the prophetic oracle is caused by the unique character of the prophetic word. God created the universe by His word. God's words of promise are more real than what is promised. When God says that something will happen, the happening itself may be in the future; but so sure is it of taking place that it can be conceived of as an event in the past.

The prophet repeats himself: "The glory of the Lord has risen upon you." In Num. 14:22, "the glory of the Lord" refers to Jahweh's mighty acts in Egypt and in the wilderness. "The glory of the Lord" is the revelation of God in divine majesty and power. It is manifested in striking interventions, judgments, and signs. "The glory of the Lord" is an expression of the will of God to save His people. In the character of Hebrew poetry, "the glory of the Lord has risen upon you" is a restatement of the previous affirmation, "your light has come." The "light" is Jahweh Himself. "Your light" is "the glory of the Lord."

14

Jahweh is Zion's hope. Jerusalem has been subordinate to the nations, but Jahweh's new resolve will effect a great reversal. The city will receive His positive attention. Nations and kings will be drawn to Jerusalem like insects to a light. Jerusalem will be light in a world full of darkness. God will reign there. Fallen but reconstituted Jerusalem will reflect the glory of the Lord.

The nations will stream to Jerusalem to learn torah according to Is. 2:2-4, but in Is. 60 the influx of the nations is less theological and more economic and political. When Jerusalem looks around, a great caravan of nations will be seen coming with heavy cargo. "The abundance of the sea shall be brought to you" refers to the maritime powers of that day, Phoenicia and Greece, bringing their riches by ship from the west. The "multitude of camels" refers to caravans loaded with produce.

"The wealth of the nations shall come to you" describes the tribute or tax money other nations will bring. Israel had been paying tribute to the Babylonians, to the Assyrians, and to the Persians as long as anyone could remember; but the process is about to be reversed. The nations will bring the best produce they have: gold, frankincense, flocks, and rams. Midian, Ephah, and Sheba are peoples of Arabia. Traditionally, the bringing of "gold and frankincense" is interpreted as being fulfilled in the coming of the Magi, cf. Matt. 2:1-12; but Matthew really does not say this. What Isaiah says is greater. What he says has a worldwide purview. Exiled Jews scattered in all parts of the world will come home. "Sons . . . from far away" and young "daughters" will "gather together."

What Isaiah announces the fourth evangelist in the New Testament says happened, cf. John 1:9 and 14. Jesus called Himself the light of the world in John 12:46. Isaiah saw the glory of Jesus, according to John 12:41.

Isaiah frequently associates "darkness" with distress, cf. 5:30; 9:2; 42:7; 49:9; 58:10. See also Lam 3:2 and Micah 7:8. "Thick darkness" is a metaphor for misery in Jer. 13:16.

We confront daily the gloom Isaiah talks about in Is. 59, experiences that darken human living. They assault us from the front pages of our newspapers and our TV screens: lies, injustice, violence, and the slaughter of the innocent. We walk in gloom so long as a million children go to sleep hungry and coloreds are second class citizens. The gloom includes our personal and individual infidelities. "We wait for light, and lo! there is darkness; and for brightness, but we walk in gloom," as Isaiah says in 59:9. We groan as St. Paul says in Rom. 8:23.

We can cause the Light of Jesus to shine in this gloom. We can reflect Jesus in our lives, although we cannot reproduce Him. We confront situations different from those with which Jesus dealt. His life was restricted to the time He lived and the people among whom He lived. He did not and could not experience all that we confront. He was a man, not a modern woman. He was a teacher but not a scholar. He did not experience old age or Alzheimer's disease. We cannot copy Jesus, but we can follow Him. We can die with Him as He did to save us. We can share His dying by sharing His cross through the whole of our lives.

Our light which is a reflection of the Light that is Jesus can "shine before others, so that they may see (our) good works and give glory to our Father in heaven," cf. Matt. 5:16. Through our lives, as people who live for others, we can reveal God and the good news of Jesus' death. We can make clear to developed and underdeveloped peoples that Christians serve by enabling deprived people to live more humanly.

We can be concerned for the babies with bloated bellies in far-off Somalia. We can deal with the problems of people in the United States, this land of power and prosperity: infant mortality, child abuse, children living in poverty, teenage suicide, teenage drug abuse, and high school dropouts. Many treat these problems of children the Child Jesus died to save like statistics. While minds are blunted and bodies stunted, we need not eat and drink, play and pray, grow rich and fat, as if "God is in His heaven and all is right with the world." We can help these people to be strong enough to live and to hope.

Ephesians 3:1-12

The Apostle Paul was commissioned to make known "the mystery of Christ." What is "the mystery of Christ?" It is God's plan "to gather up all things in (Christ), things in heaven and things on earth," to use the language of Eph. 1:10. It is that gentiles have been accepted into the people of God. Paul puts it this way: "the Gentiles have become fellow heirs, members of the same body, and sharers in the promise in Christ Jesus through the gospel." Christ Jesus, "through (His) cross," cf. Eph. 2:16, broke "down the dividing wall, that is, the hostility between (Jews and gentiles)," cf. 2:14. He "abolished the law with its commandments and ordinances, that he might create in himself one new humanity in place of the two, thus making peace, and might reconcile both groups to God in one body," cf. 2:15-16. Paul was commissioned by God "to bring to the Gentiles" this good news "and to make everyone see what is the plan of the mystery hidden for ages in God . . . so that through the church the wisdom of God might . . . be made known to the rulers and authorities in the heavenly places." At Epiphany, we celebrate Jesus' coming to save not only Jews but also the world outside of the one into which He was born.

God's plan is a "mystery," Paul says. Some think mysterion is better translated "secret." The sense the word "mystery" is intended to convey in Ephesians is different from what it is in modern society. A mystery with us is a secret no one knows or a riddle to which no one has the answer. Who committed a crime is a mystery, so long as the criminal has not been discovered. But when he/she/they are identified, it is no longer a mystery. In contrast, "mystery" in Ephesians is a secret that has been and is being revealed. God kept His purpose hidden from former ages, but He made it known through Christ Jesus, cf. Rom. 16:25-26 and Col. 1:26. God loved all people before the creation, and He still does in spite of our sins and in spite of His reaction to them, namely, our death. He loves us notwithstanding the ages long division between Jews and gentiles. The superabundant generosity and kindness of God which overwhelms our ability to understand is a mystery. We do not know this love of God as we are born into the world. "The rulers and authorities in the heavenly places" did not know it. It was hidden in God. However, it was revealed in the passion of Jesus, it is offered through the gospel, and it is to be made known to all people "through the church."

The term mystery was familiar to the Greek-speaking people of the Mediterranean world for centuries before Christ. The mysteries were the secret rites into which worshippers were initiated by the so-called mystery religions. Paul borrowed the term as a convenient way to communicate the gospel of Christ Jesus. It is not inappropriate, for it is the fulfillment of the search of the mystery religions for communion with the divine.

The good news is called "the boundless riches of Christ" in v. 8. It is called "the plan of the mystery hidden for ages in God" in v. 9. It is called "the wisdom of God" in v. 10. It is described in Eph. 2:11-16.

This may not seem like such good news or gospel to us today. Some may consider it common knowledge almost to the point of being trite. But Acts 13:44-48 describes it as really good news to the gentiles who believed it in those days. When they heard it, "they were glad."

"The boundless riches of Christ" is good news. The Greek word translated "boundless" means that we are not able to track God's plan; it is untraceable. The word "boundless" warns us against trying to rationalize it. God opens Himself up and gives Himself to us, but He does not let us make Him subject to our intellectual control. Neither God nor Christ nor what they do can be grasped by us. The god we can comprehend is always an idol. Paul acknowledges that he knows only "in part" and does not understand fully, cf. 1 Cor. 13:12. Christ's work can be admired, enjoyed, and proclaimed, but it cannot be explained or deduced. "The love of Christ . . . surpasses knowledge," Paul says in 3:18-19. Preachers, the people in the pew need to be told this! It can help them accept the gospel.

The term "the wisdom of God in its rich variety" occurs nowhere else in the New Testament. It has played hardly any role in the history and thought of the western church.

The inclusion of the gentiles into God's people is basic, but the secret is not just the plan or doctrine of the gentiles' admission into the people of God. It includes the carrying out of the plan in the realm of history. God's purpose was "carried out in Christ Jesus." He is the agent of God's plan.

The gentiles "have been brought near by the blood of Christ," cf. Eph. 2:13, that is, His death. What Christ's passion accomplished is that "in his flesh he has made both groups (Jews and gentiles) into one and has broken down the dividing wall, that is, the hostility between us. He has abolished the law with its commandments and ordinances, that he might create in himself one new humanity in place of the two, thus making peace, and might reconcile both groups to God in one body through the cross, thus putting to death that hostility through it. . . . through him both of us have access in one Spirit to the Father," cf. 2:14-18. The identifying mark of God's people is no longer racial descent from Abraham or circumcision or the observance of distinctive ordinances like the Sabbath or the distinction of meats.

Gentiles are fellow heirs with Jews. This is different from being "joint heirs with Christ," as in Rom. 8:17. They are "members of the same body," the body of Christ. They "are citizens with the saints and also members of the household of God," cf. Eph. 2:19. This has implications for our social life, according to 4:25.

Three aspects of the new situation of gentiles listed in ascending order are that they are "fellow heirs, members of the same body, and sharers in the promises in Christ Jesus."

Both Jews and gentiles have access to God in Christ Jesus. This is stated also in Eph. 2:18; Rom. 5:2; Heb. 4:16; 10:19-20. Paul encourages "boldness and confidence" as we draw near to God. Boldness enables us to talk freely and frankly with God. Timidity is the result of fear and shame. As a consequence of Christ's work, we can have holy confidence as we draw near to God. That is characteristic of faith in Christ Jesus.

The new status of gentiles comes about "through the gospel." "The gospel" means neither a book nor a specific doctrine. Rather it is the proclamation of Jesus' passion, as in Gal. 1:6-9.

"In former generations this mystery was not made known to humankind, as it has now been revealed to his holy apostles and prophets by the Spirit." On the other hand, the saints of the Old Testament period were aware of the inclusion of the gentiles in God's intention. It is stated in Gen. 12:1-3; 18:18; Is. 2:2-4; 49:6; Zech. 9:9-10; Jonah 4; and Gal. 3:8. But they did not understand it clearly enough or accept it firmly enough to act on it.

When Paul says that "the plan of the mystery (was) hidden for ages in God who created all things," he is saying that the plan always had been God's intention. The divine purpose like a golden thread runs through the ages leading to the days of fulfillment.

God gave a new revelation of the mystery "to his holy apostles and prophets by the Spirit." Paul probably is referring not to the Old Testament prophets but to the New Testament prophets mentioned in Acts 13:1-3; 1 Cor. 12:28; and 14:1-25. The mention of "the Spirit" does not emphasize a specific mode of transmission but the fact that the secret was made known to humans by God Himself. This revelation is a correlative to the mystery.

Paul says that he "wrote above" about the revelation given him. Prographo (write above) can mean to write above in the same document, or to write earlier in another letter or book, or to write up publicly. Paul is probably referring to Eph. 1:9-10 or to Eph. 2:11-22 where he talks about the revelation given him and the content of that revelation.

The words Paul wrote could have been read publicly in a worship service or some other assembly, cf. 1 Thess. 5:27; Col. 4:16; Matt. 24:15; Rev. 1:3. The great majority of people in those days could not read. There was no need to do so; few writings were available, and those available were very expensive. People were dependent on the reading out loud of written documents by others.

The Greek word oikonomia ("commission") was used of the administrative responsibility given to a servant over a household. The term is used also in Eph. 1:10 where it is translated "a plan."

God commissioned Paul "to bring to the Gentiles the news of the boundless riches of Christ, and to make everyone see what is the plan of the mystery hidden for ages in God." Paul is about to explain his status as a prisoner in Eph. 3:1 when he breaks off what he is going to say to describe his ministry in vs. 2-12. Broken sentences are found in many of Paul's letters.

Some think that he continues in v. 14 the thought he begins in v. 1, others in 4:1. Origen and Jerome thought the statement was never completed.

Paul's efforts to extend the unification of Jews and gentiles into one "dwelling place for God" through Jesus Christ, cf. 2:18-22, has resulted in Paul becoming "a prisoner for Christ Jesus for the sake of you Gentiles." He may be incarcerated in a Roman building as he writes this letter to the Ephesians, or, according to Roman practice, he may have arranged for his own accommodations with a soldier attached to him, as described in Acts 28:16 and 30-31. He was held as a prisoner in Caesarea, Ephesus, and Rome, according to the book of Acts.

Paul shows no sentimentality or self-pity as he talks about his detention brought about by Jewish and gentile opposition to his missionary work. He feels that it contributes to the progress of the gospel, cf. Phil. 1:12-26. In Eph. 6:20, he calls himself "an ambassador in chains." In 3:13, he calls his "sufferings," that is, his being held a prisoner, "your glory." He wants his readers to be at ease with his status as he is. For the Christian attitude toward such hardships, see 1 Pet. 4:15-16 and 2 Cor. 4:8-10. Paul did not envision a time when anyone would serve Jesus Christ without being conformed to His passion.

Paul calls himself "a servant . . . of this gospel." God made him "a servant." His servanthood is a gift. It is an expression of God's grace. It "was given me." God's "power" did it. His statements are redundant, but they leave no loophole for attributing to himself any honor or dignity that belongs to God alone. He gives all glory to God for what he is. It is due to the grace of God.

No one is given God's grace for his personal satisfaction and enjoyment. The grace given Paul made him an instrument of God's grace. The grace given him saved many. Grace includes "the forgiveness of our trespasses," cf. Eph. 1:7, but it includes more, too. It equips God's servants for useful work.

Paul never ceases to wonder at the commission given him. He calls himself "the very least of all the saints." The Greek word is a novel form of a Greek adjective. It is the comparative of a superlative. In English, we would do the same if we coin the word "leaster." The form describes the deepest self-abasement. It's as if the superlative "least" is too weak to express his unworthiness. Paul is not ashamed to place himself extremely low. He is not fishing for compliments.

The reason for such humility is not to be sought in Pauline passages such as 2 Cor. 4:12 and Rom. 7 where Paul describes the weakness of his flesh and the continuous rebellion of the old man against the new. Paul considers lifelong weakness, temptation, and strife characteristic of all saints. Whenever Paul gives a reason for his specifically low and suspect place among the members of the church, he speaks of his past persecution of the church, cf. Gal. 1:13, 23; 1 Cor. 15:9; Phil. 3:6.

Not all apostles and prophets were engaged in the mission to the gentiles. Paul's specific task was to announce good news to those far off, cf. Eph. 2:17. This was for him, a privilege and a burden at the same time, cf. 1 Cor. 9:16-17.

God's plan and intention is to "be made known . . . through the church." The phrase "through the church" is found nowhere else in the New Testament. It ascribes a mediating role to the church. It appears to stipulate a cosmic function for the church. The church takes up and extends Christ's prophetic ministry. She makes known the wisdom of God.

What the church makes known is not mere intellectual information or emotional propaganda. The knowledge given through the church saves people. The wisdom of God penetrates the universe and upholds it. The church is an agent of revelation. She participates in the proclamation of God's peace which began with and is continued by Jesus Christ. The church is not an end in itself but a functional outpost of God's kingdom.

Paul does not specify how the church is to convey "the wisdom of God." He probably has verbal proclamation in mind, such as preaching, teaching, liturgy, cure of souls, fraternal consolation, a pastoral letter, and a public declaration as long as Christ and the gospel are the center of them. The church is also called and equipped to be the theater of God's works. In its diverse composition made up of people who were formerly dead in sins and divided in hostility, as people who live by the forgiveness of sins, who speak to God, who suffer, struggle, are poor, and yet are rich, the church is God's display, picture window, proof, and lighthouse for the benefit of the world. When she fails to proclaim what she knows or when she condones division and sin, she belies her essence and function. The church is an instrument through which God reveals Himself. She is the revelation of God's secret in action and the manifestation of the wisdom of God.

The church is to let God's light shine. Eph. 4-6 describes in some detail how the church by sheer good conduct does this among people and powers outside the church. The secret – sometimes not so secret – yearning of ecclesiastic personnel for world domination is not supported by Ephesians.

"Through the church the wisdom of God in its rich variety (is) now (to) be made known to the rulers and authorities in the heavenly places." "In the heavenly places" occurs five times in Ephesians. It is found nowhere else in the New Testament. In 1:3, God "has blessed us in Christ with every spiritual blessing in the heavenly places." According to Eph. 1:20, Christ is seated at God's right hand "in the heavenly places." According to 2:6, God raised us up with Christ "and seated us with him in the heavenly places." In 3:10, Paul says there are "rulers and authorities in the heavenly places" to whom the church is to make known "the wisdom of God in its rich variety." "The rulers and authorities" see "the wisdom of God" at work in the church. In 6:12, there are "spiritual forces of evil in the heavenly places." We struggle against them. Christ, us, and "forces of evil" are "in the heavenly places."

"The heavenly places" are the sphere of spiritual activities. They constitute the unseen universe that lies behind the world of sense, a sort of fifth dimension. In it, great forces are at work. They oppose us and wrestle against us. They oppose the plan of God being worked out in this world. Christ rules over all these forces, and we in Him. The terminology is probably somewhat related to the Jewish view of the seven heavens. The seven heavens are 1) spirits of dominion, 2) overseers, 3) powers of the rampart, 4) holy ones, 5) angels of the Presence, 6) angels of response, and 7) thrones and authorities. The New Testament shows no real interest in this kind of ranking or naming.

In 2 Cor. 12:2, Paul refers to having been snatched up to the third heaven which he identifies as Paradise in 2 Cor. 12:4. The "air" which Paul refers to in Eph. 2:2 is just above "the darkness" which is this world. Christ defeated all these powers in His passion and resurrection.

Matthew 2:1-12

A large number of Children's Christmas pageants with troops of camels and trios of kings in exotic oriental garb have been inspired to march across the stages of Christian churches by the story of the wise men. The drama actually involves the very modern problems of vicious political intrigue and the threat of despotic power. It's the kind of story we try to protect children from today. Genocide and a family fleeing the oppression of their ruler are other sub-themes flitting in the wings. But the main theme is the birth of Jesus, our Savior. The effort made by the wise men to find Him inspires our effort to worship Him today.

The wise men arrived at least six weeks after Jesus was born. Mary and Joseph took their Baby to the temple in Jerusalem forty days after His birth, Luke 2:22 tells us. It is unthinkable that they would have done this after the warning given to the wise men in Matt. 2:12. It is reasonable to assume that the wise men told Joseph and Mary about the warning before returning to "their own country." That warning prepared Joseph for the one given him in Matt. 2:13.

The arrival of the wise men may have been as long as a year after Jesus' birth. That much time is indicated by the age of the children Herod killed according to Matt. 2:16. Two years was decided on the basis of information given by the wise men: he "learned from them the exact time when the star had appeared." Two years old would be one year according to our way of reckoning age. Jesus may have been approaching the end of His first year when the wise men came to Jerusalem.

The question may well be asked, what were Mary and Joseph still doing in Bethlehem a year after Jesus' birth? The answer may be that they chose Bethlehem as their permanent home following Jesus' birth. Perhaps they did not return to their

Nazareth home because of the scandal caused by Mary's pre-marital pregnancy. When they returned from Egypt, they planned to go to Bethlehem, according to Matt. 2:21-22, not Nazareth.

Scandal may not have been the only reason for choosing to make Bethlehem their home. The unique charge given them was the Son of God, the Messiah. They may have felt that He should be raised near the Jerusalem temple. Most Jews would have, according to John 1:46. Or being uniquely the son of David, Joseph and Mary may have felt that Jesus should be raised in "the city of David called Bethlehem," cf. Luke 2:4. Bethlehem was only six miles away from Jerusalem.

This infancy story is told in a way that resonates with the Hebrew scriptures and the great stories of Israel's past, a characteristic of Matthew's style throughout his gospel. Just as the life of Moses was threatened by Pharaoh's jealousy in the stories of Ex. 1-2, so Jesus' life is imperiled by despotic Herod. Just as a gentile seer, Balaam, predicted the rising of a star as a portent of future liberation in Num. 24:17, so gentile wise men from the east come to offer homage to the promised Savior guided by a star. Their gifts may be alluded to in Ps. 72:10-11 and Is. 60:6.

The story opens up Matthew's proclamation of the full scope of God's salvation. Later, he, a tax collector, is welcomed, in 9:9-13. So are lepers in 8:1-4 and the disabled and sick in 15:29-31. The centurion of Capernaum is the first of many who "will come from the east and west" to eat at Abraham's table, according to 8:11. The insistent faith of a Canaanite woman enlarges Jesus' mission beyond the boundaries of the "lost sheep of the house of Israel" in 15:21-28. The gospel is to be proclaimed to all nations, according to Jesus' instruction in 28:16-20.

On the other hand, Herod and the Jerusalem leaders ("the chief priests and scribes of the people") exemplify those who do not understand. Ultimately, they and many Jewish people reject Jesus, cf. 27:24-25. The wise men find Jesus, because they are responsive to the signs God gives them. The Jewish leaders and Herod know where the Messiah is to be born, but they do not go to pay Him homage.

The arrival of the wise men comes as a surprise, Matthew says. He uses the Greek word idou (behold) which the NRSV does not translate. He uses the same word in v. 9 where the NRSV translates "there," expressing surprise. Apparently, the wise men did not see the star while they were in Jerusalem. They certainly did not need it to find Bethlehem.

The term "wise men" was used in those days in an evil and a good sense. In an evil sense, it was applied to people who practiced magical arts. In a good sense, it was applied to eastern priest-sages. Their researches embraced much deep knowledge, but it is in great measure mysterious and unknown to us. It was tinged with superstition. These wise men were undoubtedly priest-sages. They were experts in astrology, the interpretation of dreams, and various other secret arts. Perhaps, they were astrologers belonging to a class of men similar to the Chaldeans mentioned in Dan. 2:2.

Popular tradition has it that there were three. Another tradition which is not so popular says that there were twelve. Luther's sermons indicate that he followed the second tradition. We do not know how many wise men there were. One way the number three may have crept into our pageants and carols is that it is a sufficient number to carry the gifts of gold, frankincense, and myrrh.

Kaspar, Melchior, and Balthasar are the names traditionally given them. It seems these names originated with the Armenian Infancy Gospel which dates from the late sixth century AD. Their names are really unknown.

That they were kings is an idea probably developed as an interpretation of Ps. 72:10-11. It is also suggested by the richness of their gifts. But Matthew says they were wise men, not kings.

Camels got into the story by way of Is. 60:6. Matthew doesn't say anything about them, and he is the only evangelist who tells the story. More logical would be the notion that they employed the beasts of burden still usually used to this day in that part of the world, donkeys.

Though legend has grown around them, nothing is known about the wise men or the circumstances of their journey beyond what is told in Matt. 2. That they came from the east suggests that they were gentiles, but they may have been Jews. If they were gentiles, their worship of the baby Jesus helps to show that the Old Testament era with its emphasis on one people as the chosen nation is done.

The wise men came "from the East," that is, east of the Jordan. We have no accurate information from where they came. Probably from Mesopotamia, although the oldest tradition says that they came from Arabia. The grounds for this tradition include the character of their gifts. At this period in history, the sacerdotal caste of the Medes and Persians was dispersed over various parts of the east. They were present also in those lands where a large Jewish diaspora existed. On the other hand, they may have been from as nearby as the land of Moab.

They "came to Jerusalem." This was the capital city of Judah, and they assume that this is where a king of the Jews would be born. At least, they suppose that the leadership in Jerusalem will know where a new king of the Jews has been born. But this is a huge mistake.

The wise men come in humility, are glad to worship Jesus, and go their way rejoicing. The scribes look up the information concerning the birth of the Messiah but seem little interested in it. At least, there is no indication that they do anything about it. Herod is hostile.

Journeys are associated with the birth of Jesus even as they are today in our celebration of it. Mary visits Elizabeth in Luke 1:39-56; Joseph and a pregnant Mary travel from Nazareth to Bethlehem in Luke 2:4-5; the shepherds journey to Bethlehem in Luke 2:16; the wise men come from the east to Jerusalem and Bethlehem; and Joseph and Mary flee with Jesus from Bethlehem to Egypt in Matt. 2:13-14. Today, Christmas is a time for getting together with parents, grandparents, siblings, and other relatives. The greatest journey of all, however, is God coming from heaven to earth for our salvation.

There is no indication whom the wise men ask in Jerusalem about the birth of Jesus. The implication is that they ask Herod or members of his court. The wise men do this in all innocence. Later, they learn that Herod is the last person they should have asked.

They don't ask if a new king of the Jews has been born. They state, "He has," and they ask His whereabouts.

"The King of the Jews" is the title under which Jesus will be crucified in Matt. 27:37. "Are you the king of the Jews?" is the question Pilate will ask Jesus at His trial, cf. Matt. 27:11; and Jesus will not respond negatively.

"The King of the Jews" was a Messianic title. The coming Savior is never called "the Messiah" in the Old Testament. "The anointed one" of the Old Testament is primarily the king.

The Old Testament concept of the Messiah-King finds its strongest foundation in God's covenant with David, cf. 2 Sam. 7:11-16. God's faithfulness to His promise to David is a common theme among the prophets, cf. Jer. 23:5-6; 33:15-16; Ezek. 34:23-24; 37:24-25; Amos 9:11; Hosea 3:5; Micah 5:2; Is. 9:7; 11:10; 16:5; Zech. 12:7-8. The New Testament provides evidence that the coming of a Davidic Messiah was normal rabbinic teaching in the first century AD, cf. Matt. 22:42-43 and 20:30.

Other Old Testament sources for the concept of the Messiah-King include the blessing Jacob pronounces over Judah giving him the rule over the Children of Israel in Gen. 49:10. Balaam's prophecy of a ruler rising out of Israel is also ultimately Messianic, cf. Num 24:17.

The New Testament writers do not lay great stress on Jesus as the fulfillment of the Old Testament Messiah-King. Jesus accepts Pilate's accusation that He is the King of the Jews in Matt. 27:11 and John 18:33-37, but He does not affirm it. He rejects every notion of a worldly kingship and asserts that He seeks no earthly crown. His throne turns out to be a cross. Matthew gives his readers clues for understanding this by describing the soldiers' mocking of Jesus in Matt. 27:29 and by informing them of the inscription placed over Jesus' head as He hung on the cross in 27:37.

The wise men bear witness that Jesus is "king of the Jews." His kingship is contrasted with Herod's. Herod's kingship is characterized by self-serving attempts to maintain his power, even to the point of taking the lives of his subjects. By way of contrast, Jesus' kingship is that of the Davidic ruler who governs by shepherding the people of God, cf. Matt. 2:5-6. The broader context of the gospel indicates what this shepherding involves: Jesus dies on behalf of His people in order to save them.

How did a star lead the wise men to Jerusalem? How did the star go ahead of them and lead them from Jerusalem to Bethlehem? What does the text mean when it says that the star "stopped over the place where the child was?" How does a star do that?

The idea of a star moving in the heavens is a troublesome detail in this story from the modern point of view. The miraculous character of the star makes it a waste of time to seek an explanation from astronomical science. The Living Bible handles it in Matt. 2:9 by simply omitting any mention of it. LB translates simply, "And look! The star appeared to them again, standing over Bethlehem." TEV says, "on their way they saw the same star they had seen in the East." When the star stopped, the wise men were filled with joy, according to Matt. 2:10. It constituted divine confirmation that they had rightly been directed to Bethlehem. It seems best to understand the statement, "it (the star) stopped over the place where the child was," as meaning over the city of Bethlehem and not over the precise house in which the family was living.

The star that led the wise men could hardly have been a phenomenon noticeable to all, because Herod and his counselors seem to have been ignorant of it until the wise men came. One thing does seem sure: it was not the kind of star you see in pictures or on Sunday School leaflets, floating about 100 feet off the ground. Everyone would have noticed that, and it seems that nobody in Palestine saw the star.

The Israelite religion forbade astrology. Nevertheless, astrology was practiced among the Jews.[1] Some rabbis computed a man's future on the basis of the constellation under which he was born.

The star could have been some peculiar phenomenon noticed only by men who studied the stars diligently. These men seem to have foretold the future on the basis of the stars. Some have suggested that it was a peculiar formation of celestial bodies which takes place about every 850 years.

The occurrence of a star or constellation at the birth of a notable person was a common association in the ancient world.

How would the wise men connect the astronomical phenomenon – whatever it was – with the coming of the promised Savior? The easiest explanation is to say that God revealed it to them. God who had revealed the coming of the Messiah to the Jews through the prophets may have revealed His coming to these gentiles through the star.

How would the wise men have heard of the coming Savior? Balaam, who lived in the east, spoke of a star rising out of Jacob, according to Num. 24:17. Daniel spent most of his life in the east. The Jewish nation spent 70 years in captivity in Babylon, and their literature probably became known to many people of the east. Only a small detachment returned to rebuild the temple and the city of Jerusalem; many remained in Babylon. The wise men could have come into contact with members of the Jewish diaspora in a number of ways. Then, too, the wise men may have been Jews.

The appearance of the star does not help in dating the birth of Jesus. We can identify the star no more clearly than we can the census of Quirinius.

When the wise men entered "the house, they saw the child with Mary his mother." The temporary shelter of the stable has been exchanged for the more permanent abode of a house. The wise men did not follow the shepherds into the stable on the night Jesus was born, as some modern representations of the story have it. A considerable period of time elapsed between Jesus' birth and the coming of the wise men. It's cute and romantic to see children dressed as wise men hurry into a stable in Bethlehem right behind the shepherds a few minutes after Jesus is born, but preachers surely know better!

The wise men came to pay homage to the child born king of the Jews. Proskuneo (to pay homage) is used to designate the custom of prostrating oneself before a person and kissing his feet, the hem of his garment, and the ground. The Persians did this in the presence of their deified king. The Greeks did this before a divinity or something holy. When it was done to human beings, they were being recognized as belonging to a superhuman realm. Matthew seems to be hinting at the submission of the gentiles to Jesus. Traditionally, the adoration of the wise men has been considered the beginning of the fulfillment of Messianic prophecies concerning the homage paid by the nations to the God of Israel, cf. Is. 49:23; 60:5-17; Ps. 72:10-15. The giving of gifts in the ancient east indicated submission and allegiance.

Frankincense and myrrh are not well known to us today. At the time the wise men came, they were as valuable as gold. Frankincense and myrrh are fragrant gum resins obtained from trees that grow only in southern Arabia and northern Somalia. Both are harvested by scraping the bark of a tree, allowing the resin ducts to ooze a thick liquid. These "tears" harden into translucent clumps in approximately a week and are ready for export ten to twenty days after collection.

Frankincense is a white gum from the Boswellia tree and myrrh from the larger Balsamodendrum myrrha tree. They both were used in medicines, mixed to form perfumes and oils, and burned as incense to propitiate the gods. The golden colored frankincense was the most important incense of the ancient world for domestic and religious purposes. Myrrh is reddish-brown in color, bitter to the taste, less aromatic than frankincense, and traditionally was used in anointing oils and as a fumigant in cooking and embalming. Myrrh was far more expensive than frankincense, and the demand for frankincense was greater.

Frankincense and myrrh were considered "spices" which in the ancient world connoted expensive, usually imported items of special distinction and value. Traffic in these as well as other spices and luxury items reached a peak during the Roman Empire and were all destined for Rome.

Gold, frankincense, and myrrh represent the wealth and perfumes of Arabia. They were the kind of treasures associated with a king in Is. 39:2. They were offerings proper for this occasion.

The church fathers said that gold was a symbol for royalty, incense for divinity, and myrrh for the passion (burial) of Christ.

Jesus was rich in infancy and in death. He was buried in the tomb of a rich man. Between times, He sometimes had nowhere to lay His head.

"When King Herod heard (about the child who was born king of the Jews,) he was frightened, and all Jerusalem with him." The Greek word, tarasso, means to unsettle, to throw into confusion. It suggests that Herod began to shake.

When Matthew says that "all Jerusalem" was frightened, too, this probably is hyperbole. The leaders of the city and the municipal workers probably are meant.

A very strong feeling existed before the wise men arrived that the Messiah was coming soon.

We think "all Jerusalem" would rejoice at the news brought by the wise men, but the coming of the Messiah, the citizenry fear, will bring unrest and change. They are satisfied with the way things are under Roman rule and don't want a change. They are afraid of change; it produces uncertainty and anxiety. They don't want even the change for good the Messiah will bring. This same sort of fear will come over the city years later when Jesus makes His triumphal entry into Jerusalem on the colt of a donkey, according to Matt. 21:10. This is the fear of revolution. Some of this fear may be expressed also in John 11:47-50. They are afraid that a Messianic pretender will bring the Romans and the destruction of the nation. The position of Herod was based on his friendship with Rome. According to popular opinion, when the Messiah came, He would free God's people from the power of the Romans. That would not benefit Herod.

Perhaps, many people in Jerusalem were afraid they would lose their jobs. Many of them probably worked for the government. They would lose their favored positions. Comfort, tranquility, and the enjoyment of material advantages were preferred above anything the Messiah might bring. A revolution could hurt business. It's the same today. If we are different, it is because God has performed a miracle in us, the miracle of the new birth. Willingness to accept change is a part of our faith. Our faith is not that the world will remain the same, but that God will guide us to His goal in all circumstances. Repentance, which means change, is a part of the daily life of

Christians. Our faith enables us to be in a constant state of change. Our solid-rock foundation is Jesus.

The gospel has always been a revolutionary teaching, cf. Acts 19:29 and 21:30. It changes people. It does not encourage violent rebellion, but the changes it produces are so radical that this is sometimes the result. This reaction sometimes brings antagonism toward the gospel. The violence is due not to the gospel but to the evil the gospel exposes. Evil will react violently to such exposure or to any attempt to change it. The only way to avoid such a violent reaction is to minimize, reduce, or ignore the gospel and support the status quo.

Herod was foolish to try to stop the inevitable. If the Messiah had been born, no sword would stop Him. In our folly, sometimes we, too, are not afraid to fight even God.

"The chief priests and scribes of the people" represent the supreme council of the Jews. The third element in the great sanhedrin is not mentioned, namely, the elders. They were mostly lay people and were not consulted because the issue at hand was of a theological nature.

Some see in Matthew's mention of the chief priests and scribes the beginning of his condemnation of the official instructors of the Jewish nation. He depicts them as standing in the service of King Herod and accessories in his plot to kill Jesus. This signals how later in Jesus' story they will prove to be murderous opponents and prime characters in His passion.

The imperfect tense of the Greek verb translated "he (Herod) inquired" adds color to the story. It suggests persistent and repeated urging to secure information: "he kept on asking," "he repeatedly asked."

Herod the Great was born in 73 BC, became governor of Galilee in 47 BC, and was named "King of Judea" in 40 BC by the Roman Senate. He was Roman governor of the whole province of Palestine from 37 to 4 BC, the year of his death. He was powerful, politically clever, passionate, and ruthless. The events recorded by Matthew fall into his last troubled years, when his suspicions and brutality were at fever pitch. The time of the story of the wise men is probably 5-4 BC.

Herod was neither a Greek, nor a Roman, nor a Jew. He

was the son of Antipater the Idumaean. The Idumaeans had been conquered and forcibly converted to Judaism by the Hasmonean prince, John Hyrcanus, who reigned 135-104 BC. Herod dethroned Mattathias Antigonus, the last of the Hasmoneans, and assumed the throne with the support of the Romans.

The title given him by some moderns, "the Great," is well deserved, for he was great in his deeds - both good and evil. His career is a study in opposites and extremes. High intelligence and an instinct for the appropriate action at the opportune moment combined and conflicted with incredible cruelty and ruthlessness and an irrepressible desire for revenge. He loved with passion and ruled with terror.

Herod was a great statesman. In the political arena, he maneuvered with shrewdness, skill, and resourcefulness. On the battlefield, he fought with courage and distinction. He resolved by compromise the incompatibility of Jewish separateness and Hellenic influence. He was liberally Hellenic in his dealings with Greeks and Romans, while taking care to be strictly Jewish in his dealings with Jews.

Herod was a cautious politician. Throughout his life, he was able to garner unstinting Roman support by catering to the desires of the rulers of Rome. This enabled him to rule without serious competition and to extend his authority over more of Palestine than any of his predecessors.

As a king, Herod aspired to glorify both his kingdom and his name. He was among the most extreme admirers of Hellenistic-Roman culture, and his desire to gain a standing for Jerusalem equal to that of the foremost Hellenistic cities led him to give his capital a decidedly Hellenistic character. This found expression in the dominant architectural style of the buildings and their monumental proportions, as well as in the life style, which included theaters, gymnasiums, hippodromes, and games. He established a cosmopolitan atmosphere and a luxurious court. This was neither entirely new nor unique in Jerusalem, where Hellenistic influence had already taken hold among the Jews of the city under the Hasmoneans.

Herod's penchant for the grandiose led to one of the most

important facets of his rule, especially for us today. He was undoubtedly the greatest builder Palestine has ever known. His craving for construction projects had no bounds. His impressive monuments included fortresses, palaces, and even whole cities. They have been revealed at various sites scattered about the country. He built the port city of Caesarea and the town of Samaria, which he renamed "Sebaste" (Greek for "Augustus"). The Temple of Augustus was the dominant structure in Samaria. These projects expressed Herod's extreme admiration for Roman urbanization, architecture, and art. In the fortresses and palaces that he built at Masada, Herodium, and Jericho, Herod gave full architectural expression to his daring eccentricity in which he sought to combine security, luxurious living, and tranquility with desert solitude. The excellence of the masonry of Herod's buildings has won the admiration of modern archaeologists. His winter and summer palaces established norms which deeply influenced the upper crust in Judea. It is noteworthy that in all these projects he strove to avoid any ornamental motifs which might give offense to the tenets of traditional Judaism.

Herod built a temple for Jahweh in Jerusalem (20 BC) which was greater than Solomon's and especially greater than the pathetic little post-exilic temple that it replaced. It was one of the architectural marvels of its time.

In his private life, Herod was a monster. He put to death three sons and a wife. He eliminated the Hasmonean family that included his wife, Mariamne. Paranoia and conspiracy formed a vicious cycle that rapidly spiraled out of control toward the end of his career. Although he lived in splendor and style, he died in agony - unloved and unmourned.

Herod went to great lengths to curry the favor of his subjects, but in their eyes he remained an Idumaean - an outsider, despised and hated. He was the object of opposition and conspiracy not only among his people but also in his own family.

The popular opinion among the Jews was that the Messiah was to be born in Bethlehem. Micah 5:2 says this. According to John 7:42, Micah seems to have been widely understood in this way. This prophecy seems to have been an important one.

It is important to identify Bethlehem as "of Judea." There

was another Bethlehem in Galilee seven miles northwest of Nazareth. The Hebrew of Micah 5:2 reads "Bethlehem Ephrathah." The LXX reads "Bethlehem house of Ephrathah." The connection of the birth of Jesus with the land of Judah is important in terms of Matthew's fulfillment theme because of Gen. 49:10.

God turned the eyes of His people away from Jerusalem, the royal residence and center of political power. Deliverance did not come by a development of potentialities present in the people. God made a fresh start in little Bethlehem. Bethlehem is a place of small beginnings, cf. 1 Sam. 16:1-13. From there, God also brought forth the new David, the Messiah. He created a new order for His chastened and restored people.

The words quoted as "written by the prophet" in Matt. 2:6 offer an interesting study in the way the evangelists employed the Old Testament. The quotation agrees completely neither with the Hebrew original nor with the LXX of Micah 5:2. The first part of the verse evidently leans on Micah 5, but the words "a ruler who is to shepherd my people Israel" come from 2 Sam. 5:2. This suggests either that Matthew is quoting from memory loosely conflating the two passages or that he is using a different translation of the Old Testament than we generally use.

The looseness with which Matthew quotes the prophecy is characteristic of the way the scribes interpreted as they quoted. The variations were designed to emphasize the proper credentials for Messiahship.

We might fault Matthew for the loose way in which he quotes the Old Testament passages, but our passion for scientific accuracy is a rather recent development. The scientific age began in the 16th or 17th centuries. In the first century AD, people were more concerned about the meaning and significance of words and events than the accuracy of quotations and descriptions.

Micah lived in the 8th century BC, when Jerusalem was threatened by the power of Assyria. God promised through Micah that He would raise up a Ruler and Deliverer who would secure freedom and lasting peace. The words of Micah are words of hope in which God opens up the future to His people. The words carried them not only through the Assyrian threat but also during the time that the great powers of Babylon, Persia, Greece, and Rome strutted upon the stage of the world.

Matthew completely changes one part of the quotation. Micah says that Bethlehem is little. Micah 5:2 in the NRSV reads "who are one of the little clans of Judah." This is what the Hebrew has. Rather than "little," the LXX has "least" (oligostos). Matthew quotes Micah as saying that Bethlehem is "by no means least." Matthew may have felt that such a change was needed as the result of Jesus' birth. At the time of Micah, Bethlehem was known only as the small home town of David. As the consequence of Jesus' birth, Bethlehem became most important. The fulfillment of the words of Micah suggests a different emphasis, from littleness to greatness. Bethlehem was "little" in human eyes but not in God's.

Bethlehem is no longer "little," "for from you shall come a ruler who is to shepherd my people Israel." "To shepherd" is used figuratively of protecting, ruling, and governing. The Old Testament describes Moses, David, and other prophets and kings as shepherding (leading) God's people.

1st Sunday after the Epiphany
The Baptism of Our Lord

Year A

Isaiah 42:1-9

When the apostle Philip joined himself to the chariot of the Eunuch of Ethiopia on the road from Jerusalem to Gaza in Acts 8:26-35, Candace's treasurer was reading one of the servant songs of Isaiah. He asked Philip, "About whom, may I ask you, does the prophet say this, about himself or about someone else?" The court official's question is asked by students of the Bible to this day. Is. 42:1-9 is one of the servant songs.

Some identify the servant as Israel, the entire community. He is so named in Is. 41:8 and 9 and 49:3. In some passages of the songs, he is only a part of the community, the remnant. He is also an individual who is called to make Israel's mission his own and to fulfill it. He is a corporate personality. For this reason, some interpreters think the servant may be the prophet or someone else from that era. But he is also an individual who, from the prophet's point of view, will come in the future.

The servant is too complex a figure to be fitted into any single category. He is the whole people, the remnant, and one person at the same time. The goal of his vicarious representation is accomplished through suffering, according to Is. 52:13-53:12.

He is the suffering servant of God. He takes the place of the "many" who should suffer. His representative work re-establishes the covenant God made with His people.

Israel's election for mission is emphasized in the book of Isaiah more than in any other book of the Old Testament. God appointed that people to be the agents of His mission in the covenant He made with them at Mt. Sinai, cf. Ex. 19:4-6. He expressed His universal concern for all nations in the words, "All the earth is mine." Israel was made the way to God for all people when God said, "You shall be to me a kingdom of priests and a holy nation."

The crucial role Israel was to play in the divine drama of salvation seems to have been only dimly understood by that people in the early days of their history. But it became explicit in Is. 2:2-4; 19:23-25; 40-55; 61:5-6; Zech. 2:11; 8:22-23; 14:16; and in the book of Jonah. God's consistent intention was to establish His redemptive sovereignty over all the earth, and Israel was made God's agent to accomplish that goal.

But at the time Isaiah is writing ch. 42, Israel is in exile and under the domination of Babylon. Nevertheless, the Lord through the prophet announces in Is. 40-41 His resolve to strengthen Israel and to make that nation His servant to accomplish His purposes. In four so-called servant songs or poems, Israel is assigned her mission again. Is. 42:1-4 is the first poem or song. The other three are Is. 49:1-7; 50:4-11; and 52:13-53:12. Their interpretation is notoriously difficult.

Many confine the first servant song to Is. 42:1-4, but the close relationship of these verses to vs. 5-9 suggests extending it through v. 9. The servant is upheld in v. 1, and whoever is addressed in v. 6 is taken by the hand and kept. The servant is chosen in v. 1, and the person addressed in v. 6 has been called. His mission is to the nations in vs. 1, 4, and 6. His mission is to "bring forth justice" in vs. 1 and 4. It is described in terms of delivering the nations in vs. 6 and 7. He is to be "a covenant to the people, a light to the nations, to open the eyes that are blind, to bring out the prisoners from the dungeon, from the prison those who sit in darkness." These phrases are rich and suggestive.

At the beginning of Is. 42, Jahweh presents His servant to an unnamed audience, possibly the divine council. God is speaking. He identifies Himself in vs. 5 and 8. Earlier in Isaiah, He says that He has been directing the course of history from the beginning, cf. Is. 41:2-4 and 25-27. The coming of Cyrus, the founder of the Persian empire, and Israel's return to Palestine are but preliminary steps in His long-range program. That program's purpose is to create a worldwide kingdom. This kingdom is not to be ushered in and maintained by force of arms. It is to be a rule assuring pardon and peace for every subject. The servant is the one who will establish this realm.

Jahweh introduces His servant at the beginning of Is. 42 in a form probably borrowed from the court. This is the way in which an emperor might have presented one of his vassal kings or a provincial governor to his nobles and legally defined the new official's duties and powers. It is something like David's presentation of Solomon in 1 Chron. 28:1-29:22. After the presentation, a statement is made about the equipment given the official to help him discharge his responsibilities, cf. v. 1. Then comes a brief description of the responsibility itself – he is to bring forth mishpat to the nations who already await his teaching. Finally, Jahweh says something about the way in which His servant will do his work. There will be no violence. His servant will spare the weak. His mission is to save. The servant's mission goes beyond Israel. He is to bring "justice" to the gentiles or to "the coastlands." "The coastlands" are the coastal region of Syria and Phoenicia. This was a remote area that the Israelites considered to be the ends of the earth.

The servant's outreach will not have the character of conquering imperialism and will not be triumphalistic. He will not sit in judgment. Rather, he will bring torah, that is, Jahweh's guidance and instruction. His aim will be that torah reach the coastlands and that the voice of justice and truth be heard.

That he is to be "a covenant to the people" is commonly taken to mean that the servant will bring people into covenant relationship with Jahweh and transform social relationships so that people are neighborly.

Jahweh has given His servant as "a light to the nations."

That is, he is the agent through whom light is to be brought to all people.

The "blind" stand for those who are helpless and groping. The servant will open their eyes. His mission is to heal a torn creation.

Isaiah describes the servant's qualifications for his mission. First, he is God's servant. To be called the "servant of the Lord" is an honor. Both kings and prophets are called "servants" in the Bible. Abraham is honored with this title in Gen. 26:24 and Ps. 105:6; Moses in Num. 12:7-8; Caleb in Num. 14:24; David in Is. 37:35; Isaiah in Is. 20:3; prophets in general in 2 Kings 17:13 and Is. 44:26; and Zerubbabel in Haggai 2:23. The nation of Israel is called "my servant" in Is. 41:8-9; 49:3; and Jer. 30:10.

The servant is pleasing to God. "My soul delights" in him, Jahweh says. "My soul" is another way of expressing what the first person singular pronoun does.

God has put His Spirit on him as He did on the judges, the early kings of Israel, and the prophets.

The style of the servant as he carries out his mission is described. He will be gentle and compassionate in contrast to the boisterous behavior of the world with its proclamations and displays of power. His style will be in marked contrast to the mighty figures of the world like kings and other powerful political leaders. He will not operate as power brokers do. He will not use violence and coercion. He will do his work with quiet determination, trusting in God who chose him and sent him.

He will not attempt to draw attention to himself or crave publicity. He will not toot His own horn. There will be no publicity in connection with the mishpat he brings. He will not "lift up his voice or make it heard in the street" as judgment.

He will focus on caring for the poor and the weak. He will have compassion for the "bruised reed" and the "dimly burning wick." A reed is a figure of weak support. Bruised reeds and dimly burning wicks refer to vulnerable people. Babylon's or any other worldly power's way is to break such people and snuff them out. The servant will do things differently.

42

The figure of "a dimly burning wick" comes from every day life. It smells bad. The smell caused because it burns dimly is in addition to the smell of the rancid oil it burns. The flickering flame doesn't give much light. Nothing is more offensive and useless. A bruised reed is also useless. To the servant there will be no useless persons. His value system will be quite different from that of every civilization. In his kingdom, success will not be a matter of the survival of the fittest.

Pastorally kind and gentle, he will promote mishpat until God's faithfulness is known among the nations. Unlike earlier prophets of doom, the servant of the Lord will bring the quiet proclamation of God's comfort to the exiles.

The Hebrew word mishpat is used three times. It is translated "justice" in vs. 1, 3, and 4. The meaning of the word is important for understanding Is. 42 and the mission of the servant. Mishpat comes from the stem shaphat which has the double meaning "to rule" and "to judge." The ambiguity raises the question whether the office of a ruler included judging or that of a judge included ruling. The Old Testament view of mishpat should be differentiated from the Roman concept of law. The mishpat of Jahweh is not dependent on a legal principle or an absolute norm of morality. Mishpat expresses relationship and regulates relationships. Thus the term mishpat is related to the idea of berith (covenant). The word zedekah (righteousness) is mentioned so often with mishpat in the Old Testament as to suggest that the two words came to be regarded as virtually synonymous.

Israel's berith with God placed her under divine blessings and curses. There was the possibility of penalty for breach of the covenant. Judgment can result in dissolution of the covenant if there is no way for restoration. However, Jahweh is characterized not only by mishpat and zedekah but also by chesed (mercy). God's chesed seems to contradict His mishpat and zedekah, and yet the activity implied in them serves the same end, namely, relationship. Thus mishpat can take on the sense of grace and mercy. Salvation is the expression of the mishpat of Jahweh. At this point, the legal content of mishpat is set aside; forgiveness is in tension with justice. The Old

43

Testament saint put his confidence both in the righteousness of God and also in His grace. Justice and grace are united through God's action in delivering His people and in this way establishing mishpat. To Israel, mishpat is grounded in God's gracious acts.

In exile, Israel knew herself a thoroughly sinful people. Her sins were a wall between herself and her God. The more clearly the sins of the people were seen in the judgment of the exile, the more their hope for the future looked to the saving action of Jahweh.

The task of the servant of the Lord is to bring mishpat not only to Israel but also to all nations. To equip him for this task, Jahweh has laid His Spirit on him. Mishpat is from God Himself. Special emphasis is laid on the extension of mishpat to the gentiles, because it was previously thought of as given only to Israel. Through the office of the servant, that limit will be transcended. The bringing of mishpat means salvation for the nations and mercy for the oppressed. It is a gracious revelation of Jahweh's will. It is the extension of Jahweh's covenant to the world which will be available to all.

The word mishpat represents the reordering of social life and social power so that the weak - the vulnerable, widows and orphans - live in dignity, security and well-being. The servant of the Lord will establish God's order in the world.

The Lord's salvation is to reach to the end of the earth, according to Is. 55:3-5; 60:1-7; 66:19-20. Jahweh's teaching (guidance and instruction) and judgment are to be brought to the gentiles. As the Levites were set apart as a priesthood to Israel, so the servant of the Lord has a priestly function to the world. The vision of Zech. 8:23 looks forward to the day when this covenant-promise will be fulfilled.

Is. 42 is addressed to Jewish exiles in Babylon about the 6th century BC. They are being crushed and demeaned by their Babylonian conquerors. They are disillusioned because Jahweh seems to be unable to protect them, and they are attracted to His rivals, the gods of Babylon, Marduk, Bel, and Nebo. Isaiah gives the exiles reason to hope in Jahweh. The message is that God is not with Babylon but with Israel.

It is remarkable that while in exile the Lord reminds Israel of their relationship, the duties He gave that nation and the obligations she is to fulfill. In exile, Israel has been preoccupied and absorbed with her sorry situation. The Lord changes the subject and directs her attention to her mission. There is work to be done, and Israel is to think about that.

Although many Messianic ideas are associated with the servant, it is probably well to keep the figures of the Messiah and of the servant of the Lord as separate as possible. Joining them together produces confusion. Certain Old Testament passages speak of the coming Davidic king who will establish a world rule of righteousness and peace. To this concept, the term Messiah or Christ came to be attached. In the days of Jesus, people were expecting the coming of this Messiah. But the servant of the Lord is a completely separate concept. Vicarious suffering was not a part of the Messianic concept. There were only faint traces of a suffering Messiah. The two figures were not closely joined before the days of Jesus. When Peter confesses Jesus as the Christ in Matt. 16:13-23, Jesus immediately begins to talk about Himself in terms of the servant. Peter does not understand what He is talking about. Both the servant of the Lord and the Messiah have the task of restoring the destroyed or distorted relationship between Jahweh and His people and of leading the people to engage in the mission God gave them through their election.

The New Testament writers assert that Jesus fulfilled the figure of the servant. When the Eunuch of Ethiopia asked Philip the identity of the servant of Isaiah, Philip "proclaimed to him the good news about Jesus," cf. Acts 8:34-35. Anchoring Christology in the servant songs probably goes back to Jesus Himself. Is. 42 plays an important role in the substructure of New Testament Christology.

If the servant songs are not a specific prediction of the life and work of Jesus, the servant of Isaiah is a figure to whom Jesus gives reality. The servant embodies not only the idea that God has given to Israel the mission to lead all people to Him, but it also identifies the character of Jesus' ministry and the means by which His mission is to be achieved, namely, through suffering, cf. Is. 52:13-53:12.

New Testament readers are familiar with Is. 42. Matthew says in 12:15-21 that Jesus fulfilled Is. 42:1-4 in three ways. One way was through His healing ministry: "he cured all of them." Matthew explains Jesus' order not to publicize His miracles, "not to make him known" by quoting Is. 42:1-4. When "the Pharisees . . . conspired against (Jesus), how to destroy him . . . . he departed," cf. Matt. 12:14-15. This action is an enhancement but very much the style of the servant. Enhancement is a characteristic of Jesus' fulfillment of prophecy.

Is. 42 may offer a clue as to why Jesus kept His accomplishments as secret as possible. The celebrity type promotes an image of superiority. His public image is one-sided: he shows only his best side, his most photogenic profile. There is no hint of his own doom. This makes the prosaic unsung lives of his hearers and readers seem insignificant. They feel out of it. Superstars, especially saintly ones, finally condemn us. Maybe that's another reason that Jesus imposed a news-blackout on His fans. He wanted to protect the little people from being overwhelmed by a superman image of Him, to keep bruised reeds from being destroyed.

The voice from heaven at the baptism of Jesus points to Him as the fulfillment of the servant in Is. 42, cf. Mark 1:11 and Matt. 3:17. The voice says, "You are my Son . . . ; with you I am well pleased." Jahweh "delights" in the servant. Another connection is that the Spirit descends on Him, cf. Mark 1:10; Matt. 3:16; Luke 3:22; and John 1:32.

To the people of the early church, there was no question that Jesus was the servant of Isaiah. This may be the force of the word "servant" applied to Jesus in Acts 3:13, 26; 4:27, 30; and Phil. 2:7-9.

Mishpat was established in Jesus' death. In His suffering and defeat on the cross, mishpat came to the earth. Until then, the "wicks" and the "reeds" were crushed by a message of doom.

When Jesus says to His hearers in the Sermon on the Mount, "You are the light of the world," cf. Matt. 5:14, He is addressing Israel. Matthew directs those words to the followers of Jesus. The gospel is to be brought to the ends of the earth, cf. Acts 1:8.

The invitation to discipleship is to go out to all nations and cultures, cf. Matt. 28:19.

Paul and Barnabas justify their mission to the gentiles by referring to 42:6 and 49:6, "I have set you to be a light for the Gentiles, so that you may bring salvation to the ends of the earth," cf. Acts 13:47. The words are echoed in Simeon's Nunc Dimittis, "my eyes have seen your salvation, which you have prepared in the presence of all peoples, a light for revelation to the Gentiles and for glory to your people Israel," cf. Luke 2:30-32.

The Christian Church today is the contemporary fulfillment of the servant. The church is the Body of Christ. God has made us responsible for the continuation of His mission.

The relationship between ancient Israel, Jesus, and the church can be thought of and maintained by calling the ancient people of God the old Israel, Jesus the true Israel, and the church the new Israel.

Is. 42 helps us understand the character the church's presence should have in the world.

When the church fails to fully comprehend her status as God's servant, as one being supported by God, as God's chosen one, as one in whom God delights, as one upon whom God has placed His Spirit, the church will not and cannot carry out God's program. This may be a contemporary problem in the church. Those who do not feel the charismatic designation need to make the appearance of success their goal.

The mandate to the servant in vs. 6-7 is framed by self-uttered doxologies of Jahweh in vs. 5 and 8-9. This sandwiching of the call of the servant makes it clear that the will of the Creator is to be carried out by the servant. It is all Jahweh and only Jahweh. All temptation to place a mortal at center stage in God's mission is removed by reference to the Ultimate Reality. Jahweh is the only One worthy of glory.

"I have called you in righteousness" is a soteriological statement. It is the principal clause in v. 6. The descriptions of Jahweh given in v. 5 dealing with creation are subordinate clauses. The statements of God as Creator are subordinate to statements about Him as Savior. The statements about Him as Creator reinforce confidence in the power of Jahweh and His readiness to help. More than that, God's saving work is a part of creation itself. Creation is a saving work of Jahweh. It is the first of Jahweh's works.

The work of the servant is called "new things." The nations are to be brought to the way of life intended by the Creator. The people of God figure decisively in the "new things" God plans to do in the world.

A preacher constructing a sermon based on Is. 42:1-9 could use the theme "the Servant Church." The church is to be a light to the nations. While we act locally, we are to think globally. The sermon might be built around the image of spaceship earth. We are none of us passengers but all crew.

Another theme might be "God's Alternate Power," namely, weakness, cf. 2 Cor. 12:8.

In times of change, we need more than ever the perspective of history. We do not determine history. The dynamic of history may be moving in a direction opposite to the one we are going. We are to be the agents of God's history.

Acts 10:34-43

The beginning of the Christian mission to the gentiles is an astonishing change in the development of the early church. This revolutionary change is revealed in Peter's speech.

The drama begins in Acts 10:1-8 in Caesarea when "an angel of the Lord" commands Cornelius to send men to Joppa to get Peter. The initiating force behind the gentile mission is not a member of the church. The beginning of the Christian mission to the gentiles is an act of God.

In the second scene, Acts 10:9-16, Peter, who is the spiritual leader of the church, resists taking the gospel to gentiles. His opposition is considerably less in the third scene, Acts 10:17-23, but he is still hesitant. In the fourth scene, Acts 10:23-33, he states explicitly the reason he is so reluctant to give the gospel to gentiles: "it is unlawful for a Jew to associate with or to visit a Gentile." Finally, in the fifth scene, Acts 10:34-43, Peter gives the gospel to Cornelius and his household. They are gentiles.

Luke follows the pattern of ancient historians in using a speech to describe the fundamental significance of an event. He uses this technique in 11:5-17; 15:7-11; 17:22-31; 20:18-35; and 22:1-21.

The universality of the salvation Jesus brought and effected seems obvious today, but it was not always apparent to the church. Paul had to fight for this truth at Galatia, according to Gal. 2:11-14. That full membership in the people of God does not involve circumcision and fidelity to the Mosaic law but only trusting faith in what God said in Christ's ministry is not apparent to Paul's fellow Christians - not even to Peter. The Antioch incident took place after Peter's encounter with Cornelius and his household and shows how slowly the universality of the gospel came to be understood. Moreover, this insight needed to be reinforced again and again. Still today, it needs to be repeated that Christ's death saves rich and poor, strong and weak, educated and illiterate, easterner and westerner, white, black, and yellow.

Much is at stake for Cornelius in the event described in Acts 10. One thing is his status as a member of an elite power group and his reputation as a loyal Roman.

Cornelius is a God-fearer, cf. Acts 10:2. This means, he is sympathetic to the claims of Jewish monotheism but he is not a convert to Judaism. He has learned some of the essentials of the Jewish faith through his contacts with the synagogue. He is a patron of the local Jewish community. He prays to the God of the Jews.

He is also a Roman soldier, a centurion, cf. Acts 10:1. As such, he has considerable military and social status and wealth. His pay is probably some sixteen times that of the basic legionary.

If Cornelius accepts Jesus Christ as Lord and King, this could jeopardize his place in the military. Roman prejudice made loyalty to Jesus Christ incompatible with loyalty to Caesar.

At stake for Peter is his status as a member of the religious elect and his loyalty to that community. Later, he is criticized by the church in Jerusalem and has to account for his acceptance of Cornelius and his family, cf. Acts 11:1-18.

The programmatic statement for the Acts of the Apostles is Acts 1:8, the words of the risen Lord to the apostles, "you will be my witnesses in Jerusalem, in all Judea and Samaria, and to the ends of the earth." The first nine chapters of the book tell about the apostles fulfilling this commission by bringing the gospel to Jerusalem, Judea, and Samaria. The fulfillment of the words, "to the ends of the earth," begins in Acts 10:1-11:18 when the gospel is preached to the household of Cornelius.

By extending the gospel to gentiles, Peter effects a fundamental paradigm shift in Christian thinking as to the kind of Messiah Jesus is. He says that Jesus is Savior beyond the house of Israel.

Peter's audience is familiar with much of what he says. The new thing is the universality of Jesus' saving work.

That God is not partial is both good news and bad. It means that Cornelius can be included in the promises God gave Israel. It also means that there no longer are insiders and outsiders. There is no longer a community of God's people maintained by prohibitions and conditions for membership. In extending the gospel to Cornelius, Peter rejects his previous understanding of the partiality of God and the limits of God's acceptance. The community of God's people becomes radically open and inclusive. All systems of preferential treatment and special status are abolished.

Religious communities are always tempted to use their self-understanding to assert moral superiority and to establish insider/outsider prohibitions. Even liberal groups try to banish racists, sexists, and other politically incorrect folk from their fellowship. Some liberal Christian communities consider themselves superior because of their inclusivity, and thereby they reject certain individuals and groups.

Luke's account of how the gentile mission began makes two important points. The first is God's impartiality; He offers salvation to all. The second is that God chose to save everyone through one man, Jesus the Christ, who is a Jew, and through His death on a cross. When divine impartiality and the universality of salvation is emphasized, it must not be forgotten that the one through whom God effected salvation is Jesus the Christ.

This Lesson shows up each church year, sometimes at Epiphany and sometimes at Easter. The Lesson offers two features: Peter's emphasis on Jesus' public ministry and the beginning of the church's mission to the gentiles.

Divine impartiality and the universality of salvation resonate with the contemporary hope that humanity will transcend the limits of culture, race, and social distinctions. It is difficult for contemporary people - even the people of the church - to deal with the scandal of the incarnation and the stumbling block of the cross. God chose to save all people through the death of One who died on a cross. Paul did not allow the congregations he founded to forget this, cf. 1 Cor. 1:23.

Jesus Christ is at the heart of Peter's speech. He was crucified by His fellow countrymen but raised by God. The cross is a sign of humiliation and loss of social status. It calls us to empty ourselves of superiority schemes and claims.

That Jesus is the "one ordained by God as judge of the living and the dead" is stated also in Acts 17:31.

When Peter says, "God shows no partiality," he is reflecting what Deut. 10:17-18 says about God. Other New Testament writers apply this aspect of God's character to other situations. Paul says that God punishes and rewards Jews and Greeks impartially in Rom. 2:11. He says that God shows no partiality to wrongdoers in Col. 3:25. He says that God shows no partiality to either slaves or masters in Eph. 6:9. Peter says that God "judges all people impartially according to their deeds" in 1 Pet. 1:17. James says in 2:1 and 9 that making distinctions between rich and poor people is contrary to the Christian faith and is sin.

NRSV translates two different Greek words in vs. 36 and 37 with the word "message." In v. 36, the Greek word is logos. This is not "the Word" of John 1:1, but the message of salvation through Jesus Christ. It is the same in Acts 13:26. This word is the story of the sending of the Son of God into the world. It announces the peace that came through Jesus Christ. "Message" in Acts 10:37 is a translation of the word hrema. It should be understood as an "event" as in Luke 2:15 where hrema is translated "thing."

The phrase "by Jesus Christ" belongs with "peace," not with "preaching" in v. 36. The Greek text makes this quite clear. Peter says that God sent peace to the world through Jesus Christ. The angels in the fields of Bethlehem said the same, cf. Luke 2:14. In sending Jesus, God declared peace between Himself and the human race. The news of this peace was spread by John the Baptist throughout Judea. Jesus made it known in Galilee by "doing good and healing all who were oppressed by the devil" after He was "anointed . . . with the Holy Spirit and with power." His healings demonstrated that God was with Him, cf. Acts 2:22. That is why the synoptists placed so much emphasis on them. Jesus' ministry extended also to Judea and Jerusalem. The reaction to His ministry was that "they put him to death by hanging him on a tree." This expressed their rejection of God's man in keeping with the directions given in Deut. 22:21-22. But God refused to accept that condemnation. Jesus' resurrection was God vindication of Jesus. God reversed the human no. This motif is quite explicit in Acts, cf. Acts 2:23-24 and 13:28-30. God commanded the apostles to continue to preach the good news of God's peace after Jesus rose from the dead by saying that God forgives sins through Jesus.

When Peter says, "God anointed Jesus of Nazareth with the Holy Spirit and with power," he may be referring to Jesus' baptism. That anointing identified Jesus as the Christ. The Holy Spirit is the Initiator of Jesus' public ministry as well as of the church's mission to the gentiles, cf. Acts 11:12.

The apostles are described as the guarantors of the tradition of the church in Acts 10:40-42. Apostolic authorship is important in establishing the canon of the New Testament.

A feature of early Christian sermons is the claim that the gospel message is the fulfillment of Old Testament prophecy. Jesus taught His disciples this, according to Luke 24:27 which may also explain what Acts 10:43 says.

Acts 10:43 is the reason some insist that the gospel of Christ, the divine message of the remission of sins by faith in Christ, is the means of grace not only for the New Testament period, but it was also for the whole era of the Old Testament.[2]

Matthew 3:13-17

In being baptized with John's baptism, Jesus expressed solidarity with the human race. He united Himself with the mankind summoned to repentance by John. He assumed that solidarity when He was born of Mary, and He confirmed it in His baptism. He accepted involvement in the guilt, burden, and fate of the human race. Throughout His public ministry, He did not identify with the self-righteous and the hyper-religious but with tax collectors and sinners, cf. Matt. 9:10-13. Because human beings need to repent, Jesus needed to repent. God's judgment rested on Him in the name of all sinners. John's baptism was a baptism of repentance, cf. Matt. 3:11. In Jesus, human disobedience was changed to obedience. Jesus was "obedient to the point of death – even death on a cross," cf. Phil. 2:8.

John did not understand when Jesus came "to be baptized by him." He asked, "I need to be baptized by you, and do you come to me?" The problem, as John saw it, was not that of the sinless Son of God accepting a baptism intended for sinners. It was essentially, according to Matthew, a matter of inferiority-superiority. The pronouns "you" and "I" are emphatic. John was aware of the contrast between himself and Jesus.

No previous contact between the two men is indicated by Matthew. No relationship is described. No explanation is given as to how John recognized Jesus as the Messiah, but he obviously did.

Perhaps the incongruity of the event caused Matthew to relate Jesus' baptism in a subordinate clause, "when Jesus had been baptized." The main clause is a very weak, "he came up from the water." "The heavens were opened . . . and he saw the Spirit of God" are also main clauses, and they are not weak statements.

John's baptism was for sinners, cf. Matt. 3:6. Jesus was

baptized as our representative. As our representative, He was a sinner. That may be something of the point Luke wants to make when he says that Jesus was baptized while all the people were being baptized, cf. Luke 3:21. This solidarity was approved and confirmed by the Voice from heaven. He said, "with (him) I am well pleased."

The Voice from heaven identified Jesus with the servant of Isaiah by echoing Is. 42:1, "with whom I am well pleased." That verse introduces the servant songs. One of those songs says, "The Lord has laid on him the iniquity of us all," cf. Is. 53:6. His life was made "an offering for sin," cf. Is. 53:10. "He bore the sin of many," cf. Is. 53:12.

Jesus explained why He needed to be baptized by John when He said, "it is proper for us in this way to fulfill all righteousness." He said that His baptism was both appropriate and necessary. The pronoun "us" refers to John and Jesus. Jesus showed obedience by being baptized by John. John showed obedience in that "he consented." In being baptized by John, Jesus accepted and affirmed John and his ministry.

Although John's baptism is nowhere prescribed in the scriptures, he was sent by God to baptize. This is what God wanted human beings to do at that time. John's baptism was a part of God's will for the human race. Jesus became a member of the human race. He came to carry out perfectly the divine will for us, as our representative. Obedience was His reason for being baptized. Isaiah says about the servant, "The righteous one, my servant, shall make many righteous," cf. Is. 53:11.

Jesus and John fulfilled "all righteousness" against the background of John's proclamation of the wrath of God on sinful people described in Matt. 3:7-12. In Matthew, "righteousness" means rightness of life in the sight of God. Righteousness is emphasized by only one other New Testament author, namely, Paul, but Matthew uses the term in a different sense. Matthew's concept of righteousness is closer to that of the synagogue with its emphasis on right human action. In Matt. 5:20, righteousness is right conduct in relationship to God and to one's neighbor. In Matt. 6:33, the righteousness of God is not God's gift, as it is in Paul, but it is human action that corresponds to the will of God. Other than James, Matthew presses more emphatically than anyone else in the New Testament toward the verification of our Christian identity through our conduct.

John says in Matt. 3:11 that Jesus will baptize with the Holy Spirit and that Jesus' baptism will be greater than his. John asks for this greater baptism when he says, "I need to be baptized by you," but Matthew gives no indication that John ever received it. This may be something of what Matt. 11:11 means.

Only Jesus saw "the Spirit of God descending." The addition of auto ("to him") – which is the best reading of the Greek manuscripts - emphasizes that only Jesus saw the heavens opened. John 1:32 says that John the Baptist also saw the Holy Spirit descending on Jesus.

Messiah or Christ means anointed. Many have identified the descent of the Spirit at His baptism with the anointing of Jesus. Acts 10:38 says, "God anointed Jesus of Nazareth with the Holy Spirit," but Peter does not connect the anointing of Jesus with His baptism. Nor does the idea naturally arise from the story of Jesus' baptism in Matthew's gospel.

Whether hosei peristeran ("like a dove") qualifies to pneuma ("the Spirit") and so means that the Spirit actually had the form of a dove or the words are adverbial modifying "descending" and refer to the manner of the Spirit's descent is unclear. Commentators disagree. Luke 3:22 is more explicit and says that "the Holy Spirit descended upon him in bodily form like a dove." It is difficult to prove what Matthew wanted to convey when he used the phrase.

A dove symbolized Israel. A passage in the Mekilta, an early rabbinic commentary on Exodus, claims that the Holy Spirit rested on Israel at the crossing of the Red Sea and that Israel was then like a dove. The dove may symbolize Jesus as the true Israel.

Some look to Gen. 1:2 to explain the significance of the dove. Three elements that appear in the story of Jesus' baptism are there: the Spirit of God, water, and the image of a bird "hovering." A passage in the Babylonian Talmud (Hagidah 15a) likens the hovering of God's Spirit at the creation to the hovering of a dove. This reflects the idea of the initiation of the new creation. The coming of a new creation can be found in both the Old Testament and the New. Readers steeped in the Old Testament scriptures would understand that the dove marked Jesus as the bringer of the new creation. At the commencement of things, the Spirit of God hovered over the face of the watery chaos, and at the beginning of the Messiah's ministry the Spirit fluttered over the waters of the Jordan. With Jesus' ministry, a new age commenced, and God renewed His great work of creation. A Jewish precedent for applying creation imagery to the end time and a clear example of the image of the Spirit hovering over human beings as opposed to hovering over the lifeless material of the watery chaos was found a few years ago in the Messianic Vision of the Dead Sea Scrolls.[3]

Because of the phrase, "like a dove," the dove is a symbol for the Holy Spirit in Christian art. Even in Judaism, there is evidence that the figure of a dove represents the Spirit of God.

The baptism of our Lord is Jesus' first act in the gospel of Matthew. It is the beginning of His public ministry.

All three Persons of the Trinity manifest themselves individually at Jesus' baptism. The Son stands in the water, the Spirit descends on Jesus, and the Father speaks calling Jesus "my Son."

God speaks at Jesus' baptism as He spoke to ancient Israel from Mt. Sinai, according to Ex. 20:22. The Voice will be heard again at Jesus' transfiguration in Matt. 17:5 and also before His passion, according to John 12:28. Matthew and the other evangelists emphasize not that God spoke but what He said.

In Matthew, the Voice says "This is my Son" to John and whoever else was around. The wording in Mark 1:11 and Luke 3:22, "You are my Son," pictures the Voice as addressing Jesus and not John and those who were with him, although the Voice may intend for John and the others to hear what He says to His Son.

The words spoken by the Voice occur in the New Testament seven times. There are the three synoptic accounts of Jesus' baptism, cf. Matt. 3:17; Mark 1:11; and Luke 3:22. The words are also spoken by the Voice from heaven in the story of the transfiguration, cf. Matt. 17:5; Mark 9:7; and Luke 9:35. The seventh occurrence is in the reference to the transfiguration in 2 Pet. 1:17.

The words were familiar to those who knew the Old Testament. The first phrase, "This is my Son, the Beloved" echoes Ps. 2:7. The second phrase, "with whom I am well pleased," echoes Is. 42:1.

With the citation of Ps. 2:7, the Voice identifies Jesus as Israel's anointed King, the Messiah. Ps. 2 is a royal psalm. The king of Israel in the Old Testament is "the son of God," because he represents the nation. God called Israel His son in Ex. 4:22-23. Qumran has supplied us with firm evidence that "Son of God" was used as a Messianic title in pre-Christian Palestinian Judaism.

The background for Ps. 2:7 is Ex. 4:22-23. Some have sought to relate the words, "This is my Son," to Gen. 22:2, 12, and 16, but the idea of sonship is probably best related to Ex. 4. The close relationship of the term with the exodus is supported by the use of the title a few verses later in Matt. 4:3 in connection with the temptation story which has a strong exodus character. It is not a reference to the divine nature of Jesus so much as to His being the true Israel.

The Hebrew of the key phrase in Ex. 4:22-23, "Israel is my first-born son," is <u>bni bchori Yisrael</u>, which literally means "my son, my first-born, Israel (is)." In Greek, it would be translated <u>ho huios mou, ho prototokos mou, Israel (estin)</u>. What the Voice says in Matt. 3:17 is very close to Ex. 4:22 in its literal form. The only variations are <u>houtos</u> for Israel, and <u>agapetos</u> for <u>prototokos</u> ("beloved" for "first-born"). The Voice from heaven is applying to Jesus the title God gave to Israel. Jerome preserves in Latin a fragment from an ancient Hebrew language gospel in which the Voice from heaven at Jesus' baptism actually says "<u>filius meus primogenitus,</u>" exactly the <u>bni bchori</u> of Ex. 4:22.

The substitution of "beloved" for "first-born" is readily explained. Judaism wrestled to interpret the term "first-born" in Ex. 4:22. It could not mean literally that the Lord would have other "sons" besides and after Israel. The term frequently gave way to interpretive paraphrases. Expressions of endearment, like <u>agapetos</u>, occur in connection with sonship in Hosea 11:1 and Jer. 31:20 and 9b. The New Testament writers picked this up in Eph. 1:6; Col. 1:13; John 5:20. "Beloved" means "only" or "only-begotten." It describes the uniqueness of Jesus' relationship to God.

Jesus was deeply conscious of His sonship in the sense of Ex. 4:22-23. The very prominence of the baptismal narrative in the gospels suggests that this event was deeply significant. The temptations, Jesus' prayers, His preaching, even His trial and the mockery as He hung on the cross point to His consciousness of sonship.

Furthermore, that the words are in the story of Jesus' baptism invites us to think of the exodus. Baptism, as it was practiced by John the Baptist as well as the baptism of Jesus, is closely related to the Red Sea experience of Israel. Paul uses the word "baptized" in connection with that event in 1 Cor. 10:1-2. At that moment, 1 Cor. 10:5 implies, they were the people "with whom God was well pleased," because later, "God was not pleased with most of them." The significance of Israel's baptism was not their getting wet with water but their "passing through" the sea. The sea was the boundary between slavery to Pharaoh and servanthood to the Lord. They crossed that boundary into the sonship of the Lord who loved them and called them out of Egypt. "All" the fathers who "passed through" belonged to the Lord as His people, even the "mixed multitude" mentioned in Ex. 12:38. In later thought, the crossing out of Egypt merged conceptually with the crossing of the Jordan into the promised land, cf. Ps. 114. Thus the "passing through" sealed the identity of Israel as the son, people, and servant of Jahweh.

In Matthew, the true Israel, Jesus, "the Son of God," unlike the old Israel, is obedient. Jesus does exactly what He ought to have done, and, therefore, He is the Son "with whom (God) is well pleased." Jesus is baptized because the old Israel was disobedient.

The word "beloved" may echo the word "chosen" in Is. 42:1. A chosen one is the special object of love. God's love is thought of not in terms of forgiveness but in terms of preference.

Matt. 12:18 quotes Is. 42:1 in this way, "Here is my servant, whom I have chosen, my beloved, with whom my soul is well pleased."

As a reminiscence of Is. 42:1-4, the words "with whom I am well pleased" point to the Suffering Servant portrayed in Is. 49:1-6; 50:4-11; 52:13-53:12. They suggest the ordination to ministry of the Isaianic servant of the Lord. The Voice from heaven reveals who Jesus is and the nature of His ministry. The servant songs point to His crucifixion as our representative. He was "stricken, struck down, and afflicted," cf. Is. 53:4. "He was wounded for our transgressions, crushed for our iniquities; upon him was the punishment that made us whole, and by his bruises we are healed," cf. Is. 53:5. "He was oppressed, and he was afflicted, yet he did not open his mouth; like a lamb that is led to the slaughter, and like a sheep that before his shearers is silent . . ." cf. Is. 53:7. "By a perversion of justice he was taken away . . . . he was cut off from the land of the living . . ." cf. Is. 53:8. "They made his grave . . . and his tomb . . ." cf. Is. 53:9. "He poured out himself to death . . ." cf. Is. 53:12.

John's baptism was not something entirely new in Judaism. No person seeking to influence Jews in any matter concerning religion would introduce something entirely new. The Mishnah and rabbinic sayings make clear how much stress was laid by Jews on the continuity of tradition. If a person could not support his ideas either from scripture or from the sayings of recognized rabbis, he could not expect a hearing.

Modern archaeology has helped us locate the baptism of John in the history of Judaism. Archaeologists have discovered numerous examples of Jewish ritual immersion baths dating to the late second temple period, prior to and during the time when John the Baptist lived. They are called miqvaot, singular miqveh.

Ritual purity was required of a Jew before entering the temple mount, before making a sacrifice, before receiving the benefit of a priestly offering, and for other similar purposes. Impurity was brought about by nocturnal emissions, sexual intercourse, or contact with a corpse. A woman was unclean after her menstrual period or childbirth. Ritual immersion was part of the process to remove such uncleanness. In most cases, the impurity ceased at sunset after ritual immersion.

Complete immersion was required. No part of the body was to be untouched by water. The pool had to contain at least approximately two gallons of water. Traditionally, the ritual immersion or bath pool held almost three cubic cubits of water, about 75 gallons. It was approximately one cubit square and three cubits deep, a cubit being about 18 inches. A height of three cubits was enough to enable a person standing in it to be completely immersed, perhaps with knees bent. Rabbinic law required flowing or living water to provide a valid purification, cf. Mikvaot 5:5. John's baptisms took place in the Jordan River.

Another predecessor of the baptism of John was Jewish proselyte baptism. This was an initiatory baptism. Three things were required of a proselyte to enter Judaism: circumcision, the offering of a sacrifice, and immersion in the miqveh. The sacrifice was no longer required after the destruction of the temple in 70 AD.

The first ancient miqvaot were identified as such by Yigael Yadin in the early 1960s at Masada. The two baths found there were not for hygienic cleansing but rather for ritual purification. Miqvaot have turned up in abundance at excavations of late second temple Jerusalem - near the temple mount, in private homes of wealthy Jerusalemites who lived on the hill opposite the temple mount, at Qumran, and elsewhere.

The role John played in baptizing is not clear. It is possible that he did not administer the washing but rather witnessed the rite. Jewish law required ritual immersion in the miqveh to be witnessed, although it is clear that the person immersed himself/ herself. A witness did not need to be a rabbi.

This Lesson ought not be used when the preacher wants to talk about Christian Baptism. Certainly, Holy Baptism can be an item in almost any Christian sermon, but there are many New Testament texts that are better suited for featuring Holy Baptism. Matt. 3:13-17 is a text for talking about Jesus who lived and died as our representative, the ministry of Jesus and its meaning, the obedience of Jesus, Jesus as the true Israel,

Jesus as the Son of God, and Jesus as the Messiah. The baptism with which Jesus was baptized was not Christian Baptism but the baptism of John. When Paul came upon "disciples" who had participated in "John's baptism," he had them baptized "in the name of the Lord Jesus," cf. Acts 19:1-7.

1st Sunday after the Epiphany
The Baptism of Our Lord

Year B

Genesis 1:1-5

"Until now there has not been anyone in the church . . . who has explained everything in (this) chapter with adequate skill" is the way Martin Luther begins his comments on Gen. 1.

He continues: "The commentators with their sundry, different, and countless questions, have so confused everything in the chapter as to make it clear enough that God has reserved His exalted wisdom and the correct understanding of this chapter for Himself alone, although He has left with us this general knowledge that the world had a beginning and that it was created by God out of nothing. This general knowledge is clearly drawn from the text. As to particulars, however, there are differences of opinion about very many things, and countless questions are raised at one point or another."[4]

Some people think that the problems between the church and the natural sciences have come about because of modern scientific research and discoveries. The truth is that the problems are as old as the church or older. In the third century before Christ, Eratosthenes of Alexandria raised problems when he calculated the diameter of the earth. Problems again revived a century later when Aristarchus discovered the heliocentric system. The theory lay dormant for 1700 years because of the influence of Aristotle, an authority no one dared to question at that time, and his geocentric theory. The Jews of Alexandria also were confronted by problems in harmonizing the scriptural account of creation with the scientific views of the day after the Septuagint appeared. The church fathers, Ambrose, Augustine, Basil, Gregory of Nyssa, and Chrysostom, coped with the problems associated with the six days of creation. Luther said about the church of his day, "apart from the general knowledge that the world had its beginning from nothing there is hardly anything about which there is common agreement among all theologians."[5] Luther also said, "Hilary and Augustine, almost the two greatest lights of the church, hold that the world was created instantaneously and all at the same time, not successively in the course of six days."[6] Walter Brueggemann begins his comments about Genesis, "The first eleven chapters of Genesis are among the most important in Scripture. They are among the best known (in a stereotyped way). And they are frequently the most misunderstood."[7]

Gen. 1 is not a scientific statement. Had the story of creation been written in the scientific terminology of the twenty-first century, it would have been unintelligible to everyone until the present. Even then, it would have been understood only by those with scientific training. Furthermore, if it had been written in accordance with the scientific ideas of today, it would most certainly be outdated and inaccurate in a century's time.

Many Bible scholars today believe that in Gen. 1 we are dealing with a poem-like story which was designed to aid memory and to teach. The ancients learned almost everything by word of mouth. Scholars have noted a pattern including the following elements: an introduction, a command, the accomplishment of the command, an affirmation of goodness, and an identification of the day. This kind of repetition may not seem like poetry to us, but such parallelism is one of the chief characteristics of the poetry of the Hebrews. The psalms contain many illustrations of this. We think of poetry as involving a repetition of sound, but the ancient Hebrews thought of it as involving a repetition of ideas.

The Bible contains many brief references to creation. Examples are Mark 13:19; John 1:3; Col. 1:16-17; Neh. 9:6; Ps. 89:11; Is. 44:24; Heb. 11:3. Four major passages that relate to the manner in which the world came into being are Gen. 1:1-2:4; 2:4-25; Job 38-41 (especially 38:4, 9-11; and 40:15); and Ps. 104 (especially vs. 2-3, 5-10, 16, 19, 24).

Christian affirmations about creation do not involve statements about the origin of the universe but about the nature of the relationship between God and people. The doctrine of creation gives us a perspective on our lives and the world in which we live. It is an affirmation about the sovereignty of God and our absolute dependence on God as creatures. To say that Jahweh made the earth is to confess that it belongs to Him; He is its Lord. Christian affirmations about creation confess that God is still the Creator today. He did not create the machinery of the world like a clock, set it, wind it up, start it, and then let it run. God is still Lord of the universe and still intimately involved in its operation. In every moment, the universe is upheld by God's creative power.

Our creatureliness means that the world is endowed with a purpose and intelligibility which we may not always be able to discern. We do not give meaning to created life, but the Creator gives meaning to us and to all things that exist.

Our creaturehood also brings home the reality of our dependence. Our existence is not necessary nor self-sufficient but dependent on many factors over which we have no control. We are not immortal but transient, here for a while and gone tomorrow.

The doctrine of creation makes God responsible for the world, and consequently there is nothing in creation that is to be rejected as intrinsically evil. The Christian faith opposes the view that the world of matter is evil in contrast to the spiritual realm, or that finite existence as such is evil and must be escaped by spiritual exercises in which a person's spirit is united with the Infinite Spirit.

The religious questions asked with regard to the origin of

the universe are quite different from the scientific questions. Science addresses how questions. Religious questions ask who and why. They wonder about meaning and destiny.

Deism operates with the idea that God created the machinery of the world, got it started, and now is removed from it. When things go wrong, deists believe that God is busy somewhere else. There are many practical deists who claim membership in the church.

Christianity also rejects pantheism. In pantheism everything that is real is God. God and the universe are conceived of as being identical. Every tree, every flower, every rock, every star, every person is a part of God. To affirm the coeternity of God and matter leads to pantheism. God and matter are the same, two names for one thing. The practical pantheists are those who are seriously engaged in the worship of the green grass of the golf course on Sunday mornings. Against such thinking, Christianity asserts in Gen. 1 that God created all things through His sovereign Word. The world is the result of His free act. He transcends the universe. It does not contain Him. He is not identical with it.

A third interpretation of the relation of God to the world is dualism. Dualism explains the universe by asserting two eternal principles in conflict with each other. The two principles are called light and darkness, good and evil, mind and matter, soul and body. This view implies two absolute and coequal principles which are engaged in an eternal struggle. The key to the understanding of life is the understanding of the nature of this conflict. The practical dualists are those who believe that the human body and the world are basically evil. Against this view, Christianity asserts that God created the universe out of nothing. All that He made was good at the beginning. Even those powers which oppose God have their source in God's creative will. They are not independent of God but are dependent on His power. The one God is Creator and Lord of all that is.

The Christian has every right to enjoy the world of matter, to love the stars and admire the majesty of the universe, to love the flowers and trees that beautify our world. The material world is not to be ignored or depreciated. As God's creation, we may love it. On the other hand, the doctrine of creation makes a clear distinction between the creation and the Creator. We may enjoy the creation, but we must never worship it.

The story of creation can offer much comfort to the child of God. In the psalms, we often find the writer comforting himself with the thought that his help comes from the Lord who made heaven and earth. That God created everything is good news, because chaos is always bubbling just beneath the surface of our lives like some mysterious blood-born pathogen that infiltrates the system, hibernates for a time, and then explodes with repercussions throughout the immune system. The wife with three young children suddenly dies. The father of a family of five suddenly loses his well-paying job. A university student massacres 32 fellow students and professors and then shoots himself. In the midst of such chaos, God offers light.

The Bible has a single plot. It is the story of God's grace. We no longer live in the original creation but in a restored one whose continued existence is guaranteed by God's grace. Israel existed not within the first covenant but in a reestablished one guaranteed by God's grace. The passion of the Christ is the story of the reestablishment of our relationship with God, a story that relies on God's grace.

Eph. 1:9-10 says that God has a purpose for His creation. Creation is not a careless, casual, or accidental matter. Its purpose is decided; it is not to be decided in the future. The Creator did not intend the world to be chaotic, fragmented, or in conflict, cf. Is. 45:18-19. He intended it to be a unity. When His intention was frustrated by human rebellion, He devised a plan "to gather up all things in (Christ), things in heaven and things on earth." God's good pleasure was accomplished in Jesus' passion.

Bishop Usher of Ireland in 1654 used Biblical genealogies and calculated that creation took place on Oct. 26, 4004 B.C. Using similar calculations, Jehovah's Witnesses set the date at 4026 B.C. Orthodox Jews have come up with the date of 3761 B.C.

A scientific study reported to the American Physical Society in 1949 that the essential creation was all done in one hour.[8]

A. J. Cronin, the famous author, once told this story: "Some years ago in London, where I had in my spare time organized a working boys' club, I invited a distinguished zoologist to deliver an evening lecture to our members. His was a brilliant address, although to my concern rather different from what I had expected. Acting no doubt on the idea that youth should be 'told the truth,' my friend chose as his subject 'The Beginning of Our World.' In a frankly atheistic approach he described how, aeons and aeons ago, the pounding prehistoric seas upon the earth's primeval crust had generated by physico-chemical reaction a pulsating scum from which there had emerged - though he did not say how - the first primitive form of animation, the protoplasmic cell. It was strong meat for lads who had been brought up on a simpler diet. When he concluded there was polite applause. In the somewhat awkward pause that followed, a mild and very average youngster rose nervously to his feet.

"'Excuse me, sir.' He spoke with a slight stammer. 'You've explained how these b-big waves beat upon the shore; b-b-but how did all that water get there in the first place?'

"The naive question, so contrary to the scientific trend of the address, took everyone by surprise. There was a silence. The lecturer looked annoyed, hesitated, slowly turned red. Then, before he could answer, the whole club burst into a howl of laughter. The elaborate structure of logic offered by this test-tube realist had been crumpled by one word of challenge from a simple-minded boy."[9]

"God created the heavens and the earth." Martin Luther said that no one will ever fully understand these words.[10]

God is referred to as being masculine. It is not that the prophets could not imagine God as female. They were surrounded by peoples who so imagined their deities. They did not use such language, because they knew from the religions surrounding them that female language for the deity results in a basic distortion of the nature of God and His relation to His creation. In religious language that identifies God as a mother, so typical of pagan mythology, the world tends to be identified with the goddess and therefore is perceived as itself divine. When the deity is a mother, she gives birth to the world out of her womb so that nature and its processes and cycles are believed to be extensions of the divine. But at the very center of Biblical monotheism is the denial of a divinized nature.

People have sometimes asked, "What was God doing before the beginning of the world? Was He in a state of rest or what?" According to Luther, Augustine responded to that question by saying, "God was making hell ready for those who ask silly questions."

It is not helpful to seek points of agreement between the schematic presentation of Gen. 1 and the data of modern science. The text seems to make use of the primitive science of the day in which it was written. The important thing to notice is that it conveys a revelation of one transcendent God existing before the world which He created. This revelation is valid for all time.

The word "create" is used five times in Gen. 1, cf. vs. 1, 21, and 27. The word "make" is used five times, cf. vs. 7, 16, 25, 26, 31. But God's characteristic action is speaking; He does it fourteen times, cf. vs. 3, 5, 6, 8, 9, 10, 11, 14, 20, 22, 24, 26, 28, 29. God's relationship to creation is determined through divine speech. God called and continues to call the world into existence, cf. Rom. 4:17 and 2 Pet. 3:5. God created all things by His word, according to Ps. 33:6 and 9 and Heb. 11:3. The word of God is the sovereign power that shapes human lives and controls the course of history. God's word is active and dynamic. It is the means by which God accomplishes His will. It is not sound or even an idea.

The Old Testament uses the same designation for "event" as for "word." God's word is an act, an event, a sovereign command that effects a result. The creation story affirms that God's word brought all that exists into being. Luther said: "(God) does not speak grammatical words; He speaks true and existent realities. Accordingly, that which among us has the sound of a word is a reality with God. Thus sun, moon, heaven, earth, Peter, I, you, etc. - we are all words of God, in fact only one single syllable or letter by comparison with the entire creation. We, too, speak but only according to the rules of language; that is, we assign names to objects which have already been created. But the divine rule of language is different, namely, when He says: 'Sun, shine,' the sun is there at once and shines. Thus the words of God are realities, not bare words."[11]

The statement "God said" is an anthropomorphism, as is "God saw." The Gospel of John opens by affirming that God's word became flesh in the person of Jesus, cf. John 1:1-18.

The chief thought to keep in mind with regard to the meaning of the word bara (create), as used in Gen. 1, is not that of the exclusion of existing material from the act. In some instances, God creates by using what exists, cf. Gen. 1:9-10, 11-12, 20-21, 24-25; 2:19, 22. The verb "create" is used exclusively of God's activity, and it expresses the effortless divine creation that surpasses any human analogy.

"The heavens and the earth" includes the whole universe, all that exists.

"In the beginning," the earth had no form. It was without rivers and mountains, without any lines of demarcation. "In the beginning," the heavens were without any luminaries.

"A wind from God swept over the face of the waters." The Hebrew word for "spirit" and "wind" is the same word.

The Hebrew word for "swept over" really means "to hover." The imagery is associated with the actions of a bird hanging in the air over its young in the nest. The same word is used in Deut. 32:11. The imagery may suggest that of the Spirit of God as the life giving principle. In the Nicene Creed we confess, "I believe in the Holy Spirit, the Lord and Giver of Life."

The design of the world is not autonomous or accidental. It came into being at God's command. It came from the will of God. Creation is what it is because God commands it.

Isaiah uses God's creation of light as an example of His lordship, cf. Is. 45:7.

Dividing, separating, and gathering together are essential elements of the process of creation. God divides the light from the darkness. He divides the water from the water, that which is above from that which is below, cf. Gen. 1:6-7. He gathers together the waters and creates dry land, cf. Gen. 1:9-10. Thus the world came into being, became a world of contrasts, of polarities and antitheses, of opposites. This is a fundamental phenomenon. No matter in which direction scientific research proceeds or how far it goes, always at the end stands a polarity. The atom is an aggregate of opposite charges. What is life but a struggle with death, and knowledge but a distinguishing between that which is true and that which is false?

Naming, to the Hebrew, involved not merely assigning a label but especially expressing the very nature of the thing.

The word "day" is used in two senses in Gen. 1:5. First, it means the period of light. The second time, it means a calendar day. Some say that a calendar day cannot mean a period of 24 hours, because there was no sun or moon. But days four, five, and six are controlled by the sun, and the same word is used for them, cf. Gen. 1:19, 23, and 31.

The evening marks the first half of the full day. The Jews began a day in the evening with the setting of the sun, and it came to an end on the following evening, according to Lev. 23:32. We often think of a day as beginning with the rising of the sun. In this, a profoundly different philosophy is expressed. The Jewish way indicates that we begin something by resting for work. We look forward. In the other way of thinking, we rest up after work. We look backward.

Acts 19:1-7

Paul meets and resolves an instance of a problem in the early church stemming from the ministry of John the Baptist. After John the Baptist was beheaded, some of his followers joined themselves to Jesus and His followers. One was a man named Apollos. Luke introduces him in Acts 18:24-28. He was a Jew who was well educated in the Jewish scriptures which included the Old Testament as well probably as some other religious writings. Apollos was an eloquent speaker, and he taught for a period of time with great enthusiasm in Ephesus. When Paul arrived in Ephesus – Apollos at the time was in Corinth – he came into contact with twelve men who were "believers." Paul asked them if they had received the Holy Spirit. They had not heard that there is a Holy Spirit. Paul asked them about their baptism. They said that they were baptized "into John's baptism." Learning from Paul about Jesus' baptism, "they were baptized in the name of the Lord Jesus."

Luke reports these things not simply because they happened. He describes them, because they were important. The important thing is the problems the early followers of Jesus had with the followers of John the Baptist.

Luke tells us how the early church dealt with these important matters without taking anything away from Apollos who was a major church figure, especially in Corinth, cf. 1 Cor. 1:11-12 and 3:3-23. Apollos was involved in the factionalism that troubled the church in Corinth. The story of the twelve men deals with the issue of the relationship between the baptism of John and Christian Baptism. The twelve who were baptized "into John's baptism" were "baptized in the name of the Lord Jesus."

Jesus said of John, "among those born of women no one has arisen greater than John the Baptist," cf. Matt. 11:11. Luke deals with the issues involving John the Baptist in a delicate way. He does not want to take anything away from John. Those issues do not exist in the church today. Today's preachers do well not to try to highlight them.

Baptism in the name of Jesus is an important step in the formation of a Christian. Our sins are forgiven, cf. Acts 2:38. We receive the gift of the Spirit, cf. Acts 1:5; 2:4, 38.

The preacher will want to take up in a sermon on this Lesson something of the dramatic change that takes place in a person in Holy Baptism as Paul describes it in Rom. 6: "all of us who have been baptized into Christ Jesus were baptized into his death. . . . we have been buried with him by baptism into death, so that, just as Christ was raised from the dead by the glory of the Father, so we too might walk in newness of life.

"For if we have been united with him in a death like his, we will certainly be united with him in a resurrection like his. We know that our old self was crucified with him so that the body of sin might be destroyed, and we might no longer be enslaved to sin. For whoever has died is freed from sin. But if we have died with Christ, we believe that we will also live with him. We know that Christ, being raised from the dead, will never die again; death no longer has dominion over him. The death he died, he died to sin, once for all; but the life he lives, he lives to God. So you also must consider yourselves dead to sin and alive to God in Christ Jesus" (vs. 3-11).

Although the twelve men were baptized "into John's baptism," "they were baptized in the name of the Lord Jesus" after Paul's instruction. John's baptism was a water baptism, cf. Acts 1:5; Matt. 3:11; Luke 3:16. It was an initiatory rite for the gathering Messianic community. It was a baptism of repentance expressing sorrow for sin and the desire to be free from it, cf. Mark 1:4; Luke 3:3; Matt. 3:11; Acts 13:24. John taught that his baptism prepared the way for the One who was coming, cf. Matt. 3:11; Mark 1:8; Luke 3:16. The twelve men did not seem to know that John's word was fulfilled with the ministry of Jesus. Paul explained that there is more in the baptism of Jesus than what they received in the baptism of John. Luke does not say that Paul himself baptized the twelve, but undoubtedly it was done under his direction.

There is no agreement as to the significance of the phrase "in the name of Jesus." The preposition eis ("in") is used in the phrase "in the name of the Lord Jesus." In Acts 2:38 and 10:48, the preposition en is used rather than eis. Some say this makes the phrases different, others think the phrases are equivalent. "In the name of" (eis to onoma) was a common expression in a commercial context. Property was paid or transferred "into the name of" someone, i.e. into his account. The meaning may be that the person baptized "in the name of the Lord Jesus" bears public testimony that he belongs to Jesus.

The absence of the Holy Spirit in connection with John's baptism seems to be one of the major differences between the baptism of John and baptism "in the name of the Lord Jesus." "When Paul had laid his hands on (the twelve), the Holy Spirit came upon them." The basic idea of the laying on of hands is the transferring of something possessed by the person performing the ceremony. In Lev. 3 and 16:21-22, sin is transferred. In Mark 5:23, healing power is transferred. In 1 Tim. 4:14, a spiritual gift is conferred. In Acts 9:17-18, physical sight is restored, and the Holy Spirit is given.

There is little New Testament evidence that the laying on of hands is a regular feature of Baptism in the apostolic church, although it is the universal and continuous tradition of the church in post-New Testament times. The matter is referred to explicitly only in Acts 8:14-18 and 9:12 and 17. The reference to "laying on of hands" in Heb. 6:2 is obscure; it may have to do with Holy Baptism or with ordination. The event described in Acts 10:44-48 and 11:15 is unusual in a number of ways.

The New Testament knows no Christian Baptism that is baptism in water only and is preliminary to some other, following ceremony in which the Holy Spirit is given. Baptism is always Baptism in the Holy Spirit. Speaking in tongues and prophesying are regularly signs that the Holy Spirit has come.

The Baptism of the twelve men under Paul's direction probably ought not be considered rebaptism, although some think it is. If it is, it is the only case of rebaptism in the New Testament. Some of Jesus' disciples were disciples of John before they followed Jesus. Nothing is said of any of them receiving Christian Baptism. Nothing is said of Apollos receiving Christian Baptism.

Many questions arise from this Lesson. Was there any kind of formal church in Ephesus? Acts 18:26 says that Priscilla and Aquila heard Apollos speaking "in the synagogue," but there is no mention of a church. No community is mentioned in connection with the story of the twelve "disciples." Nothing is said about any contact between Priscilla and Aquila and the twelve "disciples." This does not mean there was none. But if Priscilla and Aquila know them, it is strange that they have not received Christian Baptism before they meet Paul.

Where did Paul meet the twelve? They could not have belonged to a congregation in Ephesus, because this would have brought them in contact with Priscilla and Aquila from whom they would have received more instruction. Paul must have made contact with them in some place other than either the synagogue or the Christian congregation.

Why does Luke call the twelve "disciples?" Paul recognizes them as "believers." On the one hand, they are accepted as "disciples." On the other hand, their baptism is not considered valid. At other places where Luke uses the word "disciple," he means disciples of Jesus, cf. Acts 18:27; but the twelve have not been baptized in the name of Jesus. They have "not even heard that there is a Holy Spirit." Many people in the church today probably could echo their reply.

Paul's question in v. 2 suggests that he has doubts about the Christian character of the twelve. Luke does not say how or why Paul comes to have these doubts. Paul may have expected them to know that John taught that his baptism of repentance prepared the way for the coming of the One who would baptize with the Holy Spirit, but they apparently did not know this. Paul may have directed his question at a weakness in the training or instruction of the disciples of John.

Paul's arrival in Ephesus was an historic moment for the church. It may be compared to Philip's proclamation of the Messiah to the city of Samaria in Acts 8:4-25 and to Peter offering forgiveness of sins through the name of Jesus to Cornelius and his household in Caesarea in Acts 10:1-11:18. Jerusalem was the first capital of Christianity, Antioch was the second, and Ephesus became the third.

Paul's stay in Ephesus probably lasted from 52 to 55. This is the longest voluntary stay by Paul recorded in Acts.

Paul's Ephesian ministry puzzles many Bible students. He usually went to the synagogue first, and he may have this time, too; but the description of his relationship with the synagogue begins in Acts 19:8.

Ephesus was the crossroads and the chief city of Asia Minor. It was a large seaport located at about the middle of the west coast of Asia Minor at the mouth of the river Cayster. The great natural harbor gradually filled up with silt, and today there remain only the ruins of the ancient city which are located four or five miles inland from the sea.

The city had a splendid location. There was a harbor on one side and facilities for transporting materials into the interior. The great trade route went through Ephesus all the way to the Euphrates. The population of the city in the second century before Christ was estimated to have been about 225,000, and it probably was not less at the time of Paul. It had an assembly whose main function was to maintain the worship of the protecting gods of the Roman commonwealth, primarily emperor worship.

The city developed around the great temple of Diana (Artemis), and this was a great source of its pride. The temple was 360 feet in width and 180 feet in length and was regarded as one of the seven wonders of the world. The ground occupied was about four times as large as that occupied by the Parthenon in Athens and about one and a half times that of the cathedral of Cologne. It created an extensive industry in souvenirs and amulets. In general, the city, like other large Greek cities, had its stadium, gymnasium, warm baths, market-place, and above all, a colossal theater accommodating 25,000 onlookers. It was often the center of public activities.

Like Corinth, another great seaport, Ephesus was noted for its dissolute life. In the time of Paul, there were many schools of rhetoric and philosophy. However, the city was more noted for its magic and witchcraft.

Jews came to the city in the third century before Christ. They received the rights of citizenship, and the Romans protected them and generously exempted them from the obligations required by emperor worship.

Mark 1:4-11

Mark 1:4-8 is a part of the Gospel for the 2nd Sunday in Advent – Year B. We went through those verses in the Advent book. Here vs. 9-11 will be discussed.

His baptism is the first incident in the life of Jesus recorded by Mark. Apostolic preaching generally began the story of Jesus' life with His baptism. When the 120 "believers" met between the ascension and Pentecost and a replacement was chosen for Judas to keep the number of apostles at twelve, the public ministry of Jesus was defined as "beginning from the baptism of John," cf. Acts 1:22. Peter began at this point when he told the story of Jesus in the house of Cornelius in Acts 10:37-42. Jesus began His ministry by submitting to the baptism of John.

He expressed in His baptism His solidarity with sinful humanity. John's baptism was for sinners. It was "a baptism of repentance for the forgiveness of sins." Jesus was baptized not because of His own sins. He was our representative, the representative of sinful humanity. In His baptism, He formally accepted the common guilt, burden, and fate of the human race.

Nothing is said about the mode used in Jesus' baptism. When v. 10 says that Jesus came up out of the water, this, too, says nothing about the mode. Obviously, water was not brought to Jesus; He went into the water. We suppose that immersion was the mode.

A close relationship is established between Jesus' baptism and the imparting of the Spirit in v. 10. The words "the heavens (were) torn apart" make it clear that God was at work. Only Jesus "saw the heavens torn apart and the Spirit descending," as Mark tells the story. The fourth evangelist, on the other hand, omits all details of the baptism of Jesus except the testimony of the Baptist to the descent of the Spirit. He saw the Spirit descend as a dove on Jesus, according to John 1:32.

We cannot reconstruct exactly what happened on that day in the Jordan River as if the event were recorded on film. The evangelists were not concerned with that kind of precision.

Peter says that Jesus was anointed with the Holy Spirit in Acts 10:38, but Peter does not say that this happened at Jesus' baptism.

The descent of the Spirit "like a dove" is the reason a dove is a symbol of the Holy Spirit. The Holy Spirit is represented by the figure of a dove also in Judaism.[12]

Many suggestions have been offered for the significance of the dove. Some have said that in fairy tales throughout the world the action of a bird designates or reveals the true king. A passage in the Mekilta, an early rabbinic commentary on Exodus, claims that the Holy Spirit rested on Israel at the crossing of the Red Sea and that Israel was then like a dove. The dove at Jesus' baptism has been understood as identifying Him as the true Israel.

The most probable explanation is that which connects the dove with Gen. 1:2, where the Spirit broods over creation.

NRSV has "a wind from God swept over the face of the waters," but the word for "wind" (pneuma) can be translated "Spirit" and traditionally is, cf. the footnote in the NRSV. The Hebrew verb rachaph ("swept") in Gen. 1:2 can be translated "to hover" and is used in Deut. 32:11 where it is translated "hovers." A passage in the Babylonian Talmud (Hagigah 15a) likens the hovering of God's Spirit at the creation to the hovering of a dove. Three elements connect the story of Jesus' baptism with Gen. 1:2: the Spirit of God, water, and the image of a bird which is implied. Mark may be saying that Jesus initiated the new creation at His baptism.

Vincent Taylor says that the importance of what the Voice states in v. 11 regarding the significance of the event cannot be exaggerated.[13] The Voice brings together two diverse ideas from the Old Testament that were viewed separately, the concepts of the Son of God and the suffering servant of Isaiah. The Voice assures Jesus that He (Jesus) is indeed God's Son and also His Servant in the sense of the servant songs of Isaiah. The words echo what is said in Is. 42:1 and Ps. 2:7. They are not an exact quotation. With regard to Is. 42:1, huios is used instead of pais and agapetos instead of eklectos. With regard to Ps. 2:7, the second half of the saying is omitted.

The use of huios instead of pais does not reduce the relationship between the words of the Voice and Is. 42:1-4.[14] Pais can mean both "servant" and "son." The words introduce the servant songs. The servant is further described in Is. 49:1-6; 50:4-11; and 52:13-53:12. If Jesus did not know it before, the Father makes it clear to Him at His baptism that He is the servant Isaiah wrote about.

Ps. 2 is a royal psalm. Its setting seems to be the coronation of the king or a reference to his enthronement.

When Jesus became the Son of God is not at issue in this story. At His baptism Jesus is declared to be the Son of God. Taylor says: "the words are best understood as an assurance, or confirmation, of this (filial) relationship, rather than a disclosure or revelation."[15]

As an echo of Ps. 2:7, the words of the Voice from heaven

declare Jesus to be Israel's anointed King, the Messiah. The kings of ancient Israel represented God to the people and the people to God. The Voice identifies Jesus as the King of the Jews. He fulfills that role in His crucifixion as "the inscription of the charge against him read, 'The King of the Jews,'" according to Mark 15:26. He wins the world for God not by domination and conquest but by humility and death. The temptation narrative which follows Jesus' baptism makes this very clear, cf. Mark 1:12-13.

The two backgrounds for the title "Son of God" give it considerable breadth of meaning. In the New Testament, Jesus is called Son of God by various people and with different meanings. The Hellenistic derivation emphasizes Jesus' deity and His miraculous powers. He is a person who is to be radically and uniquely distinguished from all other men. Oscar Cullmann says that the most important passages of the synoptic gospels in which Jesus is identified as the Son of God do not relate to this Hellenistic background, but those in the Gospel of John do.[16]

The title "son" (of God) is used as a designation for ancient Israel in the Old Testament, cf. Ex. 4:22; Jer. 31:9; Hos. 11:1. Jahweh is understood as Israel's father in Deut. 32:6 and 18. The title is used also for individuals who represent the people of God, such as the king, cf. Ps. 2:7 and 2 Sam. 7:14. Sonship is not a biological designation but signifies selection by God for a special task.

The behavior of a son in the Old Testament is especially characterized by obedience. The witness of the synoptic writers to Jesus as the Son of God emphasizes His obedience to the task given Him, especially that of suffering.

Just as the descent of the Spirit upon Jesus at His baptism occurs as the Voice from heaven speaks, so in Is. 42:1 God says of the servant in whom He delights, "I have put my spirit upon Him."

The words of the Voice offer insight into the destiny of Jesus as the Isaianic servant. They mark out the course of His life in a programmatic way. He will be "stricken for the transgression of my people . . . although he had done no violence, and there was no deceit in his mouth," according to 53:8. He will "make many righteous, and he shall bear their iniquities," according to 53:11. "The Lord has laid on him the iniquity of us all," according to 53:6. Because He bears the sins of the world as our representative, He must be baptized with John's "baptism of repentance for the forgiveness of sins," cf. Mark 1:4. Later He will bear them in the baptism of the cross, cf. Mark 10:38-39 and Luke 12:50. As the Baptist says of Him in John 1:29: "Here is the Lamb of God who takes away the sin of the world!" Jesus' baptism is a foreshadowing of His death. As the hour of His death draws closer, the profound significance of His baptism provides the imagery with which Jesus explains the climax of His life and ministry.

The title "the Beloved" has been used to relate Jesus' baptism to the Akedah, the story of the offering of Isaac in Gen. 22:1-13. Agapetos (beloved) is used for Isaac in Gen. 22:2 and 12. Both agapetos and monogenes are used in the LXX to translate the same Hebrew word meaning "only." The "beloved" son is the only son in Gen. 22:2, 12, and 16. Jesus is also the lamb God provided for the burnt offering in Gen. 22:8.

In Mark, the Voice from heaven addresses Jesus when He says, "You are my Son." He uses the second person singular. Matt. 3:17 uses the third person. There John and the others who have come to John to be baptized are addressed, cf. Matt. 3:5-6.

1st Sunday after the Epiphany
The Baptism of Our Lord

Year C

Isaiah 43:1-7

These words articulate as forcefully and compellingly as any in the Bible, Jahweh's defining and uncompromising love for Israel. Israel in exile is reminded of the Lord's commitment that persists through and is undisturbed by any circumstance.

Israel is in exile, because God gave them up to their enemies, cf. 42:24-25. They would not behave as the people of God. He punished them, and they "did not understand." They did not take the punishment to heart.

"But" is the word with which ch. 43 begins. It is another of the Bible's big buts. God is changing the way He will treat His people. The time when this will happen is "now."

The prophet speaks for God. "Thus says the Lord," he says. The "I" used throughout the oracle is Jahweh.

If the preacher establishes the point that the church is the new Israel, the fulfillment of ancient Israel, the promises of the oracle have application for the people of God today.

Jahweh identifies Himself as Israel's Creator. This establishes His ability and His authority to do what He says He will do. His overwhelming sovereignty, power, and control is dramatically affirmed as an introduction to His soteriological proclamation, "I have redeemed you."

The early religion of ancient Israel dealt mainly with salvation. The exodus dominated all religious thinking. The religions of the Canaanite nations among whom Israel lived, on the other hand, were saturated with creation myths. The Canaanites were very concerned with protection from nature. The doctrine of creation developed later in Israel. In this oracle, the two doctrines are combined.

The two affirmations, "he who created you" and "he who formed you," support the announcement of God's saving work. Jahweh's status as Creator is repeatedly affirmed throughout the oracle, cf. 43:21 and 44:2, 21, 24.

Much of Is. 43 is Hebrew poetry which is characterized not by the repetition of similar sounds, as some of our poetry is, but by the repetition of similar ideas using different words. "He who created you" and "he who formed you" are parallel ideas. They are an example of Hebrew poetry.

Interestingly, bara ("created") is the word used for the divine creative activity in Gen. 1:1-2:4. Jazar ("formed") is the characteristic word of the second creation story in Gen. 2:4-24 and is used for the creation of Adam in Gen. 2:7.

Passing "through the waters" and "through the rivers" is the same idea. Walking through fire and not being burned uses the same imagery as "the flame shall not consume you." Giving "people in return for you" and giving "nations in exchange for your life" are the same thing. The last phrases of v. 7 repeat words of v. 1.

The oracle is built around the doubling of the encouragement "Do not fear," cf. vs. 1 and 5. Jahweh gives His people these assurances to overcome the sense of abandonment they are experiencing in exile.

Israel need not fear, Jahweh says, "for I have redeemed you." Another reason is "I have called you by name." God redeemed and called us by name in Holy Baptism.

Israel need not fear, Jahweh says, because "you are mine." That relationship can be a present help in every danger, as v. 2

says. God claimed Israel as His own in the exodus, cf. Ex. 19:5-6. God claimed us in Holy Baptism.

In claiming His people, God gives them identity. We do not belong to ourselves. God gives us shape, purpose, and perspective. He does this through His law. He defines our behavior. He does not abandon or leave us shapeless. We do well not to think of the divine law in a juridical sense. Rather, through our obedience to it, we express who we are and to whom we belong. Depression and despair are signs that God's people reject His claim on them. When we accept God's claim on us, we can be filled with hope.

Our response to what God has done for us is called "faith." Faith is a relationship in which we yield ourselves to Him. We are at His disposal. A strong, clear prophetic indictment of ancient Israel was, "You did not listen," cf. Jer. 5:21; 7:13; 11:10; 13:11; 22:21; 25:4, 8; 29:19; 35:17; 36:25. Not to listen, always to be speaking, to want to retain the initiative, always to insist on defining ourselves is to reject God. It signals that we trust no one but ourselves. It reveals a rebellious, independent spirit.

To let God have His way with us is to respond obediently. We do justice and righteousness. Paul calls this "maturity . . . the measure of the full stature of Christ" in Eph. 4:13. It is not the maturity of self – self-actualization, self-discovery, self-assertion, or self-realization. Maturity is when we say, "Father," when we do our Father's will, when we care for His other children, and when we consider this freedom. Hoping, listening, and obedience are characteristics that are the opposite of the self-grounded person who finally is hopeless and not listening to God.

Four fearful experiences are described. They recall historical events in which Jahweh saved Israel. The experiences support Jahweh's encouragement that Israel need not fear. The experiences probably are to be understood metaphorically.

First Jahweh says, "When you pass through waters, I will be with you." This may refer to the exodus when Israel passed through the waters of the Red Sea. God was with them. Seeing this as a reference to the exodus is not farfetched, because Egypt is named in v. 3.

Water reminds Christians of Holy Baptism. In that sacrament, we were inducted into the protective and sure care of God. Many have drawn a relationship between Israel's passing through the waters of the Red Sea and Christian Baptism. Jesus gave His people a greater promise than the Lord gave ancient Israel when He said: "Remember, I am with you always, to the end of the age," cf. Matt. 28:20.

Second, Jahweh says, "When you pass . . . through the rivers, they shall not overwhelm you." Israel passed through the Jordan River in Joshua 1:1-2, 10-11; and 3. The reference could also be to negotiating the rivers of Palestine which can become torrents during the rainy season.

Third, Jahweh says, "When you walk through fire, you shall not be burned." The ancients had a practice called "the ordeal." Accused persons were tested by water and fire to determine their guilt or innocence. Fire is probably a reference to personal tribulation. God's people need not fear the fire, the testing experiences of life. They can be fearless, untroubled, generous, fearing nothing as they put their trust in God's grace. Some of God's people have overcome and even made light of punishments and death. Prayers for those who are enduring personal tribulation should be not only that the trouble may be removed but especially that the sufferers may remain steadfast, faithful, and fearless.

Fourth, Jahweh says, "When you walk through fire . . . the flame shall not consume you." The hopeless plight of the exiles will be followed by a future rich in promise and good experiences. They will be tested but not destroyed.

To certify these promises, Jahweh identifies Himself again in v. 3. He reminds Israel of three names they use for Him: "the Lord your God," "the Holy One of Israel," and "Savior."

To further support His promises, the Lord refers to two historical events which may be from the past or in the future. He says, "I give Egypt as your ransom." He describes Himself as bartering for the release of His people held in bondage. He trades citizens of other countries for their emancipation and rehabilitation. This sounds rather crass. This is the language of ransom. Jesus uses such imagery in Mark 10:45: He gave His life as a ransom for us. It is an extreme expression of how Jahweh treasures His people.

The second event is, "I give . . . Ethiopia and Seba in exchange for you." The two names correspond roughly to Upper Egypt and the Lower Sudan. Together with Egypt proper, they were all of Africa known to the Hebrews. The text is generally taken to mean that Jahweh will give the African territories to Cyrus in exchange for his liberation of the exiles. No part of Africa was included in the Babylonian Empire, so Egypt, Nubia, and Seba may be thought of as extras to what Persia will gain by the conquest of Babylon. In fact, it was not until Cambyses, Cyrus' successor, that the Persians invaded Egypt.

Jahweh gives strong expressions of His regard for Israel. He still holds on to them, and He will deliver them. He has forgiven them. Jahweh's gracious turning toward Israel is a surprising turn of events.

An historical event of even greater proportions supports the promises God has given His people today: Jesus' crucifixion.

Jahweh becomes emotional as He tells Israel how He feels about them. "You are precious in my sight." "You are . . . honored." "I love you."

So strong is Jahweh's feeling for Israel that He takes sides in their favor at the expense of others: "I give people in return for you, nations in exchange for your life." The nations could be Egypt, Ethiopia, and Seba who are mentioned in v. 3.

Jahweh describes the great homecoming He will stage for Israel. He promises the return of Jews who had been forcibly removed from their homeland and made subservient to other powers. He will bring Israel's children from the east, west, north, and south. Already in the sixth century BC, the Jews were widely scattered. Some had fled to Egypt, cf. Jer. 43:1-7, taking Jeremiah with them. Others had founded a colony further south in Egypt. A substantial number from the northern tribes had been deported to Assyria. Cyrus was God's agent who effected this homecoming in the sixth century. Jer. 31:1-22 and Ezek. 37 look for a reunion of all Israelites under a ruler of the house of David. The prophets thought not of two kingdoms but of one people of God. To certify this homecoming promise, Jahweh reminds Israel that He is their Creator.

Jesus uses the language of homecoming in Luke 13:29: "people will come from east and west, from north and south, and will eat in the kingdom of God." The Eucharist is the church's dramatic ingathering of God's beloved from all of God's creation. To discouraged, troubled, despondent, and suffering people, the great love of God in Jesus' passion cannot be proclaimed too often.

In v. 1, words frequently employed in the creation stories, Gen. 1 and Gen. 2, are used. In v. 7, those words are used again together with the word asah ("made") which is used in both stories, cf. Gen. 1:7, 16, 25-26; 2:2-3, 4, and 18.

Acts 8:14-17

The dispersion of the early Christians was not the result of missionary planning and zeal. The expansion of the church's work was not an historical development. The Christians scattered because they were persecuted and could no longer remain in Jerusalem, cf. Acts 8:1.

Luke emphasizes the direction of the Spirit of God in the spread of the church. The church's mission was not planned by the apostles and the community but by God alone. The disciples simply took the next step that opened up and was shown to them. Unrelated human action that had continuity produced a plan that came to be called salvation history. No intentionality is evident in the actions that result in the establishment of the church in Samaria.

On the other hand, the Jerusalem apostles seem to have exercised general supervision over the church's work of evangelizing for some time. Luke says "the apostles at Jerusalem . . . sent Peter and John to" Samaria when they heard of Philip's success there. Apostello is the verb used. It means to send as an official authoritative representative.

Peter and John were sent to investigate the unprecedented Baptism of non-Jews, cf. Acts 8:12-13. This is a major issue in the book of Acts, cf. especially the story of Peter and Cornelius in chs.

10-11. Peter and John were sent to Samaria also because the new converts had not received the Holy Spirit. The apostles prayed that the new Samaritan Christians might receive the Holy Spirit and laid their hands on them. Then "they received the Holy Spirit."

The book of Acts describes four occasions when the Holy Spirit came to people in a spectacular manner: to the disciples on Pentecost in 2:1-4, to the Samaritans in 8:17, to the gentiles in the house of Cornelius in 10:44-46, and to the disciples of John the Baptist at Ephesus in 19:6.

The stories raise some interesting points. One is that the early Christians knew when they had received the Holy Spirit. Luke says that although some of the Samaritans had been baptized, the Spirit had not come upon any of them. It is surprising that the early Christians knew that. Paul also found twelve "disciples" in Ephesus who had been baptized but had not received the Holy Spirit, cf. Acts 19:1-2. When Paul asked them, "Did you receive the Holy Spirit?" they replied, "No." They knew. This is interesting, because 21st century Christians generally would be at a loss to answer Paul's question. Pastors generally assure their people that they received the Spirit as infants at the time of their Baptism. But such assurances are often not convincing.

One thing seems clear. The church was astonished when the gift of the Spirit did not accompany Baptism and when this gift was not manifested in some way.

The question also arises about the relationship between Holy Baptism and the reception of the Holy Spirit. Peter's Pentecost sermon links the two in Acts 2:38. But the record in Acts is inconsistent and subject to differing interpretations. There is a time-lag between the Baptism of the Samaritan Christians and their reception of the Spirit. Luke does not explain. Paul's question directed to the "disciples" in Ephesus implies that the two might not always go together. In the story of Cornelius, "the Holy Spirit fell upon" Cornelius, his relatives, and his close friends before they were baptized, according to Acts 10:44. The laying on of hands is described in Acts 8:17 as the vehicle through which the people received the Holy Spirit. The same is true in Acts 19:5-6.

One of the most difficult tasks of the church is to work for reconciliation and to build bridges of fellowship between believers of different cultures or ethnic groups that have a long history of conflict between them. The bitter animosity between Jews and Samaritans is a classic example. Jesus' attitude toward Samaritans appears to have been positive in the stories that Luke gives us in Luke 9:51-56; 10:30-37; 17:11-19. Jesus charges the apostles in Acts 1:8 to be His witnesses "in Samaria" as well as to the ends of the earth. But the first Christians who were all Jews seem to have been pushed through persecution into evangelizing the Samaritans who lived just north of Jerusalem, between Jerusalem and Galilee, cf. Acts 8:1.

Christian congregations today generally have little contact with fellow Christians from other ethnic groups much less non-Christians. Some church growth leaders advocate evangelizing only within one's own cultural comfort zone. Acts 8 seems to speak an unsettling word to this issue.

A preacher would be faithful to this text by spending part of the sermon in telling the story of Jesus' passion and its meaning. Another part could encourage the hearers to reach out with this good news and to welcome all people into the fellowship of the Crucified. They need not wait for a plan and direction.

Luke 3:15-17, 21-22

The baptism of Jesus is reported in a subordinate clause. The main clauses are, "the heaven was opened . . . the Holy Spirit descended upon him . . . . And a voice came from heaven." These things happened after Jesus was baptized and while He was praying.

Jesus' baptism was the first of His many vicarious acts. Through it, He expressed solidarity with all humankind, with sinful people. When John called for repentance and baptism, Jesus stepped forward. He who was without sin became sin for us. His baptism was an act of humility. Maybe that's why it is reported in a subordinate clause.

Luke does not say that John baptized Jesus, but Mark does,

cf. Mark 1:9. For Luke, it seems not to be important who baptized Jesus.

Luke's gospel downplays the importance of John. Instead, it stresses John's sense of the overpowering greatness of Jesus, the One who is coming. A reason for this may be that John was a part of the old age, the age of the law and the prophets, cf. Luke 16:16. Another reason may be that the followers of John caused problems for the early church.

The more powerful One is coming, John says. He is coming soon. "His winnowing fork is in His hand." Luke 3:9 says the same thing: "Even now the ax is lying at the root of the trees." The judging process is about to begin.

When Luke reports that "all the people were baptized," this should not be pressed to include every single Jew. The Pharisees and the lawyers refused, according to Luke 7:30.

The reference to Jesus praying is peculiar to Luke. The third gospel has been called the gospel of prayer. When the other gospels do not mention the prayer life of Jesus, Luke often does. He tells us that Jesus withdrew to the wilderness to pray after cleansing a leper in 5:16, before choosing the twelve in 6:12, before Peter's confession in 9:18, before the transfiguration in 9:28, before He taught His disciples the Lord's Prayer in 11:1, and as He entered His passion in 22:41. He aligned His will with the will of His Father at His baptism, at the beginning of His public ministry, and later in the Garden of Gethsemane as He began His final steps along the downward way, cf. 22:42.

As Jesus was praying, the heaven was opened, the Spirit descended, and a voice from heaven spoke. These three events seem to be Luke's focus in the baptismal story. They testify that Jesus is the Messiah.

The prophet Isaiah called out for God to rend the heavens and come down with power to save His people in Is. 64:1-4. God did this in Jesus.

Luke seems to want us to understand that the Spirit descended from the opened heaven. Mysterious as this is, that God stood on the banks of the Jordan in the person of Jesus and that He was baptized with John's baptism of repentance mystifies even more.

The physical phenomenon of the heavens being opened is

not explained. But something visible seems to have happened. John 1:32 describes it. John testifies that he saw the Spirit "descend and remain" on Jesus.

The significance of this may be explained in Luke 4:18-19. It is Luke's introduction to the ministry of Jesus. The Spirit equipped and empowered Jesus for His work of preaching, teaching, and healing.

Luke says, "the Holy Spirit descended . . . in bodily form like a dove." For this reason, the dove is a symbol of the Holy Spirit. There is an emphasis on the Spirit of God in the third gospel. Some think the dove is a motif from folklore. In fairy tales throughout the world, a bird often reveals the true king. Luke's point is that the dove is a sign that God chose Jesus.

A passage in the Mekilta, an early rabbinic commentary on Exodus, claims that the Holy Spirit rested on Israel at the crossing of the Red Sea and that Israel was then like a dove. The point may be that the dove at Jesus' baptism identified Him as the true Israel, the true Son of God.

Most commentators see Gen. 1:2 as the background for the reference to the descent of the dove. "While the Spirit of God (NRSV footnote) swept over the face of the waters" can also be translated "the Spirit of God was hovering over the face of the waters." "Hovering" is a word that describes the movement of a bird. Three elements of the creation story appear in the story of Jesus' baptism, water, the Spirit, and the dove. The coming of Jesus was the beginning of the new creation, as John 1:1 says.

The presence of the Spirit indicates divine activity. The three Persons of the Trinity are differentiated in the account of Jesus' baptism. The Son is standing in the water. The Holy Spirit descends "in bodily form like a dove." The Voice from heaven attests that Jesus is His Son.

God's voice breaks into the human realm and affirms Jesus as His Son also in the transfiguration scene, cf. Luke 9:35. In this way, here at the beginning of His public ministry and there on the eve of His turning toward Jerusalem for the climax of His ministry, His suffering and death, Jesus is empowered and equipped for the momentous events that lie before Him.

The words, "You are my Son," come from Ps. 2:7. The

90

words are directed at Jesus. Luke gives no indication that the people heard the Voice or the words. Mark uses the words of Ps. 2:7, too, in Mark 1:11. Mark and Luke have the Voice speaking to Jesus. In Matt. 3:17, the Voice may speak to the people when He says, "This is my Son."

Ps. 2 is a royal psalm in which the Lord affirms the king as His son. The king of Israel represented the nation. The psalm was never understood as Messianic in pre-Christian times, but the repeated use of the words of v. 7 referring to Jesus by the New Testament writers makes it so.

A characteristic of a son in Old Testament times was obedience to his father. This comes out strangely in our culture. God chose Israel as His son in the exodus, cf. Ex. 4:22. But Israel disobeyed. Jesus shows Himself to be the obedient Son of God when He is tempted in Luke 4:1-13. He is the true Israel.

God does not sail paper airplanes from heaven to earth with little notes of encouragement for us. He sent His "Son" in the power of the Spirit to die on a cross to save us. This is how God acts on our behalf.

The words, "with you I am well pleased," are an allusion to Is. 42:1, although the words themselves cause a problem. Perhaps they represent a Greek translation other than the LXX.

Is. 42 is the first of the servant songs. The Voice from heaven identifies Jesus as the servant of the Lord in Isaiah. He is the suffering servant of Isaiah. The fourth servant song, Is. 52:13-53:12, says of the servant that "he was wounded for our transgressions, crushed for our iniquities; upon him was the punishment that made us whole, and by his bruises we are healed. . . . the Lord has laid on him the iniquity of us all."

The word "Beloved" (agapetos) is used in the LXX to translate the Hebrew word yahid which means "only." This word connects Luke's account of Jesus' baptism with the Akeda, the account of the sacrifice of Isaac, Abraham's son, in Gen. 22. The word is used in Gen. 22:2 and 12. Isaac's life was spared, but God did not spare His own Son. Jesus was also the ram offered up instead of Isaac. The characteristic of enhancement is often noticeable in events of fulfillment.

The work of John the Baptist was the beginning of a new

era, Acts 1:22 and 10:37 seem to indicate. John's preaching filled people "with expectation." They held John in high esteem. Everyone wondered "whether he might be the Messiah." The indirect question in v. 15 is structured in Greek to imply a negative answer. Me is used not ou which would imply a positive answer.

The title Messiah is derived from Palestinian Judaism. Its origin is found in the Old Testament use of mashiach, "anointed one," which is translated in the LXX as christos. Both the Hebrew and the Greek words mean "anointed." The title "anointed" was used of certain persons who were regarded as agents of Jahweh for the service or protection of His people, Israel. It was usually applied to the kings of Israel, e. g., Saul, David, and their successors. It is never used in the Old Testament of the savior who is to come, although some point to Dan. 9:25 as an example of such use; but the interpretation of the passage is disputed.

In the last pre-Christian centuries of Palestinian Judaism, there emerged a Messianic expectation, i. e., a belief in a future David. It is found in the writings of the Essenes. The Messiah would be God's agent for the restoration of Israel and the triumph of God's power and dominion.

The later sect of John's disciples believed him to be the Messiah. John's disciples believed he was the direct forerunner of God and required no Messiah to come after him. He himself prepared the way for God to establish His kingdom. The sect apparently merged with the Mandaeans, another group of Jewish origin. This religious organization still exists today. In their sacred writings, Jesus is an impostor, a false messiah, while John is the prophet in the absolute sense.

John does not leave the people in doubt as to his identity. He affirms their negative suspicions. He clearly distinguishes between himself and the One who is more powerful and who is coming. The coming One is so much more powerful than he that he is not worthy to do the most menial job of a slave for Him, namely, to untie the strap of His sandal.

Using the metaphor of wind and fire, John characterizes the work of Jesus. The metaphor describes the sorting out of human beings according their worth done by "the one who is more powerful."

A "threshing floor" consisted of level, hard, elevated ground. Oxen would walk over the grain spread out on the threshing floor separating the kernels from the hulls. A "winnowing fork" was used to throw the threshed grain up into the air so that the wind could separate the heavier kernels of wheat from the lighter chaff. The wind blew the chaff away, and the grain fell to the ground. The piles of chaff were burned, and the grain was gathered into the granary.

The threshing floor is the world or maybe only Israel. The wheat and the chaff stand for the people of the world, good and bad. The kernels of grain stand for the people who will be saved by Him who is to come. His discriminating activity is expressed by the words "to clear" and "to gather." He will take the faithful to heaven. Matt. 25:31-46 spells this out in more concrete terms, not only the gathering but also the burning.

The image of "unquenchable fire" may be derived from the ever-burning dumps and kilns in the Valley of Hinnom, south of Jerusalem.

John uses a parallel metaphor to describe Jesus' judgmental work in Luke 3:9: "every tree . . . that does not bear good fruit is cut down and thrown into the fire." John's descriptions of Jesus' ministry as being characterized by judgment do not agree well with the character of Jesus' ministry as presented to us in either Luke's gospel or the other three.

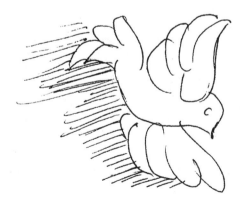

2nd Sunday after the Epiphany

Year A

Isaiah 49:1-7

This is the second of the four servant songs of Isaiah. The other three are Is. 42:1-9; 50:4-11; and 52:13-53:12.

Scholars struggle to figure out who the servant is. He seems to be an individual, but some see him as a representative person. He is called "Israel" in v. 3. On the other hand, he has a mission to Israel in v. 5. There is a debate as to whether the word "Israel" belongs in the text. It is a strange reference which many interpreters consider a later gloss. The word is deleted by some who take the servant to be an individual. But the scroll of Isaiah in the Dead Sea scrolls contains the word, and there is no metrical or textual reason for omitting it. Some resolve the conceptual problems by taking the word adverbially and translating, "my servant to Israel." Israel could have a mission to Israel in the same sense in which we say that the first mission of the church is to the church. The servant seems to fluctuate between an individual and a group. Perhaps this should not surprise us, because the identification of a group and of an individual as the representative of the group is quite common in Semitic thinking.

The most important characteristic of the servant of Isaiah is that he accomplishes the Lord's redemptive purpose for Israel and the world through suffering, cf. Is. 50:6. He takes the place of the many who are guilty, cf. 53:3-12. He is the suffering servant of God. He suffers innocently and without complaint. He lays down his life as a sin offering.

The servant was called by God before he was born. He was assigned a mission by the Lord. He was born "to bring Jacob back to (the Lord), and that Israel might be gathered to (the Lord)." He was assigned "to raise up the tribes of Jacob and to restore the survivors of Israel." The servant is to give hope to the Children of Israel who are in exile in Babylon.

The Lord equipped the servant for his mission. "(The Lord) made my mouth like a sharp sword." Hos. 6:5 describes the prophets as killing people by the words of their mouth. Heb. 4:12 in the New Testament says that "the word of God is . . . sharper than any two-edged sword, piercing until it divides soul from spirit, joints from marrow." The "sharp sword" of the servant is the word of a prophet. The word of the Lord is a formidable weapon. The servant is not a meek and mild person.

Another expression describing how the servant was equipped for his mission is "(the Lord) made me a polished arrow." An arrow consists of a shaft and a point. The servant is endowed with incisive speech, speech that goes straight to its mark.

The servant did not burst upon his world like a bright light. After calling and equipping him, the Lord "hid" him. The prophet says, "In the shadow of his hand (the Lord) hid me . . . in his quiver he hid me away." The servant does not immediately go public with his presence or his mission. Some have seen here intimations of what is called "the Messianic secret" in Mark's gospel.

The servant has not done well in carrying out his assignment. He uses a powerful triad of negatives to express frustration, discouragement, and exhaustion: "I have labored in vain, I have spent my strength for nothing and vanity." But he does not despair, and he remains committed to the Lord. His relationship to the Lord counters his futility and discouragement. He does not lose faith in the ultimate success of his mission.

The precise meaning of mishpat ("cause") in v. 4 is difficult to determine. The best commentary on it may be 1 Cor. 4:1-5 where Paul says that only the Lord judges him and that every person will receive commendation from God. The servant, too, will leave judgment of his service to the Lord. He is still resolved and prepared to do the work assigned, discouragement notwithstanding.

God renews the servant's mission. He says that the servant's mission is too small and enlarges its scope. The servant is to be a light not only to Israel but to the nations. Through him, the salvation of the Lord is to "reach to the end of the earth."

The word "salvation" means return from exile to "the tribes of Jacob," to "the survivors" of the exile. Israel is to be brought home. The homecoming is announced in Is. 40-48.

God's reign is intended for all, and to this task the servant is called. This had been Jahweh's intention from the beginning, cf. Is. 42:1-4 and Ex. 19:5-6. The servant is made the agent through whom the Lord will reach out beyond the borders of the tribes of Israel.

God chose Israel not to be an exclusive community. He drew them into a covenant relationship in order to serve as the instrument for extending His rule to the ends of the earth. Israel's mission was to bring all peoples, nations, and tongues into fellowship with God. This is the import of the blessing of Abraham in Gen. 12:3 and the point of the book of Jonah. God desires fellowship with all people.

V. 7 asserts the success of the servant's mission. The key words affirming this are "because of the Lord, who is faithful." This is the reason he succeeds.

The return from exile was accomplished following the victory of Cyrus. But the divine intention of gathering a people to Himself was not accomplished in the return to the promised land. The Children of Israel continued their disobedient ways. They even resisted and crucified the Lord when He came to them in the person of Jesus of Nazareth. But God's mission was fulfilled in Jesus' passion.

The identity of the servant is unfathomable. The expressions used to describe him are both precise and enigmatic. We cannot fully understand them. The servant cannot be identified with any historical personality of the prophet's day or earlier. The idea that the servant is Isaiah himself leaves too many questions open, especially in connection with the last song. The description of the servant makes him a prophet of the future. Jewish interpreters identify the servant as the community of Israel. The classical Christian interpretation finds the fulfillment of the servant in Jesus. Contemporary scholarship tries to identify an historical character.

The rabbis of ancient Israel had a problem in relating the idea of the servant with that of the Messiah. To them, suffering is incompatible with the mission of the Messiah.[17]

Jesus was informed by the Voice from heaven at His baptism that He was the servant of Isaiah, if He did not know it before, cf. Mark 1:11; Matt. 3:17; and Luke 3:22. The words, "with you I am well pleased," echo Is. 42:1. Jesus well understood that He was the suffering servant before His passion, cf. Luke 22:15, 22, and especially 37. He fulfilled the mission of the servant in His passion. God's will is that all people "might be gathered to Him." Jesus spoke of His passion in these terms in John 12:32.

It is unclear to whom the servant is speaking. He calls out to the "coastlands" who are identified as "peoples from far away." But the term "coastlands" is ambiguous. All peoples may be meant or the Jews who were scattered in the diaspora.

1 Corinthians 1:1-9

This study will cover only 1 Cor. 1:1-2, because vs. 3-9 are the Epistle Lesson for the 1st Sunday in Advent, Year B, and are discussed there.

The two parts of this study are easily identified. V. 1 is about Paul, the writer of this letter. V. 2 is about the people to whom he wrote, the church in Corinth. He is following the ancient epistolary form. The third part of that form, the greeting, is v. 3.

What v. 1 says about Paul is interesting from an historical point of view, but v. 2 offers more preaching material. It describes the church in Corinth. Many contemporary churches are like it in more than a few ways.

The word "church" (<u>ecclesia</u>) has three different meanings in 1 Corinthians. In v. 2, it is the local community of believers. In 10:32, it stands for the people of God in their entirety, the church catholic. The local church is a manifestation of the one church. In 11:18, it is the worshipping assembly of the community. The basic meaning is the same in all three cases.

The church is God's creation; it is "of God." It exists for Him and by His will. Its members "are sanctified in Christ." They are "called to be saints." They continually "call on the name of our Lord Jesus Christ." They are conscious that others in other places are doing the same; thus they do not think that they alone constitute the whole church or that they alone possess Christ.

This letter was intended not merely for the leadership but for all the members of the church. It reveals much about that group of people Paul calls "the church." He characterizes them in 1:26: "not many of you were wise by human standards, not many were powerful, not many were of noble birth." In 6:9-11, he says that some of them used to be "fornicators, idolaters, adulterers, male prostitutes, sodomites, thieves, the greedy, drunkards, revilers, robbers . . . ."

Paul says of the congregation at the time of his writing, "there are quarrels among you," cf. 1:11 and 11:18-19. The letter highlights some of their arguments, some of the reasons for their factions, and the differences between the various theological positions. For example, sexual immorality was being tolerated among them, according to 5:1-2. They were taking each other to court, according to 6:1. Some members lived by the conviction, "All things are lawful for me," according to 6:12. Some were eating food that had been sacrificed to idols, according to ch. 8. Some were getting drunk as they celebrated the Lord's Supper, according to 11:21.

Paul also calls these people "those who are sanctified in Christ Jesus, called to be saints . . . those who . . . call on the name of our Lord Jesus Christ." He says of them in 6:11, "you were washed, you were sanctified, you were justified in the name of the Lord Jesus Christ and in the Spirit of our God."

The first of the two lists above characterizing the congregation might cause some people to say, "I don't want to be a part of that group! I'm better than that!" But after reading the last paragraph, especially people who find themselves in the first two lists might well say, "I wish I could be like that, but it is too good to be true." The story of Jesus' passion needs to be given to them.

When Paul calls them "the church of God," this is a part of his protest against the party spirit that exists among them. He is saying that it is not the church of any individual or group of individuals but "of God."

The members of the church in Corinth "are sanctified in Christ Jesus." The tense of the Greek word for "sanctified" indicates a continuing state resulting from a past experience.

They are "in Christ Jesus," and the converse is also true, namely, that Christ Jesus lives in them, cf. Gal. 2:19-21. In Christ, they are justified, according to 2 Cor. 5:21.

The Person who called them to be saints is not the apostle but God or Christ, cf. 1 Cor. 1:9; Rom. 8:30; and 9:24-26.

The letters of Paul are rich in words and phrases that speak of Christians as a very special group. This was very important to the members of the church, because they were a minority in a hostile environment. Thereby, their status was affirmed. Their status identified them with Jesus and His crucifixion.

Some members of the church today don't want to be called saints. It puts too heavy a load on them to think of themselves as saints. On the other hand, some people who are sinners don't want to be called that. They think it puts them down too much. The saints don't have enough confidence in the gospel that lifts them up, and the sinners don't accept the law that condemns them.

Luther pointed out that as mother love is stronger than the filth on a child, so God's love for us is stronger than the sin that clings to us.[18] Although we are sinners, we do not fall from grace on account of our sin, even as we do not lose our relationship with our mother because of our filthiness.

100

The Christian religion differs from other religions in that Christians hope even in the midst of evil and sin. Islam helps people only to the extent that they are godly. All other religions encourage people to fear that they may not be good enough for God. We always lack what God wants of us, but Christ Jesus has made us complete through His cross.

The members of the church are "saints" because they were called by God not because of their holy works. We do not earn sainthood. Holiness is not a quality but a state in which we are placed by God.

The Archbishop Emeritus of the South African Anglican Church, Desmond Tutu, was asked, "What is your favorite Bible verse, and why?" He answered: "Romans 5:8. 'Whilst we were yet sinners, Christ died for us.' It sums up the Gospel wonderfully. We think we have to impress God so that God could love us. But he says, No, you are loved already, even at your worst."[19]

"Those who . . . call on the name of our Lord Jesus Christ" can also be translated "those . . . on whom the name of our Lord Jesus Christ has been called." Both statements are valid descriptions of Christians. The name of our Lord Jesus Christ was called over us in Holy Baptism. This means that we belong to Him. We call on the name of our Lord Jesus Christ in our prayers, our confessions, our doxologies, and all of the celebrations of the church. The use of the present tense, "call," emphasizes that this is an habitual activity that characterizes the life of Christians.

In linking the Corinthians "together with all those who in every place call on the name of our Lord Jesus Christ," Paul is emphasizing the unity or oneness of all Christians.

The Corinthian Christians were "called," as Paul says he was in v. 1. The parallelism is significant. He is calling on them to be "imitators" of him. He does this more explicitly in 4:16 and 11:1.

Paul says that he was "called . . . by the will of God." The word kletos ("called") is a verbal adjective with a passive meaning. In other words, Paul was called by God. It happened on the way to Damascus, according to Acts 9:1-19. God called

Paul "through a revelation of Jesus Christ." God had set him apart before he was born, and He revealed His Son to him on the way to Damascus.

"Paul (was) called to be an apostle of Christ Jesus." Apostolos ("apostle") seems to have been a commercial term. The person so designated had the same authority as the individual he represented. The closest term we have in English today may be "ambassador." A legal term that may be close is "power of attorney." An apostle had power of attorney. As Gal. 1:16 says, Paul was called to "proclaim (Christ Jesus) among the Gentiles."

Sosthenes was probably Paul's secretary who wrote this letter. The apostle did not write his letters in his own hand. While Sosthenes was the writer, he was not the author. Throughout the letter Paul uses the word "I." Sosthenes was a common name, and he may or may not be identified with the man mentioned by that name in Acts 18:17.

John 1:29-42

John the Baptist was sent to reveal Jesus to Israel. He declared Jesus to be "the Lamb of God who takes away the sin of the world." He testified that he "saw the (Holy) Spirit descending from heaven . . . and it remained on him." On the basis of that experience, he testified, "This is the Son of God."

The Baptist was a humble man. "The Lamb of God who takes away the sin of the world" was the "man who ranks ahead of me." He was "the one who baptizes with the Holy Spirit." "The two disciples heard him say this, and they followed Jesus." As John introduced Jesus to Israel, his disciples left him to follow Jesus.

The Baptist says twice, "I myself did not know him." The closest the synoptic gospels come to implying that John knew Jesus before Jesus was baptized is in Matt. 3:14. When John says to Jesus, "I need to be baptized by you," he implies that he knows who Jesus is. What the angel said to Jesus' mother Mary in Luke 1:36 makes the Baptist and Jesus relatives, but John lived apart from his family. He grew up in the desert of Judea, according to Luke 1:80. That may explain why he, although related, did not know Jesus.

The image of John the Baptist as self-effacing has led some commentators to suggest that the fourth gospel contains a polemic against a cult that venerated him exalting him to Messianic or near-Messianic status.

The Baptist's humble demeanor can serve as a model for the church and for the members of the church. Collectively and individually, we have been called to witness to Jesus as "the Lamb of God who takes away the sin of the world." John's example can help preachers and the church remember who they are and the essence of their mission which underlies – or should! - the many things in which they get involved. He provides a measure against which we can determine our priorities and evaluate our life. The decisive criterion is not the church's growth or lack of it, not her spiritual piety or her worldly secularity, but the fact and the character of our testimony in our life and our worship of Jesus.

In identifying Jesus as "the Lamb of God who takes away the sin of the world," the Baptist uses a definite article. With it, he points to a definite, well-known lamb who is expected to come in God's providential ordering of history. He does not explain that identification nor does the fourth evangelist. Apparently, the figure was well-known to the people who came to the Baptist and to the first readers of the gospel; an explanation was not necessary. But it leaves modern readers guessing.

One suggestion is that "the Lamb of God" is the lamb of Jewish apocalyptic literature. He appears in the context of the final judgment. He is a conquering lamb who destroys evil. In the New Testament, this figure appears in the Revelation, cf. chs. 6, 8, 14:10; 17:14; et al. This fits the ferocity of the Baptist's preaching and his expectations of the One to come, cf. Luke 3:9 and 17 and Matt. 3:10 and 12. But in John 1:29, the Greek word for lamb is amnos, while it is arnion in the Revelation. Nevertheless, some interchangeability of the words is evident in Jewish literature. However, the New Testament usually emphasizes the saving work of Jesus rather than His destruction of evildoers. The Baptist's understanding that the Messiah will baptize with fire and burn the chaff "with unquenchable fire" may explain his trouble believing Jesus was the Messiah, cf. Matt. 11:2-6. Jesus' meekness and lowliness did not match up to that expectation.

"The Lamb of God" may identify Jesus as the suffering servant of Is. 53:7. But there are problems with this, too. The lamb of Is. 53:7 is not a lamb of sacrifice but a lamb for shearing. There is no indication that the Baptist thought that the One who would come after him would suffer and die.

The eastern church fathers favored the interpretation that relates "the Lamb of God" image to the suffering servant, but the western fathers preferred the idea of Jesus as the paschal lamb. Passover symbolism is prevalent in the fourth gospel. The evangelist synchronizes the death of Jesus with the hour of the killing of the paschal lambs on the afternoon of Nisan 14 in 19:14. He also explains the reason Jesus' bones were not broken as He hung on the cross, while the bones of the two men crucified with Him were, by referring to the instructions regarding the Passover lamb in Ex. 12:46, cf. 19:36. The sacrificial nature of the paschal lamb had begun to infiltrate Jewish thinking by Jesus' time. Evidence for this is Paul's combination of the paschal lamb and sacrifice in 1 Cor. 5:7.

As "the Lamb of God," Jesus fulfilled all the Old Testament sacrificial lambs, the lambs offered at the evening and morning sacrifices, according to Ex. 29:38-46, and the lambs offered as a sin offering, according to Lev. 4:32-35.

Some think the Baptist has Gen. 22:8 in mind when he calls Jesus "the Lamb of God." Jewish thought increasingly came to hold that the covenant relationship with God was founded on Abraham's offering of Isaac. The Baptist is asserting that the new relationship of God and the human race in Christ came about as the result of the fulfillment of the promise of Gen. 22:8 that God would provide the lamb, and this lamb would make atonement for the sin of the world. Abraham's offering of his only son – his determination was complete - is a type of the offering of God's only Son. God's offering exceeded Abraham's in that the only Son of God died on a cross. That "the Lamb" is "of God" seems to mean that God supplied the Lamb.

The meaning of "the Lamb of God" is very complicated, but we may think of the Baptist saying, at the beginning of Jesus' public ministry, that Jesus was offering Himself as the sacrificial lamb provided by God for taking away the sin of the world. Jesus/Isaac symbolism has been discerned in John 3:16 and 19:17.

In the Old Testament, the figure of a lamb is used to symbolize many things, e.g. guilelessness in Jer. 11:19 and Is. 11:6, uncomplaining suffering in Is. 53:7, and many expiatory sacrifices. It is hardly possible to determine which idea is dominant in any particular New Testament passage. It is unwise to ask which of them is in the mind of the writer in any specific passage. They probably are all present consciously or subconsciously.

"The Lamb" came not for the pious or faithful; He "takes way the sin of the world." That He takes sin away does not mean that He takes it upon Himself. He removes it, as 1 John 3:5 also says, using the plural "sins."

The singular, "the sin," refers to the sinful human condition. Jesus took away the sin of the world in His crucifixion.

That Jesus is "a man who ranks ahead of" the Baptist may be a part of the polemic against the Baptist sectarians. They claimed superiority for John the Baptist over Jesus, because their master came first. His statement in v. 30 seems to indicate he taught that priority in time means priority in dignity. The point the evangelist makes is that Jesus was really prior to the Baptist. The fourth gospel even says that Jesus was before the world existed in 1:1-5; 8:58; and 17:5.

The Spirit's descent on Jesus marks Him as the promised Davidic king and Isaiah's servant of the Lord. The Baptist testifies, "I saw the Spirit descending from heaven like a dove, and it remained on (Jesus)." "The one who sent me . . . said to me, 'He on whom you see the Spirit descend and remain is the one who baptizes with the Holy Spirit.'" On the basis of his visual experience, the Baptist testifies concerning Jesus, "This is the Son of God." According to Is. 11:1-2, "the Spirit of the Lord" will rest on "a shoot" from the stump of Jesse. The "shoot" is the Davidic king and the "son" of God promised in 2 Sam. 7:14. God will put His Spirit on His servant, according to Is. 42:1.

The distribution of the Spirit after Jesus' death and resurrection is mentioned throughout the fourth gospel, cf. 3:5 and 34; 7:38-39; 14:16-17, 26; 15:26; 16:7-11, 13-14; and 20:22. The promise is fulfilled in Acts 1:4-5 and 2:1-4, 16-18, 33.

The Johannine account of how Jesus got His first disciples is quite different from the synoptic accounts in Mark 1:16-20; Matt. 4:18-22; and Luke 5:1-11. According to the fourth gospel, it took place at Bethany in Transjordan, cf. 1:28. The names of two of the men are the same in both accounts, cf. John 1:40. John, the son of Zebedee, may be the unnamed disciple of the Baptist who follows Jesus with Andrew in v. 37. According to the synoptics, Jesus called Peter, Andrew, James, and John on the shore of the Sea of Galilee where they were fishing.

The standard harmonization of these two accounts is that first what the fourth gospel says took place. But the men returned to their normal life as fishermen in the Sea of Galilee until Jesus called them to service as the synoptics say. There may be some basic truth in this reconstruction, but it goes considerably beyond the evidence of the gospels themselves. There is no indication in the synoptic accounts of the call at the Sea of Galilee that the men have seen Jesus before. Nevertheless, Acts 1:21-22 may give some support to the record of the fourth gospel. It indicates that the first disciples followed Jesus from the time of His baptism.

Andrew got his brother, Peter, to come and meet Jesus by telling him, "We have found the Messiah." The synoptics do not indicate that the disciples had attained such an insight of Jesus at the very beginning of His ministry. Mark goes halfway through his account of the story of Jesus before Peter confesses Jesus as the Messiah, cf. Mark 8:29. His confession is presented as a climax to that understanding of the disciples. The full understanding of Jesus by His disciples came only after His resurrection, cf. John 2:22; 12:16; 13:7.

Andrew may have told Peter that Jesus is the Messiah on the basis of his teacher's testimony that Jesus is the Lamb of God. This may mean that John the Baptist understood "the

Lamb of God" as a Messianic title. An incident that takes place while the Baptist is in prison may indicate that he did not fully understand Jesus' Messianic role, cf. Matt. 11:2-6. Nevertheless, Andrew and Peter follow Jesus, because they consider Him to be the Messiah.

When the text says that "the two disciples . . . followed Jesus," this probably means more than that they walked in the same direction behind Him. "To follow" is a technical term for discipleship, cf. John 1:43, 38, and 40; 8:12; 10:4 and 27; 12:26; 21:19 and 22; Mark 1:16-20; 2:14; Matt. 4:18-22; 19:21; and Luke 5:11.

"Jesus turned . . . saw . . . said . . . ." From the beginning, Jesus assumed the initiative in the gathering of His disciples. He made that point very clearly later in John 15:16

We might expect Jesus to be enthusiastic about His first two disciples, but He seems rather indifferent, almost suggesting that they are being nosey when they follow Him. He asks, "What are you looking for?" This is more than a question about their reason for walking behind Him. He asks why they want to follow Him.

The Hebrew word "rabbi" literally means "my great one." The evangelist's translation of "teacher" is not literal but is true to usage. This was the customary way of addressing scribes. Like a rabbi, Jesus equips Himself with a circle of followers.

Regarding the time, "about four o'clock in the afternoon," the Greek literally says "the tenth hour." Some argue that the fourth evangelist counts hours the Roman way, from midnight. That means it is about 10 AM. Others say that he reckons the night hours from 6 PM and the daylight hours from 6 AM. Then the time designation is 4 PM.

These details suggest that John, the apostle and evangelist, came to follow Jesus at this time. The event meant very much to him, and he talks about it. In other words, he was Andrew's colleague in following Jesus.

If the day is Friday and the time is 4 PM, the sabbath is about to begin. In that situation, the disciples have to stay with Jesus until Saturday evening when the sabbath will be over.

They cannot travel any distance once the sabbath begins. The sabbath begins on Friday evening at 6 o'clock.

Andrew is identified as "Simon Peter's brother," because Peter was better known in the church than Andrew at the time the fourth evangelist wrote his gospel. Peter was the early leader of the church.

The Greek word for "first" (proton) may be taken either as an adjective or an adverb. As an adjective, it means that Andrew found his own brother first and later found someone else. As an adverb, it means that the first thing Andrew did was to find his brother.

Some think the word "first" means that the other disciple, who may have been John, went to find his brother, too. That would mean that Andrew brought Peter to Jesus before John brought James. In that situation, the first disciples are the same men as those in the synoptics.

The first disciples of Jesus were former disciples of John the Baptist. Seemingly, the Baptist's disciples were a group set apart by his baptism. They had a discipline that differed from that of Jesus and His disciples, cf. Mark 2:18; Luke 7:33-34; 5:33; and 11:1. John 3:22-26 and 4:1 suggest a kind of rivalry between them and the disciples of Jesus later.

The Baptist is described as testifying to Jesus as "the Lamb of God" when "he watched Jesus walk by." This may suggest that Jesus was teaching already. Walking was the customary activity when teaching. There were no school buildings as we understand them.

"Simon" was the name given to one of the men at circumcision. He was "Simon, son of John." Jesus conferred on him the name "Peter,"

He is called "son of Jonah" in Matt. 16:17. It is not clear whether "Jonah" and "John" represent two Greek forms of the same Hebrew name or are two different names for Simon's father.

"Cephas" comes from the Aramaic kepha which means "rock." "Peter" comes from the Greek word for rock, petra. Both kepha and petra were common nouns and not names. This fact is important if we desire to judge rightly this title. "Rock" is a nickname. Maybe, we should call him "Rocky!"

The evangelist seems to say that the name "Peter" came from Jesus' insight into Simon, i.e., "Jesus . . . looked at him." Perhaps something in Peter's character caused Jesus to choose this nickname for him. Matthew gives a different explanation, cf. Matt. 16:16-18. The new name is related to Simon's key role in the church. Giving a person a new name was a significant event. Examples of this can be found in Gen. 17:5-9, 15; 32:28; Is. 62:2-4; and 65:15. See also Rev. 2:17 and 3:12.

The Lesson begins with the words "the next day." This phrase is used in vs. 29, 35, and 43. The evangelist distinguishes four consecutive days in the early ministry of Jesus. Day one is not a part of the Lesson. The second day is described in vs. 29-34. The third day is described in vs. 35-42. The fourth day is described in vs. 43-51. The evangelist seems to include 2:1-11 in the four days. He says the wedding in Cana took place "on the third day."

Luther feels that "the next day" in v. 29 refers to the day after Jesus' baptism.[20] Not the very next day, he says, because Jesus went up into the wilderness for 40 days, but one of the subsequent days.

The fourth gospel does not describe the baptism of Jesus, but the evangelist may be thinking of Jesus' baptism when he says: "John testified, 'I saw the Spirit descending from heaven like a dove, and it remained on him.'" The evidence that this is an oblique reference to Jesus' baptism is in Mark 1:10; Matt. 3:16; and Luke 3:22. The synoptists say that the Spirit descended from heaven like a dove and remained on Jesus at the time of His baptism. It is unlikely that such an event happened twice.

Why a dove should be the symbol of the Spirit is not totally clear. Perhaps the hovering of the Spirit over the primeval waters in Gen. 1:2 suggested the hovering of a bird. This observation appears in Jewish tradition.

John was sent "to baptize with water," but Jesus baptized "with the Holy Spirit." The law of Moses prescribed much water baptizing. As the result, the Jews bathed, washed, and baptized much.

There is a difference between the baptism of the Baptist and Christian baptism. John's baptism pointed people to Jesus, cf. Acts 19:4. Christian Baptism effects solidarity with Jesus in His death and resurrection, cf. Rom. 6:3-8.

2nd Sunday after the Epiphany

Year B

1 Samuel 3:1-20

One way this Lesson might be used to preach Christ crucified is this:

After God freed the Children of Israel from slavery in Egypt, He spoke to them from Mt. Sinai giving instructions as to how they should live, cf. Ex. 20. When God spoke, there was thunder and lightning, the sound of the trumpet, and the mountain smoked. The people became afraid and trembled. They said to Moses, "You speak to us, and we will listen; but do not let God speak to us, or we will die," cf. Ex. 20:19. So God spoke to Moses, and Moses relayed what God said to the people.

Shortly before Moses died, he told the people that God would continue this arrangement, cf. Deut. 18:15-20. Men called prophets would take his place. God would speak to them, and they would give the people the word from God. If the people did not heed what God said through the prophets, God would hold the people accountable. If the prophets gave the people a message in God's name which He had not given, the prophets would die.

Samuel was one of the greatest of the prophets. He was a

central character in the history of Israel. God called Samuel to be a prophet while he was learning the job of a priest under the mentoring of Eli. Samuel succeeded his teacher when Eli died at the age of 98. The story of how God called Samuel for his work is in 1 Sam. 3. His call may be compared with those of Isaiah in Is. 6:1-8, Jeremiah in Jer. 1:4-10, and Ezekiel in Ezek. 1:4-3:11. Jesus fulfilled the office of the prophet – and more! He not only spoke for God to the people of Israel, He was God Himself.

God warned Eli that his poor job performance would bring about the end of his family line, cf. 1 Sam. 2:27-36. Eli had two sons who served as priests under him. The sons blasphemed God as they carried out their duties, cf. 1 Sam. 2:12-17, 22-25, and Eli did not restrain them. God told Eli through Samuel that his sins were so great no sacrifice or offering could make up for them.

People made up for their sins against God in Old Testament days through animal sacrifices. That changed when Jesus came. Jesus was God's sacrifice for the sins of the world. That is to say, in some wonderful and mysterious way that we will never fully understand, because Jesus died on a cross, God has removed the charge that is against us for our sins.

The word naar ("boy") gives us no certain indication of the age of Samuel when he was called. The word is used for a person from the age of a newborn infant, cf. 4:21, to a man of forty, cf. 2 Chron. 13:7. It may carry the sense of inexperienced. Josephus says that Samuel was now about 12 years old.[21] At the age of twelve, Jews considered boys personally responsible for obedience to the law. Mary and Joseph took Jesus to the temple in Jerusalem at that age, cf. Luke 2:41-52.

The bad religious situation in Israel during the priesthood of Eli is indicated in 1 Sam. 3:1. The word translated "rare" is used of precious gems. The word of the Lord was prized like a precious gem, because it was so rare.

The second half of v. 7 seems to parallel the first half and to explain what is meant by the first half. "Samuel did not yet know the Lord" in the sense of receiving a personal revelation from Him.

When the Lord called to Samuel, the boy may have thought that Eli was having some problem because he was blind.

An indication of the time of day when God spoke to Samuel is given by the words, "the lamp of God had not yet gone out." The reference is probably to the seven-branched golden lampstand described in Ex. 25:31-40. The wording of v. 3 implies that the lamp would go out later. Ex. 27:20-21 and Lev. 24:1-3 seem to mean that the lamp is to burn continuously, although the Hebrew words translated "regularly" and "from evening to morning before the Lord" may not mean continuously. The lamp beside the ark was filled with enough oil to keep it lit during the night. The time must have been just before dawn.

"The ark of God" was a box described in Ex. 25:10-22. It was considered the throne of God. Where the ark was, there the Lord was believed to be.

The first job given Samuel as a prophet was to deliver a message of doom to the house of Eli. The tingling of ears was a common phrase for being struck with horror at the news of disaster or the prospect of it.

The words of Eli, "May God do so to you and more also," express a strong oath regarding punishment on Samuel if he conceals the message that came from God.

Eli was a good man who did great work for many years during a difficult and disorderly period in the history of Israel, but he was too weak to take appropriate action against his degenerate sons whom he ought to have expelled from the priesthood.

"Dan to Beersheba" is a conventional way to refer to the whole area of Israel, cf. 2 Sam. 24:15; 1 Kings 4:25; and 1 Chron. 21:2. Dan was the northernmost city of the tribal territories. It marked the northern border of the kingdom during the monarchy.

The eleventh century was a time of transition in Israel. Judges led the loosely organized tribes up to this point. After the turn of the century, kings ruled a more formally organized nation. Samuel was the last of the judges, and he anointed Israel's first two kings, Saul and David.

1 Corinthians 6:12-20

Sexual immorality was rampant in first century Corinth. Such behavior was condoned by public opinion in Greece and Rome, but Corinthians had a reputation for being immoral even according to the loose standards of paganism. Located on the Acrocorinth, the temple of Aphrodite sponsored one thousand priestesses who were professional prostitutes. They regarded fornication as consecration. The church often becomes infected with the evils of its environment as good apples in a barrel are influenced by rotten ones.

Paul says that unchastity is not acceptable for Christians, because our body is a temple of the Holy Spirit. Sexual immorality is outside the scope of Christian liberty. It is not one of those things that may or may not be all right depending on the circumstances.

Freedom is a major theme in Pauline theology. Paul says that we are free from sin, the law, and death in Rom. 6-8. The NRSV translation of the first verse of the Lesson, "All things are lawful for me," may cause a person to think that Paul's objections to the Corinthians' use of the slogan have to do with legalistic issues. But the Greek word for "law" is not in the Lesson. The tendency to think in terms of the law might be avoided if the translation "I am free to do anything" is used instead. Then it is clear that the issue Paul is dealing with has to do with Christian freedom.

Exestin means basically "it is free." It means that an action is not prevented by a higher norm or court, that it may be done and is not forbidden. In the papyri, it often means to have the right, authority, or permission to do or not to do something. It is used especially with regard to the prohibitions of the Jewish law in the later LXX writings. It is typical of Jewish legalism.[22] Paul could have appealed to the letter of the Apostolic Council which explicitly mentions fornication as something gentiles who are turning to God should abstain from, cf. Acts 15:20 and 29 and 21:25. But Paul does not mention that decision either. He uses other motivation.

Some think that the words of the slogan, "I am free to do

anything," may have been taken from Paul's own teaching about Christian freedom, because he uses it again in 10:23. If the words are not his, he does not reject them. But he does reject the way some members of the church in Corinth are using them to justify sexual immorality.

His first objection is that "not all things are beneficial" – either for ourselves or for other people. Paul is probably thinking especially of other people. We are not free to do what in itself is permissible when doing it adversely affects others. We overuse and, therefore, abuse our liberty when we hurt others. We should not be inconsiderate in the exercise of freedom. We should "take care that this liberty of (ours) does not somehow become a stumbling block to the weak," as Paul says in 1 Cor. 8:9. We should give up even what in principle is permissible, if enjoyment of it will cause another person to fall, he says in 1 Cor. 8:13. We are to "bear one another's burdens," as he says in Gal. 6:2.

We also need to give thought to the effect our actions will have on ourselves. We should not do what in itself is permissible when experience has proved that our doing it will adversely affect us. We abuse our liberty when the use of it weakens our character and lessens our self-control.

Paul's second objection to "I am free to do anything" is, "I will not be dominated by anything." There is a play on the Greek words. Exousiazein is used because of its close relationship to the word exestin through exousia (power).

An example of such domination might be drugs. We lose our liberty to do something when it makes us slaves to a habit, even if that habit involves permissible activity. When people consider sex something they need, it can dominate them.

Food seems a strange thing for Paul to bring up in a discussion of sex, but just as fornication was a feature of the heathen temples so was food, especially meat offered to idols. The heathen religions were much involved in sex and food. They were nature religions, and they focused on one of the concerns that dominated the lives of people in those days, the production of food stuffs. Fertility was a major theme, and it was celebrated through sexual immorality. Paul takes up the issue of food offered to idols in chs. 8-10 of this letter. Here, he touches on food only in passing.

The Greeks regarded sexual intercourse just as natural, necessary, and justifiable as eating and drinking. The modern sexual revolution may have gotten some of its inspiration from them. Paul destroys the parallelism. While many things – like food – are permissible and become wrong only if overindulged to an extent that is harmful to ourselves or to others, sexual immorality is simply not an acceptable use of the body. Rather, it is a gross abuse. It militates against the purpose for which we have a body.

Paul agrees that food is for the stomach, but he does not agree that fornication is for the body. The ideas are not parallel. "God will destroy" food and the stomach on the day we die, but the body is immortal. After we die, God will raise it just as He raised the Lord Jesus. The body is for the Lord. More than that, the Lord is for the body, because He dwelt in a body for our salvation and thus glorified it. God will transform and glorify our body, too, cf. Phil. 3:21.

The Greeks diminished the body in thinking that it belongs to the animal world, although they considered reason and the intellect divine. Paul says that the whole body is a member of Christ.

"I am free to do anything" can be appealed to for abandoning the Jewish restrictions on food but not for justifying sexual immorality. The body has an eternal purpose which is oneness with Christ. Fornication eliminates that destiny, cf. 1 Cor. 6:9-10. Fornicators will not inherit the kingdom of God.

The idea, "The body is meant . . . for the Lord, and the Lord for the body," is developed in connection with other matters in 1 Cor. 12 and Rom. 12:1-5.

V. 14 begins with the words "And God." The same combination can be found in v. 13. Paul is drawing a contrast. In the case of the stomach and food, their destiny is to become nothing. In the case of the body and the Lord, the destiny of both is resurrection.

That God raised Jesus is the traditional way to describe Jesus' resurrection, cf. 1 Cor. 15:15 and 20; 2 Cor. 4:14; and Gal. 1:1.

The change from egeiren to the compound verb exegerei may have little significance. In late Greek, compounds did not always have additional force. The compound may emphasize that our future rising is not less sure than Jesus' resurrection in the past. Paul's commentary on the resurrection of our body is in 1 Cor. 15.

Union with a harlot robs Christ of members that belong to Him. When Paul uses the Greek word translated "is united to" (kollao) in vs. 16 and 17, he is using the same verb that is used in the LXX of Gen. 2:24 and translated "clings to." Gen. 2:24 is involved in the institution of marriage. Kollao does not by itself mean copulation as is indicated in v. 17, but it gains this meaning through the context. The relationship that Paul implies between the marriage union and our union with Christ intensifies the significance of both. Paul calls this "a great mystery" in Eph. 5:31-32.

The basis for the statement "whoever is united to a prostitute becomes one body with her" is Gen. 2:24 which is quoted. Two people are united through sexual intercourse whether married or not. That union is the basis for Paul's encouragement, "Shun fornication!" The sanctity of the marriage relationship and of our relationship to Christ motivates such shunning. Taking away the members of Christ from Him and making them members of a prostitute is an appalling thought. We cannot be united with the Lord and with a harlot at the same time.

The phrase translated "Never!" in v. 15, me genoito, is an expression of strong dissent which is a characteristic of Paul. It expresses horror. He uses it ten times in Romans and twice in Galatians. Some translate, "God forbid!"

Paul distinguishes two kinds of sins, sins that a person commits "outside the body" and sins "against the body itself." The "outside" and "inside" phrases are related as opposites. They are difficult expressions, and commentators differ greatly as to their meaning. However, Paul's general intention seems plain: The body has an eternal destiny. Fornication takes the body away from the Lord and robs it of its glorious future. The presence of the Spirit is the guarantee of that future, cf. Rom. 8:9-11. To sin against one's own body is to defraud it of its part in Christ and to cut it off from its eternal destiny. Fornication does that.

In writing to the Corinthians, Paul appeals again and again to the principle that they are the temple of God and God's Spirit dwells in them, cf. 1 Cor. 3:16; 6:19; and 2 Cor. 6:16. In 1 Cor. 3:16, he speaks of the church as "God's temple." There he is talking about the community. In 1 Cor. 6:19, he says the same thing of each individual. The word Paul uses for "temple" (naos) is the word for the inner sanctuary itself. He emphasizes how great it is that we are temples of the Holy Spirit by saying that the indwelling of the Holy Spirit is a gift directly from God.

"I am free to do anything" is based on the idea that I am my own. Paul removes the base from that principle by saying, "You are not your own. For you were bought with a price."

Following Jesus involves surrendering the thought that we live to ourselves. When we try to achieve life on our own, we fall victim to the powers of sin and death and lose ourselves. Jesus freed us from those powers in His passion. The new self-understanding that comes with our relationship to Jesus is freedom. In this new freedom, we have life; and thereby we gain our selves. Freedom arises from the very fact that we no longer belong to ourselves. We no longer bear the care for ourselves, that is, for our own life. We yield ourselves entirely to the grace of God. We recognize ourselves to be the property of God and live for Him. Paul emphasizes this also in Rom. 14:7-9.

The reason we are not our own is that we "were bought with a price." This is not a passing thought for Paul. It is a kind of a slogan. The thought is, "You belong to God. Don't defile what belongs to God by immorality." Paul says, "we are the Lord's," in Rom. 14:8. That we belong to God is the reverse side of Paul's teaching on Christian freedom.

Paul applies to each individual Christian in 1 Cor. 6:19-20 what he says about the church in Acts 20:28. There he mentions the purchase price, namely the blood of Jesus. Although he does not say here who bought us, the numinous passive construction and the context make it clear that God is the buyer.

There does not seem to be any thought of manumission.

Manumission was a purchase to freedom. This is not ransom. No form of the word <u>lutron</u> is used. The metaphor is simply that of buying in the market place.

The Lesson concludes with an encouragement to do more than to remain free from unchastity. Paul says, "Glorify God in your body." Glorifying God is the Christian's response to the love God showed for us in Jesus' crucifixion. The encouragement is a general one and is not to be restricted to the avoidance of fornication.

The Greek <u>de</u> is an intensive particle. "Therefore" translates <u>oun</u> which is not in the Greek. A better translation might be "see to it that."

The Greek preposition <u>en</u> ("in") in v. 20 can be translated "with." Our physical body is a means of concrete service for God.

John 1:43-51

The patriarch Jacob had a dream in which Bethel was revealed as "the gate of heaven," cf. Gen. 28:12-17. "There was a ladder set up on the earth, the top of it reaching to heaven; and the angels of God were ascending and descending on it." In a similar way, Jesus tells Nathanael that He (Jesus) is the gate of heaven. He came from heaven to earth to die for us on a cross. Before Jesus' incarnation, heaven was closed. But God opened it to send His Son to the earth. He became "Jesus son of Joseph from Nazareth." Angels also came from heaven to announce the event to some shepherds, according to Luke 2:9-14. We celebrate the opening of heaven in a festival called Christmas.

"The heaven was opened, and the Holy Spirit descended" at the time of Jesus' baptism. The synoptic writers tell the story in Luke 3:21-22; Mark 1:9-11; and Matt. 3:13-17. The fourth evangelist does not, although he does record the testimony of John the Baptist to the descent of the Spirit on Jesus in John 1:32-33. He also reports that Jesus told Nathanael that he would see heaven opened. The synoptics do not tell the Nathanael story.

Since the time of Augustine, exegetes have seen a connection between Jesus' conversation with Nathanael and the story of Jacob's ladder. Some of the same words are used that are employed in the account of that event in the LXX. The dream was given to support Jacob when he felt that he was in danger from his brother who wanted to kill him. Jacob was journeying into a strange land fleeing from the wrath of Esau. God told Jacob that he would have the company of angels wherever he went and that He would bring Jacob back to the promised land, cf. Gen. 28:15.

Jesus was the fulfillment of Jacob's dream of a connection between heaven and earth. God Himself bridged the gap. Everything Jesus did, His miracles, His teachings, His actions, especially His passion and resurrection, were revelations of heaven.

It would be nice to say that Nathaniel saw all that Jesus did and heard all that He taught and that that is what Jesus meant when He said that Nathanael would see heaven opened. But we have no passage of scripture on which to base such a statement.

Besides this Lesson, the name Nathanael is used only in the list of the men who were by the Sea of Tiberias when Jesus showed Himself following His resurrection in John 21:2. The name Nathanael is known only to the fourth evangelist. It does not appear in any list of the twelve apostles.

Jewish tradition held that the stone at Bethel on which Jacob slept, called the stone of foundation, was located later in the Holy of Holies of the temple in Jerusalem. Jesus spoke not of that stone but of Himself as the place where the angels of God would be seen ascending and descending. The bridge between heaven and earth is no longer to be geographically located but is related to the person of Jesus Christ. He is "the gate of heaven."

Heaven is still open today where God's Word is preached and the sacraments administered. The angels ascend and descend serving the believers in Christ, the new Israel. They act as faithful servants, guardians, and messengers between God and His people.

Another connection with the patriarch Jacob in this Lesson is that Jesus calls Nathanael "truly an Israelite in whom there is no deceit." This is a huge compliment. Jesus says that Nathanael is worthy of the name Israel. Not only does Nathanael confirm who Jesus is, but Jesus confirms who Nathanael is.

Jacob was the first person to have the name Israel, cf. Gen. 32:28. God gave it to him as he was returning home. His deceitful dealings with his father Isaac and his twin brother Esau had made it necessary for him to leave, cf. Gen. 27:1-35. Jesus says that Nathanael, unlike Jacob, is not deceitful. It is not clear what Jesus saw in Nathanael to provoke this observation.

Nathanael is surprised by Jesus glowing evaluation. He asks Jesus where He got to know him. Jesus says, "I saw you under the fig tree before Philip called you." The evangelist underlines Jesus' ability to know things beyond normal human range.

Nathanael is impressed; he expresses great admiration for Jesus. His amazement seems to go beyond a reaction to the display of supernatural knowledge, but it is difficult to determine exactly what impresses Nathanael so. Jesus admonishes Nathanael to base his confidence in Him on more than his first impression.

Fig trees that spread their branches wide were quite common in Palestine. Rabbis often rested under them for prayer, meditation, or study. More may be involved in Jesus' remark about the fig tree than the physical location of Nathanael. The fig tree symbolized security and peace, cf. 1 Kings 4:25; Micah 4:4; and Zech. 3:10.

When Jesus tells Nathanael, "You will see greater things than these," the "greater things" probably are what Jesus refers to in the next verse, "you will see heaven opened and the angels of God ascending and descending upon the Son of Man." Some commentators think that Jesus is pointing forward to the miracle at Cana reported in John 2:1-11, but He may be pointing to more than that event.

Five titles used in this Lesson reveal who Jesus is. Philip wants Nathanael to meet "Jesus son of Joseph from Nazareth." The evangelist includes no mention of the virgin birth or of Bethlehem. Jesus is identified as a man like other men. Calling Him the "son of Joseph" was the normal way to distinguish Him from other men with the same name at Nazareth.

Philip tells Nathanael that Jesus is "him about whom Moses and also the prophets wrote." No specific prophecy is mentioned. Philip makes a general statement to the effect that Jesus is the fulfillment of the entire Old Testament. He may be referring to the prophet like Moses in Deut. 18:15-18. Philip's statement clues us in to how easily people in those days thought in terms of fulfillment and how much they were looking for the Messiah.

Nathanael expresses doubt with regard to Philip's revelation of Jesus. He is a better student of scripture and prophecy than Philip. He knows that the Messiah will be neither the son of Joseph nor a citizen of Nazareth. Micah 5:2 says that the Messiah will come from Bethlehem, the home of David. To think of Him as coming from Nazareth was offensive to Jews, cf. v. 46; 7:41-42 and 52.

Nathanael's scornful question, "Can anything good come out of Nazareth?" is filled with contempt. The implication is that any person of stature or learning has to come from Jerusalem or a city in Judea. Proximity to the temple was considered important for a religious figure.

Nathanael was from Cana, according to John 21:2. Raymond E. Brown[23] suggests that "The saying may be a local proverb reflecting jealousy between Nathanael's town of Cana and nearby Nazareth."

Nathanael is so impressed with Jesus when he meets Him that he immediately calls Him the Son of God and the King of Israel. It is difficult to suppose that Nathanael is thinking of all the implications of the title "Son of God." This may be another instance, like that recorded in Mark 15:39, in which the words of the speaker are given greater import than he himself intended. Luther thought that Nathanael may have intended merely to say that Jesus was a pious and saintly person, a man of God. But we ought not rule out the possibility that Nathanael meant "the Son of God" and "the King of Israel" as Messianic titles.

The Davidic king, the Messiah, was called God's "son" in 2 Sam. 7:14. Ps. 2:6-7 provides additional background for joining the titles "Son of God" and "King of Israel."

From the Hellenistic point of view, "Son of God" affirms

Jesus' deity and relates to His miraculous power. But the Hebrew background of the title must not be lost here. God calls the people of Israel His son in Ex. 4:22. "You are my son," the Lord says to the king in Ps. 2:7. The king represents the people. "Son of God" identifies Jesus as the true Israel. Ancient Israel was a disobedient people, but Jesus is the obedient Son of God. He was "obedient to the point of death – even death on a cross," according to Phil. 2:8. He fulfilled God's mission for ancient Israel in His passion.

King of Israel is the second Messianic title in this Lesson. The practice of anointing – to which the word Messiah points – was used especially on the kings of Israel. The title "Messiah" itself is never used in the Old Testament of the promised savior. It came into use during the intertestimental period.

When Nathanael hails Jesus as the Son of God and the King of Israel, Jesus responds by promising Nathanael and others a vision of the Son of Man. Son of Man was a way Jesus frequently referred to Himself. The Son of Man came from heaven in Dan. 7:13-14 as did the angels in Jacob's vision. He represented "the holy ones of the Most High (who) shall receive the kingdom and possess the kingdom forever – forever and ever" after "another" king arose following the ten kings and "shall wear out the holy ones of the Most High" who shall be "given into his power for a time, two times, and half a time." When judgment is given, however, "the holy ones of the Most High" will be given "the kingship and dominion and the greatness of the kingdom under the whole heaven . . . and all dominions shall serve and obey them," cf. Dan. 7:18-27. In other words, as Jesus says in Mark 8:31: "the Son of Man must undergo great suffering, and be rejected by the elders, the chief priests, and the scribes, and be killed, and after three days rise again." See also Mark 9:31 and 10:33-34. In referring to the figure of the Son of Man, Jesus foretells His exaltation following His passion. As the Representative of "the holy ones of the Most High," what happens to the Son of Man happens to "the holy ones" and visa versa.

Jesus met Philip and Nathanael when He left John the Baptist and decided to go to Galilee. The word "found" (heuriskei) is used three times in vs. 43 and 45 to explain how the three men met. Jesus found Philip who found Nathanael and explained to him that he had found Jesus. The force of the Greek verb can be understood as saying that Jesus just happened to run into Philip as He was going in the direction of Galilee. Similarly, Philip just happened to run into Nathanael although they probably knew each other before they followed Jesus.

The verb "follow" is a key word in the New Testament. It is used to express discipleship in John 1:37; 8:12; 10:4, 27; 12:26; 13:36-37; 21:19, 22.

What it means to follow Jesus is patterned in the calls of Andrew, Peter, Philip, and Nathanael in John 1:35-51. No incentive or reason is given Philip that he should follow Jesus. His response to Jesus' call is based entirely on the person of Jesus. That is of the essence of what it means to be a disciple of Jesus. Later, Jesus says to His disciples, "You did not choose me but I chose you," cf. John 15:16.

The fourth evangelist connects Philip, Andrew, and Simon Peter with the city of Bethsaida. Simon and Andrew have a "house" in Capernaum, according to Mark 1:29. The three men may have been born in Bethsaida, but the home of Simon and Andrew is Capernaum.

The evangelist thinks of Bethsaida as located in Galilee, cf. also 12:21. Actually, it was in Gaulanitis, across the border from Galilee. John's localization may reflect popular usage. Bethsaida was a fishing village on the Sea of Galilee whose location got lost. Early Christian pilgrims searched for it, but they could not find it. In modern times, three different sites north of the Sea of Galilee have been proposed. However, the ancient village of Jesus' time has been positively identified recently. It lies one and a half miles north of the current shore of the Sea of Galilee. The shoreline has drifted significantly southward over the past two millennia.[24]

Bethsaida is a significant city in the ministry of Jesus. It is mentioned more often in the New Testament than any city except Jerusalem and Capernaum. Jesus curses Bethsaida in Matt. 11:20-23, because the many miracles He performed there did not lead the people to repent.

"Very truly" is the way the NRSV translates the Greek words amen, amen that indicate firm resolve. Others use a single amen. Only Jesus ever doubles it. The phrase is reserved for Him.

Brown[25] says that v. 51 "has caused as much trouble for commentators as any other single verse in the Fourth Gospel." Some think that the saying of Jesus originally referred to His resurrection or the parousia and had another setting, but where it now stands it does not have that meaning. One reason scholars think the verse had another setting is that the word "you" in the Greek of v. 51 is a plural form. In the previous verse, the singular form of the Greek word "you" is used. In other words, Jesus is addressing Nathanael in v. 50 but a group of people in v. 51. On the other hand, the Greek word for "him" in v. 51 is a singular form and obviously refers to Nathanael.

2nd Sunday after the Epiphany

Year C

Isaiah 62:1-5

The people of Zion/Jerusalem were exploited and abused during the days of their exile in Babylon. Jahweh observed silently and permitted the oppression without intervening. In the midst of their suffering, the people implored Him to do something, but their appeal was ignored. Zion/Jerusalem was called "Forsaken" (Azubah) and "Desolate" (Shemamah).

The nations mocked Israel for the failure of their God, Jahweh, to help them, cf. Is. 36:1-37:4. In Ps. 22:1, the psalmist accuses Jahweh of abandonment. So also in Lam. 5:20. Jahweh acknowledges that He abandoned Israel and hid His face from them in Is. 54:7-8.

But a new time is coming, the prophet says in the opening verses of Is. 62. "Vindication" and "salvation" are the key words. They describe the future of Zion/Jerusalem. The city will be vindicated; she will be saved. The word "transformation" characterizes the future Isaiah describes for Jerusalem. Zion's situation will be completely different. The prophet uses a number of metaphors to communicate God's saving activity and the new relationship with God.

The return of Israel from exile in Babylon prefigures the salvation Jesus' effected in His passion. The Old Testament imagery can be used to proclaim the significance of Christ crucified.

The first three verses of Is. 62 are the final verses of the Old Testament Lesson for the First Sunday after Christmas Day, Isaiah 61:10-62:3. Material for those verses may be found there. Here we will take up vs. 4-5.

God promises to break His silence and to speak out. The prophet describes this change in 42:14. There may be a relationship between Is. 42 and Is. 62. The nations will no longer be able to mistreat Israel with impunity.

Her vindication is signaled by the new names the Lord will give her. If the name "Desolate" (Shemamah) is understood as divorce, it is the opposite of "Married" (Beulah). The imagery of divorce and widowhood is transposed into an agricultural term for a land barren and unproductive.

Another new name is "My Delight Is in Her" (Hephzibah). The imagery of marriage and delight is in dramatic contrast to the sense of abandonment, forlornness, grief, shame, and despair that characterized the exile.

The metaphor of Israel as the bride of Jahweh is common in the Old Testament, cf. Is. 49:18; 54:1, 4-8; Hos. 2:2, 19-20; Jer. 2:2; Ezek. 16:8. That the "builder" in v. 5 is "God" is supported by the poetic parallelism of the passage. John the Baptist used the marriage metaphor when speaking of Jesus and His ministry in John 3:29. Jesus used it to portray Himself as the Bridegroom of God's people in Matt. 9:15 and Mark 2:18-20. The church is the bride of Christ in 2 Cor. 11:2-4; Eph. 5:21-31; Rev. 19:7-9; 21:2 and 9. The Jewish people loved weddings, and Jesus used the imagery in His parables, cf. Matt. 22:1-14 and 25:1-13.

Jewish weddings were a time of great rejoicing. That's why the prophet uses marriage to highlight the joy that will be produced by the transformation of Israel's situation. Beyond the rejoicing of the people, the prophet describes the unrestrained delight God will experience in His saving activity. "As the bridegroom rejoices over the bride, so shall . . . God rejoice over you." The parallels to Jesus' parables in Luke 15 are clear.

1 Corinthians 12:1-11

Diversity to promote "the common good" is a part of the dynamic of the church. God gives the members of the church a variety of gifts for the welfare of all members.

Paul takes up the topic of spiritual gifts, because the Corinthians raised questions about the matter in a letter to him, cf. 1 Cor. 7:1, 25; 8:1; and 16:1. What the questions were is not clear. He refers to speaking in tongues frequently, and that suggests that this was one item. But tongues is at the bottom of Paul's list of spiritual gifts. Precedence among spiritual gifts may have been another issue. That topic is taken up in ch. 14.

Spiritual gifts are important and must not be overlooked. Paul tells the Corinthians, "I do not want you to be uninformed" about them. Other occurrences of that phrase or closely related phrases in 1 Cor. 10:1; Rom. 1:13; 11:25; 2 Cor. 1:8; and 1 Thess. 4:13 introduce important issues. The formula is always softened by the addition of the affectionate word "brothers." Sensitivity to gender issues causes NRSV to translate "brothers and sisters." Paul does not intend to be exclusive.

Old Testament prophets promised the Spirit as a gift from God to His people in the last days in Is. 32:15-18; Ezek. 37:5-14; and Joel 2:28-29. The Spirit's activity in the churches Paul founded showed that the last days had begun. The power of the Spirit was God's guarantee of His grace, cf. 2 Cor. 1:22; 5:5. Spiritual gifts are the first fruits of His love, cf. Rom. 8:23.

Paul reminds the Corinthian Christians that before Jesus happened to them they were "enticed and led astray" by pagan idols who could not speak. He is echoing some Old Testament prophets, cf. Jer. 10:5; Hab. 2:18; Ps. 115:5. The members of the church were led to Jesus by people to whom God had given the ability to speak.

However, Paul warned them that not everyone who spoke to them was moved by the Spirit of God. People moved by the Holy Spirit say, "Jesus is Lord!" Anyone who says, "Let Jesus be cursed!" is not speaking by the Spirit of God. Were such people troubling the church?

"Jesus is Lord" seems to have been the basic confession of

the Hellenistic church. It seems to have had an important place in worship. Two other occurrences of the confession are in Rom. 10:9 and Phil 2:11.

To a Jew, "Jesus is Lord" was a confession that Jesus is the God of the Old Testament, the God of the exodus. One of the central ideas of the Old Testament - if not the main one - is that God is Lord, cf. Deut. 6:4. One of the hedges Jews built around the Second Commandment to protect against violations was that whenever Jahweh - the name of God - occured in the scriptures, the name itself was not read but instead the word Adonai (Lord) was vocalized. The confession was especially important when it was affirmed in opposition to the pledge of allegiance to the Roman state, "Caesar is Lord." That involved worship of the emperor.

Speaking is not the only gift God gives the church. The Spirit of God energizes a variety of gifts, services, and activities. The one Spirit wills this variety. All spiritual gifts come from the same Spirit of God. Paul lists nine gifts, services, and activities: the utterance of wisdom, the utterance of knowledge, faith, gifts of healing, the working of miracles, prophecy, the discernment of spirits, various kinds of tongues, and the interpretation of tongues. That list is not exhaustive. Another list is in v. 28.

Gifts are given to all members of the church not just to a few. There are different jobs to do. In doing any of them, we serve the Lord. Someone has said that if two angels were sent to earth with different assignments and one was given the job of cleaning streets and the other the job of reigning as a king, both would be equally happy because they would be serving the same Lord and thus essentially performing the same work.

All spiritual gifts are given for the benefit of the Christian community. They are for practical use and ministry and not for display. They enable the members to serve each other as they make their redemptive journey together.

When people are baptized, they are made a part of the corporate life of the body of Christ. People who are strong are to bear the burdens of the weak. People who are weak can draw on the strength of those who are able to build them up.

The chastity of some strengthens others to resist the temptations of the flesh. The prayers of others plead for them.

The gifts of the Spirit are extraordinary abilities that seem inexplicable when considered in terms of merely human capabilities and powers. The Spirit is the miraculous power in what people do. To the Spirit are attributed not only miracles and extraordinary psychic phenomena but also brilliant insights and deeds of heroism and of moral power. They are regarded as gifts of the Spirit not because they are phenomena of the inner or ethical life but because they are miraculous.

The use of the Greek ho men . . . allo de ("to one . . . and to another") indicates that Paul intends that a distinction be seen between "the utterance of wisdom" (logos sophias) and "the utterance of knowledge" (logos gnoseos). But this is hard to do. Both stand for the gift of speaking instructively.

"Wisdom" is the more comprehensive term. By it, we know the true value of things through seeing what they really are. It is spiritual insight and comprehension, cf. Eph. 1:17-19. "The utterance of wisdom" is discourse that expounds the mysteries of God's counsels and makes known the means of salvation. By "knowledge," we have an intelligent grasp of the principles of the gospel. By "wisdom," we have a comprehensive survey of their relation to one another and to other things. In itself, "knowledge" may be the result of instruction guided by reason. "Knowledge" affects behavior. Our knowledge of God and what He has done and demands develops in the life of Christians as obedience and reflection. It determines the expression of the Christian faith in the life of believers. To the Corinthians, the difference between sophia ("wisdom") and gnosis ("knowledge") probably was clear, but our ignorance of the situation in Corinth makes distinguishing between the two words precarious.

The "the utterance of wisdom" is given by the instrument of (dia tou) the Spirit, while the "the utterance of knowledge" is given in accordance with (kata to) the Spirit. In the first prepositional phrase, the Spirit is the cause; in the second He is the norm or standard. Some consider the prepositions synonymous.

"Faith," as used in v. 9, is not the saving faith possessed by Christians. It is the wonder-working faith described in 13:2; Matt. 17:20; and 21:21. It is the ability to perform miracles. It manifests itself in works rather than words. It is the faith that produces martyrs. People with this gift draw their life so wholly from God and can live their life so wholly for God that they dare things others consider impossible.

That Paul separates "gifts of healing" and "the working of miracles" is significant. The two do not automatically go together. The apostles had "gifts of healing" according to Acts 4:30. It was widespread in apostolic times. The book of Acts records many examples. The plural, <u>himaton</u> ("healings"), suggests that different persons had a disease or group of diseases which they could cure. One person could not cure all sicknesses and all ailments.

"The working of miracles" might include more general works which are not healings, such as the exorcizing of demons.

"Prophecy" does not necessarily involve predicting the future, but it is preaching the Word of God with power. In 1 Cor. 14:3, Paul says of prophecy, "he who prophesies speaks to men for their upbuilding and encouragement and consolation." "Prophecy" is inspired speech through which God's plan of salvation for the world and the community and His will for the life of individual Christians are made known, cf. Eph. 3:5-6. This gift implies special insight into revealed truths and the ability to make them known to others. New Testament prophets made known to the community things hidden from former generations, cf. Eph. 3:5. The activity of two prophets is described in Acts 15:32. The nature of prophecy is made clear in ch. 14.

The prophets of the New Testament have much in common with those of the Old, but there are also differences between them. In the Old Testament, only a few people were called to be prophets. Some New Testament prophets are given prominence, but prophecy is not restricted to a few men and women in the primitive church. According to Acts 2:4 and 4:31, all believers are filled with the prophetic Spirit. According to Acts 2:16-18, it is a specific mark of the age of fulfillment that the Spirit not only lays hold of individuals but that all members of the Christian community without distinction are called to prophesy. Paul urges the Corinthians in general to strive after this gift, cf. 1 Cor. 14:1, 5, 12, 39.

Prophecy and speaking in tongues were the two gifts about which the Corinthians were especially excited. The problem regarding prophecy involved especially prophesying women, particularly in the assembly, cf. 14:33-36.

Paul rates prophecy very highly in 1 Cor. 14:1. "Prophets" are listed second directly after "apostles" in 1 Cor. 12:28. According to Eph. 2:20, the prophets with the apostles are the foundation of the church. Though Paul rates prophecy highly, it is inadequate and transitory, according to 1 Cor.13:8-10.

"The discernment of spirits" is the ability to discern whether extraordinary spiritual manifestations are from God or not. Such manifestations might be natural, or they might be from the devil. An intuitive discernment is implied without the application of tests.

Perhaps "the discernment of spirits" is closely related to prophecy, being the ability to distinguish between those who have a true prophetic gift from God and those who are seeking self-glory and who make a business of religion. The difficulty of discerning true prophets from false troubled God's people already in the days of Moses, cf. Deut. 18:21-22. Sometimes the church has set up external tests to make the distinction, but here Paul implies that such discrimination is a purely spiritual act. All rational attempts to unmask a false prophet break down, for there are no generally trustworthy criteria by which to tell if a person is a false prophet. Only the person who has the spirit or gift of discernment can judge if what is said comes from God. According to 1 Cor. 14:29, what prophets say is to be judged by other prophets.

"The discernment of spirits" was indispensable to the church at a time when false prophets abounded. John indicates that there were many in the early days of the church, cf. 1 John 4:1-3.

"Various kinds of tongues" is mentioned again in 1 Cor. 12:28. The question that follows in v. 30, "Do all speak in tongues," is probably a reference to the same phenomenon. The expression "speaking in tongues" occurs in Acts 2:4, 11; 10:46; 19:6; 1 Cor. 12:10, 30; 14:2, 4, 5, 6, 9, 13, 14, 18, 19, 22, 23, 26, 27, 39.

People speak in tongues in a trance. They exhibit the loss of conscious control and at the same time expend extraordinary energy in involuntary utterances, rapid or sudden bodily movements, profuse sweating, salivation, and so on. The organs of speech seem to be activated with enormous power by something beyond the person's will. A scientific explanation has been given. The person switches off cortical control and establishes a connection between his speech center and some subcortical structure.[26]

In some places in the New Testament, "speaking in tongues" seems to mean to speak in a human language one has not learned. In others, it means to speak in a nonhuman language or to make sounds which are not language at all in the sense of connected discourse, even if the sounds are in some way meaningful. When some Christians on the first Pentecost spoke "in other languages as the Spirit gave them ability," some foreigners present heard God being praised in their own native tongue, cf. Acts 2:4, 6-11. Acts 10:46 and 19:6 do not indicate whether the tongues were intelligible or anyone present understood what was being said. In 1 Cor. 14:2, Paul says that no one understands what is spoken in tongues, cf. also 14:9-11, 16, 23. People speak a language which is intelligible to themselves but not to the hearers, unless someone is present who has the gift of interpretation. The soul is experiencing something that ordinary language cannot express. The Spirit who produces the experience supplies also a language in which to express it. This ecstatic language is a blissful outlet for powerful emotions, but it is of no service to anyone but the speaker and those who have the gift of interpretation. From 1 Cor. 14:27-28, it seems clear that such ecstatic utterance is not uncontrollable.

Even when the one who speaks in a tongue is regarded as inspired, there remains the question of the source of inspiration. Those who claim the New Testament gift today are clearly implying that they regard what they are doing as a manifestation of the presence of the Holy Spirit. But this claim raises the same problems of discipline and order that it raised in the first and second centuries. Not all who claim contact with the Holy Spirit are able to convince all the other members of the Body of Christ that what they are doing is inspired by the Spirit of God. In 1 Thess. 5:19-22 and 1 John 4:1, Christians are instructed to weigh and test whatever is presented to them as a manifestation of the power of the Holy Spirit. What standard of judgment should be used? One does not want to misjudge and resist the Holy Spirit.

Christians today who claim the ability to speak in tongues imply that they know what is meant in 1 Cor. 12 by the expression "speaking in tongues." No sound recording was ever made of the early Christians so that it can be compared with what is called "speaking in tongues" today.

Chrysostom, who lived in the fourth century, confessed difficulty with the idea of speaking in tongues. He admitted that he had no first-hand acquaintance with the phenomenon. He believed it referred to the gift of speaking in unlearned human languages. He believed this gift was first given to the apostles and then quite generally to Corinthian believers.

Irenaeus (about 200 AD) also thought that speaking in tongues meant to speak in human languages one has not learned. He believed that Paul was able to speak many languages. He said that he had heard brethren in the church speak in all kinds of languages.

Montanus (160 AD) raised the issue in the church whether the Holy Spirit spoke through a person who was in no sense in command of himself when the Spirit spoke. Montanus might be considered a precursor of modern day charismatics. The faithful in Asia met many times and in many places before finally coming to the decision that the spirit speaking in Montanus was not the Holy Spirit of Christ.

Some[27] think on the basis of 1 Cor. 13:1 that tongues was regarded as the language of heaven.

Paul prized the gift of tongues both for himself and for the church, cf. 1 Cor. 14:5, 18, 39. But he protested an exaggerated estimate and an irresponsible, self-centered use of it. Some

Corinthians apparently prided themselves on the possession of the gift. They made a great display of it. They did not wait for one another, but each was eager to speak. The result was that several were speaking at the same time. Paul sets up controls to prevent such disorder in 1 Cor. 14:27.

He does not reject the positive evaluation the Corinthians give to speaking in tongues, but he does try to reduce the importance of it in comparison with other gifts. He ranks the people who have the gift last in the list of gifted people in vs. 8-10 and again in vs. 27-28. He may have been motivated to place this gift last by the importance that the Christians in Corinth gave to it and the problems this caused.

The gift of interpreting ecstatic utterances might be possessed by the person who utters them, cf. 14:5 and 13.

Paul rounds off this first section on spiritual gifts in 12:11 by repeating what he says in vs. 6-7. Every believer has a gift, his/her own particular one. In the economy of God's kingdom, we do not all have the same gift, nor do we all have the same amount of gifts. There are many tasks that must be done if the work of God's kingdom is to be supported and furthered. Some are less prominent than others but nonetheless important. The Spirit gives not according to the merit or the wishes of people, but according to His own will.

One of the things that makes this Lesson difficult is our lack of information about the conditions Paul is addressing. Already in Chrysostom's time, this was true. Chrysostom remarks that the whole passage is very obscure because of defective information respecting facts that took place then but take place no longer.

John 2:1-11

Wine requires aging, and "good wine" requires considerable aging. But in no time, Jesus made wine out of water. "Good wine," the chief steward judged it. When the change took place or how long it took, John does not say. But he does say that it was better wine than the guests had been drinking!

It happened at a wedding. That raises the issue of Jesus

and marriage. Jesus did not marry. Does this mean that He does not approve of marriage or that life outside of marriage is better? The Lesson does not support such a conclusion. Jesus signaled His approval of the wedding not only by attending and participating in it but also by contributing to the celebration.

This text has all the elements of a good short story: problem, conflict, suspense, surprise, and happy ending. It also highlights important elements of Jesus' ministry.

This Lesson is used in various ways. Roman Catholics base their Cana conferences on it, that is, groups meet for marriage counseling. Some use the story to make the point that Jesus was not a hermit or an ascetic like John the Baptist and the Jewish sect of the Essenes. He approved of marriage, participated in a wedding party, and even provided lots of "good wine" for the celebration. Roman Catholics emphasize marriage, Protestants note the fun, and everyone is amazed at the power of Jesus. But John uses this story for a very different purpose which is very important. He says that through it Jesus "revealed his glory" and strengthened the faith of the disciples.

John's gospel describes only seven miracles of Jesus. The synoptics tell of many more. John chose the seven "so that you may come to believe that Jesus is the Messiah, the Son of God, and that through believing you may have life in his name," according to John 20:30-31.

Three of the seven are found also in the synoptics, namely, the curing of the royal official's son in 4:46-54, the multiplication of loaves in 6:1-14, and walking on the sea in 6:16-21. Another three are of the same type as those found in the synoptics, namely, making a paralytic walk in 5:2-14, making a man who had been born blind see in ch. 9, and raising Lazarus from the dead in ch. 11. But the changing of water into wine has no parallel in the synoptics.

John says that the miracle at Cana was "the first of (Jesus') signs." It probably was not His first miracle. The chronology of Jesus' ministry is not easy to work out, but the synoptics seem to say that Jesus performed miracles before He attended the wedding at Cana.

John's use of the word "signs" is different from the way the synoptics use that word. In Luke 11:16-20, 29-30; 23:8; Matt. 12:38-39; 16:1-4; Mark 8:11-12, the adversaries of Jesus seek from Him a sign. He refuses. John uses the word "sign" for an act of Jesus which reveals that He is the Messiah, the Son of God, and that He has come to give life, cf. John 20:30-31; 2:23; 12:37. They reveal Jesus' saving work.

The story of the exodus in the Old Testament is the background for the Johannine use of the word "sign." God multiplied signs through Moses, according to Ex. 10:1; Num. 14:11, 22; and Deut. 7:19. John 20:30-31 ends the fourth gospel with a note about the signs Jesus, the true Israel, performed "in the presence of his disciples," the representatives of the new Israel, just as Deut. 34:11-12 ends the five Books of Moses with a note about "the signs and wonders" Moses performed "in the sight of all Israel," the old Israel. Num. 14:22 connects God's glory to the signs of the exodus; John 2:11 says that the miracle at Cana revealed Jesus' glory.

In the LXX, semeion ("sign") is the translation of the Hebrew oth. In the Old Testament, some oths prove that the one doing them was sent from God, cf. Ex. 3:12; 4:1-9; Judg. 6:17; 1 Sam. 10:1-10. The Old Testament designates as oths such non-miraculous but meaningful acts as Isaiah's specially named son in Is. 8:18 and the prophet's walking around for three years naked and barefoot in Is. 20:3. Isaiah's strange behavior graphically portrayed God's coming judgment or God's intervention in the life of Israel. Another example of strange behavior serving as a sign is in Ezek. 12:1-16. When Ezekiel took a stone and drew on it a picture of the siege of Jerusalem, that was a sign, according to Ezek. 4:1-5:17. An oth is a proclamation of the glory of God in Is. 66:19. It is a symbolic anticipation or revelation of a greater reality.

In John, signs are special demonstrations of the character and power of God and partial revelations of His salvation. The "six stone water jars" were not common, ordinary kitchen utensils. They were "for the Jewish rites of purification." Stone was used because it did not contract uncleanness. Jewish ordinances were very detailed regarding the washing of hands before and after eating and also the washing of the vessels used for the meal. Purification was one of the main activities in rabbinic piety. Mark 7:3-4 lists some uses for the water in the pots. The water in the six stone jars represented burdensome Jewish legalism. Jesus changed it into wine. He changed harsh Jewish legalism into joy stimulating gospel by His life and death. Wine produces gladness says Ps. 104:15.

Both the first and the last signs John reports are extreme cases. The raising of Lazarus from the dead in ch. 11 shows that there is no limit to Jesus' power to save even as the miracle at Cana shows that there is no limit to His will to give and help. The slightest need - the embarrassment of a host and the dampening of festal enjoyment – is enough to evoke His compassionate aid.

The Greek word used for "first" in John 2:11 is <u>arche</u>. That's the word used in 1:1 which is translated "the beginning." <u>Arche</u> may mean more than the first of a series. The changing of water into wine is not merely the first sign but a primary sign, because it is representative of the creative and transforming work of Jesus as a whole. Through that miracle, as well as through other signs, Jesus revealed His glory.

"Glory" is another important word and concept in the fourth gospel. It contains the full content of the Old Testament word <u>cabod</u>. The characteristic and dominant sense in the LXX and the New Testament is that of divine and heavenly power and authority that manifests the essence of God and His work. <u>Doxa</u> - the Greek word for "glory" - denotes the visible manifestation accompanying a theophany which is often bright light. In relation to people, the word "glory" denotes that which makes them impressive and demands recognition. In relation to God, it implies that which makes God impressive to people. God is intrinsically invisible. But when He reveals Himself, that manifestation makes an impression on people.

The wedding at Cana is not simply a story of Jesus' power over water. It is a manifestation and declaration of the kind of person He is. He is a Person who, when people run out of wine at a wedding celebration, provides them with "good wine" to supply their need. This gives a different picture of God than that held by many. It presents Jesus as a Person who fills people's needs. He brings joy and happiness. This is consistent with the portrait of Jesus given by all the evangelists. Jesus manifests His glory first by giving. His gifts are lavish in both quantity and quality.

This good news is certainly helpful to couples who are being married, and it may be a reason to use this Lesson at a marriage ceremony. The connection with a wedding is obvious, but the revelation of God's character is not. It takes a preacher to proclaim this good news and to tell people that Jesus came to save them by dying for them.

This is good news to newly married couples who are making plans to establish a home in a world where cities are in crisis, schools are confused, the national system of home mortgages is tottering, fears of recession abound, a burgeoning national debt threatens our future, preemptive military doctrines destabilize large regions of the world and erode international morale and morality, new technologies result in alienation and dehumanization, consumer values tend to anesthetize people, global economic policies breed resentment, rage, and despair, non-replaceable natural and cultural resources are being rapidly depleted, many communities have limited access to basic health care and safe water, indifference to savage acts of violence including torture and the systematic killing of civilians is growing, athletes appear to be as corrupt and immoral as politicians, and children are exploited as sexual toys. Not long ago, we thought that immoral acts between consenting adults of the opposite sex revealed them to be terrible people and that people who do those things are unspeakably irresponsible. No longer! It has become widely acceptable behavior.

Weddings are a frequent topic in the Bible and are used in conveying important messages about the relationship between God and His people. In the Old Testament, God's covenant with His people is described as a wedding in Jer. 2:1; Is. 54:4-8; 62:4-5; and Ezek. 16:8-43. Israel is depicted as the devoted, faithful bride of her Lord and Redeemer. Hosea depicts Jahweh as the husband who has repudiated His relationship with His wife, Israel, in Hos. 2:2. He will again betroth her to Himself when she abandons her faithless practices, according to vs. 19-20.

Jesus describes His role in the world in terms of a wedding in Mark 2:19. He Himself is the Bridegroom and His followers are the bride. John the Baptist uses the same imagery in John 3:29. Many of Jesus' parables of the kingdom involve the marriage situation, e.g. the Wedding Feast in Matt. 22:1-14, the Ten Virgins in Matt. 25:1-13, etc.

The image recurs in the writings of the apostles, cf. 2 Cor. 11:2 and Eph. 5:23-32. In the Johannine literature, the seer has visions of the end time when the marriage of Christ, the Lamb, and His bride, the church, will be celebrated, cf. Rev. 19:7-9 and 21:2.

The marriage customs of ancient Israel were different from those of western society today. A better understanding of them can intensify the significance of this Lesson. A procession of some sort was a part of the celebration. It met at a predetermined location, usually the bridegroom's house, where the wedding feast took place. There was lots of music during the procession and the feast. Wine and oil were distributed to the adults and nuts to the children. The bride covered with her bridal veil, her long hair flowing, surrounded by her companions was led to the friends of the bridegroom. Everyone rose to salute the procession or join it. It was deemed almost a religious duty to break into praise of the beauty, modesty, and virtues of the bride. When she arrived at her new home, she was led to her husband. Some such formula as "Take her according to the Law of Moses and of Israel" was spoken. The bride and bridegroom were crowned with garlands. Then the formal document, called "the kethubah," was signed. This set forth that the bridegroom would work for her, honor, keep, and care for her. He promised to give his wife a certain amount of money to increase her dowry by at least one half. Then, after the prescribed washing of hands and the benediction, the marriage supper began. At last, the friends of the bridegroom led the bridal pair to the bridal chamber and bed. In Palestine, wedding feasts often occupied seven or even fourteen days, cf. Gen. 29:27 and Judg. 14:17. Jesus participated in such a celebration and used the occasion to reveal the kind of Person He is and the significance of His ministry.

Mary is always "the mother of Jesus" in John. The fourth

evangelist never mentions her name, cf. John 2:12; 6:42; 19:25-26. This is strange, because he is not reticent to name people. He mentions a number of women by name. He names various Marys fifteen times. He never mentions his own name either. Perhaps his close relationship with Mary causes him to do the same for her. After Jesus' death, he took Mary to his own home, cf. John 19:25-27.

There is an apocryphal tradition that Mary was the aunt of the bridegroom who was John, the son of Zebedee, the author of this gospel. This is associated with the tradition that Salome, wife of Zebedee and mother of John, was Mary's sister. If all this is so, John is a cousin of Jesus. Is the wedding at Cana the story of Jesus' cousin's marriage? John may be including a portrait of himself in a corner of his gospel, as other evangelists did, cf. Matt. 9:9-13 and Mark 14:12-25 and 51-52.

It seems to have been customary when inviting a rabbi to a wedding to invite his disciples, too. Jesus was calling disciples a few days before the wedding at Cana, cf. John 1:35-51. Andrew, Simon, Philip, and Nathanael may be the "disciples" meant in John 2:2.

The bridegroom must have been embarrassed "when the wine gave out." The presence of Jesus and His disciples may have been the cause. No provision may have been made for them, because their number was not known. They were an unexpected group. Another cause may have been the poverty of the hosts; their willingness and welcome were larger than their means. The days of celebration may have been coming to an end when they ran out of wine. Some have suggested that the guests at a wedding were supposed to bring gifts. Some say that the wine supply was to some extent dependent on the gifts of the guests. Jesus and His disciples did not possess great means and may have failed to do what was expected, thus contributing to the embarrassment.

What prompts Mary to think that Jesus can do anything about the problem? Does Mary know that her son can perform miracles? How did she gain such knowledge? Has He performed other miracles? Even if Jesus has done miracles before this - as the other gospels suggest - He has done nothing like this. Perhaps Mary has learned that she can count on her Son to do what needs to be done to help people in their need without any conscious expectancy of a miracle. Is Mary asking for a miracle? The Old Testament picture of the Messiah would not have led the Jews to expect Him to work miracles on behalf of individuals, although John 7:31 may argue against that idea. Some think that Mary isn't asking Jesus to do anything; she is simply reporting a desperate situation that seems to have no solution. Yet the rather sharp response of Jesus indicates that she exerts some kind of pressure on Him. The exact nature of the expectation is not clear from the narrative. One interpreter suggests that the intent of Mary is that they should leave. Mary's next statement to the servants is founded on her understanding that Jesus' reply means that He is not going to leave. Yet, she believes He will do something to help.

There is no precedent in Hebrew or in Greek for a son to address his mother as Jesus addresses Mary. "Woman," He says to her. It is not an impolite address. It may have been Jesus' normal way when speaking to women, cf. Matt. 15:28; Luke 13:12; John 4:21; 8:10; 20:13. But it is not a way for a son to speak to his mother. It is not disrespectful, but a certain disassociation is implied; it excludes the filial relationship. Jesus repeats it when Mary stands at the foot of His cross, cf. John 19:26, and consigns her to the beloved disciple. The use of the address at that time indicates that it can scarcely be interpreted as a sign of a lack of affection. But it is a rather cold word to use in addressing His mother.

Jesus sets aside the mother-son relationship in favor of a higher one. He does this earlier in the temple at the age of 12, according to Luke 2:49. At the wedding at Cana, He is impressing on her that she has no claim on Him and His divine power because she is His mother. He does much the same in Matt. 12:46-50.

The description given here of Jesus' dealings with His mother agrees well with the total picture given in the New Testament, cf. John 19:26; Luke 2:49; 11:27-28; Matt. 12:46-50; and Mark 3:33-35. He always insists that kinship, whether it be Mary's or that of His disbelieving relatives, cf. John 7:1-

10, cannot affect the pattern of His ministry, for He has His Father's work to do.

The translations suggest a problem in interpreting the question with which Jesus responds to Mary's appeal. KJV has, "What have I to do with thee?" The RSV, "what have you to do with me?" NEB, "Your concern, mother, is not mine." The Greek literally translates simply, "What to me and to you?" It is an answer of remonstrance resisting an impatient urging.

The phrase is a Semitism and has at least two shades of meaning in the Old Testament. First, when one party is unjustly bothering another, the injured party may use this phrase, meaning, "What have I done to you that you should do this to me?" Examples are Judges 11:12; 2 Chron. 35:21; 1 Kings 17:18. Some demons reply to Jesus in this way in Mark 1:24 and 5:7.

Second, when someone is asked to get involved in something which he feels is none of his business, he may use the phrase, meaning, "That is your business; how am I involved?" Examples are 2 Kings 3:13 and Hos. 14:8. This seems to be the meaning here. Jesus may be saying, "You have no right to blame Me."

Jesus' refusal to get involved is polite. There is no rejection of Mary as His mother. But the phrase hardly adds up to anything other than a flat refusal. Jesus will not do tricks on demand. He will not act under any human pressure or compulsion. He rebukes His mother. He places Himself beyond natural family relationships even as He demands His disciples to do in Matt. 19:29.

The fact that Jesus finally supplies the wine requested makes it virtually impossible to maintain that the scene contains a harsh polemic against Mary. Rather she belongs in the general category of people who, despite their good intentions, do not fully understand Him. This agrees with what we are told in Mark 3:20-21 and 31-35.

The second part of Jesus' response to Mary's appeal is, "My hour has not yet come." The Greek can also be read as a question, "Has not my hour come?" In deciding whether the statement or the question is to be preferred, much depends on what "my hour" means. Is it the hour of His public ministry?

In that case, the question may be preferable. In the first question, He disassociated His mother's interest from His own. When He asks, "Has not my hour come?" He is offering a reason for the disassociation, namely, He has now begun His ministry by gathering disciples and has passed from a situation where family interests direct His life. The difficulty with this interpretation is that on two occasions during His ministry John says unambiguously that Jesus' hour has not yet come, cf. John 7:30 and 8:20.

In the other gospels, hora ("hour") almost always refers to the hour of the day. But it is hard to get away from the fact that in John the word usually refers to Jesus' death. Jesus' hour is the predetermined moment when He will "depart from this world and go to the Father" in John 13:1. At that hour, the disciples are scattered, according to John 16:32. It is the hour of His death when He is lifted up on the cross, cf. John 12:23, 27; 17:1. That hour is fixed by the decree of God.

As His passion approaches, John says that Jesus' hour has come, namely, the hour for Him to be glorified, cf. John 12:23. The fourth gospel leads up to that verse and 12:27. If "hour" is taken in the sense of hour for ultimate glorification, it is best to read John 2:4 as a statement.

The rhythm of Jesus' life keeps time with a clock other than that controlled by the sun. In the Gospel of John, all things are done according to a divine plan. The phrase used in Jesus' response to Mary is used again in John 7:6. There Jesus seems to say that He is bound to the divine plan even though the brothers are not. The necessity for Jesus to keep exactly to the divine schedule in order to carry out what He must accomplish is emphasized even more in John 9:4.

After Jesus rebuffs His mother, why does she make arrangements with the servants to help Him supply the needed wine? The answer is that she persists in her belief that He will help. Why does He grant her request when He has told her that her concern is not His concern?

There is a great difference between Roman Catholics and Protestants in their comments on the exchange between Jesus and His mother. A whole spectrum of interpretations concerning the role of Mary in the life of Jesus has been offered. Much of the Roman Catholic literature does not rise above the level of pious eisegesis. It suggests that people employ the intercessory power of Mary with Jesus. On the other hand, most Protestant commentators almost ignore the actions of Mary.

Roman Catholics used to say that this story encourages us to pray to Jesus through Mary. This position is scarcely held by any Roman Catholic scholar today. Raymond E. Brown, for example, says, "it must be honestly noted that the evangelist does nothing to stress the power of Mary's intercession . . . ."[28]

Mary shows some understanding of what Jesus has said to her and the reason for it, of what He is capable of doing, of His willingness and readiness to help, and of the possible reaction of the servants when Jesus tells them to do something strange. Examples of similar persistence in the face of a negative response from Jesus are in Matt. 15:21-28 and John 4:47-53. Such persistence seems to pay off.

Each of the "six stone water jars (held) twenty or thirty gallons." Neither the size nor the number of the jars is extraordinary. For an occasion like this, the family would produce or borrow such containers.

The numbers can be crunched to equal 180 gallons of water. Was all the water turned into wine? It is easy to think, as John tells the story, that it was. The miracle itself is not the most important thing; it is reported in a subordinate clause.

This was not grape juice but alcoholic wine. Greek has a different word for unfermented grape juice. The word for the fermented variety, true wine, is used. It is "good wine." We need not suppose that there was any drunkenness at this party, although the chief steward suggests that there often was at a wedding.

The servants draw some out to give the chief steward a taste. Today we would probably call him the caterer or the head waiter. He arranged the tables and the food. His job seems to have been to sample the food and the wine before they were set before the guests.

Jesus is lavish in providing wine which was the basic drink just as bread was the elemental food. Bread and wine together were the staff of life of that society. This aspect of the miracle at Cana is parallel to the feeding of the 5000 by the multiplication of loaves and the twelve baskets left over in Matt. 14:20. It is parallel to Elijah's miraculous furnishing of meal and oil in 1 Kings 17:8-16 and Elisha's supplying of oil in 2 Kings 4:1-7.

One of the consistent Old Testament figures for the joy of the final days is an abundance of wine, cf. Amos 9:13-14; Hos. 14:7; Jer. 31:12.

The wedding in Cana took place "on the third day." John's time designation has been taken by some to mean the third day in the list of days whose activities are described in John 1:19-51. Working this out is hard to do, but it is possible.

Three modern villages all bear names similar to Cana, and it is impossible to be certain which represents the ancient site. The place pointed out to pilgrims since the Middle Ages, Kefr Kenna, three and a half miles northeast of Nazareth, is probably wrong. Etymologically, the name is not a good fit.

3rd Sunday after the Epiphany

Year A

Isaiah 9:1-4

The contrasting fortunes of one geographical area are described during two historical periods. The geographical area is "the land of Zebulun and the land of Naphtali" which is also called "the way of the sea, the land beyond the Jordan, Galilee of the nations." The two historical periods are called "the former time" and "the latter time." In New Testament days, the geographical area was called Galilee. "The land of Zebulun" was lower Galilee and "the land of Naphtali" upper Galilee.

Zebulun and Naphtali were two of the twelve sons of Jacob/Israel, cf. Gen. 35:23-26. Their offspring constituted two of the twelve tribes of Israel. The tribes divided between them the land promised to their forefathers. The territory of Zebulun is described in Josh. 19:10-16 and that of Naphtali in vs. 32-39. They were in the northern part of the promised land. Naphtali included the west bank of the Sea of Galilee, and Zebulun was located to the west of Naphtali.

Canaan played a major role in the history of the Middle East, because it served as the land bridge between Egypt and the major empires to the north, e.g. Babylon and Assyria. Roads and trade routes were major historical factors. The most famous of these was the Way of the Sea which had many branches. The hub for a number of the branches was Capernaum at the north end of the Sea of Galilee.

Ever since the time of the judges, the lands in the northern part of the promised land were exposed to religious corruption from gentile influence and political subjugation by heathen foes. They suffered the most in the incessant war between Israel and the Syrians and afterwards between Israel and the Assyrians. Their inhabitants were taken into exile under Pul, Tiglath-pileser, and Shalmanassar; the land was depopulated.

The character of "the former time" is described with the words "contempt" and "deep darkness." For "the latter time," the words "glorious," "a great light," and "joy" are used.

"The former time" includes the entire preexilic and exilic experience of abuse and suffering that Judah endured under the reign of King Ahaz. He was the embodiment of failed leadership. The words "contempt" and "darkness" fit "the former time," because of "the yoke of their burden," "the bar across their shoulders," and "the rod of their oppressor," the prophet talks about. He gives other clues to the problems faced with the words "the boots of the tramping warriors" and "the garments rolled in blood." All these "shall be burned as fuel for the fire," and the situation will change "in the latter time." The prophet says that God will break "the yoke," "the bar," and "the rod."

"The latter time" was the period when Jahweh, through a Davidic king, created a new possibility for Judah. In the context of Isaiah, "the latter time" came after Ahaz when new leadership, during the enlightened reign of Hezekiah, made peace and prosperity possible. In the larger context of the book of Isaiah, "the latter time" was the time of homecoming and restoration following the return from exile. Ultimately, it was the Messianic era. According to Matt. 4:13-16, the words of the prophet were fulfilled when Christ Jesus "left Nazareth and made his home in Capernaum by the sea." The regions once called Zebulun and Naphtali were the first to receive the good news proclaimed by Him, "Repent, for the kingdom of heaven has come near," cf. Matt. 4:17.

The prophet describes "the latter time" and how the change was effected in Is. 9:2-4. These verses are a part of the Lesson for Christmas (Years ABC), Is. 9:2-7, and are discussed there.

1 Corinthians 1:10-18

Unity seems to be more important to Paul than the issues causing "divisions" and "quarrels" in the church at Corinth. An appeal for unity is the first thing he takes up in his letter to them, following his customary greeting and thanksgiving. The "divisions" and "quarrels" probably center around the items to which he gives his attention later in the letter: tolerating sexual immorality, grievances against each other that are being taken to civil courts, marriage problems leading to divorce, the eating of food offered to idols, problems in the celebration of the Lord's Supper, respect for each other's spiritual gifts, and deficiencies in their understanding of the resurrection of the dead. He appeals to them to be "in agreement" and "united in the same mind and the same purpose" before he takes up those important matters.

Unity is more important. The goal of Jesus' life and death was to unite all things in Himself, according to Eph. 1:9-10. The Corinthians' fractious quarreling did not represent the unity Jesus effected in His crucifixion and gave to them in Holy Baptism. In a similar situation today, we might try to deal with the issues first and then appeal for unity, but there may always be doctrinal differences and disagreement about practices. Perfect agreement in doctrine and practice does not save anyone, nor does unity. Jesus saved us by His death on a cross. But "divisions" and "quarrels" can hinder agreement in doctrine and practice.

"The message about the cross" is that Jesus' death unites us under God. That message says that every individual - whether man, woman, slave, servant, minister of state, merchant, barber, student, professor, or whatever - counts with God. God in Jesus suffered and died for our salvation. Now He begs and entreats us to accept Him and His saving work. The gospel says that we who find great pride in watching the President of the United States drive by at 30 or 60 miles an hour in a limousine and who reach out just to touch his hand fleetingly - we are known by God. At His invitation, we can talk to Him whenever we will. He has promised to hear us. We are invited to live with Him as His children. God has reconciled us who were His enemies to Himself. He made us one with Himself in Christ Jesus. He justified us sinners.

The cross of Christ is the means of our atonement, Col. 1:20 and 2:14 say. There Christ reconciled to Himself not only mankind but all things, earthly and heavenly things alike.

Over against factions and personality cults, Paul asserts that effective power flows from God and that God's power works through "the message about the cross." Some members of the Corinthian church organized cliques centering in people. In doing this, they espoused a theology of glory. They undermined the power and "the message about the cross." Paul combats their theology of glory with his theology of the cross. The gospel of the cross of Christ resists all self-assertiveness and marks as monstrous all clustering around people in schools and factions. It is not compatible with human boasting or with groups that center around people.

"The message about the cross" is not a demonstration of God's power nor a power of God. It is "the power of God," v. 24 says. Paul calls Christian preachers clay pots in 2 Cor. 4:7 and says that the power of "the message about the cross" is in the message itself and not in its messengers.

He asserts that God draws us to Himself through "the message about the cross." He tells the Corinthians who are engaged in a power struggle that "the power of God" works in ways very different from the usual practice of jockeying for position. It rules out factions and engages people in service to each other and to others. Divine power is self-giving love like that of Jesus, and it militates against power that tries to control, dominate, and manipulate others. God's power accomplishes His work through efforts that many consider weakness, cf. 2 Cor. 12:9.

In 1 Cor. 1:25-31, Paul offers empirical evidence of the power of "the message about the cross." He points to the experience the Corinthians themselves had. God chose them to be His people. He did this not because they were so great in a worldly sense or because they had such great insights. "The message about the cross" destroys the assertion of the greatness of all human efforts and achievements.

Paul illustrates a communal ethic of love in 1 Cor. 8. The issue of eating food offered to idols is an example of how conflicts are resolved in a community ruled by love. He makes the point in vs. 4-6 that idols don't really exist. We might anticipate logically that he will continue by siding with those who espouse the correct theology on the matter. But in v. 7, he asserts a strong alla ("however"). Where "the message about the cross" is at work, edification and unity take precedence over personal liberty and theological correctness.

People tend to be offended by "the message about the cross." To assert that the death of one man can save all people is plainly stupid. Paul acknowledges that it is foolishness to the wise people of the world, because it does not agree with the human way of thinking.

To understand the impact Jesus' cross had on the people of that day, we must understand the place of crucifixion in that society. Everyone in the Roman empire, generally speaking, was well acquainted with that form of capital punishment; they saw it often. The cross consisted of an upright post and a cross-beam. Jesus' hands were nailed to the cross-beam and His feet to the upright post, according to John 20:25 and Luke 24:39. There He hung naked until He died. This treatment was excruciatingly painful and shameful, and it was reserved for the worst kind of criminal. It was the state's declaration that the victim was good for nothing. One of the benefits of Roman citizenship was that it was illegal to crucify a Roman citizen. The word "cross" repelled Paul's contemporaries even more than the word "gallows" bothers us. To the Jews, the term "crucified Messiah" was an affront. Crucifixion designated a person as being under God's curse, according to Deut. 21:23 and Gal. 3:13. The cross was a sign of human failure and of condemnation by God. It especially provoked the righteous indignation of people who tried to live good and upright lives. To identify the powerful God with the shame of the cross is to call power weakness and weakness power. "Jews and Greeks" rejected the idea and shook their heads.

The world was and is eager to acquire knowledge of God, especially His ways and His rule. It seeks signs of the divine. Evidence of this today includes the popularity of the paranormal and the proliferation of new thought sects. But "the message about the cross" is generally viewed as folly or benignly irrelevant. Surely, a crucifixion that took place 2000 years ago in some far away land in a totally different culture cannot affect our lives today.

We resist humiliations and suffering. We look for justice, righteousness, and peace. When these do not happen, we wonder if God is truly in charge and if He is effective. We give evidence of this in our reaction to the tragedies of life. We ask, "Where is God?" Flowery words do not help to explain. Only the word of the cross offers understanding. Paul says, "the god of this world has blinded the minds of the unbelievers, to keep them from seeing the light of the gospel of the glory of Christ," cf. 2 Cor. 4:4.

"Eloquent wisdom" empties "the cross of Christ" of its power. "Eloquent wisdom" translates the Greek words <u>sophia logou</u>. The word <u>sophia</u> means wisdom. The phrase "words of wisdom" translates the same Greek words in 1 Cor. 2:4. Paul explains and elaborates on what the phrase means in 1 Cor. 2:1-5. <u>Sophia logou</u> is a way of speaking that presents human insights. God's action in the cross of Christ is emptied of its power when people use clever words and human wisdom to try to explain it. To try to justify intellectually "the message about the cross" lessens its power. It shows little knowledge of how it works. Actually, "eloquent wisdom" works against the gospel.

Corinth was a cultured and sophisticated city, and some people preferred to call themselves followers of Apollos rather than of Paul. Apollos may have had a very learned way of speaking; Paul did not. Paul's crudeness may have been offensive to some Corinthians.

Philosophical preaching that uses human wisdom to try to lessen the offensiveness of the gospel robs the cross of Christ of its content. Philosophical preaching of the cross of Christ is a contradiction in terms. The preaching of Christ crucified cannot be done with words that satisfy human wisdom, because the word of the cross is foolishness. God wants it that way!

The phrases "those who are perishing" and "us who are being saved" represent two classes of people. One group is aware of its destiny, the other is not.

The phrase "us who are being saved" describes salvation not as a completed matter but as a continuous process that is in progress. The New Testament writers use all three tenses in affirming our salvation. It is a completed event effected in the past on Calvary. It is a process taking place in the present. It will be fulfilled when Jesus comes again.

The word "us" in v. 18 embraces all believers regardless of the group they claim to be a part of, whether Paul, or Apollos, or Cephas. All "are being saved." One group is not better than another.

Paul sets the cross squarely in the center of the church. Only through "the message about the cross" will a divided church be reunited.

Paul appeals for unity in two ways. First positively, he says, "I appeal to you . . . that all of you be in agreement." Then negatively, he says, "I appeal to you . . . that there be no divisions among you." "Appeal" translates the Greek verb parakalo. Paul is not pleading with the various factions, as though they can do as they please. Actually, he is giving them a polite command.

He appeals "by the name of our Lord Jesus Christ." The various factions are using the names of different celebrated people to distinguish themselves, but Paul uses one name in his appeal for unity, "our Lord Jesus Christ."

"The name" can be omitted in v. 10, and the meaning of the verse remains the same: "I appeal to you by our Lord Jesus Christ." "For Christ's sake, brothers and sisters," Paul says, "get together. This disunity is bad." To appeal "by the name of our Lord Jesus Christ" is a phrase that is pretty much equivalent to the phrase "the message about the cross."

The phrase "that all of you be in agreement" is translated literally "that you all say the same thing." The point is not that

155

they all should use the same words. Rather, there should be harmony among them. On grave stones dating back to Paul's time, there is an expression occasionally found which reads, "So and so (husband and wife) spoke the same language." There was harmony between them.

The divisions among the Corinthian Christians seem to have to do with authority. The people did not agree on who should make decisions and who should obey and why. Each faction claimed a different leader. Instead of using conflict management to reconcile the warring parties, Paul affirmed "the message about the cross." He encouraged them all to unite under the leadership of Jesus Christ. He pointed to His crucifixion as the wisdom and the power of God.

No one knows what the structure of the church was in those days. No one knows what it should be today. Even the best church structure is misused if it becomes a tool with which people fight for dominance. Party programs are often linked with the name of an individual. They are intended to exclude certain people and do not foster unity.

The people's attachment to different people as their leader was tearing the Corinthian church apart. Paul says that there should not be divisions, because God called them all "into the fellowship of his Son, Jesus Christ our Lord," cf. 1 Cor. 1:9. The divisions will be overcome as each of them recognizes himself/herself as being anchored in Jesus Christ and His cross.

Paul appeals to his readers to mend the broken bonds of love between them. Katertismenoi ("united") is a form of the verb katartizo which is used in Matt. 4:21 for fishermen mending their nets.

Christian unity is a gift from God, cf. Rom. 15:5-6. It is not a matter of human achievement. It is not something to work at by compromise; that's the practice of politics. Rather than compromise, Paul appeals to the members of the church to adopt the same way of looking at things. They should see things through the eyes of the Lord, Jesus Christ.

Paul uses two words that are significant, nous and gnome. The fissures among the Corinthians should not be covered with a light patch. Nous ("mind") has to do with general principles.

It is the intellect in its judging function. Gnome ("purpose") has to do with the application of those principles. It indicates an expressed conviction. "The same purpose" is hardly to be differentiated from "the same mind."

A rallying point of the factionalism in the church of Corinth seems to have been who baptized whom. Paul lists the few Corinthians he baptized: Crispus, Gaius, and the household of Stephanas. We know little about them.

Acts 18:5-8 tells us that Crispus was "the official of the synagogue" in Corinth where Paul began to proclaim the gospel. The synagogue Jews "opposed and reviled" Paul, so he "left the synagogue" "in protest." Crispus followed him and "became a believer in the Lord, together with all his household." He probably was a man of some wealth and certainly a person of prestige in the Jewish community. He undoubtedly lost that status when he was baptized.

Gaius was Paul's host in Corinth, according to Rom. 16:23. Paul wrote Romans from Corinth. Gaius, too, must have been a man of some wealth, because he had a house large enough not only to put up Paul but also to accommodate all the Christian groups in Corinth meeting together. The men named Gaius in Acts 19:29 and in 20:4 are probably different people with the same name.

Entire households sometimes were baptized at the same time in the early church. Besides the household of Crispus, "the household of Stephanas" is mentioned as baptized by Paul in 1 Cor. 1:16.

More is said of Stephanas at the end of this letter, cf. 1 Cor. 16:15-18. "Members of the household of Stephanas were the first converts in Achaia." Achaia means Corinth. They "devoted themselves to the service of the saints." Their "service" seems to have been the kind given by patrons.

"Stephanas and Fortunatus and Achaicus" traveled to Ephesus to see Paul. They probably were a more or less official delegation. This may or may not indicate some wealth on the part of Stephanas. Their expenses may have been paid by the congregation.

The baptizing of households is sometimes used as a proof

for infant baptism in the early church. It certainly suggests that practice.

When Paul says, "I thank God that I baptized none of you except Crispus and Gaius," he is probably expressing happiness that he accidentally avoided involvement in that aspect of the quarrel in which people boasted about who baptized them. Such quarreling draws attention to individual people and detracts from the Lord Jesus Christ in whose name they all had been baptized.

The quarrel implies that all members were baptized. Jesus Himself instituted Baptism. Still today, all Christians are baptized. It was not simply a custom of the first Christians.

Paul is not speaking against Holy Baptism when he minimizes his baptizing activity. His thought is that the person administering Baptism should not be celebrated, but the Lord Jesus should. He emphasizes that his job is to proclaim Christ crucified.

Jesus didn't baptize either, according to John 4:1-2. The actions of Peter in connection with the Baptism of the household of Cornelius in Acts 10:48 suggest that Peter, too, did not baptize. Yet, in the great commission of Matt. 28:19, Jesus commands the apostles to "make disciples . . . by baptizing."

The story of the Baptism of the jailer at Philippi and his family in Acts 16:33 indicates the importance Paul attached to Holy Baptism. So does Rom. 6:3-4 and Gal. 3:27.

Other members of Paul's evangelistic team baptized. A period of education may have preceded Baptism already at this time. Such education was not Paul's job; it was a part of the Baptism program. He says in 1 Cor. 1:17 that his commission involves primarily evangelizing. Paul seems to have considered baptizing to be of secondary importance in relation to evangelizing. The conversion of people was his most important work. Evangelizing preceded baptizing. Baptism presupposes that the gospel has been accepted.

Paul didn't keep a ledger of his official acts as pastors do today. For that reason, he is not absolutely sure whom he baptized.

The situation in the Corinthian church was "reported" to Paul "by Chloe's people." They probably were members of the church and were disturbed by what was happening. Paul is

158

unable to doubt their report. Edelothe ("it has been reported") was used of official evidence.

It is not possible to identify "Chloe's people." They could be members of Chloe's family, her children or other relatives, members of her household, or her slaves. It is not said that Chloe is a Christian.

Paul is writing from Ephesus. Chloe and her people probably traveled from Corinth to Ephesus, or they could be citizens of Ephesus who traveled to Corinth. There was easy communication between the two cities by ship as well as by land. This was a period of great mobility in the Mediterranean area which was not maintained with the demise of the Roman empire. It was not restored until modern times.

Members of the church in Corinth are with Paul as he writes this letter, cf. 1 Cor. 16:17, but they are not connected to "Chloe's people" or to their report. In Paul's concluding messages and greetings, cf. 1 Cor. 16, he says nothing about "Chloe's people."

The ability of "Chloe's people" to travel suggests some financial resources. On the other hand, they may have traveled in the business of someone else. The "people" may be slaves who traveled on Chloe's business.

It seems strange that Paul gives the name of the people who brought the report of disunity to him in view of the way things are often done today. People tell you something only if you won't tell who told you. Pastors, in such a situation, do well to reject the information offered.

The members of each faction identify with a celebrated person. Some say, "I belong to Paul." Others, "I belong to Apollos" or "I belong to Peter." Others contradict them all by saying, "I belong to Christ." Probably, there also were others who refused to get involved in any faction. The slogans are exclusive. That is to say, they separate the people of one faction from other people. Paul rejects this factionalism. The boldness, confidence, and enthusiasm with which the people believe not in God but in their own belief and in their particular leaders and heroes is wrong. Every Christian gets his/her status from Christ and His cross. When Christians understand this, unity is maintained and restored.

We know Apollos only from a few references in the New Testament letters of Paul and from the book of Acts, cf. Acts 18:24-19:1. Apollos came to Corinth after Paul. He was from Alexandria. He was a learned expounder of the scriptures, but his theology is unknown. The mention of him indicates that he had personal success in Corinth. He was originally a disciple of John the Baptist. Through contact with Aquila and Priscilla, he learned "the way of God . . . more accurately."

The differences between Apollos and Paul may have been not so much in what they taught as in their way of expressing those teachings. Paul probably was rough and crude, while Apollos was eloquent, refined, and polished. Acts 18:24 credits him with rhetorical ability. Paul was not an attractive figure. He says he came to Corinth "in weakness and in much fear and trembling" in 1 Cor. 2:3. He acknowledges that he "may be untrained in speech" in 2 Cor. 11:6.

No blame is attached to Apollos for the divisions in the church. Some scholars today[29] think that the quarrels involved only Paul and Apollos. The jealousy between the partisans of those two great teachers stemmed from a comparison of their rhetorical abilities. This is based on Paul's disparaging comments about rhetoric in 1 Cor. 1:17.

Cephas is the name of the man we know better as Simon Peter. Jesus gave him the name Cephas in John 1:42. Cephas is the same name as Peter. Peter is a Greek word, and Cephas is Aramaic. Both names mean rock.

There is no evidence that Peter ever visited Corinth, although Oscar Cullmann offers the possibility that Peter was in Corinth at one time.[30] Peter was the early leader of the church, a great missionary like Paul, especially to the Jewish people. The Jewish element in the Corinthian congregation probably favored him.

The people in the Cephas-faction may have been Jews who came to Corinth from one of the eastern Judaic churches which Peter evangelized. They may have felt themselves to be the representatives of a more mature, more original kind of Christianity than that of the churches founded by Paul. They received the gospel from the leader of the apostles who had seen the Lord Jesus and had lived with Him. Paul, in their eyes, may have been an apostle of not quite equal rank with the twelve. They may have felt like charter members of an old, honorable club might feel toward newer members who besides being new would not be members at all if the rules had not been generously relaxed.

The quarreling may have gone something like this: Some said, "I'm a follower of Paul and proud of it." Others said, "I'm a follower of Apollos. He's a better preacher than Paul, so that makes me better than you." The Jews said, "We're followers of Peter and thus better than all of you. After all, Peter is the chief apostle." Others may have rejected all the other groups and claimed to be better than all the other people by saying that they were followers of Christ.

The preference for this or that famous churchman may have led to matters involving doctrine. What each party stood for, we can only guess. For example, some of the Peter party may have doubted Paul's apostolic credentials. Apparently, many Palestinian Christians viewed Peter's authority as supreme. The Clementine Homilies (which may be late first century documents) make violent attacks on Paul. They ascribe to Peter the office of apostle to the gentiles and not to Paul.

There is no evidence of any attempt by Peter or his agents to claim authority over the Pauline congregations. The original apostles of Jerusalem seem to have had little or no direct contact with the Pauline churches. On the other hand, "certain people . . . from James" caused a division in Galatia, according to Gal. 2:12.

Those who claimed "I belong to Christ" seem to be saying that they are the sole possessors of Christ; the others are not. Paul's words in 1 Cor. 4:18-19 may indicate that they considered Paul unnecessary. Perhaps they felt that he would never come to Corinth again. They may have rejected his authority. Paul may be talking about their arrogance in 1 Cor. 4:18-19 and their contentiousness in 1 Cor. 11:16 and 14:38. The bitter irony of 2 Cor. 11:20-21 may also relate to them.

A clique always produces cliques in reaction. The line between the church where Christ alone is Lord and the world where people head movements and command loyalty was being perilously blurred in Corinth. In a way, the first four chapters of Corinthians are a commentary on the words of Jesus in Matt. 20:25-28.

Paul's criticism of the situation begins with v. 13. He does not pit one figure against another, but he makes the community face the reality of schism. The quarreling is wrong. He asks three questions. The first is, "Has Christ been divided?" The answer is no. The church is the body of Christ. This is a good question to direct to the divided condition of the church today. There is only one church, because there is only one Christ, one body of Christ, one Spirit, cf. 1 Cor. 12:12-13 and Eph. 4:4-6.

In the Biblical view of things, there may be churches in various geographical locations, such as a church in Corinth, another in Ephesus, etc. But there are not various churches in the same place, and they do not exclude one another from their fellowship. The only words by which "denominations" can be translated into New Testament Greek is schismata (schisms) and haireseis (heresies). If we use words in their Biblical meaning only, we have to speak of the "World Council of Schisms or Heresies." There is neither sect nor sectarianism in the body of Christ. When church members separate themselves from other Christians, they separate themselves from the body of Christ.

The second question is, "Was Paul crucified for you?" Even to ask this question is highly offensive. Paul might have used the name of Apollos and Peter, but he humbly used his own, degrading only himself. The answer is the same as the first, no. The Greek word me introduces a question expecting a negative answer. Paul teaches that in Holy Baptism we all are joined to Jesus' death.

The third question is, "Were you baptized in the name of Paul?" The answer again is no. Calling the name of a person over another's head, as in Holy Baptism, signifies that they are the slave of that person, subject to his lordship and protection. Christ's name was called over the Corinthian Christians, not Paul's.

In spite of the "divisions" and "quarrels," the Christian community in Corinth still existed at the time Paul wrote. This is indicated in that the letter is addressed to the entire community. Paul calls the members of the church "saints" in 1:2. They are "brothers and sisters" in v. 10. (The Greek text uses only one word, "brothers," but NRSV is committed to inclusive language; and Paul is thinking of the sisters, too.) The church still worships together and celebrates the Lord's Supper together, according to 1 Cor. 11:17-34. Yet, there are problems between them as they do this.

The term "brothers and sisters" expresses affection. It probably implies Paul's personal acquaintance with many members. He calls them "brothers and sisters" twice in the first two verses, cf. vs. 10-11, although he criticizes them severely. Actually, because they are brothers and sisters, he criticizes them. This is a cue for how Christian admonition and encouragement can be done in a spirit of brotherliness.

Matthew 4:12-23

It is significant that Jesus began His public ministry in Galilee; in doing this He fulfilled a prophecy regarding the Messiah.

The dynamics of Matthew's gospel should always be kept in mind. The story of Jesus builds to His passion. Matthew divides Jesus' public ministry into two parts. In the first, 4:17-11:1, Jesus offers salvation to Israel in a ministry that includes teaching, preaching, and healing. The second part, 11:2-16:20, describes Israel's response; Jesus is rejected. He fixes His eyes on His passion in Jerusalem beginning with 16:21. The passion narrative begins in ch. 26.

The first disciples, Peter, Andrew, James, and John, are a strange quartet. Preachers sometimes try to make them larger than life heroes of faith. But it is important to note that Jesus enlisted rather ordinary men from the first. Nowhere do the gospels hint that descent, position, or even natural endowment qualifies anyone for Jesus' call. The kind of people who became His disciples was an expression of divine grace. That grace enables us, too, to accept His call.

The formula, "from that time," in v. 17 marks the beginning

of a new phase in Jesus' activity. It is the time for proclamation. The phrase appears again in Matt. 16:21 when Jesus begins to prepare His disciples for His passion.

I

V. 17 is a summary statement of Jesus' preaching and teaching. Each synoptic gospel includes such a statement, cf. Mark 1:15 and Luke 4:18-21. Jesus proclaimed the good news that "the kingdom of heaven has come near." In the light of this, He called on people to repent. He extended the kingdom through teaching, preaching, "and curing every disease and every sickness among the people."

Repentance is best represented by the Hebrew root shub. It is closely connected with the covenant God made with Israel at Mt. Sinai. It involves a turning or returning to Jahweh and the Sinaitic covenant. It means to assume a different mind and feeling, to change from one state of mind to another, to adopt a different spirit. The sinner hates his sin. Repentance can be equated with conversion which is the first act of repentance. The repentance Jesus calls for looks forward rather than back. Faith in Jesus empowers it and leads to discipleship and obedience.

Jesus admonished His hearers to take seriously their situation. Paul put it this way in Rom. 12:2: "Do not be conformed to this world, but be transformed by the renewing of your minds, so that you may discern what is the will of God – what is good and acceptable and perfect." Jesus called for God-centered living.

Repentance includes contrition which is self-accusation or despair of oneself. Penitents consider nothing that they are or do good in the sight of God regardless of what people say. Jesus' invitation, "Follow me!" implies forgiveness and acceptance. God's forgiveness is most strongly expressed in Jesus' death on a cross.

While the law can stimulate an awareness of sinfulness, it does not produce repentance. The gospel of Jesus does that. Repentance is empowered not by the fear of what we have done but by the gift of forgiveness in Jesus' death. Preachers cannot scare people out of hell. Jesus' death saves us.

The law of God may have the form of ordinances and commandments, but God's law also confronts us in the experiences of life like death, sickness, failure, despair, poverty, terrorism, racial prejudice, greed, pride, self-love, covetousness, lust, etc. Laws can inspire resistance and rejection, but life experiences are too valid to be set aside.

Luther began his "Ninety-five Theses" with the words: "Our Lord and Master Jesus Christ, when He said, 'Repent' willed that the whole life of believers should be repentance." Luther called repentance "hatred of oneself"[31] and "being displeased with ourselves."[32] He said it should involve the whole of life, as Jesus says in Matt. 10:39. Sincere repentance includes a longing for and a love of righteousness. Such longing flows not out of the fear of punishment but is inspired by Jesus' death. Repentance happens in the relationship of faith in Jesus.

In calling on all people to repent, Jesus declares all people sinners. That word is hard and not welcome. When, however, He says, "The kingdom of heaven has come near," that is good and longed-for news.

"The kingdom of heaven" is equivalent to "the kingdom of God," a phrase that is frequently used elsewhere in the Bible. The Jews were reluctant to pronounce the name of the holy God and therefore circumscribed it. "Heaven" was one of the customary circumscriptions. Jesus may have used both "the kingdom of God" and "the kingdom of heaven."

"The kingdom of heaven" (he basileia ton ouranon) is not a heavenly world located above the firmament into which the pious enter after death. It is the sovereign rule and authority of God on earth. It refers primarily to His rule and only secondarily to the sphere over which He rules. The preachment of the kingdom creates a community of people who live under God's rule.

Jesus does not say that there is a kingdom of God. He is not introducing a new term or idea. The kingdom of God is the subject of the Old Testament and the focus of the history of Israel. Jesus proclaims that the kingdom has come in Himself;

He personifies the kingdom. God and His rule are so near that people ought to repent.

"The kingdom of heaven has come near" is the same good news Jesus later commissions His disciples to proclaim in Matt. 10:7. John the Baptist proclaimed the same message before Jesus began His ministry, cf. Matt. 3:1-2. We are commissioned to proclaim the same message in Luke 24:47. Contemporary preachers are not to have a friendly conversation on an interesting topic with their hearers. Their job is not to entertain. The message of the kingdom is to be proclaimed.

"Proclaim" is a frequently used word in Matt. 3-4. It (kerussein) is the cry of a herald which is supported with authority.

Jesus begins preaching and teaching in the synagogues of Galilee. Jewish congregations met for prayer and praise on the sabbath and for instruction on other days. This practice began in the days of Ezra and Nehemiah and continues to this day. A visiting Jew was often asked to teach. An example of this is in Luke 4:16-28. Scriptural interpretation was a feature of synagogue worship.

The cures Jesus performed authenticated the good news He proclaimed. He cured "every disease and every sickness." Nosos ("disease") is chronic or serious disease. Malakia ("sickness") is occasional sickness. He healed people out of sheer compassion and in fulfillment of prophecy. It was a part of the credentials of His Messiahship, cf. Matt. 11:2-6.

The connection between the cures of disease and the preaching of the gospel is recognized by churches today in the establishment of hospitals and clinics.

"When Jesus heard that John had been arrested, He withdrew to Galilee." John the Baptist was arrested by Herod Antipas, son of Herod the Great, because John rebuked him for marrying his brother Philip's wife, cf. Matt. 14:1-12. Jesus feared that Herod's evil will would be directed also against Him, too, so He left that territory and "withdrew to Galilee."

The word, "withdrew" (anachoreo), means to go away, to depart, often to escape danger. What Matthew is saying is made clear by other examples of his use of the word. He uses it when he says that Joseph took the holy family to Egypt in 2:14. When Joseph was afraid to return to Judea because Archelaus was ruling there, Matthew uses anechoresen ("he went away") to say that Joseph took his family to Galilee, cf. 2:22. When Jesus became aware that the Pharisees were conspiring to destroy Him, the same word, translated "departed," is used to say that Jesus left the area, cf. 12:14-15. When Jesus heard that Herod had killed John the Baptist, Matthew says that Jesus "withdrew from there . . . to a deserted place by himself," cf. 14:13. When Jesus heard that the Pharisees took offense at what He said, Matthew uses the word again to say that Jesus "left that place and went away," cf. 15:12 and 21. Jesus left an area when He feared action against Himself until the time came for His death. Then He hurried to Jerusalem for His passion.

The place in Galilee to which Jesus went first was Nazareth where He was raised. He began His ministry there, according to Luke 4:16-30. He left Nazareth, when the synagogue there rejected Him, and went to Capernaum.

No record indicates that Jesus ever visited the great cities of Galilee, Sepphoris and Tiberias. Much of His work was done in small towns and even villages such as Nain and Cana.

II

When Jesus "withdrew to Galilee," Matthew says "that what had been spoken through the prophet Isaiah (was) fulfilled." This is the seventh Old Testament text Matthew says Jesus fulfilled. Through the citations, Matthew identifies Jesus as the Messiah. Is. 9 speaks of a time when God will send one who is called "the Mighty God" to sit on the throne of David and rule God's people forever, cf. vs. 6-7.

The background of the prophecy of Isaiah is the Assyrian conquest of the northern kingdom. In 734 and 732 BC, the Assyrian king Tiglath-pileser waged two campaigns against Israel and incorporated "all the land of Naphtali" into his empire including the areas listed in 2 Kings 15:29. Is. 9:1 refers to this disaster saying that God "brought into contempt the land of Zebulun and the land of Naphtali." The prophet speaks of this "anguish" and "thick darkness" in Is. 8:22. The people thought God was failing them. Isaiah replied that although their guilt was great and this produced the severe judgment they were experiencing, God's promises to them were still valid. God would again make glorious "Galilee of the nations." The reversal would begin precisely where His judgment first struck. A child would be given to them. The names of the child describes the blessings of His reign on the throne of David: "Wonderful Counselor, Mighty God, Everlasting Father, Prince of Peace." His reign of peace and justice would be without end.

Jesus was the "great light" Isaiah said would shine in Galilee. "Light" is new creation language. The first act of creation was when God said, "Let there be light," cf. Gen. 1:3. Jesus, the beginning of the new creation, is described as "a great light." His coming ushered in a new epoch in the history of God's dealings with the human race.

The light of God's new creation would illuminate a people who considerd themselves doomed and helpless, "sitting in darkness . . . in the land and shadow of death." This land was Galilee.

Using the metaphor of light for Jesus is common in the New Testament. When Simeon held the baby Jesus in his arms, he called Him "a light for revelation to the Gentiles and for glory to your people Israel," cf. Luke 2:32. The "Word" is called "the light" in John 1:4-5: "In him was life, and the life was the light of all people. The light shines in the darkness, and the darkness did not overcome it." John the Baptist is introduced as a witness to the Light: "(John) came as a witness to testify to the light, so that all might believe through him. He himself was not the light, but he came to testify to the light. The true light, which enlightens everyone was coming into the world," cf. John 1:7-9. Jesus called Himself "the light of the world" in John 8:12 and 9:5. During the last week of His life, He cried out, "I have come as light into the world, so that everyone who believes in me should not remain in the darkness," cf. John 12:46.

When Matthew quotes Is. 9:1-2, he uses a version other than the Septuagint. Perhaps he translated directly from the Hebrew or used a different Greek translation.

Jesus "made his home in Capernaum by the sea." Capernaum was a Roman settlement on the north shore of the Sea of Galilee. It was the center of the government of Galilee. It became strongly westernized. It became Jesus' headquarters.

Capernaum was a small village at the time with a population of about 1,000. North Galilee was largely wooded. It was a frontier region that was the first area to fall victim to any invader from the north. Capernaum was located on the crossroads of important trade routes with both the east and the west and was surrounded by fertile lands. These and the rich fishing available in the Sea of Galilee contributed to its economic development. It was quite prosperous.

A more literal translation of the phrase "on the road by the sea" is "the way of the sea" which was the name of a great trade route. A number of branches took off from the main route at Capernaum.

Galilee is "the territory of Zebulon and Naphtali." Zebulon and Naphtali were two tribes of the children of Israel. When the promised land was apportioned to the twelve tribes, Zebulon and Naphtali were given territories in the northern part of Palestine including the western shore of the Sea of Galilee, cf. Josh. 19:10-16 and 32-39.

The area is called "Galilee of the Gentiles." The contemptuous name was given to the territory because of its mixed population. The population included gentiles as well as Jews. Jesus claimed in Matt. 15:24 that He "was sent only to the lost sheep of the house of Israel," but Matthew alerts his readers to the wider significance of Jesus' Messianic mission.

Jesus located Himself in "Galilee of the Gentiles" so that He might "proclaim justice to the Gentiles," according to Matt. 12:18. "And in his name the Gentiles will hope," according to Matt. 12:21. The faith of the centurion of Capernaum - undoubtedly a gentile - caused Jesus to say in Matt. 8:11, "many will come from east and west and will eat with Abraham and Isaac and Jacob in the kingdom of heaven." During His last week, He told His disciples that they would testify "throughout the world . . . to all the nations," cf. Matt. 24:14. Finally, He sent out the eleven to "make disciples of all nations" in Matt. 28:19.

There was a large Jewish nucleus in Galilee, but adherence to Judaism was not strong. The Judaism of Galilee was different from that in Jerusalem. The gentile influence began to shape the area with the destruction of the northern kingdom of Israel. The word "darkness" should probably be understood to describe this spiritual condition. The people of Galilee resented the control of Rome; the region was a hotbed of revolt. The nationalistic Zealot movement began there. By upbringing, Jesus was a Galilean, a people who though firmly Jewish resented both Jerusalem and Rome. Isaiah said that the new creation about which he wrote would begin there.

III

The first disciples Jesus called were Peter, Andrew, James, and John. Their call was the beginning of the new people of God, the new Israel. Three of them, Peter, James, and John, later form the group of Jesus' closest associates. They were with Him at the time of His transfiguration, cf. Matt. 17:1-8, and again when He prayed in the Garden of Gethsemane on the night before His death, cf. Matt. 26:37.

The four men previously were disciples of John the Baptist, John 1:35-42 suggests, and through him they probably knew Jesus. With John in prison and soon to be executed by Herod, Jesus called them to become His disciples.

"Simon, who is called Peter" is mentioned first. Jesus gave Simon the name Peter later, according to Matt. 16:18. The name comes from the Greek word petros which corresponds to the Aramaic kepa (Cephas) and means "rock, stone."

Andrew was Peter's brother. "They were fishermen." Jesus called Peter, Andrew, James, and John while they are engaged in their fishing business. It is strange how people in the Bible become involved with Jesus while at work.

Jesus saw Peter and Andrew "casting a net into the sea." Amphiblesteron is a net that is thrown over the shoulders and spreads out into a circle as it falls on the water.

170

Some fishermen in first-century Palestine angled with hook and line, but these four fishermen were using nets. This was a hard way to make a living. They trolled though the night on a lake that was subject to sudden storms. They hauled in hundreds of pounds of fish, if they were lucky. They had to gut them for sale or transport. They had to care for the tools of the trade, their nets and boat, by washing, mending, folding, and repairing. It was grimy, smelly, back-breaking work.

Matthew describes the call of the four men in very simple language in a casual way. Jesus was walking along the Sea of Galilee when He happened to see Simon and Andrew. He called them. They followed Him. He continued walking and happened to see James and John. Yet, though simple, the narrative is very powerful.

The placement of this story immediately after Jesus' initial announcement of the kingdom enables the reader or hearer to grasp what discipleship means, not just for Peter, Andrew, James, and John, but for anyone in any age who wants to follow Jesus. As Matthew continues his narration, discipleship will be expounded through parable, miracle, and encounter. A decision for or against Jesus determines whether a person lives under God or in opposition to Him.

"Follow me" is a kind of technical term for the call to discipleship. It is a command rather than an invitation. Jesus acted in a sovereign manner. Some have called what Jesus did a confiscation. He did not negotiate.

It was a summons to become His pupil. Students who decided to become the pupils of a certain rabbi were said to have "followed him."

Matthew gives absolutely no clue of a previous knowledge of Jesus and His teachings. Matthew has no interest in explaining. He seems to intend to say that Jesus' call was a miracle. He seems to stress that the men followed Jesus because of who He was, the Messiah. The full Messianic realization, however, did not come until later. The call was based on Jesus' own decision about the men. That decision was expressed in the call. The initiative was with Jesus. The response to the call required the decision on the part of the men to follow.

No reason is given that the four men should obey the call other than Jesus Himself. He simply told them what would happen if they did; He would make them fishers of men. The disciples were not impelled by any of the human devices for making a decision. They were not played upon emotionally or psychologically and snapped up in a moment of high enthusiasm or in a mood of desperation. They were simply called.

Matthew places no emphasis whatever on their qualifications. There were no likely candidates for discipleship. All that the reader learns of these four men is that they were fishermen; and even that is recorded to enable us to appreciate the metaphor with which Jesus described their mission: "I will make you fish for people."

The list of the twelve apostles indicates that they were an odd assortment, ranging from the tax collector, who had decided to take the cash of this world and let the credit of Israel's promise go, to the Zealot, who was willing to blindly stake his life on the strength of God's promise to Israel, however mistakenly he did it. But the disciples are never really characterized very fully in the gospels. Beyond a few obvious and dramatic traits, such as the volatility of Peter, we know next to nothing about them as personalities. Martin Franzmann said: "People who write character sketches of disciples and apostles are to be admired for their enterprise; they do not have much to work with."[33]

It is not good to speak too much of the faith of the four men. They probably had not themselves a full and adequate conception of what they were getting themselves into. That would evolve in the course of Jesus' further teaching and of their learning.

The call was a very great gift. It was the Messiah's call and invitation to union and communion with Him. Later Jesus told His disciples, "You did not choose me but I chose you," cf. John 15:16. He was the only purpose, cause, and goal of the call.

The call created faith, but the response of the men to Jesus and His proclamation was not faith in the sense of the acceptance of certain things about Jesus. We are given no clue as to what they believed about Jesus at this point. As Matthew continues to tell the story, it becomes clear that most of what they initially believed about Jesus turned out to be dead wrong. Their response is better explained in terms of trust and faithfulness. Jesus' call did not cause them to change what they believed religiously so much as it enabled them to follow Him.

It was a common thing for a rabbi or teacher to gather a group of disciples about himself. Jesus' circle of disciples fit naturally into the pattern of life at that time. And yet there was a startling difference in procedure. No rabbi ever gained his pupils through the command "Follow me!" as Jesus did. In rabbinic circles, the disciples went looking for the rabbis. But Jesus went looking for His disciples. This approach is comparable only to the call to service of the Old Testament prophets.

There are similarities between the call of the first disciples and that of the Old Testament prophets. The prophets, too, were men to whom "the Word of the Lord came" without their volition and often against their volition. Moses and Jeremiah accepted the prophetic task reluctantly and only after a struggle, cf. Ex. 3:1-15; 4:1-17; Jer. 1:4-8. They were too young, they said. They were stammerers. Jonah simply ran away, cf. Jonah 1:1-3. Elijah called Elisha from his work and his father, cf. 1 Kings 19:19-21. To none of the prophets did the call come in response to self-preparation or mood-making. In the last analysis, the Word that came to them simply captivated them and left them with no alternative but to obey. Amos once said that men no more choose to be prophets than they choose to be afraid when a lion roars, cf. Amos 3:8.

The call of Paul was in this respect parallel to that of the men who were apostles before him, cf. Acts 9:1-19. The initiative was not his; he was a blasphemer, persecutor, and insulter of Christ and His church. The grace of God called him.

The call involved more than simply following Jesus. It was a summons for full commitment to Him. To follow Jesus, the men renounced the dearest and otherwise most sacred ties of family. They followed in total devotion and utter trust. Simon and Andrew abandoned the security of their vocation. James and John left both property and family.

Jesus did not permit any dreamy delusions about what following Him involved. To follow Him meant to share His lot, according to Matt. 16:24-25. Commitment to Him, which included full surrender, ruled out any looking back. Discipleship meant belonging exclusively to Him. It canceled all other ties, according to Matt. 8:19-22. Jesus was brusque with enthusiastic volunteers. To the scribe who in a moment of euphoria offered to go everywhere with Jesus, He responded by telling him that He had nowhere to lay His head, cf. Matt. 8:20. At the same time that He rejected the schooled and skillful scribe, He coolly called the tax collector from His collection booth, cf. Matt. 9:9. Every pious and self-respecting Jew kept himself at antiseptic distance from tax collectors.

Jesus' claim was not the external pressure of law. He made no rule or pattern of renunciation. His claim overrode the claim of family and home, but He founded no order of cloistered celibates. He asked that people be ready to cut off their right hands for His sake, cf. Matt. 5:30, but we hear nothing of an Order of Mutilated Martyrs. He asked that people renounce the sustaining comfort of the majority, cf. Matt. 7:13-14, but this did not mean that His followers became an isolated sect. Jesus' followers walked on a narrow way through the world, but they did not leave the world.

The renunciation required was that of the man who "in his joy" sells all that he has in order to buy the field that contains the treasure, cf. Matt. 13:44. It was not a leap into the dark with eyes closed and teeth clenched. Rather it was a leap into the arms of a loving Father who clothes the lilies and feeds the birds. Jesus is the pearl of great price for which a person gives up all other pearls, cf. Matt. 13:45-46.

The call involved a mission. The duty of ministry was upon their discipleship from the beginning. "Follow me" spelled work: "I will make you fish for people." This was not a job description but a mission statement. Jesus used this same imagery in the parable of the Dragnet, cf. Matt. 13:47-50. Some whom Jesus has called to be fishers of people have considered the invitation lightly and instead have become fishermen.

We are not attracted to Jesus' imperious way of summoning

people, but His assumption of authority over the four men was not resented by them. Their response was immediate and complete. Peter and Andrew didn't even bring in their nets. Unlike James and John, they had no one to leave in charge of their nets and perhaps their boats which were their means of sustenance. Peter talked later about how they left everything to follow Jesus, cf. Matt. 19:27.

The calling of the Christian today does not necessarily imply a change in occupation, cf. 1 Cor. 7:17-24. In this respect, it is different from that of the disciples. Following Jesus means giving up different things to different people. Some give up nets, some give up possessions, and some leave their families. Leaving the family happens sometimes in places like Japan. It also happens in the United States.

Besides the parallel in Mark 1:16-20, other examples of Jesus' call are in Matt. 9:9-13 (Mark 2:13-14; Luke 5:27); Matt. 8:18-22 (Luke 9:57-62); Matt. 16:24-26 (Mark 8:34-37; Luke 9:23-25); and Matt. 19:16-30 (Mark 10:17-31; Luke 18:18-30).

3rd Sunday after the Epiphany

Year B

Jonah 3:1-5, 10

"God changed his mind. . . . He did not do it." Who would have thought? Does God's change of mind preview the crucifixion? It certainly is the gospel of this Lesson.

Another turn around makes the story of this Lesson, by the Ninevites. We have an example to imitate.

Some people may think this Lesson is not the famous story of Jonah, because the "large fish" is not in it. The fish story must be told. However, it is only a part of the larger story.

Jonah is an intriguing, amusing, entertaining, but reluctant prophet. Actually, it is hard to think of him as a prophet. We call him that, because the Lesson says that "the word of the Lord came to Jonah." But how can we call a man a prophet who flees from what God wants him to do and from the presence of God? That's not our image of a prophet. Prophets are obedient; Jonah is rebellious. God tells him to go north and east, and he goes west.

His story is the story of our lives. God makes him face up to the issues of disobedience and rebellion, anger and frustration, life and death, and the divine sense of justice. The story of Jonah makes us face up to our prejudices, too.

God commands Jonah twice to go to the ancient city of Nineveh. The first time Jonah refuses. The story is told in Jonah 1.

God orders Jonah to "cry out against" the people of Nineveh because of their wickedness. God knows what is going on there. It is offensive to Him. Jonah is to warn them.

The road to Nineveh went north out of Israel. Instead of going that way, Jonah boarded a ship at Joppa, a port on the Mediterranean Sea, and headed west toward Tarshish. What insolence!

God's reaction to Jonah's disobedience was that He created "a mighty storm" to destroy the ship on which Jonah took passage. When the sailors realized that Jonah was the cause of their distress, they threw him overboard at his suggestion and saved their vessel and themselves.

The story of the "large fish" is the story of how God saved Jonah. The "large fish" swallowed Jonah. When he "remembered the Lord," after "three days and three nights" in its "belly," the Lord caused the "large fish" to spit him out on "dry land."

The Lesson for the 3rd Sunday after the Epiphany tells the story of the second time the Lord commanded Jonah to go to Nineveh. Giving His rebellious messenger a second chance reveals God's patience. He assigned Jonah the mission again as if nothing had happened.

Nineveh was the New York City, the Bangkok, the Rio de Janeiro, the New Orleans of Jonah's world. It was really a huge conglomeration of communities with its own spirit and an attitude of independence from the rest of the world. It "was an exceedingly large city." A more literal translation might be, "Nineveh was a vast city, even by God's standards." The word elohim is in the text and can literally be translated "according to God."

Sennacherib made Nineveh the capital of Assyria early in the seventh century BC. He began an extensive building program enlarging and beautifying it. Formerly, the circumference of the city was 9300 cubits, less than three miles, but he added 12,515 cubits. An ancient said the total circumference of the city was about 55 miles. That seems extreme.

Archeological surveys have determined that the city's circumference was seven and a half miles, an extraordinary size for an ancient city. It was an oblong shape which had on its widest axis a diameter of three miles. It may have involved an administrative region that was of much greater size.

The population was more than 120,000, according to Jonah 4:11, which is reasonable for a city that was "three days walk across." This is probably greater Nineveh and includes four cities in the area.

In many ways, Nineveh was decadent. In its day, it was the extreme case of grossness and wickedness among all the centers of world power. A description of its character is in Nahum 3.

Jonah needed no urging the second time the word of the Lord came to him. He had been saved from death as we were in Holy Baptism. He was a new man. He accepted the commission he fled from before.

Why did Jonah refuse the first time? This is how he explains it: "I knew that you are a gracious God and merciful, slow to anger, and abounding in steadfast love, and ready to relent from punishing," cf. Jonah 4:2. Jonah knew that if he went to Nineveh and issued a dire warning about "the calamity" God was going to bring on the people of the city for their wickedness, they might repent. Then God would not destroy them, and Jonah would be left holding the bag. He would be embarrassed that he had predicted that terrible things were going to happen to them. He would feel like an idiot, because what he said would happen in the name of God would not happen.

The obedient prophet walked for one day into the city. He did not reach its center. He probably felt small, one man against a vast metropolis. Feeling like a needle in a haystack in this Sodom of a city, he went no further. He shouted out the message he was to proclaim. In Hebrew, it is summarized in five words. The translation given in the NRSV is, "Forty days more, and Nineveh shall be overthrown!"

Forty is a typical waiting and testing period in the Bible.

Israel wandered in the wilderness forty years, and Jesus spent forty days in the wilderness being tested.

Scientists tell us that our days are numbered. Are they prophets God has sent to warn us? They list the wicked deeds we are engaged in. We are being overcome by environmental pollution. We are depleting our natural resources. We are digging our own grave with our nuclear physics and our biological research. The days of our mismanagement of creation are limited. We seek power for absurd goals. We lust for more pleasure and more fun. Economic doom and gloom threaten us from many directions. Houses are mortgaged for more than they are worth. People bought houses they could not afford. More is better, and most is best. Politicians do not tell the people what they need to hear but promise relief, even for those who were greedy and mismanaged. People are over their heads in debt. They look to those of us who practiced good financial management, who made some right decisions, and who are living within our means to bail them out of their extravagances. Credit is getting tighter. Still people lust for more. Their houses and automobiles must be upgraded to match their enlarged egos. When what they do fails to bring them happiness and fulfillment, they turn to drink, drugs, counselors, and divorce courts. They buy new things and establish new relationships to decorate their boulevard of unrealistic dreams.

Jonah's preaching was unbelievably successful. The people of Nineveh repented. Jonah didn't really call for that, but they did. It was a surprising reaction. Whenever we become skeptical, we should remember the story of Jonah.

Jesus referred to the repentance of Nineveh in Matt. 12:41. We Christians, like the contemporaries of Jesus, are put to shame and even brought to trial by Nineveh.

Sackcloth and fasting were the symbols of Nineveh's repentance. They are mentioned in the description of the religious activities of the people, the personal reaction of the king, and the official decree, cf. Jonah 3:6-9.

The king got off his throne in the face of the sovereign power of God revealed in Jonah's words. His throne and royal robes were exchanged for sackcloth and ashes. In stripping off his stylish clothes and donning the plain robe of mourning, he expressed humility. He issued a royal edict to regularize the spontaneous reaction of the people.

It was a Persian custom for animals to participate in mourning ceremonies. In western society, horses used to be covered with black cloth until the black limo replaced them.

Nineveh was blatantly guilty of violent injustice, especially the king, according to Is. 10:12-14. The king confessed in Jonah 3:8 on behalf of the community. We are to assume that the repentance of the Ninevites was sincere.

The forms of humble confession and of humility change and are different from society to society and from time to time. When they become formless, they really cease to exist. When honestly felt, they seek expression. Are there signs of repentance in our world? How do we show it?

Does the book of Jonah relate history? People have looked through the annals of the Assyrian kings in vain for any reference to Jonah's prophetic activity and its result. Whether this is an historical report or not, the story of the prophet confronts us with the truth regarding our weaknesses and the mercy of God. The crucifixion of Jesus documents the willingness of God to forgive. Repentance involves confessing our sins and accepting God's offered forgiveness.

God always acts in our best interests. Thus Nineveh continued to live, Jonah continued to live, and we continue to live. The cross of Christ teaches us that God wants those who are at fault to be forgiven, cf. Luke 23:34.

What follows is not a part of the Old Testament Lesson for the day, but you will want to know it and check it out. The story of Nineveh's repentance has a surprising and revealing ending.

Was Jonah happy with the success of his proclamation? God's tenderheartedness and Nineveh's repentance "was very displeasing to Jonah, and he became angry," cf. Jonah 4:1. He said to God, "I told you so!" He became despondent, cf. Jonah 4:3, 5, and 8.

Saved sinners ought to be glad when they see others repent,

but sometimes people resent having to share the blessings of Jesus' passion.

1 Corinthians 7:29-31

When Paul says, "the appointed time has grown short," he has in mind "the impending crisis" of v. 26 and the "distress in this life" of v. 28. He does not mean that relief is on the way or that the time of suffering for Christians will be shortened. Rather, he is saying that we should not invest in matters associated with this world, because the "time" of this world is short.

Ho kairos ("the appointed time") is almost a technical term for the period before Jesus' coming again, as in Rom. 13:11. Paul believed that he lived in "the ends of the ages," cf. 1 Cor. 10:11. Calvin and others think "the appointed time" refers to the shortness of life.

Jesus said in Matt. 24:21-22 that the "great suffering" which will precede the end will be so severe that "if those days had not been cut short, no one would be saved." The revelations given to John in the last book of the New Testament have more to say about this.

Schema, as in "the present form of this world is passing away," usually means outward appearance, form, shape. But here it has to do with the world itself which is always changing.

"This world" refers to the resources and the opportunities the world offers. The scope of Paul's warning is expanded in the warning of 1 John 2:15-17: "Do not love the world or the things in the world. The love of the Father is not in those who love the world; for all that is in the world – the desire of the flesh, the desire of the eyes, the pride of riches – comes not from the Father but from the world. And the world and its desires are passing away." Everything that is not of God is of the world.

Theologians are not agreed on whether "passing away" means total annihilation or only transformation. Luther taught transformation on the basis of Rom. 8:21. Gerhard argued for annihilation although he did not accuse those who taught otherwise of heresy.[34] Other passages dealing with this matter include Luke 21:33 and Heb. 1:10-12 which quotes Ps. 102:26-28.

Some[35] consider the stressful times in which Paul believed that he was living an important qualification of what he says. His opinion is determined by "the impending (or present) crisis."

Anagke ("crisis" in v. 26) has to do with external distress, as in Luke 21:23-24. For Paul, life was full of anagke, cf. 2 Cor. 6:4; 12:10; 1 Thess. 3:7. He was thinking of the dangers and disturbances in the world of his day. He was thinking also of Jesus' coming again which he believed to be very near, cf. 1 Cor. 16:22. His "opinion," cf. v. 25, might have been different if the times had been different.

Paul believed that married people will experience "distress in this life," cf. v. 28. Thlipsis is a synonym of anagke. Distress will come especially in the persecutions that precede Jesus' coming again. Marriage becomes very difficult under such circumstances. The obligations placed on us by marriage and the requirements for nurturing a family can strain our relationship with God.

Paul does not advise a change in a person's situation because of the distress, cf. 1 Cor. 7:17-24, but he does express a strong opinion as to a Christian's relationship to all earthly things.

It is wrong to emphasize only the negative side of what Paul says and to think that he is affirming an otherworldly attitude. A positive relationship toward the world is also communicated. Christians marry, weep, rejoice, and trade. Ascetic denial of the world is not affirmed nor is naïve contentment with it. God is redemptively at work in the world, and so Christians affirm it. However, the world is passing away, and so Christians should not give primary significance to the things associated with it. We should not commit ourselves to them.

Fear, mistrust, our passions (lusts), and self-love prevent us from letting God be our God, to use the language of the First Commandment of the Decalogue. Jesus says in Mark 4:19 that anxieties "choke the word." He says in Luke 21:34 that they distract us from thinking about "the day." There is a right kind of care and a wrong kind. Paul gives examples in 1 Cor. 7:32-

183

34. The marriage partner can be a representative of the Lord moving us toward Him or of the world separating us from Him. A person is in danger of neglecting one in being concerned for the other.

Paul renounces the old and continuing quest for visible security in the things of this world. Too much of our life is a pursuit for such security. We are concerned about ourselves. We hold fast to our life and property, because we fear they may slip away. But the pursuit for security in the things of this world is the way we lose our life and become the slaves of this fleeting world and the things of the world. We need to give up our hankering after tangible realities and stop clinging to visible materials so that we can become a part of God's future.

Rather than trying to carve out for ourselves a niche which we think is secure, we can surrender ourselves to God and trust Him alone because of Jesus' passion. His love for us is evident. We can accept everything He sends, because He gave His all for us on the cross.

Christians have a new orientation in Christ, a new understanding of themselves and of life. We cast our care on God, following the encouragement of 1 Pet. 5:7. We find freedom from care through prayer, as Phil. 4:6 says. God does not guarantee the fulfillment of our wishes, and He knows better than we what we need.

The world tries to lead us to apostasy through our concern for food and drink, cf. Luke 21:34. To be anxious about food, clothing, and health militates against concern for the kingdom of God and for the things of the Lord. Life is controlled by that for which, about which, and after which we strive. If, in self-concern, we place our hope in the things of this world, we fall victim to this world. Paul says that we should confront all worldly ties from the distinctive distance of "as though . . . not."

This does not mean that we give up life in this world. Paul is not thinking, as did the Stoics, of withdrawing into the safe realms of the inner life. Rather he advocates maintaining freedom in the midst of involvement. We should sow, reap, work, and spin. Paul earned his bread by work and exhorts others to do the same in 1 Thess. 2:9; 4:11; and 2 Thess. 3:10. But, we must not suppose that we can secure our life by being concerned, cf. Matt. 6:27 and Luke 12:15-21. We do not draw our life from this present world. We do not belong to this world but to the world God has prepared for us. We should structure our life after that future, cf. Matt. 6:33. We should be ready for the arrival of the world to come, cf. Luke 21:34. We should be concerned with how to "please the Lord."

Our flesh resonates with the world. We feel exhilarated by success. We are saddened by accusations and failures. We plod along as people who are not failures but never really successful. We rank ourselves in terms of our popularity. We experience victory and defeat in athletic competitions. Those who build their lives on such things are erecting houses on sand rather than rock, cf. Matt. 7:24-27, because the world is passing away.

We should measure our worth by what God thinks of us not what people think. Status is given by God; it does not depend on the opinion other people have of us. What God thinks of us is definitively expressed in the death of Jesus.

To build on rock is to know, love, trust, and fear God alone. Even death cannot destroy the future God has planned for us and prepared for us in Christ Jesus. This enables us to trust and obey our heavenly Father and to love and serve our brothers and sisters. The source of the strength to do this is the story of Jesus, His passion and resurrection.

Paul spells out pointedly what he means by not becoming too attached to the world and the things of the world. Married people are apt to become absorbed in domestic cares, mourners are apt to be absorbed in their sorrow, and buyers are apt to be absorbed in the preservation of what they bought. We should practice detachment.

We are able to be detached, because of our relationship to Jesus Christ. Although existing arrangements and duties cannot and need not be changed, the world and all that belongs to it loses some of its importance when we remember that it is not permanent.

The chapter from which this Lesson is taken deals with

marriage matters. So Paul uses marriage as his first example of how to structure earthly relationships. "Those who have wives (should) be as though they had none." Marital responsibilities make life more difficult during times of "distress."

"Those who buy (should be) as though they had no possessions." Earthly goods are a trust not a possession.

"Those who deal with the world (should be) as though they had no dealings with it." We should not try to get all we can out of the things of this world. People who remember that they are sojourners on earth are likely to remember also that worldly possessions are not everything and that worldly relationships are not permanent. They have been entrusted to us for a short time.

Paul is speaking to the Corinthians as their spiritual adviser. He is speaking with pastoral concern in view of the approaching hardships. He seeks their benefit, cf. v. 35. The "benefit" is that they will be free from anxieties, as he says in v. 32. The "benefit" is "good order and unhindered devotion to the Lord."

Mark 1:14-20

The Old Testament people of God lived in expectation of a man God would send to save them. They called him the Messiah in intertestimental times. But they misunderstood his mission. They conceived of salvation in political terms, in terms of self-rule and political control. The Messiah was an ideal king who would overthrow their foreign oppressors and restore peace and justice among them. When Jesus said, "The time is fulfilled, and the kingdom of God has come near," He claimed to be the man God had promised.

"The kingdom of God has come near" is understood by some as a direct reference to Dan. 7. The most important section of that vision is vs. 13-14 which describe a vision of "one like a son of man coming," cf. the footnote in the NRSV. The vision is explained in v. 22 and more clearly in v. 27. That the Daniel passage underlies Jesus' understanding of His mission and destiny is evident from the fact that Son of Man is His favorite term of self-identification in the synoptic gospels.

The kingdom of God is fundamentally God's rule, His reign, His sovereignty. The Christian gospel is not a proclamation of principles. It is the proclamation that God came to rule in Jesus. When Jesus said, "the kingdom of God has come near," He meant that God was at work in Him.

The kingdom theme spans Mark's gospel. Jesus' initial preaching was in terms of the kingdom, and the final question Pontius Pilate put to Him was, "Are you the king of the Jews?" cf. 15:2. The charge against Him for which He was crucified was inscribed on a sign attached to His cross, "The King of the Jews," cf. 15:26.

The idea of the kingdom of God has a political dimension. In Jesus, a power came into the world that is in conflict with the powers and policies of the world. To say that God reigns in Jesus is to say that the possibility and the opportunity to live by a different power and order than that of the dominant culture, society, and government which determine human existence is present in Jesus.

Jesus' ministry was in continuity with the prophets and their proclamation of the kingdom of God. He was the climax, culmination, and fulfillment of their preaching. What they said was coming was at hand in Him.

Jesus did not match the image of the Messiah held by the Jews of His time. He distanced Himself from the purely national and primarily political concept. On the one hand, He expressed authority and power, but, at the same time, His life was characterized by lowliness and suffering that culminated in His crucifixion. He claimed power in lowliness, sovereignty in service, and victory in defeat.

Jesus was the beginning of a new era which is sometimes called the last days. In Him, the end began to draw near. The "nearness" of the kingdom of God was the basis of His call to repentance. There is no more time. He bid people turn to the God who was turning in might and mercy to them. His preaching challenged and invited people to change their minds and come to trust and hope in God. In Jesus, God laid bare His arm, and people now are confronted with the choice of having that almighty arm for them or against them. There is no neutral corner where anyone can stand and await developments. With Him, the last days began.

Jesus met people with the demand that they deal with the power of sin in their lives. The treatment He prescribed for the problem was repentance and faith. Secular psychologists often remove from the shoulders of counselees responsibility for their condition. They attribute the counselee's difficulties to some past trauma or series of traumas done to them, to hurt feelings caused by others, or to the powerlessness of victimized people against demonic forces. Both Jesus and John the Baptist called for repentance, cf. Mark 1:4.

Metanoeo means to change one's mind. But more is involved than an intellectual exercise. It involves a fundamental reorientation of an individual's personality.

Jesus proclaimed His message against the background of the Old Testament. The burden of the Old Testament prophets was that Israel should turn to the Lord. Jeremiah recognized that people cannot do this by themselves; it is a divine work, cf. Jer. 31:18.

Jesus summoned all people to repentance, including the Pharisees. For this reason, they opposed Him.

Jesus not only announced the kingdom of God, He also set up the community in which God reigns. The establishment of that community had been the purpose of the old covenant. Jesus began to do it again when He called four fishermen to be His disciples.

Jesus began His public ministry in Galilee, according to Mark's gospel. The theme of Jesus' preaching is stated in Mark 1:15. The message Jesus proclaimed is called "the good news of God."

The positive response to "the good news of God" was demonstrated by two sets of brothers. One was Simon (Peter) and Andrew, and the other was James and John. They followed Jesus.

Jesus was the chief Actor in the calling of the first four disciples. One difference between Jesus and other rabbis of His day who assembled a following was that Jesus chose His disciples while, with the other rabbis, the pupils chose the master.

Other rabbis called their disciples to learn, but Jesus called them to enter into the fellowship of His work.

Response to Jesus' call resulted in a dramatic reorientation of the four men's lives and priorities. They illustrate an essential characteristic of discipleship, namely, absolute surrender and a change in all relationships. This characteristic is brought out also in Mark 2:14; Luke 9:57-62; and Matt. 8:19-22. The four men renounced their vocation (fishing) and their source of livelihood (their nets). Simon later reminded Jesus, "We have left everything and followed you," cf. Mark 10:28. As the Markan narrative unfolds, the reader is given episode after episode in which this demand is made of many.

The response to the call of Jesus by Simon and Andrew was immediate. "Immediately" is emphasized in v. 18 by being placed at the beginning of the sentence. Mark stresses their decisiveness. They were waiting for the coming of the rule of God. They made a radical commitment to the good news Jesus proclaimed, "the kingdom of God has come near."

Many people think the response of the four men is easier to understand if they previously had contact with Jesus, as John 1:35-42 indicates. But Mark does not suggest this.

As soon as Jesus saw James and John, He called them "immediately." Their response also is described as immediate, and it is complete: "they left their father Zebedee in the boat with the hired men." Zebedee may have had to give up his hope that his sons would take over the fishing business he established.

We know about Andrew only that he was Peter's brother, that he lived with Peter at Capernaum, and that he was one of the twelve.

Since James is mentioned before his brother, he probably was the elder. He was one of the twelve. He belonged to the inner circle of Jesus' disciples, the three. They were present at the raising of the daughter of Jairus, the transfiguration, and the agony in the garden of Gethsemane. James shared with John a desire for precedence at the parousia in Mark 10:35-37.

Zebedee is mentioned only because of his sons. He probably was the head of the fishing "company." "The hired men" continued to work for him. The world in which Jesus operated seems to have included a lot of small businessmen.

The Sea of Galilee is called a lake as well as a sea. It was twelve miles long and six miles across at its widest point. It was a natural highway between Galilee and Perea and between many towns and fishing villages on its western and northern shores.

Amphiballo is a technical term for the throwing out of the circular casting-net. It was used by a single fisherman. It was about 20 to 25 feet in diameter. The fisherman arranged the net on his right arm and threw it on the water where it was pulled down by the weights. He stood waist deep in the water at those places along the shoreline where the fish swarmed. People all around the world use such nets today.

There were two ways of retrieving the catch. The fisherman might dive down to the net if it were thrown from a boat, pull the fish through the mesh one by one, and put them into a pouch. Or he would gather all the sinkers together being very careful with the edges. Then he would take the net up into the boat with the catch inside or drag the net to shore.

The cast net was an ancient device. Complete cast nets have been found in Egyptian tombs dating back beyond 1000 BC. Two kinds were used in the Sea of Galilee, one for large fish and the other for sardines. The sardine cast net had a small mesh and a system of cords for retrieving it. The cast net for bigger fish had a larger mesh and heavier sinkers to prevent the fish from escaping before the net sank to the bottom.

A different word from that used in v. 16 is used for "nets" in v. 18, ta diktua. The word in v. 18 can refer to different kinds of nets. The men probably employed a variety.

Fishing in the lake was free to all, but there were certain restrictions. In order not to impede navigation, it was forbidden to fix nets.

Fish was one of the favorite items in the diet of the people. The market for fish was good. This may mean that fishermen were people of means and status.

Fish were eaten fresh, dried, or pickled. A kind of relish or sauce was made of them. The fish eggs also were eaten.

Large fish were carried to market slung on a ring or twine. Smaller fish were carried in baskets or casks.

An ancient boat dating back to the first century was discovered in the Sea of Galilee in 1985-1986 when the level of the lake dropped considerably because of a drought. Jutting out from the mud, the remains of a wood fishing boat appeared. The hull is 8.2 meters long by some 2.3 meters wide. The cedar and oak planking was joined by pegs and iron nails. The repairs on the boat indicate that it had an interesting history.

With a boat, fishermen could do their work anywhere on the lake. They could drag long nets through the water in those areas where schools of fish were located. Using this technique, they were able to secure a larger and more rewarding catch than with casting nets.

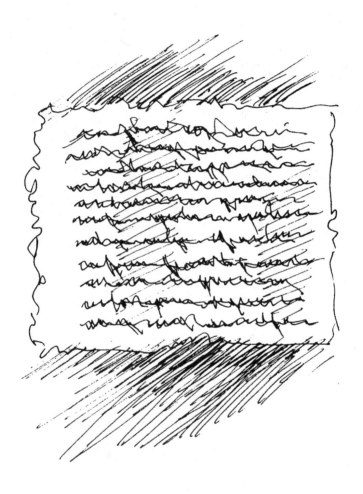

3rd Sunday after the Epiphany

Year C

Nehemiah 8:1-3, 5-6, 8-10

The foundation for the nation of ancient Israel was the covenants God made with Abraham and his descendants, cf. Gen. 15; 17; 18:10; and 22:15-18, with the Children of Israel through Moses at Mt. Sinai, cf. Ex. 19-34, and with David, cf. 2 Sam. 7:8-16; 23:5; Pss. 89:3, 28-29. God promised Abraham, in what He called "an everlasting covenant," that He would make him the ancestor of a multitude of nations and that his descendants would be so numerous he would be unable to count them. He gave Abraham's descendants all the land of Canaan from the Nile River to the Euphrates River. He said that all the nations of the earth would be blessed in him. At Mt. Sinai, God made the Children of Israel "a priestly kingdom and a holy nation." God told David that his kingdom and the rule of his descendants over that kingdom would last forever.

But disaster struck in 587 BC. The Jerusalem temple where God lived among His people was destroyed. The Davidic monarchy ended, and the nation ceased to be a political entity. The best elements of the population were deported to Babylon.

These developments stimulated a radical reassessment by

Israel of her identity and her relationship to God. How should they understand what had happened? Had God sent them into exile, or had the gods of Babylon overwhelmed them? Were they still the chosen people of God, or had God abandoned them? Was God able and willing to deliver them? Did He remember the promises He made to Abraham and David and through Moses?

The conclusion reached was that the events were God's judgment on an unrepentant people in fulfillment of the warnings issued by the prophets. The calamity was just.

But was this God's final word? Hope began to grow that the promises to Abraham, Moses, and David might still be realized. The anticipation of eventual restoration was never completely given up.

Babylon was destroyed by Cyrus the Persian who early in his reign issued an edict of restoration to the exiled Jews. He encouraged them to go home. The Israel that emerged from exile was not the same that had been deported.

With the return from exile nurtured by Cyrus, institutions began to develop that mediated the promise and heritage that had created the old Israel. The leaders of the restoration were Zerubbabel, Ezra, and Nehemiah. Zerubbabel took up the task of rebuilding the temple. Ezra reinstituted the law of Moses. And Nehemiah rebuilt the walls of Jerusalem. The traditional view is that Ezra preceded Nehemiah, but many scholars question this sequence.

The Lesson for the 3rd Sunday after the Epiphany describes a scene of joyous covenant renewal led by Ezra and Nehemiah.

Thus the history of the old Israel continued until the birth of Jesus. In His crucifixion, the covenants God made with Abraham and David and through Moses were fulfilled, and He made the new covenant described in Jer. 31:31-34. When John the Baptist was born, his father, Zechariah, talked in Luke 1:69-73 about how God was keeping the oaths He swore to Abraham and David. He said in Luke 1:76-79 that John would "go before" and "prepare" the way for Him who would bring salvation to God's people. The angel Gabriel told Mary in Luke 1:32-33 about the son she would conceive by the Holy Spirit, "the Lord

God will give to him the throne of his ancestor David. He will reign over the house of Jacob forever, and of his kingdom there will be no end." Mary, the mother of Jesus, said in Luke 1:54-55 that in her son's birth the Lord was acting "according to the promise he made to our ancestors, to Abraham and to his descendants forever."

Some of the key features of the Lesson for the 3rd Sunday after the Epiphany may offer useful points for the preacher:

There was solidarity among the people. The phrase "all the people" is used in vs. 1, 3, 5 (three times), 6, 9, 11, and 12. Not only men but also women took part in the ceremony of covenant renewal. "All who could hear with understanding" may be a reference to the children who were of age. "All the people gathered together" to hear the law of Moses. Ezra did not summon them. The people wanted to hear "the book of the law of Moses." Ezra did not impose it on them. They "were attentive." They "worshipped the Lord," when Ezra opened the book to read.

What is included in the phrase "the book of the law of Moses" is not certain. Perhaps the entire Pentateuch is meant, especially Deuteronomy. It would have taken a long time to read all five books of Moses. Ezra may not have read every single section, and the reading may have continued over a number of days, cf. v. 18.

Understanding was important. The phrase "all who could hear with understanding" is used in vs. 2 and 3. The Levites interpreted what Ezra read, cf. v. 7. They may have translated the Hebrew Ezra read into the Aramaic the people spoke. "The people understood." This is repeated in v. 12: "they had understood the words that were declared to them."

Ezra is called "the scribe" in v. 1 and "the priest and scribe" in v. 9.

"All the people wept when they heard the words of the law;" they were so moved. But Nehemiah encouraged the people to rejoice, because now they knew how to live under God. Before, they had not known. Deut. 16:14 and Lev. 23:40 encourage rejoicing.

Nehemiah told the people that the day must be kept as a

festival. They must eat the best of food and share their good things with those who could not afford them.

1 Corinthians 12:12-31a

The church is not a club in which like-minded individuals have banded together, although seen from outside it may seem so. The church is not a conglomerate of Spirit-filled individuals each of whom has a private relationship to Christ. The church is the body of Christ. St. Paul says not merely that the followers of Christ are like the body of Christ but that they are the body of Christ. The uniqueness of this phrase is not the word "body" but the qualifying genitive. The body is not "the body of Christians" but "the body of Christ."

Paul is the only New Testament writer who uses the term "body" for the church and "members" for Christians, cf. Rom. 12:4-5; 1 Cor. 6:15; Col. 1:18, 24; 2:19; Eph. 1:22-23; 4:4, 12, 15-16.

Christians think of "the body of Christ" in three ways: as our crucified Lord; as Christ present in, with, and under the bread of the Lord's Supper, cf. 1 Cor. 11:29; and as the followers of Christ.

The point of the Lesson is stated in v. 12 and restated in v. 27: all the members of the church are individually the one body of Christ. He is addressing the church of Corinth in its disgraceful divisions and pride, cf. 1 Cor. 1:10-17

Paul is talking about more than the social nature of people and the organic nature of a community. He uses for the church not just the metaphor of a body but of "the body of Christ." In Rom. 12:5, he talks about the church as being "one body in Christ." The words "of Christ" and "in Christ" indicate that Paul has in mind more than what sociologists and psychologists talk about.

The term emphasizes that the church's nurture, direction, and growth is in, by, from, and to the crucified Lord. That the growth of the body is from and to the Head (Christ) is stated in Eph. 4:15-16. The story of the incarnate and crucified Son of God is not merely the retelling of a past event or fact of salvation but a present, lasting, spiritual power that gives life, feeds, inspires, controls, and directs the members of the church.

The great events of Jesus' birth, death, resurrection, and ascension are events in earthly history as much as any battle or enthronement; but they are different from other historical events. The term "the body of Christ" says that they are a part of our life. He lived for us, and we live in Him. We are not Christ, but we are His body. As "the body of Christ," we are ruled by Christ; and He uses us who are the church as His instrument.

We were incorporated into Christ through Holy Baptism and the Lord's Supper. "We were all baptized into one body," Paul says also in Gal. 3:27 and Rom. 6:3-5. "We were all made to drink" is a statement parallel to "we were all baptized." Paul is referring to the Lord's Supper which he talked about earlier in 1 Cor. 10:16.

The body of Christ does not come into existence through Baptism. The members do not constitute the body; Christ does. We were made a part of the body through Baptism. The body existed before we were baptized. Christ is there not through and in the members but before their incorporation.

Baptism involves participation in the death and resurrection of Christ Jesus, cf. Rom. 6:3-11. We do not know Jesus truly until we know that He died, rose, and lives for us. We do not know who and what we are until we perceive and confess that His life is a part of our history. We are not lonely, forlorn creatures but adopted prodigals, sinners condemned and saved at the same time.

Christ continues to live in this world in us. The members of the church are the members of Christ, His mouth and His hands. There are many members.

The life of the members of the body of Christ is not identical with the life of Christ. The life of Christ is shared with the members. The life of the members is a response to that sharing. His lowliness enables us to be God's children. His poverty makes us rich. His death is our life. The foolish word of His cross is our wisdom. His kingship at God's right hand is reflected in our life in this earthly body. One day, as the body of Christ, we will share in His rule.

In the actions of the members of the body of Christ, the Head Himself acts. His love for the church is displayed in a man's love for his wife. His care for people is shown by the honor we give to our weak brothers and sisters. Our redemption through Christ is manifested in the forgiveness we grant to offenders.

There is no imperative need to be met and no advantage to be gained by speaking of a mystical, invisible, extended, sacramental, re-presented, re-enacted, or actualized body of Christ. Such terminology complicates the concept more than it needs to be. In Christ's body, the curse, guilt, sin, and division of mankind is summed up, gathered together, and put to death. By reference to that body, we are the body of Christ.

The body of Christ or the church is one and at the same time varied. It is a unit consisting of all racial, national, and social classes of people. As we individually are bound to Christ, we are bound to each other. "In Christ," is a phrase Paul often uses, cf. Gal. 3:27-28; 2 Cor. 1:21; Rom. 16:7; 1 Cor. 1:30.

The metaphor of the interdependence of the various members in the body was frequently employed in the ancient world. It encourages a view of the church that is inclusive of its broadest constituency.

The words of vs. 14-18 protect and strengthen the place of inferior people in the body of Christ. The dynamic of those words pushes against their self-assessment and destroys their isolation and individualism. "The body" in v. 14 is any human body.

Paul conjures up a false dialogue in which members of the body exclude one another. In both situations described, the exclusion asserted is rejected. First, in vs. 15-16, members of the body exclude themselves from the body. No one in Christ can say that he/she does not belong to the body, because God makes individuals members of the body of Christ. In v. 21, one member of the body excludes another. Rejection of such exclusion is valid for the same reason. No one can exclude another, because God makes individuals members of the body of Christ. The conditional clauses in v. 17 are unreal conditional clauses. They conjure up images of a monster, the whole body as an eye and as an ear.

C. S. Lewis celebrates the varied character of the body of Christ and the dependence of one member on another: "When you find yourself wanting to turn your children, or pupils, or even your neighbors, into people exactly like yourself, remember that God probably never meant them to be that. You and they are different organs, intended to do different things. On the other hand, when you are tempted not to bother about someone else's troubles because they are 'no business of yours,' remember that though he is different from you he is part of the same great organism as you. If you forget that he belongs to the same organism as yourself you will become an Individualist. If you forget that he is a different organ from you, if you want to suppress differences and make people all alike, you will become a Totalitarian. But a Christian must not be either a Totalitarian or an Individualist."[36]

Beginning with v. 19, Paul protects and strengthens the right and place of modest people in the body of Christ. In v. 19, he emphasizes the validity of the differentiation and in v. 20 the unity.

The dialogue between members of the body is picked up again in v. 21 and is directed especially against those who feel that they are better than others and think that they can be independent because of their superior abilities. They exalt themselves over the weak. But even in their weakness, the weak are still part of the body. They should not be pushed aside; but they should be nurtured, restored, and strengthened.

The head and the eye are generally recognized as the outstanding parts of the body. That the eye and the head should say to the hand and the feet "I have no need of you" is not only impossible, it is absurd.

The head of the body is Christ in Eph. 4:15, but in 1 Cor. 12:21 it is simply one member of the body with no special status.

With the words "the members of the body that seem to be weaker" Paul may be thinking of the delicate organs such as the eye and the invisible organs such as the heart. "Those members of the body that we think less honorable" may be our private parts, such as the genitals. Paul uses present tenses to state what is generally true.

The word "we think" and "we clothe" in v. 23 might suggest that we give status to the members of the body, but Paul insists in v. 24 that "God has . . . arranged the body."

By "giving greater honor to the inferior members," God creates confusion in the body. He does this in order that the body might function harmoniously. He wants the members to "have the same care for one another."

The cells of the human body do "care for one another." The ordinary person does not know how to manufacture adrenalin, but the cells of the body do. It requires skilled technicians and an expensively equipped laboratory to produce an antitoxin against scarlet fever, but the cells of the body know how to fight the disease. We have never learned how to make red blood cells, but the tissue which we call marrow in the bones knows how to make them. Certain cells in the ear know what compounds to take from the blood stream in order to make wax. Glands related to the gastro-intestinal tract take from the same blood stream the elements necessary to produce hydrochloric acid. These and hundreds of other chemically complex compounds are being produced continually within our bodies. Each of the millions of cells within the body knows instinctively what is needed to maintain its own health. The nervous system is a complex interrelationship of communication that automatically integrates all of the many functions required to keep the body strong and healthy. Every change in external temperature sets in motion a complicated procedure which maintains the body temperature of the normal individual at a constant level.

The inter-relationships of the members of the body are so complex that the disorder of one organ can seriously affect the entire body. The interrelation finds expression not only in suffering but also in rejoicing with one another. It should be so in the body of Christ.

The translations of vs. 18 and 28 can cause the reader to miss the correspondence between them. Exactly the same Greek verb is used in each verse, but it is translated differently. First it is "God arranged," and then it is "God has appointed." If the word in both instances is translated the same in English, the parallelism can be recognized.

The words of v. 28, "in the church," show that Paul is thinking of the body of Christ as a whole and not merely of an individual congregation.

He lists the order in which God has arranged the gifts given to the members of the church. Apostles are listed first here and in Eph. 4:11. This gift involves proclaiming the gospel and establishing congregations. Apostles saw the risen Lord, cf. 1 Cor. 9:1-2 and Acts 1:21-26.

The list of apostles should not be restricted to the twelve. Paul asserts his status as an apostle in 1 Cor. 9:1-2. "James the Lord's brother" seems to be called an apostle in Gal. 1:19. Paul says that "Andronicus and Junias (or Junia) . . . are prominent among the apostles" in Rom. 16:7. NRSV considers Junia to be the best reading. In that case, she is a female apostle.

Prophets are described in 1 Cor. 14:3 as speaking "to other people for their upbuilding and encouragement and consolation." Sometimes they also predicted the future, as in the case of Agabus, cf. Acts 11:27-28 and 21:10-11.

"Teachers" might be applied to apostles and prophets as well as to the special class of teachers. How the gift of teaching was recognized is impossible to determine. James 3:1 suggests that it was a matter of personal choice. Apostles and prophets probably instructed both the converted and the unconverted, but teachers probably ministered only to settled congregations.

The first three gifts are explicitly listed in the order of eminence. They are outstanding. "Then" may simply mean that the next two come after the first three. We should not count the "thens" as equivalent to fourthly or fifthly. The classification ends with "teachers."

The gifts that follow after the first five are not connected with particular persons but are distributed for the profit of the whole congregation. "Forms of assistance, forms of leadership" are a pair and refer to general management of an external character.

"Forms of assistance" (antilempsis) occurs nowhere else in the New Testament. The root of the word means to take firm hold of someone in order to help. It probably has to do with the care of those in need, that is, the poor, the sick, widows, orphans, strangers, travelers, etc.

"Forms of leadership" (<u>kuberneseis</u>) probably refers to those who superintended the externals of organization. The term is found nowhere else in the New Testament. The word is derived from the idea of piloting a ship. It acquires the sense of directing with skill and wisdom. The figure of the helmsman was very popular for ruling. Paul is talking about gifts rather than the offices that grew out of the gifts.

"Various kinds of tongues" was purposely placed last, because it was too highly regarded in Corinth. The Corinthians probably were shocked to hear the last five brilliant gifts declared to be inferior to teacher, but "then" (<u>epeita</u>) can mean that.[37]

To emphasize the need for variety in the church/body, Paul poses a series of questions in 1 Cor. 12:29-30. Each question begins with the word <u>me</u> in the Greek text which implies that a negative answer is expected.

Strangely, although all the gifts listed in 1 Cor. 12:28-30 are gifts given by the Spirit, Paul encourages us to "strive for" them. He does the same in 1 Cor. 14:1, 12, and 39.

Luke 4:14-21

Luke introduces Jesus' public ministry with a report of Him preaching to the people of His hometown, Nazareth. The text Jesus uses is Is. 61:1-2. His message is that He is the fulfillment of the prophecy of Isaiah; He is the Messiah. The word "Messiah" is not used, but that title can be translated "the Anointed One." "The spirit of the Lord . . . has anointed me" is a reference to the Messiah. Jesus said to the people of His hometown, "Today this scripture has been fulfilled in your hearing." Is. 61:1-2 characterizes Jesus' ministry.

Peter says in Acts 10:38 that "God anointed Jesus of Nazareth with the Holy Spirit and with power." Luke says that "the Holy Spirit descended upon" Jesus at the time of His baptism, cf. Luke 3:21-22. The anointing with the Spirit made Jesus the Messiah and gave Him the endowments for the fulfillment of His Messianic task. Jesus was consciously aware of the Spirit's power in Himself.

Isaiah said that the Anointed One would "bring good news," and He would "proclaim." He would offer 1) "good news to the poor," 2) "release to the captives," 3) "recovery of sight to the blind," and 4) He would "proclaim the year of the Lord's favor."

In His preaching, Jesus said, "Blessed are you who are poor, for yours is the kingdom of God" in Luke 6:20. "The poor" include "the captives," "the blind," and "the oppressed." They are people who have nothing and are nothing in their own estimation. Such self-judgment is found most often among poverty-stricken people, because that is the way society evaluates them. The rich are thought by others to be something; and they are inclined, therefore, to come to that same conclusion about themselves. But wealthy people, too, may be nothing in their own estimation. Furthermore, some poor people may be rich in spirit. Jesus' preaching and His ministry gave clear evidence that God has not rejected anyone – not even the poor – but values everyone.

Another group to whom the Messiah would give relief is "the captives." The word obviously has to do with prisoners, but other kinds of people have lost control of themselves, too. The whole Jewish nation was bound up by the man-made laws of the scribes and Pharisees, cf. Luke 5:33-6:10. Many people possessed by demons were released by Jesus, cf. Luke 4:33-37; 4:41; 6:18; and 7:21.

The liberation given by the Messiah included freedom from sin. Jesus forgave sin in Luke 7:36-50. All mankind is under the rule of the devil and the slavery of sin. Luke shows throughout his gospel how this release takes place in Jesus' encounters with those around Him. In His cross and resurrection, the chains of sin and death that opposed mankind were once for all time broken; and the forgiveness of God proclaimed. Jesus demonstrated His authority to forgive sins when He healed a paralytic in Luke 5:17-26.

Luke refers to Jesus healing the blind in 7:21. In all of His preaching, Jesus gave people the opportunity to see God.

The words "to let the oppressed go free" are taken from Is. 58:6; they are not in Is. 61. The word "free" (aphesei) connects Is. 58:6 to Is. 61:1-2. The word is used in both passages in the sense of release. Luke also uses the word aphesei in the sense of forgiveness in 1:77; 3:3; 24:47; Acts 2:38. Jesus healed and forgave a paralyzed man in Luke 5:18-26, and He cured a man with a withered hand in Luke 6:6-11.

The quotation of Is. 61:1-2 in Luke 4:18-19 is a fairly free citation from the LXX. Some parts of the passage are omitted. The omissions accent what is included. It was not uncommon in first century Judaism to pull two or more passages out of their original literary context and read them together as Jesus did. This was usually done when each passage had at least one word that was the same. In this case, it was the Greek word aphesis. The anointed one was to preach aphesis to the captives, according to Is. 61:1. The Lord wants the oppressed to go in aphesis in Is. 58:6. The Hebrew shemitta in Deut. 15 and deror in Lev. 25 are translated aphesis in the Greek. The two passages provided legislation for the year of Jubilee which is called "the year of the Lord's favor" in Is. 61:2. Is. 61 was composed leaning on the Jubilee traditions.[38] So when Jesus added Is. 58:6 to the quotation of Is. 61:1-2, He was not wildly picking an Old Testament passage. He was doing so fully in the spirit and even the letter of Is. 61. The central concept of Jubilee was periodic release or liberty: letting the land periodically lie fallow, release of debts, release of slaves, and repatriation of property. Some believed that the real Jubilee would be introduced by the Messiah.

The age/period of Jesus is called "the year of the Lord's favor" or "the acceptable year of the Lord." Some consider this an allusion to the year of Jubilee described in Lev. 25:10-34. Jesus said, "This time is now."

Isaiah is cited, alluded to, and otherwise appears in the New Testament more than any other Old Testament book. It apparently was the most helpful single book of the Old Testament in assisting the early church to understand Jesus' life, especially His passion. Five hundred and ninety references, explicit or otherwise, from 63 chapters of Isaiah are found in 23 New Testament books (239 from Isaiah 1-39; 240 from chs. 40-55; 111 from chs. 56-66).[39] Passages such as Is. 42, 49, and 53 illuminated for the first Christians the crucifixion in such a way that they could see how God worked the salvation of the world through Jesus' death. Jesus Himself may have taught this to His disciples, cf. Luke 24:27. Isaiah 61:1-2 was one of the favorite passages of Judaism in the time of Jesus.[40]

The people of Nazareth had heard many rumors about what Jesus did and His teaching in nearby synagogues. "A report about him spread through all the surrounding country." He "was praised by everyone." When He finished reading from the Isaiah scroll, the people of Nazareth wondered what He would say, what comments He would make. They probably wanted Him to answer chiefly two questions: who do you claim to be and what are you doing. They waited eagerly. Luke says, "The eyes of all in the synagogue were fixed on him."

The words of Luke 4:21 are not all the words Jesus spoke on this occasion. They are a summary.

The prophet's words were originally addressed to the exiles returning from Babylon. The consolation for Zion promised by Isaiah was given by Jesus in a fuller sense and in a fuller way to the descendants of the exiles. Isaiah's words were fulfilled.

Fulfillment is the theme of the first sermon of Jesus Luke presents. Jesus said that He was fulfilling the prophecy of Isaiah. He was the Messiah about whom the Old Testament prophet spoke. This was an important message. It is a dominant message in Luke's gospel and in the entire New Testament. Luke restates it at the end of his gospel, cf. Luke 24:27.

Jesus alluded to Is 61:1-2 again in Luke 7:22 as He talked about His mission in response to the question from John the Baptist. Between 4:21 and 7:22, Luke describes how the prophecy of Isaiah was fulfilled by Jesus. Some of this is outlined above.

Luke emphasizes the fullness of the Holy Spirit in Jesus. The Spirit "descended upon Him" at His baptism, cf. Luke 3:22. He is "full of the Holy Spirit" and "led by the Spirit" in Luke

4:1. He taught in the power of the Spirit in this Lesson. The Spirit is a dominant figure in Luke's description of Jesus' ministry and has a dominant role in Lucan theology.

Luke describes Jesus as a teacher in 4:31; 5:3, 17; 6:6; 11:1; 13:10, 22, 26; 19:47; 20:1, 21; 21:37; 23:5. He does not say what Jesus taught as do Mark, cf. 1:14-15, and Matthew, cf. 4:23. The story of Jesus in the Nazareth synagogue offers an example of His teaching regarding the fulfillment of the scriptures on one occasion.

As a teacher, Jesus spoke the language of the people. He used terms and images that were close to and germane to their lives. The materials of His parables were taken from the world every Palestinian knew: the garden, the farm, the kitchen, the fisherman's trade, the relationship between master and slave, weddings, feasts, fastings, going to court, wineskins, patched clothing, the son who left home, and the dangerous road from Jerusalem to Jericho. Jesus used no metaphors drawn from athletics. There were amphitheaters, stadia, and hippodromes in Palestine, but the world of Graeco-Roman athletics remained remote from the life of the average Jew. In Paul's writings, on the other hand, there is a free use of athletic imagery, e. g., 1 Tim. 4:7-8; 2 Tim. 4:7-8; 1 Cor. 9:24-27, despite the fact that the great athletic festivals, such as the Olympian and the Isthmian games, were pagan religious celebrations.

Luke says that Jesus "went to the synagogue . . . as was his custom." He may be referring to a family custom or to Jesus' habit as He traveled around. He lived the life of a pious Jew. Synagogue attendance was expected of every devout Jew.

Christians early gave up the observance of the sabbath and established Sunday as the Lord's day, cf. Col. 2:16-17 and Acts 20:7. Sunday became the official day of rest with an edict by Constantine in 321.

The origin of synagogues is shrouded in mystery. There is no way to know when or how they came into existence. It may be that they developed during the Babylonian captivity when the people did not have access to the temple in Jerusalem. It is not until the beginning of the Christian era that we are fully informed about synagogues.[41]

The institution remained even after the return from exile and the reconstruction of the temple. At the time of Jesus, it was the regular place for religious gatherings. The pious met there every Sabbath and usually on Mondays and Tuesdays, as well as on other special occasions.

Synagogue buildings were used for prayer, for reading the scriptures, and for instruction. Sacrifices were not performed there. Such places became more important as the prominence of the law increased. The law had to be read and taught to the people.

Every synagogue had a chest in which the rolls of the scripture were kept, a platform with a reading desk from which the scripture of the day was read, lamps for lighting the building, and benches or seats for the congregation.

Every synagogue had a library of sacred scrolls, especially scrolls of the law and the prophets and perhaps also related literature. They were hand-copied on sheep or goat skins or on papyrus from Egypt. The language of the community and of commerce was generally Aramaic, but Hebrew remained the language of the scriptures.

The Isaiah scroll from Qumran is a good example of the sort of scroll that Jesus might have used. It is complete and dated to about 100 BC.

The word "synagogue," like the word "church," can be either a gathering of people or the place where the people gather.

Worship in a synagogue was led by laymen. Leadership responsibilities were divided among the adult males of the congregation.

Worship consisted of the recitation of the Shema, a prayer, a fixed lection or reading of the law, a free lection from the prophets, an explanation, an application of one or both scriptural passages to the contemporary situation, and a blessing by the priest, or a prayer by a layman.

The ruler or elder presided over and directed the synagogue service. Rabbis in Israel still do not conduct the service or have leadership in the synagogue. They are not even in the paid employ of the synagogue. They hold a position as teacher. Priests and Levites had no recognized position in the synagogue.

Their functions were confined to the temple and to the duties prescribed by the law.

Jesus "began to teach in their synagogues," Luke says. The use of the plural indicates that Jesus went from place to place. This seems to have been His mission method. Paul followed it later.

Any stranger could be invited to address a synagogue assembly. When Jesus "stood up to read" in the synagogue of Nazareth, He may have been invited by the president of the synagogue assembly.

The holy scrolls were always read standing in the synagogues. First, a lesson from the law was read and then one from the prophets. The liturgies of today's so-called liturgical churches are a direct descendant of synagogue worship. What Jesus did may be compared to the reading of the Lessons and the Gospel.

After the lesson was read in Hebrew, it was interpreted/ translated in Aramaic or in Greek. This was done verse by verse in the law; but in the prophets three verses might be taken at a time. Then followed the exposition or sermon. The worship of the church in the apostolic age seems to have followed a similar order, cf. 1 Tim. 4:13. When this is done in worship today, a tradition going back to the time of Jesus and before is being renewed.

Although the synagogue officers had fixed duties, no one was especially appointed either to read, to interpret, to preach, or to pray. Any member of the congregation might do that. If a visitor known to be competent was present, the synagogue officials might ask him to read and to expound a passage. The reader, interpreter, and preacher might be one, two, or three separate persons. In Nazareth, Jesus was both the reader and the preacher. Possibly, He interpreted as well. When He became famous as a teacher, it was always easy for Him to address a congregation. He was often invited to do so.

Jewish tradition traces the practice of reading portions of the sacred writings in worship back to the time of Moses and Ezra, cf. Deut. 31:10-12; 2 Kings 23:1-3; Neh. 8. But synagogue traditions are in dispute. Jewish pericope books are extant only from the tenth to the twelfth centuries AD, although they probably represent earlier practices. It is likely that the reading of the torah was fixed at least as early as the century before Christ. Readings from the prophets at the end of the service came later. Isolated chapters rather than continuous readings seem to have been the rule.

For Jesus to sit down after He read from the Isaiah scroll may sound strange. It was not as though He did not anticipate talking to the people. He sat down, because He wanted to talk to them. The reading of the scriptures was done standing, but teachers and preachers in those days sat as they spoke. Perhaps the hearers stood.

That "the scroll of the prophet Isaiah was given to" Jesus has been understood by some to mean that Is. 61:1-2 was a part of the assigned reading for the day. Some explain heuren ("found") to mean that He located a prescribed passage which had been marked in the scroll. But vs. 18-19 do not strictly follow the Old Testament text. Is. 58:6 has been incorporated into what Jesus read. And the evidence for a cycle of prophetic readings in first-century Palestine is debatable.

Lectionaries have played an important role in Judaism and Christianity. They are orderly sequences of selections from scripture which are read at public worship. A lectionary can be put together by an individual for a local community to be used for one season only, or it can be the product of many minds and be used throughout a broad region for centuries. Its selections or pericopes may be a few verses in length or many. They may be for festivals, Sundays, or weekdays. There may be one or several readings for each occasion.

Many people in their private devotions welcome following some plan. In the same way, a system is useful for public readings. Lectionaries follow an orderly succession of passages which reflect the calendar, fit the public worship pattern of a group, and cover passages of scripture which are important to a community. They provide uniformity so that wherever a person worships, the same lessons can be expected. They provide continuity from generation to generation. A lectionary gets beyond the subjectivity of a local preacher and allows lessons that might otherwise be avoided to come up naturally.

Lectionaries may be arranged for the continuous reading of Biblical books or isolated excerpts may be selected for various reasons.[42]

Jesus gave the scroll "back to the attendant." It is probable that he was the man who gave Jesus the scroll to read.

Luke says that Jesus "returned to Galilee." Hupestrepsen can mean either "returned" or "withdrew." The word may indicate that Jesus was living in Nazareth before He went to the Jordan to be baptized by John the Baptist, cf. 3:21-22, and to the wilderness where He was tempted, cf. 4:1-13.

Visiting the Nazareth synagogue may not have been the first thing Jesus did in Galilee. V. 15 says that He began to teach in the synagogues. V. 23 refers to a ministry in Capernaum before He addressed the people of Nazareth.

Galilee was a fertile area thickly crowded with towns and villages. Josephus says that the smallest community contained more than 15,000 inhabitants. He numbered 204 cities and villages in Galilee.

Jesus' parents came from Nazareth. This is where He was raised. The town that Jesus knew has been obliterated. It was a struggling farm community located near a spring. It consisted of little more than small scattered structures of fieldstones and mud with thatched roofs. What remains are a few cisterns, storage bins, presses carved in the bedrock, and small caves. The population may have been less than 400.

A comparison with the gospels of Matthew (13:54-58) and Mark (6:1-6) suggests that the story of Jesus' visit to the synagogue in Nazareth is probably not correctly placed chronologically in Luke's gospel. Matthew and Mark seem to have Jesus preaching in His hometown on a different occasion. Mark uses the account of Jesus' preaching in Nazareth as a transitional unit. It comes at the end of His Galilean ministry. Matthew presents the story of Jesus at Nazareth as the climax of His Galilean ministry. Luke's lack of concern for chronological precision indicates that he is not interested simply in an accurate recounting of the events of Jesus' ministry. The third gospel is not simply a biography.

Some think that the event recorded in Matt. 13:54-58 and

Mark 6:1-6 is different from the one in Luke 4:16-30. One difference is that Mark 6:1 says that "his disciples followed him." In Luke, Jesus seems not to have any disciples. Nevertheless, it seems clear that the event recorded in Luke was not the beginning of Jesus' public ministry. A ministry in Capernaum is mentioned in v. 23, cf. also vs. 14-15.

4th Sunday after the Epiphany

Year A

Micah 6:1-8

This <u>rib</u> ("case" or "controversy") contains one of the most famous passages of the Old Testament: "He has told you, O mortal, what is good; and what does the Lord require of you but to do justice, and to love kindness, and to walk humbly with your God?" It sets the parameters for Godly behavior. It is a classic definition of the duty of one person toward another and toward God.

The first stipulation lays down social and moral standards in one's relationship with the people with whom one lives: "to do justice." Commitment to Jahweh includes commitment to them.

Justice (<u>mishpat</u>) is the word often used by the prophets to sum up this social obligation. It covers and transcends a number of negative precepts, such as the prohibitions of oppression, perjury, and bribery. It calls for a sense of responsibility toward the weaker members of society. It insists on the rights of others.

Justice must be understood in more than a legal sense and involves more than a legal process. It means showing God's regard for people and their needs, especially for people who do not have the necessities of life.

When public speakers today talk about justice, its meaning and value are often assumed. The Old Testament prophets often do not analyze, justify, or explain it. In all of western culture, justice connotes meanings like equal, fair, right, and good. When someone cries out for justice, something has gone wrong in the relationship between society and its members. Amos issues such a call in Amos 5:21-24. He connects justice and the worship of God. He says that because there is no justice, there is no acceptable worship of God. Another cry for justice is in Is. 5:1-7. The goal of Israel's entire history is justice and righteousness.

Justice is rooted in the knowledge of God who Himself is just. It is a moral value that frequently is mentioned synonymously with righteousness. Righteousness is a quality that describes people who are fair and favorable to other people. To do justice is to love good and to hate evil.

In contrast to a view too generally held in modern legal systems, the Old Testament prophets believed that justice can be done in the courts and in the economy. Concrete acts, decisions, and policies that effect justice are attainable. Too many people today consider justice an impossible goal for the courts. Two or more contenders who represent different positions present the evidence for their position and against the other. The goal of both is not justice but winning. When one side wins the approval of the judge or jury, that is called justice. But such justice depends much on the ability of the presenters. In that kind of justice, greed is a great motivator for both sides; and genuine justice takes a back seat. Injustice too often is the result. Too many people consider it the best that can be done.

The prophets articulate a notion of justice that has relevancy beyond their time and place. They believe that all citizens should have a share in the control of society's basic economic good, providing them access to basic rights and freedom. The administration of order should protect and support their status against economic and political processes that oppress them. Wealth that endangers the welfare or the rights of others is unjust. Good treatment of the least favored in society is the fundamental criterion of the achievement of justice.

In their cry for justice, the prophets attack the problem

associated with ownership of the land and the rights and privileges that go with it. Land was being accumulated into estates and used as a basis for status and to generate more wealth than people could use. Those who lost their land were deprived of status and economic support. The rights of the widow, the fatherless, and the weak and their protection against economic oppression were widely ignored. The result was a growing gap between rich and poor. Amos, Isaiah, and Micah considered the situation critical, and it caused them to cry out for justice. Their cry was addressed to the people with authority and power in the social and administrative structure.

A redistribution of land was the primary target of the prophetic indictment in Micah 2:1-2. Land was a person's inheritance from God. God was the real Lord and Owner. To lose one's inheritance was tantamount to losing one's identity as a member of the people of God and the privileges that went with it, cf. 1 Kings 21. For ownership of land to become the basis for the control of one citizen over another was a violation of God's intention.

Micah and other prophets point repeatedly to what was happening in the courts, in the local assembly in the gate of each town, and in the legal apparatus created by the monarchy, cf. Micah 3:1-3; Amos 5:7-12; Is. 1:21-26.

The levying of taxes and fines, the enforcement of creditors' rights, foreclosure on land and crops, the commitment of persons to bond servitude and slavery may have been legal according to the definition of the term at that time; but by the criterion of the values and the social goals in which Israel believed and to which they were committed, they were a travesty of justice and unrighteousness. Justice should be the foundation and the criterion of laws; laws should not be the foundation and the criterion of justice. Because of their close relationship the prophets often speak of justice and righteousness at the same time.

As wealth grew, the difference between the rich and the rest increased, and those who were rich could afford more justice than the others. Micah talks about the corruption of judges through their love of money. Amos speaks of bribes. Isaiah says

215

all officials run after fees. Just laws require righteous people for whom the social well-being of others is a higher priority than gain.

Wealth, the pursuit of it and the possession of it, is a subject that appears repeatedly in prophetic indictments. Amos paints a verbal picture of a group who built houses of hewn stone and owned large vineyards, kept summer and winter palaces, collected furniture inlaid with ivory, were gourmets who ate the best meat and drank the best wine. Both he and Isaiah satirize perfumed and bejeweled women who pester their husbands for more and more and a leisure class who are heroes at drinking wine and famous for lavish entertainment. Micah accuses the leaders and professionals, including priests and prophets, of the prostitution of their vocations to the lust for wealth.

The prophets do not reject prosperity and the pleasure that comes with well-being. They see no virtue in the poor or in being poor. Amos seems to have been a successful sheep-breeder. Isaiah belonged to the upper circles of Jerusalem's urban society. But there is a kind and degree of wealth which they hold to be incompatible with justice, and the nature of its incompatibility can be inferred from the way in which they describe it. If its acquisition and possession cost the economic freedom and welfare of others, they call it violence and oppression. If it fosters conspicuous consumption at a level of luxury that is enjoyed without concern for the needs of others, it is wrong. If it sets profit above personal relations, it is iniquitous. If wealth is the dominant motivation of those who hold power and thus control social well-being, that is sin.

The motif in the social sayings of the prophets that is probably best known is their concern for the weak and the poor. "The fatherless and the widow" are a specialty of Isaiah. There will always be some who, by reason of misfortune or handicap, are unable to maintain their own support and status. The situation of a family that has lost its husband and father is particularly desperate. The narrative of Ruth is a famous illustration. The prophets make the treatment of the poor and the weak the functional criterion of a just society, cf. Is. 3:14-15.

They offer no solutions, no programs, no detailed approaches that can be directly adopted and applied to modern problems. They advocate no program of new laws or administrative correction. They do not call for revolution or for the overthrow of the existing order in favor of something else. They issue no summons to one class to seize power.

The prophets appeal to the faith and conscience of their hearers, cf. Is. 1:16-17. They call for righteousness. They appeal to people to change when they are confronted with a contrast between what they do and the way of righteousness. The powerful should use their power for the welfare and rights of others. The courts should uphold justice. The cause of the poor should be recognized and met. There is a naïve character to the idea of doing justice, loving mercy, and walking humbly with God. Where that naïve character is lost, the alternative is a society based on the self-justification of whoever can seize and hold power.

The prophets speak of God exercising His wrath and enforcing His purposes in the world. Misused power will be displaced. Wealth and luxury gained from oppression will be dissolved. The continuity and institutionalization of injustice will be interrupted. The ground will be cleared for a new beginning. Amos looks for the end of the northern kingdom. Isaiah foresees a purging and cleansing of Jerusalem. Micah expects the elimination of officials and leaders along with their estates and power. The prophets say that divine judgment will break through and break up the dominance of injustice in the society of Israel. Their demand for change in the lives of people and their trust in the work of God in overturning the old to make way for the new is very powerful.[43]

The second thing the Lord requires is "to love kindness." The Hebrew word is chesed. It expresses the moral aspect of love, the fulfillment of an obligation, and the acceptance of a responsibility. It describes the loyalty of Jahweh toward Israel. God tied Himself in a covenant to Israel and took upon Himself obligations. That is chesed.

God's chesed inspires human chesed. The dynamic is like that of love in the New Testament. Hosea indicts the northern kingdom for failure to practice chesed in Hos. 4:1-2. He exposes the disparity between the community spirit that Israel is supposed

217

to have and the wretched reality. Micah calls the southern kingdom to a higher ethic. He wants the people to reflect God's concern in every area of their society.

The first two elements in what Micah calls "what is good" and says the Lord requires are oriented toward the way people treat each other, but they are based on God's character and will. This is brought out especially in the third element, namely, "to walk humbly with your God."

To live with God is to humbly go along with what He wants. It is the opposite of self-centeredness and everyone going his/her own way. Calling God "our God" implies that we are "His people," cf. Lev.26:12; Ps. 50:7; Hos. 2:23; 4:12; Jer. 11:4.

The response God wants from His covenant partners is recognition of His grace in the past and of His will for the present. It is a readiness to be guided by Him in all that they do.

Walking with God includes obedience to ritual laws as well as ethical behavior toward others. Jesus calls for this in Matt. 5:24. Micah is not calling for a change in ritual but a shift in emphasis from acts of worship to life. As it is vain for a person to give all of his/her goods to feed the poor and give his/her body to be burned without love, so it is vain to offer thousands of rams if there is no chesed, cf. 1 Sam. 15:22.

Micah 6:8 comes at the end of a covenant lawsuit called in Hebrew rib. Jahweh accuses Israel of breaking the covenant He established with them through Moses at Mt. Sinai, cf. Ex. 19:3-6. The lawsuit reveals elements that were a part of ancient Near Eastern treaties between a sovereign ruler and his subject people. One important thing is the role of a covenant mediator whose prototype was Moses.

Rib is a controversy or accusatory pronouncement. The word is used three times by Micah, once in v. 1 where it is translated "case" and twice in v. 2 where it is translated "controversy." Other examples of the rib form are in Is. 1:2-31; Jer. 2:4-3:5; Pss. 50 and 81.

First, the prophet addresses his audience to prepare them for the drama that follows. Then he addresses Jahweh, the Accuser, and tells Him to present His rib. He summons the witnesses of the covenant to be present, cf. v. 2, the mountains, the hills, the enduring foundations of the earth. A similar thing is done in Deut. 32:1 and Ps. 50:4-5.

The Lord states His charge against Israel in vs. 3-5. A similar charge is made in Deut. 32:4-18. Israel's ingratitude is emphasized.

At the beginning of His speech, Jahweh allows for the complaint that somehow He has given His people reason for a charge against Him. The point is that they have no reason for their failure to keep the covenant.

He begins His rib with a self-identification rooted in the covenant preface, cf. Ex. 19:4. "The saving acts of the Lord" which constituted the people of Israel are recited. Four items are stressed. He rescued them from slavery in Egypt; He "redeemed" them. The idea is that of release. No payment is envisioned. Leadership was provided. He led them for forty years under Moses, Aaron, and Miriam. The mention of Moses and Aaron is a part of the traditional language of covenant remembrance, cf. Josh. 24:5 and 1 Sam. 12:6. Miriam is added. Jahweh was with them and protected them to the end of their journey. The encounter with Balak and Balaam which came toward the end demonstrated this. The story is told in Num. 22-24. The Lord gave them entry into the promised land of Canaan. "What happened from Shittim to Gilgal" is the crossing of the Jordan River. Shittim was the last stopping point before crossing, and Gilgal was the site of the first encampment on the west side, cf. Josh. 3:1 and 4:19. That miraculous event was commemorated in subsequent years at Gilgal, cf. Josh. 4:19-24.

Israel is called on to remember these historic events, her salvation history. The relationship between Jahweh and Israel was quite different from the relationship between the gods of the religions of the ancient Near East and their followers. That relationship focused on events in nature while the relationship between Israel and Jahweh centered on events in history.

Remembering involves more than recall of what happened in the past. Every Israelite in succeeding generations shared in the experience of the exodus through ritual. All the annual festivals were occasions for such remembering. The worshippers participated in the history of Israel through the ritual, cf. Deut. 26:1-10. Those events shaped their lives.

Israel had not been remembering. She had been looking for Jahweh elsewhere than where Jahweh manifested Himself and was involved with her. The point is that Israel should have responded to Jahweh's faithfulness by being faithful to Him.

The prophet gives Israel's reply to the Lord's charge in vs. 6-7. On the one hand, the people were offended and felt that the divine charge was unwarranted. They appeared to be penitent, submissive to Jahweh, and ready to do whatever was necessary to make up for their sins. On the other hand, Israel's response has an arrogant and sarcastic tone. This touch is given through the ridiculous suggestions: "calves a year old," "thousands of rams," "ten thousands of rivers of oil," and the sacrifice of "my firstborn for my transgression, the fruit of my body for the sin of my soul."

The acts of atonement grow larger in size as they are listed. In "burnt offerings," the whole animal was consumed by fire on the altar. In other types of sacrifice, part of the animal was eaten by the worshippers at the cultic meal.

Calves were eligible for sacrifice from the age of seven days, cf. Lev. 22:27, but yearlings were regarded as the greatest sacrifice. Obviously, the older the animal got the more the worshipper had invested in it. A yearling was a greater economic sacrifice than an animal that was only a few weeks old.

"Thousands of rams" was the mammoth offering Solomon and other kings sometimes made, cf. 1 Kings 3:4; 8:63; 2 Chron. 30:24; 35:7.

Oil accompanied some of the offerings. Usually, it was given in relatively small quantities. "Ten thousands of rivers of oil" is a gross amount.

Sacrificing their firstborn would be a desperate quest for forgiveness and covenant renewal. It was an offer highly offensive to Jahweh.

Human sacrifice was known in the ancient Oriental religions, but it was exceptional. Usually and in Israel, an animal was substituted as a means of redemption. However, cases of child sacrifice are found in 2 Kings 16:3; 21:6; 23:10; Jer. 32:35.

The people no longer understood God and were no longer intimately acquainted with Him. They asked God, "How much do you want?" They had forgotten who Jahweh was and what His nature was. The questions they addressed to Him were an insult.

Israel offered ritual sacrifice to heal the breach between them and God. Micah rejected their offer. Isaiah also condemned that idea in Is. 1:10-17. God's covenant with Israel involved ritual, but the prophet expected more. He called for the proper behavior toward other people.

Micah did not pretend to offer Israel anything new: "He has told you, O mortal, what is good." His answer was quite traditional. He had nothing new to say with regard to what God wanted.

He said that ritual did not replace an obedient life or make up for a disobedient life. He denounced as pointless the hypocrisy of cultic solicitation of Jahweh's favor by a society that was morally corrupt. He urged a change in conduct.

An individual represented Israel: "O mortal."

The prophet cut Israel down to size after her arrogant response in vs. 6-7: "He has told you! You know better!"

"What is good" is not an achievement but activities. Jahweh did not want to regulate life by law. His desires were described by the general term "good," cf. Hos. 8:1-3; Amos 5:14-15; and Is. 1:17.

Christian preachers today can follow much the same outline as that used by the prophet. They can confront their hearers' injustice, unmerciful behavior, and pride with "the saving acts of the Lord," the passion of Jesus. God has done more for us in Jesus Christ than He did for Israel in the exodus.

We are made participants of what Jesus did in the Lord's Supper. As we eat and drink, we do more than simply recall what happened. We become involved. The Lord's Supper is an <u>anamnesis</u>, a remembrance meal, cf. 1 Cor. 11:24-25. Although it is not wrong to describe its dynamic by saying that through eating Jesus' body and drinking His blood together with the bread and the wine He becomes a part of us, a different description may be as powerful – or more so – if we say that through the eating and drinking, we become a part of Jesus and what He did. The Greater does not become a part of the lesser, but the lesser becomes a part of the Greater.

Our special relationship with God was established when we were baptized. Paul calls for a response to this relationship in accordance with "what is good" when he appeals to us "by the mercies of God, to present your bodies as a living sacrifice, holy and acceptable to God" in Rom. 12:1, when he encourages us to "live your life in a manner worthy of the gospel" in Phil. 1:27, to "lead a life worthy of the calling to which you have been called" in Eph. 4:1, and to "be careful . . . how you live" by "understand(ing) what the will of the Lord is" in Eph. 5:15 and 17. The New Testament is full of models the preacher can use in making such an appeal.

1 Corinthians 1:18-31

The first verse of this Lesson is the final verse of the Epistle Lesson for the 3rd Sunday after the Epiphany (A). We will try to avoid repeating here the discussion of it there.

This Lesson is a major resource for the premises of this study, "Preaching the Passion." Paul asserts that the power of God is in "the cross of Christ," cf. 1:17, and that the power of God comes to us and saves us through "the message about the cross." This is true although "the message about the cross is foolishness to those who are perishing." "The message about the cross" is not for those who consider themselves wise, and it does not save them. Those who are being saved are not the "powerful" and those "of noble birth." Those who are being saved let the power of God work in them.

Paul is appealing to the Corinthian Christians to give up their arrogant boasting that produced and is sustaining a divisive party spirit among them, cf. 1 Cor. 1:11-13. He urges them to be united in Jesus Christ and His cross.

People are continuously trying to acquire knowledge of God and His ways and a closer relationship to Him. The New Age religions are very popular these days. Even Madonna, the pop singer, is practicing Kabbalah "which involves the attempt to more directly understand God through contemplation and arcane

222

textual study."[44] The tradition has its roots in Judaism and stretches back centuries. But all effort to know God through human research is futile. Human thinking does not agree with the wisdom of God. "God made foolish the wisdom of the world."

"The cross" is a code word Paul uses for Jesus' death by crucifixion. The apostle is the only Biblical author to use the term in this way. He describes God's way of saving people in his Letter to the Romans using the terminology of justification by faith. In this letter to the Corinthians, he says the same thing using the terminology of "the cross."

Paul does not describe the historical event of Jesus' death in his New Testament writings. Rather he proclaims the saving value of Jesus' crucifixion. The people to whom Paul proclaimed "Christ crucified" were all too familiar with the bloody details of that capital punishment. They were frightened by them. They saw too many people put to death in that way.

A man was suspended in the air on two pieces of wood, one positioned vertically and stabilized in the ground. The other was attached to the vertical piece horizontally. He was fastened to the wood with crude, hand-made nails driven through his hands/wrists into the horizontal piece, and one nail was driven through both feet into the vertical piece. He hung there until he died. The place of execution was usually beside a busy road where a lot of people could observe and learn that they should not do what that man had done. The slow and excruciatingly painful process of dying often took two or three days. The victim hung naked and exposed to the taunts of all who passed by. Crucifixion is considered one of the most awful forms of capital punishment ever devised. Many people considered the portrayal of Jesus' crucifixion in the movie "The Passion of the Christ" overdone, but it is very hard to make crucifixion more terrible than it was.

It was considered so awful that it was illegal to punish a Roman citizen in that way. Cicero said, in a speech on behalf of Rabirius Postumus in the Roman forum, "The very name of the cross should never come near the body of a Roman citizen, nor even enter into his thoughts, his sight, his hearing." Cicero said that Postumus could not be defended if the indictment were true that he had had Roman citizens crucified. Until the fifth century, Christians hesitated to depict Jesus suffering on a cross. Doing this on a large scale became customary only in medieval Gothic times. The word "cross" repelled Paul's contemporaries probably more than the word "gallows" repels us today.

The oldest portrayal of Jesus' crucifixion in existence dates back probably to the third century. It was found on the Palatine, the imperial residential district in Rome. Jesus on a cross is represented under an ass's head. Below the depiction is the sarcastic scribble: "Alexamenos worships his God." It would be impossible to say more strongly that "the message about the cross" was anything but edifying to the ancient world. It was worse than a bad joke.

D. T. Suzuki, the prominent Zen Buddhist, highlighted the offensiveness of crucifixion: "Whenever I see a crucified figure of Christ, I cannot help thinking of the gap that lies deep between Christianity and Buddhism."

Neither ancient Jew, Greek, nor Roman would have thought of giving a positive, religious meaning to the cross. It was for outlaws. A devout Jew considered the cross a curse from God. It was a symbol of condemnation by people and by God, cf. Gal. 3:13.

"The message about the cross" is that through Jesus' death God saved the world. Paul does not blame the Romans, the Jews, or any people for crucifying Jesus. God decided to save the world through "Christ crucified."

How Jesus' death accomplished that goal is hard to understand. But God has declared that because of the crucifixion of His Son the sins of the world have been forgiven.

God's decision to save the world in this way was His response to the world's rejection of Him in favor of "images resembling a mortal human being or birds or four-footed animals or reptiles," Paul says in Rom. 1:21-23. God revealed Himself in creation, but the world exchanged the truth about God for a lie by calling its images God. God could have given up on the world, but instead He "decided" to save the world through "Christ crucified."

The crucified Christ exposes the radical discontinuity between God and the world. Jesus' crucifixion reveals why the world needs to be saved. The chasm between God and humanity is now bridged by a message that does not make sense.

"The message about the cross is foolishness to those who are perishing." The Greeks consider it foolishness, and Paul accepts their judgment of that proclamation. Something is foolish when it does not agree with the human way of thinking. "The message about the cross" does not. People are confused and offended by it.

Today, the cross symbolizes for Christians redemption, liberation, and salvation. It is a prized piece of jewelry. But in the days of Jesus and Paul, it was a symbol of pain, shame, humility, and condemnation. God, by definition, is the ultimate in power, wisdom, strength, honor, glory, and dominion. To say that He humbled Himself, became a human, and died on a cross to take away the sins of a world that rejected Him doesn't make sense. He can do anything; He could have chosen a better way to save the world.

Christian preaching holds God up before the world not only in His majesty but also as a humble man who was executed in an ignominious way. It says that God established His reign in the world through the humiliation, suffering, and death of Jesus of Nazareth. The human mind cannot conceive of God's kingdom being established in this way. God has destroyed "the wisdom of the wise."

"The message about the cross" must be preached as foolishness, because "God decided" to save the world through such foolishness.

"To us who are being saved," "the message about the cross" is "the wisdom of God." There is a close relationship between "the wisdom of God" and "the foolishness of our proclamation." "The foolishness of our proclamation" is how God now reveals Himself to the world. This revelation is not formal communication of new knowledge about Him but a way of salvation which can be accepted only by faith.

"Proclamation" (kerugmates) in v. 21 is not the act of preaching but its content. The reference is to the divine plan involving "Christ crucified." Paul says, "We proclaim Christ crucified."

"The message about the cross" is the lens that enables believers to see things rightly. Luther said, "A theology of glory calls evil good and good evil. A theology of the cross calls the thing what it actually is."[45]

"The message" is not a power but "the power of God" through which He saves people. But Paul's contemporaries must have been shocked when he told them that the means God uses to exercise His power is "the message about the cross." The cross seems to be weakness. To the Jews, the very term "crucified Messiah" was offensive. To assert that Jesus' death on a cross effected salvation evidencing the power of God is not acceptable.

But the cross of Christ is the way of human atonement with God, according to Col. 1:20; 2:14; and Eph. 2:16. Christ reconciled not only humans but all things, earthly and heavenly things alike. The means He used is His blood shed on Calvary's cross. It has universal expiatory power. God erased "the record that stood against us with its legal demands. He set this aside, nailing it to the cross," cf. Col. 2:14. The cross is where God did away with sin that separates us from Him.

Because "the message about the cross is foolishness," Christians might be afraid or ashamed to proclaim it. But Paul was not. He says, "I am not ashamed of the gospel; it is the power of God for salvation" in Rom. 1:16. Even if "the message about the cross" is "foolishness" and "weakness," it is "wiser than human wisdom, and . . . stronger than human strength." Through it, people come to know God and His love for them.

The foolishness of "the message about the cross" ought to make the church humble and keep her from developing arrogant "divisions" and engaging in boastful "quarrels." The character of "the message about the cross" does not agree with the character of the party spirit that developed among the Christians in Corinth. It proclaims a divine humility so great that, according to human standards, it is foolishness. The church ought to reflect the character of the God she represents.

The Corinthian Christians were trying to establish power

blocks, that is, factions and preacher personality cults to gain power over each other. They were trying to elevate themselves to a high status on the basis of the strength of their leader. Apollos is better than Paul, Cephas is better than Apollos, and Christ is better than all. They claimed these men as their leaders and claimed status on the basis of their association with them. Paul rejects such thinking and uses the Corinthians themselves as an example of why it doesn't work. God's choice of them to be His people was as foolish as the message He used to claim them.

Many think the early Christians were low on the social scale of that day. They base such thinking on what vs. 26-28 say. It has probably been more influential than any other single text in promoting that idea. On the other hand, some think the early Christians were members of the middle class of antiquity up to the time of Emperor Constantine. They were primarily free workmen, craftsmen, small businessmen, and independent farmers. As time went on, more and more members of the upper classes entered the church, but it was not until after the conversion of the emperor himself that the aristocracy converted in large numbers. It is easy to believe that this is what happened in that hierarchically organized society. At the beginning of the second century, Pliny noted that the Christians in Asia Minor were members of every class and were primarily city dwellers. Pliny was disturbed because they were beginning to penetrate the countryside.

Paul uses the word "foolish" to describe the Corinthian Christians. He employs three negative statements: "not . . . wise by human standards," "not . . . powerful," and "not . . . of noble birth." This is followed by three positive statements saying the same thing: "foolish," "weak," and "low and despised."

Modern church planners would have chosen a different kind of people to form the foundation of the church in Corinth. God worked, as only God does, when He called the people He did, the weak, the lowly, and the despised. In the same way, modern church planners would have chosen a different messenger than Paul, cf. 1 Cor. 2:3-4. God's work excludes human self-assertion.

The words "not many" are used repeatedly and indicate

that Paul excluded no class of people. There were some but "not many."

"Not many (of them) were powerful." The word "powerful" emphasizes political power. "God chose what is weak in the world to shame the strong." Before God no one is small, since before Him no one is great. The Bible is one long record of how God uses "weak" people as the agents of His power. Paul's description of how He worked in Corinth expresses the truth Mary stated in her Magnificat: "he scattered the proud in the thoughts of their hearts. He has brought down the powerful from their thrones, and lifted up the lowly," cf. Luke 1:51-52.

"Not many (of them) were of noble birth." This has to do with social status. The Corinthian church included people from all levels of society. There were some from the lower levels as well as some from the upper. Not many were nobility.

"God chose what is low and despised in the world, things that are not, to reduce to nothing things that are." The use of the neuter gender for the Greek words referring to people emphasizes what Paul is affirming. A more contemptible expression, according to Greek thinking, than "things that are not" was not possible. Being was everything to them.

Paul puts down the Corinthians when he says that not many of them were wise, powerful, or of noble birth and when he calls them foolish, weak, low, and despised. On the other hand, when he says that "God chose" them, he makes them a very special group. Their status is established by their relationship to God and what He did for them.

God's ultimate aim in choosing the people He did was, "so that no one might boast in the presence of God." In Christ crucified, people discover a completely different way of looking at themselves. Their dignity takes a quite different form.

The words "became for us" refer to Jesus' passion. In His passion, "Christ Jesus . . . became for us wisdom from God, and righteousness and sanctification and redemption."

Christ is the true wisdom. He was made so by God. In union with Him, Christians are made wise. They possess God's wisdom. Paul is pointing forward to 1 Cor. 2:6-8 where he develops further the idea of Christ as "wisdom from God."

Paul wants to curb the intellectual and spiritual snobbery in the Corinthian church. His main point is that no philosophical subtlety or intellectual ability can arrive at true wisdom. Wisdom is found in what the philosophy of this world calls foolishness. In the cross of Christ, God Himself reveals as wisdom what is in contrast to the wisdom of this world. It offers not intellectual acumen but righteousness, sanctification, and redemption.

"Righteousness" is the status of being in the right with God. It is God's gift and always remains an object of hope in this world, cf. Gal. 5:5. Salvation is our expectation in the final judgment based on our justification in the present, cf. Rom. 5:9-10 and 13:11.

We are God's righteousness in Christ Jesus. Christ was made sin by God for us, cf. 2 Cor. 5:21. Ours is an alien righteousness, cf. Phil. 3:9.

If the Corinthian Christians want to boast, Paul admonishes them to "boast in the Lord." They should boast about what God has done for them. They should glory in the cross of Christ, cf. Gal. 6:14, foolish though it is judged by the wisdom of the world. Paul talks at length about Christian boasting in 2 Cor. 11:16-12:10. If, in their boasting, the Corinthian Christians would follow the example of Paul and boast of their weakness, the church's "divisions" and "quarrels" would end.

When Paul uses the term "Jews and Greeks," he means all people, especially the human race at its best, the religiously favored and the intellectual elite. Paul was a Jew and was aware that the Jews were God's chosen people. Jews were distinguished from Greeks by language, descent, and culture. The culture of the Mediterranean lands was essentially influenced by the Greek tongue and Greek civilization. The Romans conquered the Mediterranean world militarily and politically, but the Greeks conquered it culturally. The word "Greeks" changes to "Gentiles" in v. 23.

The Jews of the New Testament time demanded a sign when a person asserted that something came from God. They wanted powerful proof from God, divine certification, some miraculous happening. Biblical examples are numerous, cf. Mark 8:11-12;

Matt. 12:38-40; 16:1-4; Luke 11:16; John 6:30. Jesus' remark, "Unless you see signs and wonders you will not believe," in John 4:48 indicates how prevalent the demand was. It had precedents in the Old Testament, cf. 2 Kings 20:1-11; Judges 6:36-40; and Ex. 4:1-9, 27-31. The sign God offered to certify Jesus was His cross. This was something completely different from what the Jews wanted.

Jews considered the cross not powerful proof from above but a display of weakness. It was "a stumbling block." They considered it scandalous to link God with weakness. The defeat Jesus experienced, the disgrace, and the ignominy was the "stumbling block." The Jews expected a triumphant Messiah who would set up a glorious kingdom. They could not relate to the Christian proclamation that the Messiah established God's kingdom by being tortured and crucified.

The cross of Jesus still remains a scandal and an offense to Jews and pagans insofar as it exposes the human illusion that we can deal with God, that we can work out our salvation by our strength, wisdom, piety, or self-love, that we can dispute with God and call Him into question.

The Jewish demand for signs and the Greek demand for wisdom have in common that they call for proof from the human point of view in support of divine truth. In doing this, Jews and Greeks set themselves up as authorities who pass judgment on what is of God. God must submit Himself to their criteria. God's revelation has to present itself as a factor belonging to the world. God is the possession of human beings. The Jewish demand for signs and the Greek demand for wisdom reduce the Creator to a manageable creature.

God was taken hold of also by the Corinthian Christians. Their boast of a Pauline, Petrine, or Apollonian relationship resulted in party strife. They put human beings in the limelight where honor is proper for God alone.

Paul did not consider miracles to be signs. He never mentions the miracles of Jesus. Apparently, miracles were taking place in the Corinthian community, cf. 1 Cor. 12:9-10. Paul says that he himself possessed the gift of working miracles, cf. 2 Cor. 12:12.

The distinctive characteristic of Greeks, according to Paul, is wisdom. No one denies the high intellectual perception of the Greek philosophers, but their wisdom was the obstacle to their believing reception of the gospel. "Christ crucified" is foolishness to seekers after wisdom, because human wisdom uses different norms than those of the gospel of God.

An example of the Greek's reaction to the proclamation of "Christ crucified" is Paul's discussion with the Athenians on the Areopagus in Acts 17:18-32. He was rejected by them, because the gospel of Jesus' death and resurrection was not acceptable. They desired philosophical and theological arguments and oratory.

"God decided" to "destroy the wisdom of the wise" and to "thwart" "the discernment of the discerning" through "the message about the cross." In this way, He fulfilled the words of Is. 29:14. Paul seems to be quoting that passage in v. 19 in support of what he says in v. 18.

The phrase "the wisdom of the wise" is equivalent to the phrase "the wisdom of the world." The opposite is called "the wisdom of God" which the wise call foolishness.

"Wisdom" (sophia) and "discernment" (senesis) refer not only to theoretical knowledge but also to attitude, in this case hubris. "Discernment" is the ability to put two and two together.

The frequent occurrence of the word "wisdom" (sophia) in the early chapters of 1 Corinthians suggests that Paul is employing a key word used by the Christians in their quarrels. The word is used sixteen times in 1 Cor. 1-3, perhaps only three times in the rest of the Pauline literature.

Probably, no distinction should be sought between "the one who is wise," "the scribe," and "the debater of this age." "The one who is wise" is the person who claims to know and who ought to understand. The Jewish scribes claimed knowledge of God. The phrase "of this age" probably applies to all three terms. The phrase "the wisdom of the world" sums up all that is included in the three. "The message about the cross" mocks human self-confident pretensions.

Human striving can do no better than Roman law and the Hebrew religion, both the highest of their kind in the ancient world. They combined to crucify the Son of God. That is the ultimate foolishness.

The foolishness of God is wiser and the weakness of God stronger than the very best that humans can muster. "Has not God made foolish the wisdom of the world?" is a rhetorical question expecting an affirmative answer.

"The world" is a fallen creation that is hostile to God's ways. Paul here places the world in antithesis to God.

When Paul uses the term "the wisdom of the world," not all human knowledge about every topic - physics or medicine, for instance - is being considered - at least not primarily. The words "the wisdom of the world" apply specifically to the human ability to comprehend God. The wisdom of the world led men of wisdom to make "images resembling a mortal human being or birds or four-footed animals or reptiles" and call them god. That is foolishness.

Paul establishes a contrast between God and "the message about the cross" on one hand and "the wisdom of the world" on the other. Using its wisdom, the world is perishing. Through the foolishness of "the message about the cross," the world is being saved. This makes the wisdom of the world foolish.

Paul is not saying that it is impossible by means of reason to draw up doctrinal statements about God from observation of the world, but he is saying that it is not possible by means of reason to achieve a relationship to God as God, as Creator, to honor Him as God. "The message about the cross" is set against the backdrop of the world's failure to know God through human wisdom. The world's norms for knowing are totally inadequate and result in not knowing God. God eludes and confounds the world's way of thinking that associates Him with power, majesty, honor, and glory. Over against "the wisdom of the world" as exemplified by Jews and Greeks, God set "the message about the cross." By choosing to reveal Himself in Christ crucified, God contradicts all human notions of greatness. By saving the world through Jesus' crucifixion, God makes foolish that wisdom of this world which understands greatness to be the ability to inflict suffering and to escape from it. Jesus' cross makes us think in a different way. "The message about the cross" forces us to adopt a new logic, a new way of living as well as thinking, a way that rids the Corinthian church of the party spirit.

The world's rejection of God was active refusal, according to Rom. 1:18-23. God revealed Himself in nature, Paul says, and in the history of Israel. He tried to lead the human race to know Him in ways that are compatible with human thinking. But humanity was so rebellious that it refused to acknowledge Him in that way.

"The world did not know God" when using the categories of "the wisdom of the world." So God chose another way to make Himself known. Now He reveals Himself through the cross of Jesus and "the message about the cross."

God is the most obvious reality in the world, yet the one most violated. God condemns human wisdom by accomplishing His will apart from human norms of wisdom. In effect, God says, "You people will not understand me. You refused to accept me when I came to you in understandable ways. So now, your understanding be damned. I will do my saving work apart from your understanding."

To "know God" is to recognize Him and His work and to live with Him.

We resist humiliations and suffering. We think that where God is at work, there is justice, righteousness, and peace. Where those things are lacking, we wonder if God is at work at all and if He is being effective. We evidence this in our reaction to the tragedies of life. When they happen, we ask, "Where was God?" Fancy words do not explain. Only "the message about the cross" gives understanding.

The preacher today must grapple with the hearers' instinct to hear good teaching, discuss a nice philosophy of life, and engage in interesting ethical debates while resisting the notion that the death and resurrection of Jesus is the final answer to anything.

Although Paul draws a contrast between the way the Greeks sought after wisdom and "the wisdom of God," the two grew together as Christianity became a part of the Hellenistic world.

A new discipline developed called theology. It was the achievement of the Greek and Latin fathers. For them, philosophy, too, came from God, though not in so direct a way as the law of the Jews. They found the same truths in the philosophers and the scriptures such as the teachings regarding the unity of God, the attitude toward the worship of images, the attitude toward certain evil religious practices, and the problem of the righteous and virtuous conduct of people.

They explained the similarities between the prophets and the philosophers in three ways. One, they said that the philosophers borrowed from the scriptures. Another explanation was that the philosophers came to their discoveries of the truth through the power of reasoning which God had implanted in them. Sometimes they explained that the discoveries of the philosophers were God's special gift to the Greeks by way of human reason as scripture was to the Jews by way of direct revelation.

Their attempt to identify with the philosophers was motivated in part by their desire to protect Christianity from the attacks of Hellenism. They tried to show that in opposing polytheism, idolatry, and the various forms of heathen worship, they were following in the footsteps of the best pagan philosophers. Their doctrines were in agreement with the teachings found in philosophy.

When those who opposed what the fathers were doing quoted Paul's warning against being "taken captive through philosophy and empty deceit" in Col. 2:8, they argued that the warning was only against the use of that kind of philosophy which is "empty deceit" but not against true philosophy which conforms, or at least can be made to conform, to the teaching of scripture. They took over many technical terms from philosophy in order to define and defend the concepts of the Christian faith, terms like "substance," "essence," and "hypostasis."

The phrases "those who are perishing" and "us who are being saved" represent classes of people. One group is aware of its destiny, the other is not.

In the phrase, "us who are being saved," salvation is thought of as not completed during this life.

Paul mentions only believers as being saved in v. 21. "Christ crucified" did more; He saved "the world," according to 2 Cor. 5:19.

Matthew 5:1-12

No portion of the scriptures was more frequently quoted and referred to by Christian writers during the first three centuries of the church than the Sermon on the Mount. It may still be the most popular section of the Bible today.

The Sermon on the Mount is the example par excellence of Jesus' teaching, but teaching was not His chief mission. Jesus came to the world to save us by dying on a cross. He said of Himself, "the Son of Man came . . . to give his life a ransom for many," cf. Mark 10:45.

The Sermon on the Mount in the Gospel according to Matthew begins with a series of Beatitudes. The exact number is debated. They are reckoned as being seven, eight, nine, or even ten in number. There is no dispute that there are seven Beatitudes in Matt. 5:3-9. V. 10 may be a distinct Beatitude. That vs. 11-12 should be regarded as a Beatitude is confirmed by its being among the four in Luke, cf. Luke 6:22-23. V. 12 by itself does not seem to be a Beatitude. The word "blessed" is not used, and it should be joined with v. 11.

In the Beatitudes, Jesus outlines the style of life that is the mark of His disciples. The Beatitudes do not describe different kinds of people but different characteristics that make up the Christian person. The poor in spirit are meek. Those who are merciful are peacemakers. Those who hunger and thirst after righteousness are pure in heart.

Jesus "went up the mountain" where "he began to speak." The use of the definite article, "the mountain," correctly reflects the Greek original. The same place is referred to in Matt. 15:29 and 28:16. It is possible that there was some spot where Jesus often met with His disciples which they called "the mountain." The place is not identified in the Bible. From the 13th Century on, the name was given to the Horns of Hattin that lies ten miles from the Sea of Galilee. The Horns of Hattin really is not a mountain but only a hill 60 feet high. The name derives from its twin peaks. It is on the road from Tiberias to Nazareth, about one and a half hours in walking time northwest of Tiberias. Modern guides point to a spot at the northwest corner of the Sea of Galilee overlooking the lake as the place where Jesus delivered the Sermon on the Mount. The term "the mountain" may have theological rather than geographical significance. Matthew may be saying that "the mountain" was a new Mt. Sinai and that Jesus was the new Moses, cf. Deut. 18:15.

Jesus "sat down" as He "taught." Sitting was the customary posture for a teacher. Another example is Luke 4:20-21. Matthew's great chapter on parables begins with Jesus sitting in a boat beside the Sea of Galilee, cf. Matt. 13:1-2. Other examples are in Matt. 15:29; 23:2; and 24:3.

Who "his disciples" were is hard to say. We probably ought not think simply of the twelve apostles. Matthew tells the story of the calling of the twelve later in Matt. 10:1-5. "Great crowds . . . from Galilee, the Decapolis, Jerusalem, Judea, and from beyond the Jordan" were following Jesus, according to Matt. 4:25. The presence of such a large following caused Jesus to go up "the mountain," Matt. 5:1 says. Then "after He sat down, his disciples came to Him." We probably should think of Him as teaching "the crowds" and "his disciples." At the end of the sermon, Matthew says that Jesus was speaking to "the crowds," cf. Matt. 7:28.

The evangelist may have in mind a procedure used when speaking to a large group in those days. Jesus spoke directly to His disciples, and they relayed what He said to the crowds. This was before PA systems were available.

1

The human eye sees everything upside down; but that poses no problem, because we have learned to make the adjustment so that everything looks right-side-up. That adjustment can be likened to our moral situation. The world is upside down if we think of how God intended it to be. It is totally corrupted by sin. But we have become so accustomed to the upside-downness of the world that we consider it right-side-up. As a result, we resist efforts to change it.

The upside-downness of the world is the human problem. Jesus came to save us from this situation. He came to turn us right-side-up, to enable us to live as God intended. He walked in this upside down world right-side-up. The people who lived with Him found this intolerable. When they could not get Him to walk upside down the way they did, they killed Him. But some did believe Him and let Him turn them right-side-up. They followed Him. They were His disciples. After Pentecost, they went about preaching what He taught them. The Jews in Thessalonica called them "people who have been turning the world upside down," cf. Acts 17:6.

The difference between a life that is right-side-up and one that is upside down is made clear in the Beatitudes. Some people are blessed whom others consider to be getting the short end of the stick.

The word "blessed" is the origin of the name "Beatitudes." The Latin word is <u>beatus</u>. Some translators like to replace the word "blessed" with the word "happy," because it is easier to understand. But the word "happy" can hinder rather than help us understand what Jesus is talking about.

Happiness is sometimes mistakenly linked with a fine home, a good income, security, health, and reputation. Some people assume that those whose material concerns are provided for are among the happiest people in the world. If a family moves from a $200,000 home to a $600,000 home, or if their income increases from $6,000 a month to $20,000, some people think their happiness will triple. External factors and materialistic considerations can contribute to happiness and contentment, and a lack of sufficient material things can cause problems. But external factors in themselves are not the basis of lasting happiness. Some people are happy with little, while others are not happy with much. Some poor people are among the most contented people in the world. Some people with much in terms of material possessions never find happiness, because they keep looking for it in the wrong places.

We should not think that we can shop for happiness at

Tiffany's or a BMW dealership. The good feelings we experience in acquiring things at such places dissipate as quickly as vanilla ice cream sitting in the sun. They are great at the first taste, but they quickly lose their ability to satisfy. The Beatitudes are clearly eschatological.

Jesus is more than a teacher; He is the Giver. He declares "the poor in spirit" blessed. That declaration indicates that God has acted, is acting, or will act in their favor. Jesus breaks into and transforms the dark present of "the poor in spirit" with this word. He conveys to them what His words say. Whomever He blesses is blessed indeed.

To grit our teeth and clench our fists in order to survive what is happening to us, to be strong and hard can make us unable to receive what Jesus wants to do for us and in us. The same steel that prevents us from being destroyed can also prevent us from being opened up and transformed by the power of God. We may survive on our own. We may even grow strong on our own. But we cannot be "blessed" on our own. A clenched fist cannot accept the blessings God wants to give us.

"In spirit" following "the poor" shifts the emphasis of "the poor" from the material sphere to the spiritual. "Spirit" refers to the human spirit. It denotes a quality in a person. The interest of the Beatitudes in Matthew is not the problem of physical want, although that may be present. Those who are materially poor are not necessarily "poor in spirit." Those who are wealthy can nevertheless be that kind of people.

"The poor in spirit" are neither poor in courage, nor poor in the Holy Spirit, nor poor in spiritual awareness. They are disciples of Jesus who stand before God with no illusions of self-righteousness or self-sufficiency. To be "poor in spirit" means to be somewhat downcast, some might even call it a little depressed. "The poor in spirit" are those who have a humble opinion of themselves. They are sensitive to their own inadequacies and their sinfulness. They know how unimportant they are. They feel a great need and depend entirely on God to supply that need.

The characteristic Jew in Jesus' day was just the opposite; he was proud, vain, and ambitious. The Pharisees, the scribes, and the chief priests resisted and resented what Jesus taught. They wanted nothing to do with His kind of world, because they had succeeded in carving out for themselves a very advantageous niche in a different one. So they put Him to death.

We tend to reject the first Beatitude. We have been taught to think, "Blessed are those whose spirits are high, for they sit on top of the world." Blessed are they who have dignity, who respect themselves and have the respect of others, who are self-confident, who feel adequate for what they are doing.

Life is a pursuit of dignity. A craving for wealth is one expression of it. When people have money, they can present themselves to the world as the center of a beautiful, respected, and dignified picture. Their rich home, their car, their clothes, and the vacations they take are parts of it. Physical things do influence our spirit.

Our passion for dignity moves us to conform. Do what others do; never be odd. That's the way to be accepted. Acceptance is an awfully important factor in dignity.

We will not allow an attack on our dignity. We devise evasions and excuses to cover ourselves. If we fail, we find comfort in casting the blame elsewhere. Why should we blame ourselves when we can blame another person? We seek the comfort of association with our own kind. There we find at least some degree of respectability, some hope of being accepted, some signal that we are not utterly worthless. Sin covers sin, lie covers lie, evasion covers evasion until we have constructed around ourselves a world in which we have some respect and some dignity. In this world we hide, and our greatest dread is to have our cover shattered and taken from us. Faced with that reality, some people commit suicide.

Self-esteem is considered an essential ingredient for human happiness. It is thought to be the single, most important personality trait human beings can develop. Self-esteem is the belief that we are lovable and capable. It is the way we rank ourselves and our status in comparison to others. It means feeling good about ourselves.

Secular humanism rejects humility. Humility has been replaced by dignity. Dignity is the primary value of the secular age. Women demand equality with men. Blacks demand equality with whites. Young people demand equality with old people. Even children talk about their rights.

God knows all about our need for dignity. He wants us to have it. What He condemns is the way we seek it, and the illusory quality of the dignity we manage to achieve. The fact is that we cannot create or achieve our own dignity. We can build only illusions of it. We can long for flattery, delight in the giddy satisfactions of success, and be courageous in our battle against threats to our self-respect. But we acquire only a little dignity, and that only once in a while. We keep it only a short time. To be dignified is a dream; it is like a glittering soap bubble; it disintegrates as we grasp for it. We need something more real, a dignity we can really have and keep and on which we can build our life so that it is neither a delusion nor an evasion of reality.

Whenever dignity is considered to depend on human achievement, pride rises high. Competition is exalted and pits person against person to fight, exploit, envy, and despise. Even religion is turned into a tool for the pursuit of dignity and superiority. The girl who is elected "queen" of something or other, the young man who receives a citation as a superior student, the man who enters politics and wins an election, the athlete whose brilliant performance carries him or his team to victory - such people have dignity.

Pride is the opposite of spiritual poverty. It is a spiritual cancer. It eats up the possibility of contentment, love, and even common sense.

True dignity is God's gift; it is not our achievement. Jesus gives dignity to those who claim none. He fills our need for dignity when He says, "Blessed are the poor in spirit." He did that, too, when He lived on this earth among us, cf. Luke 7:36-50. The forgiveness Jesus secured for us on the cross sets us free from all that shames us. He gives dignity in this Beatitude to us who have accepted that forgiveness.

The spiritually poor do not place their confidence and trust in temporal goods. Temporal goods are good and to be used, but we should not identify ourselves with them as though we felt that they would be with us forever. Our thoughts and emotions, loves and loyalties should so be fixed that we are able to leave house and home, spouse and children, jobs and community. Even though we continue to live among people and serve them out of love, we should be able, if necessary, to give them up at any time for God's sake.

Rich people may be "spiritually poor" without discarding their possessions. But when the necessity arises, they let God take them. They do this not because they want to get away from spouse and children, house and home. They would rather keep them and thereby serve God. But they do not find security in possessions. They do not call home, in the full sense of that term, any foot on earth. No earthly society claims their complete allegiance. They are poor and place their hope in Him who called them to be His disciples.

When dignity is conceived of as a gift from God, we are set free from the pursuit of it. Recognizing that they have no righteousness of their own, "the poor in spirit" are willing to be saved by the rich grace and mercy of God. They are willing to be where God places them, to bear what He lays on them, to go where He bids, and to die when He calls. "The poor in spirit" cherish the dignity of the name son/child of God. This is greater than any honor that a person can achieve or the world can confer.

Since we need not pursue our own dignity, we are free to be used for the glory of God. We can love others.

We will never lose the dignity God confers. What we gain on our own, we can lose. What God gives, no one can take from us.

Jesus demonstrated the truth of this Beatitude. He was crucified in a most undignified way. Yet He never lost His dignity, the dignity that matters. He was the Son of God, no matter how many people denied it, no matter what they said. God raised Him on the third day. That was a powerful declaration of His Sonship in the face of every rejection.

The word "heaven" is a circumlocution for "God." "Kingdom of heaven" and "kingdom of God" are identical in meaning.

The word "kingdom" indicates not a place so much as an activity. The kingdom of God refers to God's ruling activity.

Jesus says that "the poor in spirit" are blessed, because God is working for them. They have God as their King. They do not rule. The Ruler of the kingdom is God. That they are a part of His kingdom means that they have accepted His will as the only rule in their lives.

"The kingdom" is not merely a promise for the future. Jesus does not use the future tense but the present. This is a declaration regarding the present situation of "the poor in spirit." God in His grace is their King, and they enjoy and share in His reign.

The first and the eighth Beatitudes are in the present tense. The promises of the other Beatitudes are in the future and portray the ultimate blessings of the kingdom, the final fruit of Jesus' royal ministry, cf. Matt. 25:34.

While the Beatitudes promise and grant the kingdom, we petition God for it in the Lord's Prayer, cf. Matt. 6:10.

One place we begin to experience the promise of this Beatitude is in the Holy Communion. Sometimes Satan keeps us away from the blessed Sacrament through a feeling of unworthiness. But Jesus does not reject the person who is "poor in spirit." People who acknowledge their unworthiness are the worthy ones. Those who feel worthy of it are really unworthy. People who are secure, proud, puffed up, and feel no need to repent are unworthy.

2

The second Beatitude follows easily from the first. Jesus calls "blessed . . . those who mourn." In their relationship to God, they are very near those who are "poor in spirit."

Mourning is misery. It seems to be the opposite of blessedness. The world tries to avoid it. With each Beatitude, Jesus widens the gulf between His disciples and all other people. The call to be different becomes increasingly clear.

We mourn because we are not recognized. We are ignored, forgotten, and taken for granted. We mourn because we are very ordinary and can make no exceptional claim. We mourn because we did not get our way, or we were defeated in battle. The materials of nature controlled us and mocked our efforts to do something creative. We have no confidence in ourselves. We mourn our inadequacy.

The world refuses to mourn. Philosophies of pessimism may be reasonable and realistic, but they are never popular. We must be optimistic. No matter how depressing reality may be at any given moment, we search until we find some thread of hope. We seize it in desperation, build our life with it, and ignore everything else. We exercise the power of positive thinking.

The result is that much of our life is a massive strategy of evasion. Any evidence that we are not strong, not beautiful, not wise, not honorable, and not better than others is simply ignored. When some dreadful event strikes us, we take refuge in unbelief. "I can't believe that's true," people say. "I can't believe it happened to me. I feel as though it happened to someone else."

Another device we use is to assure ourselves that the dreadful reality is not really dreadful. "That's life!" "We all have to go sometime!" "Time heals all wounds." "You'll get over it." "This, too, shall pass." Or we cover up the reality with jokes. One of the effective ways to evade what we ought to fear or to escape the guilt of something of which we ought to be thoroughly ashamed is to deny that we made a mistake, to reject failure, or to make it the subject of humor. We joke about it. We escape reality by keeping busy, by pursuing pleasures, by being entertained, by traveling and forgetting, by wild parties, by drink, by drugs, or by acting as though we were happy.

Evil must not be allowed to be real. We must not mourn. If there is no solution for evil, we must forget it, drown it, ignore it, deny it, disguise it, philosophize it, be bigger than it, or pretend that it doesn't hurt. "Keep a stiff upper lip," we say. "Big boys don't cry!"

In the end, such efforts are in vain. They are a useless expenditure of energy. If happiness depends on being important, we aren't. The joy of success is fleeting. It quickly fades into only a memory. If happiness depends on being right, how can we be right when so much of our life is sheer pretense? A tiny germ or a single malfunction can kill us. A small stupid mistake can wreck our whole world.

The world regards the words of Jesus, "Blessed are those who mourn" as nonsense. Yet Jesus means exactly what He says. He means that they are blessed who acknowledge sorrow. This is so, because they are open to a new possibility, the comfort and the salvation of God in Jesus.

Sin is real! Death is real! It makes a mockery of the life that is conceived in terms of achievement. We leave this world as naked as we come into it. Jesus knows this, and He urges His disciples to face up to it. His realism comes through in the way He approaches sinners. He does not say, "Everybody sins!" as though that should reduce the guilt. He does not try to dismiss sin by saying, "Lots of people have done what you did." He does not let the guilty off the hook with the concession, "It's human nature."

The human situation demands mourning, the honest despair of self. Only to such as do that can the promise of deliverance and blessing be given. Death is awful! It is an expression of the wrath of God for sin. When Jesus says to those who are experiencing the death of a loved one, "Do not weep!" it is because He is prepared to offer the only real comfort, the resurrection that overcomes death. Nothing less than that can comfort. Anything less than that is escapism. Our weakness is real, and our boast of power is self-deception! To mourn is to confess our helplessness to deliver ourselves from evil. It is to acknowledge the hopeless futility of all our self-saving devices - our lies, our illusions, our escapism.

"Those who mourn" does not mean all who are crying. Much depends on the cause of the mourning and the spirit of the mourners. Those who lament earthly losses are not assured of comfort. But those who mourn their own shortcomings and sins and those who lament the wickedness of the world may count on divine blessing. By "those who mourn," Jesus means disciples who grieve over the sin and evil in the world.

God's consolation is Jesus. The passive, "be comforted," indicates God's action. Jesus came "to comfort all who mourn," cf. Is. 61:2. He is the Messiah, our Savior. He died for us!

Relief is not to be understood exclusively in terms of the day when "(God) will wipe away every tear from their eyes," which Rev. 21:4 describes. In this life, too, there is comfort for the mourners Jesus is talking about.

What Jesus offers is the antidote for sin. He came to this world not to teach us how to win friends and succeed in business, how to be magnetic personalities and likable companions, how to have peace of mind and forget our fears, how to feel good about ourselves and to have self-esteem. Sin is not cured by cushioning ourselves against its consequences. Jesus came to comfort those afflicted by their sins. In Jesus, those who mourn their sins with a penitent spirit become better rather than bitter. God's gift to those who mourn is Jesus Himself and His death. The mourners are comforted with the joy of God's victory. Jesus was not a loser. He rose from the dead. He broke the power of sin, the sting of death.

The mourner is offered comfort from a loving and forgiving Father. When we are faced with our weakness, we should not make a pretense of strength or try to disguise it so that nobody can see. When we face defeat, when the pains of old age come, when we are frustrated and feel inadequate, then we should weep and mourn. It is the truth. Comfort comes from the Lord Jesus who offers us His strength.

When we are lonely, we should not pretend courage. It is dreadful to be lonely, to be forgotten, to feel unwanted, unimportant, or ignored. It is a time for weeping, not for defiance and strength. Jesus gives us the strength to rise to seek out others who are lonely and forgotten and to comfort them in the name of Jesus.

When we face death - a loved one's or our own - that is not the time for heroics or a brave show. It is a time to mourn, to acknowledge the horror of it, to hear in it the message of the judgment of God on all human rebellion, pride, independence, and resistance. Comfort comes from the cross on which Jesus died, the grave from which He rose, and the reality of His promise of eternal life.

3

The world considers no statement of our Lord to be more ridiculous than "Blessed are the meek." The world rejects that idea: "No! Rather, blessed are the aggressive, for they dominate the earth." Any disciple who takes Jesus' call to meekness too literally will never get very far. "Blessed are the aggressive!" is the way life is.

Not only do we consider it irrational to be meek, we become irritated with people who are. "Don't be such a Mr. Milktoast!" "Don't be such a spineless weakling!" "For once in your life, stand up for your rights!" "Tell him where to head in!" "If you are so chickenhearted, people will continue to walk all over you."

The commencement speaker sends another class into the world with the admonition, "Be ambitious! Know what you want and set out to get it! Have the courage to assert yourself! Defend your rights! Demand your due! Be strong and alert! Dream big dreams! Seize every opportunity!" Such a philosophy is the source of the aggressive competitiveness, the division of person against person which we call modern business.

Those who take this kind of philosophy most seriously are prime candidates for fear, tension, and ulcers. The self they present to the world is bigger than the self they really are. It takes a lot of puffing to maintain the proper inflation.

The exact difference between "the poor in spirit" and "the meek" is hard to state. Meekness commonly means a disposition towards people, but here it also has to do with a disposition toward God.

People who hold an office, like parents, government officials, etc., are not to be meek. This Beatitude is not for them. The government is to "bear the sword," cf. Rom. 13:4, and to punish those who do wrong, cf. 1 Pet. 2:14. Those who hold an office must be sharp and strict at times. They must get angry and punish when that is called for. Jesus is talking about individuals in their relation to others: husband to wife and neighbor to neighbor.

Nor does this Beatitude have anything to say about how we ought to be when others are being oppressed or treated unjustly.

Meekness then should cause us to neglect our own well-being to resist injustice and to defend the oppressed, even if we must act against great odds.

There is a natural meekness and a Godly meekness. Natural meekness loves to be at ease, avoids controversy at all costs, and lacks firmness and decisiveness. It is timid and pliant, easily persuaded to go either way.

Jesus' disciples realize that they have no inherent rights, and they do not claim them. When reproached, they hold their peace. When subjected to violence, they endure patiently. They leave their rights to God. In serene and confident dependence and trust in the Lord, they wait patiently for Him. They trust God and serve their neighbors rather than dominate them. They do not argue against God. They do not complain about the things God does. Whatever the Lord requires is right, and whatever He does is wise and good. They may have many and great trials, and in them they bow in humble submission. They live under the rule·of God, and they consider it gracious even as do "the poor in spirit." They are kindly disposed toward others, gentle, and forgiving.

Jesus' words are practically a quotation of Ps. 37:11. That psalm describes the meek in such a way as to exclude those milk-and-mush connotations which the word "meek" has acquired. The meek "trust in the Lord, and do good" in v. 3. They "take delight in the Lord" in v. 4. They "wait patiently for Him" to act in v. 7. They "refrain from anger, and forsake wrath" in v.8. They "do not fret" in v. 8. They are "generous and keep giving" in v. 21. They "depart from evil, and do good" in v. 27. They "utter wisdom . . . and speak justice" in v. 30. They "wait for the Lord, and keep to his way" in v. 34. They believe that "The salvation of the righteous is from the Lord; he is their refuge in the time of trouble. The Lord helps them and rescues them; he rescues them from the wicked, and saves them, because they take refuge in him," cf. vs. 39-40.

Abraham, when he divided the land with Lot, is an example of meekness, cf. Gen. 13:2-12.

Jesus went the meek way of serene and confident dependence on God. He invited people to follow Him as One who is meek and lowly in Matt. 11:29. He entered Jerusalem with no means of power, no trappings of royalty, on a borrowed beast, with nothing and no one but God to depend on. He was the meek Messiah, cf. Matt. 21:5 and 1 Peter 2:21-23. Even His enemies said of Him, "He trusts in God" in Matt. 27:43. The meek Messiah said, "All authority in heaven and on earth has been given to me" in Matt. 28:18. This Beatitude is an autobiography of Jesus. He was the meek Teacher and meek King. He was crucified. Disciples slowly learn to walk the downward way after Him, the way of humility, self-sacrifice, and death.

The words, "they will inherit the earth," point to physical blessings. "The earth" represents security. That's what we want. To the extent that we control the things that happen to us, we feel secure. We use all of our vision and ingenuity to acquire and maintain security. We try to anticipate. We prepare for every emergency and stay away from every threat to our well-being: college education, a savings account to tide us over for six months of expenses against a rainy day, an insurance program that covers fire, flood, medical expenses, catastrophes, liability, collision, and death. What is security? When do we have enough? There is little if any correlation between the amount of wealth people have and the security they feel.

Jesus offers a completely inverted kind of security when He says, "Blessed are the meek, for they shall inherit the earth." The sons of God do not need to fight to possess the earth. It is already theirs as an inheritance. It is not won by hard battle. God gives it to those whom He has chosen to be His own in Holy Baptism. They do not fear that what is theirs will be taken from them. Their Father is alive, active, and alert. He knows what is going on and is quite capable of handling any one who wants to assert a claim to the property He has bequeathed to His children.

The meek have faith and trust in the heavenly Father. Grasping and striving for security, imagining that we must assume responsibility for our own life and survival demonstrates a fundamental distrust in the God whom we call our Father. When we do not trust Him, we meddle in His business. Our Father will do the worrying and the giving. We can attend to the business He has assigned to us. See Matt. 6:24-34.

Jesus' meekness was not weakness. Even His enemies knew that. Never a compromise, never a concession to deceit or distortion, never a knuckling under for the favor of people or in fear of suffering. He was strong in His meekness, strong in doing the will of His Father. His strength was in His heavenly Father and His security in His identity as the Father's Son.

His disciples throw themselves on the mercy of God. He made us His children in Holy Baptism. He holds us in His hands as a parent holds his child. His strength does not threaten us; rather it is our security. His promises will not fail.

The disciples of Jesus show by their manner of life that they do not belong to this earth. Yet Jesus says, "They will inherit the earth." The earth they stand on so precariously now is their earth. They claim nothing but God, and they receive everything from God. Security is given them as a gift.

This does not mean that we should quit working, cash in our insurance policies, close out our savings accounts, and empty our pantries and freezers. We can see and use all of these things properly if we recognize them as gifts of the Father and evidences of His grace and if we do not hang on to them because they represent our hope and safety. If necessary, we can let them go; for we have the promises of our Father and our status as His children.

Life on this earth is a training ground in the art of trusting the Father. One day our Father will say in finality, "All right, now is the time! Come, let it all go!" On that day, some will cry out in fear, desperately trying to have security in this earth, to be strong, to hang on, and to save themselves. They will not be able to save anything. But God's children will let it go. They know that they cannot lose their inheritance. Jesus says that such meek people are "Blessed." They are blessed indeed!

4

"Those who hunger and thirst for righteousness" have a good appetite. They not only renounce their own rights, as in the preceding Beatitude, but they renounce their own righteousness, too. They yearn for the salvation God gives in

Jesus' death. The world disagrees and says, "No. Rather, blessed are those who are satisfied with their righteousness." But being satisfied is humanity's great problem.

It's a relief to know that our Lord's promise, "they will be filled," is not for those who do righteousness but for those who long for it. We may be anxious to please God yet find in ourselves much rebellion against God, much spiritual pride, much rejoicing in ourselves and our own achievements. We are saddened by this.

Our Christian education may deprive us of qualifying for this Beatitude. The longer we are Christians the more we take righteousness for granted. The greatness of what God has done for us in Jesus Christ becomes common-place. By way of Holy Baptism and the Confirmation process, we are assured and reassured that we have the righteousness of God through Jesus Christ. Our respectable Christian lives also can cause us to feel pretty good about ourselves. Christian satisfaction is worse than hungry heathenism. Our Confirmation process so emphasizes the confidence of faith that we fail to leave room for doubt. Doubters are made to feel guilty. Those who hunger and thirst for righteousness wonder if something is wrong with their faith; they have doubts. This Beatitude says that they ought to thank God for their hunger and thirst. Even that is God's gift.

Some Christians consider faith the big thing in our religion. It makes us righteous. This attitude encourages people to have faith in their faith. But faith is not the big thing. The big thing is the cross of Jesus Christ. Faith is letting God give us what He wants to give us through the cross of Jesus.

Our hunger and thirst have to do with the goals of our life. They control what we do. Our large goals may involve our career, our marriage, our family, etc. Immediate goals may be to escape a difficulty, some danger, suffering, sickness, a state of depression, or even a feeling of boredom. Our goals may involve escape from something that is inconvenient, painful, or uncomfortable The disciples of Jesus desire that God's will be done. This desire is their hunger and thirst.

Righteousness is not a series of fragmentary right actions.

250

Our hunger is a part of our joyful agreement to the purpose of God. Jesus' promise is that we "will be filled." God gives us righteousness in Jesus Christ and His cross.

Biblical scholars have centered much discussion around the differences in the concept of righteousness in Matthew's gospel and in the letters of Paul. Matthew encourages the disciples of Jesus to righteous behavior. Paul emphasizes that we have been made righteous in Jesus Christ and His passion. We become righteous not through our behavior but through Jesus and His death, cf. Rom. 5:1. But Paul also encourages hunger and thirst for righteous behavior. He says in Rom. 6:19, "just as you once presented your members as slaves to impurity and to greater and greater iniquity, so now present your members as slaves to righteousness for sanctification." Faith inspires us to do righteousness. Paul was commissioned an apostle "to bring about the obedience of faith," cf. Rom. 1:5.

Paul insists that no one can achieve righteousness before God, cf. Rom. 3:20. Matthew would not disagree. We are justified by faith, cf. Rom. 3:21-25, 28; 10:9-10. Instead of using words like "hunger and thirst for righteousness," Paul talks about walking by the Spirit, cf. Rom. 8:4-6, 12-14.

The promise of the fourth Beatitude, "they will be filled," is another instance of the numinous passive. The unmentioned agent is God. TEV reads, "God will satisfy them fully." "Those who hunger and thirst for righteousness" are declared righteous by God. Righteousness is not our achievement but God's gift.

Faith is so little a thing. It is simply taking God at His Word. It is letting God have His way with us. The story of Jesus' cross proclaims God's Word. It became a part of our story when we were baptized. We are the children of God. We do not have to ask, "Do I please God?" Our status in the family of the Father does not depend on our achievements but on our incorporation into the promises of God in Baptism. God washes us clean every day. He disciplines us, but He does not disown us. He shares with us His vision, His goal for this world, and rejoices when we live out our character as His children in righteousness.

The verb of the promise, "will be," is future. Jesus is talking about the future consummation of the kingdom. In our present hunger, we are sustained by the Bread of Life in the Lord's Supper which is a foretaste of the Messianic Feast at the consummation.

5

The first four Beatitudes form a unit. Jesus is giving to those who have nothing and need everything that which answers their every need - the kingdom, comfort, the earth, and righteousness. The last four Beatitudes bring into view the last judgment and the new world God has created.

"Blessed are the merciful." One aspect of mercy is gladly to forgive the sinful and the weak rather than to condemn them. We should not immediately raise a rumpus and start a riot if something is missing or if things do not go as they should, as long as there is still some hope for improvement. One characteristic of counterfeit piety is that it does not have pity or mercy for the frail and weak. It insists on enforcement. As soon as even a minor flaw shows up, there is anger and impatience. True holiness is merciful and sympathetic, but all that false holiness can do is rage and fume. It does so out of a zeal on behalf of righteousness. Counterfeit saints are so proud that they despise everyone else and cannot be kind and merciful.

We can be free from the frantic pursuit of and concern for the punishment of the guilty. We can be free to fulfill the purposes of God. We can love people whether or not they are lovable, nice, clean, or even grateful. Disciples love the oppressed, the sick, the wronged, the outcasts, and all who are tortured with anxiety. When people fall into disgrace, we can shield them and even take their shame on ourselves. Jesus did this for us. He became our brother, and He bore our shame even to death on a cross.

Another aspect of mercy is to do good to those who are poor and in need of help. An example of such mercy is the Good Samaritan in Luke 10:30-37.

"The merciful" in this Beatitude are not people who want

recognition for humanitarian accomplishments. The Pharisees, too, were merciful in the sense that they gave monetary contributions; but the way they practiced their mercy made it clear that their goal had to do with self-realization not the welfare of their neighbor, cf. Matt. 6:2-4. They became indignant at Jesus' ministry, because they missed the point of what Jahweh says in Hos. 6:6: "I desire steadfast love and not sacrifice." Twice Jesus told them to go and learn what Hosea says, cf. Matt. 9:12-13 and 12:1-7.

The promise, "they will receive mercy," is another numinous passive. The agent is not explicitly identified but is understood to be God. God will show them mercy in the judgment, as Matt. 7:2 says. The merciful receive the mercy of God through Jesus.

Many worldly-minded people think it is a waste of time and money to give gifts to the poor, to visit those who are sick and try to comfort and alleviate them, to show hospitality toward those who have some need, and to go to the aid of those who are in distress. The world does not agree with this Beatitude.

In His person and work, Jesus made the mercy of God visible. That God is merciful means that God gives and loves because that is His nature, not because people have a claim on Him or are deserving. We cannot bargain, negotiate, or argue claims with God. Our hope lies solely in His mercy. We ought to be merciful as our Father is merciful, cf. Luke 6:36.

6

"Blessed are the pure in heart." The phrase, "in heart," in v. 8 is exactly parallel to the phrase of v. 3, "in spirit." The heart is the innermost part of a person in the Old Testament. It is the seat of spiritual powers and capacities. The heart stands firm when a person is brave and courageous. It is the seat of rational functions. From the heart come planning and motivation. Religious and moral conduct is rooted in the heart.

The heart is the most common of all anthropological terms in the Old Testament. The heart is the point where all impressions from outside meet: sorrow in 1 Sam. 1:8 and Ps.

13:2 and joy in 1 Sam. 2:1; Ps. 16:9; and Prov. 15:13. What people see and especially what they hear enters the heart. The ways of life have their origin in the heart. The divine commandments are written on the tablets of the heart. Since these commandments make a person pious and intelligent, piety and understanding reside in the heart. This is the most common use. The heart, however, does not merely record and keep impressions that it receives. It also forges plans by which the impressions are changed into acts. By nature, the heart is not absolutely pure. It inclines to falsehood and is divided and proud.

God is concerned about the heart. He examines it and tests it, according to Ps. 17:3 and 1 Chron. 29:17-19. He knows it as it really is, according to Prov. 15:11. He makes it pure and firm and causes it to be one with Him.

New Testament usage of the word "heart" rests largely on the Old. Feelings and emotions, desires and passions dwell in the heart. The heart is the seat of understanding, the source of thought and reflection. It is the seat of the will and the source of resolves. It stands for the whole of the inner being of people in contrast to their external side.

"The pure in heart" are disciples who are undivided in their allegiance to God. Purity of heart includes such things as chastity, modesty, and sincerity. People who are "pure in heart" are innocent of evil not only in fact but in intention. They have no desire to offend either God or people. Cleanness of mind and sincerity of purpose are their characteristics.

To the scribes and Pharisees, purity consisted in outward cleanliness of body, skin, hair, clothes, and food. They did not touch a dead body or have a scab or rash on their body. To maintain such purity, they avoided other people. Jesus says they made "clean the outside of the cup and of the plate, but inside they are full of greed and self-indulgence," cf. Matt. 23:25-28.

To be "pure in heart" means to think about what God says and to change our way of thinking to conform to what He thinks. Common laborers, grease monkeys, furnace men, and foundry workers may be dirty and grimy and smell because they are

254

covered with dirt. Still they may be "pure in heart." They may say, "My God has made me a man. He has given me my house, wife, and child and has commanded me to love them and to take care of them. He has given me a job through which I can do good to other people." Although such people stink outwardly, they are pure incense before God inwardly. Doing dirty and repulsive jobs like hauling manure or washing and cleaning children can be pure work and flow from a "pure heart." This is the kind of purity that is blessed.

Pureness in heart does not mean never thinking about the world or the evil things in the world. It does not mean being unconcerned about worldly affairs and business and thinking only heavenly thoughts. Whatever goes in accordance with God and His ways must be called clean, pure, and white as snow.

The person who looks at his wife and fondles her may be considered dirty and disgusting by some, but he has good precedence for this in the patriarchs, cf. Gen. 26:8.

"The pure in heart" have learned that sonship means obedience. They have learned that singleness of devotion which lives by every word that proceeds from the mouth of God. They have an aversion to sin and desire to cultivate the virtues described in Phil. 4:8: "whatever is true, whatever is honorable, whatever is just, whatever is pure, whatever is pleasing, whatever is commendable, if there is any excellence and if there is anything worthy of praise, think about these things." "The pure in heart" shun falseness and deceit, cf. Ps. 24:3-4.

The promise of the sixth Beatitude is that "the pure in heart" "will see God." We cannot by nature see God, because we are impure and dishonest. Moses asked to see God but was denied, except for a glimpse of His departing glory. No one can see God with physical eyes in this life, cf. John 1:18. We are satisfied with the Father's disclosure of Himself in His only Son. Seeing God will have its complete realization when the kingdom comes in its fullness.

But even in this world, we can see God. Through faith in Jesus, "the pure in heart" see the graciousness of God. The eyes of faith enable us to see God in his fatherliness and friendliness. The person who is "pure in heart" is open to the nearness of God and is prepared for God's presence. That person sees God while others are altogether unconscious of His presence. That person sees Him in every good experience and in every cross. God's wisdom, goodness, love, mercy, and faithfulness are always before that person's eyes. He can trace God's counsels in the course of history. To "see God" is to see His intention in our station as husband, wife, child, neighbor, or friend. The vision of God is not mystical but eschatological; it is the ability to see the reality of things.

The verb of the promise, "will see," is future. In the world to come, we will see God face to face, cf. 1 John 3:2-3 and 1 Cor. 13:12.

7

"Peacemakers" are disciples who work for the wholeness and well-being that God wills for a broken world. No one will argue the desirability of peace. War is hell. But conflict is not limited to weapons and armed warfare. The battles and tensions between individuals and families, between a wife and her husband, between parents and children, between brothers and sisters are terrible. Conflicts and jealousies, taunting and hatred develop among students at school and between people thrown together at work. Beyond this, there are rivalries and competitions, cliques that exclude, the bitter animosities that resent exclusion, and divisions into races and cultures. Even more are the tensions and stresses that arise within people, the depression of spirit, and the war inside us. We want peace. The exhausted mother, with so much to do and with her children constantly pestering her and getting in her way, gives vent to the unbearable irritation. "Stop it! Get out, all of you! I need a little peace!"

Jesus is our peace. Having been given peace, disciples of Jesus are dedicated to spreading it. They seek peace not only for themselves but also for other people. They try to settle ugly and involved issues. They endure squabbling and try to avoid and prevent war and bloodshed. They overcome evil with good. They adjust, reconcile, and settle quarrels and tensions between husband and wife and between neighbors.

People enjoy hearing and telling the worst about their neighbor, and it tickles them to see a fault in someone else. A woman may be most beautiful; but if she has one little spot or blemish, you are expected to forget everything else and to look only for that spot and to talk about it. If a lady is famous for her honor and virtue, some poisonous tongue will come along and defame her in such a way as to destroy all her praise and honor. All some people can notice about other people are the faults they can denounce, but what is good about them they do not see. No person is so bad that there is not something about him/her that is worthy of praise. But we are so inclined to leave the good things out of sight and feast our eyes on the evil.

Luther tells the story of a married couple who lived together in such love and harmony that it was the talk of the whole town. When the devil was unable to undermine this in no other way, he sent an old hag to the wife. The hag told the wife that her husband was having an affair with another woman and planned to kill her. She embittered the wife against her husband and advised her to hide a knife on her person in order to beat him to it. When the hag had done this, she went to the husband and told him the same, that his wife planned to murder him. As proof, she told him that he would find a knife next to her in bed at night. He found it and cut off his wife's head with it. Whether this story is fact or fiction, it shows what wicked and poisonous mouths can do even to people who love each other deeply.

Disciples of Jesus are on their guard against trouble-makers and neither listen nor pay attention to them. They put the best interpretation on what they hear about their neighbor. They conceal what bad things they hear so that they may establish and preserve peace and harmony. The Eighth Commandment teaches us this.

Jesus did this by reconciling us to the Father, bringing us into the Father's favor, and interceding on our behalf. We should talk about the best of others and keep quiet about their bad side.

If disciples hear evil about another, they do not talk about it to others; but they go to the one who has done it and admonish him/her. If that does not work, they take it to those who have the job of punishing.

The followers of Jesus do not start wars or create unrest. They work for peace. If they are the victim of injustice and violence, they do not immediately start getting even and hitting back. They think it over, try to bear it, and maintain peace. If that is impossible and they cannot stand it, they go to the proper authorities for legitimate redress. To start a war, we need more than a just cause.

However, when someone is being hurt or the public welfare is in danger, disciples are no longer quiet. They defend the public good and attack the evil. This is especially incumbent on those whose task it is to teach and to warn everyone. Such people have been commissioned and charged to see to it that no one is misled. They must give an account at the last judgment, according to Heb. 13:17. St. Paul warns the pastors of the churches in Ephesus to watch and guard their whole flock against the wolves who will appear among them, cf. Acts 20:28-29. This duty is incumbent on all pastors. In the Beatitudes, Jesus is not talking about public office, but about all Christians in general as they deal with each other in their common, daily life.

How does a person make peace? One method to try is sweet reason, but that does not always work. It has not helped much in international politics. Disarmament negotiations have been going on for a long time. That nations should reduce their armaments and work at improving the lot of their people is certainly reasonable. Our national debt skyrockets under the burden of military expenditures, while we reduce monies available for easing the plight of the elderly, the sick, the poor, and the unfortunate people of our society. Reason plays at best a limited role for those who want to be peacemakers.

Another method to use to make peace is force and law. This is the way of police, courts, judges, and jails. On an international scale, this would mean a world court and a police force of nations. But people would not trust such a force. Independent nations would not submit to it if their own interests were involved. The way of force and law helps toward maintaining order, but it is not the final answer to the desire for peace.

Another method is to use moral force. The fear of being isolated, exposed, condemned by public opinion is great. But, self-interest asserts itself against everyone sometimes.

Another method is trying to dominate the situation. The strong man is king of the hill, and no one dares attack him. This is the way the international game is played. America must be strong and alert everywhere to maintain peace in the world. This forceful pacification is clearly distinguished from what Jesus is talking about here. Pacification by force is what Pres. Ronald Reagan had in mind when he called the MX missile "peacemaker."

All these methods may help toward peace to a degree. But this is not the peace God intends for the human race. This is not the peace of God. It does not transform lives or change the nature of people. It does not get at the root of the problem.

The root of the problem is the delusion we all live under that we must create our own lives and achieve and defend our own worth. A man tosses in his bed at night, unable to sleep because he remembers how he was insulted or how he made a fool of himself. He tries to think what brilliant words he might have used to save himself or to make the other person a fool. He plots how to get even. He is filled with indignation; he is miserable and has no peace. But he would be more miserable to surrender, to admit defeat, and to give up the battle. The peace people seek is success, victory, and control over others. This, of course, is the dilemma of the world and the reason it has so little peace.

The peace Jesus brings is remarkably different. Jesus rejects as wholly incompatible with His kingdom the peace of the conqueror. The sons of God do not use power to impose peace like some dictator or like the warden of a prison, even as Jesus, the Son of God, does not force people to be good. When humans had declared their independence of God, when they split apart from each other, God became the Peacemaker. He became a man in the person of Jesus of Nazareth. Jesus' goal was simple,

259

not to dominate us but to win us back to God. He came to reconcile us to God by dying on a cross. The kind of peacemaking Jesus is talking about has to do with love, humility, and self-denial.

"The peacemakers" should try to reconcile each of the contending parties to God before trying to reconcile them to one another. The new relationship God established with the human race through Jesus lays the foundation for a new relationship of people to people.

"The peacemakers" are "the sons of God." Its inclusive policy caused the NRSV to translate "children of God," and certainly females are also "peacemakers."

"The peacemakers" are not afraid of the world, because they know their Father and rest secure in what Jesus has done for them. They confront a world in conflict by simply being "the sons of God." They bring the love and peace of God to the poor, the despairing, and the depressed and invite them to the new life. They expose the hypocrisy of a world that refuses to see or acknowledge evil in itself but rejoices in its arrogance. They endure the consequences. They absorb the evil of the world without throwing it back and without retaliation. They love their enemies and pray for those who persecute them, cf. Matt. 5:43-48.

Jesus is the "Prince of Peace." The kingdom He came to establish is a kingdom of peace. All "peacemakers," therefore, are spreading His sovereignty and the rule of the Father. God calls "the peacemakers" His sons because they are like Him.

The agent who will call them "sons of God" is obviously not the world which may abuse them for interfering in its domain. The agent is God Himself and His Son. The numinous passive verb says this.

8

Vs. 10-12 will be dealt with as one Beatitude. What these verses teach is taught also in 1 Pet. 3:14. Disciples of Jesus who experience persecution on account of Jesus are blessed.

Non-Christians cannot understand this Beatitude. The world

says, "No! Rather, blessed are you when people like you, say nice things about you, want you for their leader, and even consider themselves fortunate to know you. Rejoice and be flattered, for great is your prestige on earth; for so people treated the conformists who were before you."

We tend to suppose that the person devoted to righteousness and the other characteristics Jesus has been describing in the Beatitudes will be very popular, but Jesus teaches us that the reaction really is just the opposite. The demonstration of this is Jesus Himself. Other examples are Paul, Peter, and John the Baptist.

It is dangerous and misleading to talk to disciples of Jesus as though suffering and difficulty are something they can prevent or that they can escape, say for example through prayer. Christians do suffer pain. They do have spiritual torments. They are not always well-adjusted. They are not always able to keep smiling. They are not always unperturbed by the things that happen to them. The cost of discipleship is very high. The life and death of Jesus teaches us this as do the lives of many great Christians. Consider the apostle Paul, as he describes some of his experiences in 2 Cor. 11:31-12:10. Dietrich Bonhoeffer, who wrote The Cost of Discipleship, was murdered by his Nazi jailers in the concentration camp at Flossenburg, Germany.

The salt of God burns like fury in the open wounds of an insipid and dying world, cf. Matt. 5:13-16. The light of God's truth and hope can only be interpreted as an enemy by those it blinds. Such activity will always produce conflict. We will be persecuted.

The disciple grows in grace through suffering, cf. Rom. 5:3-5 and James 1:2-3. This is paradoxical and goes against the grain of every human. It is often through suffering - physical suffering but especially spiritual suffering - that we become aware of our relationship to God and of God's to us.

Luther said, "this is the most dangerous trial of all, when there is no trial and everything is and goes well; for then a man is tempted to forget God, to become too bold and to misuse the times of prosperity."[46] Peace and tranquility often bring out the worst in us.

A great deal of suffering is inflicted on those who resolutely, without fear of people, walk the path of righteousness, condemning what is evil, protesting wrongdoing, and upholding the principles of Christian living. The world wants religion but not a religion that demands change. The world believes that everything is right the way it is - basically at least. The world can be improved, but there is nothing wrong with its foundations, its premises, or the direction in which it is moving. Let no one insist too loudly or confront the world too directly with the proposition that this is not so. The only salvation the world wants is to be declared right and to be assured that at the end of its road is solid and enduring success.

The followers of Jesus must expect antagonism from the people of the world. John 3:20 teaches us that the world hates Christians, because Christians condemn the world. It is vain for the children of God to suppose that by discretion or tact they can silence the clamors and hatred of wicked people. The scribes and Pharisees said that austere John the Baptist had a devil and the sociable Jesus was a wine-bibber, and their words carried much weight. Paul says, "all who want to live a godly life in Christ Jesus will be persecuted," cf. 2 Tim. 3:10-13 and John 15:20.

Martin Luther said: "If you live in order to have a good time here without persecution, then you will not get to heaven with Christ, and vice versa. In short, you must either surrender Christ and heaven or make up your mind that you are willing to suffer every kind of persecution and torture in the world. Briefly anyone who wants to have Christ must put in jeopardy his body, life, goods, reputation, and popularity in the world. He dare not let himself be scared off by contempt, ingratitude, or persecution."[47]

A variety of false accusations was made against the early Christians. They were accused of engaging in bloody sacrifices, of feasting on human flesh, of being atheists, of looking for another kingdom, of prostitution, and of sodomy. This is not the form that religious persecution usually takes today. But reviling and slanderous statements are still frequent.

When the disciples of Jesus refuse to join in the sinful amusements of the world, this may result in their being charged that they are proud, selfish, clannish, unsocial, lacking in courtesy, conceited, etc. The disciples are unwanted, and the demand lies heavy on them to conform or get out.

We resist all wrong done to others. This means particularly to fight against the wrongs done to the poor, the despised, and our enemies. It is very simple to fight against the wrong that is done by those who have no power. Anyone can do this, and almost everybody does. We get into trouble when we fight the wrongs done by the powerful, the rich, and our friends.

Sometimes, persecution consists merely of sneers and ridicule. At times, it extends to the inflicting of financial and other material loss. Disciples provoke the world to insult, violence, and slander by their meekness. In suffering, they are too patient and too silent.

The only surprising thing about the persecution of Christians is that Christians are surprised when they encounter it. Our Lord warned us plainly that it will come in Matt. 10:16-39 and John 15:18-21.

Luther said, "Things neither can nor should run peacefully and smoothly. How could things run smoothly, when the devil is in charge and is a mortal enemy of the gospel? . . . If he were to let it go ahead unhindered, it would soon be all over and his kingdom would be utterly destroyed. But if he is to resist it and hinder it, he must rally all his art and power and arouse everything in his might against it. So do not hope for any peace and quiet so long as Christ and His gospel are in the midst of the devil's kingdom. And woe upon the peaceful and smooth situation that used to be, and upon those who would like to have it back! This is a sure sign that the devil is ruling with all his might and that no Christ is there."[48]

This Beatitude enables us to console ourselves when we are persecuted for righteousness' sake. Constant threats to life and property can wear a person down physically and spiritually. But faith can lift us up so that we hear this Beatitude and receive strength to continue.

People often refer to the opposition they meet and the persecutions they undergo as proof of their rectitude. This has resulted in the tendency by those who wish to be counted as

Christians to behave in such a way toward non-Christians that they provoke their hatred or at least have little care to avoid it. But persecution in itself is no proof of rectitude. The opposition must result from righteous acts. The blessing falls on those who endure for righteousness' sake. One can also suffer justly, as 1 Pet. 4:15 says. Therefore yelling and bragging about how one suffers is worthless. Godless people may do this too. We must see to it that we have a genuine divine cause for which we suffer persecution.

The promise – stated in the present tense - given "those who are persecuted for righteousness sake" is the same as that given "the poor in spirit," cf. v. 3, "theirs is the kingdom of heaven." In persecution, "those who are persecuted for righteousness sake" are the equals of "the poor in spirit."

We are not only to accept persecution and reviling but also to rejoice in it, James 1:2-3 says. We are not to pity ourselves for what we must endure. No greater invitation or challenge has ever been offered to humans than to be a disciple of Jesus Christ. Luke encourages a physical expression of joy in the face of persecution. "Leap for joy," he says in Luke 6:23.

The strength to rejoice comes from the story of Jesus and the sacraments, from the Spirit of God as the community of saints gather to worship their Lord, to remember again who they are, to be forgiven failures, to be freed from Satan's accusations, to start clean again, and to strengthen one another in temptation. The disciples do not hide, nor do they try to save face, nor do they try to make an impression. They simply try to be who they are, children of God, reflecting the character of their Father.

The disciples' hope for the future enables them to keep up their courage and Christian morale. Disciples do not cling to the world and do not feel abused if the injustice of people snatches away from them benefits God has given. Disciples do not despair if they suffer oppression, if affliction and evil befall them. The valley of the shadow of death itself becomes the instrument of God's purposes. They wear faith, that is, their confidence in the Father's care and leading, as a shield.

The persecution Christians endure must not be regarded by

them as a sign that they are following the wrong course or are not God's children. The prophets of old were persecuted, and they certainly were God's servants. The prophets whose persecutions are recorded are Moses, David, Elijah, Elisha, Jeremiah, Micaiah, and Daniel.

The world is haunted by the promises Jesus offers in the Beatitudes, but it hesitates to accept the program He outlines. His program has not been tried and found wanting. It has been found difficult and generally not tried. The world says, "A bird in the hand is worth two in the bush." But, in the Beatitudes, Jesus encourages us to let everything go for a promise.

4th Sunday after the Epiphany

Year B

Deuteronomy 18:15-20

A prophet was a person to whom God spoke and who spoke God's word to people. "I will put my words in the mouth of the prophet, who shall speak to them everything that I command." Sometimes what God said had to do with the future. Then the prophet became a predictor. But the primary job of a prophet was to communicate messages from God.

The Canaanites had other ways to determine the will of their gods and to know the future. Moses listed them in Deut. 18:9-10: divination, a soothsayer, an augur, a sorcerer, through spells, through consulting ghosts or spirits, and oracles from the dead. While the general meaning of these practices is clear, the precise distinction between is not. Moses seems to have piled up terms to include everything. He almost exhausted the Hebrew vocabulary in designating the religious practices of the Canaanites. Divination, soothsaying, and auguring have to do with the future. Sorcerers conjure up magic spells. Consulting ghosts or spirits and seeking oracles from the dead are various ways of trying to consult the spirit world. The number of regulations in the Pentateuch against the cult of the dead and the rites pertaining to it indicate that this cult was quite popular among ancient people, cf. Lev. 19:28, 31; 20:6, 27; 21:5; Deut. 14:1; 18:11; 26:14; etc. Moses called these rituals "abhorrent practices" in 18:9. He said in 18:12 that it was because of these practices that God was driving the Canaanites out of their land.

In his farewell address to the Israelites before they entered the land of Canaan, Moses told the people that God would continue to speak to them as He had through him. But he warned them not to get involved in the practices of the Canaanites. God would not "permit" that, cf. 18:14. Living in Canaan would constitute a great change for Israel. The temptation would be great for them to adopt the worship practices of the inhabitants of the land. Moses said that God would raise up a prophet for them like him through whom He would speak to them. The prophet would speak authoritatively for God. He said the prophet would be one of them.

This was in line with the request Israel made at Mt. Sinai - which is also called Horeb - when God established His covenant with them. After God spoke to the assembly of Israel and gave them the Ten Commandments, the people were filled with great fear. They were afraid that they would die if they listened to the voice of God again. "When all the people witnessed the thunder and lightning, the sound of the trumpet, and the mountain smoking, they were afraid and trembled . . . ." They asked Moses to listen to the Lord and then tell them everything that He said. They "said to Moses, 'You speak to us, and we will listen; but do not let God speak to us, or we will die,'" cf. Ex. 20:18-19 and Deut. 5:22-27. The Lord agreed with this suggestion and made Moses His prophet.

God also placed on Israel a responsibility. The people would have to heed the words that the prophet spoke in God's name. God said that He would hold them accountable if they did not. This responsibility was placed also on the new Israel represented by Peter, James, and John on the mount of transfiguration, according to Matt. 17:5. The Voice from the cloud said, "Listen to him!" referring to Jesus. The implication was that the disciples should listen to Jesus from now on instead of Moses. Jesus was the prophet Moses had said God would raise up. In fact, Jesus was the fulfillment of the role Moses played in Israel.

When Moses talked about "a prophet," the singular noun pointed to an individual. But, as he continued speaking, he evidently was talking about a succession of men. He refers to "any prophet." Many interpreters have seen in Moses' words a double reference. There was a preliminary fulfillment in a body of prophets who served Israel through the centuries. "A prophet" was a collective figure individualized in men like Samuel, Elijah, Isaiah, etc. Like Moses, they communicated messages from God. Through the centuries, the Old Testament names many prophets whom God raised up to speak for Him to Israel. Many of these men wrote down what God said, and their names are attached to some of the books of the Old Testament. Other prophets did not write down the word given them, and their names are learned as the books of the Old Testament are read. Among the non-literary prophets were men like Elijah and Elisha.

The prophets, too, had to be responsible. "Any prophet who speaks in the name of other gods, or who presumes to speak in my name a word that I have not commanded the prophet to speak – that prophet shall die."

The writer to the Hebrews began his letter, "Long ago God spoke to our ancestors in many and various ways by the prophets, but in these last days he has spoken to us by a Son. . . . he . . . made purification for sins . . . ," cf. Heb. 1:1-3. The Son was Jesus of Nazareth who spoke words of divine forgiveness to those who would receive it and "made purification" by His suffering and death.

Matthew told the story of Jesus in his gospel using as his outline the life of Moses. Like Moses, Jesus' life was in danger when He was born. He escaped by going down to Egypt. Through an angel, God called Him out of Egypt to save His people. As Moses received God's commandments on Mt. Sinai, so Jesus proclaimed God's will in the Sermon on the Mount recorded in Matt. 5-7. Matthew tells of ten miracles Jesus performed just as Moses did ten miracles in Egypt. The writer to the Hebrews says that Jesus was like Moses, only greater, cf. Heb. 3:1-6.

In Jesus, the prophetic role was fulfilled. Through Jesus, God spoke His final word. However many and varied the ways God spoke by the prophets, the same God spoke. What He said by His Son was the same message of salvation He spoke by the prophets.

1 Corinthians 8:1-13

These are sharp words. Their incisiveness may be felt more if they are rephrased.

The real issue is not eating "food sacrificed to idols." That's the occasion that brought the issue to the surface. The problem has to do with the attitude some strong members of the church in Corinth have toward members whom Paul describes as "weak." The strong are "destroying" the weak, people for whom Christ died. They are "sinning" against fellow Christians. They "are sinning against Christ." Their confidence in what they know makes them arrogant.

Here is a rephrasing of the text: You strong people say that the weak are as knowledgeable as you. You do not yet know enough. What you do know makes you arrogant. You need to know love. Love builds up people. Then God knows you.

What you strong people know is that idols are simply pieces of wood, stone, or metal. They are not gods. And you are right! There is only one God, the Father, and one Lord, Jesus Christ.

But the weak are not like you in their understanding of this. Having been reared and trained all their lives to think of idols as gods, they have not yet completely rid themselves of their attachment to idols. As the result, if they see you strong people eating in the temple of an idol, they might think you are doing what they used to do. Before they became Christians, they thought that they were drawing close to and uniting themselves with a god. They might think that is what you are doing. Seeing the example of you strong and knowledgeable Christians, they might think it is all right to worship an idol. They might do what they consider to be such worship. Your example might lead them to a gross violation against the First Commandment and to the destruction of their relationship to Jesus Christ. The love of Christ for them – He died for them! – should keep you from doing this. That's the reason I never do it.

"I'm not going to let what other people think inhibit what I do" is an attitude many people have, even many in the church. "But love does!" Paul says to the Corinthian Christians. Love for Jesus and love for other people lets what other people think influence what we do.

Christian freedom is the issue. It is sometimes called libertinism. The strong Corinthians seem to interpret Christian freedom as license to act within the parameters of their faith without regard for others. Paul takes a firm position against such thinking. 1 Cor. 8:1-11:1 is a classic exposition on the use and misuse of the freedom we have in Christ Jesus.

Paul founded the church in Corinth. The story is told in Acts 18:1-17. A number of issues developed in the church that the Corinthians were not resolving. They wrote to Paul for help. He took up one of the matters in 1 Cor. 8.

He answered the questions put to him by the Corinthians beginning with ch. 7. The issues involve such practical matters as marriage, eating food sacrificed to idols, incest, taking legal disputes to pagan law courts, patronizing temple prostitutes, hair styles for men and women, conduct at Eucharistic meals, and speaking in tongues. Paul seems to follow the order of the questions as posed. The first, covered in ch. 7, has to do with marriage problems. "Food sacrificed to idols" is the second.

Ch. 8 describes the problem and Paul's answer. In ch. 9, Paul points to his own ministry as an example of self-denying, self-giving love. Free as he is, he practices strict self-discipline. He makes himself slave to all. He sobers the confidence the libertines have in their knowledge by reminding them in 10:1-12 of what happened to Israel in the wilderness. He warns them in 10:14-22 against too close an association with idol worship and reminds them of the Lord's Supper which they do. Finally, Paul sums up in 10:23-11:1 with a series of rules formulated as imperatives introduced by his modification of a Corinthian slogan. He describes how love for a neighbor influences what a person does.

What Paul teaches in 1 Cor. 8:1-11:1 is much the same as what he says in Rom. 14-15. Dealing with food offered to idols in letters to two different churches - as well as references in Acts 21:25 and Rev. 2:14 and 20 - indicates how necessary such instruction was in the early days of the church.

Jewish thinking on the matter may have been involved. Jews were forbidden by the law of Moses to eat food sacrificed to idols. They were not to touch it. If a Jew came into contact with such food in an enclosed space, he was as unclean as when he touched a corpse.

The issue is clearer if we understand how people sacrificed food to idols. Only a part of the sacrifice was actually consumed by fire or given to the deity. Two things might happen to the rest. Either it was eaten by the worshippers at a festal meal or sacred banquet with the deity as the honored guest, cf. v. 10, or it was sold in a public market, cf. 10:25.

The sacrifices made in the temple in Jerusalem were dealt with in a similar way. Only the whole burnt offering was consumed on the altar. In the other sacrifices, some of the food was given to the priests for their daily nutritional requirements. The rest was eaten by the worshippers in a festal meal that was a part of their worship.

Much, if not most, of the meat sold in the markets of Corinth probably came from sacrifices made in the heathen temples. During festival periods, there must have been a huge amount of meat for sale in the public markets, food that had been sacrificed to idols. The temples probably had a near monopoly on meat, because they did not pay for what they sold.

Opportunities to eat food sacrificed to idols probably were prevalent in Corinth. Unless the first Christians were vegetarians, they could scarcely avoid eating meat that had in some way been involved in a religious rite dedicated to a heathen deity.

Furthermore, the Christians had associates, relatives, and friends who worshipped the heathen gods. Through them, they probably were invited to participate in meals that included idol-food. Invitation cards have been found among the papyri. Friends would send them a part of their sacrifice. They attended family marriages, the funerals of their pagan relatives, club parties, banquets in pagan temples to which they were invited, public festivals during which idol-food was distributed to all, etc. Paul admonishes the Corinthians in 1 Cor. 10:14-22 not to participate in the feasts in the temples of pagan gods.

Some new Christians had not yet gotten rid of the feeling, probably nurtured in them from birth on, that the idols are gods. They thought that eating food sacrificed to the gods was food received from them. Some Christians in Corinth were sensitive to these feelings. They did not think that Christians should eat idol-food. Other Christians were not troubled by it, because they rejected the basic premise of the matter, namely, that the idols were gods. There was no involvement with the idol through eating food that had been offered to it, because the idol actually did not exist. The new Christians remembering the comfort and security experienced from their worship of idols from childhood on had deep feelings for them.

Their feelings are described by Paul. They are still "accustomed to idols." "They still think of the food they eat as food offered to an idol." As the result, "their conscience . . . is defiled" if they eat. That is to say, they think that through the eating they come "close" to the idol.

The more mature Christians boasted of their knowledge and the freedom they had in Christ by riding roughshod over the scruples of the weak members. They ate temple food freely and publicly. This encouraged the weak to do the same. The leaders of the church came to Paul asking for help.

The matter had been dealt with in the earliest days of the church. The recommendation of James at the Apostolic Council was that Christians should abstain from eating food that has been sacrificed to idols, cf. Acts 15:29. That's what the letter sent to the church at Antioch by the Council said, cf. Acts 21:25. Eating such food is strongly condemned in letters to the churches of Asia Minor in Rev. 2:14 and 20.

Paul does not use the ruling of the Council as a club on the Corinthians. Instead, he deals with the matter in a pastoral way by reviewing the theological issues involved. First, he affirms the freedom of Christians. Because we live under the lordship of Christ, no idol has a claim on us or power over us. Other people may call idols gods, but Christians do not. V. 6 states what Christians believe. But the issue in Corinth is larger than this. It involves also love.

Paul does not seem to be so strict in this letter as was the Apostolic Council and the Lord of the church in His letters to the churches of Asia Minor. According to 10:27-28, Paul allows for the eating of idol-food under certain circumstances.

Paul describes two kinds of Christian strength. The one is strength of knowledge or theology and the other strength of love. He says that showing loving strength is more important than demonstrating theological strength. This is also what he says in 1 Cor. 13:2.

Paul defends the conscience of the weak Christians. He forbids activities that can look like participation in the worship of pagan gods. But he is careful to preserve the freedom of Christians to use the pagan meat markets and to accept invitations to meals in pagan homes, cf. 10:25-31.

We today have no experience involving the eating of food sacrificed to idols, and yet there are parallels in other aspects of life which call for sacrifice to protect fellow Christians.

"All of us possess knowledge," Paul says. What everyone involved in the Corinthian discussion – strong and weak - knows is that "no idol in the world really exists" and that "there is no God but one." That "an idol has no real existence" is a conclusion drawn from "there is no God but one." The idea is the basis for the freedom claimed by the strong.

The words "all of us possess knowledge" were probably a slogan being used in the discussions at Corinth. Other slogans may be the words: "no idol in the world really exists" and "there is no God but one." Paul rejects the slogan in v. 1 when he says in v. 7 that "not all possess this knowledge."

Paul highlights the danger of knowledge: it puffs up. Knowledge is not genuine and good if it produces pride. Then it blocks love. Knowledge, especially knowledge that knows that it knows and by implication takes pride in the fact, is a menace. The person who is puffed up "does not yet have the necessary knowledge" which, Paul says, is love. The Greek word translated "puffs up" is translated "arrogant" in 5:2.

The puffed up people were probably socially prominent in the Corinthian community. They may have gotten and accepted invitations to dinner where food sacrificed to idols was served, perhaps even in the shrine of a pagan deity. They may have had some social or business obligations that were important in their roles in the larger society. People of lower economic status may also have been involved. If they were clients of non-Christian patrons, they would surely also sometimes have found themselves in such situations. Public servants found restrictions on what they could eat limited their social intercourse and reduced their effectiveness in their career.

Knowledge alone is a questionable gift. The strong Corinthians were proud of their knowledge and consequent freedom. Paul says that love is greater. He speaks of the relationship between knowledge and love in 1 Cor. 13:2 and 8-9.

Paul explains how the lack of love can affect others. The weak "might . . . be encouraged to the point of eating food sacrificed to idols." "By your knowledge those weak believers for whom Christ died are destroyed." "You . . . sin against members of your family." "You . . . wound their conscience."

There is a difference between knowing God and being known by Him. The greater thing is being known, that is, being loved, chosen, and called by God. The importance of being known by God is brought out also in 1 Cor. 13:12 and Gal. 4:9.

That they are "known by God" gives Christians a distinctive identity. It sets us apart from other people. To be known by God is to be welcomed and acknowledged. The opposite is that He does not know us. That is the worst possible thing, according to Matt. 7:23. It is to be utterly and absolutely outside, repelled, exiled, and ignored.

Paul describes what Christians believe in vs. 4-6. While others may believe in many gods and lords, Christians acknowledge only one. Paul identifies the one God as the Father who created all things and us. He identifies Jesus Christ as the one Lord through whom all things, including us, were created. The conclusion is that, in the final analysis, there is nothing behind the food that has been offered to idols. But Paul goes on to plead the case of the people who do not have this knowledge.

The slogan "there is no god but one" reflects the Great Shema of Deut. 6:4 and the First Commandment. The idea is basic to the Christian faith. Other gods become gods when other people believe in them. Paul accepts the idea that idols exist, because some people believe they exist. But they really are not gods, cf. Gal. 4:8.

On the basis of coins minted in Nicomedia, a city in western Asia Minor, we know of more than forty deities who were worshipped there. Acts 17:16 describes the city of Athens as Paul found it. By the reckoning of the ancients, there were more than thirty thousand gods.[49] When the early Christians looked at the religious behavior of their fellow citizens, they saw shrines to local deities and temples to the Olympian gods, small domestic altars to serve the family and huge platforms to serve the city, statues of Apollo and pictures of Venus, processions to the Thracian goddess, and festivals to honor the emperor's birthday, a landscape teeming with life and variety.

Religious practices varied greatly. Some people worshipped crocodiles, others honored birds, some considered goats divine, and others adored calves. Some people worshipped fire. These practices were traditional and had been handed on from earlier times, so they were upheld and respected by the citizenry.

In the ancient world, religion was a matter of observing inherited rituals, of preserving values handed down from the past. We think of religion on the model of the great religious traditions of the world: Islam, Judaism, Buddhism, Hinduism, Christianity, et al. We compare and contrast the beliefs of those religions with each other and with Christianity. The ancients spoke of "having gods" in the sense of "having customs or laws" rather than of "believing in the gods." Religion was less a matter of holding beliefs than of observing annual festivals or public rituals, less concerned with conversion than participating in local cults, of identifying with the traditions of the city in which they lived. Seldom did it require conscious choice.

In the Roman Empire, there was no term corresponding to our word "religion" meant as a set of beliefs, a form of ritual, a code of behavior, or an organization. Piety was the word used most frequently to designate religious acts and feelings, but it was not used to designate a religion or a particular form of piety. Whatever religious observances in a particular city or among a specific people were traditional and authenticated by ancient texts or established customs were considered pious and god-pleasing.

Sophisticated thinkers of that day believed in one god, a spiritual being, supreme and transcendent, who rules over all and to whom all other rational beings give honor and adoration. They recognized also many lesser gods or intermediary beings. The lesser gods were subordinate to the one high god. His honor was not diminished but enhanced if one also prayed to the intermediary beings. In contrast, Christians claimed that the one God has revealed Himself at a particular time and place and in a specific person, Jesus of Nazareth, cf. John 14:6.

Paul says that God is the Creator and end of all things, and Jesus Christ is the Mediator and Means of Life for the world and for ourselves. Some say that v. 6 is an early Christian confession of faith that was involved in the development of the Apostles' Creed. Similar statements are in Col. 1:15-17 and Rom. 11:36.

"The Father" explained to pagans the content of the words "one God." The words made known the nature of the one God as the Creator. They did not describe Him here as the Father of our Lord Jesus Christ.

Both "God, the Father" and the "Lord, Jesus Christ" have to do with creation. The distinction between them lies in the prepositions: ex ("from") and eis ("for") in connection with the Father and dia ("through") in connection with Jesus Christ. John 1:3 and Col. 1:16 also ascribe creation to Jesus Christ. The strongest statement is Heb. 1:10.

To say that all things are "from" the Father is to say that He is the origin of all things. To say that we exist "for" the Father is to say that He is the goal of all things.

Jesus is the Mediator of creation. His existence prior to His birth at Bethlehem is presupposed. He mediates the action of the Father. All power in heaven and on earth has been given to Him, cf. Matt. 28:18. The heathen lords are not lords. The other powers and authorities have been conquered by Jesus and are subject to Him.

Unlike the words "the Father" which explain the word "God," "Jesus Christ" does not explain the content of the word "Lord." "Jesus Christ" names the "one Lord." The pagans understood the word "Lord."

Throughout the Hellenistic world, kurios (lord) was used to denote the divinities of the mystery cults. It was also the title for the divine emperor. Kurios designated deity with respect to its absolute power and superiority. Both the national and mystery religions of Asia Minor, Egypt, and Syria called gods and goddesses kurios or kuria. Kurios is used in the LXX to designate Jahweh. The earliest confession of the Christian faith may have been simply "Jesus is Lord," cf. 1 Cor. 12:3; Rom. 10:9; Phil. 2:11. The revelation of the one God in the Lord Jesus excludes all others.

As we read Paul's words to the Corinthians, we might anticipate that he will side in the dispute with those who espouse a correct theology, those who know there is only one real God and that idols are not gods. This should settle the question with regard to eating food offered to idols. But then comes v. 7 with its big "but" (alla). Love works differently. Edification takes precedence over personal freedom and theological correctness, cf. Phil. 2:4.

Paul continues by saying that knowledge must be exercised with regard for the knowledge of the Christian brother and sister. The exercise of knowledge must be controlled by love. The man with knowledge has no inalienable right to exercise his knowledge at the expense of another. At the same time, he does not have to submit for no reason to the other's scruples. But there is a reason here, namely, the thinking and practice of some people. Before they became Christians, they believed the food they were eating was in honor of and worship to an idol, and they still have some feeling for the idols.

Eating and drinking things offered to idols may have no significance to the person who knows that idols are not gods, but it may be disastrous for the Christian who has not yet assimilated this knowledge. True knowledge includes assimilation into one's behavior. The person with mature knowledge must care in love for the weakness/immaturity of the other. He must not flaunt his knowledge arrogantly.

The slogan, "all of us possess knowledge," is contradicted in V. 7. V. 7 shows that the words of v. 1 are a slogan probably used by the strong, and they are not Paul's. The ones who think that eating food offered to idols is actually nothing use the slogan.

The knowledge everyone does not have is stated in the slogans of v. 4. Everyone has not yet assimilated this knowledge. They still associate idol-food with worship of the pagan gods.

There is great variety in the way translators treat the phrase in v. 7 that is translated in the NRSV "Since some have become so accustomed to idols until now." But what Paul says seems clear enough. "Until now," the weak were idol worshippers. "Now" they are Christians. But they have been so accustomed to regard an idol as a god that even now, in spite of their conversion, "they still think of the food they eat as food offered to an idol."

The weak do not lack knowledge, but thought patterns followed for years or even decades cannot be changed in a short time. It takes a while to assimilate new knowledge. The idols gave the weak some security and hope in the past, and the weak are still under their influence somewhat. They should follow their conscience. They should not be encouraged to engage in conduct that their conscience condemns.

In today's world, well-instructed Christians may be influenced by the practice of witchcraft against their reason long after their conversion. Folk-wisdom may influence people's behavior long after they have come to know Jesus Christ.

The Greek word suneidesis like the English word "conscience" consists of two words meaning "joint knowledge." Originally, suneidesis meant joint knowledge with another, but by Paul's time it had long since come to have the meaning of knowledge shared with one's self.[50]

The term denotes the relationship of a person to himself. It is a person's understanding of his own conduct. It is a state of mind in which a person reflects on and scrutinizes the intent of his own mind. Conscience judges. It is knowledge about one's own conduct in respect to a requirement which exists in relation to that conduct. This knowledge may have to do with something that is still to be done, a duty to be fulfilled, as well as something that has already happened.

Their conscience forbids the weak to eat food that has been offered to idols. If they eat it, their conscience will be defiled; they will have a bad conscience. Through the example of the strong, the weak "might . . . be encouraged to the point of eating food sacrificed to idols." They associate the eating of idol-food with participation in the cults of pagan gods. For them, idolatry is real and dangerous. Paul worries that the example of the strong will destroy the weak. Their conscience will be wounded. They may fall.

The principle involved is stated in Rom. 14:14: "it is unclean for anyone who thinks it unclean." It is also stated in Rom. 14:23: "those who have doubts are condemned if they eat, because they do not act from faith; for whatever does not proceed from faith is sin."

The strong needed no barriers between the idols and themselves in order to protect their Christian faith, because they knew that idols were nothing. They were proud both of that knowledge and of the power and freedom it gave them. They wanted to practice it and not give it up. But love should control what they do.

Paul gives no advice either to the strong or to the weak on the question of how weak consciences can be strengthened. Each person should hold to the position in which he finds himself. Rom. 14:4 says that we are not to pass judgment on the weak.

Actually, the strong do not yet have "the necessary knowledge" either. They need to learn the practice of love.

"Food will not bring us close to God," Paul says. The NRSV text places these words inside quotation marks, suggesting that this is another slogan. It sounds like what Paul would say, not the strong. It may be a slogan Paul inserts into the discussion. The words that follow may either be a part of the slogan, as the NRSV suggests in a footnote, or an explanation of it.

Paul continues to shift attention away from the rights and freedom of the strong to the responsibility freedom places on them for the weak. Paul talks about "this liberty of yours." The word translated "liberty" is exousia which is sometimes translated "right," "capability," "power," and "authority." The translation "liberty" gives to exousia concrete shape and meaning, but it does not have a good connotation. "This liberty of yours" is liberty that doesn't care about the effect its practice has on others. It can "become a stumbling block to the weak." It can destroy the "weak." The exousia of the strong is legitimate. It is based on knowledge. It is shared by Paul. But it can be evil. It can empower a person to "sin against members of your family." It can empower a person to "sin against Christ." The sin is committed not only against the brother but against the Lord. The brother represents Christ, according to Mark 9:37; Matt. 10:40; 25:45.

Love will lead the strong to avoid becoming a stumbling block. Love gives up freedom for the sake of the other. The behavioral principle – avoid giving offense - is stated in 1 Cor. 10:32. The ultimate concern is the salvation of people and not to destroy "believers for whom Christ died."

Paul does not forbid visiting a temple restaurant. But if "others see you" there, that may create a problem. It is not the conduct of the strong that affects them, but the weak seeing them there. The immature knowledge of the weak makes the uncaring behavior of the strong sin.

"Might they not . . . be encouraged," Paul wonders. The Greek word ouchi indicates that he expects an affirmative answer.

The strong who, claiming liberty, eat meat offered to idols may argue that their example "builds up" the weak, encouraging them to become equally free. Paul rejects this idea. He says that quite the opposite happens, the weak are strengthened to defile their conscience. They are encouraged to engage in what they think is idol worship. In the eyes of the weak the gods are still powers, and by eating food offered to them the weak would honor them as such.

By "eating in the temple of an idol," the strong exercise

their freedom without consideration for the weak. Even if the strong do this out of contempt for the idols, the weak think they do it out of veneration for the idol. The weak, too, may come to their conclusion without consideration for the knowledge of the strong. Nevertheless, the strong are exercising their freedom in such a way that they destroy the weak.

Instead of building up the weak, the strong are destroying them "by your knowledge." The en ("by") may be instrumental, or it may mean "by reason of" your knowledge.

They are destroying "believers for whom Christ died." Paul is not using the word "love" as a subjective feeling. It is determined by the saving work of Christ Jesus.

There is no discussion on how God will deal with the weak person who has fallen due to the behavior of the strong. The issue is not so much the weak as the strong. What have the strong done, and what should the strong do?

It is hard to get away from the idea that when Paul uses the word "destroyed," he is talking about eternal damnation. This idea is supported by Rom. 14:15. Christian faith is an extremely fragile thing that can be destroyed by the actions of other people. Christians can lose their salvation. Christians need to protect each other's relationship to God.

In the summary statement of this chapter, cf. "therefore" in v. 13, Paul uses himself as an example. Statements to the same effect are in Rom. 14:21 and Mark 9:42.

In the statement, "I will never eat meat," the Greek contains a very strong double negative, ou ma. It is uncertain as to whether Paul is referring only to meat sacrificed to an idol or abstinence from meat altogether. Some argue that the Christians in Corinth were never sure whether they were eating idol-meat, but there may have been Jewish and even Christian butchers.

Mark 1:21-28

Why does Jesus rebuke the unclean spirit, telling him, "Be silent?" The unclean spirit knows who Jesus is, and he tells other people. Isn't that helpful to Jesus and His ministry? Isn't that what we are supposed to do?

282

Jesus is portrayed in Mark's gospel as trying to keep people from telling other people who He is and what He has done, cf. 1:34, 44; 3:12; 5:43; 7:36. This feature is sometimes called "the Messianic secret."

A variety of reasons have been offered to explain this phenomenon. One is that Jesus does not want unclean spirits or demons promoting Him. That would not help His ministry. Of course, the word is out by the time Jesus silences the unclean spirits, and the people in the synagogue have heard their testimony. Furthermore, this explanation can't be used to explain the prohibition that follows the raising of the dead girl in 5:43 or the healing of the deaf mute in 7:36, because unclean spirits are not involved.

Another improbable explanation is that Jesus wants to keep the crowds from turning Him into a sideshow and getting Him to perform more miracles. One miracle follows another in Mark's account. Another idea is that Jesus shunned the reputation of being a wonder-worker so that He would not be diverted from His true calling as a teacher. Some say that Jesus is not clear in His own mind as to whether He is the Messiah. But the impression is that Jesus knows who He is and does not want it to be made known. Some think that Jesus fears the Romans will try to stop His work if He is known too early as the Messiah. But the opposition to Him does not come from the Roman authorities. They do not crucify Him on their own initiative but at the instigation of the Jewish leaders. It is hard to prove that Mark is aware of any of these explanations.

Some think the Messianic secret is a literary device used by ancient and modern writers who want to reveal to the reader significant information that is not known to the characters in the story. That explanation doesn't seem to ring true either.

The Messianic secret may be a dramatic device used by Jesus and/or a literary device used by Mark to say that the miracles are not the important events about Jesus, that people ought not focus on them to learn who He is and what He is trying to do, and that His real identity is to be found somewhere else. The somewhere else, of course, is His passion. His crucifixion is the focal point, the main thing, and the climax of

Mark's presentation of "the good news of Jesus Christ, the Son of God," cf. Mark 1:1. Jesus' character and identity are seen not in His miracles and teachings but in His suffering and death. He saves the world on the cross and inspires us to follow Him in a life of humility and self-sacrifice.

Misunderstandings of Jesus' power arise when people focus on His miracles or His displays of authority. More than that, His crucifixion reveals and confirms the true character of God's dominion against the backdrop of human misconceptions of power and control.

Neither Jesus' exorcisms, His authoritative pronouncements, His miracles, nor His teachings lead anyone to recognize Him as the Son of God. Even the disciples do not understand Jesus fully until after His resurrection. The secret is revealed when He dies on the cross. The first to get it is the officer under the cross, cf. Mark 15:39. The point of the so-called "Messianic secret" is that Jesus can be understood only in His passion.

Jesus' miracles should not be made the focal point of His story, because they are ambiguous. They do not prove that He is the Messiah. Some people, as a matter of fact, saw them as the work of the devil, cf. Mark 3:22, 30; et al. Others saw and did not believe. The miracle in the synagogue is typical. What Jesus did aroused temporary wonder and amazement, but Mark does not describe the reaction in v. 27 as producing the faith that changes sinners into obedient children of God who trust God instead of themselves and forgive their enemies. Jesus did not make disciples by displays of power.

Still, miracles play an important role in Mark's presentation of "the good news of Jesus Christ." There are eighteen in his gospel: four exorcisms, cf. 1:21-28; 5:1-20; 7:24-30; 9:14-29; nine healings, cf. 1:29-31, 40-42; 2:1-12; 3:1-6; 5:21-43; 7:31-37; 8:22-26; 10:46-52; two feeding stories, cf. 6:34-44 and 8:1-10; two stories of rescue at sea, cf. 4:35-41 and 6:45-52; and one prophetic sign, cf. 11:12-14, 20. In addition, there are summaries of Jesus' healings and exorcisms in 1:32-34, 39; 3:7-12; and 6:53-56, as well as incidents that refer to His mighty deeds in 3:22-30; 6:1-6; 8:14-21; and 15:29-32.

Mark uses the miracles to reveal Jesus' divine authority.

Mark 1:27-28 tells us that people were amazed at Jesus' authority. When He enabled the paralytic to take up his pallet and go out, "they were all amazed and glorified God, saying, 'We have never seen anything like this!'" cf. 2:12. The disciples were "filled with great awe" in 4:41 and exclaimed, "Who then is this, that even the wind and sea obey him?" The herdsmen were "afraid" in 5:15, when they saw what Jesus did for the man whose name was Legion. The man who was possessed with demons proclaimed what Jesus did for him, and "everyone was amazed" in 5:20. Jesus raised the ruler's daughter from the dead, and the mourners were "overcome with amazement" in 5:42. Mark tells us in 6:2 that the people of Jesus' hometown were astonished at Him. They asked, "Where did this man get all this?" Another exclamation expressing the same surprise is, "What deeds of power are being done by his hands!" Herod's remarks in 6:14-16 also imply that Jesus had a supernatural character. Jesus stepped off the surface of the water into the boat with the disciples, and the wind ceased. They were "utterly astounded" in 6:51. When Jesus made the deaf man with an impediment in his speech both hear and speak, the people were "astounded beyond measure" in 7:37.

Miracles played a prominent role in the original pattern of God's saving activity, the exodus. God eliminated the enemies of His people in the ten plagues and the destruction of the armies of Egypt and of Amalek. Jesus did the same, using His divine power for the welfare of God's people. The enemies of God's people in Mark are the demons and unclean spirits. Mark tells how Jesus used His special authority and power to exercise divine domination.

The ultimate power in heaven and earth is not the devil, the Caesar, a Prime Minister, the Congress, the almighty dollar, or the threat of nuclear destruction. The ultimate authority is Jesus. He shows this authority by commanding an "unclean spirit" to come out of a man.

Jesus came proclaiming, "The time is fulfilled, and the kingdom of God has come near," cf. Mark 1:15. The proclamation of the kingdom of God by its very nature arouses opposition. Forces in the world that resist God do not easily yield. First, the demons oppose Jesus and His teaching, cf. vs. 21-28. He meets this opposition by ordering the "unclean spirit" out of the man. In Mark 2, opposition begins to come from the religious authorities, the scribes and Pharisees. He rejects the charges they make against Him. In the second half of Mark's gospel, the major opposition that Jesus faces comes not from His enemies but from His disciples. The disciples resist the notion that He must suffer and die, because they do not understand His mission, cf. Mark 8:31-32 and 9:30-32.

Jesus, Simon, Andrew, James, and John "went to Capernaum," a town at the northern end of the Sea of Galilee. It was the center of Jesus' Galilean ministry. He may have made Simon's house His headquarters.

With the miracle at the Capernaum synagogue, Mark begins a series of events that is well titled "A Day in the Ministry of Jesus." Four events appear to take place on a sabbath within a period of 24 hours. They are held together by location, the city of Capernaum. When the sabbath began about 6 PM, Jesus, as a pious Jew, went to the synagogue. There He ordered an unclean spirit out of a man, cf. vs. 21-28. Leaving the synagogue, He went to the house of Simon and Andrew where He healed Simon's mother-in-law, cf. vs. 29-31. At sunset, "they brought to Him all who were sick or possessed with demons," and He cured them, cf. vs. 32-34. In the morning, while it was still dark, He went out to "a deserted place" and prayed. Then He and His "companions" left the Capernaum area and went on a mission throughout Galilee, cf. vs. 35-39.

An aspect of Jesus' life style was that He went to a synagogue on the sabbath. Synagogues were meeting places of the religiously oriented Jews. They went to the synagogue to learn. Even small towns and villages where Jews lived had synagogues where they gathered for worship, prayer, and the reading and exposition of the law and the prophets.

Jesus did much teaching in the synagogues, cf. Mark 1:39. He was a rabbi. Any member of the congregation might be invited by the president of a synagogue to expound the law and teach. Jesus adapted Himself to synagogue practice, according to Luke 4:16-20. Emphasis is laid on Jesus' teaching ministry in Mark, cf. 2:13; 4:1; 6:2, 6, 34; etc.

Jesus' teaching style was radically different from that of the rabbis. The scribes were teachers of the law of Moses. Many belonged to the party of the Pharisees, but some were also Sadducees. In interpreting the law, their teaching lacked spontaneity. They based their teaching entirely on tradition. Their expositions consisted of expressions or quotations from famous rabbis and scholars. They refrained from promulgating a novel interpretation until they were satisfied that they had secured for it an informal consensus among their colleagues.

Mark describes the reaction of the people to Jesus' teaching in v. 22: "They were astounded." This means that their senses were struck out of balance by some strong feeling such as fear, wonder, or even joy. They were astonished, because "he taught them as one having authority, and not as the scribes." The authority of Jesus is mentioned twice. His style of teaching exuded authority, according to v. 22. His miracles substantiated His authority, according to v. 27.

Usually, the clause "with authority" in v. 27 is taken with the following phrase, but it may be preferable to take it with the preceding phrase, "a new teaching." What arouses astonishment is not only the freshness of Jesus' teaching but also His evident authority. "He commands."

According to the thinking of that time, the demon had Jesus at a disadvantage because he knew Jesus' name. That gave the demon power over Jesus, so people thought. But Jesus was able, despite that disadvantage, to call the demon out. That would have struck the people of that day as a demonstration of incredible power.

The theme of Jesus' teaching is reported in Mark 1:15.

The appearance of "a man with an unclean spirit" in the synagogue is surprising, because the Jews did not allow people who were regarded as unclean to contaminate the synagogue premises much less to participate in their worship. The surfacing of this unclean spirit is related to the teaching of Jesus which must have provoked the spirit. Up to that time, the people were probably unaware of the unclean spirit.

The behavior of the man cannot be explained psychologically. He recognized who Jesus was while people in general did not. The experience Jesus had with the man is characteristic of His ministry. Mark says it happened frequently in 3:11-12.

Luke uses the word "demon" instead of "spirit" in his record of the event, cf. Luke 4:33 and 35.

Jesus believed in demon possession. There is no indication that He accommodated Himself to an idea of demon possession held by the general population.

It is difficult to say whether the loud cries of v. 24 are those of the man or those of the unclean spirit in him. Not the man but the demon living in him recognized Jesus. The unclean spirit spoke through the man. The voice referred to himself in the plural. Perhaps the man identified himself with the demon and spoke in the name of the class of demons to which the demon belonged. In v. 24, he changed from the first person plural to the first person singular.

In Hebrew, the question, "What have you to do with us?" means, "Why are you bothering us?" The unclean spirit was telling Jesus to mind His own business.

The demons recognized that in Jesus their enemy had appeared. They asked, "Have you come to destroy us?" They felt a sense of menace in the person and teaching of Jesus. Usually, the Greek words are translated as a question, but they can be understood as an assertion, too: "You have come to destroy us!" A decision cannot be made on the basis of the original manuscripts, because they do not have punctuation marks.

What Mark means in v. 26 by the word "convulsing" is given additional clarity in Luke 4:35. The man fell down in a convulsion.

The word "amazed" (thambeomai) is a strong word. So strong a reaction is remarkable, because exorcists were active in those days. Jews were not unfamiliar with the practice. The exorcists often used quite elaborate incantations.[51] The astonishment of the people may have been due to the fact that Jesus cast out the unclean spirit with a word. He did not use magical formulas. The comments of the people indicate that they thought the teaching of Jesus was somehow involved. There were many secrets in those days. Apparently, the people thought that Jesus' power was based on some special knowledge. It was quite usual to speak of different torahs or teachings. For example, there was a torah of the Hillelites, a torah of the Shammaites, etc. The people wondered if He was the author of a new torah, cf. v. 27.

Palestine never lacked people with new and strange doctrines. Nor did Palestine lack wonder-workers and magicians. But the crowds perceived that Jesus was different. The full significance of His uniqueness, however, was not apparent to them.

The news about what Jesus had done spread quickly. He was an overnight celebrity. V. 28 recapitulates the preceding section and anticipates what is to come.

4th Sunday after the Epiphany

Year C

Jeremiah 1:4-10

The salient features of Jeremiah's call are that he was predestined for the prophetic office before he was born, God overruled his objections to the call with the promise of divine aid, and God placed His word in Jeremiah's mouth. His call had its origin in the eternal counsels of God. Isaiah said much the same about himself in Is. 49:1.

Jeremiah tried to decline his call. In this, he was unlike Isaiah who volunteered his service, cf. Is. 6:8, but like Moses, cf. Ex. 4:10, Gideon, Ezekiel, Hosea, Amos, and others before him who also were reluctant. Characteristic reasons for denial were fear and a sense of unworthiness.

Jeremiah claimed to be "only a boy." The Hebrew word translated "a boy" denotes a young person from the age of infancy to manhood, including all who are not yet able to take the full responsibility of a given profession. Jews were not permitted to be public figures before they reached the age of 30. Jeremiah was probably a little younger than that.

God did not respect the Jewish age requirements. He overcame Jeremiah's declination by promising to be with him, cf. v. 8. This promise is repeated in Jer. 1:19 and 15:20.

After he was called, Jeremiah had two reinforcing experiences, cf. 1:11-13. They can be thought of as confirmations of his call.

When God touched Jeremiah's mouth, He did something different from what He did to Isaiah in Is. 6:7. God cleansed Isaiah's mouth, but He empowered Jeremiah's.

The prophet understood himself quite literally to be the mouthpiece of Jahweh. He reported what he heard Jahweh say in the heavenly council, cf. Jer. 23:16-22. Dozens of times, he introduced or concluded his oracles with formulas such as "Thus says the Lord."

Jeremiah was "a prophet to the nations." The word he spoke affected not only him and his people, but it changed the course of history. Four words are used in v. 10 to describe the destructive power of what he would say: "pluck up," "pull down," "destroy," and "overthrow." Two words are used to describe the construction that would follow the destruction: "build" and "plant."

The time was probably 626 BC. The nation of Judah was in the midst of the reformation initiated by King Josiah. With his death in 609 BC, his reforms began to unravel. Judah began a downward spiral that led to destruction and exile in Babylon. During this chaotic period of national destruction and personal disorientation, Jeremiah was called to speak for God.

His message was like a two edged sword. On the one hand, he was to prophesy the certainty of divine judgment on the inept and disobedient political and religious establishment of Judah and the religious corruption of the time. At the same time, he was commissioned to give the nation hope in God. It was a critical time.

Judah existed between two military powerhouses. To the north were the mighty armies of Assyria and Babylon, and Jeremiah was concerned about being invaded by them. To the south was the army of Egypt. Judah occupied a precarious position for a tiny nation. She was a small land bridge between competing civilizations.

Most of the political and religious leaders in Jerusalem

rejected both Jeremiah's message and his credibility. His message of doom went against their patriotic and religious conviction that God had guaranteed the throne to Israel's Davidic ruler.

Consequently, Jeremiah suffered much. He spent time in a private dungeon, a military prison, and a miry pit. Ease, comfort, peace, and prosperity do not characterize his ministry. He proclaimed God's Word at great personal expense, but he persevered.

The Word of the Lord became for the prophet a divine compulsion, cf. Jer. 20:8-9. It was more than the almighty speaking to him. It was also divine power at work in him. This dynamic aspect of the Word of God is described in Is. 55:11. In the New Testament, it is affirmed in Heb. 4:12.

God's powerful Word is at work in the church today. It sets the church apart from earthly organizations. It is the channel through which God confronts the world. Thus the church is more than a world-wide organization dedicated to the high ideals of Jesus Christ, the Teacher, in the same category with organizations like Rotary International. It is more than a charitable organization like the Red Cross for the alleviation of human misery. The church proclaims God's saving work in Jesus Christ and offers hope to the world. The Word it proclaims fulfills the Word published by Jeremiah.

1 Corinthians 13:1-13

These words about love are well-loved. They are also well-used – even when they are misused in the sense that the author did not intend them to be applied to the situation in which they are being used. They are most often read at weddings probably. But Paul specifically directed them to the church in Corinth in response to questions put to him about problems that had developed between and among the members of the church, cf. 1 Cor. 7:1 and 12:1. One of the matters has to do with the marriage relationship, cf. 1 Cor. 7, but the section that includes 1 Cor. 13 has to do with spiritual gifts, cf. 1 Cor. 12-14.

Greek employed three words for love: <u>eros</u>, <u>philia</u>, and agape. Agape is the word used in 1 Cor. 13. The differences between the words are important.

Eros shows up in the English language in words like "erotic." It is not connected with agape in any way. It is not a preparatory stage for agape. Agape is not a purified form of eros. Rather, the two words refer to attitudes that move in the opposite direction. We love either one way or the other. There is no compromise. The New Testament avoids the term eros. The reader of the New Testament is not even reminded of that kind of love.

Eros is a grasping, taking, possessing, and enjoying love. It should not be understood only as sexual. Sexual love is included, but it does not indicate the depth of eros and its dangerous opposition to agape. Eros is love that claims, that desires and tries to control. It is self-love. Eros, although it can show considerable warmth and intensity, thinks not of the other but of itself. The other is seen as a gain, an acquisition, a booty, a prey to be used for oneself. Eros is basically rejection of the other person.

Philia shows up in the English language in a name like "Philadelphia," which is made up of two Greek words sometimes translated "brotherly love." Occasionally, the New Testament uses the word phileo, but the usual New Testament term for love is agape which is unknown in classical Greek and is used sparingly in Hellenistic Greek.

"Caring" may be the best translation for the almost untranslatable agape. The KJV translates with "charity," but to modern ears that means philanthropy and not much more. "Caring" may be useful, because it has not been over-sentimentalized the way "love" has. "If I speak in the tongues of mortals and of angels, but do not care, I am a noisy gong or a clanging cymbal."

Many people think that agape is a human virtue. But what is described in 1 Cor. 13 is really beyond human ability. It has its origin in God. It is the highest gift God gives. It is greater than faith and hope. It is the power of God at work among people. It is not a mere feeling but a new kind of existence. We should not say, "I am loving." Rather we should more accurately say, "I am giving love." Our Christian faith lets God work through us. That is love. We "have love."

Is Paul talking about love for God or love for people? Words like "patient" and "kind" indicate that love for people is included. The close connection between love, faith, and hope shows that love for God is involved, too. Love for God and love for the neighbor is really one, as Jesus teaches in Matt. 22:34-40.

The greatest heresy says that religion is an individual affair, a one-to-one relationship between God and an individual. In its extreme form, this heresy says that communion with the neighbor is a hindrance to the attainment of perfect union with God. This way of thinking leads to the divisions, the segregations, the egocentric spirit of condescension, and the disregard of other people that was at the bottom of the problems at Corinth. This way of thinking produces the kind of people that inhabited the monasteries and cloisters Luther emptied. It produces hermits and recluses. Love surrenders oneself to other people. To effect that kind of surrender, a person cannot be isolated.

Love is voluntary and selfless giving to others for their welfare. It may not be preconsidered or calculated, because, in that case, we would calculate our own risks and, therefore, our own welfare. When a patrolman lifts a fallen wall off a boy, this can hardly be the calculated action of a man who needs to use his back the rest of his life. When a man waiting on a platform with his two young children jumps into the path of a train arriving at the station to hold down between the tracks someone who has fallen off the platform as the train passes over them, he has not calculated this act. Moreover, he knows that something beyond him has responded to the need of the other person. We all are called to this kind of existence by God's love for us.

Love means that we have died, and now God uses us as His instrument. No deeds, however splendid, are Christian unless they are rooted and grounded in love. Human existence is Christian only where love acts.

Love begins with God's love for us as demonstrated in Jesus' passion. It gives itself as Jesus gave Himself for us. It identifies with the interests of the other in independence of their attractiveness and what they have to offer. Agape gives itself without expectation of a return, at the risk of ingratitude or refusal to make a response.

Agape is from God. It is a reaction to God's love. We give ourselves to God not for what He will give us in return, nor for the sake of some purpose that can be achieved with His help, but because of what He has done for us. If we think the meaning of life is to seek ourselves, to find ourselves, we lose; and our life is meaningless. As we Christians love, we find ourselves.

1 Cor. 13 is a self-contained unit with a distinctive literary character arranged in three strophe-like parts, vs. 1-3, vs. 4-7, and vs. 8-13. The words and lines have a parallel structure. The chapter has a rhythmic movement. Adolf Harnack rejected the idea that it is poetry or a hymn. C. Spicq stated that it is neither a psalm nor a hymn properly speaking.

Five conditional clauses form the major part of the first section. Three times the condition ends with the identical phrase, "but do not have love." The concluding clauses of each sentence convey self-condemnation like "I am nothing" and "I gain nothing."

As the words elevate the value and importance of love, they diminish all other spiritual gifts. Speaking in tongues or even more speaking the language of angels, prophesying, knowledge, faith that can move mountains, great acts of charity and philanthropy, and martyrdom are the highest and loftiest things people can do. But Paul says that if each is not motivated by and does not express love, it is noisy, nothing, and profitless.

Spiritual one-up-manship was a problem in the Corinthian church. Boasting, envy, and strife had created factions, cf. 1:10-17. The members took their grievances against each other to heathen magistrates for resolution. The rich despised and embarrassed the poor at the eucharistic love feasts which were a travesty of selfishness. Paul checkmates that game of one-up-manship by saying, if you "do not have love," you are wasting your time in all you think you are good at.

The game did not end or run out of players in Corinth when

Paul served there. We still try to score with different forms of religious ostentation and personal pretension.

I

Vs. 1-3 contrast love with other religious actions and attitudes. Ean ("If") introduces a condition which may be possible, "supposing that." The conditional clause presupposes that people in the Corinthian church are doing great things

Paul follows the Corinthian order of merit for spiritual gifts: first tongues, then prophecy in v. 2, followed by understanding mysteries, knowledge, and faith. Charity and martyrdom are mentioned in v. 3.

The gift of tongues was highly valued in the church at that time. The Spirit enabled some in a state of ecstasy to utter the wonderful works of God with superhuman oratory or in strange languages. Some gloried in this unusual gift and felt superior because they possessed it.

Some people today claim to speak in tongues. This implies that they know what is meant by the New Testament word "tongues." It implies also that what they are doing is the same as what the early Christians did.

The exact meaning of what the New Testament calls "tongues" is not clear, plain, and simple. In some places, "tongues" seems to refer to human language, as in Acts 2:4 and 6-11. In other places, it seems to mean nonhuman language. In Acts 10:46 and 19:6, no indication is given as to whether the tongues were intelligible or if those who were present understood what was being said. In 1 Cor. 14:23, Paul says that outsiders entering a church where the people are speaking in tongues might think that the church people are out of their mind.

Chrysostom, in the fourth century, confessed ignorance regarding tongues. He called them "things which happened then but do not now occur."[52] Both Irenaeus (about 200) and Chrysostom thought that tongues meant speaking in human languages one has not learned.[53]

"A noisy gong" (chalkos echon) may not refer to a musical

instrument. Chalkos means "copper, brass, bronze." It can be used for a variety of objects cast from bronze or brass: armor, knives, cauldrons, mirrors, and money. When used with echon, it indicates a gong. Echon is a present active participle of echeo which means "to sound, to ring, to echo, to roar." Some think that Paul is referring to a bronze sounding vase or a bronze echoing vase. These were used in the Greek theater for the amplification of voices. Paul is saying that without love what a person says is as dull and lifeless as the acoustic amplifiers used on a Greek stage.[54]

The kumbalon ("cymbal") was a well-known musical instrument of the period. The heathen cults used clanging cymbals, especially the cults of the goddess Cybele and Bacchus. They may have been thought to attract the attention of the gods or to drive away demons. Cymbals played a part in Jewish worship, too. The term is used in Ps. 150:5 as an instrument on which to praise God.

The gift of "prophetic powers" may refer to extraordinary revelations and insights into the divine mysteries or to the ordinary gift which some today have of dipping deeply into Christian theology and being able to understand and expound the scriptures. Whatever, the meaning remains pretty much the same.

What Paul means by propheteia (prophecy) is brought out in 1 Cor. 14:1-5. The word there is translated by TEV "proclaiming God's message." Prophecies may include both prediction and declaration. Prophesying is one of the highest Christian activities, according to 14:1, but it is nothing without love.

"Mysteries" such as those Paul talks about in v. 2 may have to do with the after-life as mentioned in 1 Cor. 2:7 and 15:51. Musteria is translated with the word "secret" in 2:7.

Knowledge was evaluated highly by the Corinthians, cf. 8:1-3, but Paul degrades it by saying that our present knowledge is only partial and by making it worthless without love.

When Paul talks about faith, he is not talking about a kind of faith which is different from that of faith in Jesus. He is writing to people who have the faith relationship to God through which they have received the blessings of Jesus' death and resurrection and who need urging to bear good fruits. Faith is useless, no matter how great it may be, if there is no love. People with "all faith, so as to remove mountains" draw their life so wholly from God and can live their life so wholly for God that they dare things deemed impossible by other people. Faith that moves mountains is a proverbial expression meaning to do what seems impossible. Jesus uses it in Matt. 17:20.

Paul is no belittler of faith, yet he insists that without love faith is nothing. Love is not a competitor to faith. Rather without love, there really is no faith, no relationship with God. John also says that, in 1 John 4:7-16. If we use our gifts in conceit and vainglory rather than in loving service to others, we are nothing. No deeds, however splendid, are commendable if they are not rooted or grounded in agape.

Giving to charity was held in high esteem by the Jewish rabbis and thought to gain great merit, but there were restrictions prohibiting a person from giving away all of his goods. For example, in a year he was not to give more than 20% of all his possessions. So giving away all one's possessions, as Paul says, was way above board.

There is a strange conditional clause in the NRSV text of v. 3, "if I hand over my body so that I may boast." The footnote of the NRSV offers a different clause, "if I hand over my body to be burned." There is considerable manuscript evidence for the reading of the NRSV text, but it is generally rejected. The next phrase, "but do not have love," really doesn't make sense with that reading. The reference probably is to persecution and martyrdom, cf. Dan. 3:19-21. Burning was a form of capital punishment. It was similar in certain respects to the offering of a sacrifice. Paul speaks of his martyrdom as a burnt offering in 2 Cor. 2:14-16. He doesn't use the word "sacrifice" but refers to the "aroma" or "fragrance" of a sacrifice, the smell of burning flesh, the same that comes from our backyard grills. The burning could also be burning oneself to death as an ascetic act. This Indian custom was known in the ancient world. A heroic attitude in the face of death by fire is a standard theme in Greco-Roman philosophy. So is the voluntary burning of oneself.

II

Vs. 1-3 make the point that no deed, however splendid, is commendable if there is not love. Vs. 4-7 describe the nature and activity of love. With the change in subject comes also a change in style. The style of vs. 4-13 is quite different from that of vs. 1-3.

Vs. 4-13 present the passive and active dimensions of love demonstrated in the life, death, and resurrection of Christ Jesus. Love is contrasted with human existence. This is how love behaves. Vs. 4-7 open with two positive statements and close with five. In between are eight negatives.

The traits of love described are in contradiction to the character of the Corinthian church. The members of the church are not patient with each other. They are not kind to each other. They are arrogant. They are rude. The strong insist on their rights.

Pastors are tempted sometimes to ask, "How can I be the pastor when the people under my care will not be the church?" But we are called precisely for that reason. We are called to deal with God's people in their faithlessness and brokenness. Envy, boasting, conceit, egocentricity, cherishing inflated ideas of one's own importance, keeping a score of wrongs, and gloating over the sins of others are often evident.

Love is revealed in forbearance. The idea of makrothumei (to be patient) is that it takes a long time before fuming and breaking into flames. It is patient with those who do wrong. The present tense emphasizes a continual and habitual state or action.

People who are "slow to anger" are people "with good sense," according to Prov. 19:11; 14:29; 16:32; 17:27. This is a characteristic of God in His dealings with people, according to Ex. 34:6-7; Num. 14:18; Ps. 86:15; 103:8; Joel 2:13; Jonah 4:2; and Rom. 9:22. The makrothumia of God is displayed in His saving work for Israel. Divine restraint postpones the fulfillment of wrath until something takes place to justify the postponement. If a new attitude does not develop, wrath is fully visited.

Patience is a fruit of the Spirit, according to Gal. 5:22. It is defined as "bearing with one another in love" in Eph. 4:2 and Col. 3:12-13. It is the main theme of James 5:7-11.

Love serves others graciously and with good humor. It does good in return for evil.

Boastfulness involves ostentation. A person is "boastful" who talks a lot and, according to J. B. Phillips, is anxious to impress.[55] Ostentatious boasting easily leads to the next item, "arrogant."

Puffed up are the words used in 1 Cor. 8:1 to refer to the "arrogant." Phillips paraphrases by saying that they "cherish inflated ideas of (their) own importance."[56] Danker says that they are conceited and put on airs.[57] Arrogant people tend to assume that the earth revolves around the spot where they are located.

To be rude is to behave disgracefully, dishonorably, indecently, and shamefully. Love is tactful and does nothing to make a person blush. Phillips says, "Love has good manners."[58] Scholars point to 1 Cor. 11:2-16 or 1 Cor. 14, especially v. 23, for examples of disgraceful behavior in the Corinthian church.

The opposite of insisting on your own way is seeking the way of Christ. Paul writes in Phil. 2:4 that each person should "look not to (his) own interests, but to the interests of others." Conzelmann translates "does not seek its own advantage."[59] An example is given in 1 Cor. 10:24 and 33.

Conzelmann says that paroxunein points predominantly in the direction of inciting to anger.[60] Love does not do that. Phillips paraphrases, "It is not touchy."[61]

Love does not store up resentment and bears no malice. It does not compile statistics of evil. Logizesthai is a word that was used in keeping accounts.

Some have pointed to v. 7 as describing the attitude of Jesus in His passion. His passion demonstrates and inspires Christian love.

Love "bears all things." The Greek word stego comes from

the word for "roof." It has been used to mean "cover, withstand, bear, protect." The meaning is either to cover in the sense of to protect as a roof or to bear up as in supporting a roof. The idea of covering is brought out in 1 Pet. 4:8 and Prov. 10:12.

Love "believes all things." Phillips paraphrases, "Love knows . . . no end to its trust." Love "endures all things." Phillips: "It can outlast anything." Rom. 15:1 calls for that. Love is revealed in forgiveness.

III

The third and final section begins with the words "Love never ends." Vs. 8-13 explain that statement and its significance. Prophecies, tongues, and knowledge will end; but love never will.

The Greek text literally says that prophecies "will be put to an end." The passive verb is another example of the numinous passive. God Himself will bring prophecies to an end, when Christ comes again.

"Tongues . . . will cease" represents the future indicative middle of the verb pauo. This means that tongues will make themselves cease or automatically will cease of themselves.

What Paul means when he says that knowledge "will come to an end" is explained in vs. 9-12. Our knowledge now is fragmentary, indirect, and darkened. It is as incomplete and immature as the life and ways of a youth in comparison with the attitudes and actions of a mature man. Mature Christians do not put themselves at the center of their world as immature children tend to do.

We know and can know very little of God. A few people have gained a little understanding of Him from their study of the scriptures or in other ways. They have the appearance of being enlightened, but their superior knowledge is only relative. Some may think of it as absolute knowledge not because it really is but in comparison with the little understanding of others. When we see God face-to-face, we will realize that we all were more or less wrong in our understanding of Him.

Our knowledge of human beings and of the universe is growing by leaps and bounds, but the more we come to know the less we understand. Life was simpler and clearer for our forefathers who lived in a tidy little world that was flat than it is for us who see images of our earth from the perspective of outer space on the flat TV screens attached to our den walls. People were easier to understand before we learned about the strange complex of genes, glands, instinctive drives, and the unconscious and subconscious surges that control human behavior. The more we learn the more we understand how little we know. Paul speaks of a time when our knowledge of God will be as complete and perfect as God's knowledge of us. "Then we will see (him) face to face."

The illustration involving a mirror brings out the disparity between what we know about the future now and what we will know then. Paul is probably thinking of the mirrors produced by the manufacturers of bronze goods in Corinth. Corinth produced a fine quality of bronze known for its unusual color.[62] He is not thinking about the fuzzy image in the mirrors of his day in comparison to the sharp images reflected by today's mirrors. The ancients thought their mirrors reflected a very good image. The contrast Paul makes is between the object itself and the sight or reflection of it in a mirror. The "dimness" of the visual image in a mirror is a reference to the fact that the object is seen indirectly. The opposite of seeing things "dimly" is seeing them "face to face." The Greek word (ainigma) translated "dimly" is the source of the English word "enigma." The apostle is saying that we see now indirectly, but then we will see firsthand.

Some say the word "now" in v. 13 is an adverb of time, and others say that Paul is drawing a logical conclusion. The meaning doesn't change much.

Faith, hope, and love will still have relevance and be important in the age that is to come. Faith has to do with our relationship to the past. Love is active in the present. Hope focuses on the future part of our story. The future is partly known, because we know the past. God who acted in Jesus Christ is Lord of the future. If we let ourselves be held in God's hands now, we will not fall away.

Faith is the way we receive the righteousness of God. God

justifies us through the cross of Christ. Faith is a decision we make about the cross of Jesus. Not just that it happened, but that it happened for us. Faith is the way we receive the benefit of Jesus' cross. Our faith in God is a response to the death of Jesus. It is saying that when Jesus died, something happened that affects human despair, human sin, and human death. Faith is our decision even though the grace of God is the dynamic of that decision. Faith is God's gift. It involves a decision He empowers us to make.

Faith says that because of the cross of Jesus God can be trusted. We commit ourselves to Him completely. Our sin is no longer an obstacle between us and God, and nothing can separate us from Him. We can trust Him completely in the present and into the unknown future. Faith is grounded in an act of God in the past, it is at work in the present, and active in our anticipation of the future so that it is almost indistinguishable from hope.

Hope is about the future. Faith is our conviction of the trustworthiness of God, and so we know something about the future. We know that God controls the future, although we do not know what form or quality that future will have. Moving into the future, we are confident that God will be there before us.

Hope feeds on faith, cf. Rom. 15:13. Dealing with the unknown future depends in part on dealing with the past. Hope is freedom for the future and openness toward it. We turn over our anxiety about ourselves and our future to God in obedience.

Hope is indispensable – like oxygen. It gives breath to our life. Dante pictures hell as a place of utter hopelessness. Christian hope depends on Christian faith. Faith is the root, hope is the tree that springs from faith, and love is the fruit of the tree.

Human hope depends on progress. Progress was once generally regarded as automatic and inevitable. The many modern wars and the prevalence of terrorism have convinced some that the cards are stacked against us. Many have turned to science. If progress through science is not automatic, at least it is possible. But our confidence in science has been diminished by the frightful circumstances it has created. Science both frightens us and gives us hope for the future. Many people are afraid that the findings of science have given us the ability to destroy ourselves. We want more than natural human hope. Such hope is inadequate, because it begins and ends with human ability, with human wisdom and skill. The human temperament does not foster confidence with regard to the future.

The decisive difference between the hope Paul is talking about and hope in general is that Christian hope is centered in God. It is based not on what humans are able to do, but on what God has done. It is produced by faith in God. This is God's world. He created it. He controls it. His Son, Jesus, saved it by His life and death.

Paul was not by nature an optimistic person. His life included stonings and imprisonments. One of the sources of hope for Paul was the Old Testament scriptures, cf. Rom. 15:4. One of the truths Paul learned from scripture is that the unseen is real: "What can be seen is temporary, but what cannot be seen is eternal," cf. 2 Cor. 4:18. Paul believed that behind all the changes and the fleeting phenomena of life is the hand of the eternal God. God inspires hope even when things seem most hopeless. Especially then.

Another truth Paul learned from the scriptures is that God does not work in a hit or miss fashion but purposefully. The thing that drives some people to despair is the haunting suspicion that everything is just sound and fury signifying nothing. But Paul learned that life makes sense. It has a purpose. He saw this purpose unfold in the history of Israel. There things did not always happen on the main stage of history, but through them God was at work saving people – the call of Abraham, the exodus, the establishment of the monarchy, the building of the temple, the exile in Babylon, the return from there, and the climax in the life, death, and resurrection of Jesus.

Paul saw purpose in his own life, even in his afflictions. "We boast in our sufferings," he wrote in Rom. 5:3. Suffering develops endurance, character, and hope. His thorn in the flesh served a purpose; it kept him humble so that he would not become too elated, cf. 2 Cor. 12:7. He said that the jealousy his preaching provoked in the Christian preachers in Rome served a purpose; it resulted in the furtherance of the gospel, cf. Phil 1:12-18. Paul said, "We know that all things work together for good for those who love God," cf. Rom. 8:28.

Paul believed that God has a purpose for the human race. He said, "We know that the whole creation has been groaning in labor pains" in Rom. 8:22. A woman in travail is hopeful despite the pain, because new life is being produced. So Paul believed that history is going somewhere. "The creation waits with eager longing for the revealing of the children of God," cf. Rom. 8:19.

Life is like a voyage. As we engage in this voyage, the primary question is not the size of the ship or her speed, the kind of weather, the menu, the congeniality of the passengers, or the competence of the crew. The question is, How does the journey end? What difference does it make how we travel if the ship like some proud Titanic ends up on the bottom of the ocean? Christian hope centers not around the ship and her accommodations but around the Pilot. It springs from the faith that the God who loves us is at the helm. Never mind how bad the weather. Despite piracy, even mutiny, nothing can destroy or defeat God's purpose for our voyage.

Christian hope always has the dimension of eternity. These are words from the writings of Paul: "We know that if the earthly tent we live in is destroyed, we have a building from God, a house not made with hands, eternal in the heavens," cf. 2 Cor. 5:1. "This slight momentary affliction is preparing for us an eternal weight of glory beyond all measure," cf. 2 Cor. 4:17. "I consider that the sufferings of this present time are not worth comparing with the glory about to be revealed to us," cf. Rom. 8:18. "To me living is Christ and dying is gain," cf. Phil. 1:21.

Love is the Christian's posture in the present that is formed by faith, by the character of God revealed in the cross of Christ. The image of a cross is a symbol of God's love.

We love, because God loves us. Our love is provoked by faith and supported by hope.

Luke 4:21-30

It was the sabbath, and Jesus was worshipping in the synagogue at Nazareth where He was raised. He was asked to read a lesson from the scroll of the prophet Isaiah. It was Is. 61:1-2. He told the people that the prophecy was fulfilled that day. V. 22 seems to say that the home town people reacted favorably to what He said. But their reaction turned into "rage" in v. 28, and they tried to kill Him. What happened? It takes some doing to work it out.

What happened is tersely described in John 1:11: "He came to his own home (see the NRSV footnote), and his own people did not accept him." Luke places this story at the beginning of Jesus' public ministry and uses it to characterize His entire ministry. It prepares the reader for Jesus' passion.

Some details of this story have already been discussed in connection with the Gospel for the 3rd Sunday after the Epiphany (C). The story begins in v. 16. The discussion of the Gospel for that day includes v. 21.

The words of Jesus quoted in v. 21 are not all the words He spoke in commenting on Is. 61:1-2. This was the theme of His message. Perhaps He interpreted to them in detail on the basis of the prophecy "the things about himself" as He did to the two disciples on the way to Emmaus following His resurrection, cf. Luke 24:27.

Is. 61:1-2 outlines the program of the Messiah. What the prophet announced to the exiles returning from Babylon, Jesus proclaimed to the poor, the prisoners, the blind, and the downtrodden of His day. What Isaiah said was being fulfilled in the person, words, and deeds of Jesus. Jesus proclaimed the year of the Lord's favor.

The prophecy of Isaiah was very important to the first century Jews living under Roman oppression and rule. When Jesus read the prophecy, He omitted one line: "and the day of vengeance of our God," cf. Is. 61:2. The people understood those words to promise God's judgment on the gentiles and His victory for Israel over her enemies. They may have been disappointed when Jesus omitted that line.

The first response to Jesus' teaching/preaching seems to have been agreeable. The report had reached the hometown people that Jesus was a remarkable preacher, and they were seeing that this report was true. This seems to be a success story: hometown boy makes good.

Actually, the word translated "amazed" (ethaumazon) can express either admiration or amazement coupled with criticism, doubt, and censure. Some scholars think that the phrase "the gracious words" does not mean that the words of Jesus were charming but that He talked about the mercy of God directed toward gentiles. The Greek word is charitos which fundamentally has to do with beauty and charm but can also be translated "grace," referring to the love, the mercy, and the forgiveness of God. The people may have protested "the gracious words" coupled with the omission of God's "vengeance" on gentiles.[63] The question, "Is not this Joseph's son?" may have been a dismissal. The words of Mark 6:3 are a little stronger: "Is not this the carpenter, the son of Mary and brother of James and Joses and Judas and Simon, and are not his sisters here with us?"

The future tenses used in v. 23 indicate that Jesus anticipated what the people would say next. He quoted a proverb. The Greek word parabole ("proverb") has a wide breadth of meaning, and here it means a proverb.

The point of the proverb is disputed. Some take it to mean, "Heal the ills of your own town." It means much the same as "Charity begins at home." But the proverb exhorts the prophet to heal himself. The meaning of the saying is explained in the second half of v. 23. The people asked for some sign to support Jesus' claim that He was the Messiah. They wanted Him to do some miracles such as, according to what they heard, He did in Capernaum. The demand for signs proceeded from skepticism and doubt. Also the people did not believe that Jesus had done the things He was reported to have done in Capernaum. "We have heard you did" them are the words Jesus used to express the skepticism they felt.

Luke does not report "the things" Jesus "did at Capernaum." Mark 1:21-2:12 may describe some of them.

The people thought that Jesus had neither the background – He was a carpenter or a carpenter's son - nor the authority to skip the words about God's vengeance in His presentation of Isaiah's prophecy. He was abusing the text. Also He had no authority to talk about God's goodness to gentiles. He sounded to them like a gentile lover instead of being the fulfillment of Isaiah's prophecy.

The force of the introductory words in v. 24 may be expressed more strongly by translating, "But instead of granting their request, He said."

Jesus called Himself a prophet. Luke leaves it to our imagination to hear the people respond, "You, Jesus, are no prophet! You are the carpenter's son!"

Various proverbial sayings express what Jesus says in v. 24. A current one is, "Familiarity breeds contempt." Because He grew up among the people of Nazareth, it was difficult for them to perceive His special character.

If the people's objection to Jesus' quotation of Is. 61:1-2 is His omission of God's vengeance on gentiles, He began to take up the underlying issue of that objection in v. 25. The issue was their prejudice against gentiles. To counter this prejudice, He reminded them of the ministry of two of the greatest prophets, Elijah and Elisha.

There were many widows in Israel who could have been helped by Elijah, but God sent the prophet to a gentile widow living at Zarephath in Sidon. The story is told in 1 Kings 17:8-16.

"Elijah was sent to . . . Zarephath." This is a numinous passive; God sent Elijah. "Was shut up" in v. 25 and "was cleansed" in v. 27 are the same kind of passive.

The story of Naaman and Elisha is in 2 Kings 5:1-19. Naaman was the commander of the army of Syria and was sent by the Syrian king to the king of Israel to be cured of his leprosy. The Israelite king interpreted the Syrian king's request to cure Naaman as a pretext for starting war. But Elisha asked the king to send Naaman to him. He told the commander to bathe seven times in the river Jordan. The commander complained that the Syrian rivers Abana and Pharphar were "better than all the waters of Israel," but he bathed in the Jordan and was cured.

In the stories of Elijah and Elisha, Jesus was saying that God's favor is directed not only to Jews but also to gentiles. This contradicted the people's understanding of God's unique relationship with them and His relationship with gentiles. Jesus said that the grace of God was not inhibited by the traditional boundaries of culture and ethnicity. It was not limited to "our kind of people." That Jesus is the Savior of all people including gentiles is one of the strong themes in the writings of Luke.

The reaction of the people to Jesus' references to the stories of Elijah and Elisha was that they "were filled with rage." They considered Jesus' expression of divine favor for gentiles blasphemy. The Jews were fanatically nationalistic. Jews today are still very sensitive about real or imagined slights committed against their nation and their superiority to other people. What Jesus was saying was unpatriotic and against their religion. Paul met the same reaction from the Jews at Jerusalem when he told them that the heathen would receive the divine blessings they despised in Acts 18:4-16; 21:27-22:23.

The people "drove (Jesus) out of the town." These were Jesus' neighbors, family, relatives, and friends! He grew up with them! Luke describes the rejection of Jesus by the people of Nazareth as total. Mark and Matthew are not so harsh. Mark 6:5 concludes the story, "he laid his hands on a few sick people and cured them." Matt. 13:58 concludes, "he did not do many deeds of power there." Both Mark and Matthew bemoan the "unbelief" of the hometown people.

Attempts to locate "the brow of the hill" from which the people wanted to "hurl him off the cliff" have not been very successful. The village must have been quite small at the time, although the presence of a synagogue suggests some size. Perhaps the modern village has been built over "the cliff." There is a precipice that varies from 80 to 300 feet in height about two miles from the city. It is called "the hill of precipitation" and since the ninth century is pointed to by guides as the place to which the people hustled Jesus. But the distance from the city seems too great. Another hill directly overhanging the town has about a 50 foot drop and seems more likely. Luke is generally regarded as not too sharp on Palestinian geography.

A false prophet was to be put to death, according to Deut. 13:1-5. The people of Nazareth thought that Jesus was guilty of that charge. Hurling a person off a cliff was preparation for stoning him to death.

No miracle is asserted or necessarily implied when Luke says that Jesus "passed through the midst of them." Jesus' majesty and dignity may have been enough to overawe those who thought that He should be executed. But what Jesus did was a miracle. It may be considered the sign the people asked for.

Jesus' "way," cf. v. 30, eventually led to Calvary. So far as we know, He did not return to Nazareth. It is not likely that He would after the attempt on His life.

Although Luke uses this story to introduce Jesus' Galilean ministry, this is not the beginning of Jesus' preaching, teaching, and healing. Matthew 13:54-58 and Mark 6:1-6 seem to tell the same event. But Matthew and Mark have Jesus preaching in His hometown at a different point in His ministry. Mark uses the account of Jesus in the synagogue at Nazareth as a transitional unit. It comes at the end of Jesus' Galilean ministry. In the first major section of the second gospel, Mark 1:21-5:43, Jesus is depicted as mighty in deed and word. Mark ends the section with the story of Jesus' rejection at Nazareth, a theme that continues until he tells the story of the crucifixion when Jesus is rejected by the Jews, His disciples, and even God. The story of Jesus in Nazareth is a part of the theme of suffering, death, and resurrection that dominates Mark's gospel. Matthew presents the rejection of Jesus at Nazareth as the climax of His Galilean ministry.

Some think the event recorded in Matt. 13:54-58 and Mark 6:1-6 is different from the one in Luke 4. One difference is that Mark 6:1 says that "his disciples followed him." In Luke's account, Jesus seems not to have any disciples. In any event, this is not the beginning of Jesus' public ministry. v. 23 says that He worked in Capernaum before He came to Nazareth.

In telling the story of Elijah, Jesus says "the heaven was shut up three years and six months." Rain falls when the windows of heaven are open, and it stops raining when they are closed. This cosmology is the same as that in the Old Testament, cf. Gen. 1:7; 7:11-12; and 8:2.

"The third year of the drought" is mentioned in 1 Kings 18:1. This does not represent a discrepancy between the gospel and 1 Kings, because not only does the original Hebrew lack the words "of the drought," according to the NRSV footnote, but also the story indicates that some time elapsed before and after 1 Kings 18:1. Jas. 5:17 confirms what Jesus says in Luke, that the drought lasted three years and six months.

Jesus says that the "severe famine (was) over all the land." The words may or may not be intended to include the whole world. Only the land of Israel may be meant.

The mention of Joseph in v. 22 really says nothing about whether he was alive or dead at this time.

The existence of lepers in Israel is attested by 2 Kings 7:3.

In extra-Biblical Greek, the word lepra usually designates something like psoriasis. It refers to several inflammatory or scaly skin diseases. The descriptions in Lev. 13-14 conform much more to true leprosy which today is called Hansen's disease. In the Old Testament, "leprosy" caused ceremonial defilement. Persons so afflicted were excluded from normal intercourse with others and had to live outside of the towns, cf. Num. 5:2-3; 12:10-15; 2 Kings 7:3-9.

By reporting how Jesus dealt with the anti-gentile prejudice of the people of Nazareth, Luke gives strong support to the Christian mission to gentiles. The book of Acts documents the difficulty the early church had in starting this work. Luke provides justification for the mission to gentiles from the Old Testament.

In the stories involving Elijah and Elisha, Jesus said that God is not limited to helping Jews. That is like a preacher today saying that God helps not only Christians. God is the

God of all people, and Christians do not have a corner on Him and His favor. He is the Creator and Redeemer of all people. He is free to bestow His grace where He wills. Grace is a form of divine injustice anyway; it is undeserved. God has His own agenda. He forgives and dispenses His grace to any and all of His creatures.

5th Sunday after the Epiphany

Year A

Isaiah 58:1-12

This prophecy has been called "A Diagnosis of Religious Sin."[64] The prophet bemoans a lack of integrity in worship, because the people are guilty of economic exploitation and social injustice.

Although the prophecy is directed to "the house of Jacob," it applies to all God's people of all ages, because God does not change. The God who castigated the house of Jacob has made us His people through the passion of Jesus Christ, and so the warnings of the prophecy speak to us, too. To worship God requires an attitude of humility and caring for the hungry, the homeless, and those who do not have adequate clothing.

"The house of Jacob" is charged with hypocrisy in worship. God sides with the oppressed, the poor, and the weak. Those who genuinely worship Him do, too, as James 1:27 says: "Religion that is pure and undefiled before God, the Father (includes) to care for orphans and widows in their distress . . . ." Furthermore, Jesus identified Himself very closely with the hungry, the thirsty, strangers, the naked, the sick, and those in prison when He said, "Just as you (helped or did not help) one of the least of these who are members of my family, you (helped or did not help) me," cf. Matt. 25:40 and 45.

The nation must stop oppression; the people must free those who are oppressed. "Then your light shall break forth like the dawn," the prophet says. Then God will answer their cries for help.

God's people today need to be confronted with this same message. The American psyche includes a strain of evil that praises selfishness as a virtue and ignores or rejects charity. Some people champion unbridled capitalism, individual rights, ruthless self-interest, and disdain for the poor as being in the best interests of our country. They try to terminate state-sponsored welfare and social programs. Some of these people occupy high places in our society. They sit on the Supreme Court and hold positions of great importance in the realms of high finance and politics. They have a great influence on the priorities of our nation. They are an embarrassment to the human race and to the God whom some of them claim to worship.

The prophecy begins with God authorizing the prophet to condemn "the house of Jacob" for its hypocrisy, the gap between the actual worship of the people and what they pretend to do. This deep-seated variance must be overcome before the nation will prosper.

God wants the condemnation to be a public event. The problem is important. The prophet is instructed to use his voice like a trumpet, which in those days probably was not a metallic instrument but a horn from an animal like a sheep or a goat.

Hypocrisy is called "rebellion" and "sin" in v. 1. It is described in these words: "they seek me and delight to know my ways, as if they were a nation that practiced righteousness and did not forsake the ordinance of their God . . . they delight to draw near to God." Worship life is strong. The people enjoy worship. They do it "day after day." But the words "as if" identify what they do as hypocrisy. They act "as if" they were a people whose righteous action and faithfulness to the commands of God warranted good from Jahweh.

Genuine worship focuses people's behavior on what is important to Jahweh, but the nation does not have this focus.

In their worship, they pretend concern for the things of God, but their behavior is not affected by what concerns Him.

How deeply the sin infects them is evidenced by the complaint made against God in response to His charge of hypocrisy. They say, "we fast, but you do not see" and we "humble ourselves, but you do not notice." They are firmly convinced that they are glorifying God.

God rejects their defense by making clear how hypocritical their piety is. He tells them that even the intent of their worship is hypocritical. He says, "You serve your own interest on your fast day." While they fast, they carry on their daily business. The spiritual character of the day is absorbed by their selfish desires. Their worship is calculated and manipulative. They worship with hope of personal gain. They fast to draw Jahweh's attention to themselves. They try to use God instead of worshipping Him. They use the time of worship to plot ways to acquire more for themselves. It is not worship at all. Calculating worship is hypocrisy.

When we experience the mercy of God, we are merciful to others; but, the prophet charges, you "oppress all your workers." The meaning may be that they push the workers in their work on days of worship more than at other times, so that there is no loss of production because they have taken time off to worship God.

"You fast only to quarrel and to fight and to strike with a wicked fist." When they fast, they are irritable and bad-tempered. Being focused on themselves, they quarrel and fight with each other. They even strike each other with an angry fist.

Their worship is a distortion. They are hiding their self-righteousness and their unrighteousness behind a façade that they call fasting.

Jahweh exposes their delusional thinking by describing the character of true fasting and what accompanies it in v. 5. V. 5 may also be a continuation of the castigation of their pretense. Fasting is an expression of humility, but they only pretend to be humble. They feign humility by walking around with bowed heads and lying in sack cloth and ashes. Fasting is a time for prayer, but it accomplishes nothing when it is accompanied by oppressive behavior toward other people.

The worship of God involves people's attitude and behavior toward other people. God is concerned about people, especially people who are hurting; and His people have the same concern. They represent Him.

A nation that genuinely practices righteousness will "loose the bonds of injustice" and "undo the thongs of the yoke." The term "the yoke" is used twice in v. 6. It probably refers to indebtedness. Some people are in hock. "To undo the thongs of the yoke" probably means to cancel paralyzing debts.

The Lord wants His people to "let the oppressed go free." Jer. 34:8-22 gives an example of hypocrisy along this line. When the Babylonians were besieging the city of Jerusalem, a general emancipation of Hebrew slaves was proclaimed. This was supposed to be done regularly, but the ordinance had not been kept. The general emancipation was intended to rectify this negligence. But as soon as the Babylonians lifted the siege, the liberated slaves were brought back into servitude.

Fasting involves more than abstinence from eating. It involves also self-denying love and help for the needy. God's people "share (their) bread with the hungry." A true fast involves doing without and giving up things to help others: shared bread, houses, and clothing. These things are necessary for life.

The charity encouraged may refer to public policy as well as helping individuals. The point is that life should not be preoccupied selfishly with one's own needs and passions. We should get involved in the needs of others both individually and in public policy decisions. Especially, we should help hungry, homeless, and inadequately clothed relatives.

"The afflicted" in v. 10 may refer to people who are humiliated, exploited, and demeaned by their social situation.

God promises "the house of Jacob" a change in their fortunes when they change their ways. V. 8 describes great well-being. Everything good that is hoped for from Jahweh will come to them. In v. 3, the people want to be noticed by Jahweh in their worship, and Jahweh promises that He will see them and care for them in v. 8.

This can be seen as a quid pro quo matter, Jahweh making a deal with His people. Or it can be seen as instruction on how social security works. When people get along with each other and help each other, a nation prospers. Selfishness, greed, indifference toward people who are suffering, and exploitation produce the opposite result.

If they change, God promises His people security. He says that He will go before them, and "the glory of the Lord shall be your rear guard."

He promises them His attention, His availability, and His presence. The deepest religious need and craving is the presence of Jahweh. It is the assurance that in risk and danger we are not alone. If people attend to their neighbors, God will attend to them.

"The yoke" is referred to again in v. 9. It probably refers to heavy economic requirements. If "the yoke" is removed, good things will happen. Genuine relationships with people involve just and compassionate economics in contrast to exploitation. A good relationship results in well-being.

The people must stop pointing the finger at and speaking evil of each other. The prophet probably is referring to social recriminations, accusations, slander, and gossip. These destroy relationships.

God will give "light" to people who practice justice and compassion. He will give their nation good leadership.

The greatest need of people "in parched places" is water. Water is a really great thing in a place like Palestine. It is promised in Is. 35:6-7 and 41:17-18. Ps. 23:2 speaks of the Good Shepherd who "leads me beside still waters."

The reference to the rebuilding of "your ancient ruins" suggests that the prophet delivered this message during the rebuilding of Jerusalem. When the people mend their ways, the nation will have the energy, strength, and resources to rebuild. These characteristics will come as the people invest in each other. The nation will be honored by being called "the repairer of the breach" and "the restorer of streets to live in." A restored nation does not rise primarily from the bureaucracy, the technology, high finance, or ingenuity. It begins with people caring for each other and treating each other with dignity.

319

1 Corinthians 7:1-16

Sex and marriage are always of interest. Some instruction Paul gives in this Lesson might better be discussed in a format other than the sermon in a worship situation.

The newly converted Christians in Corinth were troubled by a number of things. They wrote a letter to Paul requesting help. In 1 Corinthians, he takes up sex and marriage in 7:1-24, celibacy in 7:25-40, food sacrificed to idols in 8:1-11:1, head coverings in 11:2-16, problems in connection with the Lord's Supper in 11:17-34, spiritual gifts in chs. 12-14, the resurrection of the dead in ch. 15, and the collection for the saints in 16:1-4.

Paul may take up sex and marriage first, because they were first on the list of "the matters" about which the Corinthians wrote. But Paul may be led to deal with sex and marriage in ch. 7, because he says in the final verses of ch. 6, "your body is a temple of the Holy Spirit within you . . . you are not your own. For you were bought with a price; therefore glorify God in your body." To go from there to marriage is an easy step. Jesus' death is the motivation for sexual morality.

1

Speaking generally, Paul says, "It is well" if a person does not marry; but he concedes that a person should marry to avoid sexual immorality.

Orthodox Jews generally regarded marriage as a duty, and they opposed celibacy. A strong reason for this was God's promise to send a savior. This promise was fulfilled when Jesus was born. He saved us by His death and resurrection. Jews structured their lives around waiting for the promised son of David, cf. 2 Sam. 7:11-14. But no one knew whom God would choose to be the Messiah's parents. Therefore, they organized their lives so that God might use them. Celibacy was unproductive. The procreation of children was the purpose of marriage. The new Christians in Corinth may have wondered if they were expected to conform to such thinking, or if they could remain unmarried.[65]

In a city filled with immorality like Corinth, some Christians seem to have felt that the safe thing was to abstain from the company of women altogether. It appears from 1 Tim. 4:3 that there were people in the early church who forbade marriage. They saw it as an impediment to the Christian life. They did not recognize the moral dangers involved in making the church an association of celibates. They apparently also permitted married people to separate in order to be free for the Lord, especially when the spouse was an unbeliever. Paul warns them against the danger of licentiousness in 1 Cor. 5 and 6, and in ch. 7 he takes a position against asceticism.

Paul's first answer on the matter of marriage, "It is well for a man not to touch a woman," may be male oriented, because the issue was formulated that way as presented to him. The discussion of sex and marriage in the rest of the Lesson generally respects the principle of equal rights, cf. vs. 2-4, 10-11, 12-14, and 16. Paul deals with the subject of the relationship between the sexes in 11:2-16.

The phrase used to affirm celibacy, "it is well," means that the unmarried estate is not wrong. It is laudable. The Greek word kalon ("well") means useful, pleasing, suitable, or appropriate for a situation.

The touching Paul talks about has been interpreted by some so narrowly as to forbid touching the hands or the skin of a woman. Those who forbad touching the hands or skin of a woman admonished men to keep themselves so far removed from women that they neither saw nor heard them, thinking that in this way they were promoting chastity. They kept boys away from girls and girls from boys. This kind of thinking led to the foundation of monasteries and nunneries. Luther says, "How this turned out and how they made room for the devil in so doing – this would be awful to hear and tell."[66]

Wherever the sexes are together, they are attracted to each other and temptations come. The problems that arise are not helped by separation. The crucial factor involves thoughts and desires, and separation does not eliminate that.

On the basis of v. 1 and Rev. 14:4, some people in the early church seem to have required celibacy as a condition for Baptism and membership. Tertullian represented the extreme form of this notion; he condemned marriage and sex. He said, "Marriage and fornication are different only because laws appear to make them so; they are not intrinsically different, but only in the degree of their illegitimacy."[67]

Although Paul goes on in 1 Cor. 7 to talk about marriage and the problems that can arise, his preference for the unmarried state is clearly stated in vs. 7 and 8. He wishes that everyone had the gift of celibacy, so that they might be relieved of the burden and cares of marriage and might be concerned only with God and His Word as he himself is. But he acknowledges the impossibility of commanding everyone to be celebate, because God has not granted this gift to everyone.

He allows for marriage "because of cases of sexual immorality." The phrase has been variously translated. The Greek simply says, "because of immoralities (or fornications)." The Greek word is porneia, the word for fornication. The term is used for all sorts of illicit sexual relations. If people want to make a distinction between pre-marital and extra-marital sex, porneia may be broader than moicheia and include pre-marital sex. Paul is talking to the unmarried. NEB has caught the meaning nicely: "because there is so much immorality." JB, which has a Roman Catholic orientation, reveals a doctrinal bias: "but since sex is always a danger." It is not certain that Paul would have agreed with that.

Fornication is to be avoided, according to 1 Cor. 6:9, 18; 10:8; Gal. 5:19; Acts 15:20, 29; 21:25; Eph. 5:3, 5; Col. 3:5.

The city of Corinth was famous throughout the ancient world for its immorality. The nickname for a loose-living person was "Corinthian." The situation in that port city may have been much like it is in the U.S.A. today.

The apostle is not discussing marriage as an ideal state or in a vacuum. He is answering questions put to him by Christians who were living in the city of Corinth. The application can be made quite directly from the then-and-there to the here-and-now. In a society so full of temptations, Paul advises marriage. He does not describe marriage as the lesser of two evils but as a necessary safeguard against sin. Marriage is not wrong, as some

Corinthians are thinking; but it is a necessity for many people. A positive reason for marriage is not given only a negative one, the avoidance of "sexual immorality."

Some have criticized Paul on the basis of this passage for having a low regard for marriage. But the man who likens marriage to the relationship between Christ and the church in Eph. 5:22-23 and 32-33 cannot validly be accused of having a low estimate of marriage.

Paul's statement, "each man should have his own wife, and each woman her own husband," rules out polygamy.

This passage of 1 Corinthians is used in the Augsburg Confession (Art. XXVII, 19) to justify breaking the vows of celibacy. The church at the time the Confession was written said that vows made contrary to papal canons were not binding. The Augsburg Confession says, "How much less should they be binding or have legal standing when they are contrary to God's command!" (23)[68]

The relationship between wife and husband is discussed in vs. 3-5. The NRSV calls sexual intercourse "conjugal rights" in v. 3. The Greek simply says "her due." What "her due" means, is spelled out in v. 4. The obligation has to do with sexual intercourse.

Nevertheless, sexual intercourse should happen voluntarily. Each should serve his/her partner. In this matter, too, Christians are to be governed by Christian love. Erotic love seeks only its own interest in the other. But Christian love does not seek its own, according to 1 Cor. 13:4-7 and Phil. 2:3-5. With Christians, spouses exist for each other.

Paul did not envision marriage as a sexless relationship. He specifically directs in v. 5 that withdrawal from sexual relations is to be only by mutual consent, for a limited time, and for a specific purpose.

Some people think that the only or the prime purpose of sexual intercourse is the procreation of children, but Paul seems to indicate that sex has a place by itself and in its own right.

He emphasizes unity in marriage. He refers to one's spouse as one's self in Eph. 5:28. Each feels completely, entirely, and totally a part of the other, and hence each gives himself/herself completely, entirely, and totally to the other. The aim is not self-gratification but the fulfillment of a duty that each owes the other.

The wife's body is the private property of her husband and vice versa in marriage. A husband and a wife give their bodies to their spouse. No husband or wife should even think of letting other people violate this sacred trust by laying hands on or allowing hands to be laid on that which does not belong to them. A proper attitude of jealous possession may help the spouse maintain this trust.

The phrases create a paradox. On the one hand, the woman's body is called "her own" and the man's "his own;" and yet he/she "does not have authority over" it. How can it be one's own if one cannot do as one likes with it?

Sexual life has its seat in the soma ("body"). Homosexuality is the degrading of the body, according to Rom. 1:24, 26-27. Soma belongs to the very essence of a person. A person does not have a soma but is soma.

Jerome cited as the saying of a heathen man, "He who is too violent in love commits adultery with his own wife." Luther ignores this saying and says it is not true. On the contrary, Luther says, "Certainly no one can commit adultery with his own wife unless he did not think of her as his wife or did not touch her as his wife."[69] Paul says that marriage is intended to be a help and means to avoid unchastity. Whoever uses marriage to avoid fornication has St. Paul as an advocate and patron. Luther disagrees with all those who try to make rules and laws concerning when there should and should not be sexual intercourse between married people. He says, "How many laws this little saying of St. Paul repeals: 'No one rules over his own body'! . . . God's permission is greater than mankind's prohibition . . . ."[70] He says, "The bride is the bridegroom's and not the ruler over her own body . . . one should let the matter rest there and not try to do everything better."[71]

It is evident that refusal amounts to fraud, a withholding of what is owed. The word translated "deprive" (apostereo) means to rob, steal, to take from people what belongs to them rightfully. The Greek form is a present imperative which may imply that some Corinthians had been doing this. Paul says to them, "Cease to defraud!"

Marriage is essentially a commitment, really several commitments. One is the commitment to sexual intercourse. A spouse who refuses, holds back, or is not responsive fails in a moral obligation which one assumes when marrying. Deceit is too often practiced here. Anger and dissension can play a role. Excessive spirituality is sometimes involved. But St. Paul says that there should be agreement, and no one should try to change what the apostle says. Some form of conscious or unconscious fraud is at the bottom of much marital tension.

What should be done when people overestimate their capacity to meet their spouse's sexual needs? At this point, some persons start what may be a completely unconscious process of deception. They develop an illness, or fatigue, or a nervous state which they think excuses them from their marital duty. Many marriage problems stem not so much from actual adultery as from this form of unfaithfulness.

Abstinence must be by mutual consent. Eccl. 3:5 also allows for abstinence. Joel 2:16 does, too, for a very severe situation.

The rabbis taught that abstinence from intercourse was allowable for generally one to two weeks, but disciples of the law could continue abstinence for 30 days against the will of their wives while they occupied themselves in the study of the law.

Married people may exercise abstinence from sexual intercourse at times in order to give themselves to prayer, Paul says. Why is abstinence necessary for this? Paul may be thinking of continuous prayer carried out with the persistence of a rabbi's study of the torah. Paul may make this statement influenced by this Jewish custom.

Self-restraint is not regarded by Paul as a superior state of life, as some Roman Catholics have interpreted. He allows for abstinence, because he knows that in the present life we too seldom think of God. Our everyday affairs claim us so completely that we forget that God is our Lord and that all our hopes and fears must center on Him alone. Luther is supposed to have said, "It is not possible to pray in the marriage bed."

When Paul says that husband and wife should "come together again," he refers to being sexually together. Luther says: "St. Paul has very little confidence in (human) chastity because he well knows the devil and his tricks and the weakness of the flesh too."

The reason for coming together again, Paul says, is "because of your lack of self-control." This thought agrees well with the idea that people should be married "because of cases of sexual immorality."

"Your lack of self-control" should be understood in the sense of irrepressible desire for sex. Other translations include "incontinence" and "unrestrained desire."

Paul obviously is not hostile to sex.

Paul says that his instruction is a "concession." It is not a "command." How much the word "this" covers is not clear. Probably the whole of what he says in vs. 1-5.

What he says is not a binding rule but is allowable. His statement has the feeling of "forbearance." There is no example that suggnoma ("concession") means personal opinion. "By way of concession" does not mean the same as "I give my opinion" (gnomen), cf. v. 25. Other similar expressions are in vs. 12 and 40 (gnomen).

The "concession" is made probably because of the situation in Corinth at the time to which he refers in the phrase "because of cases of sexual immorality." Paul seems to be coming back around to his initial thought on the subject of marriage: "It is well for a man not to touch a woman." He is telling people that they may marry, not that they must. Whatever v. 6 means, it must be understood in the sense of v. 7. What he says in the previous verses must be understood against the background of v. 7. Marriage is not required. It is a free choice. But once married, the individual is to honor the conjugal rights of the spouse.

When Paul wishes "that all were as I myself am," he expresses satisfaction with his life and no regrets. His desire is not only that all would be unmarried, but also that all would be able to control themselves.

There is not total agreement as to what Paul's situation was at this time. The possibilities are that he never married, that he was a widower, or that his wife left him and returned to her family because of his conversion to Christianity. Paul seems to say clearly in v. 8 that he is unmarried. Many think that 1 Cor. 9:5 indicates that he never married. Tertullian said that was the case.

But Jeremias suggests that Paul seems to classify himself with the widowed rather than the unmarried. This idea is supported by the fact that marriage was required of rabbis, and Paul was a rabbi at the time of his conversion. Celibacy was allowed but only with special permission and as an exception made by God.

Luther, too, believed that Paul was married in his youth.[72] Luther understood 1 Cor. 9:5 to say that Paul had a wife but didn't want to take her with him as the other apostles did; or Paul did not now have a wife, but he would have liked to have one. Some think "my loyal companion" in Phil. 4:3 refers to Paul's wife. Luther concluded that Paul had been married and was living as a widower.

Marriage is as much a gift from God as celibacy. There is not "the" Christian way of behaving. We do not do our duty by binding ourselves to a rule and thus evading responsibility for our behavior. Each person has a particular kind of behavior in his/her situation. That opposite courses may both be right for different individuals is said also in Rom. 14:1-2; 12:6-8; and 1 Pet. 4:10.

Those who forbid marriage forbid what has been given by God. Origen said this. Luther objected to calling certain states "religious orders" and marriage a "secular order." He said it should be the other way around. Marriage is the real religious order, and the other orders should be called secular. He rejected the idea that nuns call themselves "brides of Christ." He said, "They are rather the brides of the devil . . . ." They do not use chastity as it should be used. They use it to pretend to be better in the eyes of God than other people. But they should use it to make people freer and more able to give attention to the things of God and His Word. Marriage by its nature drives, impels, and forces people to faith which is the highest spiritual state.

We must daily look to God for food, shelter, and clothing for those who are dependent on us. The religious orders were most securely provided with all the necessities of the body. People would not join the orders unless their bodily needs were guaranteed for life. That which drives people to rely on God and His Word is certainly the higher spiritual state. This does not mean that all people use the order of marriage in faith. On the other hand, some may use the religious order through faith. Faith makes all things good. Lack of faith makes all things bad.

The "gift" to which Paul refers in v. 7 is not being unmarried but continence without which it is disastrous to remain unmarried. God gave him this gift. He wished that all people had it, but he recognized that all people do not.

II

In vs. 8-16, Paul groups people according to their sexual situation. The first group is "the unmarried and the widows."

The Greek form for "unmarried" (<u>tois agamois</u>) is in the masculine gender. It covers both single men and widowers. Unmarried females are dealt with in vs. 25-38, because the question under discussion here is whether they should be married. In that society, they would not have had much to say in the decision about their marital status.

The word translated "widows" (<u>tais cherais</u>) is in the feminine gender, but there is conjecture that the feminine form should be dealt with as a masculine. The masculine form is not found anywhere in the New Testament, and the masculine intention is more suitable when considering the phrase "as I am" and the masculine gender of the word "them" (<u>autois</u>).

Apparently, some in the Corinthian church were not practicing self-control. In Greek, <u>ei</u> ("if") with the indicative introduces a condition that is assumed to be true. The wording may imply reproach.

What is meant by this failure to have power over themselves is explained by the phrase "to be aflame with passion." A prolonged and painful struggle seems to be intended, a condition fatal to spiritual peace and growth.

Those who "are not practicing self-control . . . should marry." The Augsburg Confession says (AC, XXIII, 3-4): "Scripture clearly proclaims that the married state was instituted by God to avoid sexual immorality, as Paul says that to avoid immorality, 'Each man should have his own wife' [1 Cor. 7:2], and again, 'For it is better to marry than to be aflame with passion' [1 Cor. 7:9b]. When Christ says, in Matthew 19[:11], 'Not everyone can accept this teaching,' he shows that he knew human nature quite well, namely, that few people have the gift to live a celibate life. For 'God created humankind . . . male and female' (Gen. 1[:27])."[73]

Paul is attacking a refined doctrine of righteousness by works that regards abstinence from sexual intercourse as meritorious before God. His point is that marriage is not a way of life that earns less merit with God than celibacy. Paul resists the imposition of celibacy on anyone. God Himself will make plain to people whether they are fit for celibacy. If God gives people that gift, they should use it and remain unmarried.

Luther says: "St. Paul gives but this one reason (for marriage), and I know of none fundamentally stronger and better, namely, need. Need commands it. . . . If this need were not there, all the other reasons (for marriage) taken together would make very poor marriages."[74] The instruction Paul gives in v. 9 agrees with that given in vs. 2 and 5 and in 1 Tim. 5:11-15.

Paul says, "It is better to marry than to be aflame with passion." The verb puromai means "to burn." Paul uses it in a transferred sense "to be enflamed with passion." Here it means "to be consumed with the fire of sexual desire."

Explaining that phrase, Luther says: "There can . . . be no doubt that those who have the grace of chastity still at times feel evil desires and are tempted. But it is transitory, therefore their problem is not this burning. In short, 'aflame with passion' is the heat of the flesh, which rages without ceasing, and daily attraction to woman or to man; we find this wherever there is not desire and love for chastity. . . . Some among them suffer so severely that they masturbate. All these ought to be in the married estate."[75]

Luther says: "I have no doubt that everyone who wants to

live chastely, though unmarried and without special grace for it, will understand these words and what they convey. For St. Paul is not speaking of secret matters, but of the common, known feeling of all those who live chastely outside of marriage but do not have the grace to accomplish it. For he ascribes this flaming with passion to all who live chastely but without the necessary grace, and prescribes no other medicine than marriage. If it were not so common or if there were some other advice to be given, he would not have recommended marriage."[76]

"Why" is it better to marry? asks Luther: "Because this burning, even if no act were to result from it, is still lost chastity, because it is held to not from desire and love, but with great dislike, unwillingness, and pressure. Before God this will be counted as unchastity, because the heart is unchaste and the body simply was not permitted to be unchaste. What use is it that you hold with such enormous, sour, unwilling effort to a lost and unchaste chastity? It were better to marry and rise above such unhappiness. For although in marriage there is also much trouble and unhappiness, still one can enter into it with good will and at times have peace and happiness. But outside marriage, where there is no grace, it is impossible to have good will toward chastity and live happily in it."[77]

III

"To the married," Paul directs a strong prohibition against divorce. But, the parenthetical phrase in v. 11 speaks to the situation of divorce.

The instruction is a command of the Lord. In classical Greek, paraggello ("I command") is used for the military word of command.

How did Paul get the "command" from the Lord? Scholars are universally agreed that the gospels were not yet committed to writing at the time Paul wrote. He obviously is referring to a collection of sayings of Jesus, either oral or written. Other statements in the New Testament support the idea that such collections existed, cf. 1 Cor. 9:14; 11:23-25; 1 Thess. 4:15-17; and Acts 20:35. Individual sayings of Jesus transmitted outside the canonical gospels are called agrapha. Some 200 to 300 of them can be found in the form of quotations in the works of early Christian authors, in textual enlargements in gospel manuscripts, or in the apocryphal gospels. They do not significantly increase the sayings of Jesus recorded in the Bible.[78]

There is no need to assume that Paul had received a direct revelation from the Lord on the matter of divorce. Christ's statement was well known. The saying of the Lord that supports Paul's "command" may be Mark 10:9, 11-12.

In the statement, "the wife should not separate from her husband," Paul allows for no exceptions. But in the very next statement, the next verse, the conditional clause does allow for it. V. 15 gives another allowance. Christians are not bound to the rule if they have an unbelieving spouse who does not consent to live with them.

Paul's reference to the unusual situation of a wife divorcing her husband suggests that such a thing had actually occurred or was mentioned in the Corinthians' letter as likely to occur. Under Jewish law, a woman could not sue for divorce; but under Roman law she could.

In a culture where the relationships between husband and wife were neither strong nor reliable and divorce might be obtained at the whim of people, prohibiting divorce provided some stability and protection for women.

The words, "if she does separate," Luther says, concede "that man and wife may separate, provided that they do not marry again. In so doing (Paul) repeals the law of Moses according to which the man could send away his wife if he were displeased with her or tired of her and take another. And she, too, could take another, according to Deut. 24:1ff. Now although Moses gave such a law . . . to people who were hardheaded and heathenish, still such actions are not fitting for a Christian, and therefore Christ himself revoked it in Matt. 19:8-9.

"Where there are no Christians, or only crude, false Christians, there even today it would be good to hold to this law and allow them, like heathen, to divorce their wives and marry others, so that they would not set up two hells in their disunited lives, one here and one there; but they should know that by separating they are no longer Christians but heathen and in a damnable condition.

"The apostle refers to one cause of divorce: anger – when a man and his wife cannot live together in harmony but only in hatred and dispute, so that they can neither pray nor do any other good work. The text clearly states this by admonishing them either to be reconciled and not separate or to live without marriage if they cannot be reconciled and wish to separate. Where reconciliation is recommended, there anger and disharmony are indicated. The apostle certainly permits such separations by being lenient over against the weaknesses of Christians when two people simply cannot get along together. In all other cases everyone is obligated to carry the burden of the other and not to separate from him. That is also the reason why he does not permit divorced persons to change their status, that they may have the opportunity to come together again; yes, he may even thereby urge and force them together, for they may not have the grace of chastity.

"But what if one party did not want to be reconciled with the other but remained quite separate and the other could not control himself and needed a mate? What should that party do? May he change his status? Answer: Yes, without doubt. For since he is not (sic?) commanded to live in chastity and he does not have the grace to do so, and his spouse will not return to him, taking away the body he cannot do without, therefore God will not demand the impossible because of the disobedience of the other, and he should then act as though his spouse were dead. This is particularly true because it is not his fault that they cannot be reconciled. But the one who does not want reconciliation must remain unmarried, as St. Paul points out here."[79]

Paul does not approve of remarriage, unless it is to the former spouse. Some consider v. 9 to state an exception to this prohibition. Jesus allows for remarriage in Matt. 19:9 and 5:32, but He does not approve of it. Some think that Jesus' exception may have been unknown to the apostle. Matthew is the only evangelist to have it. A woman is free to remarry after the death of her husband, according to 1 Cor. 7:39-40.

IV

The instruction Paul gives "to the rest" deals with the problems of mixed marriages, the marriage of a believer and an unbeliever. Paul deals with two questions: May Christians and pagans live together in marriage at all? and What should a Christian do when the pagan partner gets a divorce? May the Christian marry again?

The qualification Paul puts on what he says in this section is the opposite of what he says in v. 10. He is making a distinction between precepts that Jesus gave during His earthly life and were being circulated among the first Christians and precepts that had not been proclaimed by Jesus Himself but were now being enunciated by an apostle. The marriage of a Christian and a non-Christian is a situation that did not confront Jesus for obvious reasons. It is a situation on which He for that reason had never commented.

As far as the authority with which Paul speaks is concerned, William Arndt in <u>Does the Bible Contradict Itself?</u> says, "not with one syllable does the Apostle hint that his words as given in verses 12-15 are less binding upon the Christians than those found in verses 10 and 11."[80]

On the other hand, Luther says: "Because St. Paul here bears witness that these words are not from the Lord but from himself, he indicates that these things are not commanded by God but are left to the individual to choose in one way or another. For he distinguishes his own words from the Word of the Lord, that the Lord's Word is to be a commandment, but his own words advice."[81]

Luther's comment is strange. St. Paul is speaking with apostolic authority and not as a private individual. Paul is not saying that what he says does not count for much or that it may be dismissed, cf. v. 40. He is distinguishing between his own inspired utterances and the express commands of Jesus. The contrast is not with his own private views and his inspired utterances.

Marriages between a believer and an unbeliever posed a problem at that time. It often happened that a person converted whose spouse remained a heathen. Ordinarily, the subordinate members of a household shared the religion of the paterfamilias but not always. If the wife did not share the religion of her husband, the question arose whether the converted party should continue to live in marital union with such a person?

Luther takes the words "she consents to live with him" to mean that "the non-Christian is content and willing to stay with the Christian spouse and allows him to do all things proper to a Christian. For marriage is an outward physical thing that neither promotes nor hinders faith, and the one partner may well be a Christian and the other non-Christian, just as a Christian may eat with a heathen, Jew, or Turk, or drink, buy from him, and have all ordinary commerce with him. In the same way one marriage partner may now be a true devout Christian and the other an evil, false Christian; still it is not necessary to dissolve the marriage because of piety or malice.

"But if the non-Christian should not let his spouse be a Christian and live a Christian life and should hinder and persecute him, then it would be time to keep these words of Christ also physically: 'He who loves wife or child (footnote: Luther provides an extension of the meaning of the passage by substituting 'wife or child' for 'father or mother'.) more than Me is not worthy of Me' (Matt. 10:37). Then divorce is in order; but once the divorce is effected, then there must be reconciliation, or that partner must remain unmarried who will not be reconciled, while the other is permitted to change his status . . . . For one must honor Christ, the spouse of the soul, more than the spouse of one's body; and where the one will not tolerate the other, one must stay with the spouse of the soul, who is eternal, and let the physical one go and take another who will tolerate the eternal spouse alongside himself."[82]

The phrase "to live with" means in marriage.

The "woman" in v. 13 is a Christian woman.

The principle enunciated in v. 14 is valid in every situation, but it is not easy to establish what the principle is. Luther explains by saying, "all things are holy to him who is holy." In support of this statement, he quotes Titus 1:15 and Rom. 8:28. Then he goes on to say, "A Christian spouse may not be divorced but can live with a non-Christian mate and even conceive and raise non-Christian children. The reason is this: if the non-Christian spouse does not prevent the Christian mate from leading a Christian life, then faith is such a mighty thing that no hurt will come from living with a non-Christian; it will make no difference whether he associates with religious or irreligious people, for even death, that most terrible thing of all, is still a holy thing for a Christian."

"If this were not so, no Christian could live, for he is forced to live among evil and non-Christian people. But if he does not follow them but puts them to good use, he may live with or among them to the end that they may gain piety and become Christians.

"To a Christian, therefore, the entire world is holiness, purity, utility, and piety. . . . believers can use all things in a holy and blessed way to sanctify and purify themselves. But the unholy and the unbelievers sin, profane, and pollute themselves incessantly in all things. For they cannot use anything in a right, godly, and blessed way, so that it might serve their own salvation.

"In the same way children are also holy, even though they are neither baptized nor Christians. They are not holy in themselves (St. Paul is not discussing <u>this</u> holiness here) but are holy to you, so that your own holiness may associate with them and raise them without profaning you, just as though they were holy things. St. Paul also wants to convey this: If a Christian spouse should have grown children with a non-Christian mate (as often happened in those days) and the children should not want to be baptized or become Christians, then, inasmuch as no one should be forced to believe but only willingly be drawn by God through His Gospel, the father and mother should not abandon the children or withdraw or fail in their motherly or fatherly duties, as though they could thereby sin and pollute themselves in unbelieving children; rather they should guide and care bodily for these children as though they were the holiest of Christians. For they are not impure or unholy, Paul says; that is, your faith can demonstrate itself in them and thus remain pure and holy."[83]

Again Luther says with regard to the children: "Where children do not want to accept the Gospel, one should not therefore leave them and send them away but care for them and support them like the best of all Christians, commending their faith to God, so long as they are obedient and upright in all other things having to do with outward living. For parents can and should resist and punish outward evil acts and works. But nobody can resist and punish unbelief and an inwardly evil nature except God alone."[84]

Is Paul saying that the pagan husband is, whether he wills and knows it or not, a partner in a Christian marriage; and in that respect, he is consecrated by the divine grace which is over that marriage? Is Paul saying that holiness is transferable without faith and even Baptism being necessary? Oscar Cullmann says that non-Christian members of the family are taken into the body of Christ.[85] Johannes Schneider objects by saying that then the body of Christ has unbelieving members. That doesn't make sense. Does Paul mean that because of the parent's faith, the children, too, have become holy? He assumes as axiomatic that the child of a parent who is holy must be holy.

Haggai 2:11-14 seems to say the opposite of what Paul is affirming. The Lord, through the prophet, says that uncleanness is communicated and consecration is not. Today people would probably use the analogy of apples in a barrel. Good apples do not make bad apples good, but bad apples make good apples bad.

Cullmann understands Paul's statement about children being holy to imply that the children of Christian parents do not need to be baptized, because they belong automatically to the body of Christ by reason of their birth. He says that in this respect the situation is parallel to the practice of proselyte baptism in Judaism. The children of proselytes were baptized along with their parents, but the children born to such parents after their reception into Judaism did not need to be baptized. If Cullmann is right, Christian baptism would be limited to the baptism of converts, as Jewish baptism was limited to proselytes. The post-apostolic church did not share this idea. The children of believing parents were, as a matter of historical fact, always baptized.

There is no thought of a state of innocence with regard to the children.

Actually, the Lesson contains plenty of preaching material, and the preacher may be able to avoid preaching on vs. 14-16. What Paul is saying is not entirely clear.

When Paul talks about the unbelieving partner separating, he is talking about divorce. <u>Chorizetai</u> is used in the papyri as a technical term for divorce.

When Paul says that "the brother or sister is not bound," does he mean that the believer may remarry? Luther argues that he does.[86] Luther speaks of a situation in Eisenach where a wife was unwilling to live with her husband and repeatedly left him without cause. He says that he permitted the husband to remarry but not the wife.[87]

Luther rejects the teaching of the Roman church that the Christian mate must wait before remarrying until his non-Christian spouse comes back or dies. He says: "Now, what if the runaway mate should return and wanted to make amends, should one permit him to do this and accept him? Answer: When the one who has remained behind has not changed his status, he may accept the returning mate, and it is advisable that they again sit down together. But where the one has already changed his status, he should let the other one go and not receive the returning spouse. Here we may profit from what is written of the rejected wife in Deut. 24:3-4, that the first man cannot take her back again, even though she is separated from the second by death or a bill of divorce. One should do the same today, so that the runaway is punished. And if one were to do so, there would doubtless be less running away."[88]

Luther: "We should live peaceably with one another. . . . a Christian spouse should not quarrel with his non-Christian mate concerning belief or unbelief nor separate from his mate if that non-Christian mate permits him to lead a Christian life. Each one should leave the other to his faith and commend the whole matter to God. For no one can be driven or forced to believe; instead, God must draw him in grace, and we should teach, admonish, and supplicate, not force. And so a Christian spouse should conduct the outward forms of the married state peaceably with his non-Christian mate and not threaten or defy his partner either with running away or turning him away."[89]

It would have been very difficult in those days to live with a non-Christian who wanted a divorce, because the animosity of the heathen toward Christians was great. The difficulties with the children would have been very great. "In such a case the brother or sister is not bound." The believer should let the divorce happen.

With regard to v. 16, Luther says: "it is not your work or within your power that anyone should believe, but that is solely in God's power. But since you do not know whether you are worthy that God should save your spouses through you, you should live in peace with them; and no husband should put pressure on his non-Christian wife or quarrel with her concerning faith, nor should any wife do so with a non-Christian husband. If God wants to convert them through you, He will help you to achieve this and distribute among you the grace and gifts for that purpose. This seems to me to be the proper understanding of St. Paul in this passage, that he wants nobody to be forced into faith or piety but that we should live in peace with all men until God with His grace converts through us those whom He wants converted, as St. Peter also teaches in 1 Peter 3:1f.

"One should also treat a spouse who is falsely Christian in the same way; that is, one should tolerate in peace his evil life and not defy him or force him toward the good, but instead, one should in peace and friendliness help him toward it. For you are perhaps not worthy to bring anyone to piety. If you should be worthy, however, God will assign and lend you the grace for it according to His will. Meanwhile you may be certain that you should live with your non-Christian or evil mate, so long as you do not follow or approve of his unbelief or evil life, and he on his part does not force or hold you to it; and you should tolerate such unbelief and injustice from your partner just as one has to tolerate them from the rest of the world and from devils, and you should use kind words to him and live in peace until God grants His grace, so that he, too, may be converted."[90]

Matthew 5:13-20

The metaphor "You are the salt of the earth" conveys the idea that Jesus' disciples are indispensable for the existence of the earth. The metaphor "You are the light of the world" establishes their mission.

Teaching was not Jesus' chief achievement. He came, He said in the Sermon on the Mount, to fulfill the law and the prophets and, at another time, "to give his life a ransom for many," cf. Matt. 20:28. Perhaps, a sharp distinction ought not be made between the two statements. He came to take away the sins of the world, cf. John 1:29, by dying on a cross.

I

Before opening up the penetrating metaphor "the salt of the earth," the preacher will help the hearers get it by explaining a little about the importance and value of salt in the ancient world. Today, we take it pretty much for granted. More than that, it is our number one food fear. There is good reason for such concern. Too much salt can raise your blood pressure and with it the risk of heart attack and stroke – events that kill about 800,000 Americans a year.[91] Cutting down on salt is the primary medical advice given by doctors for the control of high blood pressure. Americans tend to use more salt than is good. Some have proposed banning it in any form in the preparation of any food in a restaurant. Government officials are looking for ways to reduce the quantity of salt in processed and restaurant foods. Salt is the target of government officials eager to encourage healthier eating habits.

But people who lived closer to the age of Jesus spoke of salt in glowing terms. Homer called salt "divine." Plato hailed it as "a substance dear to the gods." Salt has many valuable qualities; it purifies, seasons, and preserves.

It was used in the Jerusalem temple offerings as an element in Israel's worship, as a part of the sacrifices. It was sprinkled on or mixed into the sacrifices, according to Lev. 2:13 and Ezek. 43:24. It was an element of the holy incense, cf. Ex. 30:35.

Newborn infants were rubbed with salt, according to Ezek. 16:4, both to cleanse them and perhaps also to ward off demons. Covenants were made through salt, according to 2 Chron. 13:5. Bedouin traditionally will not attack a man whose salt they have eaten.

In a Roman religious ritual, grains of salt were placed on an eight-day-old baby's lips. This is some of the background for a part of the Roman Catholic Baptismal ceremony in which a morsel of salt is placed into the mouth of the child to symbolize purification.

Salt was rare and expensive in the ancient world. Salt routes crisscrossed the globe. One of the most traveled led from Morocco south across the Sahara to Timbuktu. Herodotus describes a caravan route that united the salt oases of the Libyan desert. In the 6th century, in the sub-Sahara, Moorish merchants traded salt ounce for ounce for gold. Ships bearing salt from Egypt to Greece traversed the Mediterranean and the Aegean. Venice's wealth was attributable not so much to exotic spices as to the salt that the Venetians exchanged in Constantinople for the spices of Asia. In 1295, when Marco Polo returned from the far east, he delighted the Doge with tales of the prodigious value of salt coins bearing the seal of the great Khan. Twentieth-century Ethiopia still used salt disks as money. Stacks of them were salted away in the treasury. More wars have been fought over salt than over gold.

Rome built a highway, the Via Salarium, to transport salt from Ostia which was located on the shore of the Etruscan Sea. Roman armies were paid partly in salt. This salt money was called "salarium" from which we get the English word "salary." That may suggest the origin of the expression about a person being worth his salt. Or it may go back to the purchase of slaves with salt by the Greeks and Romans.

One of the major factors leading to the French Revolution was the government's monopoly of salt. The French people had to buy all their salt from royal depots for centuries. To smuggle salt was to risk the death penalty; yet, an average of 500 salt smugglers were executed each year.

In protest against the high British tax on salt in India,

Mahatma Gandhi in 1930 led a mass pilgrimage of his followers to the sea to make salt.

Salt is used to flavor and preserve food, and it is considered a good antiseptic. This is why the Latin word for salt, sal, is related to Salus, the goddess of health.

Indians used salt to keep away evil spirits, and Orientals still use it for that purpose. During the Middle Ages, spilled salt meant bad luck. To reverse the evil consequence, the spiller would throw a pinch of salt over his left shoulder, because the left side was thought to be a place where evil spirits tended to congregate. In Leonardo Da Vinci's painting of the "Last Supper," Judas is shown with an overturned saltcellar in front of him.

Salt had social symbolism in medieval etiquette. The rank of guests at a banquet was gauged as late as the 18th century by where they sat in relation to a saltcellar on the table. The host and distinguished guests sat at the head of the table - above the salt. People who sat below the salt were of lesser esteem.

Salt is a humble compound whose basic makeup defies logic. It is a blend of sodium and chlorine, the first, a metal so unstable that it bursts into flame when exposed to water; the second, a lethal gas. When we swallow the blend, it forms hydrochloric acid in our stomach. And it does not kill us.

Our life depends on it: our blood, sweat, tears, and the very beating of our heart. Sodium chloride is essential to all living things. Each person contains about eight ounces of salt. It is involved in muscle contraction, including heartbeats, nerve impulses, and the digestion of body-building protein. The tissues of the human body are constantly moistened by a briny solution. The balance of salt to water must be carefully maintained. Virtually all vital functions depend on it. Salt regulates the exchange of water between our cells and their surrounding fluid that carries food in and wastes out. All body fluids of mammals are salty solutions. Red blood corpuscles burst when placed in fresh water; they remain stable in a salt solution.

Built-in controls regulate the body's salt content. Keeping the proper balance of salt to water is the work mainly of the kidneys. Take in too much, and the kidneys will excrete it.

Ingest too little, and they will give up water but virtually no salt. Through perspiration the body constantly loses both water and salt. Without replenishment, the body dies. The healthy body needs and can use about 200 mg of sodium per day.

When our ancestors were hunters, they got the salt they needed from raw meat. Roasted meat keeps its salt, boiling leaches it out. When people began to farm, cereals did not give them enough sodium chloride; and the great salt hunt began.

When Jesus says, "You are the salt of the earth," He is referring to something that is very expensive and very precious. Salted with the blood of Jesus' disciples, the earth again becomes the good earth God created. God's kingdom comes.

Jesus' words are a declaration of the power of His disciples and of their obligations and responsibilities. Salt gives taste to whatever it touches. It is a positive influence even as the Christian character is a positive force in the world. Some characteristics of "the salt of the earth" are listed in the Beatitudes. People of this character sustain the earth.

Salt prevents putrification, corruption, and decay. It keeps foods fresh and palatable. Sodom and Gomorrah could have been saved by ten salters. The disciples of Jesus oppose the corrupting power of sin in the world.

The disciples' thoughts are not fixed on heaven. They are "the salt of the earth."

Salt stimulates thirst. The disciples of Jesus give people a thirst for the things of God.

Salt bites. The world knows that its outwardly gross sins like stealing and murder are evil. It needs to learn that its most precious and highest assets, its wisdom and goodness are not of God.

Paul wrote to the Colossians, "Let your speech always be gracious, seasoned with salt, so that you may know how you ought to answer everyone," cf. 4:6.

Salt cannot salt itself. It cannot salt the food on the table while it remains in the saltshaker. It must be scattered.

Jesus does not say that His disciples have salt but that they are salt. His disciples need not be concerned with how to become salt. They are salt. Nature and function are one with salt. Salt salts because it is salt. Salt that does not salt is not salt. The person who does not salt the earth is not a disciple.

How does salt lose its saltiness? In Jesus' day, salt was obtained from evaporated pools by the shore of the Dead Sea or from the small lakes on the edge of the Syrian desert which dry up in the summer. The salt crust is never pure. It contains magnesia, lime, and vegetable remains which, when the salt is dissolved by moisture, remain as useless refuse. Jesus sternly warns that when salt loses its saltiness, "It is no longer good for anything, but is thrown out and trampled under foot." The passive verbs are probably intended to be numinous passives; that is, the active agent is God.

II

The Old Testament background of Jesus' saying "You are the light of the world" is strong. The metaphor emphasizes the mission of Jesus' disciples.

Light was the first expression of God when He created the earth in Gen. 1:3. Is. 9:2 speaks of "the great light" that will come into the world. The prophet speaks of the Servant of the Lord who will be "a light to the nations" in Is. 42:6 and 49:6. See also Prov. 4:18 and Is. 60:1-3.

John 1:4-9 says that Jesus is "the true Light" who has come into the world. Jesus says of Himself, "I am the light of the world," cf. John 8:12. The life that came into being in Him "was the light of all people," according to John 1:4.

Jesus did not say, "You are to be the light of the world." He did not say, "You have the light of the world," as though "light" is put into the disciples' hands like the gospel or preaching. He who called Himself "the light of the world" said of His disciples, "You are the light of the world." Having removed His physical presence from the world, He is now represented here by His disciples. He still shines in the world through them. Another way to say this might be that Jesus' disciples shine in the world through reflecting His light.

The world estimates Jesus Christ not by the Beatitudes, not by the Sermon on the Mount, but by the lives of His disciples whom they see and know. The Beatitudes and the Sermon on the Mount are guidelines for the disciples. Their mission is to do them, not merely proclaim them. As they do them, they shine.

Disciples are visible in the world as though they were a city on a high mountain. "A city built on a hill cannot be hid." They shine freely and publicly without regard to honor or shame, riches or poverty, disfavor or popularity, death or life. They know that they serve Jesus who made them "the light of the world."

Placing a lighted lamp – a lit candle not an electric bulb - under a bushel basket is not a rational act. The light soon goes out. It is like salt that has lost its saltiness. When the lamp is put on a lampstand, it gives light to all in the house. Jesus uses the term "house" for Jerusalem, the center of Israel, in Matt. 23:38.

"The bushel basket" was a utensil in every house in Palestine used for the purpose of measuring grain. It was a wooden container in which the day's bread was measured. It held about a peck.

The disciples of Jesus are to let their light shine in the world in order to glorify God. People are not to see the disciples but their good works which can include meekness and peaceableness. Disciples bear the cross of Jesus.

Jesus does not say that people will see God. They will see the good works of the disciples and glorify God for them. The cross and the works of the cross are the things that will be visible. Their works reveal the kingdom of God. Their works can include feeding the hungry, giving drink to the thirsty, receiving strangers, clothing the naked, and visiting the sick, cf. Matt. 25:35-45. What disciples do demonstrates whose they are.

The purpose of the good works of the disciples is that God is praised, cf. 1 Cor. 10:31 and 1 Pet. 2:12. Disciples exercise great care that in their good works they do not seek their own honor and good name. Few people are able to remain indifferent and unchanged when they are being honored and praised. When people want to glorify the disciples and not Jesus in them, the disciples do not permit it. They flee as from a grievous sin.

How radically Jesus removed doing good from the idea of reward is evident in Luke 14:12-14.

Jesus often referred to "your Father," cf. 5:16, 45, 48; 6:1, 4, 6, 14, 15, 18, 26; etc. He often referred to "my Father," cf. 7:21; 10:32, 33; 11:27; etc. But He never included Himself when He referred to "our Father." He did not join in the words of the Lord's Prayer, cf. Matt. 6:9. He said, "You pray."

III

Having established the character and mission of His disciples, Jesus, in the third part of this Lesson, talks about His own mission. Understanding these verses depends on the meaning of the key words, "the law" and "the prophets." Jesus says that He has come to fulfill the law and the prophets. Many people pick up on Jesus' assertion that He came to fulfill the law, but they miss that He came to fulfill also the prophets.

V. 17 implies that the mistaken impression was circulating among the Jews that Jesus was trying to abolish the law and the prophets. Because the gospels depict the Pharisees as Jesus' chief enemies, the idea is easily accepted that they were the ones accusing Jesus of trying to do this, because He disregarded the oral tradition which they held to be equal in authority to the written law. He violated the sabbath. He did not keep the weekly fasts or observe the elaborate distinctions between clean and unclean. He associated with tax collectors and sinners. Above all, He spoke as if He Himself were an authority in interpreting the law and as if He were above the law.

The term "the law and the prophets" is a reference to the Hebrew scriptures which today are called "the Old Testament." The third part of the Hebrew scriptures is the wisdom literature which is not mentioned. The term, "the law and the prophets," is used in Matt. 7:12; 11:13; 22:40; Luke 16:16 and 24:44 (where "the psalms" also are mentioned).

Judaism used nomos (the Greek word for law) and torah (the Hebrew word) very broadly. Torah was the word for both the Pentateuch (the first five books of the Old Testament) or the scriptures and also as that which governs what we should do and not do. Torah was the foundation of the world, the rabbis said. It had been involved in creation. Even God Himself studied torah. In Matt. 22:36, nomos is used referring not to the Pentateuch but to the commandments in the context of the law. It is hard to make a clear cut distinction in the usage of the terms.[92]

"The prophets" refers to the Old Testament books of Joshua to 2 Kings and Isaiah to Malachi.

The law says that the relationship of humans to God is achieved through certain behavior. That behavior demonstrates the proper attitude toward God. The history of Israel describes the various stages of the nation's relationship with God. Sometimes it was good, sometimes very bad. God sent the prophets to bring the people to Himself. The preaching of the prophets was fundamentally the offer of a good relationship with God. Jesus fulfilled the law and the prophets in His life, death, and resurrection. He satisfied every claim upon the human race as our representative. We are not dependent for our relationship with God on anything we do. God gives it to us in Jesus.

"The law and the prophets" chiefly tell the stories of the exodus and of the return from exile in Babylon. In the fullest sense of the term, they are the same event. In them, God sought to establish a people for Himself on the earth. Israel's rebelliousness prevented that. God's good pleasure was accomplished through Jesus and His passion. He fulfilled "the law and the prophets."

Although Jesus made it very clear in His preaching that He was bringing and inaugurating something radically new, He also asserted that He was not destroying the old religion. Rather He was fulfilling it.

Jesus committed Himself to the law as no rabbi, moralist, or legalist had ever done or would ever do. No one ever took the law with such absolute seriousness as did Jesus. A more literal translation of a phrase in v. 18 is: "not one iota (cf. NRSV footnote), not one stroke of a letter, will pass from the law." What is probably meant by the NRSV translation "letter" is the

Hebrew equivalent, the yodh, for the Greek iota. In both cases, the letter is the smallest in the alphabet.

The Greek word (keraia) translated in the NRSV "stroke of a letter" usually means "horn." It refers to a tiny mark that distinguishes one Hebrew letter from another. An example might be the dot that distinguishes the letter shin from the letter sin. Other suggestions are that it describes the difference between yodh and waw, daleth and rho, he and cheth, beth and kaph.

It has been suggested that Jesus has the written page in His mind's eye when He refers to the iota and dot of "these commandments." Others have seen "these" as a reference to the commandments of Jesus which follow. No antecedent for "these" is available.

To "be called least in the kingdom of heaven" means simply that the person will not be in the kingdom at all. "Heaven" is a circumlocution for "God," a common phenomenon in Matthew.

The righteousness that exceeds that of the scribes and Pharisees is not piety and ritual but being salt and light in the world. V. 20 is the most important verse in Matt. 5:17-20. The greater righteousness is the theme of the Sermon on the Mount.

How the greater righteousness is lived is spelled out with regard to the Fifth Commandment in vs. 21-26, the Sixth Commandment in vs. 27-30, divorce in vs. 31-32, oaths in vs. 33-37, retaliation in vs. 38-42, and love of others in vs. 43-47. It is summed up as a law of perfection in v. 48. The quality of obedience from disciples must surpass that given by the scribes and Pharisees.

Some interpreters suggest that the demands Jesus set forth in the Sermon on the Mount are so radical that He did not intend them to be taken literally as commandments for life. They think that the extreme expression of the law is to expose our sin and so make us despair of our merit. The greater righteousness is God's gift received through the transforming encounter with the righteous Jesus Christ. A confession of utter helplessness sets the stage for receiving that righteousness.

Our righteousness must be greater than that of the scribes and Pharisees in that it must involve the complete surrender of our will to God's. It must involve more than outward performance. The law leads us into sin. Our will remains opposed to the law and would prefer to do something else if it were allowed to, even though we may outwardly do what the law commands. We desire things that are forbidden. We desire what is denied. What is given is not appreciated, and what is not permitted entices. We often obey the law from fear of punishment not from love of righteousness. We would prefer to sin if that were possible without punishment. Ps. 1:2 describes the greater righteousness, "Their delight is in the law of the Lord." We are credited with that righteousness in Jesus through His passion.

In referring to "the scribes and Pharisees," Jesus is speaking about the best people in that society, the paragons of virtue, the models for Godliness. In the whole nation, no class was so highly praised and no title so highly honored as that of the Pharisees and scribes. If you wanted to call a man holy, you called him a Pharisee.

Undoubtedly, the disciples of Jesus themselves supposed that no greater holiness was to be found than the holiness of these men. Nothing was farther from their minds than that Jesus would attack them and their piety. Instead, they supposed that He would support them in what they were doing. The Pharisees thought so, too. That Jesus condemned them rather than joining forces with them caused the Pharisees and scribes to reject Him as the Messiah. This is the reason for the sharp conflict between them.

Especially after the strong affirmation Jesus makes of the law and the prophets, one would expect Him to praise the scribes and Pharisees. They were the group in Israel that promoted the law and the prophets. They observed the law more than others. They were considered the most accurate interpreters of the law. Jesus concedes that the Pharisees and scribes have a righteousness and that they lead upstanding lives, but He so utterly rejects that life as counting with God that it accomplishes nothing.

Jesus criticism of the Pharisees is similar to that of the Qumran people. The Essenes said that the Pharisees made the law practicable for themselves. By their casuistry, they broke the ultimate and radical demands of the law. Jesus criticizes the Pharisees not because they are not good but because they are not good enough.

"The scribes and Pharisees" are frequently spoken of together in the New Testament, and the impression is created that they are closely allied if not identical groups. The impression is not false, although it needs to be clarified. The scribes were authoritative custodians and interpreters of the law before the appearance of a distinct group called "the Pharisees." Not all Pharisees were scribes. The scribes did not constitute a sect of Judaism. Most of them apparently belonged to the Pharisees. That accounts for the fact that they are usually bracketed with them. Some may have belonged to the Sadducees. Others may have belonged to neither.

The name "scribe" indicates a professional writer. The scribes copied the scriptures, but they did many other things, too. They were the teachers and the intellectual guides of the nation. Some scribes were law experts to whom people came for advice in legal matters. Some were scholars who gave counsel and enlightenment on a variety of questions. Some were teachers of the law who gathered pupils about themselves.

The scribes constituted an authority side by side with the temple and its priestly aristocracy. At first, they were priestly scholars who specialized in the law, but gradually the torah came to stand in opposition to the temple and to be taught and applied by people who owed no allegiance to the temple hierarchy and were prepared to resist its rule and enactments. The development of this situation was probably post-exilic. Lay lawyers may have functioned in Israel during the exile and at the time of the restoration. The Pharisaic movement took its rise among the ranks of these lay lawyers. The task of the scribes was taken up by the Pharisees.

The word "Pharisee" seems to come from a Hebrew word which means "separated." The Pharisees urged separation from the heathen and those Jews who lived like heathen - that is, those who did not bind themselves to the law the way they did. Contact with such people polluted a person, the Pharisees thought.

The history of the Pharisees is obscure. The seeds of Pharisaism were sown during the exile. Deprived of the temple and its cult, the law became the center of the Jewish religion and supplied the pattern of Jewish life. Even after the temple was rebuilt and the ritual restored, the law continued to be the soul of the nation.

Very likely, the Pharisees stemmed from the Hasidim, or "pious ones," whose allegiance to the nation and the law gave impetus to the Maccabean revolt in the second century before Christ when the Jews were struggling desperately to maintain their national identity. The Pharisees said that what was distinctive about the nation was that God had given them the law. Pharisaism was fundamentally a lay movement.

The Pharisees encouraged their fellow Jews to keep the law of Moses as written in the first five books of the Old Testament. They did this by teaching the law, interpreting it, and setting themselves up as examples of how to keep it. They also imposed on the people the traditions established by the rabbis. In this respect, they differed from the Sadducees who followed a more literal interpretation of torah. The Saducean interpretations tended to be conservative, static and fixed, incapable of adjusting to new conditions. The tradition of the Pharisees, because it was oral, remained flexible and adjustable.

The Pharisees applied the law to every aspect of life. They continued and expanded the traditional interpretations. Their work is the so-called rabbinic literature, a large body of material from the early centuries of the Christian era. The basic document of the rabbinic literature is the Mishnah.

In their interpretation of the law and observance of it, the Pharisees were fanatical. The word "strict" does not accurately describe them, because they did not strictly observe the law of Moses. They went beyond it, laying greater burdens on the people than the law did, thus supposedly making the people more pious and more holy. They made more stringent the sabbath law, advocating that one abstain even from the appearance of work. They carried the matter of tithing to a ridiculous point, tithing even wild herbs. They strained their drinking water for fear of swallowing an impure gnat. They observed many ceremonial washings, made large contributions to the temple even at the expense of their own parents' welfare, and the like.

The Pharisees wore distinctive clothing. They did literally what Deut. 6:6-8 and 11:18 say. They made phylacteries which were pieces of calf skin wrapped and worn on the forehead and left arm. Wrapped in the skins were confessions of faith. The Pharisees made their phylacteries broad so that everyone could see their piety. They still do. They are very visible in modern Israel. The law of Moses says that the Israelites should wear tassels on the corners of their clothing as a reminder of God's commandments to them. The Pharisees made their tassels conspicuously large.

The Pharisees were loved by the masses of the Jewish people for their religious zeal and patriotism. The people felt that no greater holiness was to be found anywhere than the holiness of these men.

The number of Pharisees never exceeded 6000, but they had a great influence on every phase of Jewish life. They were a religious-political group.

In Matthew, Jesus strongly condemns Pharisaism. He and the Pharisees are always irreconcilably opposed to each other. Jesus' preaching, according to Matthew, begins with the blessing on the poor in spirit of the Beatitudes and the demand for a righteousness that exceeds that of the Pharisees. It concludes with a very strong indictment against them in Matt. 23.

The Pharisees are the chief opponents of Jesus in Matthew's gospel, cf. 9:11, 34. After the Pharisees "conspired against him, how to destroy him," cf. Matt. 12:14, they accused Him of healing with the aid of Beelzebub, cf. 12:24. It is then that Jesus calls them a "brood of vipers," cf. 12:34 and 23:33, and uses the figure of the tree that produces good or rotten fruit to pass judgment on their speaking "against the Holy Spirit," cf. 12:32-33.

5th Sunday after the Epiphany

Year B

Isaiah 40:21-31

The prophet extols the greatness of God and calls on Israel to hope in Him and trust Him. The words of v. 31 are a classic formulation of Old Testament hope.

Israel in exile thought that God either didn't care what was happening to her, or He didn't notice, or He was not able to help, or He had forsaken and forgotten her. Removed from the homeland God gave her for a perpetual inheritance, she was depressed and despondent. She wondered if the gods of Babylon were greater than Jahweh. They seemed to be more powerful, because Babylon defeated her, destroyed Jerusalem, and carried many inhabitants into exile. The people were full of self-pity. Their complaint, expressed in v. 27, was an implied judgment against Jahweh. Another expression of her despair is in Is. 49:14.

The Lesson breaks into the prophet's oracle. The theme of his doxology is the sovereignty of Jahweh. Jahweh is the Creator who rules the universe. The questions with which the Lesson begins are rhetorical.

God is the subject of the great verbs of creation the prophet uses in vs. 22 and 23: He "sits above the circle of the earth," He "stretches out the heavens," He "spreads them," He "brings princes to naught," and He "makes the rulers of the earth as nothing." Everything else is an object of the verbs. Earth and the heavens were established by Jahweh. Princes and rulers are like the gods they serve. The inhabitants of the earth are like grasshoppers.

"It is he who sits above the circle of the earth" extols the omnipotence and omniscience of God. He controls the rulers of the earth. The prophet's language changes in v. 24, and he uses an agricultural metaphor. "They" refers to the "princes" and "the rulers of the earth" of v. 23. Earthly rulers are as fragile as new plants. One gust of God's breath makes them wither and carries them off. Reliance on them is foolishness and sure to fail.

The prophet quotes God Himself in v. 25 in his polemic against the gods of Babylon. The Babylonian people consider their idols to represent powerful beings. Their success as an empire makes their power very clear, they think. But God challenges His people to compare the Babylonian gods to Himself.

What the prophet wants everyone to "see" in v. 26 is the stars. Babylon was the home and center of star-worship. The Babylonian gods were mostly star-gods. The prophet insists that they do not rival God. Rather, they are witnesses to His great strength. God created the stars. "He . . . brings out their host" - every night. He calls on the stars to rise in the sky. Therefore, not one of the innumerable host remains behind. "Not one is missing." He numbers them to be sure they are in the right place. He calls them by name. No Babylonian god, no idol can make a similar claim.

The followers of Him who died on a cross for the salvation of the world can add to that comparison by saying that a star led the wise men to worship the Son of God, Jesus, the Babe of Bethlehem.

Numbering the stars is imagery borrowed from the military. It conjures up the image of a commander leading his army onto the field of battle. As a general musters his army, so God brings out the stars.

Modern people have tried to count the stars. Dr. Hubble, who used to study stars at the Wilson Observatory, once said that there are 100 million stellar systems scattered in the universe at an average distance of 2 million light-years. One light-year equals six trillion miles. The distance is twelve plus fifteen zeros miles away! The prophet, of course, has no feel for such distances, although he knows the numbers are large.

We can see about 2,000 stars with the naked eye. Using the Hubble telescope in outer space, astronomers are able to see many times that. They are able to see billions. The new telescopes being developed suggest that there really are many more.

If something can be numbered, it is under control. Only God knows the number of the stars. Humans do not. The patriarch Abraham was not able to number the stars, according to Gen. 15:5.

God's intimate knowledge and concern for all things is evidenced in that He calls the stars "by name."

If God has numbered and named the stars, His people may be sure that He has not forgotten them and has not given up His concern for their well being. Jesus emphasized this in Matt. 10:29-31. How many hairs are on our head? Someone has said that a blond person has approximately 104,000 hairs on his/her head, a brunet has 102,000, and a red head 88,000.

The Creator God knows each one of His people, although they may be a mere cipher among the millions of citizens in the world. "He's got the whole world in His hands." In Him, their security is certain.

In response to the two complaints Israel makes in v. 27, Jahweh's prophet asks two questions in v. 28. They imply a reprimand. He repeats what he says in v. 21: they should know better.

What they should know is that Jahweh's work as Creator is not a one shot effort. There is no night or day with Him, no time out or time off. He works continuously. He does not become exhausted. He does not wear out.

The prophet calls on Israel to stop running, to stop scurrying about in frantic but futile efforts to get out of their mess and misery. All their schemes will not work. No matter how hard and long they run, they will drop exhausted and done in. Even youths and young men become fatigued and weary. The youth represent those who are confident of their own strength; youth are often very brash and cocky.

The solution to Israel's problems is to be found not in running but in waiting for God. He will rescue them. He will come in His own time and according to His own carefully and lovingly laid out plans for their welfare to rescue them from exile. They should wait. Then their strength to endure will be renewed. The Lord will give them the wings of an eagle to rise up and to fly above their troubles. They will run and not become weary. They will walk and not become faint.

This long doxology is intended to glorify Jahweh. Its function is pastoral and political. Pastorally, the exiles are told that they are not alone. Jahweh is still with them, and He is their source of power and energy. Politically, He rejects the authority and power assumed by the rulers of Babylon.

The encouragement can help us, too. He who created the earth is still active. His power to help and save has not diminished, and He is not running down. He who parted the waters for His hemmed-in people at the Red Sea long ago, who made for them a path of safety from their enemies through the sea, and who brought them back to the promised land from exile in Babylon, can do the same for His people who today are surrounded by disappointments, failure, losses, and sufferings. He can part the waters for us, too, and make a way of escape. The greatness of His concern for us was demonstrated definitively in Jesus' passion. He has saved us.

Natural strength becomes exhausted, but those who wait for God look to Him with faith in the midst of their weakness and impotence and are renewed with a strength that never fails.

An important point that needs to be kept in mind is stated in v. 29: "The Lord gives power to the faint, and strengthens the powerless." As one cannot pour water into a glass already full, so God cannot fill with His power people who are full of themselves. First, they must be emptied of self-reliance. God empties us through suffering. We must become nothing before He gives us consolation and strength.

The gospel proclaimed by the prophet needs to be heard today. God is not obsolete. He is still the One who gives strength and who rules. The claims made by the prophet must have seemed as outrageous to ancient Israel as they do to us.

Hope anticipates good in the future. The righteous man does not endure in his own power. His hope is in God.

Hope trusts God. Ps. 25:1-5 links waiting for the Lord and trust in Him. Such trust is encouraged in Jer. 17:7. What sustains us is that God has made us righteous in Jesus Christ and His passion.

Godly hope is not directed to anything specific and does not project its own view of the future. It is simply confident of God's protection and help. Jer. 29:11 describes God as giving hope rather than help. In Biblical declarations of hope, what is hoped for is less frequently named than the basis for hope, namely, God and His faithfulness.

The distinction between hope and trust is small. Both involve quiet waiting for God, cf. Is. 30:15; Ps. 27:14; 37:5-7.

Those who wait for the Lord receive a superhuman, miraculous power that makes the impossible possible. Youth may grow weary and exhausted, and young men may break down; but those who wait for the Lord do not. There is a difference between physical strength and the energy of a living faith in God. A faithful relationship to God overcomes all temptation and weakness, even the most serious afflictions of life including death itself.

Some understand the word the NRSV translates "they shall mount up" differently. Iaalu can mean "to grow." Then the translation is, "they shall grow wings." That's how the LXX reads. Some have seen here an allusion to the popular belief that the eagle renews its plumage in old age. This is rather fanciful, although Ps. 103:5 talks about renewing one's youth as the eagle does. The strength of an eagle is suggested in Ex. 19:4 and Deut. 32:11. The birds called "eagles" are really griffon-vultures. The point may be that God strengthens those who wait for Him so that they are able to maintain their ideals.

The prophet lists two other kinds of strength the Lord gives. The words "they shall run and not be weary" may promise the strength to meet crises. "They shall walk and not faint" may promise the strength to cope with our daily routine. For most of us, the Christian life is something we maintain not by exciting and adventure filled feats of extraordinary daring but by carrying out the humdrum duties of each day. With people as with an automobile, the chief test often comes in low gear. To walk and not become fatigued is sometimes more difficult than to run and not be weary. We want to jet out of trouble and tour the world. We want to go to another city and start life over. We want to run out of the house, when there is trouble. We want to run away. But God wants us to walk beside Him. He wants to turn our sorrow into joy. He has done this in Jesus and His passion.

1 Corinthians 9:16-23

"A Christian is a perfectly free lord of all, subject to none. A Christian is a dutiful servant of all, subject to all." Martin Luther expounds these propositions in "The Freedom of a Christian," one of the three important tracts he wrote in 1520 to explain Christian living. Citing 1 Cor. 9:19, he says, "Both are Paul's own statements."[93]

We are obliged to serve all people. When we accept this obligation willingly, we are free. We serve others without thought of benefit for ourselves but only in response to their need and to what God has done for us. Paul is an example.

God laid on Paul the obligation to "proclaim the gospel." He carried out this obligation willingly. Therefore, he considers himself free.

God changed Paul from being a persecutor of the church to being an apostle in Acts 9:1-19. Being an apostle was not his decision. He says in Gal. 1:15, "God . . . set me apart before I was born and called me through his grace." His call was like that of Jeremiah, cf. Jer. 1:5. Paul says, "An obligation is laid on me . . . . I am entrusted with a commission."

His keen awareness of his commission is brought out clearly in the Greek. Epikeitai ("is laid") and pepisteumai ("I am entrusted") are perfect indicative passive forms that emphasize his state or condition.

Oikonomia ("a commission") is a word that was used for the task given a faithful servant who was appointed over a particular area of responsibility in the household. The word stresses the responsibility and faithfulness of the servant to his master in carrying out his assigned task.

Paul has the firm conviction that he is an instrument of God's plan of salvation which is spelled out by Jesus in Mark 13:10: "The good news must be proclaimed to all nations." Paul repeatedly emphasizes that he is called to preach especially to the gentiles, cf. Rom. 11:13; 1:14; Eph. 3:7-8.

Paul considers himself "a slave to all." The exercise of his freedom and that of all Christians involves service. Human beings are at their best when they dedicate their life to serve others. Jesus showed us what it means to be a slave to all, cf. Phil. 2:5-8. He gave His life on the cross to save the world. Losing one's life in service to others is the way to find it, Jesus says in Matt. 10:39.

Paul's understanding of his apostolic work is closely related to the Greco-Roman world's understanding of an ambassador in that he exercises political flexibility. The changeless gospel empowers him to change his approach to meet the circumstances of the people he serves. Although he denies the validity of the different viewpoints of Jews and gentiles, he adjusts his behavior to the situation in which they live. This does not mean that he is a Judaizer in one place and a pagan in another, but he is flexible in dealing with different situations.

Paul's intentionality in doing this is indicated by the behavioral choices he makes. He has the salvation of everyone in mind, cf. 1 Cor. 10:33. When he talks about winning people, he has in mind winning them to be followers of Jesus Christ. He says, "I have become all things to all people, that I might by all means save some." In restating Paul's behavioral choices, Luther used the familiar proverb attributed to Ambrose by Augustine: "When in Rome, do as the Romans do."[94]

Strangely, Paul says, "To the Jews I became as a Jew." This is strange, because Peter was designated to proclaim the gospel to the Jews, according to Gal. 2:7. Paul and Barnabas were to proclaim the gospel to the gentiles. But this arrangement did not prevent Paul from bringing also Jews to Jesus. His policy was to proclaim the gospel in cities where it had not been proclaimed. When he entered a new city, he regularly went first to the synagogue and proclaimed the gospel there.

He seems to have practiced Judaism all of his life. He claimed to be a Pharisee during his last visit to Jerusalem in Acts 23:6. He joined with four men in effecting ritual purification according to the law that all might know that he observed the law, cf. Acts 21:23-24. He had Timothy circumcised, according to Acts 16:3. He cut his hair, placing himself under a vow in Acts 18:18.

As a Jew, Paul followed the practices of Judaism while teaching that the law is not a way of salvation. He lived as a Jew, because he knew that once he forsook the observance of the law Judaism would close its door against him. He could even accept Jesus as the Messiah, but once he deliberately gave up the practice of the law he would forever forfeit the right to be seriously listened to by other rabbis. If he was regarded as an outcast by his own group, the Jews, he would also have little prestige among gentiles.[95]

When Paul says that he "became as one outside the law," he does not mean that he lived in an unregulated and irresponsible way. His freedom from the law was not lawlessness. "God's law" is wider and more inclusive than law in the sense of torah. The term "Christ's law" is influenced by the parallelism with "God's law." The meaning is that he was obliged to be obedient to Christ.

There is no hos ("as") before asthenes ("weak") in v. 22 as there is before the situations referred to in vs. 20 and 21. The word is found in some manuscripts perhaps because some considered it offensive to think of Paul as weak. "The Jews," "those under the law," and "those outside the law" probably were non-Christians; but "the weak" were members of the Corinthian Christian community. Paul talks about them in 1 Cor. 8:9-13.

The earliest model of Christianity was a Jewish one. The earliest Christians accepted Jesus as their Savior in essentially Jewish terms. They were all Jews by birth. Everything about

Jesus made sense for them in terms of Jewish history and Jewish destiny. The Jerusalem temple seems to have been their regular meeting place, and the temple liturgy was used in their worship. There is no trace of any program to transform the proclamation of Jesus to make it intelligible and applicable to non-Jews.

The movement of the church to Antioch opened the way to a Hellenistic understanding of Jesus. The gentile mission developed there rather than in Jerusalem. Paul became the leader of this movement that produced a new model of thought and life. The gospel was presented in terms of Hellenistic language and thought. The conceptual vocabulary of the Hellenistic world was used. The gospel was translated into the language of gentiles. More cautious and conservative Christians recoiled at the syncretistic possibilities that opened up. The process continued in the work of Origen, Augustine, Anselm, and Luther. It is still going on.

The majority of Christians today are Africans, Asians, Latin Americans, and Pacific Islanders – and the proportion is rising daily. Christianity is now primarily a non-western religion, and all present indications are that it will steadily become more so. We can expect Christian theology to move in that direction, too.[96]

Mark 1:29-39

Jesus proclaimed, "The time is fulfilled, and the kingdom of God has come near," cf. Mark 1:15. In Him, God came to the earth to establish His rule and to fulfill the promises He made to His people in the Old Testament. The miracles Jesus performed made Him very popular, but they did not fulfill His mission.

The miracles play a strong role in the four gospels. Mark tells about eighteen, nine of which are miracles of healing, cf. 1:40-45; 2:1-12; 3:1-6; 5:1-13; 7:31-37; 8:22-26; 10:46-52. It is easy to be attracted to Jesus' miracles, but they are not what He came to do. His mission was to die on a cross.

Toward the beginning of His public ministry, Jesus went to Capernaum where He taught on a sabbath. The first thing He did on leaving the synagogue was to enter the house of Simon Peter and Andrew. They were brothers and apparently lived together.

John 1:44 says that the two brothers were from Bethsaida. Some think that their "Bethsaida" was the fishing quarter of Capernaum.

"Simon's mother-in-law was in bed with a fever." Jesus was told of her malady. The seriousness of her illness cannot be determined. Luke 4:38 says that she had a "a high fever." The usage of the time distinguished great and small fevers.

Mark does not tell us that anyone asked Jesus to heal the lady, but the request probably was made. Taking her hand, Jesus lifted her up; and she was healed.

The rapidity and completeness of the cure is indicated in that she then served the sabbath meal. She was not prevented from doing this by the exhaustion and debility generally following a severe fever. The feat was significant enough to cause the evangelist to note it.

When the sabbath ended at sunset, the citizens of Capernaum could move their sick and those who were possessed with demons without violating the sabbath law. So they brought them to Jesus together with those who were possessed with demons. Jesus drove an unclean spirit out of a man in the synagogue earlier that day, cf. Mark 1:21-28. The imperfect tense of the Greek verb, epheron ("they brought"), describes a steady stream of people being brought to Jesus.

When the evangelist says, "they brought to him all who were sick or possessed with demons," that is typical Markan hyperbole. Another example of such hyperbole is in 1:5: "all the people of Jerusalem were going out to (John the baptizer), and were baptized by him." Certainly, every single person was not baptized. Another example is Mark's description, "the whole city was gathered around the door." The author is simply emphasizing that a large group of people surged around the door of Simon's house.

Mark consistently makes a distinction between those "who were sick" and those who were "possessed with demons," cf. vs. 32 and 34. The way Jesus dealt with demons revealed His divine authority. They were expelled by a word of command. To emphasize this authority seems to be the reason Mark has so many demon stories. Jesus came to destroy the power of the devil and to establish the reign of God. Thus the healings of the demon-possessed are an essential part of the gospels.

They were of special significance to the church as proofs that Jesus was the Messiah. They are frequently emphasized in the summaries of Jesus' miracles, cf. Mark 1:34 and 39; 3:11; Matt. 4:24 and 10:8; Luke 7:21. Besides the summary reports, Mark tells about three exorcisms, cf. 1:21-28; 5:1-13; 9:14-27. Matthew also includes two stories in 9:32-34 and 12:22-24.

The demons had a knowledge of Jesus that they expressed verbally when He confronted them.

Two reasons generally given that Jesus did "not permit the demons to speak" are the feeling that a person who had a demon should not be heard, and Jesus did not want to be identified with demon possessed people. But the command for silence may also be an example of the secrecy motif in Mark's gospel. Silence was enjoined also after other miracles in 1:44; 5:43; and 7:36. Jesus sternly ordered silence also after Peter's confession in 8:30 and at the descent from the mount of transfiguration in 9:9. Jesus' withdrawal from the crowd in 1:35-37 may be another instance of the secrecy motif.

The phenomena may be a way in which Jesus tried to keep His miracles from becoming the dominant factor in His ministry. Or it may be a literary technique used by Mark to downplay the spectacular character of the miracles. They attracted many people to Jesus in that day, and they are popular among Christian people today; but they do not further the heart of the matter in Jesus' ministry. Mark downplays miracles, which must be a part of the story of Jesus, in order to try to keep the readers' attention fixed on Jesus' passion, cf. Mark 10:45.

The secrecy motif may also help to explain Jesus' refusal to return to Capernaum, although "Everyone is searching for (him)." More than His natural, humble character and His rock-star popularity is involved.

"Simon and his companions" thought that the healings and exorcisms presented a valuable opportunity for Jesus to promote

His ministry and that He did not realize how widely He was being sought. But carrying out the mission He received from the Father was the reason He left Capernaum. The disciples did not understand that mission until after Jesus' resurrection.

When Mark says in v. 34 that "many" who were sick and possessed with demons were cured, although in v. 32 he uses the word "all," it is doubtful that he wishes to say that not all were cured. "Many" may be a Semitic way of saying all. Luke removes the ambiguity in 4:40 saying that Jesus cured each of them.

The next morning, Jesus "went out to a deserted place." Eremon topon here is not a desert place, because the district around Capernaum was cultivated at the time. The meaning is a lonely and quiet spot.

The imperfect, proseucheto ("he prayed"), describes what Jesus was doing when Simon and his companions were hunting Him down. Katedioxen ("hunted for") is a strong word.

The prayers of Jesus are mentioned in 6:46 and 14:35-39. Luke speaks frequently of Jesus' prayers, cf. 3:21; 5:16; 6:12; 9:18, 28-29; 11:1; 22:41-44.

"He went throughout Galilee." The strongest reading of Luke 4:44 is "Judea," with "Galilee" a strong variant.

The house of Simon and Andrew became the headquarters for Jesus' ministry when He was in Galilee, cf. "at home" in Mark 2:1 and 3:19 and "in the house" in 9:33 and 10:10.

A visitor to the area of Capernaum in 385 said that a church was made out of the house of Peter and that the walls still stood as they once were. In 570, another visitor to the city said that the house of Peter was a basilica. This may suggest that the church seen in 385 had been made larger.

Archeologists have discovered an octagon-shaped Byzantine church probably from the fifth century. Underneath are the remains of a first century fisherman's quarters. Some rooms were adapted for Christian worship as colored ornamentation and graffiti show already in the second and third centuries and continued in such use through the fourth century. After that, the basilical church was built with its octagon directly over the earlier prayer room.

364

Simon was married at this time. His wife accompanied him later on his missionary journeys, according to 1 Cor. 9:5.

The Talmud prescribes a magical remedy for "a high fever" such as Simon's mother-in-law may have had. The principal part of the remedy is to tie a knife wholly of iron by a braid of hair to a thorn bush and to repeat on successive days the words of Ex. 3:2-3, then v. 4, and finally v. 5. After this, the bush is to be cut down while a certain magical formula is spoken. What Jesus did to heal the lady was radically different.

Jesus proclaimed His message in the synagogues of Galilee. The word "synagogue" basically means "a bringing together." It came to mean "an assembly," especially a Jewish religious assembly. It is used of a Christian assembly in James 2:2.

At the beginning of His ministry, Jesus used the opportunities provided by the synagogue, cf. 3:1 and 6:2. St. Paul followed the same method in his later missionary work, cf. Acts 9:20; 13:5 and 14.

Even small towns and villages had their synagogues where people gathered for worship, prayer, and the reading and exposition of the law and the prophets. The synagogue was a lay institution. Not only scribes and elders, but any member of the assembly might be invited by the president of the synagogue to expound the law and teach. The presence of priests was not mandatory, not even for worship. The synagogue also served as a place for communal discussions and meetings. Public decisions and announcements were made there. Synagogues were also used as hospices where Jews from abroad stayed. Rabbis especially found rooms and slept in synagogues. The great opportunity this offered Jesus naturally disappeared as the breach between Him and the rabbis widened.

Miracles and proclamation are closely associated in the ministry of Jesus. When Jesus sent out His disciples in Mark 3:14-15 and 6:7-12, He charged them also to preach and to heal. In preaching, God is at work. His rule becomes a reality. Signs and wonders attested to this.

Preaching is not giving a lecture; it is proclamation, the declaration of an event. As a herald went before the chariot of the king and announced the approach of the ruler, so preachers travel throughout the world crying, "Make ready, the King is near!" The proclamation is a divine Word, and as such it is an effective force that creates what it proclaims. Preaching is no mere impartation of facts or interesting talk. It is an event. What is proclaimed happens.

5th Sunday after the Epiphany

Year C

Isaiah 6:1-13

What a negative mission God gives Isaiah! He is to "Make the mind of this people dull, and stop their ears, and shut their eyes, so that they may not look with their eyes, and listen with their ears, and comprehend with their minds, and turn and be healed."

Is. 6 is one the most startling chapters of the Bible. Its vivid descriptions stimulate universal interest. It is very difficult to understand because it is so dark, but it is one of the most frequently used passages of the Old Testament. It projects overwhelming divine anger. Who knows anything about seraphim?

The chapter is theologically rich. It has been used as the basis for discussions on the holiness or incomprehensibility of God, on sin and forgiveness, on the nature of worship, on the call of God, on the power of the Word of God, on "the hardening of the heart," on election, and even on the doctrine of the Trinity. Preachers find in it a wide variety of themes.

The vision has two parts: Isaiah's calling to be a prophet in vs. 1-8 and his mission in vs. 9-13. His message is spelled out in vs. 9-10. God has tried His people, found them guilty, and will punish them. A hint of gospel finally comes at the end with the words, "The holy seed is its stump." Resurrection is promised. If God has to kill His own Son and raise the dead to accomplish His purposes, He will do it.

The harsh judgment is directed against Judah. They are "a people of unclean lips." God has decreed their hard-heartedness and willed Jerusalem's destruction. Oftentimes He had called them "my people," but now He refers to them as "this people."

Many have said on the basis of Acts 28:25-27 that the voice giving the prophet his mission is that of the Holy Spirit. He is to lead the people of Judah not to salvation, but he is to harden their stubborn wills. Three expressions are used: "Make the mind of this people dull, and stop their ears and shut their eyes." The order is reversed in the reason given for the message that reveals the extent of God's displeasure.

Isaiah will be God's agent. In the Old Testament, hardening of the heart is always represented as an act of God and not a result of human nature.[97]

Isaiah is purged of his own guilt with a burning coal, so that he might harden the people with his word. If he does not harden them, they might "turn and be healed." He must see that this does not happen.

Ezekiel is given a similarly difficult and even hopeless assignment in Ezek. 1-3. His commission is hedged about with words that prepare him for failure.

Some have rationalized that the judgment Isaiah proclaimed was Judah's deliberate choice. They themselves stubbornly refused to hear God. God predicted their response; He did not ordain it.

Others have believed that God permitted the people to be overwhelmed by the accumulated consequences of their own free decisions. God concluded Israel in unbelief that He might have mercy on the gentiles. The text celebrates the mercy of God rather than God's wrath. Neither the freedom of the human will nor the mercy of God is in question.

Others have believed that Judah was blind, because she deserved to be. The participation of God in this blinding was permissive rather than active. When the Word of God is continually rejected, the capacity to hear and understand it dies. Deliberate neglect of God's Word and habitual deafness to it inevitably bring indifference to it. "Will not" is punished by "cannot." There comes an end to God's patience and His willingness to forgive. It is possible to push Him beyond that limit.

Isaiah asks how long his service of hardening and the state of hardness will continue. He expresses sympathy for the nation. He believes there will be an end to God's anger. The Lord's answer describes a situation of utter desolation, without inhabitant, without human, only emptiness. Even if only ten per cent of the people are left, there will be another wave of burning and destruction. The idea of exile seems to be implied.

Hope is held out when the destruction of the nation is likened to that of "a terebinth or an oak whose stump remains standing when it is felled." Those trees have the peculiar ability to grow again from the root when they have been cut down. The root stump represents the remnant that will survive the dire judgment. It will be the seed from which a new Israel springs up after the old has been destroyed. The words were fulfilled in Jesus' suffering, death, and resurrection. He was the "shoot . . . from the stump of Jesse," Is. 11:1 talks about.

Jesus quotes Is. 6 in all four gospels, cf. Mark 4:12; Matt. 13:14-15; Luke 8:10; and John 12:37-43. In the synoptic tradition, the words are quoted as judgment upon those who do not properly understand and receive Jesus. In the fourth gospel, Jesus uses the same words to comment negatively on those who suffer from spiritual blindness and do not properly discern who He is and what He requires.

Acts 28:26-27 uses the same words to explain Jewish resistance to Paul's preaching of Jesus. Jewish refusal to believe opens the way for Paul's mission to the gentiles. The early church sees the rejection of Jesus as parallel to the rejection of the prophets. In both cases, there is an awareness that the resistance is initiated by God. As God decreed Israel's hard-heartedness and the consequent destruction of Jerusalem, so He decreed Israel's resistance to Jesus and Jesus' crucifixion.

The purposes of God are carried out in the world, even through resistance to Him.

Isaiah's message sounds ominous to a society narcoticized not only by chemical dependence but also by a host of numbing dependencies: poverty and wealth in the extreme, self-indulgence, brutality, militarism, and injustice. The prophet spoke against these things. Not paying attention to God and His will leads to termination that comes like a thief in the night, too quiet to be noticed until it is too late. There is no easy gospel, no cheap grace, no good word of a quick and comfortable deal with God.

The passive of "be healed" in v. 10 is changed to an active "I would heal" when Jesus quotes the passage in Matt. 13:15 and John 12:40. Jesus implies that He is God. Mark 4:12 retains the numinous passive.

The vision takes place "in the year that King Uzziah died." Isaiah is allowed to see and hear what is happening in the heavenly council assembled around the throne of Jahweh. The vision is echoed in Rev. 4:6-11.

Micaiah in 1 Kings 22:19-23 and Ezekiel in Ezek. 1-3 also are commissioned by God as He sits enthroned in the midst of the heavenly entourage. The situation of Micaiah's call in 1 Kings 22 seems to be a regular session of the assembly "with all the host of heaven standing beside him to the right and to the left of him. . . . one said one thing, and another said another until a spirit came forward" with a suggestion. The prophet is then dispatched to carry out the suggestion.

Many have thought that the vision is not corporeal but imaginative and intellectual. When the prophet saw, he did not see with his eyes but with his mind. That is to say, no one standing beside him saw what he saw, as everyone at King Belshazzar's feast saw the handwriting on the wall in Dan. 5. The images Isaiah saw were implanted in his imagination by God. He was also given an understanding of their significance.

In describing what Isaiah saw, many church fathers adopted the principle of accommodation. When God reveals Himself to people, He does not appear as He actually is but such as people can receive. The vision of the throne, the robe, and the bodily appearance of the Lord were adapted to the capacity of Isaiah to perceive the inconceivable majesty of God.

What is true of Isaiah's vision is true of all human knowledge of God from whatever source. No human being knows God as He is but only as He has adapted Himself to the limitations and capacities of people. All knowledge of God is accommodated knowledge.[98]

Isaiah does not dare to lift his eyes. He sees only the hem of the Lord's robe.

Many have believed on the basis of John 12:39-41 that Isaiah saw Jesus.

The king is dying when Isaiah has his vision, but God lives. The fall of King Uzziah is the point at which Isaiah recognizes Jahweh's righteous rule as lord of history and sovereign of the nations. Isaiah sees not Uzziah's son, Jotham, who succeeded his father on the throne of Judah, but "the Lord sitting on a throne, high and lofty." Jahweh rules not Jotham.

This is the only place seraphs are mentioned in the Bible. They are six winged heavenly beings who praise God. They are fiery serpents, not naked cupids. They are popular ancient near eastern creatures, part human and part beast. In ancient near eastern cultic circles, they are used to signify the power and majesty of Jahweh. Their humility and their awe at the divine glory is expressed by covering their faces with two of their six wings. With two others, they express their reverence by covering their feet. Some consider "feet" a euphemism for genitals. Their readiness to serve is expressed by flying with their two remaining wings. They hover about God. They are in attendance on Him. The seraphs form an antiphonal choir engaged in continuous praise. They cry not the "Unclean, unclean, unclean!" of lepers – the king has become one of those people - but "Holy, holy, holy is the Lord of hosts!"

The trisagion ("holy, holy, holy") is the Hebrew way of saying most holy. To the Hebrew mind, holiness is not one of many attributes of God; it expresses the very nature of God Himself. The basic meaning of <u>kadhosh</u> ("holy") is separate from sin, removed, exalted. The word does not always have the sense of meeting moral demands. The holy commands respect. It is acknowledged inwardly. It is not simply fear in the face of what is absolutely overpowering, but it is a faltering confession of divine supremacy that recognizes and extols a value beyond all conceiving. The object of such praise is not simply absolute might; but God is acknowledged to have the right to make the highest claim and to receive the highest praise, because He is worthy of it. To say this, Rudolf Otto suggests using the word "numinous."[99] The favorite name of God in Isaiah is "the Holy One of Israel." That name is an echo of the seraphic praise.

God is everything. He calls people to be. He is above all, but He exercises that power in the human sphere. He is the ultimate authority. He is holy.

"The glory of God" is His power, status, and honor. God's glory fills the whole creation. It is perceived in the world in various ways. It is experienced in history, according to Ex. 14:4, 17-18; and Ezek. 28:22.

It probably is pretty hard to use Is. 6 to preach on the holiness of God or His glory. "The man upstairs" is about as close as most moderns can get to those ideas.

In Hindu thought, the holiness of God gives Him a hands off quality. In Christian and Hebrew thought, God does not withdraw because of human sin. On the contrary, He yearns over His people. He touches their sin and removes it. He redeems us. He saves us through Jesus' passion.

Some see in the trisagion a reference to the Trinity. Many have believed that this vision, in one way or another, involves the whole Trinity. "The Lord sitting on a throne" is the Christ, according to John 12:41. The voice giving Isaiah his instructions is that of the Holy Spirit, according to Acts 28:25-27. The Father is involved in that the Son is the image of the Father. The "us" in v. 8 implies the three Persons in the Godhead. The idea of the Trinity is strengthened by the three-fold repetition of "holy."

The triune God of the New Testament is Jahweh in the Old Testament, but it is a stretch to see the doctrine of the Trinity expressed in the Old Testament. There is no evidence that the Jews thought of Jahweh in Trinitarian terms. God's Trinitarian character is a part of New Testament theology.

372

The word sabaoth ("hosts") is often used in the Old Testament and has to do with the military and armies.

Isaiah receives his vision in the temple. The building itself is seized with reverential awe to its deepest foundations. The thunder of the seraph's trisagion makes the place shake. The temple was usually filled with smoke as the result of the burning of incense and the many sacrifices; but, on this occasion, it is filled with smoke as the result of the seraphs' praise.

God told Moses, according to Ex. 33:20, "no one shall see me and live." Isaiah reflects this sentiment when he says, "I am lost." The holiness of God is to the sinner a consuming fire, cf. Is. 33:14. At his direct encounter with supreme holiness and in the atmosphere of sheer adoration, Isaiah becomes conscious of his own sinfulness and is appalled. He becomes acutely aware of his inadequacy, his lack of qualification to be in the divine presence.

The prophet senses first not the people's failure but his own. His vision of God causes him to sense his unworthiness. He may have recognized that he had put too much hope in Uzziah, but he is not here giving expression to an uneasy conscience. He describes his unholiness with the words "unclean lips," because he is in the midst of a choir of beings who are praising God with pure lips.

When Peter became aware of the presence of God in Jesus, like Isaiah he said, "Go away from me, Lord, for I am a sinful man!" cf. Luke 5:8. In both cases, the self-depreciating response is immediate, instinctive, and spontaneous. It is not based on deliberation. It is a direct reflex stimulated by the awareness of God's presence. It does not spring from the consciousness of some committed transgression. It belongs to a special category of valuation and appraisal. It is more deep seated than the feeling of a transgression of the moral law. It is hard to describe, but it comes with piercing acuteness and is an uncompromising judgment on one's very existence as a creature.

Isaiah's sense of personal unholiness is especially great because of the closeness of his connection with an unholy nation. The condition of the nation is described by the prophet in other passages. He talks about the vain trust in ostentatious wealth and physical beauty on the part of the prancing women of Jerusalem in Is. 3:16-17 and 32:9-11. He decries the confidence in military preparation and political alliances on the part of the royal court in Is. 22:8-11; 30:1-5; and 31:1-3. The holiness of the Lord of hosts means that Jahweh alone is to be feared, cf. Is. 8:12-13.

To be effective, preachers must have a deep awareness of personal sinfulness. If they take a position standing with the seraphim around the throne of God as they preach, they will not communicate well. Preachers who consider themselves morally superior to their hearers, even if they have by God's grace made progress in achieving holiness of life, will not relate well to the hearers. When God began His good work in us, we were spiritually blind, dead, and enemies of God, along with the rest of the human race. There is no room for superior feelings in anyone who is trying to apply the gracious work of God to people.

The confession by the prophet of his uncleanness is not met with denial: "No, you are not!" Rather his guilt is removed. He is cleansed by a seraph who touches his lips with a live coal. His sense of unworthiness is taken away. He is made fit to do the work that will be assigned to him.

Then the purpose of the heavenly vision is revealed. A new situation is developing. The Lord says, "Whom shall I send (to speak for us), and who will go for us?" Some have seen the plural "us" as a reference to God, the seraphs, and the assembly, while the question, "Whom shall I send?" identifies the Lord.

Isaiah hears the question. A decision has been made in the heavenly council with regard to Judah. The decision involves invasion, destruction, and disaster for Judah. The decision must be announced in human society.

Isaiah offers himself as the messenger before the heavenly assembly can begin a discussion of the question. The immediacy and the joy with which he volunteers is a direct consequence of the purging he has received. In striking contrast to his previous despair, he now engages boldly on a divine mission during a crucial period of his nation's history.

What happens in worship leads to a change of life. Worship is important for remembering who we are. Worship always ends with dedication to service. Sometimes the announcements made at the end of a contemporary worship service do not encourage this.

Isaiah is an example of the effect worship should have on us. The purpose of Isaiah's vision is not to give an understanding of what God or the throne room of God looks like. Other prophets similarly perceive their mission. They leave untold so much that interests us. Amos is an example. He says that he sees Jahweh holding a plumb-line to a wall. But when Jahweh asks him what he sees, he says that he sees a plumb-line, cf. Amos 7:7-8. He says nothing of what Jahweh looks like. When he sees Jahweh standing on the altar, he shows an astonishing lack of interest in Jahweh's appearance, cf. Amos 9:1. The first prophet to attempt a detailed picture of the glory of Jahweh is Ezekiel in Ezek. 1:26-28. The job of the prophets was to tell about coming events of a spiritual sort that were also concrete realities. They were not concerned with the appearance of God but with events that were about to occur in this world.

The time of Isaiah's commissioning is identified as "the year that King Uzziah died." Gerhard von Rad says, "The way in which the prophets give the exact time at which they received certain revelations, dating them by their character as real historical events, has no parallel in any other religion."[100] The writers of both Testaments assert that they are talking about real events that happened in history. The Old Testament provides the pattern for the historical statement of the New Testament that Jesus "suffered under Pontius Pilate."

The ministry of Isaiah under Uzziah was very short. He was called "in the year that King Uzziah died." Isaiah wrote a history of the reign of Uzziah, according to 2 Chron. 26:22.

Uzziah reigned 783-742 BC, although some say that he died in 746.[101] He was a good king at first. His reign was a time of great prosperity and peace and a high point in the history of the divided kingdom. Uzziah's successes caused him to become haughty. God punished him for this with leprosy. The development of leprosy really brought his reign to an end. It ended in tragedy. He had to be removed from society. He eked out his last days in ignominy. Without him, the key to the period of prosperity and peace was gone. Some interpreters have suggested that the "death" of Uzziah referred to in Is. 6:1 is, in fact, the civil death created by his leprosy.

The story of Uzziah's illustrious reign is passed over rather quickly in 2 Kings 15:1-7 where he is called Azariah. A fuller account of his building enterprises and military exploits is given in 2 Chron. 26.

Isaiah grew up during the 41-year reign of Uzziah. He must have been filled with a sense of pride as the might of Judah grew during Uzziah's early years. He grew up in proximity to the court having been born of princely lineage. But his confidence in Uzziah burst like a bubble when God marked the king with leprosy as an arrogant sinner. The juxtaposition of the two phrases "King Uzziah died" and "I saw the Lord" may be significant. The king is near death, but God lives.

Isaiah may have gone to the temple where he has his vision in grief because of the king's health. The vision impresses on him that the situation of the kingdom is not hopeless. He sees the ultimate Ruler high and lifted up. He still reigns.

Isaiah's call is connected with the beginning of Assyrian expansion. In 745, Tiglath-Pileser came to the throne of Assyria and initiated an aggressive military policy against his neighbors. Judah became involved with the Assyrians and slowly but surely lost all of her territories and a great deal of her prosperity. Judah was but a little buffer state. She was threatened with extinction as the world powers of Egypt and Assyria struggled for domination.

Jotham (742-735 BC) followed his father Uzziah. Under Jotham, Judah became a satellite of Assyria.

Ahaz (735-715 BC) followed Jotham. Ahaz had plans for rebellion. During Ahaz' reign, the nation was alternately pious and syncretistic. Ahaz led the people to more and more apostasy followed by reliance on foreign alliances. This signaled the end of trust in Jahweh. In 721, Samaria fell. Babylon leveled Jerusalem in 587 BC.

1 Corinthians 15:1-11

The death of the Son of God is a most mysterious event, but His resurrection makes sense of it. Some consider Jesus' death and resurrection individual events with independent theological meaning. Others consider the two a linked pair; when one is mentioned, the other is always implied. Jesus' resurrection implies His death. More than that, Jesus' resurrection reveals the saving character of His death.

Jesus' resurrection was not an issue at Corinth. The problem was that some considered it unique. Paul reestablishes the validity of Jesus' resurrection in vs. 1-11 before he takes up matters involving the resurrection of believers.

There is still a lot of opposition to the idea of Jesus' resurrection - even in the church. Those who oppose it say that a physical resurrection could never have happened, because it violates the laws of nature. The dead are not raisable today, and they never were.

Modern people ask, what actually happened? The ancient writers of the scriptures did not ask that question and did not try to explain. They were evangelists not historians.

Scholars today generally agree that the starting point for any investigation into Jesus' resurrection lies not in the narratives at the ends of the four gospels but in 1 Cor. 15, because it is the earliest written record. Paul wrote to the Corinthians about 55 AD, or some 20 to 25 years after Jesus' resurrection. This account is at least 20 years older than the written record in Mark's gospel.

Jesus' empty tomb is not a part of Paul's proclamation of the resurrection, nor does Easter faith rest on it. Paul emphasizes the appearances of Jesus.

Earlier in this letter, Paul took up a variety of topics, because the Corinthian Christians directed questions to him, cf. 1 Cor. 7:1 and 25; 8:1; 12:1. But in 1 Cor. 15, the typical word "concerning" is missing. Unlike the earlier topics, Paul does not talk about the resurrection because of a question from Corinth. Rumors seem to have reached Paul about some things Christians in Corinth were saying regarding the resurrection.

He says in v. 12, "some of you say there is no resurrection of the dead." He begins to deal with that matter by rehearsing "the good news" he had given them when he was in Corinth.

"Good news" (euaggelion) or "gospel" is an important term in 1 Cor. 15:1-2. The frequency of its use can be demonstrated with the translation, "the gospel which I gospelled to you . . . in what words I gospelled it to you . . . ."

A valuable verse for the Old Testament background of the term "gospel" is Is. 52:7. Isaiah anticipates a great victory for Jahweh. The messenger does not say that the rule of God will soon commence. He proclaims God as reigning. Through that announcement, it happens. Salvation comes with the word of proclamation. The word does not just provide information. It is power. The effect of the proclamation is liberation.

Among the Greeks, a messenger came from the field of battle by ship, by horse, or as a swift runner and proclaimed to the anxiously awaiting city the victory of the army and the death or capture of the enemy. Often the news was sent by a letter. The news was called "gospel," and the person conveying the news was "an evangelist." Political or private communications that brought joy were also called "gospel." So were the words of the birth of a son and the news of an approaching wedding.

The Greeks often associated salvation with chance and fortune. A Greek commander achieved victory over the Persians through fate, good fortune, or luck. He feared the gods and sought to protect himself from their power. Such an idea is completely foreign to Christian thinking. God is in control of events.

Paul begins by repeating what the Corinthians already know, although they have not fully grasped it. Later in the chapter, he talks about things that may be new to them. To have to remind them what he taught them implies a gentle rebuke.

He uses several kinds of authority in this chapter to assert the validity of the good news he proclaimed to them. He makes a very strong appeal to tradition in vs. 1-3. The authority implied in v. 11 is similar but also a little different in that it is more contemporary. He insists that what he proclaims agrees with what all the other apostles who were witnesses of the resurrection proclaim.

At the outset, the apostle leads his readers away from all argumentation or reason about the resurrection and directs them solely to the good news he proclaimed to them. To believe in the resurrection of the dead does not depend on human investigation. Reason merely observes facts as they appear to the human eye. The world has stood for a long time, people die one after another, remain dead, decompose, and turn to dust. No one has ever returned from the grave. Sometimes people are burned to ashes. Some ashes are spread over water. Some people have a leg resting in one place, an arm in another, and their skull in still another. One day, probably, some astronaut will be launched into outer space and not return. When reason reflects on these facts, it is entirely at a loss. So many odd, peculiar, and absurd ideas present themselves that reason decides there is nothing to the idea of resurrection. Faith must learn to adhere to the good news even though it is against everything that our senses feel and comprehend. The resurrection is an article of faith, not one of reason or wisdom.

Paul lists three reactions the Corinthian Christians made to the resurrection of Jesus as he proclaimed it to them. First, they "received" it.

Paul uses two terms in vs. 1 and 3 that are the technical terms of early Judaism for the passing on and the reception of tradition. The two words are paralambano ("to receive") and paradidomi ("hand on"), cf. 1 Thess. 2:13; 4:1; Gal. 1:9; 1 Cor. 11:2; 15:1, 3; Phil. 4:9; Col. 2:6; 2 Thess. 2:15; 3:6; Jude 3; 2 Pet. 2:21. The words are used also in connection with another block of Christian tradition in 1 Cor. 11:23-25. Paul is telling the Corinthians not merely what he believes and teaches, but what he is telling them is the normative and valid Christian proclamation. In the past, they received this proclamation. Parelabete is an aorist and looks to the past.

In the present, they "stand" in the good news he proclaimed to them. Hestakate ("stand") is a present tense form. Paul commends the Corinthian Christians for maintaining the traditions handed on to them in 11:2. Their recognition of the traditional Christian creed provides a common basis for discussing the resurrection.

They "are being saved" through the good news Paul proclaimed. <u>Sozesthe</u> ("you are being saved") is a present passive form that indicates continuous action and points to the future. The phrase "us who are being saved" is found also in 1 Cor. 1:18; Acts 2:47; and 2 Cor. 2:15.

The salvation event includes both Jesus' death and resurrection. He who died is also He who was raised. Strictly speaking, the incarnation is also a part of that one salvation event. He who gave Himself up to die is none other than the pre-existent Son of God who became a man.

In the final analysis, neither Jesus' manner of life, nor His ministry, nor His personality, nor His character, nor His message are as basic as His death and resurrection. Paul does not remind the Corinthians of those other things, although it seems certain he told them those things, too.

Salvation is God's gift. It happens through God's initiative. We do not achieve it by our own efforts. It is given to us as a gift by God in Jesus' death and resurrection.

Paul encourages the Corinthian Christians to hold firmly to the good news he has proclaimed. The possibility of falling from such faith is implied here and in 1 Cor. 10:12. A person may not at his/her pleasure accept or not accept the good news.

Paul emphasizes strongly that he did not invent the good news. He received it. The Christian gospel was handed on by word of mouth in the same way that the traditions of Judaism were conveyed through the generations.

Vs. 3-5 seem to be a part of a Christian creed. Paul is rehearsing some of the primitive Christian tradition. This is one of the first written records of the apostolic tradition. Paul says that this <u>kerygma</u> has been the content of both his and the earlier proclamation. This passage may have supplied material for the formulation of the three ecumenical creeds, the Apostles', the Nicene, and the Athanasian.

The primitive Christian tradition apparently starts in v. 3. Where it ends is more difficult to determine. It seems certain that it goes at least to the end of v. 5. It is there the word "that" (<u>hoti</u>) last occurs. Vs. 3-5 contain a series of four that's. The word <u>hoti</u> may introduce a quotation in Greek. Ancient Greek did not have quotation marks. The apostolic tradition Paul quotes may or may not have had a written form.

Paul's proclamation which he believes the Corinthian Christians "hold firmly" goes to v. 8. He expands the apostolic tradition to include Jesus' appearance to him. The appearances following the one to him could have come from a list separate from the apostolic tradition. The word "they" in v. 11 may indicate that the apostles proclaimed all the appearances Paul lists.

What Paul says in v. 3 seems to contradict what he says in Gal. 1:11-12. There he claims to have received the gospel by divine revelation. In v. 3, he seems to emphasize that his proclamation follows an historic tradition. There he rejects the idea that he received "it from a human source, nor was I taught it, but I received it through a revelation of Jesus Christ." Here it is tradition, there it is revelation.

Paul does not mean that the content of the gospel, the facts about Jesus' life, especially His crucifixion and resurrection, were given to him apart from any human action or agent. We know little or nothing about the exact nature of the Christian instruction Paul received, but in v. 3 he indicates that he was given and has given a traditional presentation of the gospel. Paul gave the Corinthians a commonly shared gospel. The tradition he passed on predated him.

Actually, the tradition and the personal revelation belong together. They were combined by Paul. On the way to Damascus, the exaltation of the crucified One was revealed to him and thereby Jesus' significance in history. But he was already familiar with the basic story of Jesus; and because he did not believe it, he was persecuting those who proclaimed it.

The traditional message of the church is basically historical. The first part seems to be, "You killed Jesus, but God raised Him up," cf. Acts 2:22-36; 3:13-15; 4:11; 5:30-31. The second part is, "This happened according to scripture," cf. Acts 2:25-31; 3:18; 4:11. The third part is, "We are witnesses," cf. Acts 2:32-36; 3:15b; 5:32.

Jesus' death displays the love of God for us, cf. Rom. 8:32, and the self-giving love of Jesus, cf. Gal. 2:20; Eph. 5:2 and 25.

Some think that the Moriah scene in Gen. 22:1-14 was in

Paul's mind.as He developed the doctrine of the atoning power of Jesus' sacrificial death.[102] The Letter of Barnabas (7:3) is the earliest evidence of drawing out the Isaac-Christ typology according to which Isaac on Moriah was an Old Testament type of Christ. Clement of Alexandria, Tertullian, Irenaeus, and Origen were familiar with the theme that Christ was the Isaac of the gospel.

In Christian art, the sacrifice of Isaac (called Akeda) played a role from the 4th century onwards. It occurs in the frescoes at Dura. In the case of both Jesus and the Akeda, it is the sacrifice of a son flowing from a divine command. In one case, the sacrifice is made by One whom God sent and who knows Himself to be the Messiah. In the other, it is a man who is to sacrifice his only son, not God Himself. But Abraham acts at the divine command. On that son depends the fate of Israel and the world. But the sacrifice of Isaac does not reach completion.

The early Christian formula contains more than bare historic fact. Not only did Christ die, but He died "for our sins." This idea is probably taken from the Suffering Servant Song of Is. 53, cf. vs. 5, 6, 8, and 12. There is an element of interpretation in the tradition. Furthermore, it happened "in accordance with the scriptures," as did the resurrection, according to v. 4.

The logical connection between Jesus' death and the forgiveness of human sins is beyond our comprehension. It can only be explained in terms of love.

Huper ("for") includes the meanings "to our advantage," "in our place," or "as our representative," cf. 2 Cor. 5:14-15 and Gal. 3:13. The huper formula occurs frequently in the writings of Paul. It is huper with the genitive. Occasionally, peri with the genitive or dia with the accusative is used. Huper and peri are interchangeable in kerygmatic formulations. The meaning has to do with Jesus' vicarious atoning death.

Rabbinic Judaism knows nothing of a suffering Messiah who would take upon Himself the burden of humiliation and death for the sins of the world. Some have felt that it might have existed in smaller Jewish communities, but others consider it highly improbable that this notion existed anywhere in pre-

Christian Judaism. Wherever the relationship of people to God is based on law, wherever righteousness by law is the fundamental consideration and no way of salvation is known except that of law, no room remains for a suffering Messiah who takes upon Himself the guilt of others. It must have shocked the Jews to hear it said that Christ died "for our sins."

The double appeal to scripture in so brief a statement, cf. vs. 3 and 4, is deliberate and important. The agreement between prophecy and fulfillment is made.

The Old Testament testimony of what took place is appropriately placed before the apostolic testimony. The apostolic testimony begins in v. 5. "The scriptures" Jesus fulfilled by His death and resurrection must be Is. 53. Paul is not the creator of the doctrine of the atoning death of Christ.

Jesus' burial is recorded in all four gospels. It was evidently regarded as important. It is evidence that a genuine death and a genuine resurrection took place.

The resurrection is proclaimed with a passive construction, "He was raised." This appeals to Jewish sensitivities, because it avoids the use of the divine name. The passive construction is equivalent to saying that God raised Jesus.

All events listed in the creed Paul proclaims were witnessed except the resurrection. No one saw that. God raised Jesus.

The tense of "he was raised" in Greek (egegertai) is different from that of the preceding two verbs, "died" (apethanen) and "he was buried" (etaphe). It is a present perfect that indicates completed action with enduring results. Christ was brought back to life in past time and in the present continues to live. Paul is emphasizing that the resurrection of Christ is of enduring force and significance.

Jesus' death and burial witness to Jesus' true humanity. He lived out a human life at our level. By His resurrection, Jesus raised us up to His level.

Jesus' resurrection witnesses to the nature of the ultimate victory over death. At His resurrection, Jesus was translated into an entirely new mode of existence. His resurrection was quite different from the kind of resuscitations experienced by Jairus' daughter in Luke 8:40-42 and 49-56, the widow's son at

Nain in Luke 7:11-17, or Lazarus in John 11:1-44. They died again. Jesus did not and will not die again. All who are baptized into Jesus' death share in His resurrection, cf. Rom. 6:3-9.

The resurrection of Jesus means removal from human time and space into another dimension, that of God. Jesus is the prototype of Christian existence after death. In His victory over death, we see our victory. It was not an escape from His human perishable frame. It was a bodily existence in which marks that allow for the recognition of individuality remain, cf. John 20:24-29, but it was not subject either to death or to the normal constraints of bodily existence as we know them in this world, according to Luke 24:31 and 36 and John 20:19 and 26. After He rose, Jesus appeared to many who touched Him and saw Him consume food, cf. Luke 24:41-43.

In the world in which Paul lived, beliefs and hopes about the after-life varied considerably. On the one hand, belief in personal immortality was not very common in Roman paganism. There was not even much longing for it. Tombstone epigraphs repeat a joke about death: "I was not, I am not, I care not." On the other hand, the literature of the philosophers seems to assume widely held beliefs in personal immortality. Even in Judaism, beliefs about a future life varied from one group to another.

Old Testament/Jewish apocalypticism spoke of the new life given in the end-time, cf. Is. 26:19. The disciples announced that this took place in Jesus.

When Paul says "that (Jesus) was raised on the third day," this does not mean that He lay dead in His tomb for three days as western civilization counts three days. Jesus was buried about six o'clock on Friday evening, and He rose about six o'clock on Sunday morning. That amounts to thirty-six hours or a day and a half. But the people of Paul's time counted a part of a day as a whole day. Jesus was in the tomb a few hours on Friday, all day Saturday, and a few hours on Sunday. That's three days, the early church said.

The phrase "on the third day" was a part of the earliest tradition. It is hardly less firmly rooted in the tradition of the church than the resurrection itself. It is a part of the passion predictions in Mark 8:31; 9:31; 10:34; and Luke 24:46.

The church very consciously tied itself to early formulas as a way of avoiding the intrusion of false doctrine. One problem with this kind of policy is that later generations may misunderstand terminology that is divorced from its setting.

In the first century, the soul was thought to remain in the neighborhood of a dead person for three days. In the Jewish view, on the fourth day, the separation of soul and body was final.

The scriptures say that the Messiah is "to rise from the dead on the third day," according to 1 Cor. 15:4 and Luke 24:46. But it is difficult to find an Old Testament passage that prophesies Jesus' resurrection on the third day. Peter points in Acts 2:25-28 to Ps. 16:8-11 as prophetic of Jesus' resurrection; the burden of Peter's citation seems to be v. 10. But none of these passages speaks of a resurrection on the third day. Some have suggested 2 Kings 20:5 which speaks of Hezekiah being healed on the third day, but relating the healing of Hezekiah to the resurrection seems to be a stretch. Hos. 6:2 talks about the restoration of Israel on the third day after the punishment for her infidelity. The New Testament thinks of Jesus as the new Israel, punished for our sins and raised for our justification. Talking about His resurrection, Jesus refers to Jonah 1:17 in Matt. 12:40, but Jesus wasn't in the tomb "three days and three nights," only 36 hours. The plural "scriptures" in the phrase "according to the scriptures" suggests that Paul may have in mind the totality of the Old Testament.

While the phrase occurs twice in vs. 3-5, it appears nowhere else in the Pauline corpus. Some consider this more evidence that Paul is quoting some sort of creedal statement.

He testifies to Jesus' resurrection through references to His appearances not through a description of His rising. These were real visible manifestations.

Paul does not mention any appearance to women, although the four gospels indicate that Jesus appeared to some women first. The reason for this may be that a woman's testimony was not considered valid in law at that time. Their testimony was useless for attesting to the resurrection.

At best, only two of the appearances Paul lists are mentioned also in the gospels. One is the allusion to the appearance to Peter in Luke 24:34. In Matt. 28:16-17, it is to eleven rather than the twelve that Jesus appears; but the term "the twelve" was a technical term for a certain group of Jesus' followers. That group had been diminished by one due to Judas' suicide.

Not included in the gospels are the appearances Paul lists to more than 500 brethren, to James, to all the apostles, and to Paul himself. The appearance to all the apostles in v. 7 may be a reference to the ascension. If included, it would add to the appearances mentioned both by Paul and the gospels.

Six appearances Paul does not list include the one to the women on their return from the grave in Matt. 28:9-10, to Mary Magdalene in John 20:14-17, to the two disciples on the way to Emmaus in Luke 24:13-31, and to the disciples that evening in Luke 24:36-49 and John 20:19-24. This group of disciples includes more than "the twelve," according to Luke 24:33. Thomas was not present, according to John 20:24. Thomas was present a week later in John 20:26-29. Another appearance Paul does not list is to the disciples at the Sea of Tiberius in John 21.

There is considerable difficulty in harmonizing the details of the various resurrection narratives.

Paul mentions Cephas first as one to whom Jesus appeared following His resurrection. The passive verb, ophthe ("he appeared"), indicates that this is something that happened to Peter. The active party is Jesus. This is not a vision. Cephas sees Jesus with his eyes. This can be said also of the other appearances.

Ophthe seems to have been a technical term already when it was used for the appearances of Jesus. The LXX uses it when God addressed Abram in Gen. 12:7. It is used also in Acts 7:2, 30, and 35. In His post-resurrection appearances, Jesus came to His disciples as God to renew His fellowship with them.

The order in which Paul lists the appearances seems to be significant. When the risen Christ appeared to Peter first, He put His seal, so to speak, on the distinction He had given Peter during His lifetime by naming him Cephas, cf. Matt. 16:13-20.

One reason the appearance to Peter is only alluded to in the gospels and that only in Luke 24:34 may be that Peter was alone at the time. This would tend to make Jesus' appearance suspect as being only a vision. It would not tend to support the resurrection as would those appearances made to more than one person. In the church, however, the fact that Jesus appeared to Peter first probably contributed greatly to his authoritative position.

Another significant thing is that the "that's" end with the appearance to Peter. Some say this means that Paul ends what he "received" at this point. He supplements the data he received. The word "that" is replaced with the word "then." Eita and epeita ("then") may have either temporal or logical significance.

Some identify the appearance "to more than five hundred brothers and sisters at one time" with Pentecost, although the story of Pentecost in Acts 2:11-41 does not mention an appearance by Jesus.

By pointing out that even witnesses of the resurrection die, Paul provides in advance an argument for his thesis that believers who die during the time between the resurrection and the parousia receive life. Paul is writing 20 years or more after the resurrection.

James is called the Lord's brother in Matt. 13:55-56; Mark 6:3; and Gal. 1:18-19. He was not a full brother, since Joseph was not the father of Jesus. James did not believe in Jesus before the resurrection, according to John 7:2-5. Jesus' appearance to James is frequently understood as the conversion of James. He is a "pillar" apostle in Gal. 2:9. He became the head of the Jerusalem church after Peter had to leave Jerusalem. He suggested the compromise between the Jerusalem church and those preaching to the gentiles in Acts 15:12-29. His importance is indicated also in Acts 21:18.

When Paul says that Jesus appeared "to all the apostles," he seems to refer to a group larger than the twelve. He says that Jesus appeared to the twelve in v. 5. He does not say that Jesus appeared "to all the apostles" at one time. There may have been a number of appearances. The important thing is that all the apostles saw the risen Lord. That was one of the stipulated requirements when the replacement was chosen for Judas, in cf. Acts 1:21-22.

This requirement was met by Paul. He claims that the risen Christ appeared to him, too. Later the exalted Christ appeared also to Stephen, cf. Acts 7:55-56. This was an apocalyptic vision, is not counted as an appearance, and is not listed by Paul.

Paul did not come to apostleship in the normal way. He was not with Jesus from the preaching of John the Baptist to the time when He was lifted up. His conversion appears as an abnormal and violent birth. It is described in Acts 9:1-19; 22:6-11; and 26:12-18.

Paul calls himself "one untimely born." Ektromati is the Greek word for a miscarriage, an abortion, or a premature birth. It indicates that which is incapable of sustaining life on its own and requires divine intervention if it is to continue.

Paul equates the appearance to himself with the appearances to Peter, the twelve, and others. He uses the same verb that he uses in v. 5 to talk about the appearance to Peter. He thought of himself as having experienced an appearance of the risen Lord just as the other apostles did, cf. 1 Cor. 9:1.

Paul characterizes his persecuting activity as violent with the intent to destroy the church in Gal. 1:13. This is the reason he considers himself "unfit to be called an apostle." But he insists that he is an apostle "by the grace of God." God's grace toward him has not been "in vain." It was not empty and without success. He says that He "worked harder than any of them."

Paul describes the extent of his work in Rom. 15:18-19. He preached the gospel from Jerusalem to Illyricum. It is customary to divide Paul's activity into three great missionary journeys. The first was to Cyprus and southern Asia Minor in Acts 13-14. The second was to Macedonia and Greece in Acts 16-18. The third was to western Asia Minor in Acts 19.

His claim that he "worked harder than any of them" is illustrated in 2 Cor. 11:21-29. The word ekopiasa ("worked") means to work hard, to work to the point of exhaustion.

Paul's boasting to the Corinthians, as well as in other places, is not to seek praise for what he has personally achieved. Rather his boasting is in praise of God for what He has done through Paul. His accent lies not only on the laborious effort but also on the result.

Regarding the statement that he "worked harder than any of them," Luther said: "he does not wish to belittle the true apostles, among whom he also numbers himself, but he is attacking the others, the false apostles, who are criticizing him and finding fault with him. But if someone wishes to apply these words . . . to all the apostles, he may interpret them to mean that Paul's work was more extensive than that of all the others. . . . Paul penetrated the entire Roman empire with the Word . . . . he traveled farther in his apostolate . . . he got in touch with and covered more countries and people with his preaching than the others. . . . lest some one find reason to suppose that he is arrogant with his boasting and that he wants to exalt himself over all the other apostles . . . he is quick to add 'though it was not I, but the grace of God which is with me, etc.'"[103]

Luke 5:1-11

Akoloutheo means to follow and is a technical term in the New Testament for becoming a disciple of Jesus, cf. 5:27-28; 9:23, 49, 57, 59, 61; 18:22, 28. Simon Peter becomes a disciple of Jesus after he sees Jesus cast out demons, cf. 4:33-36, and heal people, cf. 4:38-41; after he hears Him teach, cf. 4:31-32 and 5:3, and "proclaim the good news of the kingdom of God," cf. 4:43-44; and after he is involved in a nature miracle, cf. 5:4-7. Andrew, Peter's brother, cf. Mark 1:16, probably was with Peter in doing these things. James and John, Peter's fishing partners, followed Jesus, too.

Peter is acquainted with Jesus when Jesus boards his boat. Peter probably was in the synagogue when Jesus taught there and commanded an unclean demon to come out of a man. When Jesus finished teaching in the synagogue, He entered Simon's house and healed Simon's mother-in-law. Jesus probably stayed with Simon overnight, cf. Luke 4:38-42. The miracle with the fish happened some time later.

When Jesus taught in the synagogue at Capernaum, "He spoke with authority," that is, like a king, according to Luke 4:32. Following this statement, the evangelist gives other examples of Jesus' verbal authority. He drove out of a man "the spirit of an unclean demon" in 4:33-35 and rebuked the demons in v. 41. He healed Peter's mother-in-law in 4:38-39 by rebuking her fever. He got Peter to row out into deep water and let down his nets despite a recent frustrating experience. He assuaged Peter's fear and made him a disciple. Jesus' word was very powerful.

"The crowd was pressing in on (Jesus) to hear the word of God," is the way the story begins. The people did not come to hear the scriptures. They came to hear Jesus. Some people think "the word of God" always means the Bible, but here it means the teaching of Jesus. "The word of God" can be understood as the word that comes from God, subjective genitive, or as objective genitive, the word about God. The word of God Jesus proclaims is called "the good news of the kingdom of God" in Luke 4:43. It is "the good news" that God came to the earth in the person of Jesus of Nazareth to assert His reign as king. Jesus is the Messiah God promised to send. He assumed the divine reign in His passion, cf. Luke 22:69 and 23:38 and 42. To work with Jesus, Peter, Andrew, James, and John left their occupation as fishermen to catch people, to use the metaphor of Jesus.

The miracle of fish led Peter to a better understanding of Jesus and caused Peter to fall "down at Jesus' knees, saying, 'Go away from me, Lord, for I am a sinful man!" He realized that Jesus lived in a realm or sphere which he himself could not attain. He was amazed. The emphasis is on Jesus and what He did and not on the sinful things Simon has done. The main point is missed if Simon's confession, "I am a sinful man!" is traced to a sudden awareness of great sins he committed in comparison to the sinlessness of Jesus. Peter's upbringing and religious training made him very sensitive to the difference between the holy and the sinful. He realized that he did not belong in holy circles. Luke plainly says that Peter's confession was prompted by amazement "at the catch of fish that they had taken." It was not produced by remembrance of sins he committed.

Jesus' words, "Do not be afraid," are often associated with theophanies. Peter's reaction was not unusual from people who came into the presence of the holy. They recognized the great distance between what is holy and what is human. Peter became aware of the holiness of Jesus.

Peter had seen Jesus perform miracles before, cf. Luke 4:31-41. What was different this time was that the miracle happened in a realm with which Peter was very familiar. Peter was a fisherman by profession. That explains his amazement. People just don't do what Jesus did.

Luke says that "all who were with him" were similarly "amazed." Who were these people? We may assume that Andrew is one, cf. Mark 1:16. James and John cannot be counted among "all who were with him," because they are mentioned separately in v. 10. We do not know any others. It is strange that the word pantas ("all") is used. The difficulty must have been noted early. The phrase "all who were with him" is omitted in an important manuscript, namely, D.

Is. 6:5 records an experience by the prophet Isaiah similar to that of Peter. Isaiah's "Woe is me!" is not evoked by the consciousness of sins he committed but is a reaction to his awareness of the numinous. It is an immediate and spontaneous reflex that devalues everything that exists. On the other hand, it expresses appreciation for that which is holy. It is not a moral judgment but a reaction to a confrontation with that which is transcendent. A natural person cannot know or imagine such a feeling but only a person who is in the Spirit.

Peter's response to the numinous has been called creature-feeling or creature consciousness by Rudolf Otto.[104] It includes the diminution of self into nothingness. It is very different from the littleness, weakness, or dependence of which we may become aware under other circumstances.

Just as the angel purged the prophet by touching "a live coal" to his lips and mouth in Is. 6:6-7, so Jesus purges Peter when He makes him a partner in His enterprise.

Luke 5:1-11 characterizes Jesus' ministry to "tax collectors and sinners." In His teaching/preaching and by His actions, He makes it clear that divine favor is not extended on the basis of what a person does. Jesus bridges the gap between sinners and the holy God in His own person.

Peter's regard for Jesus grows in this story. He calls Him "Master" in v. 5 and "Lord" in v. 8. Epistates ("Master") means overseer, director, or master. It implies that the person addressed has authority. It is used here of one who has the right to give orders. The word is used for Jesus only by Luke in 8:24, 45; 9:33, 49; 17:13. With the exception of Luke 17:13, the word is used only by disciples. The usual term employed by people outside Jesus' immediate circle is "teacher," didaskalos, cf. 7:40; 8:49; 9:38. "Lord" (Kurios) represents a higher degree of respect and awe than "Master."

It is idle to speculate whether what Jesus does is a miracle of omniscience or creation.

There is an air of extravagance about the catch of fish just as with many of Jesus' nature miracles, cf. John 2:1-11 and 21:1-11.

"They left everything and followed," Luke says. This is the price of discipleship also according to Luke 5:28 and 14:33. No one has more than enough; no one has too little. Everyone has just the right amount to become a disciple of Jesus: it costs everything. For other examples of this message, see Matt. 13:44-46. Disciples are called to renunciation and ministry. Peter describes his commitment and that of the other apostles in Luke 18:28 and Matt. 19:27.

What can be said about the faith of the four men? There is little indication that they understood Jesus, His ministry, or the assignment He gave them. Yet their trust was unquestioning, simple, and complete. Later would come the teaching. At this point, they had the experience of the great draught of fishes, Jesus' teaching, a number of healing miracles, and a number of times He cast out demons. Their confidence in Jesus was already indicated when they pushed out into deep water and let down their nets. They had been working all night and had caught nothing.

Jesus gives Peter a directive: "you will be catching people."

That phrase in a story about fishing, if detached from the actual context, may conjure up a false image, namely, that of an individual sitting relaxed beside a lovely lake casting a baited hook into the water, waiting for a nice sized fish to grab the hook, and then reeling it in. In this sense, fishing is a sport. The reality of Peter's fishing was quite different. It was a cooperative effort of several people and often more than one boat. No attempt was made to lure the fish or trick them. The individual skill involved was knowing where the fish were and either dragging a net or casting a net there. Then the fish were hauled in. Peter's fishing was a commercial effort to secure his livelihood and support his family.

If this story is used as a metaphor for evangelism – as the church has often used it – evangelism is a group project with several people coordinating their efforts. The men had no choice as to what they were going to do. Jesus did not take note of their special skills and abilities. He simply confiscated them and announced how He would use them. People-catching is not a matter of strategy. It is Jesus' work, and He directs the people whom He uses. Their fellowship with Him involves the work they do.

Mark 1:16-18 is the second evangelist's account of the call of Peter, Andrew, James, and John. It is quite different from the story Luke tells in 5:1-11. While Jesus says, "Follow me," to the four men only in Mark's story, the men leave their fishing occupation and follow Jesus in both.

This is a remarkable story. The men experience their greatest professional success, and then they leave everything to work for Jesus. Jesus gives Peter great material prosperity. Two boats loaded with fish must have been worth quite a bit. Then Jesus assigns him a different job, "catching people."

Many consider the metaphor "catching people" strange, because what fishermen do to fish is not salutary. The metaphor is to be explained on the superficial level of gathering in. The implication is that people are saved from death and given life as they are gathered into the kingdom of God. Disciples are nets Jesus uses to catch people.

Luke shows considerable regard for Peter in his gospel. He

lists him first among the twelve in 6:14. Peter is the spokesman for the disciples in 9:20, 33; and 18:28. He, James, and John are closely associated with Jesus, according to 8:51 and 9:28. Luke tells of Peter's denial of Jesus in 22:33-34 and 54-62. But Luke omits Jesus' rebukes of Peter which Mark gives in 8:32-33 and in 14:37.

The fish were probably white musht. The five species of this group have a long dorsal fin that looks like a comb. The biggest and most common is the Tilapia Galilea which can reach a length of 1.5 feet and weigh about 4.5 pounds. The body has a silvery color. With the cooling of the waters of "the lake of Gennesaret" as winter begins, the musht congregate and move in shoals, especially toward the northern part of the lake where there are warm springs. The musht is the only large fish in the lake that moves in shoals. Its flat shape makes it especially suitable for frying. The skeleton consists of an easily detachable backbone and relatively few small bones, and thus the fish is easy to eat. It has long been known as St. Peter's fish. The name is good for tourism. The fish is good eating, and many tourists enjoy them.[105]

Other names for "the lake of Gennesaret" are the Sea of Tiberias and the Sea of Galilee. It is formed by the Jordan River and is about 680 feet below sea level. The lake is 14 miles long and 6 miles wide. The land along the shore is remarkably fertile. At the time of Jesus, it was surrounded by a number of flourishing towns. Gennesaret was a small, fertile, and heavily populated district west of the lake. It lay south of Capernaum.

Tradition has identified the place where this event took place as Tabgha.[106] In the winter, fishermen from Capernaum worked there. Several warm mineral springs attracted fish. Tabgha is a corruption of the Greek for "Seven Springs."

The boats that plied the lake of Gennesaret were open craft some 20 to 30 feet in length. When Jesus approached Peter and his fellow fishermen, they were cleaning their nets of seaweed and other foreign matter.

According to Jewish custom, teachers sat while teaching. Jesus teaches sitting in Simon's boat.

6th Sunday after the Epiphany

Year A

Deuteronomy 30:15-20

Moses probably did not have abortion in mind when he spoke these words to Israel on the east side of the Jordan, although some church people use a few words from this pericope today as though abortion is the major issue. The issues of life and death Moses is addressing involve worshipping God and obeying Him in a broad way.

It is a mistake to say that the words "If you obey the commandments of the Lord your God . . . you shall live . . . and the Lord your God will bless you . . ." make ancient Israel a nation of law, as though she earned her special relationship with God by obedience. Obedience was not a prerequisite for God's choice of Israel as His special people. The order was rather the reverse. First, Jahweh chose Israel. Then He gave that people His law and called on them to obey it.

When Israel was chosen, she had not yet had the opportunity to obey. This is clearly expressed in Deut. 27:9-10: "This very day you have become the people of the Lord your God." Afterwards comes the command for obedience: "Therefore obey the Lord your God, observing his commandments and his statutes that I am commanding you today."

God's choice was to motivate Israel's obedience, cf. Deut. 14:1-2. Love motivated God's choice of Israel, cf. Deut. 7:6-8 and 11. Israel's response to the divine love given her should be love for Jahweh and clinging to Him alone. That would mean life for her. Obedience to the commandments is what it means to love Jahweh.

Deuteronomy calls itself torah, but the term cannot be translated by the English word "law," because "law" has a dark side. Deuteronomy is often called the book of the law or a law code, but this designation misses the essential characteristic of the book which is life. The Deuteronomic term torah means Jahweh's saving will.

However, there are a number of places where the reception of the blessings of salvation is in actual fact conditional and made dependent on Israel's obedience, cf. Deut. 6:18; 7:12; 8:1; 9:8-9; 16:20; 19:8-9; 28:9; and elsewhere. These imperatives are motivated by final clauses: "do this, that you may remain alive, that it may be well with you, that you may enter into the land." Still Deuteronomy's great offer of grace is not annulled and a legal way of salvation proclaimed. Even those cases that seem to make salvation conditional and dependent on Israel's obedience are prefaced by a declaration of Jahweh's election and His love. Preceding the imperatives stand Deuteronomy's indicatives: "you are now the people set apart for Jahweh," cf. Deut. 7:6, 14:2, 21, 26:18. The commandments do not call into question those indicative statements. The imperatives bid Israel to accept the blessings given and to take her place in that relationship with obedience and gratitude. They are exhortations directed to those who have already received the word of salvation.

Some have summed up the message of Deuteronomy with the phrase "become what you are." The form is called paraclesis. Paraclesis is an exhortation in view of the indicative fact of salvation. This form is extensively developed in the New Testament epistles.

The setting of Deuteronomy is the plains of Moab just before srael enters the promised land of Canaan, cf. Deut. 1:1; 4:45-6. The generation that experienced the original covenant eremony at Mt. Sinai, cf. Ex. 19:1-8, has died as punishment or their disobedience. Moses addresses a new generation of sraelites. The promises of God are about to be realized.

Deuteronomy is an appeal for exclusive loyalty to Jahweh, he God of their fathers, the God who brought the nation into being, redeemed her from bondage, revealed His holy will, guided, protected, and disciplined her, and willed for her peace and prosperity in the good land He allotted to her. In view of what Jahweh did for the nation, the worship of any other god or gods would be ingratitude. God's love should be reciprocated with love, and this love should be manifest in obedience to His righteous will in all areas of personal and national life. Other saving events in Israel's history are also used to motivate obedience in Deut. 10:20-22; 15:15; 16:1; 24:17-18.

Moses reviews the journey that Israel made from Egypt to the east side of the Jordan River. He draws from this history conclusions about the power and nature of Jahweh. Jahweh has controlled the whole process and thus loyalty is owed to Him.

At Sinai - Deuteronomy always calls it Horeb - Jahweh gave much more law to Moses than Moses gave to the people, cf. Deut. 5:22-31. The people were incapable of listening to the whole law. Moses proclaimed the entire revelation of the divine will before his death. It was to be Israel's rule of life in the land of Canaan. Deuteronomy regards itself as the full revelation given at Sinai. A later appendix is given in a special covenant made in the land of Moab, cf. Deut. 29:1-15.

Israel is to be a holy people, a different people. They are to live in righteousness and brotherly love before God. Other nations will notice and marvel, cf. Deut. 4:7-8. Through their response of obedience to God's will, Israel will find life, peace, and prosperity. But if they lust after other gods, if they practice injustice and oppression, if they gloat over their achievements and trust in their own strength, they will perish from the earth.

Deuteronomy stands between promise and fulfillment. The election has occurred. God has revealed His saving intention and His determination to lead the people of Israel into the land of Canaan. But entry is still in the future. Israel is still on the way to the land of salvation, the promised land, the land of Canaan: "you have not as yet come into the rest and the possession that the Lord your God is giving you," cf. Deut. 12:9. The Israel addressed by Deuteronomy is still waiting for the fulfillment of that promise. In this "not yet" situation, many dangers threaten. Much can still happen, even disaster. A deep concern runs through the Deuteronomic paraclesis that Israel can lose her salvation in the last minute before the fulfillment.

God redeemed Israel from bondage in Egypt. The question is, what will be her response? Will she love and serve Jahweh in thankful response, or will she go after other gods and thus lose her life and her good? Jahweh sets before her the choice of life or death. The people of God can fail to possess their final inheritance. They can fail to enter into the promised fulfillment. Israel stands at a critical and decisive moment in her history.

With the occupation of Canaan, a new period in her history will begin. Anticipating her needs in her new environment, Moses explains the law that will determine her status as a covenant nation. Each generation is to obligate itself to the same basic principles of the covenant the fathers entered at Mt. Sinai. Only minor adjustments will be necessary to meet the needs of life in Canaan. The idea is often expressed, "These are the statutes and ordinances that you must diligently observe in the land that the Lord . . . has given you to occupy all the days that you live on the earth," cf. Deut.12:1; 17:14; 18:9; 19:1; 21:1; 26:1. The goal of the book of Deuteronomy is to make Israel listen to the revelation of the will of Jahweh in all circumstances. Covenant renewal is a frequently repeated event in the life of Israel. Joshua repeats the injunction to choose in Joshua 24:14-24.

Faithfulness to God is motivated in three principal ways: 1) an appeal to God's love that should inspire the response of love; 2) a call for thanksgiving in view of what God has done; 3) the use of rewards and punishments. Life, peace, prosperity, and prestige among the nations are among the rewards promised for faithfulness. Death, disease, drought, famine, oppression, captivity, and national extinction are held up as deterrents to unfaithfulness.[107]

The Hebrew word tov ("prosperity") means good. In Deuteronomy, the word "good" is used primarily for the gracious actions of Jahweh and not for the actions of Israel. Deuteronomy emphasizes the goodness of God toward His people. The people are to focus not on doing good but on receiving good. The outpouring of God's goodness is set in a covenant context that assumes obedience.

The scope of the goodness of Jahweh is extremely inclusive. It functions as a synonym for shalom in its most wholistic sense. In Deut. 30:15, "good" or "prosperity" is a synonym for "life." There is no sorting out or separating of the spiritual and the material, cf. Deut. 6:10-12 and 8:12-17. God's goodness includes cattle, children, produce, and rain in Deut. 28:11, life in 5:16 and 33 and 6:24, length of days in 4:40; 5:16; 22:7, the land in 5:16, 33 and 6:18, and the promise of many offspring in 6:3. For this reason, NRSV translates the word tov with "prosperity."

Love for God is acted out in obedience to God's commandments. Love in Deuteronomy is a verb, an action, and not an inner emotion. God's love toward Israel consists in His deliverance of her out of Egypt, His guidance of her through the wilderness, and His gift to her of the promised land, cf. 26:5-9. Israel's love toward God is to be active obedience in response.

The laws of Deuteronomy are intended to spell out the content of that obedience. The commandments are designed as guides for the life of the redeemed. They do not establish the relationship with God but give guidance about how to live in the relationship that has already been effected by God. Preachers have a wealth of subjects with which to deal and can select from among the commandments materials to fit the situation of their congregation. Many of the commandments of Deuteronomy are no longer relevant to our lives, cf. 18:1-8; 22:12; 23:12-13. Some laws have been countermanded or transformed and deepened by our Lord, cf. Mark 10:2-12 vs. Deut. 24:1-4; Matt. 5:21 vs. Deut. 5:17; Matt. 5:27 vs. Deut.

5:18; Matt. 5:38 vs. Deut. 19:21. Yet often the intention of the commandments remains valid for Christians and is confirmed by the teachings of Jesus.

To love God means to show liberality and kindness toward the poor, cf. Deut. 15:1-18; 23:19-20; 24:14-15, 19-22. It means to respect the neighbor's property, cf. 19:14; 23:24-25, and his dignity as a human being, cf. 24:10-11, even if he is a criminal being punished, cf. 25:1-3. It means to protect the neighbor against accidents, cf. 22:8, and to help him out when he has suffered loss, cf. 22:1-4. It means to practice justice in a court of law, cf. 16:18-20; 19:15-21; 24:17-18, and in all business and commerce, cf. 25:13-16. It means to recognize that there is a sphere of justice belonging to God that is beyond human justice, cf. 19:1-10. It means to protect the realm of nature as stewards of God's creation, cf. 20:19-20; 22:6-7; 25:4; 5:14. It means to foster the well-being of the family, cf. 24:5; 22:13-21, 22, 30, and to protect the chastity of the unmarried, cf. 22:23-29. It means to construct a society that reflects the justice, the love, and the mercy of God, cf. 5:15; 15:15; 16:12; 24:18, 22. The affirmation of 1 John 4:19 characterizes most of Deuteronomy's laws.

To love God is also to worship Him in sincerity and truth. It means to offer Him worthy and costly sacrifices, cf. 17:1 and 23:18, and to intend sincerely in one's heart what one says and vows to Him, cf. 23:21-23. It means to acknowledge with one's gifts God's ownership of creation, cf. 15:19-20; 26:1-11, and to thank Him with grateful hearts for His bounty.

Worship is above all a joyful occasion. With one of the three great, yearly, pilgrimage feasts, cf. 16:1-17, the payment of a vow, a tithe, or a freewill offering, cf. 12:1-19; 14:22-29, a special day of commemoration, cf. 27:1-8, or the offering of the first fruits, cf. 26:1-11, the thought always is that Israel shall "rejoice before the Lord," cf. 12:7, 12, 18; 14:26; 16:11, 14; 26:11; 27:7, because she is worshiping a God who first loved her.

Christians, too, face life or death. Jesus died on a cross for our salvation, and He made us His own people in Holy Baptism. He talks about the narrow way that leads to life and the broad way that leads to destruction in Matt. 7:13-14. The juxtaposition of indicative and imperative statements is evident in the New Testament writings.

The New Testament church was in a situation similar to that of ancient Israel. She expressed her own consciousness of election and the joy of being accepted by God as the people of His possession with the very same words as Deuteronomy, cf. 1 Pet. 2:9. The Epistle to the Hebrews also sees the distinctiveness of the situation of the church in that she is journeying toward the final fulfillment. It retains the conception of the wandering people of God and speaks, too, of the fulfillment of the promises as an entry into rest.

Nevertheless, we are not the people of Israel addressed by the preaching of Deuteronomy. We are not an earthly people with a king and an army that goes to war. We are not administered by elders, priests, and prophets. We do not celebrate Passover or the Feast of Tabernacles.

Israel has been delivered from slavery in Egypt, led through the wilderness, and brought to the eastern shore of the Jordan. Israel is underway, at midpoint between her redemption out of Egypt and her final fulfillment in the promised land. So, too, is the church. We have been redeemed out of slavery to sin and death and set on a pilgrimage toward the final fulfillment of God's promises to us of eternal life in heaven. All along the way, there are texts from Deuteronomy that tell what God is doing on the journey and how we are to respond to Him, Deut. 5:1-27; 7:6-11; and 8:1-10.

When preaching from Deuteronomy, the preacher does well to pair its text with a passage from the New Testament to acknowledge the mediation of Deuteronomy through the work of Jesus and to proclaim the New Testament outcome of Deuteronomy's words. Deuteronomy is not general moral law but instruction for a specific people with a particular history. The preacher must say that God's act in Jesus Christ was the final interpretation of the Old Testament. The final shape of the sermon must set forth Christian theology that accords with the apostolic witness of the New Testament. The preacher needs to explain how the congregation's relation to God is analogous to that of the covenant people's relation to God in Deuteronomy.

God gave only one nation, ancient Israel, instruction on how to live harmoniously with all the powers that are at work in the world. That knowledge is one of the greatest things people can possess. One cannot enjoy life by fighting the powers at work in the world. Israel did not understand the Decalogue as a prescription for ethical living. Rather it was a divine revelation through which God gave her the gift of life.

1 Corinthians 3:1-9

Six terms are used by Paul to describe the church at Corinth: "brothers and sisters," "spiritual people," "people of the flesh," "infants in Christ," "God's field," and "God's building." The terms give direction to the church for becoming the kind of people God wants them to be.

"Brothers" is the only Greek word in the text, but Paul means women, too. So the NRSV's inclusive translation gives the meaning accurately. "Brothers and sisters" describes the relationship between the members of the church. Fellowship is an issue in the church at Corinth.

"Spiritual people" is the kind of people the members of the church should be, but the term cannot be applied to the Corinthian Christians. Spiritual people are not jealous and do not engage in quarrelling as they are doing. Spiritual people do not behave "according to human inclinations." They "understand" and "receive the gifts of God's Spirit," cf. 1 Cor. 2:14, that include "love, joy, peace, patience, kindness, generosity, faithfulness, gentleness, and self-control," according to Gal. 5:22-23.

Paul says in 1:7 that the Corinthians "are not lacking in any spiritual gift;" but he still cannot speak to them as spiritual people, because they are acting "as people of the flesh." They are divided into cliques. Some of them claim to be followers of Paul and others of Apollos. Why Cephas (Peter) is not mentioned is not clear. The three factions are mentioned in 1:12, together with one more.

It is impossible to reconstruct the makeup or tenets of the

factions. The people were quarreling about their favorite preacher. The issue seems to have centered largely around personality. The tone of the letter suggests that Paul was mainly concerned that his authority and the gospel of Christ crucified that he preached, cf. 1 Cor. 2:2, were being undermined.

Acts 18:24-27 provides information about Apollos. He is a cultured Jew from Alexandria who has some knowledge of Christianity. He came to Ephesus and received more accurate instruction from Aquila and Priscilla. He wanted to go to Corinth. Paul, Aquila, and Priscilla had recently come from there. The church in Ephesus recommended Apollos to the church in Corinth. He apparently attracted a considerable following among the Corinthians.

One factor that led to the party spirit seems to have been that the Corinthians were fascinated with the concept of wisdom and with rhetorical skills. Neither Paul nor his gospel of Christ crucified depends on those things, cf. 2:1-5. The quarreling threatens to empty the gospel of its power. The dissension endorses the wisdom of the world. But the gospel does not conform to the wisdom of the world; it is foolishness to unbelievers.

Paul appeals for unity. The conversion of the Corinthians confirmed the truth that God chooses foolish things to shame the norms of the world, cf. 1:26-31. God was the source of their new life in Christ. Their faith rests not on human wisdom but on divine power; it rests on Christ crucified, cf. 2:1-5.

Eris ("quarrelling") and zelos ("jealousy") are difficult to distinguish.[108] They are listed in Gal. 5:20 as "works of the flesh" together with fornication, impurity, licentiousness, idolatry, sorcery, enmities, dissensions, factions, envy, drunkenness, and carousing. The works with which they are associated help to establish their evil character. Paul is thinking of ecclesiastical quarrels, cf. 1:11-13 and 3:5-9.

"People of the flesh" orient themselves around themselves. They pursue their own ends in self-sufficient independence of God. They behave according to human inclinations. They are controlled by human motives and feelings. They shape their life according to human standards and after models taken from the world. While quarrels characterize the relationship of people in the dog-eat-dog society of secular Corinth, they should not exist in the church.

Jealousy and quarreling are only a part of the damage being done by the "people of the flesh." Their view of the church and of the relationship of the preachers to the church is a greater problem. They think that the preachers own the church. They identify with the leader whose wisdom and oratory most clearly shows his authority.

Ouchi in v. 3 is a strengthened form of ou. It introduces a question that expects the answer yes.

Their "jealousy and quarreling" demonstrates that they are "infants in Christ" and not mature people. For this reason, Paul has been giving them baby-food instead of solid food. He has been feeding them milk. Their "jealousy and quarreling" shows that they are not ready for solid food. The writer to the Hebrews uses this same metaphor in Heb. 5:12-14.

Calling them "infants in Christ" is intended to deflate the Corinthians' arrogant quarreling just as is the term "people of the flesh," but it also softens that characterization. It tends to excuse their jealousy and quarreling. They are just babes in Christ. They are beginners in the area of Christian living.

Paul humiliates them when he calls them "infants in Christ." No one likes to be called a baby or immature. His words are aimed especially at the people who claim a high status as Christians, because the preacher they are associated with is greater than the other preachers.

Those who are newly born of the Spirit retain their natural desires for a time. This is not blameworthy. But to remain that way, that is, still using the judgments of the world, is worthy of rebuke.

The Corinthians immature behavior is a serious matter. That's why Paul makes an issue of it. They are abandoning the simple gospel for something that looks like solid food but has no nutritional value. It is a Corinthian brand of wisdom; it is not Christian. They are acting like unbelievers. They do not comprehend the "message about the cross."

The apostle speaks wisdom to "mature" Christians, but to

those who are still "babes" he explains the basic elements of the faith, as described in Heb. 5:12-14. "Mature" Christians have "come to the unity of the faith and of the knowledge of the Son of God," cf. Eph. 4:13. "Children" are "tossed to and fro and blown about by every wind of doctrine, by people's trickery, by their craftiness in deceitful scheming," cf. Eph. 4:14. Mature Christians "grow up" into Christ by "speaking the truth in love," cf. Eph. 4:15. When the body of Christ is working properly it grows; it builds "itself up in love," cf. Eph. 4:16.

In the early church, the newly baptized were given three sips from a cup of milk sweetened with honey. Tertullian called it "a foretaste of peace and fellowship."[109] The "milk" represented the elementary Christian instruction that offers the basic facts of salvation. "Solid food" is the wisdom of God that only the spiritual or mature Christians can receive.

It is not always possible to tell some people at once the whole matter of Christianity and of Christian living. They must have certain experiences and a certain amount of faith before they are able to accept some things. Giving people the proper instruction takes judgment and pastoral experience. Errors can be made in presenting too much too soon - or too little. The aim must always be to develop the person. However, as they are being built up, Christian people must be recognized as the church, as Paul does the Corinthians in 1:2.

Is it possible that the "solid food" Paul feels he cannot yet feed the Corinthian Christians has to do with the theology of the cross as opposed to the theology of glory?

Pneuma (spirit) is the miraculous divine power that stands in contrast to all that is human. Spirit is contrasted with "the flesh" or "behaving according to human inclinations" in v. 3. Paul says that "people of the flesh" who argue who is best among their spiritual leaders "are . . . merely human." He expresses a little frustration when he says, "Even now you are still not ready." That judgment had to cut the Corinthians deeply!

The terms "God's field" and "God's building" are used by Paul to address the Corinthians' wrong conception of the church. The metaphor of God's building is developed in vs. 10-17 and is outside of our first interest here. Vs. 5-9 use the language of God's field and are a part of the appointed Lesson. The metaphor makes the point that God, not the preachers, owns the church.

Paul establishes his and Apollos' relationship to God's field when he says that they are servants of the Lord. This makes the point that God directs the preachers, not the church. The Corinthians think that Paul and Apollos are their masters, but Paul says they are only God's servants who have been assigned the job of bringing them to faith. They were sent by the Lord not to be served but to serve them as Jesus did.

In calling himself a servant of the Lord, Paul does not give up his apostolic authority. He actually claims supreme authority. He says that he speaks for the Lord.

Paul and Apollos played an important role in the Corinthians' relationship to the church. Through the work of the two men, the faith of the Corinthians developed. Paul planted, and Apollos nurtured their faith. The story of the beginnings of the church in Corinth is in Acts 18:1-18.

God assigned Paul and Apollos their jobs. He set the goal, too, which was the growth of the church. The preachers are not rivals but share a mutual purpose that unites their efforts.

The RSV translation, "fellow workmen for God," is good. The preachers do not work with God so much as they work together for Him, and He works through them. They are His instruments.

In the ancient world, plant germination and growth were considered a divine miracle. Paul is stressing God's power that brought the church into being.

The metaphor must not be pressed too hard, as though only Paul planted and only Apollos watered, or Paul only planted but did not water and Apollos only watered and did not plant, too.

Jesus uses the metaphor of sowing seed for preaching the Word in Matt. 13:3-9, 24-30. Paul uses the agricultural metaphor again in Col. 2:7.

"Planted" (ephuteusa) and "watered" (epotisen) are aorists expressing completed action in past time. "Gave the growth" (euxanen) is imperfect denoting continued action. Paul is

406

referring to the planting and watering he and Apollos did in the past. But growth is continuing.

Paul says that what he and Apollos did is nothing. They were only farm hands. "God gave the growth." God made them the church. The work of Paul and Apollos, though different, were parts of the same effort. The important thing is not the work they did but the church, God's field.

The Corinthians should not try to reward Paul and Apollos. God will determine their pay. He will reward them based on what they accomplish. God's judgment will come later, and the Corinthians should wait until He gives it, cf. 4:5.

Other metaphors for the church Paul uses in his writings are the temple of God in 1 Cor. 3:10-17; Rom. 15:20; Col. 2:7; and Eph. 2:20-22 and a vineyard and the flock of God in 1 Cor. 9:7.

A sermon on this text could focus on the attitudes of preachers and congregations toward each other as they relate to "the message about the cross." In this world of hi-tech religion, huge Sunday crowds squint under the glare of spotlights as "their" preachers dazzle viewers with wisdom and rhetorical charm. The Christian public admires TV evangelists and big-time clergy. "I like to listen to ____." "He's OK, but I like ____ better." Everyone has their favorite preacher these days. "Preacher religion" is in. The result is an increasingly fragmented church. It sounds like the church in Corinth: "I belong to Paul, and you don't." Corinth may have been tame by comparison.

Actually, we may be more subtle than that. "He's my preacher" may be a cover for pride. We idolize effective leaders, dynamic preachers, good organizers, successful church-growth entrepreneurs, and successful fundraisers. Congregations like to brag about their ministers. It is a backdoor way of exalting themselves.

Preachers will not be outdone. They like to talk about "my church." It gives them a sense of power to pastor certain congregations. They think, "Only someone with my smarts and skills could do this."

There also are denominational claims. "I belong to Luther."

"I belong to Calvin." "I belong to Pope ___." No wonder the church is divided. Quarrels and party spirit are undercurrents in all the church does.

"Babies!" Paul says. "You are acting like babies!" The world is too much with us. We act like "people of the flesh." We behave "according to human inclinations." We are "merely human." We may think we are spiritual, but our behavior betrays us. We apply human standards to the Christian life. Competition and ownership have become working principles in the church. We bypass the theology of the cross which is difficult to accept in favor of a theology of glory.

So how should we think of the leaders of the church? They are servants assigned by God to do His bidding. They are called to promote Christ crucified, not themselves. Each has a God-given task. Apart from that task, they are nothing. All are equal in the eyes of God. People should not idolize or degrade them. They are not rivals for the loyalty of a congregation. Only God can praise or blame them for the work they do.

At the same time, the church should let herself be nurtured by God's servants. She should let the servants cultivate God's field. On the one hand, she ought not glorify her preachers for the work they do, but, on the other hand, she ought to acknowledge God's goodness when He sends her good preachers. The servants are sent for her good.

God alone gives life to the church. Preachers may labor long and hard using their many gifts, but, in the end, God gives the growth. Aside from their tasks, servants are nothing; God is everything. The church is His. The servants ought not regard the church as theirs. Neither should the people regard the church and its workers as theirs, no matter how much they have invested in it.[110]

Matthew 5:21-37

Murder, sex, divorce, and perjury are topics that fill the front pages of our daily newspapers and provide grist for the news mills of the television stations. They may not be the topics of a lot of preaching in the church these days. The prohibition of such matters may be taken for granted, or they may be considered too sensitive to deal with in a sermon. But Jesus takes them up in the Sermon on the Mount, and they are brought to the attention of the church in the lectionary.

The strictures expressed by Jesus in the Sermon on the Mount may be politely declined by many contemporary Christians, but they spell out the life of those who are in the kingdom of God. Jesus came to establish the kingdom of God on earth. He made it possible for everyone, including the worst offenders of what He teaches, to become a part of God's kingdom.

The Pharisees and scribes, who were the teachers in the Jewish synagogues, took the commandments of God's law seriously; but they applied them only to outward behavior. Jesus called for a greater righteousness from His disciples, cf. Matt. 5:20, a righteousness that involves the inner thoughts, desires, and intentions of people as well as their deeds. He uses several commandments as examples. God forbids not only the acts of murder, adultery, divorce, and perjury but even things that precede those acts, such as anger, name-calling, evil desire, etc.

Each of the four topics dealt with in Matt. 5:21-37 is introduced with some part of the formula, "You have heard that it was said to those of ancient times." Jesus then briefly states what the synagogues of His day taught. Following this, He announces what He teaches on the matter beginning with the phrase, "But I say to you."

The disciples heard the law read and expounded in the synagogue. Most teaching there was done orally. The synagogues did not have a lot of tracts and books. When Jesus addresses highly educated and cultured people like the Pharisees, the scribes, and the Sadducees, He begins, "Have you not read etc.," cf. Matt. 12:3, 5; 19:4; 21:16, 42; 22:31.

"It was said" is a passive construction; it is the numinous passive. It is a circumlocution for the name of God. It means, "God said."

People thought that Jesus was pitting His word against the law that had been given at Mt. Sinai through Moses. Actually, Jesus was doing more than that; He was claiming authority as the Author and Giver of that law. The law received at Mt. Sinai had been changed by the scribes and Pharisees. Jesus reinstated the law.

Matthew presents Jesus as the new Moses who assumes the place occupied in Judaism by the law and as One who stands above the law. He speaks with authority and not like the scribal and Pharisaic interpreters of the law. The people were able to tell the difference, cf. Mark 1:22. With the phrase "But I say to you," Jesus claims to be God.

I

On the matter of killing someone, the synagogue taught, "'You shall not murder'; and 'whoever murders shall be liable to judgment.'" The Fifth Commandment is recorded in Ex. 20:13 and Deut. 5:17. The killing of animals, insects, and plants is not forbidden. Hebrew has a special word for killing human beings, and that is the word used in the Fifth Commandment.

The Mosaic law said that whoever committed murder was to be put to death. The murderer was to be brought for judgment before the local council that met in the synagogue and was subordinate to the Great Council of Seventy, or the sanhedrin, at Jerusalem.

The scribes and Pharisees understood "kill" to mean "strike dead with the hand." According to them, the Fifth Commandment does not forbid anything beyond that. If a person's victim dies three or four days after being hit on the head, the person has not committed murder. Death is due to complications. Also a person is not guilty of murder if he can get another person to kill for him.

An example of this kind of thinking long before the Pharisees were organized as a sect in Judaism is in 1 Sam. 18:17. King Saul wants to get rid of David, so he sends him to fight against the Philistines hoping that he will be killed by them. He thinks that with such duplicity he will remain innocent of wrongdoing.

David's treatment of Uriah in 2 Sam. 11:14-17 is another example. Nathan makes very clear to David the wrong he did in 2 Sam. 12:1-9.

410

The Pharisees considered themselves pious even though they harbored anger, hatred, envy, pronounced curses and blasphemies on their enemies, and concocted evil schemes to get rid of people. In effect, Jesus says that a person may find as many ways to kill as he has organs. He may use his hand or his tongue. He may use signs and gestures. He may use his eyes to look at someone sourly or to begrudge him his life. He may even use his ears if he does not like to hear the other person mentioned. His hands may be still, his tongue quiet, his eyes and ears muffled; but he will be happy if the person is dead. Because he wants the other person out of his life, he is as guilty before God as a murderer.

"Judgment," "the council," and "the hell of fire" represent ascending jurisdictions. Anger, insult, and name calling are offenses of descending seriousness according to human estimations. Jesus assigns a higher court to what people consider lesser offenses. The human way of thinking does not agree with the way God judges.

Jesus is not saying that the person who is angry should be brought before the council. He is saying that such a person is as guilty as a murderer from the point of view of divine justice, cf. 1 John 3:15. The punishment that He pronounces on anger is the same the synagogue pronounces on murder.

The phrase translated in the NRSV "if you insult a brother or sister" can more literally be translated "whoever says to his brother, 'Raca.'" Raca is a casual angry word. It means fool or empty headed. Such words seek to hurt and to destroy people. It is doubtful that the council would have regarded it an offense to say "Raca" to someone.

The person who speaks a casual angry word against another has committed a more serious offense, Jesus says, than the person who becomes angry. He doesn't mean that such a person should be hauled before the higher court, but that his offense in the eyes of divine justice is as great.

Calling another person a fool is an insult. It openly disgraces the person in the eyes of other people and hopes others will despise him.

"The hell of fire" may be intended to be a reference to God's

411

own court. The NRSV footnote says that the Greek reads "the fire of Gehenna." Gehenna was the Hellenized form of the name of the valley of Hinnom at Jerusalem in which fires were kept burning constantly to consume the refuse of the city. It had come to signify the place of fiery torment reserved for the punishment of the wicked. Gehenna is a frequently used reference to the future, final punishment in Matthew, cf. 5:29, 30; 10:28; 18:9, 23:15, 33, and their footnotes.

The greater righteousness that Jesus teaches calls for love. Love wishes the other person well and seeks to effect the other's welfare. Anything less than that with regard to another's physical well-being is a sin against the Fifth Commandment.

Anger is not good. Holding on to anger leads to vengeance. When we seek vengeance, we put ourselves in the position of the highest Judge. But "Vengeance is mine, I will repay, says the Lord," cf. Rom. 12:19 and Deut. 32:35.

People who know what Jesus is talking about when He forbids anger prove thereby their own guilt. What adultery and homicide are, one can learn from others. Anger and evil desires, one cannot know at second hand. People must experience them personally before they know what they are.

In forbidding anger, Jesus gives profound insight into its nature and human nature. More destructive than an act done in anger is the inner feeling of anger when held in and unresolved. It can harden into resentment, hostility, and hatred. If intense or if allowed to become chronic, anger makes love impossible. It also gives people a sense of insecurity and emptiness. Human relationships grounded in such feelings are like poison. Anger aims to destroy its object. It also prevents us from receiving what we most need, namely, love. It is therefore self-destructive.

Jesus' point that it is important to be reconciled "quickly," is an insight of modern psychology. When we temporize with anger and hatred, we intensify it. When we defend and justify anger, it tends to take us over and control us. The inner structure of our personality becomes sick through holding onto and fostering hostile, destructive feelings. The day may come when this process cannot be reversed. We may literally become imprisoned by our own hostilities.

The opposite of anger, hatred, and murder is love which moves us to help our neighbor in every physical need. Helping people meet their physical needs is a lifetime occupation. To busy ourselves with other great things that God has not commanded and so to become unable time wise to help our needy neighbor is to fail in following God's direction.

Collective hatred, strife, and conflict, be it between a husband and wife or between Iran and the United States, the hatred of one family for another, of one nation for another, of one race for another is sin. That relationship is sick in which people are joined to each other by a common hatred of another person or of other people. Nothing has really been gained when a husband and wife become reconciled and continue to hate the neighbors or the mother-in-law.

Anger is not always bad; it is sometimes necessary and proper. Pious parents become angry and even punish their children to keep them from evil, and they should. The government must sometimes be angry. Pious judges should get angry with criminals, even though personally they wish them no harm and would rather let them off without punishment. But we must be sure that our anger is Godly. When another person is being attacked, oppressed, or injured, we must get angry with the attacker, even though no injury is done to us personally. We must not get angry for an injury done to us.

The greater righteousness calls for reconciliation. Church people inevitably become angry. To protect their anger and allow it to become divisive represents failure.

To be reconciled is hard. It is difficult to forgive. It requires humility and calls for enduring personal insult. But it is the way of the greater righteousness. Our need to be angry is diminished as we seek to meet the needs of others.

Jesus does not say that the person who attempts reconciliation is the guilty party. He may be entirely innocent. Whether the other is justified or not is not at issue.

Jesus presents two brief examples of subduing anger by reconciliation. The first involves ritual and the second law. Jesus wants us to take the initiative in becoming reconciled with those who are angry with us.

413

The first example results from the conjunction of two happenings. A person is making an offering, and he remembers that someone has something against him. Anger is related to worship. When we get angry with other people and swear at them, when we insult or slander them, we erect a barrier not only between ourselves and them but also between ourselves and God. Our sacrifices, worship, and prayers are no longer acceptable to God.

Worship cannot be divorced from our relationship to other people. If we despise another, our worship is fake. So long as we refuse to love another, so long as we make another the object of our contempt or let another harbor a grudge against us, our worship and sacrifice are unacceptable to God. Love for other people is one way we express our love for God, cf. Matt. 25:40.

The Pharisees taught that a sacrifice could be interrupted only for ritual reasons. To interrupt it simply on account of a neighbor would have been inconceivable, because the goal was the offering of a pure and perfect ritual. According to the greater righteousness of Jesus, one's attitude and proper relationship with one's brother/sister are essential for effective worship.

When a person must attend to both an ethical and a ritual duty at the same time, Jesus places ethics before ritual. After attending to one's ethical obligation, a person is to return and complete his/her ritual obligation.

Real worship can pose serious difficulties. At times, it can be a painful experience, and at times it is joyous. At times, it can be disturbing and at times comforting. At times, it can be upsetting, and at times it brings peace. At times, it can be very frustrating, and at times it is very satisfying. At times, it can leave us confused, and at other times it clarifies the vision and purpose of our life. What happens in our experience of worship is indicative of our inner condition. Real worship involves facing ourselves in our relationship with others and with God.

When we understand this, we can understand why so many people avoid worship and why others turn it into an empty form. In order to worship, to grasp our relationship with God and to make an appropriate emotional, intellectual, and volitional response to what God has done for us in Jesus, we have to face and work through the emotional obstacles within ourselves. Worship brings us face to face with ourselves in the presence of God. Such an experience can make us aware of potentialities in ourselves that we would like to ignore and avoid. It can make us aware of weaknesses and sins that we want to cover up, because they are painful to admit.

Many times the church fosters unhealthy worship. We urge people to come to worship, but we do not help them find reconciliation with others before they come.

Some people find it necessary to go through a counseling experience or a psychotherapeutic experience in order to free themselves from intense antagonisms toward others before they find worship possible. Under some conditions, others find such growth taking place through worship itself.

In Mark 11:25, Jesus seems to say much the same thing He says in Matt. 5:23-24. We should not expect to receive divine forgiveness if we do not forgive our neighbor. The petition for forgiveness in the Lord's Prayer is similar, cf. Matt. 6:12 and Luke 11:4.

At the time Matthew wrote vs. 23-24, their literal meaning had become impossible. The temple had been destroyed, and bringing an offering was impossible therefore. The validity of the words does not depend on their literal meaning.

Jesus' words have been used in the Order of the Holy Communion at the very beginning of the meal. But they should not become a part of an order of worship. They make their point through insisting on the disruption of the orderly. The worship of God is to wait on reconciliation.

What would happen, if after worship began on a Sunday morning, all who felt that another had something against them quickly left? It would upset the service, no doubt; but worship would become dynamic! To avoid such upset, we conform to custom and become unhealthy. Persons who have been helped with hostilities through pastoral counseling report that they suddenly and spontaneously find new meaning and freedom in worship.

There is little background for Jesus' second example of the need for reconciliation, the legal situation. It corresponds to nothing in Roman usage and has an un-Greek ring to it. Imprisonment for debts and as punishment in general were unknown in Jewish law. Jesus seems to be deliberately referring to non-Jewish legal practices.[111] The accuracy Jesus describes in accounting serves to illustrate how severely the divine sentence will be executed.

Only one motive needs to be promoted to cause us to forgive those who wrong us, that is being forgiven by God. For that, it is required that we forgive. If we refuse, the throne of mercy is inaccessible. Jesus died in vain for us.

II

With regard to sex, the synagogue taught, "You shall not commit adultery," cf. Ex. 20:14 and Deut. 5:18. Adultery is sexual intercourse with anyone other than your spouse.

Sex is an immense power. Every society surrounds itself with rules in an effort to harness the power and to prevent it from becoming harmful.

With their literalistic interpretation of the law, the scribes and Pharisees did not see that the Sixth Commandment refers to a person's inner thoughts as well as to his deeds. The desire to commit adultery is equivalent in the eyes of God to committing the deed. Jesus says that lust is adultery. Both constitute rebellion against God. He does not depreciate the body and its natural instincts, but His disciples do not allow free rein to their desires.

Jesus' saying about the eye and the hand in vs. 29-30 is repeated in Matt. 18:8-9.

The eye is a very valuable member of our body. The right eye, some say, has a little preference over the left.

Eye here could stand for anything that is precious and dear to us. People, too. If they are causing us to sin, we ought to cut off our association with them. Jesus' words about the right eye and the right hand teach us that our Lord is not given to exceptions.

Origen used Jesus' words about the eye to show that the meaning of the gospels is not a literal one. Why should one tear out only the right eye, when presumably both offend? The words of Jesus can be ridiculed or their intention can be sought out. The follower of Jesus does the latter.

Does Jesus want us to tear out our eyes? The question does not seem to allow for an answer. If we do not take Jesus' words literally, we are evading the seriousness of Jesus' commandment. If we decide to take it literally, our Christian position seems absurd. We are left in a situation where the only thing to do is to obey.

One of the methods Jesus used in teaching was to speak in extremes. He does not want us to mutilate ourselves. He wants us to stop sinning. Some people say, "I can't help myself. That's the way I am." Jesus' word gives us the answer to that situation. If we have a choice between stopping the sin and lopping off a limb, we are going to put forth every effort to stop the sin and keep the limb. That's what Jesus wants. The demand to cut off the hand and to pluck out the eye is a drastic expression of the imperative to control our sexual desires.

Jesus' word seems very strong, but He accepted even prostitutes forgivingly and without placing conditions on them for entrance into His fellowship and into the kingdom of God, cf. Luke 7:36-50. That is the significance of His passion.

The prohibition of lust does not forbid desiring one's spouse or the person one is going to marry. Luther said: "When a suitor loves a girl, desires her for his wife, and marries her, he does not commit adultery, even though the Law forbids desire; for matrimony was divinely instituted and commanded for those who cannot live a chaste life without it."[112]

Luther points out that we must "distinguish between looking and lusting. You may look at any woman or man, only be sure that you do not lust. That is why God has ordained for every person to have his own wife or husband, to control and channel his lust and his appetites. If you do not go any further than this, He approves it, He even pronounces His blessing upon it, and He is pleased with it as His ordinance and creature. But if you do go further, if you refuse to be content with what God has given you for your desires, and if you leer at others, you have

417

already gone too far and have confused the two, so that your looking is corrupted by your lusting.

"When a man does not look at his wife, on the basis of the Word of God, as the one whom God gives him and whom He blesses, and when instead he turns his gaze to another woman, this is the principal cause of adultery, which then is almost inevitable. Soon the heart follows the eyes, bringing on the desire and appetite that I ought to reserve for my wife alone. Flesh and blood is curious enough anyway. It soon has its fill and loses its taste for what it has, and it gapes at something else. With the devil's promptings, a person sees only his wife's faults, losing sight of her good and laudable qualities. As a consequence, every other woman seems more beautiful and better to my eyes than my own wife. Indeed, many a man with a truly beautiful and pious wife lets himself be hoodwinked into hating her and taking up with some vile and ugly bag.

"As I have pointed out more fully in my other discussions of marriage and married life, it would be a real art and a very strong safeguard against all this if everyone learned to look at his spouse correctly, according to God's Word, which is the dearest treasure and the loveliest ornament you can find in a man or a woman. If he mirrored himself in this, then he would hold his wife in love and honor as a divine gift and treasure. And if he saw another woman, even one more beautiful than his own wife, he would say: `Is she beautiful? As far as I am concerned, she is not very beautiful. And even if she were the most beautiful woman on earth, in my wife at home I have a lovelier adornment, one that God has given me and has adorned with His Word beyond the others, even though she may not have a beautiful body or may have other failings. Though I may look over all the women in the world, I cannot find any about whom I can boast with a joyful conscience as I can about mine: "This is the one whom God has granted to me and put into my arms." I know that He and all the angels are heartily pleased if I cling to her lovingly and faithfully. Then why should I despise this precious gift of God and take up with someone else, where I can find no such treasure or adornment?'

"Thus I could look at all women, talk with them, laugh, and

have a good time with them, without experiencing any lust or desire and without letting any of them seem so beautiful or desirable to me that I would be willing to transgress the Word and commandment of God . . . . But because a person does not give this Word of God a glance or a thought, it is easy for him to get tired of his wife and to despise her; he finds his love drawn to another, and his lust and appetite for her are irresistible. For he has not learned the art of looking at his wife correctly, according to the beauty and adornment with which God has clothed her for him. He cannot see beyond what his eyes see, that his wife seems to have a poor shape or other faults, while another one seems prettier and better. Thus you understand when it is a sin and when it is not a sin to look at a woman, namely that you should not look at another woman the way a man should look only at his wife."

"It is impossible to keep the devil from shooting evil thoughts and lusts into your heart. But see to it that you do not let such arrows (Eph. 6:16) stick there and take root, but tear them out and throw them away. Do what one of the ancient fathers counseled long ago: 'I cannot,' he said, 'keep the bird from flying over my head. But I can certainly keep it from nesting in my hair or from biting my nose off.' So it is not in our power to prevent this or some other temptation and to keep the thoughts from occurring to us. Just be sure that you let it go at that and do not let them in, even though they knock on the door. . . . It is still sin nonetheless, but it is included in our common forgiveness; for we cannot live in the flesh without a great many sins, and everyone must have his devil."

"This argument and inquiry has come from some: 'Is it sinful for a man and a woman to desire each other for the purpose of marriage?' This is ridiculous, a question that contradicts both Scripture and nature. Why would people get married if they did not have desire and love for each other? Indeed, that is just why God has given this eager desire to bride and bridegroom, for otherwise everybody would flee from marriage and avoid it. In Scripture, therefore, He also commanded man and woman to love each other, and He shows that the sexual union of husband and wife is also most pleasing to Him. Hence this desire and love must not be absent, for it is a good fortune and a great pleasure, if only it continues as long as possible. Without it there is trouble: from the flesh, because a person soon gets tired of marriage and refuses to bear the daily discomfort that comes with it; and from the devil, who cannot stand the sight of a married couple treating each other with genuine love and who will not rest until he has given them an occasion for impatience, conflict, hate, and bitterness. Therefore it is an art both necessary and difficult, and one peculiarly Christian, this art of loving one's husband or wife properly, of bearing the other's faults and all the accidents and troubles. At first everything goes all right, so that, as the saying goes, they are ready to eat each other up for love. But when their curiosity has been satisfied, then the devil comes along to create boredom in you, to rob you of your desire in this direction, and to excite it unduly in another direction." [113]

III

With regard to divorce, the synagogue taught, "Whoever divorces his wife, let him give her a certificate of divorce." The synagogue law according to which it was possible for a man (but not a woman) to get a divorce by giving his wife a certificate of divorce was Deut. 24:1-4. That document removed any ambiguity about the wife's status, declaring her legally free to remarry. The intention was to protect the woman.

The abbreviated nature of the introductory words in v. 31 in comparison to vs. 21 and 27 may be explained by the close connection between the statements regarding divorce in vs. 31-32 and those regarding sex in vs. 27-30. The two sections form a unit on the Sixth Commandment.

Deut. 24:1 prohibits divorce, but the prohibition is not absolute. A reason is allowed, namely, "because he finds something objectionable about her." The Pharisees tried to make that loophole as big as possible. The phrase can be translated "because he has found in her some scandal of a matter" or "some scandalous matter." That broadens the loophole considerably.

The rabbis worked the exception in different ways. The School of Shammai stressed the word "scandal." They regarded adultery and moral misconduct as the only acceptable grounds for divorce. In the case of such unchastity, the man was compelled to divorce his wife.

The School of Hillel, which was that of the Pharisees, emphasized the word "matter." They held that any cause of offence, even quite trivial ones, were sufficient grounds for legal divorce. Examples of such permissible grounds were that the wife had spoiled a dish by letting the food burn, she had a physical deformity, failure to care for the family, the husband had found another, more beautiful woman to be his wife, or she spoke too loudly in the house.

Perhaps the Jews of Jesus' day could see that what they were doing was frequently quite frivolous and not good. The prophet Malachi already had bemoaned the prevalence of divorce: "I hate divorce, says the Lord the God of Israel," cf. 2:14-16.

The form of divorce was simple. The husband made out a declaration contradicting that which had sealed the marriage contract. In the Jewish colony at Elephantine, the practice was that the man pronounced in front of witnesses the words, "I divorce my wife." In Assyria, he said, "I repudiate her" or "You are no more my wife." In Israel, Mesopotamia, and Elephantine, the husband had to draw up a writ of divorce that allowed the woman to remarry. Such a writ of divorce has been found dating back to the second Christian century.

In contrast to the Pharisees, Jesus reestablishes the divine intention. The Jews understood the Mosaic regulation wrongly and on the basis of this misunderstanding made divorce easy. God's original intent had been to make the bond between a man and a woman unbreakable. Jesus sanctifies marriage and affirms its indissolubility.

Jesus explained the "loophole" of Deut. 24:1 in Matt. 19:3-9 as something that was permitted "because you were so hardhearted." In other words, it was to preserve them from worse excesses. God did not intend it to be that way. What He has joined together, He does not want separated. Jesus reaffirms the intention of the Old Testament law. He protects marriage and the home.

That Jesus here speaks exclusively of a man divorcing his wife is due to the fact that in Israel the procuring of a divorce by a woman through charges against her husband was almost unthinkable. Salome, the sister of Herod, sent her husband a letter of divorce. Her action was held to be against Jewish law.[114] The husband alone had the right to dissolve the marriage not the wife.

Nevertheless, divorce was difficult for a man. The woman retained the right to her bridal gift, and so the man suffered financially if he dismissed his wife.

The phrase "except on the ground of unchastity" in v. 32 has produced much controversy. The meaning is the same as the phrase in Matt. 19:9, "except for unchastity." Jesus' sayings on divorce are reported in slightly different versions and contexts in Matt. 5:31-32; 19:9; Mark 10:2-12; Luke 16:18; 1 Cor. 7:10-11. Only in the passages of Matthew is there any mention of the exception.

Several explanations have been advanced. The traditional one is that used by the translators of the NRSV. As they construe it, the Greek expression means "except on the ground of unchastity." The contention of this interpretation is that Jesus, though He forbids divorce in principle, nevertheless allows it in the event that a spouse is unfaithful or commits adultery. Against this interpretation is the objection that since the Greek moicheia ("adultery") is used, it is unlikely that porneia ("unchastity") is to be understood as a mere synonym of moicheia. Jesus seems to make the two words distinct in Matt. 15:19.

According to this interpretation, the qualification blunts the saying. It seems to reflect the intention of Deut. 24:1. It has become the loophole in the church corresponding to that in the law of Moses. Here, too, the people of the church are trying to make that loophole as large as possible.

There is no directive as to what should be done in the case of the exception clause, that is, in the case of "unchastity" (porneia). It does not demand that marriage remain indissoluble under all conditions. In the case of infidelity, a divorce may be necessary. If a man gets a divorce because his wife engaged in unchaste activity, he does not cause her to commit adultery by divorcing her.

Another interpretation uses a different translation: "But I say to you that whoever divorces his wife, except on the grounds of an incestuous marriage, makes her an adulteress." With this translation, Jesus forbids divorce in every case except one. Should a gentile couple join the church, whose marriage is adjudged to be incestuous according to Lev. 18:6-18, that couple would be required to divorce. This may have been the intention of the apostolic advice recorded in Acts 15:20 and 29.

Matthew was writing for Jewish Christians. Some have tried to explain Matthew's exception clause by saying that for Jews adultery was an unforgivable sin, punishable by stoning. When adultery happened, the husband sought God's righteousness. To Jewish ears, the idea of remaining with an adulterous wife was obscene and absurd. The husband was legally forced to divorce his wife. An example of this is the story of Mary and Joseph in Matt. 1:18-19. So if a Christian husband gets a divorce under those circumstances, he should not be criticized. Matthew may have adjusted the saying of Jesus to fit the legal situation that existed, but the saying is more accurately reported by Mark and Luke and faithfully reflected by Paul.

This explanation obviates the exclusion for Christians in most cases. For Christians, God is glorified when we forgive each other. Thus the offended Christian spouse seeking God's glory communicates divine forgiveness to his wife. Of course, if the spouse spurns that forgiveness, the marriage is dead.

Some scholars think that the exception clause was originally not a part of the text of Matthew and that it was added as the result of changes made in church law. But the manuscript evidence strongly supports inclusion of the phrase in the original.

The NRSV translation brings out a point which may or may not be significant for the meaning of the clause. The word translated "unchastity" is <u>porneias</u>. The word "adultery" is used four times in vs. 27-33 and is used to translate a form of the verb <u>moicheuo</u>. <u>Porneia</u> may be a broader term than <u>moicheuo</u>. It may refer to any sexual irregularity.

When Martin Luther was asked about the causes of divorce, he listed two: "The first is adultery. Here one should make an effort to reconcile the couple again after the guilty party has been sharply rebuked. The second cause: when one deserts the other, thereupon returns again, and finally goes off for the third time. Generally such good-for-nothings are on a seesaw; they have a wife elsewhere, return after a couple of years, make that wife pregnant again, and then go away without consent. Men like this ought to have their heads chopped off." [115]

"Anyone who divorces his wife causes her to commit adultery, except (when the divorce takes place) on the ground of unchastity." If a man divorces his wife, he makes her commit adultery; unless she has already committed adultery. Some understand the words to mean that he causes her to become the victim of adultery. If she is compelled to marry somebody else, the new marriage is an adulterous relationship.

When Jesus speaks of "a divorced woman" in v. 32, He may be referring to a woman who was divorced on the grounds of adultery. He may also be presupposing that she is unrepentant of her sin. Would this also be true of a woman who was divorced wrongly, that is, she was not divorced on the grounds of unchastity?

Jesus was not adjusting what He said to the social thinking of His day. How opposed to the prevailing Jewish notions on divorce Jesus' stand was, we easily see from the reaction of the disciples. They consider it better to remain single under such circumstances than to marry, cf. Matt. 19:10.

There is a difference between the Christian conception of marriage and that held by others. Christian marriage is marked by discipline and self-denial. Jesus liberates marriage from selfish, evil desire and consecrates it to the service of love.

Luther: "What is the proper procedure for us nowadays in matters of marriage and divorce? I have said that this should be left to the lawyers and made subject to the secular government. For marriage is a rather secular and outward thing, having to do with wife and children, house and home, and with

424

other matters that belong to the realm of the government, all of which have been completely subjected to reason (Gen. 1:28). Therefore we should not tamper with what the government and wise men decide and prescribe with regard to these questions on the basis of the laws and of reason. Christ is not functioning here as a lawyer or a governor, to set down or prescribe any regulations for outward conduct; but He is functioning as a preacher, to instruct consciences about using the divorce law properly, rather than wickedly and capriciously, contrary to God's commandment. Here, therefore, we will not go beyond an examination of their situation and a consideration of the proper behavior of people who lay claim to the name `Christian.' The non-Christians are no concern of ours, since they must be governed, not with the Gospel, but with compulsion and punishment. Thus we shall keep our ministry clear and not claim any more right than we are authorized to have."

"They asked Christ, Matthew 19: `Is it lawful to divorce one's wife for any cause?' His answer to them is a severe sermon . . . coming to the conclusion as He did here: Except for the cause of fornication, both he who divorces a woman and he who pays court to a divorced woman are guilty of adultery and are making her guilty of adultery, too, if she takes another man; for if she did not have a man again, she could not be guilty of adultery. So He not only rebukes them for their frivolity in the question of divorce, but He teaches them not to get a divorce at all, or if they do get one, to remain unmarried on both sides. And He comes to the conclusion that divorce is always an occasion for adultery.

"They asked (Matt. 19:7): `Why, then, did Moses permit such divorces?' He answers (Matt. 19:8): `For your hard hearts Moses allowed you to divorce your wives. It is still not a good thing to do; but since you are such wicked and unmanageable people, it is better to grant you this much than to let you do worse by vexing or murdering each other or by living together in incessant hate, discord, and hostility.' This same thing might even be advisable nowadays, if the secular government prescribed it, that certain queer, stubborn, and obstinate people, who have no capacity for toleration and are not suited for married

425

life at all, should be permitted to get a divorce. Since people are as evil as they are, any other way of governing is impossible. Frequently something must be tolerated even though it is not a good thing to do, to prevent something even worse from happening.

"So it is settled now. Those who want to be Christians should not be divorced, but every man should keep his own spouse, sustaining and bearing good and ill with her, even though she may have her oddities, peculiarities, and faults. If he does get a divorce, he should remain unmarried. We have no changing and exchanging. But the rule is the one Christ pronounces (Matt. 19:6): `What God has joined together, let no man put asunder.' The only source of trouble here is the fact that marriage is not thought of on the basis of the Word of God, as His work and ordinance, and that His will is ignored. He has given every man his spouse, to keep her and for His sake to put up with the difficulties involved in married life. To them it seems to be nothing more than a purely human and secular state, with which God has nothing to do. Therefore they tire of it so quickly; and if it does not go the way they would like, they immediately want a divorce and a change. Then God so arranges things that they are no better off as a consequence. A person who wants to change and improve everything and who refuses to put up with any inadequacies, but insists on having everything clean and comfortable, will usually get in exchange something twice as uncomfortable or ten times as uncomfortable. This is a general rule, not only in this matter but in all others as well."

"If you want an undertaking of yours to be blessed and successful, even a temporal undertaking like getting married or staying home or accepting a position, lift up your voice to God, and call upon the One who owns it and who has to grant it. It is not a small gift from God to find a wife who is pious and easy to get along with. Then why not ask Him to make it a happy marriage? For your initial desire and your curiosity will not give you either happiness or stability, unless He adds His blessing and success and helps you to bear the occasional troubles. Those who do not do this, therefore, who rush into things on their own as though they did not need God's help, and who do not learn how to make certain allowances - they get exactly what they deserve. They have sheer purgatory and the torments of hell inside them, and that without any help from the devil. They do not bear their trouble patiently. They have selected only what seems to be just right to them, and they have tried to abolish and annul the article called 'forgiveness of sin.' Therefore their reward is a restless and impatient heart; thus they have to suffer double trouble and have no thanks for it. But we have said enough about this elsewhere.

"But you ask: 'Then is there no legitimate cause for the divorce and remarriage of a man and his wife?' Answer: But here and in Matthew 19:9 Christ sets down only one, called adultery; and He cites it on the basis of the Law of Moses, which punishes adultery with death (Lev. 20:10). Since it is only death that can dissolve a marriage and set you free, an adulterer has already been divorced, not by men but by God Himself, and separated not only from his wife but from his very life. By his adultery he has divorced himself from his wife and has dissolved his marriage. He had no right to do either of these, and so he has brought on his own death, in the sense that before God he is already dead even though the judge may not have him executed. Because it is God that is doing the divorcing here, the other partner is set completely free and is not obliged, unless he chooses to do so, to keep the spouse that has broken the marriage vow.

"We neither commend nor forbid such divorces, but leave it to the government to act here; and we submit to whatever the secular law prescribes in this matter. To those who really want to be Christians, we would give this advice. The two partners should be admonished and urged to stay together. If the guilty party is humbled and reformed, the innocent party should let himself be reconciled to him and forgive him in Christian love. Sometimes there is no hope for improvement, or the reconciliation of the guilty one and his restoration to good graces is followed only by his abuse of this kindness. He persists in his flagrant and loose behavior and takes it for granted that he is entitled to be spared and forgiven. I would not advise or prescribe mercy for a person like that; rather I would help to have such a person flogged or jailed. For one oversight is still pardonable, but a sin that takes mercy and forgiveness for granted is intolerable. Anyway, as we have said, we know that no one should be compelled to take back a public prostitute or an adulterer if he does not want to do so or is so disgusted that he cannot do so . . . .

"An additional cause for divorce is this: when one spouse deserts the other, when he runs away out of sheer peevishness. For example, if a pagan woman were married to a Christian man, or as happens sometimes nowadays, if one spouse is an Evangelical and the other is not, is divorce legitimate in such a case? Paul discusses the matter in 1 Corinthians 7:13-15 and comes to this conclusion: If the one partner consents to remain, the other partner should keep him; even though they may not be one in matters of faith, the faith should not dissolve the marriage. If it happens that the other partner simply refuses to remain, then let him go; you have no duty or obligation to go with him. But it sometimes happens now that one of these good-for-nothings deserts his wife without her knowledge or consent, leaving his house and home, wife and children, and staying away two or three years or as long as he feels like staying away. When he has sown his wild oats and squandered his property he decides he would like to return home and pick up where he had left off. And now the other partner should be obliged to wait for him as long as he feels like staying away and then to take him back?! Such a good-for-nothing should not only be barred from his house and home, but also banished from the country. If he refuses to come after summons and a decent interval of waiting, the other partner should be set completely free. Such a person is worse than a heathen and an unbeliever (1 Tim. 5:8); he is less tolerable than a wicked adulterer, who fell once but can still improve and be as faithful to his wife as he had been before. But this person treats marriage just as he pleases. In his wife and children he does not recognize the obligations of domestic life and duty, but takes it for granted that he will be received if the notion takes him to return. This is how it should be: Whoever wants to have a wife and children must stay with them; he must bear the good with the ill with them as long as he lives. If he refuses to do so, he should be told that he must; otherwise he will be separated from wife, house and home permanently. Where these causes are not present, other faults and foibles should not be a hindrance to marriage nor a reason for divorce, things like quarrels or other trouble. But if there is a divorce, says St. Paul, both partners should remain unmarried."

"As I have said, the best way to prevent divorce and other discord is for everyone to learn patience in putting up with the common faults and troubles of his station in life and to put up with them in his wife as well, knowing that we can never have everything just right, the way we would like to have it. Even the condition of your own body can never be any different or better. You have to put up with many kinds of filth and discomfort that it causes you every day; and if you were to throw away everything about it that is impure, you would have to start with the belly, which you need to nourish you and to keep you alive.

"Now, you can stand it when your body emits a stench before you realize it, or when it festers and becomes pussy and completely pollutes your skin. You make allowance for all this. In fact, this only increases your concern and love for your body; you wait on it and wash it, and you endure and help in every way you can. Why not do the same with the spouse whom God has given you, who is an even greater treasure and whom you have even more reason to love? For the love among Christians should be the same kind of love as that of every member of the body for every other one, as St. Paul often says (Rom. 12:4, 5; 1 Cor. 12:12-26), each one accepting the faults of the other, sympathizing with them, bearing and removing them, and doing everything possible to help him. Hence the doctrine of the forgiveness of sins is the most important of all, both for us personally and for our relations with others. As Christ continually bears with us in His kingdom and forgives us all sorts of faults, so we should bear and forgive one another in every situation and in every way. Whoever refuses to do this, may God grant him no rest and make his misfortune or plague ten times as bad."[116]

IV

With regard to perjury, the synagogue taught, "You shall not swear falsely, but carry out the vows you have made to the Lord." The Old Testament passages are Lev. 19:12; Num. 30:2; and Deut. 23:21-23.

In interpreting vs. 34-37, commentators have oscillated between rejecting every oath as a sin and rejecting only frivolous oaths and perjury. In the early church, the commonest interpretation was that perfect Christians were forbidden to swear at all, but the weaker brethren were allowed to swear within certain limits. Even Augustine allowed for this latter view. The Lutheran Confessions allow for oaths exacted by the state in a court of law. St. Paul frequently employs expressions of an oath-like character. God Himself swore, cf. Luke 1:73; Acts 2:30; Heb. 3:11, 18; 4:3; 6:13-18; 7:20-21. The oath of God is likened to the oath of men by which all disputes are ended in Heb. 6:16. Jesus allowed Himself to be put under oath before the Sanhedrin in Matt. 26:63.

An oath is an appeal made in public to God calling on Him to witness a statement made in connection with an event or fact, past, present, or future. Oaths are intended as a barrier against lies. But they can be used to protect, maintain, and conceal lies. Plenty of evidence exists for saying that oaths do not guarantee the truth.

Furthermore, no one has an infallible knowledge of the past. Taking an oath regarding something in the past, does not mean that any statement we make is free from error. It says something about the integrity of our mind and conscience but not about the truth. If the oath has to do with the future, we are not lord of our own future. We must be extremely cautious about making oaths with regard to the future.

Jesus is speaking here in opposition to the thinking that only promises made under oath need to be kept, and not all of them. The Jews of His day maintained that it did not matter if they failed to do something which they had not sworn to do. They were used to swearing oaths for every little thing in the daily routine, at home, in the kitchen, and in the shop. The result was that the potency of the oath was diminished.

The Jews in those days also made a distinction between oaths that are valid and those that are not. They held that perjury is not sinful, unless the oath is taken in a particular form, cf. Matt. 23:16-22. For example, if someone were to swear by heaven, or by Jerusalem, or by his head, those were little oaths which were not very binding as long as one did not invoke the name of God. Casuistic discussion on the validity of oaths occupies the entire Mishnah tractate Shebuoth. That tractate said that swearing by the heavens and by the earth is an oath which is not binding on witnesses. The rabbis said that a vow made "by Jerusalem" was nothing unless it was sworn "towards Jerusalem." One had to be facing in the direction of Jerusalem. False swearing was especially common among the Jews outside of Palestine engaged in trade.

Jesus sweeps away all such sophistry. He says that all oaths are to be avoided. Everything a person says should be considered sacred and binding. We live in the presence of God. For this reason, oath-taking is not necessary. When we say something as though God is not present, that is ungodly. The greatest sin is not taking a vow but rather regarding the making and fulfilling of vows as something which can be done apart from the presence of God. This teaching of Jesus is repeated in James 5:12.

An oath tends to cause doubt about the truthfulness of all other statements we make. The reason we need to swear that we are telling the truth is that we tell so many lies. If we always told the truth, we wouldn't have to swear to what we are saying. People would believe what we say.

When Jesus calls Jerusalem "the city of the great King," He is referring to what Ps. 48:2 says.

When He says, "you cannot make one hair white or black," we have to remember that He lived long before Clairol Preference or Excellence were available.

Jesus does not assert that saying more than yes or no is evil, but that it comes from evil or from the evil one, cf. NRSV footnote. It is impossible to tell if Jesus is referring to "the evil one" or to "evil" in v. 37. The masculine and the neuter forms of poneros ("evil") are the same. The same uncertainty exists in Matt. 6:13 and 13:38. Jesus says in John 8:44, "the devil . . . is . . . the father of lies."

It is right to swear, when the government requires, when the truth needs to be confirmed, or when peace and harmony require it. Another cause is love. An oath may be necessary for the good of our neighbor.

When we swear, we should swear by the name of God, cf. Deut. 6:13; 10:20; and Jer. 12:16. Moreover, when we swear, we should always tell the truth.

Conclusion

When people say they like the Sermon on the Mount, they may not be listening to what Jesus is saying. The Sermon on the Mount has been called the most terrible indictment of the human race in all of literature. It holds a mirror before us and reveals the kind of people we are. It requires of us a radical change in the way we live. Its moral demands cannot be met.

In the pre-Reformation period, the church taught that Jesus did not intend everything in the Sermon on the Mount to be regarded as a command for all to observe. He gave much of it merely as advice to those who want to become perfect. This in spite of the fact that Jesus never tells people simply to do the best they can. He says in Matt. 5:19 that anyone who teaches others to break one of the least of His commandments will be called least in the kingdom of heaven. That means God does not rule them at all.

The Sermon on the Mount was quoted and referred to by Christian writers more frequently during the first three centuries of the church than any other portion of the scriptures. It may still be the most popular section of the Bible. It may be known by more people than any other part of the Bible except the Ten Commandments.

6th Sunday after the Epiphany

Year B

2 Kings 5:1-14

God can use unimportant people and simple material to accomplish great things. His great accomplishments are sometimes hidden behind insignificant developments so that people do not see that He does them. When we humble ourselves under His mighty hand, He may use us for His great purposes.

Two kings and the commander of the army of the Arameans are important people in this story. Aram is Syria, a strong and influential nation in the Middle East, while Israel is a small, buffer country recently defeated by Aram. A slave girl, Naaman's wife, his servants, and the prophet Elisha are unimportant people who drive the story. The rivers of Damascus, Abana and Pharpar, the victorious military man boasts, are a lot better than the Jordan River of Israel. The mighty warrior has leprosy and goes to Israel to be cured. He anticipates that someone will do something spectacular in a grandiose manner to heal him, something befitting his status. But the greatest thing that happens to this man who is in high favor with the king of Aram is that he comes to know the God of Israel in a life altering experience.

He marches up to the palace of the king of Israel in Samaria with a mighty contingent from his great army, including horses and chariots. He wants to make an impressive introduction of himself, and he is in enemy territory. He recently defeated Israel. He carries a written request from the king of Aram to the king of Israel. The request is that the king of Israel should cure this military hero of his leprosy. The king of Israel is upset and panics. In dismay and confusion, he sends Naaman to the prophet Elisha.

The commander prances up to the house of Elisha in full regalia with his entire retinue. But the prophet is so unimpressed, he doesn't even come out to greet him. He sends a messenger to tell the hero of Aram to go wash in the Jordan River. Naaman feels ignored and humiliated. He goes away in a rage.

Naaman's servants plead with him to do as the prophet directs. They support Naaman's hurt feelings and agree that what Elisha is asking him to do is beneath his dignity. But, their argument is, "if the prophet had commanded you to do something difficult – something corresponding to your power, stature, accomplishments, and ability - would you not have done it? How much more, when all he said to you was, 'Wash, and be clean'?"

So Naaman swallows his pride, goes down to the Jordan, and immerses himself seven times in the river as Elisha instructed him. He is cleansed. "His flesh was restored like the flesh of a young boy." But that's less than half of it! A radical change takes place in him. He is converted!

The hero who initiated this entire complex series of events is a young girl who served Naaman's wife. She is an Israeli slave who was captured on one of Aram's raids into Israel. She urged Naaman's wife to have her husband go see Elisha so that he could be cured.

That's how God uses insignificant people and material to accomplish His great purposes. It is an important lesson to learn.

God did something even greater many years later. He chose a young girl from a small village called Nazareth to be the mother of His Son. The Son of God carpentered with His step-father as He grew up, a man named Joseph. One day, Mary's son,

Jesus, left home and saved the world. Although at times people followed Him and praised Him, in the end no one stood with Him or defended Him as the religious leaders of Judaism maligned Him, ridiculed Him, and condemned Him. They turned Him over to their Roman rulers and insisted that He be killed. The Roman governor didn't want to do it, because Jesus didn't seem to be a dangerous man. But the Jews forced the issue, and Pilate gave in. After the Roman soldiers enjoyed their perverted kind of fun with Jesus, they beat Him up, scourged Him, and crucified Him. That's how God saved the world! That's how Jesus took away the sin of the world.

Today, God still operates that way. Jesus' saving work is credited to us through people who are sometimes too big for their britches, sometimes arrogant, and sometimes overbearing and manipulative. Their job is simple enough; they are to tell us what Jesus did and give us Jesus' salvation. The minister's job is to pour a little water on us in the name of God. In this way, we are born again through the power of the Holy Spirit. The minister's job is to give us in remembrance of Jesus a little bread which is also Jesus' body and a little wine which is also Jesus' blood. Through words, water, eating, and drinking, God comes to us, lives in us, causes us to live in Him, forgives our sins, and gives us heaven. Through these simple things, God remakes and renews our life. We live with God as we let Him have His way with us.

The setting of the story of Naaman is very complex. The story is related in few words and with little detail.

In the ancient world, leprosy referred to many different skin diseases that marked a person with a variety of social stigmas. A person suffering from leprosy in Israel was barred from the worship of Jahweh, cf. Lev. 13-14. In certain circumstances, a leprous person might be ostracized from normal life in the community. The text does not give any information about the nature of Naaman's disease or the social consequences resulting from it. Nevertheless, his response when he hears there is a cure suggests that it bothers him a great deal. He is willing to travel to Israel to be healed.

When the king of Israel tore his clothes, it was a gesture of grief. He is known to have been a negative person who usually feared the worst, cf. 3:10.

Jesus knew about Naaman. He refers to this story in Luke 4:27.

We should not despise God's little people – not even ourselves – nor His little things – not even what He has given us. But we should use them and let ourselves be used by Him to accomplish His gracious purposes in the world.

1 Corinthians 9:24-27

How does a winner run? Paul says, "Run in such a way that you may win." He is not saying that Christians have to be better than every other runner to win. But runners who win do have style. The prize Christians receive does not recognize superior competitive achievement. It has already been won for everyone. Jesus ran the race representing all people. There was only one competitor who opposed Him, the devil, who represented the forces of evil. Jesus defeated them in His suffering and death. Paul wants the Corinthian Christians to follow Jesus as winners. Paul wants the Corinthians to imitate him as he imitates Christ Jesus, cf. 11:1.

That Paul is not drawing a contrast between all the runners and the single winner becomes clear in 10:1-5. All the people who followed Moses out of Egypt in the exodus participated in the miraculous wilderness events that followed. But all of them did not enter the land God promised to give them, because they were rebellious. Most of them died in the wilderness, because God was not pleased with what they did. They did not run in a winner's way.

Sports talk must have been popular in ancient Greece. Sports were a feature of city life. Still today, the world pays homage to the great Greek interest in athletics every ten years when the nations gather for the Olympic Games.

Paul capitalizes on this interest in some of his letters to the churches he founded in Greece. He even describes himself as a Christian athlete - a runner and a boxer.

When he uses sports' language, he is talking to the

Corinthians on their level. Corinth was located on an isthmus - that is, a narrow stretch of land - that connects the Peloponnese to the mainland of Greece. In the sixth century B.C., the city of Corinth began to sponsor a Panhellenic festival that was called the Isthmian Games. The festival was held every three years about ten miles northeast of Corinth.

How does a winner run? Paul describes how he is running in 8:13-9:23. He says he will never eat meat so that he does not cause one who is weak to fall. He has not made use of his right, cf. 9:12 and 15, to live off of the work he does, cf. 9:3, 6-14, and to be accompanied in his mission travels by a wife, cf. 9:5. He has made himself a slave to all, cf. 9:19-23. He does not put any obstacle in the way of the gospel, cf. 9:12. He spreads the gospel free of charge, cf. 9:18. He wants to win as many people for Christ as possible, cf. 9:19-22. He wants to share in the blessings of the gospel, cf. 9:23. Paul wants the Corinthian Christians to imitate him as he imitates Christ Jesus. That's the style of a winner.

The idea of winning a prize is a common New Testament metaphor. All who long for Jesus' coming again win"the crown of righteousness," according to 2 Tim. 4:8. "The crown of glory" will never fade away, according to 1 Pet. 5:4. The Lord has promised "the crown of life" to all who love Him, according to James 1:12. All who are faithful unto death will receive "the crown of life," according to Rev. 2:10.

Paul contrasts the "perishable wreath" of the Isthmian Games with the "imperishable one" that Christians run for. The Isthmian prize was a wreath of pine leaves and some money. The winner might also be rewarded with a statue. He received fame and popularity.

Winning takes self-control. Winning athletes follow strict training programs. The intensive training period for a Greek athlete lasted some ten months. Paul is talking about the style he is working on when he says that he does not run aimlessly. He has a fixed goal.

He is not like a boxer who beats the air; his blows land; he hits his mark. He punishes himself and makes himself a slave to the prize. He avoids everything that might disqualify him.

Paul is not boasting, but he wants the Corinthians to imitate his determination in serving Jesus.

Mark 1:40-45

"See that you say nothing to anyone" is called the Messianic secret. It is a characteristic of the second gospel, cf. 1:24-25, 34; 3:11-12; 5:43; 7:36; 8:30; and 9:9. It plays a greater role in Mark's gospel than in the other three. Why does Jesus tell the leper to say nothing?

Judaism expected the Messiah to heal lepers. When John the Baptist sent his disciples asking Jesus if He were the Messiah, Jesus gave him an affirmative answer by pointing to His cleansing of lepers, cf. Matt. 11:5 and Luke 7:22. The gospels emphasize Jesus' healing of lepers. But why, then, does He command this leper to saying nothing to anyone? Wouldn't it help Him to be recognized as the Messiah?

Many explanations have been offered for Jesus' command to silence. More is involved than His desire to avoid the impression of being a miracle-worker, or to avoid undue publicity in order to have more moments of peace with His disciples, or because He wishes to act modestly, or to withhold the truth about His person from the world until after His resurrection. More is involved than a desire to avoid recognitions from an undesirable source, as in the case of healing people possessed by demons. Some say that Jesus commands silence to avert the danger of revolution. Taylor says that Jesus imposes silence because of the nature of Messiahship as He conceives it.[117] The silence motif is sometimes associated with Jesus' conflict with the official leadership of Israel.[118]

Mark says that Jesus' Messianic goal primarily involves the cross, cf. Mark 10:45. The climax of the second gospel is reached in 15:39 when the centurion at Jesus' cross makes his great confession, cf. 1:1.

The commands to silence are a literary device intended to subordinate the role of miracles in Jesus' ministry. The work He came to do is accomplished in His passion. Miracles are not the most important things He does. Mark keeps the readers'

438

focus for Jesus' ministry on His passion with the injunctions to be silent about the miracles.

The Old Testament defines leprosy in Lev. 13:1-44 and 14:33-47. The restrictions placed on lepers are given in Lev. 13:45-46. The procedure by which a leper could be declared clean and return to society is spelled out in Lev. 14:1-32.

What is called leprosy in the Bible is probably not what is called leprosy today. Modern leprosy manifests itself in paralysis, the rotting of fingers and toes, facial deformity, and the loss of feeling. Today's leprosy is also called Hansen's disease. Biblical leprosy was a skin disease such as psoriasis or ringworm which was characterized by bright white spots or patches on the skin and white hair. The white patches grew depressed, and the disease produced a scab that spread.

Remarkably, Jesus touched the leper. Mark seems to make a point of this. In touching the leper, Jesus Himself became ceremonially unclean.

A leper was banished from society and could not associate with non-leprous people. He was considered among the "living dead," cf. Num. 12:10 and 12. He was required to go about with torn clothes, bared head, and a covering on his upper lip and to give warning of his polluted presence by crying, "Unclean! Unclean!" He was felt to be under the judgment and punishment of God.

It is strange that a leper approached Jesus. Lepers were more likely to flee from a rabbi, because rabbis tended to be antagonistic toward them. But this man probably had heard Jesus preach or had seen or heard about Him healing all manner of sick people. That together with his desperate situation probably led him to approach Jesus. His words, "If you choose, you can make me clean," express not doubt but faith in the power of Jesus.

Mark describes Jesus as the new Moses, cf. Deut. 18:15-18. Moses stretched out his hand in executing some of the plagues in Egypt, cf. Ex. 4:4; 9:22-23; 10:21-22; 14:16, 21, 26-27. Mark may be drawing a correspondence between Jesus and Moses when he says that Jesus stretched out His hand to heal the leper. The idea of a relationship between Jesus and Moses is triggered by the mention of Moses in v. 44. One difference between the two reveals Jesus as being greater than Moses. Moses acted only on the direct command of God while Jesus acted on His own.

No one had probably touched the leper for some time. The effect on him of Jesus' touch must have been very great. Mark emphasizes the instantaneous cure and associates it with Jesus touching him.

Only rarely in the gospels are the emotions of Jesus described and His reaction to people indicated, but Mark says that Jesus sternly warned the leper. Embrimesamenos ("sternly warning") indicates a strong inner feeling. It is difficult to find an adequate English equivalent. It indicates feeling that boils over and expresses itself. Included is the idea of agitation. Translations that suggest anger, although closely related to the meaning of the verb, are not satisfactory if they suggest that Jesus was angry with the man; for there is nothing to indicate this.

A variant reading is orgisthesis which means "being angry." D is the only major manuscript to contain this reading. Taylor accepts the variant, Plummer rejects it as a marginal gloss, and Swete says that at this stage in the story there is nothing to suggest anger. Its use may have been influenced by the word embrimesamenos.

If the variant is accepted, the cause of Jesus' anger is difficult to explain. It may be Jesus' reaction to the disease; He recognizes it as a manifestation of evil. Another suggestion is that Jesus is expressing indignation at the evil in the world that can reduce a man to the plight of this leper. That Jesus is indignant at the interruption of His preaching ministry is hard to believe. However, it is possible to think that the leper interrupted Jesus' intention to "go on to the neighboring towns" and to "proclaim the message there," cf. 1:38. Others have suggested that the leper's statement to Jesus in v. 40 suggests that while he admits Jesus' power he doubts His good will. Another suggestion is that in touching the leper, Jesus Himself became unclean and unable to enter the towns in which He intended to preach.

In healing the leper, Jesus indicted the priestly establishment.

They would have to recognize the healing, but they would refuse to acknowledge the Person and the power of the Healer. This may be the meaning of the phrase "as a testimony to them," cf. v. 44. It was necessary for the man to go to the priest and to make the required offering in order to again participate in society.

6th Sunday after the Epiphany

Year C

Jeremiah 17:5-10

The Lord blesses the righteous and those who trust in Him as their strength. He curses wicked and foolish people who rely on human ingenuity and human strength. Even beyond trusting in the Lord is making the Lord and only Him your trust. The message of the Lord through Jeremiah needs to be proclaimed especially in times of stress, but really all the time.

From time to time, great achievements empower people and cause them to trust human ability. Periods of prosperity can corrupt our faith in God. Periods of adversity can deflate people and cause them to renew their trust in God. Times of adversity can cause us to think more about the nature and meaning of life and to turn to God.

Faith is always imperiled on the one side by despair and on the other by optimism. Of the two, optimism is the more dangerous. Optimism and self-sufficiency go together. Optimistic people believe in their nation, their culture, the goodness of their church, the goodness of pious people, the capacity of human reason for infinite growth, the human ability to shape a civilization that will be free of the evils by which all previous civilizations destroyed themselves. Victories can be more deadly than defeats. When we conquer, we tend to engage in self-praise that causes our destruction. Human pride is a root of human failure.

Cursed are those who trust in people, even if they are pious people or, perhaps, especially if they are pious people. Cursed are those who trust in the church. Even God's people are sinful, and the church people build is a very human institution. The church is directed by faulty insights and the sinful ambitions of cliques, special groups, and classes. The money needed to maintain the church comes from earthly sources. The church easily becomes dependent on people from those classes of society that can most easily afford it, that is, from those who benefit most from the injustices of society.

The church should not be equated with the kingdom of God. Wherever religion is mixed with power and wherever religious people achieve power, whether inside or outside the church, they are in danger of claiming divine sanction for the very human and frequently sinful actions they take. Human sin corrupts all enterprises of the church. When there is no distinction between church institutions and the gospel, the church itself falls under the curse the Lord pronounces through Jeremiah.

Christians are seldom conscious of the way they mix faith in God and trust in people. Religious faith is often confused with faith in our Christian civilization. Luther opposed such thinking and saw the peril of human self-confidence. Christians do not believe that people can achieve the kingdom of God through their virtues. Christians do not believe that the church should be identified with the kingdom of God, although they frequently do that in various practical way.

Christians are not free from the temptation to place their trust in people. They, too, tend to trust pious people. Pious people know God's will and do it. Pious people sometimes suggest that if only pagans were as good as they, the kingdom of God would come. Sometimes the moral code of lower middle-class life is dignified as the sign and the proof of a God-fearing person. Sometimes the ethics employed in accumulating money is sanctified in the same way. "Cursed are those who trust in

444

mere mortals." The Christian faith in the goodness of God is not to be equated with confidence in human virtues.

Some highly educated people have come to the conclusion that what makes human beings dangerous, unjust, and unreliable is their religious faith. Christianity has made many false claims and frequently defended the indefensible in the name of God.

Cursed are those who trust in young people as the hope of the future. Old people are shrewd, designing, and cowardly. They are so full of ancient vices that they are not able to create a new situation free from evil. Trust young people! They are heroic and self-sacrificing. They are outraged by the evils their elders have accepted for so long.

Trust no one! All people have strengths but also weaknesses. Every historic group makes its own unique contribution to society, but there is no form of human goodness that cannot be and will not be corrupted, especially in the day of success. The victory of good over evil is not guaranteed by anything in human nature or human history.

It is significant that the most fanatic disciples of fanatic religions are young people. What is more pitiful than the corruption of the youth! They frequently do not realize that the intensity of their dedication is the direct consequence of the emptiness of their head. They lack experience. Cursed are those who trust in young people as the hope for the future.

Human optimism is a variation of trusting "in mere mortals and (making) mere flesh their strength." So great is the power of human pride and so pervasive its blindness that the illusions it creates do not become apparent until they have destroyed their source. A modern version of what the Lord says through Jeremiah might be, Cursed are those who trust in collective people and believe in the immortality of their nation.

A new version of human pride is the modern confidence in science and education. Some people believe that universal education will solve all the problems of mankind. Education will eliminate religious prejudice and superstition and all the injustices that flow from them. Some people hold that reason can adjust all human conflicts and arbitrate all conflicts of interest. But history shows that reason turns out to be the servant

445

of prejudice as much as its master in even the best people. Science can sharpen the fierce fangs of people as much as it can alleviate human pain. Ignorance is not to be preferred to education and science, but cursed are those who trust in mere humans even if they are intelligent people or perhaps especially if they are intelligent people. Intelligence increases the power of people for both good and evil. Our inner self exhibits an incomprehensible duplicity, characterized by self-deception. It is incurable. We are prisoners of our own opposition to God.

The Lord through the prophet compares "those who trust in mere mortals and make mere flesh their strength" to "a shrub in the desert." The identity of the arar ("a shrub") has puzzled translators. The KJV translates "heath," the RSV and NRSV "shrub," the Good News Bible "bush," NEB "juniper," and "tamarisk" is in the 1978 translation of the Jewish Publication Society. Recent study has come to the conclusion that it is the famous Sodom apple.[119]

As a shepherd, Jeremiah was familiar with the plants, vegetation, and trees of the wilderness and desert regions and of a number of oases. A short distance away from Anatoth where he lived is the harsh, barren landscape of the Arabah in the Valley of Jericho. The contrast in vegetation is dramatic. The lush foliage of the wadi gives way to parched, partially salty flatlands, sparsely dotted with vegetation. In the middle of the barren, arid, salty plain, the desolate Sodom apple stands out in stark relief against an empty landscape. It is a small tree reaching a height of about ten feet. From a distance, it appears to bear juicy, thirst quenching fruit. But its appearance is deceiving. The Bedouin call it "cursed lemon," and they explain the name with a story.

Before the destruction of Sodom and Gomorrah, when the citizens of those two cities still followed God's commandments, the arar was a tree that produced juicy fruit for the comfort and relief of thirsty desert travelers. But when the people of Sodom and Gomorrah turned away from God, He destroyed their cities and dried up the arar so that it shriveled, producing only fibers and seeds. The legend ends with the idea that when people once again return to the ways of God, the <u>arar</u>'s original sweet juiciness will be restored.

"Those who trust in mere mortals and make mere flesh their strength . . . shall be like a shrub in the desert." <u>Arabah</u> ("the desert") is a general term as well as a specific geographic designation for various areas in the Afro-Syrian Rift. The region of Eilat is called Arabah in Deut. 2:8. The Dead Sea is called "the sea of the Arabah" in Joshua 3:16. In Joshua 11:2, the area south of Lake Chinneroth is called Arabah. The Arabah Valley of Jericho is mentioned in 2 Kings 25:4 and other places.

"Those who trust in mere mortals and make mere flesh their strength . . . shall not see when relief comes." They will not recognize the good times when they come. They will not feel prosperous even when conditions are favorable. Prosperity offers no relief for those who lack trust in God.

Some of the fruit trees near the lower springs in the wilderness and desert regions familiar to Jeremiah remain green and bear fruit even in winter while trees of the same species growing in the vicinity of Anatoth are still dormant and leafless. The trees near the lower springs are not troubled when there is drought or when devastating heat sweeps over the Judean desert.

We ought not place our hope in another world, because we find this world evil. The goodness of creation can be discerned beneath the corruptions of human sin. We should not be driven to despair by sin. Christians believe that life is worth living, and this world is not merely a vale of tears. God is not only our Creator but also our Redeemer. The greatest work He has done since creation is the passion of Jesus. Jesus saved the world.

The evil other people do is not very different from the evil we ourselves do. It is false to equate our ideals with our achievements and regard other people with bitterness, because they fail to measure up to our ideals. We need to be conscious of our own shortcomings. The best antidote for the bitterness of a disillusioned trust in other people is disillusionment in ourselves. Such disillusionment may be true repentance.

The Christian trusts only God. He created a good world. Although humans have corrupted it through sin, God will finally destroy the evil that people do and save them from their sins.

Such faith is not optimism. It does not come until human optimism breaks down, and people stop trusting in themselves that they are good. History teaches that human life is subject to decay, and virtue is subject to corruption.

The prophet contrasts trust in the Lord with trust in human strength. He encourages the people of God to rely wholly on the unseen despite what appears to be real, true, and factual. Jahweh is the unseen God of the universe, ever present yet beyond the reach of our sensory perception. Reason encourages us to depend fully on what can be perceived, what is visible, what can be touched, and what is real. We value empirical data, evidence, and proof that is certain.

Jahweh admonishes us not to be deceived by what appears to be real. We are challenged to depend on the imperceptible, giving it priority over that which is evident. What we perceive to be real and therefore worthy of our trust is not as certain as the unseen truth. This is hard to swallow in our contemporary context. God is the only reality that is dependable and trustworthy, cf. Prov. 3:5. Reliance on the Lord brings a blessed and fruitful life.

The contrast between the wicked and the righteous is illustrated by comparing the struggling Sodom apple tree in the Arabah with one planted "by water." A fruitful tree planted by water is a picture of blessing.

Depicting prosperity in material terms is in keeping with one of God's principal promises to the people of Israel in Ex. 3:8 to give them a fertile land, flowing with milk and honey.

Knowing that the God of the universe cares deeply for us gives us strength. Knowing that God has actively intervened in our lives in Jesus and His passion gives us great confidence. "Those . . . whose trust is the Lord" are "blessed" in times of plenty and times of adversity.

What does this say to those dedicated but poor Christians around the world? Do they trust less? Is there a factor that confounds simple trust and blessing? Jeremiah's own experiences seem to challenge the truth that "those . . . whose trust is the Lord" are "blessed," cf. Jer. 12:1-3.

Life continues in a delicate balance in the part of the world where Jeremiah lived. "Those . . . whose trust is the Lord . . . shall not fear when heat comes." The blessed experience adversity. The Lord does not shield them, but He provides them ability to overcome when difficulties abound. Trust in the Lord fosters life and life more fully in spite of the inevitable times of distress.

The questions created by the tensions between the curses and the blessings pronounced by the Lord through the prophet Jeremiah are resolved in the passion of Jesus, but they are not solved there. The Son of God endured cruelty, injustice, oppression, and the death of an innocent man. When we experience these things, we can think that we are being cursed. But what Jesus experienced shows divine love for us. In some wonderful and mysterious way that we will never fully understand, through His passion He took away the sin of the world, cf. John 1:29; 3:16; and 2 Cor. 5:18-19.

Jeremiah was called to be a warner to God's people. As Jer. 1:10 says, the Lord appointed him to tear out and to pull down, to ruin and to destroy. Like a modern wrecking crew, he was to break down all human achievements so that the will and way of God might prevail and people might make the Lord their trust and be blessed.

Jer. 17 seems to be a collection of odds and ends. John Bright called it "Jeremiah's miscellaneous file."

Some of the thoughts of Ps. 1 parallel those of Jer. 17:5-10.

1 Corinthians 15:12-20

Christ as "the First Fruits" is an incredibly apt metaphor to proclaim the resurrection of Christians. The matter of a universal resurrection is not at issue in 1 Cor. 15:12-20, only the destiny of those who have died in Christ.

The term "first fruits" comes from the ritual for the Feast of Unleavened Bread in Lev. 23:9-14. It was a harvest festival. "The first fruits" was the first sheaf of the harvest.

Christ died during the Feast of Unleavened Bread. Passover is the first day of the Feast, cf. Mark 14:12 and Matt. 26:17.

The last supper Jesus ate with His disciples in an upper room somewhere in the city of Jerusalem was the Passover meal. The following afternoon He died.

The first fruits offering was made to the priest on the third day of the festival. The completion of the harvest was celebrated seven weeks later at Pentecost. Christ was raised on the third day as the "first fruits of those who have died." He was the first instance who established the character of the entire harvest and what will happen to all. The fulfillment of His resurrection or the completion of the harvest, will take place at the parousia.

Paul uses the term aparche ("first fruits") for the first converts to Christianity in a geographical area in 1 Cor. 16:15 and Rom. 16:5. He also uses it in Rom. 8:23 and 11:16. But only in 1 Cor. 15 does he use it of Christ.

"The first fruits" implies a community of nature. The first sheaf is the same in kind as the entire harvest. The consecration of the first fruits involves the consecration of the whole even before it is fully developed, cf. Rom. 11:16.

The metaphor signifies both something incomplete and something hopeful. Christ is the beginning and the guarantee of the full harvest of those who have died in Him. Two resurrections are seen as one revealed in two temporal stages. In the resurrection of Jesus, the beginning of the end is apparent. The powers of the age to come are at work. The last times, the age to come has begun.

The resurrection of all who belong to Christ is strongly affirmed when Christ is called "the first fruits of those who have died." As the "first fruits," Christ's resurrection guarantees that those who are in Christ will rise from the dead with Him. It portrays the idea that Christians are "united with (Christ) in a resurrection like his," a fact Paul states in Rom. 6:5. Such solidarity is effected in Holy Baptism, cf. also Col. 2:12 and 3:1-4.

In Jesus, the bonds of death over the human race were loosened, Peter says in Acts 2:24 on Pentecost. If death was not able to hold in its power the representative Man, Jesus, its power over mankind is broken. Even though others must still die, the omnipotence of death is ended. Jesus has taken from death its power to doom the human race, cf. 2 Tim. 1:10.

Jesus' resurrection is a fact of the past, it promises what will happen in the future, and it radically changes the present. A different situation has come into being through the fact that one resurrected Person lives. The power of resurrection, the Holy Spirit, has entered the realm of the physical.

With the same expression, "first fruits," that he applies to the risen Christ, Paul speaks of the Holy Spirit at work in us in Rom. 8:23. The resurrection of Christ and the work of the Holy Spirit are closely related. This is the reason the resurrection of the dead is in the Third Article of the Apostles' Creed.

Salvation is a divine work in three tenses, past, present, and future. Through Christ and His crucifixion, God reconciled us to Himself, cf. 2 Cor. 5:18 and 1 Cor. 6:11. Our salvation is an accomplished fact, already completed. Christ lived, died, and rose not merely as an individual but as the corporate representative of the human race. As a present experience, we "are being saved," cf. 1 Cor. 1:18; 15:2; 2 Cor. 2:15. We are being transformed into the likeness of Christ, cf. 2 Cor. 3:18. But past fact and present experience will have their culmination in the future: we live in expectation of the parousia. Then death will be swallowed up in victory, and God's universal purpose will be fully realized.

We need not let death, misfortunes, distress, and misery terrify us. Nor should we regard what the world has done and can do, but we should balance all these things against who we are and what we have in Christ. We have life with Him, and we are no longer under the power of death. The devil aims his poisonous darts at our conscience. He afflicts us with all sorts of trouble. But against all of these things, our defiant affirmation is that Christ is our "First Fruits," "Christ has been raised from the dead." The resurrection has begun. He has burst through the devil's kingdom, through hell and death. Christ rules and has rescued us from the prison of death.

Paul's joyous and authoritative proclamation of Christ as the First Fruits in v. 20 is in sharp contrast to the dreary picture he has been rejecting through the use of reason in vs. 12-19.

451

The source of those dreary pictures is the position of some in the Corinthian church that "there is no resurrection of the dead." Paul says in v. 20 that what they say simply is not true! Christ has been raised, and His resurrection includes all who are His!

The resurrection of believers is at issue in 1 Cor. 15:12-20, not the resurrection of Jesus Christ. But the resurrection of Jesus Christ establishes the resurrection of His followers; so the resurrection of Jesus is the basic issue. Vs. 12-19 deal with the consequences of rejecting the resurrection of believers.

The people who say, "There is no resurrection of the dead," probably downgrade physical existence as the result of their upbringing in Greek philosophy. The Greeks considered the body unimportant. A physical resurrection was an absurd notion to them. God may be able to raise a corpse, but, as Greeks they asked, "Why?" Matter is evil, and it is incredible that a soul, once set free from the body by death, wants to return to its unclean prison. Instead of resurrection, some of the Christians in Corinth may have said that souls ascend to heaven at the moment of death. Another possibility is that they believed the resurrection had already taken place, cf. 2 Tim. 2:18. The Sadducees also denied the resurrection of the dead, cf. Matt. 22:23. Some of the people Paul is talking to could be Jewish Christians.

Paul is more gentle with the Corinthians than he is with the Galatians in Gal. 1:6 and 3:1. This is probably because the Corinthians have to overcome the culture of which they are a product. There is no thought of excommunication, but Paul does not want them to upset the faith of their fellow Christians any more.

He draws seven deductions from their erroneous position. One, if "there is no resurrection of the dead, then Christ has not been raised." Two, "if Christ has not been raised, then our proclamation has been in vain." Kene ("in vain") means empty, hollow, devoid of reality.

Three, "if Christ has not been raised . . . your faith has been in vain." Paul is appealing to them as committed Christians who accept the Christian faith as recounted in vs. 3-5. They believe Christ "was raised on the third day." If Christ has not been raised, their faith has no foundation in fact because it is based on something that didn't happen.

Four, "if Christ has not been raised . . . we are . . . found to be misrepresenting God." "We," first of all, includes Paul himself; but it includes even those who say there is no resurrection of the dead and the entire church, because all of them have been a part of the Christian proclamation that Christ "was raised on the third day," cf. v. 4. The words "misrepresenting God" can be translated literally "false witnesses of God." As an objective genitive, the meaning is "false witnesses about God." As a subjective genitive, the meaning is that God inspired the apostles and the others to tell lies about Him.

Five, "If Christ has not been raised, your faith is futile and you are still in your sins." Jesus' atoning death is revealed, supported, and affirmed by His resurrection. The resurrection is essential for validating Jesus' passion.

Sometimes there is little difference in the meaning of the word kene ("in vain") used in v. 14 and the word mataia ("futile") used in v. 17. In this passage, kene means wanting in reality, and mataia means wanting in result or fruitless.

What Paul means when he says, "your faith is futile," is "you are still in your sins." The two phrases are not separate ideas. The word "and" is not a part of the original Greek text.

The gospel says that "Christ died for our sins," cf. v. 3. The same thing is said in Rom. 4:25. Denial of Jesus' resurrection makes untenable the idea that He has taken away our sins. A dead Jesus does not save us from death, the penalty for sin. A risen Jesus saves us by His death.

Six, "If Christ has not been raised . . . then those who have died in Christ have perished." Not being liberated from sin, they remain a prey of death. This does not mean merely that they are not alive. It means that they are at the mercy of the power of death.

Seven, "If for this life only we have hoped in Christ, we are of all people most to be pitied." Monon ("only") qualifies either the word elpikotes ("hoped") or the whole clause. The meaning is: "If all that we Christians have got is hope in Christ, without the possibility of life with Him hereafter, that is pathetic?" In that case, our hope will not be realized; and, as Paul says in v. 32, we ought to eat, drink, and enjoy ourselves.

Another possible translation is, "If in this life we have only hoped, etc." Christians should be pitied for having only hope and not the fulfillment of that hope. The Christian hope is not only for this life. The fulfillment of our hope will be realized at Jesus' coming, cf. v. 23.

We are to be pitied if there is no resurrection, because we now endure all kinds of troubles and misfortunes for our faith. People despise and vilify, revile and slander us. The world is hostile to us. Our faith is in vain and futile if Christ has not been raised and there is no resurrection of the dead.

The NRSV footnote points out that the Greek really says in v. 20 "those who have fallen asleep." Christ rose from the dead. Thereby He destroyed death. For this reason, Paul does not speak of us as having died but having fallen asleep; but He is referring to death. Since Christ passed from death to life, death is no longer death; it has become sleep. Christians who lie in the ground are no longer dead but sleepers, people who will rise again. The word "sleep" implies awakening, resurrection.

The Greek word <u>nuni</u> ("in fact") in v. 20 does not have temporal but logical meaning.

Luther says, "No one who . . . claims to be a Christian or a preacher of the Gospel may deny (Christ's resurrection)."[120]

Luke 6:17-26

How shall we understand these words that pronounce a blessing on the "poor" and a woe on the "rich," a blessing on those who are "hungry now" and a woe on those who are "full now," a blessing on those who "weep now" and a woe on those who are "laughing now," a blessing on those who are hated, excluded, reviled, and defamed on account of the Son of Man and a woe on those who are popular? The words seem upsidedown and contrary to common sense.

Appreciation for these sayings requires more than a surface

understanding of Jesus' character and His mission. He came not to be served but to serve and to give His life as a ransom for the world, cf. Mark 10:45. He did not try to accumulate wealth or to be popular. He died on a cross to take away the sins of the world. He walked the downward way, the way of humility, self-sacrifice, and death. His disciples follow Him along that way, because it is the way to eternal life. He teaches and shows how God made us to live.

What Jesus did and teaches does not reflect the life-goals of most Christians. Our initial reaction may be rejection. The words are clear and straightforward, and their meaning can hardly be missed. But when we try to give them to other people, we begin to fumble and to stammer. We know how difficult it will be for them to accept what Jesus says, because we have difficulty with it, too.

The goals Jesus proposes are certainly what His disciples want, but Jesus says that the way many of us are trying to reach these goals will not get us there. Disciples want God to be their king, but striving for wealth will not lead to that goal; nor does the acquisition of riches mean that we have gotten there. Wealth may hinder us. Disciples of Jesus want to speak the truth for God; but when people like us and what we say, that does not mean we are giving them insights into the truth of God. The Old Testament prophets were not always well received by the people of their day, and many people were attracted to the false prophets. The blessings Jesus points to are what God has in mind for us: "yours is the kingdom of God," "you shall be filled," "you shall rejoice," and "your reward will be great in heaven." The disciples of Jesus want these blessings most.

Jesus does not say that those who are poor, those who lack what is needed for a pleasant life, and those who suffer are guaranteed heaven on earth. The beatitude addressed to the poor says that God is ruling them. As the poor believe this, their situation changes. They become capable of helping others without thought of prestige or envy of those who have more than they do. Because they are confident of God's favor, they can trust in God's providence and look forward to a joyous future. They need not worry about food, clothing, or anything at all for the next day, as Jesus says in Luke 12:22-31.

One of the harshest effects of poverty is a loss of self-esteem. Because other people regard poor people as unimportant and out of favor with God, they tend to think of themselves that way. They feel that they count for nothing and tend to be rather hopeless. To such disciples, Jesus speaks really good news: "You are a part of God's concern. You count! God rules you! You can be happy!"

Of course, things were different in Jesus' day. Because of the agrarian culture and the climate, little clothing was required, finding a home presented no great problem, and food could be obtained if necessary in the fields. It was possible to live practically from hand to mouth.

Matthew talks about "the poor in spirit" in Matt. 5:3. This rules out pretensions, immodest arrogance, and anxious concern that can be found even among disciples who are materially poor.

That Jesus is talking about the poor in the literal sense is underscored by the "woe" over the rich. How the blessing and the woe are intended is made clear in the parable of the Rich Fool in 12:16-21 and the story of Lazarus and the Rich Man in 16:19-31. The rich person is not lost because he is rich, and the poor is not blessed because he is poor. Instead, the conclusion is stated in the introduction and conclusion of the parable of the Rich Fool, cf. 12:15 and 12:21. Life is lost for the person who thinks he can live on what he has gotten for himself. The entire world began to experience some of the effects of greed in 2008.

Jesus is on the side of the poor. The rich who heap up for themselves treasures that rust and moths consume and that thieves can steal and who give their heart to wealth, He presents in all their miserliness. Success and social advancement mean nothing to Jesus. Anyone who exalts himself will be humbled and vice versa, cf. Luke 14:11. Disciples who are secure and sheltered, attached to the transitory goods of this world, do not live in God's realm.

On the other hand, Jesus does not require His followers to

renounce material things. There was no renunciation of possessions in the primitive Christian community. A number of Jesus' followers had houses of their own. He approved Zacchaeus' distribution of only half of his possessions in Luke 19:8. What He demands of the rich young man in Matt. 19:16-22, if he wants to follow Him, He does not require generally and rigidly from every disciple in every situation. Jesus was supported by those of His followers who had money, especially by the women who followed Him, cf. Luke 8:1-3. Sometimes He accepted invitations both from rich Pharisees and from rich tax collectors.

On the basis of the beatitude on the poor, early Jewish Christians called themselves "Ebionites" from the Hebrew word for poor. The name appears in the lists of sects provided by the church fathers. It was an honorable name that deteriorated. The remnant of the primitive church adopted it probably after their flight from Jerusalem. The sect that emphasized the ideal of poverty continued into the second century. They believed that there was an inner connection between righteousness and poverty, and this belief hardened into law. Later church fathers (Hippolytus, Tertullian, Epiphanius, and others) mistakenly supposed that there was a father or godfather of the sect named Ebion. According to Epiphanius, later Ebionites on Cyprus about the year 377 appealed to the position taken by their ancestors in Jerusalem who had laid all their possessions at the feet of the apostles. They maintained that Jesus had promised the kingdom of God to the poor. Their social conditions became extremely impoverished and wretched. Later, the hatred and satire of opponents reduced Ebionite to a nickname and term of abuse so that the Jewish Christians themselves avoided using it. They did, however, continue to associate their voluntary disposition of possessions, following Acts 4:34-35, and their poverty with the ideal of holiness. Paul may have been referring to some early Ebionites in Rom. 15:26 when he refers to "the poor among the saints at Jerusalem." Other Ebionite passages in Luke include 12:33; 14:33; and all of ch. 16.[121]

Isaiah's suffering servant says, "The Spirit of the Lord . . .

has anointed me to bring good news to the poor," cf. Luke 4:18. The first beatitude proclaims that good news.

Whenever possessions come between God and us, whenever people are slaves to money and make the accumulation of it their goal, the curse of v. 24 applies. Jesus' warning is crystal-clear: it is easier for a camel to go through the eye of a needle than for someone who is rich to enter God's kingdom, cf. Mark 10:25. All attempts to modify that saying - a small gate instead of a needle's eye or a ship's rope instead of a camel - are of no avail. Wealth is extremely dangerous to salvation. The intended goal of this warning is not condemnation but repentance.

Luke spends considerable time talking about the rich, more than Matthew and Mark do. The rich are more than possessors of material goods. There is a contrast between the rich and the poor in 21:1-4 and 16:19-31. This is preceded by another considerable discourse on the use of wealth in 16:1-15.

A rich tax collector is held up as an example to follow in 19:1-10. That Jesus does not object to wealth per se is suggested in the parable of the Pounds, cf. 19:11-27. The one coin is taken away from the man who has only one and given to the man who has ten. The rich, in the estimation of Jesus, according to these passages, are those who love money not those who only have great wealth.

Being rich is apparently a hindrance to discipleship, cf. 18:22-27; 12:21; 8:14. For this reason, Zacchaeus who gave half of his belongings to the poor and returned four times as much as he had taken to the people he had cheated, cf. 19:8, is held up as an example for Christians. See also 16:9; 14:12-14; 18:28-30.

The word translated "you have received" in v. 24 is apechete. It was a Greek commercial term that acknowledged full payment. Beyond their present possession of riches, rich people have nothing to hope for. They can expect nothing more from God.

Those who are described as "laughing now" in v. 25 might be people who are considered to be cool.

The words of v. 26 may have something to say to disciples

who think the church must never do anything to cause people to become unhappy with her. What does it say to those who insist that the church must not become involved in the social and economic problems of the day, because this will turn people away from the church, the church will get into trouble, and the church might be wrong some times? Some disciples feel that the church should not mess around in the common life of people, because she might get hurt.

The beatitude that speaks a blessing on the hungry brings into being that which it describes. In other words, Jesus' statement that they are blessed conveys blessedness to them.

Jesus is not referring to an existing social or religious group. The hungry are those who both outwardly and inwardly are painfully deficient in the things essential for life as God means it to be, and who, since they cannot help themselves, turn to God. People who do that find divine help in Jesus.

This world is a time of unequal distribution. We should be ready for hardship. Hunger is an elemental expression of impotence. Sometimes, it is difficult to understand why some people suffer hunger, poverty, disaster, the ravages of war, illness, etc. The ways of God are often inscrutable. Still, we can trust God and believe in Him. The hungry are forced into a situation where they must learn to wait for God. The hunger experienced by Israel in the wilderness is described in Deut. 8:3 as a historical means of instruction.

Luke 16:19-31 makes the point of the beatitude on hunger in parabolic form. The woe of 6:25 is incorporated into the parable.

The disciple who is ready to live by God's grace will receive everything essential for true life, according to Luke 12:22-31. When Jesus says, "you will be filled," He is talking about what God will do. This is a numinous passive. God is the agent.

Four outrages are listed in the beatitude of v. 22: hatred, ostracism, denunciation, and denigration of one's name. Ostracism probably was experienced by the Jewish Christians of Luke's day; they were excluded from the synagogues. Ostracism can also be exclusion from social intercourse. Defamation probably refers to the name Christian, cf. Acts 11:26;

26:28; 1 Pet. 4:16, more than to personal names. The NRSV footnote translates more literally, "cast out your name as evil." To revile someone is to heap insults on him or her.

A part of the reward of the fourth beatitude is being linked with the prophets. The reference could be to the prophets of the New Testament church but probably Old Testament prophets are meant, cf. 1 Kings 19:10; Jer. 26:20-24; 38:6-13; Luke 11:50-51; Acts 7:52; 1 Thess. 2:14-15. Prophets of old who enjoyed the esteem of their contemporaries sometimes turned out to be deceivers, cf. Is. 30:9-14; Jer. 5:30-31; 6:13-14; 23:16-17.

This collection of Jesus' words is called the Sermon on the Plain. It is very similar to Jesus' Sermon on the Mount, but there are differences, too. These words are called the Sermon on the Plain, because Jesus "came down . . . and stood on a level place." Jesus was on "the mountain" praying, cf. Luke 6:12. In Matt. 5:1, "he went up the mountain; and . . . sat down" to teach. That's why Matt. 5-7 is called the Sermon on the Mount. Like Moses, cf. Ex. 19:14, 20-21, 24-25; 32:15; 34:29, Luke describes Jesus descending the mountain to speak to His disciples.

The "great multitude of people" that gathered to hear Jesus was from Judea, including Jerusalem, and "the coast of Tyre and Sidon." Tyre and Sidon were two ancient and important cities of Phoenicia on the coast of the Mediterranean. They lay in Syria in ancient times but are in Lebanon today, south of Beirut.

Power for healing "came out from (Jesus)" according to v. 19 "and healed all" who had diseases. This power is also mentioned in 5:17 and 8:46.

The beatitudes of Matt. 5:3-12 are not exactly the same as those of Luke. Matthew has eight; Luke has four which match the first, second, fourth, and ninth of Matthew. In Matthew, Jesus uses the impersonal third person plural, while in Luke He directly addresses His disciples. The Sermon on the Plain has only 30 verses; the Sermon on the Mount has 107. Some count 109.

Despite many differences in the two sermons, there is a basic similarity. The subject matter is the same; they give directions to Jesus' disciples in their behavior. Both sermons conclude with the parable of the Two Houses that challenges the listeners and readers to become not only hearers of His words but doers, too.

Jesus did not originate the beatitude form. Macarisms can be found in Egyptian literature, classical and Hellenistic literature, and in the Old Testament.

7th Sunday after the Epiphany

Year A

Leviticus 19:1-2 and 9-18

Two familiar commands, "You shall be holy, for I the Lord your God am holy" and "You shall love your neighbor as yourself," and the familiar refrain, "I am the Lord" or "I am the Lord your God," constitute the burden of this Lesson.

God chose ancient Israel to be His special people among the nations of the world in the exodus. He gave them instructions as to how they should worship Him and how they should live. This attempt to establish a people of God on the earth failed because of Israel's disobedience. So God decided to accomplish His goal in a different way.

The Son of God became Jesus of Nazareth to fulfill God's good pleasure. He established the new people of God through His passion. The followers of Jesus are the new Israel. To the Christians in Asia Minor "who (were) chosen and destined by God the Father and sanctified by the Spirit to be obedient to Jesus Christ," according to 1 Pet. 1:2, 1 Pet. 2:9-10 says, "you are a chosen race, a royal priesthood, a holy nation, God's own people . . . . Once you were not a people, but now you are God's people . . . ."

The book of Leviticus is a record of the instruction God gave His ancient people. We distinguish between moral law and ritual law, but that distinction would not have been intelligible to ancient Israel. They made no such differentiation regarding duties to God. For example, if a person did not know better, he might assume that the passage, "You shall love your neighbor as yourself," is moral law and is to be found somewhere in the prophetic material of the Old Testament; but it is found in Leviticus which includes mostly ritual law.

Jahweh declared Israel to be "a holy nation" at Mt. Sinai, cf. Ex. 19:6. Even though the word <u>kadosh</u> is usually translated "holy," its primary etymological meaning is "set apart for God," "separate," "different." God's people are to be holy as He is holy.

To define the holiness of God is impossible. We can only point to it with negatives. The holiness of God excludes all that is unjust, incomplete, unclean, and impure. God is holy in His being, His attributes, His works, and all His dealings and judgments.

The God of Israel and of the church is different from anyone or anything. So, too, His people are to be holy, that is, they are to be different from all other peoples. The Israelites were hallowed by being consecrated to Jahweh's service through their election, their entry into covenant with Him, and their obedience to His commandments, cf. Ex. 19:5-6. The church's consciousness of her differentness – that is, her holiness - is vital to her nature and identity as she confronts the world.

It is impossible to apply all the rules of an agricultural society that ancient Israel was to the complicated conditions of an economic society that we are. Nevertheless, the basic elements of the stipulations can be applied. For example, God is concerned about the poor and aliens, cf. vs. 9-10. His people should be concerned about them, too. We represent Him on the earth. Poverty is as real in the USA today as it was in ancient Israel. Many aged people are among the poor. Wealthy nations ought to share their resources with the poor ones. The Christian countries of the West own most of the world's wealth. We can have a concern for the poor nations.

Resident aliens were non-Israelites who lived in the land of Israel. They were expected to obey certain cultic regulations, cf. Lev. 17:15-16. They could even celebrate Passover if they were circumcised, cf. Ex. 12:48-49. Still resident aliens were distinct and lived at some disadvantage. For example, while they were not slaves, they did not possess full civic rights. They or their children could be made slaves, cf. Lev. 25:45-46. As a rule, the resident aliens were poor and were grouped with the poor, that is, with the widows and orphans who were economically weak, cf. Jer. 7:6; 22:3; Zech. 7:10. They also were under the protection of God, cf. Deut. 10:18; Ps. 146:9; Malachi 3:5. The people of Israel were to help the resident aliens remembering that they themselves had once been aliens in Egypt, cf. Ex. 23:9; Deut. 24:17-18, 21-22. They were to love the aliens as themselves, cf. Lev. 19:34 and Deut. 10:19. There may be a correspondence between the resident aliens in ancient Israel and the illegal aliens who populate the USA, but the fit probably needs to be debated.

Dealing falsely and lying are dealt with under the rubric of stealing in v. 11. Maybe this can be applied to today's company prospectuses and to modern advertising. Suppression of truth may be a form of lying. This may say something to businessmen and salesmen.

In a socio-economic society in which many people lived hand-to-mouth, to retain a servant's wages overnight meant that his family did not eat that evening, cf. Deut. 24:14-15.

Some say that v. 14 means that we should not take advantage of anyone's physical weaknesses or handicaps.

There is not to be one law for the rich and another for the poor. Money and social standing should not make a difference in the courts.

There are to be no whispering campaigns. We should not try to get our neighbor into trouble.

The Hebrew of v. 16 literally translates, "you shall not stand against the blood." This means that we should not try to get our neighbor put to death.

"You shall reprove your neighbor" is a far cry from the current widespread idea that loving one's neighbors means not judging them but rather accepting them as they are. We are to be genuinely concerned for our neighbor's spiritual and temporal welfare. This concern is called for by Jesus in Matt. 18:15-20.

There are eight direct references in the New Testament to the command, "You shall love your neighbor as yourself," cf. Mark 12:31; Matt. 5:43; 19:19; 22:39; Luke 10:27; Rom. 13:9; Gal. 5:14; and Jas 2:8. In Hebrew, the command consists of only three words, but it has evoked a virtual torrent of commentary and exegesis.

The Lesson gives specific suggestions as to what it means to love our neighbor. God's people are to be generous to the poor in the gleaning of their fields, cf. vs. 9-10. Lev. 19:34 says, "You shall love the alien as yourself."

"Love your neighbor as yourself" describes an aspect of what it means to be holy. It is a key part of Jesus' message. It is a statement of His basic teaching on our obligation to others. Jesus did not invent this idea as many Christian people tend to suppose. Jesus declared it the second commandment in Matt. 22:39, but He said it is like the first which teaches us to love God. Jesus says that on this command and on the command to love God, cf. Deut. 6:4-5, hang all the scriptures, cf. Matt. 22:37-40. The disciples of Jesus should interpret all of scripture on the basis of these two commandments. The scribe says and Jesus agrees that loving God and our neighbor "is much more important than all whole burnt offerings and sacrifices" in Mark 12:33. All duties toward our fellow human beings are summed up in this command, according to Rom. 13:9.

Three questions arise. The first is, what is love? The second, who is my neighbor? has been asked for a long time. Jesus answered it in the story of the Good Samaritan in Luke 10:29-37. The third question is, what is meant by loving my neighbor as myself?"

God wants more than the abstract feeling in our hearts toward others that is suggested to some by the word "love." Webster's definitions don't cover the meaning of the word for Christians. Such an abstract idea would have been alien to an Israelite world characterized by concrete commandments.

The Hebrew words involve an unusual construction. Ahab

("love") is typically used with the direct object marker et. An example is Gen. 29:18. But in this passage, the Hebrew construction is different. Ahab is used with an indirect object marker, the preposition la, usually translated "to." This construction occurs only three other times in the Old Testament, cf. Lev. 19:34; 1 Kings 5:1; and 2 Chron. 19:2. There is an interesting parallelism in 2 Chron. 19:2. The first phrase contains the verb azar which means "to assist" or "to help." The parallel in the second phrase is ahab. This suggests that ahab can best be translated "to provide assistance to," "to be useful to," "to help." Accordingly, v. 18 might be translated "be useful to your neighbor as to yourself." This translation works also in the other places where the same construction is found.[122] It eliminates the abstract aspect of love and gives it a more concrete and pragmatic context. Love involves action, doing good, not mere feeling.

Jesus' story of the Good Samaritan in Luke 10:29-37 illustrates that neighbor-love. There is no indication that the Samaritan kisses the fallen man's cheek or embraces him warmly. Although he is "moved with pity," his love is described in bandaging the stranger's wounds, pouring oil on his lacerations and bruises, placing him on his animal, paying for his convalescence, and assuming responsibility for his debt.

In classical Judaism and among present day Orthodox Jews, the commandment to "love your neighbor" means to love your fellow Jew. The context is clearly parochial: "your people" and "your neighbor" in v. 16, "your kin" and "your neighbor" in v. 17, and "your people" in v. 18. The text reflects our common human nature to love those who are close to us and not outsiders. To maintain peace and order within the tribal family and community, it is essential that people who are related maintain strong bonds of love towards each other. This ensures not only peace but also the unity, solidarity, and strength of the community. Jesus called for more. He pointed out the unimpressive value of love which is parochial in Matt. 5:46-47: "If you love those who love you, what reward do you have? Do not even tax collectors do the same? . . . Do not even the Gentiles do the same?"

Loving a stranger is counter to human nature. Freud wrote: "If this grandiose commandment had run 'love thy neighbor as thy neighbor loves thee,' I should not take exception to it." "If he is a stranger to me . . . it will be hard for me to love him."

Some say that Jesus gives this passage universal application, but it does not have that in the Old Testament. The context lists a number of people for whom we are to care: the poor (ani) and the alien in vs. 10 and 15, a laborer in v. 13, the deaf and the blind in v. 14, and fellow citizens (amit) in vs. 15-17. Jesus expands the category of neighbor to include even our enemy.

The commandment broadens out in Lev. 19:33-34. It does not, however, give aliens right to the land. That comes in Ezek. 47:21-23. When the exiles returned to the holy land from Babylon, the land was not empty but was occupied by other people. The exiles were to be tolerant toward the aliens. Although they were still considered aliens, everyone must enjoy human and political rights as equal citizens and share the land on an equal basis.

In Israel today, more than a million people are known as Israeli Arabs. They are Israeli citizens. But, they are not considered nationals. The distinction between citizenship and nationality is one of the contested issues in Israel.

Three million Palestinians live under Israeli occupation in the West Bank and the Gaza Strip. They are considered "resident aliens." The land belongs to the Jewish people, and the Palestinians have no rights to it. Religious Jews consider the Leviticus text to be more binding than the text of Ezekiel, because it comes from the heart of the torah.[123]

Who is our neighbor is influenced by our answer to the question, who is our God? Jesus makes this very clear in Matt. 22:37-40 where love for our neighbor elucidates our love for God. Luke 10:27 indicates that the combination was commonly understood in Jesus' day. If our God is exclusive, our neighbor is exclusive. If we define neighbor in a narrow and exclusive way, it is because we believe in an exclusive God. But God is the loving Creator of all people, and we all stand before Him on an equal basis. He is the God of justice, mercy, and love. The relationship between God and our neighbor is brought out in 1 John 4:20-21.

The English word "neighbor" has the connotation of being one who lives next door. But Jesus' story of the Samaritan teaches that our neighbor is everyone who needs our help and our compassion. The cultural tension between Jews and Samaritans is an important aspect of Jesus' story.

Some think, on the basis of the phrase "as yourself," that love is to be ego centered. If a person does not love himself, the command justifies the mistreatment of others. This is a modern idea and is not in agreement with the worldview of the people of the Old Testament. It is an aberration of Biblical thought. Paul's words to the Philippians can help interpret the phrase in a Christian way: "Let the same mind be in you that was in Christ Jesus, who, though he was in the form of God, did not regard equality with God as something to be exploited, but emptied himself, taking the form of a slave, being born in human likeness. And being found in human form, he humbled himself and became obedient to the point of death – even death on a cross" (Phil. 2:5-8).

The refrain "I am the Lord" or "I am the Lord your God" is used 15 times in Lev. 19, cf. vs. 3, 4, 10, 12, 14, 16, 18, 25, 28, 30, 31, 32, 34, 36, and 37. It is found primarily in motive clauses following the presentation of cultic or ethical requirements. The refrain emphasizes that the commands and prohibitions have been established by the Lord.

God is presented as an authoritarian rather than a loving God. The motive clauses must be understood in the context of Israel's relationship to God who acted redemptively on her behalf: "I am the Lord your God, who brought you out of the land of Egypt," cf. Lev. 19:36. The instructions extend the benefits of God's redemptive activity.

The repetition of the motivating clauses suggests that the commandments of Lev. 19 were used in the liturgies of Israel.

1 Corinthians 3:10-11 and 16-23

Some statements of this Lesson are pretty dramatic: "you are God's temple," "God's Spirit dwells in you," "all things are yours," "all belong to you, and you belong to Christ." In English, the word "you" may be singular or plural. The context determines. But in Greek, the form of the word itself usually informs us. In every case listed above, the word "you" is plural. Paul is talking about the church. He says some pretty amazing things about the church in Corinth, a troubled church, a church divided by factions!

The factions are his target. The members of the church are divided and quarreling about who is their greatest leader: Paul, Apollos, or Cephas (Peter). They are finding personal status in being followers of that leader. They are determining who is the best or the greatest on the basis of "the wisdom of this world" which Paul says "is foolishness with God." He encourages them to "become fools so that (they) may become wise." According to the wisdom of God, he says, "all things are yours . . . all belong to you, and you belong to Christ."

To those claiming personal status because they are followers of Paul, Apollos, or Cephas, Paul responds, "Let no one boast about human leaders." Already you are more than you can become by being involved with a human leader. "You are God's temple and . . . God's Spirit dwells in you."

Paul initiated the metaphor of the church as God's building in v. 9. He calls himself "a master builder" of the church in Corinth and says that he laid the foundation of that church. The Greek word is <u>architekton</u> from which obviously is derived the English word "architect." Paul calls himself "a skilled master builder," because he used the right means and materials.

The foundation he laid is Jesus Christ. "No one can lay any foundation other than" that, he says. He provides greater insight into the foundation he laid in 1 Cor. 2:1-5 where he says that he proclaimed to the Corinthians nothing except "the message about the cross" which is "Jesus Christ, and him crucified," cf. 1:18. He calls this message "the gospel" in 1:17.

Paul is not engaging in personal boasting. "The grace of God" gave him the ability to do the work of "a master builder." He is praising God for what he did.

Preachers today can take this same attitude toward their work as they evaluate it on the basis of their preaching of Christ crucified. This attitude can allay over-anxiety about how much good they are doing and also inspire them with the great dignity of their work.

Ordinary Greek usage allows the word <u>themelios</u> to be used for the foundation of a house or for that of a philosophical system. The word is used for laying the foundation of a community here and in Rom. 15:20 and for fundamental Christian doctrines in Heb. 6:1.

Some churchmen say that the foundation of the church is the Bible. They say this without any reference to Jesus Christ. For example, one church leader wrote: "Our church has taken for the foundation on which she stands the Holy Scriptures, and on it she stands honestly and squarely; from this foundation she will not depart one finger's breadth." Another wrote: "the Church of the Reformation stands on the rock of Holy Scriptures, on the <u>Sola Scriptura</u>."[124]

A popular hymn confesses what Paul wrote to the Corinthians,

> "The Church's one foundation Is Jesus Christ, her Lord;
> She is His new creation By water and the Word
> From heav'n He came and sought her To be His holy bride;
> With His own blood He bought her, And for her life He died."[125]

Another hymn:

> "My hope is built on nothing less
> Than Jesus' blood and righteousness;
> . . . On Christ, the solid rock, I stand;
> All other ground is sinking sand."[126]

Some church people have difficulty with the statement, "The gospel gives the scriptures their normative character, not vice versa," meaning "the gospel" in the sense of everything that God has done for our salvation in Jesus Christ. They want to make the Bible the foundation of the church rather than Jesus Christ. The Bible is an "other" foundation distinct and different from Jesus Christ.

Many Christians are confused by the distinction between "believing in Christ" and "believing in the Bible." They think the phrases are identical. But one refers to a person and the other to a book. Some think that believing the Bible from cover to cover distinguishes a Christian from other people. Faith and unbelief, orthodoxy and heresy are made to turn not on what people think of Jesus Christ but on what they think of the Bible. They change Paul's insistence on taking "every thought captive to obey Christ," cf. 2 Cor. 10:5, to taking every thought captive to obey the Bible.[127]

This is what the familiar song says, "Jesus loves me. This I know, for the Bible tells me so." That which supports Jesus and His love is the Bible, a book with which the people to whom Paul is writing were not familiar, because it did not exist for at least another 50 years.

In order to maintain the idea that the Bible is the foundation of the church, the correct interpretations and the correct readings of disputed Biblical texts are determined by taking a vote at a denominational convention. After this, conformity is enforced to the convention's decrees. Dissidents are brought under the power of institutional discipline and compelled either to yield or to get out. The oneness of the church, as the result, consists in conforming to the interpretations adopted by a modern convention's votes.

In Corinth, others were building on the foundation Paul laid for the church. He warns "each builder" after him to "choose with care how to build on (that foundation)." He warns them to use quality materials in 1 Cor. 3:12, and he warns against shoddy work in vs. 13-15.[128]

He raises the metaphor of the church as God's building to an even higher level by calling it "God's temple." The church not only belongs to God, He lives in her.

The metaphor of the church as God's temple came out of the Old Testament. Other metaphors for the church from the Old Testament include the planted field of God in 1 Cor. 3:5-9 and Col. 2:7, a vineyard and the flock of God in 1 Cor. 9:7, the Israel of God in Gal. 6:16, and the descendants of Abraham in Rom. 4:13, 16, 18.

The church is God's temple, because "God's Spirit dwells in (the members)." Paul's "Do you not know" seems to imply that he taught the Corinthians this at an earlier time. He uses the phrase with regard to things he thinks are obvious to the Corinthians also in 5:6; 6:16 and 19. The question implies a rebuke. The negative, <u>ouk</u>, introducing the question shows that the apostle expects the answer yes. The Corinthians have failed either to grasp or to retain this doctrine he taught them.

Although the definite article is not used with "God's temple" in v. 16, it should be understood. The church is not merely a temple of God but the temple of God. There is only one. The term "God's temple" encompasses the church as a whole, each local church, and each individual Christian. There is only one temple of God and yet each Christian is a temple.

<u>Naos</u> is the Greek word translated "temple" not <u>hieron</u>. The <u>naos</u> contained the Holy of Holies. The <u>hieron</u> included the whole of the sacred enclosure in Jerusalem.

Pagan temples featured an image of a god. The Jewish temple was inhabited by a symbol of the divine presence, the shekinah. The Christian temple is inhabited by the Spirit of God Himself.

Paul will pick up again the idea of the church as God's temple when he speaks about Godly living, especially proper sexual conduct in 1 Cor. 6:19. He uses it in his second letter to the church at Corinth to warn against religious unionism in 2 Cor. 6:16. The metaphor is applied to individual Christians in 1 Cor. 6:19, but in 3:16 it refers to a local church.

The warning in v. 17 is stronger than the one in v. 15. What it means is difficult to work out. Eternal destruction is eliminated by v. 15. But terrible ruin and eternal loss of some kind seems to be meant.

When Paul says, "God's temple is holy," he means that it is set apart from all that is worldly. Its members have no home here; our citizenship is in heaven, cf. Phil. 3:20. We wait for the city that is to come, as Heb. 13:14 says. While in this world, we are away from our home on a pilgrimage.

Paul tells the Corinthians that they are deceiving themselves if they think following either him, Apollos, or Cephas gives them personal status. The situation in Corinth is not pretty. The words, "If you think you are wise in this age," constitute a first-class conditional clause in which the condition is assumed to be true. Competing groups have plunged the community into strife, cf. 1:10-11 and 3:3-4. Each group praises its own preacher, cf. 3:21-22; 1:12, and correspondingly disparages the preachers of the other parties, cf. 4:6, 3 and 5.

The Corinthians apparently value "the wisdom" of their own preacher. Sophia is probably a key word in their competing claims. Sophia is used sixteen times in 1 Cor. 1-3 but otherwise appears seldom in the writings of Paul.

The members of the parties believe themselves to be wise, because their preacher is wise. They may pride themselves on the wisdom they demonstrate in evaluating the preachers. Their arrogance with regard to their wisdom may be linked to the party disorder.

Self-deceit easily leads people to make a wrong estimate of themselves. We always believe that we are wise, because in our own eyes and before some other people we are. Our self-understanding should be rejected, because it can cause us to misjudge ourselves badly.

We trust our wisdom. Our sins and our mistakes are not always apparent to us. We are confident that we know the difference between good and evil. We live according to that understanding. It is what hardens us against God. It is the basic evil in us, the original sin.

People who are unwilling to endure criticism against themselves, their actions, or their ideas do not believe that they are sinners. They tend to think that they are truthful, well-intentioned, and have been falsely accused.

But "the wisdom of this world is foolishness with God." Worldly wisdom is made absurd by the word about the cross. The wisdom of the people quarreling in Corinth is not superior to that of the rest of the world. It will come to nothing, Paul says in 2:6.

If they really want to be wise, they must become fools. Paul talks about the foolishness of the gospel in 1:20-25. Christ crucified is the wisdom of fools. It is the wisdom of God.

In the conclusion stated in vs. 21-22, Paul contrasts the confidence some of the Corinthian Christians have in their leaders with what God has given them in Christ. They have developed confidence trusting in the estimate they have made of their leaders using the wisdom of the world. This confidence which is the basis of the party spirit demonstrates shallow arrogance.

Human wisdom leads them to think that they are something, because they can claim a close relationship to a great man. But they have it all backwards. They do not belong to certain leaders, cf. 1:12. The leaders belong to them. Paul inverts their factional slogans.

God has given them more than the leaders: "all things are yours, whether Paul or Apollos or Cephas or the world or life or death or the present or the future – all belong to you." The love of God in Christ Jesus is stronger even than "life or death," Paul says in Rom. 8:38-39. "The present" and "the future" includes all that lies before them.

When we live according to the human understanding of good and evil, we lose ourselves. Faith produces an understanding of ourselves which sets us free. We do not belong to ourselves; we have been ransomed by Christ in His passion, cf. 1 Cor. 6:20; 7:23; and Acts 20:28. We no longer bear the care for ourselves, for our life. We should let such care go.

To belong to one's self means to conduct one's life according to standards and perceptions of worldly wisdom, while belonging to Christ means conforming one's life to the new identity given us in Christ. Through Baptism, we were made one with Christ. We are the body of Christ. Everything that belongs to Christ belongs to us - not only all people but all creation. God made us His agents to rule the earth.

After making the point "all belong to you," Paul emphasizes that we are not the ultimate owners of anything. The real Owner is God – even of Christ.

V. 23 is one of the few places in which St. Paul expresses his conception of the relation of Christ to God, cf. Col. 1:15. This subordinationism is expressed also in 1 Cor. 15:28.

The image of the church as a building occurs several times in Paul's letters. The foundation of the building is people, either Jesus Christ as in v. 11 or "the apostles and prophets" as in Eph. 2:20. In Heb. 6:1, "the foundation" is more doctrinal: "repentance from dead works and faith toward God, instruction about baptisms, laying on of hands, resurrection of the dead, and eternal judgment."

The structure depends for its coherence and stability on Jesus Christ as "the cornerstone" in Eph. 2:20. The Old Testament writers called the Messiah "the chief cornerstone" that had been rejected by the builders in Ps. 118:22. He is "a foundation stone. . . a precious cornerstone, a sure foundation" in Is. 28:16.

The growth of the "temple-house" is not only quantitative as more stones are added, but it is qualitative as the stones become intimately joined together in a common life. Individual Christians are referred to as "living stones" in 1 Peter 2:5. They are exhorted to "encourage one another and build up each other" in 1 Thess. 5:11 and Acts 20:32.

Victor Paul Furnish suggests that the building boom going on in Corinth at the time may have influenced Paul to use the metaphor of the church as a building. Many of the great buildings of Corinth had lain in ruins or disrepair for a century or more before the city became a Roman colony in 44 BC. After colonization, this changed rapidly. Archaeologists continue to find evidence of major construction activity during the first century AD. When Paul arrived about 50, he would have seen a number of the city's official, commercial, and religious edifices being restored and many new ones under construction.

Some members of the church may have been skilled stonemasons or otherwise been employed in the building trades. Surrounded as they were by public buildings in various stages of repair or construction, the members of the church could hardly have failed to appreciate the apostle's point about his role in their existence as the church and how to build on the foundation he laid.

Paul uses two passages from the Old Testament in vs. 19-20 to emphasize that "the wisdom of this world is foolishness with God." The first is Job 5:12-13. The verb, "he catches," describes the strong grasp or grip which God has on the slippery cleverness of the wicked. "Craftiness" is the readiness of the wicked to do anything to gain their own end.

Paul establishes the point that "God made foolish the wisdom of the world" in 1 Cor. 1:20-21. He insists in 2:6-7, "we do speak wisdom, though it is not a wisdom of this age or the rulers of this age, who are doomed to perish. But we speak God's wisdom . . . ."

The second passage is Ps. 94:11. Paul changes "the thoughts of humankind," cf. the footnote, to "the thoughts of the wise." In this way, he adapts the meaning of the psalm to the subject he is discussing. Tous dialogismous ("the thoughts") is used of questioning or opposing the ways of God in Ps. 56:5; Luke 5:22; 6:8; Rom. 1:21; and James 2:4.

Matthew 5:38-48

It is difficult to agree with all that Jesus directs us to do and to say that it is wisdom. We just do not think that way.

Many have tried to make the words of this Lesson more agreeable. For example, the Roman Catholics at the time of Martin Luther maintained that what Jesus says is not intended for every Christian but only for those who wish to achieve a special degree of perfection. They called Jesus' words "evangelical counsels." The Romans felt it is an error to say that they are intended for all followers of Jesus.

The twelve evangelical counsels are: 1) do not retaliate evil treatment, 2) do not practice vengeance, 3) turn the other cheek when someone strikes you, 4) do not resist an evildoer, 5) let someone have your cloak as well as your coat if they take you to court, 6) when someone forces you to go one mile, go with them two, 7) give to every one who asks, 8) lend to every one who wants to borrow, 9) pray for your persecutors, 10) love your enemies, 11) do good to those who hate you, and 12) pray for those who spitefully misuse you.

But Jesus says nothing in the Sermon on the Mount to suggest that these instructions are meant only for a special class or group of people. They are addressed to all His disciples. The whole idea of evangelical counsels has no basis in the scriptures. As a matter of fact, Jesus says just the opposite in Matt. 5:19.

Others have gone to the other extreme. They apply Jesus' words to every human relationship, for example, family life, the state, and the relations of nations with each other. They say that Jesus' words direct governments in their treatment of criminals and the course they should follow when war threatens. But Jesus is not addressing the governments of the world telling them how to conduct their political affairs. He is speaking to His disciples.

A third position was taken by Albert Schweitzer. He advocated the idea that Jesus' words were not meant for all time. They were intended only for the time between when He spoke them and the time when He would come again. The disciples thought that Jesus would come during their lifetime. But Jesus suggests no such limitation. He is illustrating in a practical way what He means by the greater righteousness of Matt. 5:20.

If the followers of Jesus have not realized it before, it is clear from what He says in Matt. 5:38-48 that the life He wants from them is impossible. Salvation comes not through obedience to the laws of Jesus but as a gift through His passion. His directives are gifts, too, teaching us how best to live. They describe the way He lived.

We should restrain the vindictiveness not only of our fist but also of our feelings, our thoughts, and all our powers. If only our own person is involved or an injury or injustice is done only to us, we should not resist. Jesus' words put us at odds with our natural inclination to seek revenge. We should not do that. If we see violence and harm being done to others, we should help to defend and protect them.

Jesus encourages an attitude toward other people that requires a high level of emotional and spiritual maturity. It cannot be practiced by immature or neurotic people. They respond to being hurt either with hostility or with a kind of submissiveness that perverts Jesus' meaning. He is indicating what our general attitude should be toward those who do evil to us. We should love them. We should be quite willing to suffer wrong.

Rhapizo refers to striking another on the face with the back of the hand. It might be translated "slaps." Such action was regarded as a very great insult in those days. Some feel that

478

slapping on the cheek involves not so much violence as insult. Jesus is saying that if a person insults us, we should let that person do it again rather than seek reparation. Moreover, Jesus is not optimistic. He does not promise that if we turn the other cheek, we will not be slapped again.

Some say that Jesus did the opposite in John 18:22-23. When an officer of the high priest struck Him, He did not offer the other cheek. On the contrary, He declared His innocence and rebuked the officer. Did Jesus violate v. 39?

Patient endurance of evil does not mean that we grant it rights. We are not to condone or justify evil done to us. The attack, the deed of violence, and the act of exploitation are evil. Disciples should bear witness to that as Jesus did. We should let the evil intention play itself out and overcome it by patiently enduring it.

To turn the other cheek is to take the initiative in seeking to form a relationship. It is to return love to those who hurt us. To be sure, we may get hurt again. Being hurt may be necessary for the other's redemption. Jesus was hurt for us in His passion!

Many pacifists use v. 39 to support their position that Jesus forbids the waging of war. Luther disagreed. He said that Christians can be regarded from two points of view. First, they are disciples of Jesus. As such, they must not defend themselves against injury but meekly suffer whatever is done to them. Secondly, Christians have a place in this world and society. In so far as they are fathers, they must govern their family. Only a very bad father would permit his son to strike him without punishing him. In so far as they are the heads of a family, they are responsible for the well-being of their family. They must resist the person who tries to hurt the members of their family, set the house on fire, destroy the crops, cause them to be fired, put them out of business, or inflict some other damage. In so far as they are citizens, they must help the government preserve law and order. If circumstances require it, they must use a weapon to ward off those who want to hurt the community. When the holy martyrs were called to arms even by heathen emperors and lords, they went. In all good conscience they killed and in this respect were no different from the heathen.

They did not sin against v. 39. They were doing this as obedient subjects under obligation to secular authority.

The idea of krino ("to sue") is to take a person to court or to go to the law with someone. The chiton ("coat") was a long close-fitting undergarment, a sort of shirt. To himation ("cloak") was a term for clothing in general, but probably in this case refers to the outer garment.

Luther appeals to vs. 39-40 and to 1 Cor. 6:7 to restrain Christians from instituting legal proceedings on account of earthly things. Anthistemi can mean to oppose or to take action against. It also has a juridical meaning, to resist in a court of law or to oppose before a judge.

To the objection that if we do not resist evil, we will get hurt, Luther replies that this is just what scripture would have us endure. Only the weak are allowed the privilege of applying to the civil authorities for the avenging of wrong. To strong Christians, it is forbidden. The requirement of the renunciation of self and the world is here carried to an extreme. Jesus removes from the disciples' life a whole battery of defenses that provide security in this fallen world. He bids us live more dangerously than people ever lived. He tells us to do only what He Himself is doing.

Jesus calls those who follow Him to share His passion. We cannot convince the world to follow Jesus through our preaching of the passion when we shrink from that passion in our own lives. Jesus grants His disciples participation in His cross when He calls on them to follow Him.

If we do not resist or take to court for punishment people who attack us, will they not be encouraged to attack other people? Do we not protect society when we have such people removed from society? Must we suffer all sorts of things without defending ourselves? Do we have no right to plead a case or to lodge a complaint before a court or to claim and demand what belongs to us? If all these things are forbidden, a strange situation develops. It is necessary to put up with everybody's insolence. Personal safety and private property are impossible, and finally the social order will collapse.

We may not go to court to defend ourselves, but we do

have a house and home, a wife and children. We must do what these relationships require. If we do not support our house, our wife, and our children and protect them, we do wrong. It will not do for us to say that we are Christians and forsake or relinquish everything. Emperor Julian the Apostate made fun of the Sermon on the Mount by taking whatever he wanted from the Christians.

There is a limit to how closely we are able to follow Jesus, and we are inclined to underestimate our ability along this line. But we should not suppose that our salvation depends on how far we go. Rather, our ability is inspired and strengthened by our confidence in the salvation Jesus secured for us through His crucifixion.

Jesus' words, "if anyone forces you to go one mile, go also the second mile," is said in the context of the practice of the government or the military to commandeer a service or property for public use. A non-Roman civilian could be compelled to carry a Roman soldier's gear for a mile. An example is Simon of Cyrene whom Pilate's soldiers compelled to carry Jesus' cross. The same word used in v. 41, a form of aggareuo ("forces"), is used in Mark 15:21 and Matt. 27:32. The Roman mile was a thousand paces. It became a fixed measure of about 4,854 feet.

Jesus points to three ways we should suffer with regard to our temporal possessions: we should let them be taken away, we should be happy to lend them, and we should give them away.

Jesus is not laying down rules for the world of finance. Out of love, we should aid the poor. That a number of questions of a practical nature arise when we try to live according to what Jesus says is of course true. If there is any doubt as to our action in certain situations, the cardinal principle should be that all things be done in love.

We should be generous. We should be willing to lend and to give to everyone who asks. Yet if the others are evil people, we are not obliged to give to them. Jesus is not telling us to give what we have to any scoundrel who comes along and to deprive our family or others who may need it and for whom we are responsible. We should not fling our gifts into the wind without looking to see who is getting them. But we ought to give to one who really needs it. There are plenty of needy people. Deut. 15:11 says, "There will never cease to be some in need on the earth. I therefore command you, 'Open your hand to the poor and needy neighbor.'"

We need to be prudent in our contacts with other people, to recognize the poor, and to see the kind of people with whom we are dealing and those to whom we should or should not give. If we see a genuine seeker, we should open our hand and lend to him or her. There are pious people who would like to work and support themselves, their wife, and their children but who never prosper and occasionally get into debt and difficulty. For the benefit of such people, we need procedures to determine who they are and to help them. However, we should not encourage any lazy bum to become a burden to other people.

"You shall love your neighbor and hate your enemy," Jesus says His audience was taught in the synagogue. The exact statement cannot be found in the Old Testament. The command to love the neighbor is joined nowhere in rabbinic Judaism with the addition "and hate your enemy." Not until the Dead Sea Scrolls were discovered was an instance of the saying finally found. According to the Qumran Manual of Discipline, new members of the sect swore an oath "to love everyone whom God has elected, and to hate everyone whom he has rejected . . . to hate all the sons of darkness."[129] Some scholars have deduced from this saying that Jesus opposed the Essenes or whoever the authors of the Dead Sea Scrolls were.

But the idea can be found scattered throughout the book of Deuteronomy where the enemies of Israel, Moab, Ammon, and Amalek, are named. Although Deuteronomy does not expressly say that God's people should hate their enemies, such a conclusion follows from statements like the one in Deut. 23:3-6 that they should never do anything good for the Ammonites and the Moabites. They should not even wish them good fortune or success.

The scribes of Jesus' day gave validity to human lovelessness by haggling with the law, as people under law invariably do. By asking questions like "Who is my neighbor?"

cf. Luke 10:29, they sought and found areas where a person does not have to love. Only the people of God qualify as neighbors according to the Old Testament context of Lev. 19:18.

"You shall love your neighbor" is a reference to that passage. The words are quoted seven other times in the New Testament. Jesus quotes them twice more in Matthew's gospel, cf. the story of the Rich Young Ruler in 19:19 and the great commandment in 22:39. Only one of these citations is found in Mark, cf. 12:31. In Luke 10:27, it is the lawyer who cites the Leviticus passage before Jesus uses the story of the Good Samaritan to answer the question, "Who is my neighbor?" cf. 10:29-37. James, too, recalls the Levitical command in 2:8. Paul invokes it in two different settings, Rom. 13:8-10 and Gal. 5:13-15.

Agape or agapao ("love") enters the vocabulary of the Sermon on the Mount and the Gospel according to Matthew for the first time in v. 43. The love Jesus is talking about is not a matter of sentiment and emotion, but it involves action. We are a channel through whom God pours His love on the members of the human race.

Freud said that loving a stranger is counter to human nature. "If he is a stranger to me . . . it will be hard for me to love him."[130] The German poet Heine said that it is not hard to forgive one's enemies, but only after they have all been hanged. The idea of loving an enemy is an intolerable offense to us as we are born into the world. It is beyond our capacity. It cuts right across our ideas of good and evil. Modern people have a hard time with it. No one is so unlovable as the one who wants to hurt us. Our impulse is to hit back.

Enemies are people who hate us, not those whom we hate. We should hate no one.

Love of the enemy, by the very nature of the situation, is always one-sided love. The nature of real love is made clear by the existence of an enemy. Love of the enemy is the acme of love. Love of our neighbor can be allied with our own welfare. Fraternal love receives as much as it gives. But love of an enemy is purposeless love. It reveals whether love seeks its own or not. Enemies profit us nothing. If our prayer for them is answered, they reap the benefit; and we are hurt.

The person who feels no inward resistance against Jesus' instruction to love our enemy does not know what enemies are and, therefore, does not know what it means to love them. We who feel some antagonism have already shown by our hostile feelings that we are guilty.

Preachers need to be careful as they proclaim this teaching not to help their hearers evade Jesus' plain command. They need to take care not to blunt Jesus' message.

We may have heard and mouthed the statement "Love your enemies" so much that we are no longer conscious of how impossible it is. We should not blind ourselves to its impossibility, for that very impossibility recalls the heart of the matter. Human love is based on sympathy, sentiment, attraction, and goodness. It is inspired by a lovable object. Love for our enemies is possible only as God's love in us and through us. It is possible only with a faith that lives by the love of God. God loved and gave His Son to die for us while we were His enemies.

Love is more easily done toward those who are far from us than toward those who are near to us, but love begins at home. Love for one's neighbor must be exercised in what lies close at hand. We need to be reminded to remain faithful under the trials of family life and of our vocation.

Everyone says love is a wonderful idea, until they have something to forgive. Such is the situation in war-time. To mention the subject of love and forgiveness toward the enemy at such a time solicits expressions of anger. But the term "enemies" applies even to people with whom we are at war. We should love even those who are making attacks on our institutions, our prized possessions, and our liberty. This does not mean that we should give in to them and that we should not oppose them in war if this is necessary. But we should have feelings of kindness toward them and intentions of extending them aid.

Jewish moral writings of that time also contain encouragements to love those who do us evil. One such statement is this: "And if any one seeketh to do evil unto you, do well unto him, and ye shall be redeemed of the Lord from all evil."[131] Judaism had its "golden rule" both in a negative and in a positive form, to treat one's fellowmen as one would wish to

484

be treated. Hillel (c. 20 BC) described this golden rule as being almost the sum total of the written law. But in Judaism, hatred of enemies was considered more or less permissible. Personal enemies formed an exception to the obligation of love. The monks of Qumran expressly commanded hatred toward outsiders, the sons of darkness.

Confucius mentioned "love of man." By this, he meant simply deference, magnanimity, sincerity, diligence, and kindness. He expressly rejected love of enemies as unfair. He said that we should repay goodness with goodness, but wrong must be repaid with justice not with goodness.

Jesus is talking about what we as Christians should do. We should not respond to someone's hate or envy, slander or persecution with more hatred and persecution, slander and curses. Rather we should love and help, bless and pray for them. Jesus is not optimistic. He does not say that if we love our enemies, they will no longer be our enemies.

Why we should love our enemies is stated in vs. 45-48. The love of the disciple has its root and source in the love of the heavenly Father. We should love our enemies not because of our common human nature. Rather we are to love them, because then we will be like our heavenly Father. Paul says in Rom. 12:21 that in this way we overcome evil with good. God wants us stamped with the divine likeness just as human parents want their children to replicate their values and their style or achieve a higher level. Our love of the enemy derives its standard from the love of God. God's love is extravagant, risky, and an offense to common sense. We are to love like that, too. Forgiveness of enemies makes Christianity distinctive. It also makes it difficult.

Sonship is always the gift of the Father. It cannot be claimed or won. It is not through showing love toward our enemies that we gain possession of the status of children of God. Through such love, we prove or demonstrate that we are the children of God.

Our heavenly Father is the pattern for our love toward others. He loves all people. He loves His enemies, those who hate Him, us. He loved us while we were still His enemies. The Father's love is love to the loveless, love to the evil and the unjust. When we love like that, we show ourselves to be His children.

In loving, we should not take account of gratitude or ingratitude, of praise or blame, of gain or loss. We should not love to put others under obligation. We should not distinguish between friends and enemies. We should not anticipate thankfulness or unthankfulness. Most freely and most willingly we should spend ourselves and all that we have, whether we waste all on the thankless or gain a reward. That's what our Father does. He distributes all things to everyone richly and freely. As His children, we should do the same.

The sun and the rain epitomize all the earthly blessings God gives. If it were not for these two things, or even one of them, the whole world would long since have become a wasteland, desolate, and destroyed.

In our conceit, we sometimes think that God is gracious to us because of our goodness, our wisdom, our cleverness, or our ascetic life. People who imagine that they will be saved on the basis of their goodness deceive themselves.

A practical question. Two farmers had adjoining fields. One farmer was a God-fearing man who went to church every Sunday. Sometimes he could be seen stopping his tractor at the end of a row, kneeling on the ground, and praying. He was a good family man. The other farmer drank a lot – and not infrequently too much. On Saturday evenings, he could be seen in the local bar carousing with the boys until the early hours of Sunday morning. In such a condition, he could not attend church. He could often be heard cursing and swearing as he drove his tractor around his fields. He did not treat his wife well – nor his children. Question: which farmer will raise the better crops? The answer: they will be pretty much the same, because their fields are adjoining. God "makes his sun rise on the evil and on the good, and sends rain on the righteous and on the unrighteous."

Jesus comments on those who love those who love them: "if you love those who love you, what reward do you have?" How often we fail to do even this! Clement of Alexandria said: ". . . when the heathen hear God's oracles on our lips they marvel at their beauty and greatness. But afterwards, when they mark that our deeds are unworthy of the words we utter, they turn from this to scoffing and say that it is a myth and a delusion. When, for instance, they hear from us that God says, 'It is no credit to you if you love those who love you, but it is to your credit if you love your enemies and those who hate you,' when they hear these things, they are amazed at such surpassing goodness. But when they see that we fail to love not only those who hate us, but even those who love us, then they mock at us and scoff at the Name."[132]

The Greek particle ou in v. 46 indicates that Jesus expects a positive answer to His question about tax collectors doing the same.

Christians are not different in the sense that they serve their neighbors while other people do not. Christians have no monopoly on service, not even, in a sense, on love. Gentiles and tax collectors are quite capable of loving, as Jesus says here. They can greet the people they meet in a friendly way. Lives of service can be produced completely within and by the knowledge of good and evil apart from a good relationship with God.

The tax collectors at Rome auctioned off the taxes of various sections of a country. Subordinates let out the taxes to local collectors who extorted all that they could. The Jews regarded these collectors as traitors, and their name became a byword for all that was vile. They were looked on with contempt by the average Jew both because they were willing to serve a foreign power which was occupying their land and also because they had a reputation for personal dishonesty.

Earlier in the Sermon on the Mount, Jesus said that our righteousness should be greater than that of the very pious scribes and Pharisees, cf. 5:20. Now He wants us to do more than tax collectors and gentiles. He begins with wanting us to do better than people who are considered the best. Now He wants us to do more than those who are considered the worst.

Greetings were more meaningful among Orientals and were of a much more formal nature than in our society today. To greet someone was a sign of friendship and kindly interest. It was an expression of a desire for the peace and welfare of the other.

When Jesus says, "Be perfect," He is drawing a contrast between gentiles and tax collectors on the one hand and His followers on the other. The word "you" is explicit in the Greek text. "In contrast to tax collectors and gentiles, you, my disciples, be perfect!" Jesus wants His followers to be more than righteous.

This is the ultimate demand. No higher requirement can be imagined. We must not try to explain Jesus' words away. We might be tempted to say, "This doesn't really mean perfect; it means try to do the best you can!" But we should take Jesus' words seriously.

V. 48 has always presented a kind of exegetical knot to Biblical scholars. The underlying meaning is related to goals and targets, to growth and ripening maturity, to coming of age. To be perfect means to grow up into full stature as a woman or man of God. Being perfect means being wholehearted more than it means being flawless. It means having no inner dividedness, full-grown, mature. It does not mean sinless. Rather it means complete consecration to God. It has to do with discipleship.

Jesus' final words annihilate any search for loopholes. They keep us from measuring ourselves in a statistical way, supposing that because we keep most or almost all of the directives of Jesus, we are better than others. Jesus' claim on His followers is total and complete. These words show how necessary was Jesus' passion.

7th Sunday after the Epiphany

Year B

Isaiah 43:18-25

"I am about to do a new thing" is one of Isaiah's most spectacular assertions. Vs. 18-21 describe the salvation Jahweh is about to effect for His chosen people who are in exile. The verses are a part of a new exodus oracle.

The Biblical account of the history of salvation centers mainly around three events. The first is the exodus from Egypt and the establishment of Israel in the land of Canaan. The second is Israel's return to the promised land from exile in Babylon. The third is the passion of Jesus the Christ. The second and third events are illuminated and the divine intention in them is revealed by using elements of the first.

The new exodus oracle emphasizes the "new thing" God will do. He says that He will do it "now." He will bring Israel back from exile in Babylon and reestablish her in the promised land. This saving act points ultimately to Jesus' passion when God's intention to have a people of His own on earth will be fulfilled.

The pattern of Israel's history has the form of a cycle consisting of a new beginning, defiance or rebellion, a lack of faith, sins, and renewal. The cycle is repeated again and again. In a sense, we are in such a cycle now. The saving event we anticipate is Jesus' coming again.

As he describes the new thing Jahweh is about to do, the return from exile, the prophet encourages his contemporaries to forget the events that gave their faith its content. "Do not remember the former things," he says. He wants them to concentrate on the new. The new is more dazzling, more overwhelming, more massive. It will not develop out of "the things of old." It is not connected to the past. However, "the former things" are a type of the new. "The things of old" refers to the saving history that began with the call of Abraham and the exodus from Egypt and ended with the destruction of Jerusalem.

The "new thing" like the old will be a massive miracle that will transform life. It will be a new exodus like the emancipation from Egypt. In the former exodus, Jahweh made a way in the sea. He will effect the new thing by making a path in the wilderness. An arid landscape will become a fountain of water that will make life possible. The rhetoric recalls the words of Is. 35:5-7 and 41:17-20.

The new thing cannot be understood apart from the old. The old provides categories for understanding the new. Israel is still "my chosen people, the people whom I formed for myself so that they might declare my praise."

Biblical faith is geared to the future. It looks forward to God's coming miracle that will exceed what He did in the past.

Jatzar in v. 21 denotes the activity of the potter as he shapes and fashions vessels and figures with his hands. The term expresses the relation of Israel to the Creator. It brings out the distinction, superiority, and higher wisdom of the One who fashions in relation to what He creates. It expresses the absolute dependence of "the people" on God.

The purpose for which God chose Israel, to recount Jahweh's praiseworthy acts, in the manner of the Hallelujah psalms, cf. Pss. 105-107 and Deut. 10:21, is ascribed to the new Israel, the church, in 1 Pet. 2:9. The Hebrew word for praise comes from the same root as the word "Hallelujah."

Christians believe that Jesus is the ultimate "new thing" from God. God is always moving on to a fresh present that is different from what was. Yet what He will do cannot be known apart from the past, things that are old, remembered, and treasured. Ancient miracles will be reenacted in fresh ways.

The failures of Israel in her relationship to Jahweh are recounted in vs. 22-24. They failed to worship God with their prayers, sacrifices, and offerings. Jahweh expected these things from Israel. He expected to be called on, to be counted on, to be served, to be given generous gifts; but Israel turned to other gods. They did not acknowledge their relationship to Him. The emphasis in the Hebrew text is on "not . . . me." The implication is that they called on other gods. They made sacrifices but not to Jahweh.

The reason Jahweh will save Israel in spite of her rebellious relationship with Him is given in v. 25. God blots out transgressions. That is the reason the "new thing" will happen. In His mercy, God blots out the past as He creates the new. He is endlessly committed to Israel and offers her forgiveness for her sins.

The Persians led by Cyrus destroyed the Babylonian empire in 539 B.C. and brought Israel's exile to an end. He permitted the Jews to return to the promised land and rebuild the temple at Jerusalem, cf. Ezra 1:1-4. This led to the restoration of the kingdom of Judah.

2 Corinthians 1:18-22

Once I rejected the opportunity to kiss the Blarney Stone in Ireland. I explained that it is not fitting for a preacher to have people say that he kissed the Blarney Stone. I did not realize how valid that statement is until I was studying this Lesson.

Paul's relationship with the Corinthian church was troubled by their feeling that his word could not be trusted. He told them that he would come to Corinth, and he did not come. He tries to explain why he did not come in 2 Cor. 1:15-17 and 1:23-2:4. He defends his veracity in vs. 18-22. He uses the words "yes," "promises," and "Amen" and makes reference to

Holy Baptism. He says, "God is faithful." He uses Christian theology to defend himself. He says that his truthfulness in dealing with them is assured by his preaching of Christ to them.

Vs. 18-22 are set apart in Paul's explanation by two things. One, he uses the first person plural instead of the first person singular used in the verses that surround it. Two, he focuses on the faithfulness of God and the fulfillment of God's promises in Jesus Christ. God's faithfulness in Christ is the theme of these verses.

The phrase "God is faithful" is a simple description of God in 1 Cor. 1:9; 10:13; 1 Thess. 5:24; and 2 Thess. 3:3. But in v. 18, it is followed by a hoti clause, and so it needs to be understood as an oath. Paul uses oaths in his letters frequently and with great variety, cf. 2 Cor. 1:23; 2:10; 11:10, 11, 31; Rom. 1:9; 9:1; Gal. 1:20; Phil. 1:8; 1 Thess. 2:5, 10.

When Paul talks about "our word to you," he has in mind two things. He promised to come to Corinth two times, on the way to and from Macedonia. He fully intended to keep that promise. The other thing is the gospel he, Silvanus, and Timothy preached on their first visit to Corinth: in Christ, all the promises of God have been fulfilled.

Paul's argument is that his word about such a practical matter as his visit is guaranteed by the dependability of the gospel he gave them. He does not vacillate, even as God does not.

Paul summarizes his preaching in Corinth in 1 Cor. 2:2 and 1:23 as "Jesus Christ, and him crucified." In 1 Cor. 15:1-8, he uses a creedal statement of the church which has an accent on Christ's death to summarize his preaching. These passages are typical of many others in which the apostle identifies the center of his proclamation as the cross and its meaning, cf. Gal. 3:1; 6:14; Rom. 5:6-11; 2 Cor. 5:14-15. But in v. 19, he says that what he proclaimed to the Corinthians is "the Son of God, Jesus Christ." This theme has a relatively minor place in Paul's thought as a whole. He uses it here, because he wants to remind the Corinthians that Jesus Christ as the Son of God is the very embodiment of God's faithfulness.

The title "the Son of God" occurs only three other times in the writings of Paul, cf. Rom. 1:4; Gal. 2:20; and Eph. 4:13.

The combination used in v. 19, "the Son of God" and "Jesus Christ," appears nowhere else in Paul's letters.

Jesus Christ is the one in whom the divine "yes" has been spoken and in whom all the promises of God have been fulfilled. Using the word "yes," Paul affirms the unchanging character of God's dealings with His people. He does not say that Christ is the "Yes," but he says that God's promises have their "Yes" in Him. In Christ, a new age was inaugurated and salvation decisively established.

Paul uses the plural "promises" in Gal. 3:21 to speak of the promises to Abraham and his descendants. The plural is used also in Gal. 3:16; Rom. 9:4; and 15:8. More often, Paul uses the singular, cf. Rom. 4:13, 14, 16, 20; 9:8; Gal. 3:14, 18, 22, 29; 4:23, 28. In the singular instances, the reference is almost always to the story of Abraham and Sarah. When the plural is used, the reference is probably more general. God's promises are associated specifically with the passing away of this world and the coming of the next, the final judgment, God's rewarding of the righteous and His gift of eternal life. In rabbinic literature, God's promises are associated especially with His faithfulness to the covenant with Israel. Paul is saying that such promised blessings of God have been fulfilled. Christ is the irrefutable proof of God's faithfulness, cf. Rom. 15:8, and the word of those who preach Christ is fully dependable.

Amen is a liturgical act of praise by which glory is ascribed to God and confirmed, as in Gal. 1:5; Phil. 4:20; 1 Tim. 1:17; 2 Tim. 4:18; Heb. 13:21; 1 Pet. 4:11; 2 Pet. 3:18; Jude 25; Rev. 1:6; and 7:12.

When Paul says, "We say the 'Amen,'" he probably has in mind more than himself and his two associates, Timothy and Silvanus. He probably is thinking of the entire church, including the Corinthian church.

The use of the article "the" with "Amen" means the customary Amen. It is clear in 1 Cor. 14:16 that the reference is to a liturgical acclamation. In synagogue worship which served as the initial pattern for Christian worship, Amen was spoken as the assent to benedictions and to the praise of God.

Amen is a formula of confirmation, the expression of

ultimate certitude. The Hebrew root amen means to be firm or sure. In the Old Testament, the word is used both by the individual and the community to confirm the acceptance of a task in the performance of which there is need of the will of God as in 1 Kings 1:36, to confirm the personal application of a divine threat, curse, or blessing as in Num. 5:22; Deut. 27:15-26; Jer. 11:5; and Neh. 5:13, and to attest to the praise of God in response to a doxology as in 1 Chron. 16:36 and Neh. 8:6. It is used at the end of the doxologies of the first four books of the Psalms, cf. Pss. 41:13; 72:19; 89:52; and 106:48. It is the acknowledgement of a word that is valid and binding.

In Judaism, the use of amen was widespread. Great value was attached to saying it. In synagogue though not in temple worship, it occurred as the response of the community to the praises uttered by the leader with the prayers. In this way, the community affirmed the praise of God. It was also the response of the community to each of the three sections into which the priests divided the Aaronic blessing of Num. 6:24-26 and by which the community made the blessing operative. It was used in response to any prayer or praise offered by another person. The concluding Amen signified concurrence. When used at the end of one's own prayers, it expressed hope for what was requested.

In the New Testament world, the Hebrew amen was usually taken over as it is. It is a liturgical acclamation in Christian worship, cf. 1 Cor. 14:16, as in the heavenly worship of the four creatures in Rev. 5:14. Christian prayers and doxologies mostly end with "Amen," cf. Rom. 1:25; 9:5; 11:36; 16:27; Gal. 1:5; Eph. 3:21; Phil. 4:20; 1 Tim. 1:17; 6:16; 2 Tim. 4:18; Heb. 13:21; 1 Pet. 4:11; 5:11; Jude 25.

In Rev. 1:7, it occurs in close proximity to nai which is translated "So it is to be." In Rev. 22:20, it is the answer of the church to the divine Yes. Amen acknowledges the divine promise that is the basis on which the petition is made. The nai ("yes") of God in v. 20 is declared in Christ, because He is the fulfillment of God's promises. The divine Yes forms the sure foundation of the church, cf. v. 21. Christ Himself is called ho Amen in Rev. 3:14. He is "the faithful and true witness."

Jesus places Amen before His sayings in the synoptic gospels: 30 times in Matthew, thirteen times in Mark, and six times in Luke. It is used 25 times in John, liturgically doubled. With the word Amen, Jesus asserts that what He says is true and reliable.[133]

Both Paul and his readers were acquainted with the Amen as a solemn liturgical response by which an act of praise was affirmed as one's own. Paul is suggesting that with the Amen of their own worship, the Corinthians themselves are affirming Christ as the sign of God's faithfulness. They are thereby also affirming the dependability of those who brought Christ to them.

Three baptismal images are used in vs. 21-22 through the use of the words "anointing," "seal," and "guarantee." The word "Baptism" is not used, but many scholars - not all - believe that Paul has this sacrament in mind. Paul may be looking back to the Baptism of the Corinthians and their conversion with the words "has anointed us." The aorist participle concretizes God's saving work in a specific act. Paul uses the verb chriein (to anoint) nowhere else. He may have used the metaphor to create a wordplay on the name "Christ." On the other hand, the practice of anointing with oil at the time of Baptism is not attested until the late second century.

Ho bebaion ("who establishes") is used in the papyri for making a legal guarantee and appears often in the guarantee clause of a bill of sale. The present tense emphasizes the continuing action of God.

The phrase "us with you in Christ" includes Paul and his associates as well as the Corinthians. All of them together are being incorporated into the body of Christ.

No other proper noun approaches the frequency of usage by Paul of Christos. In its root, it is a Jewish honorific designation. But it changed from being a primitive Christian title to a personal name. The word occurs for the most part without the article, but it is found sometimes with the article as well. Personal names are linked with the article in both Greek and Hebrew.

In the ancient world, a seal performed a double function. It kept secure and secret what was intended for public disclosure at an appropriate future time, cf. Rev. 10:4; Dan. 8:26; 12:4, 9. It also served to attest and confirm what otherwise might be uncertain or under question, cf. 1 Kings 21:8; Jer. 32:10-14; Esther 8:8, 10. It marked something as property belonging to a certain owner.

By the time of Hermas and 2 Clement (second century), the "seal" of the Christian was being identified specifically with Holy Baptism. There is the possibility that already at the time of Paul there was an actual rite in the liturgy of Baptism by which a person was sealed.

Arrabon ("a first installment") is a loan word from the Semitic. It is used in Greek commercial papyri as a technical term for the first installment of a total amount due. It functions both to establish the contractual obligation and to guarantee its fulfillment.

Silvanus is the Latinized form of the name Silas which is the name used for him in Acts. Silvanus was from Jerusalem and a leader in the church, cf. Acts 15:22 and 27. He was known as a prophet, according to Acts 15:32. He was with Paul in Syria, several districts in Asia Minor and Macedonia, cf. Acts 15:40-17:10, including Corinth, cf. Acts 18:5. He is listed as one of the co-senders of both letters to the Thessalonians, cf. 1 Thess. 1:1 and 2 Thess. 1:1, which may have been written from Corinth. He is known to have worked also with Peter. He is named in 1 Pet. 5:12 as the amanuensis of 1 Peter.

Timothy assisted Paul in founding the church in Corinth, according to Acts 18:5. It is probably to Timothy's work at that time that Paul is referring in 2 Cor. 1:19. Timothy was from Lystra in Asia Minor. He was the son of a Jewish mother and a gentile father, according to Acts 16:1. He and his mother were already Christians when Paul met them. Paul enlisted him as an associate and had him circumcised, according to 16:3, before taking him along into Macedonia. He was with Paul in Athens, cf. Acts 17:13-15, and then again en route from "Greece" (presumably Corinth) to Macedonia, cf. Acts 20:4. He preceded Paul to Troas, cf. Acts 20:5. He was one of Paul's most trusted associates, cf. Phil. 2:22. The close relationship that existed between them as well as the good reputation he continued to enjoy in the later church is attested by the two letters from Paul to Timothy in the New Testament. Paul sent Timothy to Corinth to help straighten out the situation there, according to 1 Cor. 4:17 and 16:10. Some scholars question whether Timothy ever got to Corinth, because no mention is made of his visit in 2 Corinthians. Paul writes in 1 Cor. 16:10, "If Timothy comes, etc." But ean can be translated "when." Paul says that he sent Timothy in 1 Cor. 4:17.

The listing of the three men in the NRSV is proper English, but actually Paul refers to himself first in the Greek. He does this to emphasize the part he played.

Mark 2:1-12

This is more than a miracle story. It is an event which teaches that Jesus has the power to forgive sins. The scribes questioned "in their hearts" and discussed "among themselves" whether Jesus had this power. Mark reports the discussion in vs. 6-10. He sets these verses off from the story of the miracle itself with the phrase, "he said to the paralytic" in v. 5b and again in v. 10. Interesting and informative as the discussion of the scribes is, it is not necessary for the miracle story; and yet, it played a major role in the event.

Jesus could have been using the numinous passive when He said to the paralytic, "your sins are forgiven." This would have been a reverent way of avoiding the use of the name of God that was frequently used by the Jews. Or Jesus could have beeen implying that He Himself was forgiving the man. This ambiguity is in line with the indirect way in which Jesus often revealed Himself as God. The scribes understood Jesus as forgiving the man's sins by His own authority. They called what He was doing blasphemy.

How monstrous what Jesus did was may not be immediately apparent to us today. There is no Old Testament/Jewish analogy for what He did. The Old Testament emphasizes that God is gracious and forgives, cf. Ex. 34:6-7; Is. 43:25; and Ps. 103:3, but only He does so. Occasionally, forgiveness is proclaimed through prophetic utterance, cf. 2 Sam. 12:13; Is. 44:22; and

497

43:25. The priestly rites of atonement and the formulas of absolution involved are hardly comparable to what Jesus said. Contrary to all of Israel's traditions, Jesus did what only God can do. In this way, He asserted His identity as God.

The major point of Mark's gospel, Jesus' passion, is beginning to become clear already. Casting out demons, curing a fever, cleansing a leper, and making a paralytic walk are incredible events; but they are acceptable. However, it is not acceptable for anyone to assume divine authority, the authority to forgive sins. The consequence of this assumption was that the scribes considered Jesus guilty of blasphemy.

They reacted to what Jesus did with contempt for Him. They referred to Him as "this fellow." The charge of blasphemy was not expressed audibly. Jesus "perceived in His spirit" that the scribes were "questioning in their hearts." Neither the scribes nor Jesus named the charge. From their point of view, the scribes were right. Jesus' words were an extravagant personal claim going beyond that of usual prophetic authority. He said much more than Nathan did in 2 Sam. 12:13. Although His language may have been ambiguous, the scribes were eager to find fault.

The penalty for blasphemy was stoning, cf. Lev. 24:15-16; 1 Kings 21:13; John 10:33; and Acts 7:58. Mark implies, if he doesn't actually say, that at this point already the scribes had a reason to plot the death of Jesus. He states this explicitly in Mark 3:6.

Jesus did not contradict what the scribes were "questioning in their hearts" and "discussing . . . among themselves." He used what they were thinking and discussing to identify Himself to them. The two phrases, "your sins are forgiven" and "Stand up and take up your mat and walk," involve things that only God can do. When the paralytic walked, this was proof that Jesus could forgive. His power was visibly demonstrated by His ability to make him walk. The scribes were right; Jesus was claiming to possess the power of God.

Paul J. Achtemeier comments: "When . . . ministers (today) reach the point in the worship liturgy, after the confession of sin, where they announce forgiveness of sin in the name of Jesus, how often do they ponder the awesome power of that act? . . .

Matthew preserves a saying in which that power is conveyed to the church (18:18-20). . . . Ministers should be aware of the power inherent in the words they use, miraculous power. Such awareness would keep us, I suspect, from cheapening the words and would restore some of the seriousness to what we do in the liturgy."[134] The power of the absolution is reduced when the minister expresses doubt that he has such authority.

Blasphemy is the charge the high priest makes against Jesus in the passion story, cf. Mark 14:64.

Jesus answered the unspoken question of the scribes with a counter-question, "Which is easier, etc." He did not ask for a definite answer. Rather He wanted to stimulate their reflection by asking a question that was not easy to answer. If they recognized the truth, they would know that both forgiving sins and healing display the reign of God. The claim to forgive cannot be substantiated by a demonstration, but the power to heal was demonstrated immediately. The healing confirmed what Jesus asserted, namely, that He was from God, that He was God. The healing took place not for its own sake but as a demonstration that the Son of Man had the power to forgive sins. This is the language and intention of the text. Jesus' authority to forgive was attested by His authority to heal.

Jesus referred to Himself as "the Son of Man." Some think the title relates to men in general. That idea is supported by Matthew's statement of the response of the crowd to Jesus' miracle in Matt. 9:8.

This is the first use of "the Son of Man" in Mark's gospel. It is used 13 other times, cf. 2:28; 8:31, 38; 9:9, 12, 31; 10:33, 45; 13:26; 14:21 (twice), 41, 62. It is usually used in connection with Jesus' suffering, death, and resurrection. Mark may be implying that connection when he uses the title in 2:10.

"Son of Man" is an enigmatic title that both arrests the attention of Jesus' disciples and leaves them puzzled as to the nature of what He is doing and saying. Only after His death and resurrection do they understand. The paradox between His suffering, death, and resurrection and His power as God is expressed in the Old Testament background which is Dan. 7:13-14. In Dan. 7:21-22 and 25, "the holy ones" of God suffer; "the

Son of Man" represents them.[135] What can be said of "one like a son of man" can be said of "the holy ones of the Most High," the people of God, and visa versa.

"Son of Man" is a Messianic term. Jesus may have been making a Messianic claim even as He hides His Messianic character. Mark seems to use the title this way.

The scene is set for the miracle in vs. 1-2. It is Capernaum. The word "again" is omitted in the NRSV translation of v. 1. It is probably meant to be included in the word "returned." Literally, the Greek reads, "And coming into Capernaum again after some days, etc." The words point back to Mark 1:21. Jesus left Capernaum, according to Mark 1:38-39, to engage in a preaching and healing ministry in Galilee. His return may have taken place a matter of days or even weeks later.

The "home" of Jesus may well have been the home of Peter which Jesus used as His headquarters when He was in Capernaum, cf. Mark 1:29 and 3:19-20. Some take this as a reference to Jesus' own dwelling.[136]

Jesus was very popular at this time, cf. Mark 1:33; 2:15; 3:20; 6:31. That doesn't mean that everyone who came to hear Him supported Him. This story indicates that the religious leadership, for example, objected to what He said and did.

The content of "the word" Jesus spoke to the crowd is given in Mark 1:15.

The problem is described in vs. 3-4. We can only make an educated guess as to the nature of the man's paralysis. It is not described. That four men carried him suggests paralysis of the legs at least. The paralysis could have been more extensive. V. 11 agrees with whatever is deduced from v. 4.

The problem of getting the paralytic to Jesus was compounded by the presence and the size of the crowd. The description of how this was done is full of local color and much action. The account in Luke, cf. 5:19, describes the roof as made of tiles and suggests that the men removed the tiles to let the paralytic down. The root of the verb used by Mark relates to digging. It suggests that they made an opening in the roof by digging through the clay. The ex prefix indicates that they put the debris to one side so that it did not fall on the heads of those in the house. Both digging and removing tile may have been involved in letting the man down before Jesus. The roof was flat and may have been formed by beams and rafters across which matting, branches, and twigs were laid. This then was covered with earth pressed hard. This may have been paved with tile. First, the men removed the covering of tiles, and then they dug out an opening through the dirt underneath. All this, done by four strong men, could have been completed in only a few minutes.

An outside stairway may have given them access to the roof. Or they may have reached the place above Jesus along what the rabbis called "the roof of roofs." Houses on the same street sometimes were joined to each other, and a person could walk from roof to roof. The roofs were surrounded by a balustrade that, according to Jewish law, was at least three feet high.

Jesus saw their faith in their effort to get the paralytic to Him. "Their faith" probably did not include the full scope of what we call the Christian faith today. Not even the disciples had that before Jesus' resurrection. The group with the paralytic trusted Jesus and His ability to help. Their faith consisted in their confidence that God was at work in Him.

"Their faith" includes the four friends carrying him and the paralytic. Perhaps the parents of the invalid, too, ought to be included. But some think that the reference is only to the four men carrying him. Clearly, the faith of the paralytic is not a precondition for his healing. The story is about the power of Jesus not the virtue of the paralytic. The proof of the miracle is the bystanders' reaction of amazement.

When Mark says that "all" were amazed and glorified God, he probably is engaging in a little hyperbole. It is hard to say that the scribes glorified God for the healing when we consider the stories that follow culminating in the statement of Mark 3:6.

All who were amazed and glorified God probably did not believe in Jesus as God. Some of them probably were amazed and praised God as when a person responds to seeing some grand natural phenomenon, like Crator Lake in Oregon or Old Faithful in Yellowstone National Park.

The healing of the paralytic demonstrated Jesus' power over the forces of evil arrayed against God in this world.

The rabbis taught that suffering was a way of expiating sin. They believed that a person could not recover from an ailment until he received forgiveness for his sin. When Jesus announced forgiveness, He dismissed the rabbinic idea that the man's paralysis was the consequence of a sin he committed. Jesus also rejected this idea in John 9:1-7. The blindness of the man in that instance was not to be traced either to his sins or to those of his parents.

The order in which Jesus assured the man first of forgiveness and then healed him is important. After He pronounced the paralytic forgiven, he was still lying on his mat. The preacher must be careful not to make too close a relationship between the man's physical well being and his sins. That is not a part of Mark's message. If Mark had wanted to say that, the man would have gotten off his mat when Jesus proclaimed him forgiven. He did not do that. To read and preach the healing of the paralytic in such a way that the paralysis is the result of his sins and that by forgiving his sins Jesus healed him, is to misread the text and to violate New Testament teaching on the subject. Jesus has something to say about the relationship between human sin and disastrous events in His reference to the collapse of the tower of Siloam in Luke 13:4-5.

Religious people generally tend to rely on their own righteousness before God. Jesus' preaching of the free grace of God provoked opposition from the religious people of His day.

The hostility of the scribes and Pharisees grows throughout Mark's gospel. In ch. 2, Mark begins describing five disputes in Galilee between Jesus and the scribes and Pharisees emphasizing the issues between them. In 2:1-12, the scribes and Pharisees object to Jesus forgiving the sins of a paralytic. In 2:13-17, they object to Jesus' fellowship with sinners. A discussion about fasting and the incompatibility of the old and the new is recorded in 2:18-22. Twice in 2:23-3:5, they object to Jesus' disregard of sabbath rules and regulations as they understand them.

In Mark, Jesus' teaching takes place primarily in debates with the Pharisees who are His enemies or with His disciples who are His friends. The debates with the Pharisees and the scribes have parallels with debates in the writings of the rabbis. Mark 2:1-17 is a good example of this. Forgiveness is at the core of Jesus' teaching. But rabbinic Judaism had no word of forgiveness and no word of welcome to speak to the person burdened with sin.

Research into the kind of literature Mark wrote and the pattern he used has consistently produced little. He seems to have followed no formal models used in either the Jewish or Greek cultural circles of the early to mid-first century. He collected the material about Jesus circulating in the church into stories with a minimum of editorial comment. The form is apparently his creation.[137] Rather than interlacing the stories with comments as to how an incident is to be understood, Mark chose to let the incidents speak for themselves.

The key for understanding the stories about Jesus in Mark is Jesus' death and resurrection. This is clear in the collection of stories in Mark 2:1-3:6. Mark has done little to integrate these stories with one another. What he is interested in is the result of the conflicts reported. That result is indicated in the last verse of the last story. Mark 3:6 reads: "The Pharisees went out and immediately conspired with the Herodians against (Jesus), how to destroy him."

The conflict portrayed in any one of the stories could have led to Jesus' condemnation by the religious and civil authorities. The point is made less by editorial comment than by the cumulative effect of the five stories. Mark does much the same thing in 12:13-37.

The central element in Mark's gospel is the passion, including the resurrection. All that Jesus did and said become clearer when we realize that in Jesus God carried out His plan for the salvation of the human kind. Following His resurrection, what Jesus of Nazareth did and said took on importance undreamed of by those who heard and saw Him. The cross and resurrection are the key to understanding Jesus for Paul, cf. 1 Cor. 15:14 and 17. The Gospel of Mark is dominated by passion week. More than a third of it is devoted to Jesus' last week in Jerusalem with the remaining two-thirds pointing to that climax.

Jesus' crucifixion changes the way we look at ourselves and our future. Humanity did not become sinless or less self-centered because of Jesus' crucifixion, but sin and self-centeredness were stripped of their potency. What Adam did, Jesus undid. We are no longer prisoners of our past. We have been freed of its burden and can face with confidence a future under God's benevolent control.

The future is in God's hands, despite all the evil humans might do. Those who follow Jesus know that the future is assured. Those who follow Him know that finally life is not a tragedy but, in the classic sense, a comedy in which the final resolution is not pain, despair, and defeat but joy, victory, and sunny laughter. We can stride confidently into the future, because it is in the hands of a merciful God. In the confidence that God cannot be defeated, preachers do what they can in word and deed to spread this good news.

Mark says that "Jesus perceived in his spirit that" the scribes were charging Him with blasphemy "in their hearts." How the phrase is interpreted depends on whether it is important to emphasize His deity or His humanity. That Jesus answered questions that had not been voiced suggests that He is God. But the point ought not be stressed too much. Every good teacher is able to feel the questions the students are asking before they vocalize them. Nor does it help the main point of this story which is that Jesus has the power to forgive sins. What the scribes were thinking may have been visible on their faces. Nevertheless, Jesus' power to know what people were thinking is affirmed in John 2:25. The rabbis regarded the reading of thoughts as the fulfillment of Is. 11:3. They considered it one of the marks of the Messiah.

When Mark says "Jesus perceived in his spirit," no reference is intended to the Holy Spirit.

The central teaching of Mark 2:1-12 is the power of Jesus to forgive sins. Since most parishioners have little doubt about this, the preacher might be tempted to turn to peripheral matters and to other needs of the congregation. Must a sermon deal with the central teaching of a text, or may its focus be on peripheral matters?

Through the centuries, powerful evangelical sermons have been preached on peripheral issues. An image the preacher might work with in this text, one that might even be made to produce a little humor as an aid to drive home the message, is who repaired the roof after the crowd went home. Some might say Jesus did, since preachers often are left to clean up after they proclaim the Word of God.

Another peripheral matter is the four who brought the paralytic. They could be compared to the faithful members of the church who bring others to Jesus. This is what should happen. When the four find the doorway jammed, they go up on the roof, tear it apart, and lower the man. This could be used to describe the problems that sometimes need to be overcome to bring others to Jesus.

However, the gospel writer uses this miracle story to proclaim the power of Jesus to forgive sins through His suffering, death, and resurrection. It is a message that needs to be proclaimed and reinforced again and again. It need never be boring and should never be taken for granted. It is the heart of the matter.

7th Sunday after the Epiphany

Year C

Genesis 45:3-11 and 15

"I am Joseph" must be one of the most startling statements in all of the stories told in the Bible. It is almost on a par with the statement of the angels in Mark 16:6, "He has been raised."

One of the most powerful men in the world said it. He was "a father to Pharaoh, and lord of all his house and ruler over all the land of Egypt." He was "lord of all Egypt," the dominant super power in the world, a country on the verge of becoming much more powerful in the next five years under his wise leadership.

Joseph went from favorite son of Jacob to a desert pit to the slave market to a prison. From there, he was raised up to the right hand of Pharaoh. He was tried, humbled, and raised up so that he could rule over the whole world. He became Zephenathpaneah the Great, husband of Asenath, the daughter of the priest of the great temple at Heliopolis. Luther says that Joseph was raised to such heights because he was mortified, brought down to hell, slighted, and driven to despair. Yet, in his time of trial, he retained great faith and great hope.

In the same way, Joseph disciplined and humbled his

brothers so that he might exalt them. Luther says, "He is a perfect and outstanding example of the governance of God, 'who did not spare His own Son but gave Him up for us all' (Rom. 3:22) . . . . we are not humbled to render satisfaction but to be cleansed."

The final cause of afflictions is "mortification and getting rid of sins and of that original evil which clings to nature. And the more you are purged, the more you will be blessed in the life to come. For glory will undoubtedly follow the misfortunes and vexations which we endure in this world. But the main purpose of all these is the cleansing, which is altogether necessary and useful, lest we snore and become dull because of the laziness and sluggishness of our flesh. For when there is peace and quiet, we do not pray. Nor do we meditate on the Word, but we treat the Scriptures and all things that belong to God coldly or finally slip into fatal smugness.

"Therefore we must be troubled and humbled, if not by bloodshed and imprisonment . . . at least through spiritual trials, sorrow, grief, and anguish of heart. Otherwise we shall perish in our sins. For the flesh is corrupt, filled with poison, leprous, and has need of a physician to counteract that rottenness by means of cross, martyrdom, sadness, confusion, and disgrace. These, you see, are the medicines with which God purges away sin.

"Holy Scripture is full of such examples."[138] The story of Joseph shows us the mysterious way God rules His people.

The depth of the emotion and the drama in this Lesson cannot be realized until the preacher rereads the story of Joseph. It's called "the story of the family of Jacob." Jacob was the patriarch. Through him, the promises God made to Abraham were passed on. But the story of Jacob in Gen. 37-50, except for ch. 38, talks mostly about what happened to Joseph and what he did.

The story of Joseph is didactic narrative. It makes a great contribution to the theology of history. The subject is divine guidance. God Himself causes all things that happen to us to work out for our good. He uses even the dark aspects of human nature to accomplish His goals. The text says this explicitly.

When Joseph asked, "Is my father still alive?" it was a different question from the one he posed in 43:27-28, although they sound the same. The point is made in 44:18-34 that Jacob is still alive. Nevertheless, the question, "Is my father still alive?" is not unnecessary. In ch. 44, Joseph asked as a stranger. In ch. 45, he asked as a brother and son. He may have been seeking reassurance, too. The health of his father was a matter of great importance to him.

The brothers did not recognize Joseph because of his dress, his language, and his high position. Also there seems to have been some physical distance between him and them in the audience room. Suddenly, the brothers heard the Egyptian speak Hebrew. They had not expected that.

Although the Egyptians heard Joseph weeping, he did not want them to hear about the bad things his brothers had done to him. That would have caused the Egyptians to think badly of the brothers and complicated things greatly. Joseph hid the sins of his brothers. He called them closer to himself. He spoke more softly as he identified himself by reminding them what they did to him. He not only forgave them, but he covered for them, too.

The words, "whom you sold into Egypt," positively identified him to his brothers. No one knew what they did to their brother except their brother himself.

Luther more literally translates the Hebrew of v. 5, "Let no anger be in your eyes." Joseph's anger is what is meant not that of his brothers. They were very much afraid and needed to be strengthened. He had been pretending ill will and anger toward them, but now that was not what he wanted them to see. In effect, he said, "I am not angry with you, nor do I enjoy your confusion and shame. I know that all these things happened in accordance with God's plan." Later in Gen. 50:19-20, he says this very specifically.

Joseph absolved his brothers from their sins against him. This was not done explicitly but is implied. No desire for vengeance is apparent in Joseph's words, no ill will or desire to hurt his brothers, but only mercy and goodness. Joseph is an example of what it means to forgive a brother his fault, as Matt.

18:35 requires. Joseph's forgiveness also gave his brothers courage.

They had much reason to be concerned about their situation after all the tricks Joseph had played on them. But now Joseph wanted them to put the past behind them. He wanted to make a new beginning. That they were not able totally to do this is evident in 50:16-17.

All the terrible things that happened to Joseph were used in God's plan for saving Israel and the world from the famine. God was with Joseph in all the disastrous things that happened to him: in the hatred of his brothers, in being sold, in prison, in disgrace, and in all his misfortunes. Ps. 105:16-22 reviews this history.

Luther says, "these things should be set before the church of God, in order that by such examples the godly may be stirred to faith and patience, and learn to believe in God, the almighty Father, the Maker of heaven and earth. With God we can lose nothing when we believe, but every loss is a hundredfold gain."[139]

"This example . . . teaches that we, too, are not being destroyed when we are afflicted and under a cross, but that we are being saved, provided that we believe. For faith must be present. Unbelief thinks nothing of those things . . . . let us consider diligently and impress on our hearts that it is a 'sending' and a salvation when Joseph is sold into Egypt."[140]

Three times Joseph repeated the point "God sent me," cf. vs. 5, 7, and 8. "God sent me before you to preserve life" is the key to the entire Joseph narrative. Joseph himself may not have been aware of this during his wretched experiences. Or he may have kept this awareness to himself.

There is no evidence in the Bible that Joseph made an attempt to contact his father and his family during the nine years he had been ruling Egypt. There is no evidence that he tried to check out his brothers. Before Joseph revealed himself to his brothers, there is no hint that what happened to him was being used for God's purposes, or that he was aware of God's plan. Joseph's insight, "God sent me," gives the story of Jacob and his family new meaning. The purposes of God were being worked out in the sordid actions of Jacob's dysfunctional family.

510

Joseph explained to his brothers what God had been doing and what He had in mind. The brothers envy, betray, sell, and kill their brother; but Joseph said that their selling him was the salvation and life of their family, of Egypt, and of the world.

This story is an example of what Is. 55:8-9 says. We should learn to follow not our own thoughts in trying to understand our misfortunes, works, and experiences. The regions of heaven and earth are different. The way of speaking in each is different. Luther says, "Before the world Christ is killed, condemned, and descends into hell. But before God this is the salvation of the whole world from the beginning all the way to the end.

"Therefore in every work and thought, especially in sufferings, when Christians are afflicted, if you are a believer, do not reach a conclusion about your life and actions. Otherwise you will err. You are mute, foolish, tried, and a captive; and you can neither speak nor judge correctly concerning your affairs. The psalmist says: 'Wait for the Lord (Ps. 27:14), and do not be offended, murmur or despair.' For you do not give the right name to your works or sufferings. Your judgment is false; your speech is erroneous; your wisdom is folly. But it is God's will that the old man be destroyed and the flesh be mortified; but while it is being destroyed and mortified, it speaks falsehoods and makes foolish judgments.

"In this manner God allows Joseph to be crucified, hurled into prison, and to suffer reproach . . . . For all these things do not happen otherwise in the world. But before God that same thing is to send him for salvation.

"This way of speaking is peculiar to and customary for God. . . . it is a theology of promises; they are the words of God . . . . We, however, do not understand them until His counsels are carried out."[141]

The story of Joseph is not a secular story, a wisdom tale, or the account of a royal person. The story has explicit theological purposes. The God of Abraham, Isaac, and Jacob accomplishes His purposes in a rather secular context. God's saving work is done in the arena of human choice. The proper perspective seems to be that we do not work in the realm where God is working, but God works in the realm where we function. He makes what we do serve His ends. The family of Jacob worked freely. But, in the end, God caused what they did to produce life. Paul seems to say something like that in Phil. 2:12-13. Rom. 11:36 may state it best. God uses even the dark side of human planning and action for His glorious purposes.

"God sent me . . . to preserve life." Joseph repeated the idea and enlarged on it in v. 7 to calm the troubled spirits of the brothers and to assure them of his forgiveness. Their envy and hatred were used by God for a beneficial sending. Joseph repeated God's plan in 50:20. From a horrible deed, God produced a great heap of blessings and life. God's purposes are gracious. He used all the dark things that happened to Joseph. God's power is so great that He is able to turn evil into good. Paul puts it this way: God "gives life to the dead and calls into existence the things that do not exist." The apostle is specifically referring to the story of Abraham, but what he says also describes the story of Joseph. The people who play a leading role in the story of Joseph were refined through suffering.

"God sent me" is the attitude and the faith all Christians should have about their lives whether good things come or bad. As God controls the world, He makes everything turn out for our good. He has a good purpose toward all of us. The evidence of this is that He sent His Son to die for us. If He made this great sacrifice, He is not going to withhold from us lesser things. We may not always be able to discern God's purposes. Joseph may not have until he revealed himself to his brothers. Then everything fit into place. "God sent me to preserve life," he said.

Each day we should simply do that which we know God wants us to do without thought for the consequences. When we let God lead us, this is peace. When we try to be the masters of our own fate, we have nothing but frustration and unhappiness awaiting us. We should commit our way to the Lord, do His will, and believe that good is happening whether the way leads up or down.

God's purpose is hidden and mysterious even to the participants in the things that happen. There is no clue in

Joseph's story that anyone saw what God was doing as things happened. What God wants to accomplish does not depend on human resolve, willingness, acceptance, or understanding. There is no hint as to how God is working out His plan. The way of Biblical narrative is that the story never lingers to explain God's purpose and method as it progresses. This is how a blind man sees in John 9:1-7 and the way of Jesus' resurrection in Mark 16:1-8. Nevertheless, it is through people that God's purposes are worked out in history.

The ways of God are decisive but invisible. In Is. 9:7, after the promise of a new king and a new power arrangement, the poem ends, "The zeal of the Lord of hosts will do this." Yet, God does not act. Everything proceeds "naturally." Is. 14:24-27 explains. Is. 55:8-9 affirms that the ways of God fit none of our preconceptions. God does not intend that we should understand Him and what He is doing, but He wants us simply to praise Him, cf. Rom. 11:33-36.

Joseph issues commands in vs. 9-13. God has made him father, lord, and ruler of Egypt. The family of Jacob may have been on the brink of starvation, but its fortunes are sharply reversed. The family can count on Joseph. He will fill the role of provider. That is how the story develops. But the real provider is God.

Joseph's words, God "has made me a father to Pharaoh," may be either a figurative expression indicating that Joseph had care for all of Pharaoh's business, or, as many scholars think, "father to Pharaoh" is a lofty title employed by the Egyptians.

Luther says, "Just as Christ commands His disciples, saying: 'Go into all the world preach the Gospel,' (Mark 16:15), so Joseph sends his brothers, saying: 'Hurry. Do not tarry, but spread abroad without delay what you have heard.' For when we have learned to know God in the Son after apprehending the forgiveness of sins and the Holy Spirit, who clothes our hearts with joy and with the freedom from care because of which we despise sin and death, what is left? 'Go, and do not keep silence, in order that the rest of the multitude may be saved too, not you alone.'"[142]

Joseph gave careful instruction to his brothers as to what

they should say to their father. He knew that it would be very hard for Jacob to believe what they would tell him. The patriarch had been mourning the loss of Joseph for 22 years and must have given up all hope of ever seeing him again. He would find it hard to believe that his son was lord of all Egypt.

The brothers had to tell their father an incredible story. It was like the story of the angel at the tomb of Jesus in Luke 24:5. It was like the story the women gave to the apostles later in Luke 24:8-11. It was like the story of the church today. We are experiencing so many troubles and disasters. It is hard for us to believe that boundless joy and the greatest glory awaits us and an unfading crown that we cannot now see. But we must believe, hope, wait, pray, listen to the Word of God, and cling to it. The psalmist encourages us to do that in Ps. 55:22 and so does Paul in Phil. 4:4-6. It has already been determined by God that He wants to turn our pains, troubles, and crosses into everlasting and supreme joy.

Joseph did not tell his brothers to tell their father about selling him to the Ishmaelites, cf. Gen. 37:28. He told them to tell their father only that he was the ruler of all Egypt and the father of Pharaoh. Nevertheless, Jacob must have wondered what happened. He must have gotten the whole story from them. Joseph's forgiveness may have given them the strength to confess to their father what they did to their brother.

Goshen, where Joseph wanted to provide for his family, was probably an unsettled district, loosely attached to Egypt.

The Lesson ends with the words, "after that his brothers talked with him." I should think so! Probably for hours! We can only surmise what they talked about. We are not told. They probably confessed to Joseph the grief they caused their father and talked about many family matters.

1 Corinthians 15:35-38 and 42-50

This is the most complete description of the risen body in the Bible. Paul takes up the subject, because some members of the church in Corinth doubted the possibility of resurrection.

One of the cardinal doctrines of Christianity is the

resurrection of Jesus Christ. Paul succinctly states the heart of the Christian faith at the beginning of 1 Cor. 15: "Christ died for our sins . . . he was buried, and . . . he was raised on the third day . . . ," cf. vs. 3-4.

The resurrection of Jesus Christ is not an issue in Corinth but the resurrection of believers. Paul is writing to Christians, and that means by definition they believe the resurrection of Jesus Christ. But they consider Jesus' resurrection a unique event. Paul says in 1 Cor. 15:12, "some of you say there is no resurrection of the dead." Paul links the resurrection of Jesus Christ with the resurrection of believers in the next verse when he says, "If there is no resurrection of the dead, then Christ has not been raised."

Two questions raised by those who doubt the resurrection of the dead are stated in v. 35: "How are the dead raised? With what kind of body do they come?" Scholars debate whether someone in Corinth was posing these questions, or if they reflect Paul's suppositions regarding the situation there.

Paul could have answered the "how" question by simply appealing to the omnipotence of God, but "some people have no knowledge of God," he says in v. 34.

The second question supports the first. Will it be the same body as the one that died? Will it be a different kind of body? If it is different, is that a resurrection? What will be the nature and the properties of the raised body? The Talmud gives us reason to think that the rabbis believed the particles of the body that died would reunite at the resurrection and form the same body again.[143]

Paul has little sympathy for the two questions. He calls the objector a "fool." <u>Aphron</u> ("fool") is someone who is ignorant and who does not have or use understanding. His questions seem to be clever, but they are really foolish. Paul uses daily experience to answer them.

Paul's first point is that the dissolution of the body in the grave is not only possible but necessary for life. There can be no resurrection without a death. Dissolution frees the life principle. There is no way around it. If there is no dissolution, there will be no new life.

Paul is not talking about how the dead are raised. He is not saying that the resurrection of the body is dependent on the matter that decays in the grave. He probably uses the analogy of seed, because it was a rabbinic commonplace. Rabbi Eliezer said: "All the dead will arise at the resurrection of the dead, dressed in their shrouds. Know thou that this is the case. Come and see from (the analogy of) the one who plants (seed) in the earth. He plants naked (seeds) and they arise covered with many coverings; and the people who descend into the earth dressed (with their garments), will they not rise up dressed (with their garments)?"

Queen Cleopatra asked Rabbi Meir: "I know that the dead will revive, for it is written, And they (the righteous) shall (in the distant future) blossom forth out of the city (Jerusalem) like the grass of the earth. But when they arise shall they arise nude or in their garments?" He replied, "Thou mayest deduce by an a fortiori argument (the answer) from a wheat grain: if a grain of wheat which is buried naked shooteth forth in many robes, how much more so the righteous, who are buried in their raiment?"

The analogy of seed implies continuity as well as discontinuity. Only by the dissolution of the material particles in the seed is the germ of life, which no microscope can detect, made to operate. The new living organism is not the old one reconstructed, although it has a necessary and close connection with it. But it is not identical with the former. The seed and the plant that rises from it are so far from being the same that the one must die in order for the other to live. Dissolution and continuity are not incompatible. How they work is a mystery. But the fact that they do work together is evident. Death, which sets free the mysterious power of life, is a part of the how.

It is not the earthly body that rises. Nature shows that there is no necessity for the body that dies to be the same as the body that rises. There is discontinuity between the present life and the future.

The question of how the dead can be recognized if they do not wear their old body does not concern Paul. The important point is that neither the seed nor the sower provides the new body. God does. God will give the seed the kind of body that is proper for it. He will also give to every human body a proper resurrection body.

From the first, vegetation has had its laws, cf. Gen. 1:11-12. Great as is the variety of plants, the seed of each has a body in which resides the vital principle that is brought into action by death and decay.

Beginning with v. 42, Paul applies to the questions posed in v. 35 the remarks he makes in vs. 36-38. He emphasizes the differences, the discontinuity, and the miraculous character of the future life. The victory over death will be total and complete.

He presents six contrasts between the body that dies and the body that is raised. One, what is sown corruptible is raised incorruptible. The raised body will no longer be liable to disease or decay. In the animal world, death precedes burial. But with vegetation, the burial of the seed precedes its death. In vegetation, death is necessary for life, cf. John 12:24. In human existence, what precedes the death that prepares the way for the resurrection of the body is life in this world. Life in this world is what is meant by "sown" in vs. 42-44. Death sets the vitality free to begin a new career under far more glorious conditions.

Two, what is sown in dishonor is raised in glory. The risen body will be glorified, radiant and shining like Christ's glorified body, cf. Phil. 3:21. The "dishonor" is that the dead body rots and smells.

Three, what is sown in weakness is raised in power. Mankind's fall into sin produced weakness, disease, aging, and death. The weaknesses that cause people to tire and need rest will no longer hinder them at the resurrection.

Four, what is sown a natural body will be raised a spiritual body. The risen body will no longer function according to its natural instincts, but it will live completely under the power and direction of the Holy Spirit. "Spiritual" may mean simply "supernatural," or it may designate a body that is the perfect dwelling and instrument of the Holy Spirit, cf. 1 Cor. 6:19.

"Spiritual" for Paul does not mean immaterial. The "spirit" has a physical nuance such as it often had for his rabbinic contemporaries. In Hebrew, <u>ruach</u> is not only spirit but also wind. That the Hebrew word can have those two meanings does not suggest that the spirit is immaterial. The wind is in fact material. And so is the spirit. The rabbis conceived of the Holy Spirit as light, fire, and sound.[144]

The change of the risen body to a spiritual body is necessary, because "flesh and blood cannot inherit the kingdom of God, nor does the perishable inherit the imperishable."

Five, the Christian's body which now bears "the image of the man of dust" will then bear the image of Christ, cf. Rom. 8:29 and Col. 3:10.

The concept of "the first man, Adam" and "the last Adam" is worked out further in Rom. 5:12-21. The two are representative figures; this is made clear in v. 48. When v. 45 says, "The first man, Adam, became a living being," Paul is quoting Gen. 2:7.

"The last Adam" refers to Jesus the Christ. This is the only place in the Bible where this term occurs. Paul may have invented it to correspond to the "first Adam." The two Adams were alike in that they came into being without father and without sin. Paul uses the word "last" rather than the word "second," because Jesus is the supreme Adam. The first Adam was in a sense the head of the human race. Jesus is the Head in a different sense. There will be no third head.

The term "the spiritual" is explained by the phrase in v. 47 "from heaven." The term "the physical" is explained by the words "from the earth." What the phrase, "the first man was from the earth, a man of dust," means is explained in Gen. 2:7.

Six, now already, we are "seated . . . in the heavenly places in Christ Jesus," according to Eph. 2:6. When Jesus comes again, He will transform our body to "be conformed to the body of his glory," according to Phil. 3:21. The mortal nature will put on immortality, cf. vs. 53-54. It will no longer be subject to death.

"Flesh and blood cannot inherit the kingdom of God." The phrase "flesh and blood" means our present mortal nature. It does not have to do with our evil tendencies. Our present bodies

518

are unfit for the kingdom of God. There must be a transformation.

The term "the kingdom of God" seems to be used differently than in the gospels. The meaning is clearly other-worldly. "The kingdom of God" is more a power than a place in the gospels. Here it seems to be a place. It is used in much the same way in 1 Cor. 6:9-10.

Luke 6:27-38

So strong is the theme of love in Christian teaching that many Christians know the Greek word for love, agape. Love is the chief behavioral characteristic of the children of God. It reveals whose we are. Jesus shows us what love is in His passion; He laid down His life for us to make us acceptable to God. Jesus' love for us inspires our love for others.

The ancient Greeks had three words for our complex, single English word "love." One word was eros. From it has come the English word "erotic." It is the love stimulated by sex. Eros is passionate love that desires the other for itself. Eros was the name of one of the Greek pantheon of gods. The worship of Eros involved prostitution. The god Eros was compelled by none but compelled all. Eros love puts an end to reflection or thought; it involves intoxication. It leaves no room for choice, for will, or for freedom. It is tyrannical. The bliss it offers comes from being mastered by it.

A second word, philia, is the love of friends. It is love of humanity. It is not an impulse or intoxication as eros but a relationship that a person may either recognize and respond to or evade.

The third word is agape. Among the ancient Greeks, it had nothing of the power or magic of eros and little of the warmth of philia. Its meaning was weak and variable. Often it meant little more than to be satisfied with something. It conveyed the idea of preference or seeking after something. Perhaps because its meaning was imprecise, it came to be used to communicate the special characteristics of Christian love. When the ancient Greeks used the word on its highest level, it had certain points of contact with Christian thought. Eros is impulsive; agape is a decisive act. Eros seeks satisfaction wherever it can. It seeks from others the satisfaction of its own hunger. Agape gives and is active on behalf of others. Agape is the word used in this Lesson.

Like us, the Hebrews had only one word for love. The LXX almost always renders the common Hebrew word for love (ahav) by agape. It is used for the passionate love between a man and woman in Song of Sol. 8:6, for the selfless loyalty of friendship like that between David and Jonathan in 1 Sam. 20:17, and for resolute adherence to righteousness in Ps. 45:7. For the Hebrews, love for God and for the neighbor involved not intoxication but activity. Agape was able to be filled with Hebrew significance, because among the Greeks it was so imprecise. With it, the Hebrews were able to give expression to the nuances of selection, will, and action. It was once thought that agape was a completely new word coined by the LXX. This no longer is considered likely.

Love for the enemy is the attitude of the people of God. They accept anger and rejection. Paul calls on us to bless those who persecute us in Rom. 12:14 offering himself as a model in 1 Cor. 4:12 after the likeness of Jesus, according to 1 Pet. 2:23.

The word translated "strikes" in v. 29 may indicate not merely a contemptuous slap but a violent blow with the fist. "The cheek" (siagon) can mean the jawbone. "Coat" (himation) is the outer garment. "Shirt" (chiton) is the undergarment worn next to the skin.

The word "everyone" in v. 30 excludes consideration of the person's background or condition or the purpose of the begging. Need must not be met with selfish reserve.

The word translated "takes away" (airein) is used in the sense of stealing by stealth or force.

God's people love without expecting anything in return. They lend where there is little hope of repayment. Such an idea would have been considered outlandish to a Greco-Roman audience.[145] In the Roman household, gifts brought with them the expectation of reciprocity. Jesus discourages running a household according the principles of debt and obligation.[146]

One thing unusual about Jesus' call for love is that He considers the impossible Christian life style as self-evident. He describes this impossible behavior as though it were something that every person should and can do. It is possible for us to do it because of what He was doing, His ministry and His passion. He was creating a new world situation. His demonstration and proclamation of the love of God for all humans placed people in a completely different situation. Jesus was bringing divine forgiveness of sins. In experiencing it, a new and overflowing love is released, cf. Luke 7:47.

We easily love those who love us. God does not give credit for that kind of love. Paul pronounces a terrible judgment on people who do not help their relatives or members of their own household in 1 Tim. 5:8.

The forgiveness of God is the foundation for a new relationship between people. Jesus wants us to be ready unconditionally to help and to forgive. He wants us to renounce all hatred and force and resolve to love in the face of animosity. Then we are behaving like the children of God. We will receive a great reward.

Since the 18th century, v. 31 has been labeled the Golden Rule. Others in the ancient world stated this principle in a negative way. For example, Rabbi Hillel who was a contemporary of Jesus said, "What is hateful to you, do not do to anyone else; that is the whole Law, all else is commentary. Go and learn." Parallels can be found also in classical Greek writers.

Mercy is often predicated of God in the Old Testament, cf. Ex. 34:6; Deut. 4:31; Joel 2:13; and Jonah 4:2. Jesus encourages God's children to cultivate this quality. Mercy is love toward those in distress. Merciful people are not quick to pounce on evildoers or to demand the last ounce of flesh, even if they have a legal right to do so.

When Jesus says, "Do not judge," He is not referring to the judicial decision of a legally established judge but to the human tendency to criticize and find fault. He is not implying indifference to the moral condition of others or blind acceptance of those with whom we have to live. Feelings of superiority, hardness, and blindness to our own faults lead us to be judgmental. A readiness to forgive reduces that tendency. Fault-finders and nit-pickers create the impression that they share none of the flaws of humanity. Jesus' admonitions are not to be used by someone who is caught in a wrongdoing and then says to the one who admonishes him, "Remember, 'Judge not!'"

The passive verbs in vs. 37-38 are numinous passives. That is to say, the agent is God. It is one way the Jews referred to God without using His name. In this way, they built a hedge around the Second Commandment. They avoided using the name of God lest they misuse it.

The reward we will receive for lending and expecting nothing in return is "a good measure." The imagery is taken from the oriental grain market. The analogy is to a measure of grain.

"Into your hands" is probably what we would say today instead of "into your lap." But "lap" conveys a more generous giving than the little that can be contained in the hands. The flowing material of an oriental cloak or a tunic served as a pocket or a bag for carrying things.

Joachim Jeremias describes "a good measure." "The measuring of the corn is a process which is carried out according to an established pattern. The seller crouches on the ground with the measure between his legs. First of all he fills the measure three-quarters full and gives it a good shake with a rotatory (sic!) motion to make the grains settle down. Then he fills the measure to the top and gives it another shake. Next he presses the corn together strongly with both hands. Finally he heaps it into a cone, tapping it carefully to press the grains together; from time to time he bores a hole in the cone and pours a few more grains into it, until there is literally no more room for a single grain. In this way the purchaser is guaranteed an absolutely full measure . . . ."[147]

8th Sunday after the Epiphany

Year A

Isaiah 49:2-16a

The first seven verses of this Lesson comprise the Old Testament Lesson for the 2nd Sunday after the Epiphany (A). The comments on those verses can be found there. We begin with v. 8 here. The return from exile the servant of the Lord promises in vs. 1-7 is celebrated. The Lesson concludes with one of the most touching images in the Bible of the love of God for His people.

The Lord assures the servant in v. 8 of His support and solidarity. The words are quoted by St. Paul in 2 Cor. 6:2 to strengthen the confidence of the Corinthians that he and his associates are working together with God. The emphasis, however, is on the mission of the servant. The Lord has given him "as a covenant to the people." This point is made also in the servant song of Is. 42 in v. 6.

It is difficult to elaborate on the phrase, "as a covenant to the people," because the meaning of the Hebrew is uncertain, cf. the footnote in the NRSV, and the sense of the phrase is not clear. But this much can be said: the servant is an agent of God. He is identified with the people. He is the guarantee of a new future for those who are in exile.

The mission of the servant is described as "to establish the land, to apportion the desolate heritages." The returning exiles will repeople the land Jahweh gave Israel as her inheritance, according to Deut. 4:21; 15:4; and 19:10. Israel did not conquer Canaan by her effort or plan its conquest. God gave Israel the land. Possession of the inheritance was not automatic but depended on the faithfulness of the people to the covenant with God, cf. 1 Chron. 28:8; Deut. 4:25-27; and 1 Kings 14:15. The sign that the divine favor was being renewed was that the people of Israel were brought back from exile and lived again in the land God promised them.

Israel in exile in Babylon is given a variety of descriptive names, "the desolate," "the prisoners," "those who are in darkness," "his suffering ones," and "Zion."

The servant is empowered to command the exiles, "Come out!" and "Show yourselves!" Exile produced despair. Israel lost her sense of being a special people. She lost her sense of purpose, hope, and what was possible. The servant is to stimulate and inspire her with a new sense of courage. The exilic community is summoned, authorized, and empowered to assert themselves, to throw off their despair, and to claim their God-given freedom.

"Come out!" is an exodus command. The exiles are to leave Babylon as their ancestors left Egypt. Their departure is further described in Is. 52:11.

The return journey to the promised land will be long and hard. The Lord describes it in pastoral terms. That imagery is very comfortable for Israel, because shepherding was their occupation.

Her shepherd who will lead her in the return is not named, but He is the Lord who is called "he who has pity on them." The flock will be safe and well cared for, because the shepherd will have pity on them. He will guide them and see that they have adequate water. The description reminds the reader of Is. 40:11 and Ps. 23. The imagery anticipates the parable of Jesus concerning the shepherd who seeks the lost in Luke 15:3-7 and the passage in John 10:10 of the shepherd who gives his life for the sheep.

The exiles filled with new courage are described as they make their way to their homeland: "They shall feed along the ways, on all the bare heights shall be their pasture; they shall not hunger or thirst, neither scorching wind nor sun shall strike them down . . . by springs of water (he) will guide them. And I will turn all my mountains into a road, and my highways shall be raised up." They will be protected from the dangers of weather and environment that always threaten a flock of sheep. They will be spared the onslaughts of wind and sun and of a shortage of water and food. The imagery is that of a flock of sheep moving under the supervision of a caring shepherd.

"Mountains" will be turned into roads. "A road" is a prepared path that is safe, speedy, and well protected, cf. Is. 35:8 and 40:3. In those days, they did not have earthmovers, interstate highways, and signs that give directions. The roads may have been made by and used primarily by sheep.

The shepherd will gather the sheep that have been scattered to many places. Jeremiah spoke of this same process in Jer. 31:10. The people will come home from wherever they are - "from far away," "from the north and from the west, and . . . from the land of Syene." The imagery depicts a complete reversal of fortunes. Jesus spoke of the gathering of the people of God in Luke 13:29.

The cosmos is called on to celebrate the return of the exiles. V. 13 is a liturgical refrain. The summons to rejoice is in lines one and two of the hymn. The reason for rejoicing is given in lines three and four.

Heavens, the earth, and mountains are frequently called on in the Old Testament as witnesses to the Lord's indictment of Israel for her covenantal faithlessness. Here they are called on to testify to God's compassion as He works toward renewal. The idea of all nature rejoicing in God's redemptive work is a common theme in Isaiah, cf. 44:23; 52:9; and 55:12.

The Lesson concludes with the Lord reaffirming His unending love for Israel. He recalls the complaints of the Israelites in exile that the Lord "has forsaken" and "has forgotten" them. To forget means more than a temporary lapse in attention. Coupled with the charge of abandonment, it points to a callous disregard. Actually, God did not abandon and forget Israel, but Israel abandoned and forgot God. The prophets routinely charge the people with abandoning God in favor of other gods and of forgetting the One who rescued them and constituted them a people and a nation, e.g. Hosea 2:13.

The Lord compares his love for Israel to that of "a woman" for "her nursing child" and "for the child of her womb." These are images of the most intense mother love.

Other similes and metaphors in the Bible depict God's love for His people. God likens Himself to an eagle carrying its young on its wings in Ex. 19:4-6. Jesus likens His love for God's people to a hen gathering "her brood under her wings" in Matt. 23:37. God's love is most strongly presented in the New Testament not in a simile or metaphor but in an historical event, the crucifixion of Jesus Christ.

The only answer to the question of v. 15 is, "Of course not!" That a nursing mother would forget her nursing child is improbable, although it is not impossible. The bond between a mother and her infant is very strong. Infant care is one of a woman's primary functions. Nursing mothers are physically required to be attentive and to nurture. The physical needs of both mother and child are almost impossible to ignore. The idea of a nursing mother abandoning her infant is universally repugnant.

Nevertheless, mothers do forget and abandon their children. A cursory scan of the daily newspaper offers proof that mothers today are capable of neglect and great cruelty to their own infants and small children even as they were then. Lam. 4:2-4 describes such cruelty.

The Lord insists that such forgetting and forsaking is not a possibility for Him. His commitment and compassion are stronger and more intense than that of a nursing mother for her nursing child. The nation of Israel has a unique relationship to Him. Contrary to what the exile suggests, He has not forgotten and has not abandoned Israel. And He will not.

As evidence of His commitment, the Lord shows Zion the tattoo of the city "on the palms of (his) hands." The practice of tattooing is referred to also in Is. 44:5. Israel wrote Jahweh's name on her hands. The Lord says that He has inscribed Zion on the palms of His hands. The attentiveness of the Lord is assured in this way.

The object of "I have inscribed" is not a name but "you," Zion, the city of Jerusalem. The next phrase in the verse is a parallel. "You" corresponds to "your walls." The Lord's stigmata are sketches of the city He loves and of which He is reminded whenever He looks at His hands.

1 Corinthians 4:1-5

"I don't care a fig for what any of you thinks of me," Paul says in effect to the church in Corinth. "I am answerable to God!" If some pastor said that today, it would immediately get the attention of the congregation. It would probably also get the attention of whatever ecclesial body has oversight of that pastoral position.

In 1 Corinthians, Paul addresses two serious problems. One is that the Corinthian church is split into factions. The spiritual leader each group claimed is named in 1 Cor. 1:12. What lay behind these factions is not clear, but the situation concerns Paul. The theological implications of the factionalism are grave. By aligning themselves with different leaders the people have lost sight of who should be the ultimate and only object of their loyalty, God in Christ Jesus.

The second problem is not as theologically significant as the first, but its ecclesiological implications trouble Paul nonetheless. Paul founded the church in Corinth, and he is their father in Christ, cf. 1 Cor. 4:15. That some of the Corinthians exalt Cephas and Apollos as their spiritual leaders can only be viewed as an implicit criticism of Paul's ministry and a rejection of his authority. Not only is the effectiveness of Paul's leadership being undermined, but his understanding and presentation of the gospel are also being challenged.

As he addresses these problems, Paul uses two common words to describe his status in the church, as well as that of Cephas and Apollos. The two words are "servant" (huperetes) and "steward" (oikonomos).

The Greek word <u>huperetes</u> ("servant") suggests a rower on a large ship, a trireme. He rows in the lower tier. It came to mean those who do anything under another, an underling, a servant, or an attendant. It was used to express all kinds of subordinate relationships: a physician's assistant, the priest's helper, the servant who attended each man-at-arms and carried his baggage, his rations, and his shield. It was used of staff officers in immediate attendance on the general, aides-de-camp. It was also used of servants of a board or court, or of the Sanhedrin, as well as of a synagogue attendant.

Paul claims to be a servant of Christ. That means that Christ is the object of his service. In the same way, today's ministers serve Christ by serving their congregation. They make the mind of Christ apparent to the people. Being the servants of Christ to the congregation does not place them under the judgment of the congregation; they are the servants of Christ.

Paul also claims to be a steward of God's mysteries. The <u>oikonomos</u> in an ancient household was a superior kind of slave who bore great responsibility for the day-to-day management of household affairs, accounts, etc. He assigned to each slave his duties and was entrusted with the administration of the stores. The word emphasizes that he has been given great responsibility and has to be accountable. He is a slave in relation to his master, but in relation to the workers he is an overseer, cf. Luke 12:42. In the same way, Paul, Cephas, and Apollos are stewards of the revelation of God in Christ. The stores entrusted to them are the mysteries of God.

Paul describes some qualifications of God's steward (<u>oikonomos</u>) in Titus 1:7-9. He "must be blameless; he must not be arrogant or quick-tempered or addicted to wine or violent or greedy for gain; but he must be hospitable, a lover of goodness, prudent, upright, devout, and self-controlled. He must have a firm grasp of the word that is trustworthy in accordance with the teaching, so that he may be able to preach with sound doctrine and to refute those who contradict it."

The words <u>huperetes</u> and <u>oikonomos</u> were taken over from the language of administration. Underlings of Christ and overseers for God - these two phrases capture the paradox of the apostolic call. Humility and exaltation are united in one office.

Paul says that he, Apollos, and Cephas should be thought of "in this way." He may refer both to the words that precede in 1 Cor. 3:18-23 as well as to the words that follow in 1 Cor. 4:2-5. Ultimately, what he says applies to all who are charged with the ministry of the new covenant.

Luther used v. 1 to discount the use of the word "priest" for "those who are in charge of Word and sacrament among the people." He said, "I think . . . we neither can nor ought to give the name priest to those who are in charge of Word and sacrament among the people. The reason they have been called priests is either because of the custom of heathen people or as a vestige of the Jewish nation. The result is greatly injurious to the church. According to the New Testament Scriptures, better names would be ministers, deacons, bishops, stewards, presbyters (a name often used and indicating the older members). . . . He does not say (in 1 Cor. 4:1), 'as priests of Christ,' because he knew that the name and office of priest belonged to all. Paul's frequent use of the word 'stewardship' or 'household,' 'ministry,' 'minister,' 'servant,' 'one serving the gospel,' etc., emphasizes that it is not the estate or order, or any authority or dignity that he wants to uphold, but only the office and function. The authority and the dignity of the priesthood resided in the community of believers."[148]

The genitive phrase, "of God's mysteries," expresses what God's steward is entrusted with and what he is to administer. Jesus speaks of God's reign as a secret or a mystery in Mark 4:11. It is a reality that is hidden. St. Paul speaks in 1 Cor. 2:7 of the Christian knowledge of God as "God's wisdom, secret and hidden". He uses the term "mystery" to refer to the great truths of the Christian religion. They became known to the human race through divine revelation. In the New Testament, there is also a mystery of the person of Christ and a mystery of the divine plan of salvation.

A mystery in this Biblical sense is something quite different from a secret. A mystery is not something that must be kept secret. On the contrary, it is a secret that God wants known and that He has charged His apostles to make known to all people. When Paul calls himself a "steward of God's mysteries," he is not thinking of himself as having the custody of secret and unknown rites but as an evangelist who has been entrusted with proclaiming the gospel of Jesus Christ.

God's mysteries do not cease to be mysteries when they have been revealed, whereas a secret then ceases to be a secret. When the mystery of the person of Christ is revealed, it is not less mysterious than before. A mystery is not laid open to public inspection even when it is preached from the house-tops. An example: the superscription Pilate had placed on the cross of Jesus may have made public the news that Jesus was the King of the Jews. But the inward mystery of the kingship of Jesus is not disclosed by means of a public bulletin board. God's being is a mystery that can be perceived only by faith. Revelation discloses the hidden God. But even after He has been revealed, God's being still remains inaccessible to our understanding. God revealed Himself in His saving acts, but He remains hidden from us.

The paradox of the Biblical concept of revelation is that God veils the brightness of His glory as He reveals Himself. This veiling is a gracious act of divine condescension. The true Light as He appeared on earth was veiled so that we humans might see Him. Otherwise, we would have been blinded by His brilliance. God revealed Himself by hiding Himself in our humanity. The divine splendor was at once veiled and revealed in the flesh that Christ took from the Virgin Mary, His mother. The Son of God wore His human robe so perfectly that people in every generation since have looked at Him as merely one of themselves and have failed to penetrate the guise He assumed. So, too, the divine life of the church involves a veiling of the inner mystery of its existence, cf. Col. 3:3. It will be fully revealed in its glorious reality at the manifestation of Christ, cf. Col. 3:4. Similarly, the sacraments are veils penetrable only by faith. Even the words of the scriptures themselves are veils. Luther called them the swaddling-clothes in which Christ is laid. All forms of revelation are veilings of the truth and examples of the infinite condescension of God who accommodates His divine majesty to the capacity of our human weakness.

Paul was aware of the meaning of "mystery" in the pagan religions of his day. Yet he did not set forth the mystery of the gospel in the guise of a new mystery-cult. The gospel of Jesus Christ was proclaimed in the market-place to all who would listen. It was not whispered to the initiates in superstitious ceremonies behind locked doors. It was clearly a different kind of mystery from the pagan mysteries.

The mysteries St. Paul proclaimed were not a secret gnosis magically conferring immortality on the few. They included the plan of salvation for the entire world, Jew and gentile alike. God's plan is to "unite all things in Christ," cf. Eph. 1:9-10. It was prepared from the creation of the world, cf. 1 Cor. 2:7. It was hidden in God through the ages until the present age, cf. Eph. 3:9-10; Rom. 16:25-26; Col. 1:26. God has revealed it now in the last time in Christ to His elect. He has revealed it more particularly to His apostles and prophets who are its stewards.

Paul's mission is to make God's mysteries known, cf. Col. 1:25-26 and Eph. 3:8-9. That includes Christ Himself, cf. Col. 2:1-3. He requests the prayers of the churches that he may reveal the mystery clearly, cf. Col. 4:3-4 and Eph. 6:19-20.

Luther was describing God's mystery when he talked about the theology of the cross. Until one understands the theology of the cross and understands that true Christianity is not a theology of glory, one does not have a true understanding of reality. The theology of glory speaks of pomp and ceremony, majesty, might, and power. It is embarrassed by the figure of a suffering Savior as well as by the suffering God places on the shoulders of the followers of Christ. According to human standards, the cross, suffering, and weakness are to be avoided as unworthy of a mighty and benevolent God. But God chose to offer His grace in a form that was foolishness to the Greeks, a stumbling block to the Jews, and an offense to our good common sense. What a bystander at the scene of Jesus' crucifixion saw was the dying Jesus of Nazareth, the final defeat of a religious fanatic. In reality, it was the event of history, as God's revelation testifies. God's Son was conquering the forces of evil and making the salvation of mankind possible. To know Christ is to know God hidden in suffering. A person who does not know Christ prefers works to suffering, glory to the cross, strength to weakness, and wisdom to folly. But God can be found only in suffering and the cross. Friends of the cross call suffering good. Friends of the theology of glory prefer humanly devised good works to suffering. They want to attain God's favor by works that they decide please God. Through the cross, works are dethroned and the old Adam is crucified, the old Adam that is edified by works.

The theology of the cross leaves little room for human pride. According to it, we must despair of our own ability. Only after we have learned to accept the fact that it is presumptuous for us to strive for grace on the basis of our own strength are we ready for God's grace in Christ. We will always be puffed up by our good works unless we have first been deflated and destroyed by suffering and evil, until we know ourselves to be worthless and that our works are not ours but God's. This radical revelation of reality is possible only by faith. It appeals neither to reason nor to common sense. It is the foolishness of God that is wiser than men, cf. 1 Cor. 1:17-31.

Paul highlights especially one specific aspect of the metaphor of a steward, namely, his trustworthiness. Luther is off the mark with his translation, "Now no more is required of stewards save that . . . ." Faithfulness is a lofty demand. Stewards must be accountable. This is one of the criterion of a steward.

The present tense, "it is required," states that which is always true. Paul makes a statement specifically about "stewards of God's mysteries," but it is a general statement that applies to all stewards. We all are stewards of the things God has given us. A faithful steward is one who is ready when his Lord comes, according to Luke 12:42-43.

The apostle had been commissioned by God for his task of proclaiming the gospel, and only God could evaluate his performance of it. The church is not a competent judge, for it is at one and the same time the object and the fruit of this apostolic work.

Actually, Paul does defend himself "to those who would examine" him in 1 Cor. 9:3-23. His defense is that he has not profited from his apostolic ministry and rejects the idea of getting a "living by the gospel." His "boast" is that he proclaims the gospel "free of charge."

The arrogant in Corinth had mounted a quasi-judicial investigation of Paul. Paul rejects their judgment. The only investigation that really counts with Paul is the one the Lord will make when He comes.

Paul does not consider even himself to be a competent judge of himself. His conscience does not accuse him, but his unaccusing conscience does not per se mean the absence of guilt. His vision is limited to the past and present and does not include the eschatological results of his labor.

Paul is not being arrogant. He does not consider himself beyond all responsibility. He recognizes that he is engaged in his apostolic ministry "by God's mercy," cf. 2 Cor. 4:1.

In v. 5, Paul moves from the evaluation of his own ministry to the judgment God will give everyone for everything they have done on the last day. Even the activities of the division leaders and those who are quarreling in Corinth will be judged. Those who claim to speak for God will one day be judged by God on their faithfulness.

A person cannot judge himself/herself. Judgment belongs to the Lord, cf. 2 Cor. 5:10. It cannot be anticipated by humans. We are either too lenient or too harsh on ourselves.

"The time" for judgment is when "the Lord comes." He will know all things. He "will bring to light the things now hidden in darkness and will disclose the purposes of the heart." The heart was considered the organ of thought, the seat of the will, and the source of resolves.

The expectation when the Lord comes is not judgment with condemnation but salvation. The judgment will be based not on merit but on reward. It will be "from God."

In the New Testament, praise is important when it does not represent a general human judgment or popular evaluation but when it is approval by God, cf. Rom. 2:29. At the last judgment, the conduct of believers will be approved and vindicated by

God. This is in contrast to what will happen to the wicked. A person may receive much, little, or no praise at that time. However, it probably will be different from the praise humans will give.

Matthew 6:24-34

The root of much of our unhappiness is our divided mind. We want God - but just a little. We don't want God so much that He disturbs our lives or causes us to change our ways. We also want money, pleasure, and the favor of people. The little of God we accept makes us uneasy.

Part-Christians tend to feel a kind of envy for thoroughgoing worldlings. Children of the world are not inhibited in their attempts to wipe out a competitor. They are not bothered by sentimental things like loving other people and contributing time and money to the poor. They can cheat on their taxes or engage in a minor adulterous affair without being disturbed too much by their conscience. But we part-Christians have inhibitions, scruples, and troubled consciences. When we pray, we do not concentrate on God. We make plans for the meeting that's on our schedule this evening. We worry about our business. We cannot be red-blooded sinners like other people, but we also have not given up sin for God. We have neither in the real sense, and this is our trouble. We are torn between two life styles. That's why we are so unhappy.

Part-Christianity leads to dejection that has its roots in our divided nature. Only the single-minded are happy. Only the single-minded person has a clear direction, a clear goal. People who want only a little of God always find God to be a brake, an impediment, and a pain. On the other hand, people who wholly want God learn that He is the source of power, that He gives His people freedom and strength, that following Him is the most joyful thing in the world. They discover that God frees us from the things that tempt and torment part-Christians. When we struggle with sadness and depression, we ought to ask ourselves whether the reason may be this division in ourselves.

That we cannot have two bosses, as Jesus says, is hard for

us to understand. In our society, that is very possible; we do a lot of moonlighting. Jesus is talking about slavery, and we don't really understand that institution. Douleuein ("serve") means to be a slave to. A slave is at the complete disposal of his master. In our society, a person can work for two employers, but no slave can be the property of two owners.

When Jesus says, "No one can serve two masters," He means two masters who are opposed to each other. There is no contradiction involved if people serve both God and their parents, their governor, their president, or their boss. But we cannot serve two masters who are opposed to each other the way God and the world are.

Some people think that God is satisfied with a half-hearted commitment, if they attend church regularly and contribute to the church and some charities generously. Meanwhile, they carry on their business dealings as the people of the world do. It is no sin to have money, property, wife, children, house, and home; but we must not let those things master us. Elijah said to the Children of Israel, "How long will you go limping with two different opinions? If the Lord is God, follow him; but if Baal, then follow him," cf. 1 Kings 18:21. There can be no spiritual fence sitting. Jesus wants wholehearted service of God from His people. James 4:4 and 1 John 2:15-17 encourage this, too.

Some people think it is all right to have wealth as long as they share some of it with those who are poor. Jesus, on the other hand, does not focus His attention first on the conduct of the wealthy toward other people but on the First Commandment. What/who controls our life? Who is our god?

Worry is self-concern with regard to the future. It can be concern for the things that maintain life, like food, drink, and clothing. It can be concern for our own life. Worry is based on the illusion that we can secure our life by our concern about it. Actually, worry is futile, because the future is not in our hands. Jesus' statement in v. 27 refers mockingly to the fact that a person can achieve ridiculously little by worry much less be secure.

Earthly things tempt us into thinking that they make us secure, but they are the source of our anxiety. When we try to insure tomorrow, we create uncertainty today; and we detract from today's pleasure and happiness. We should leave tomorrow in the hands of God. "Today's trouble is enough for today." Tomorrow is beyond our control. It is senseless to pretend that we can make provision for it. God rules. When we worry, we are acting like God; we are acting as though we rule the world.

Worry is the style of heathen people, of "the Gentiles," Jesus says. Being anxious and being a believer are incompatible postures. When we worry about food and clothing, we lose God. Things can separate us from God. This is true not only with regard to the person who loves luxury but also with regard to the person who is willing to settle for security. Ultimately, the question is not how much does a person want to have - Jesus is not imposing a rule of poverty on His disciples - but how deeply is a person concerned about having.

Among the outward and coarse vices, none opposes the gospel and holds back the kingdom of God as much as anxiety for the things of life. It causes preachers to keep quiet when they should speak. It causes laymen to avoid doing what they know they should do. It keeps people from supporting the work of the gospel. It inhibits the extension of the kingdom of God.

Some people think that worry is good, because it shows responsibility. Some parents, for example, think they should worry about their children. The world does not regard anxiety as a sin but as a virtue.

Worry kills more people than work. It affects our ability to function properly. It prevents us from doing our best. It weakens our inner strength. It keeps us from responding appropriately to difficult situations. It makes us suspicious of others. It causes us to live constantly on the edge of pessimism and gloom. Worry does not relieve tomorrow of its problem, but it saps today of its strength. "Worry is an old man with a bended head, carrying a load of feathers which he thinks are lead."

On the other hand, we should be concerned about some things. Every office and station involves taking on certain concerns. The head of a household has to be concerned about whether the children are being brought up properly. Similarly, it is the concern of a minister or preacher to preach well and to administer the sacraments properly, to comfort the sorrowing and the sick, to lead the wicked to repentance, and to pray for needs of every kind. Government officials have to be concerned about the proper administration of their office. Servants/hired people should be concerned about serving their masters/bosses well and saving them from any loss. Such concern should be sharply distinguished from worry. It is concern for the neighbor's welfare. It does not seek its own interests but even neglects them and forgets them in order to serve another.

When does care become worry? Concern is undue when it involves tomorrow. If our care for food, drink, and clothing extends into tomorrow, then our care has become anxiety/worry.

Worry is a habit. It is formed or broken like all other habits. It does not happen against our will. We are not powerless against it. We need to learn to trust God.

Worry is unnecessary. Whatever happens is under God's control. Jesus gives the secret for overcoming worry in the admonition of v. 33. People who are concerned about themselves and who try to find security in the things that maintain life are admonished to make the lordship of God their first concern. Then anxiety about life will wither away.

Neither Jesus nor His disciples accepted the basic presupposition of an economic order by taking part in the acquisition or holding of possessions. When Jesus commissioned the twelve, He abandoned them to total insecurity, cf. Matt. 10:9-10; 19:27; Mark 1:18-20. When later He asked them if they lacked anything, they answered, "Nothing," cf. Luke 22:35.

The early church tried a dangerous alternative to the popular economic attitudes and practices in Acts 2:44-45 and 5:1-4. What Matt. 6:19 says is even more dangerous. It may indeed be a new piece of cloth that cannot be sewn on the old garment or new wine that cannot be put into old bottles, cf. Matt. 9:16-17.

The injunction, "do not worry about your life," is the unique proclamation of the gospel of the glorious liberty of the children of God. We have a Father in heaven, a Father who has given us His beloved Son. Having given Him to us, He will give us all good things. Only Jesus' disciples can receive this word as a promise of His love, as deliverance from the slavery of things. Care does not free us from care, but faith in Jesus Christ does. We can be confident of God's care because of Jesus' death for us on a cross. The alternative to being anxious is described by Paul in Phil. 4:6-7. Peter encourages us to trust God in 1 Pet. 5:7. See also 1 Tim. 6:6-10.

Jesus often turned to the realm of nature for His illustrations and parables of how God works. There He found His illustrations ready made. The birds of the air glorify their Creator not by industry, toil, or care but by daily unquestioning acceptance of His gifts. Jesus encourages us to operate as the birds do. They would die if they did not search for food, but the food they find does not come from their work; it is a gift of God. He puts the food there for the birds to find.

Jesus makes the birds our teachers. A sparrow preaches to the wisest person saying, "Look, you have a house and home, money, and property. Every year you raise a field full of grain and other plants of all sorts, more than you need. You have a salary or a good paying job. Yet, you cannot find peace, and you are always worried about starving. You do not trust God to give you food for one day. Though we sparrows are many, none of us spends his days worrying. Still God feeds us every day." In other words, we have as many teachers and preachers as there are little birds. Their living example should be an embarrassment to us. Whenever we hear a bird singing and proclaiming God's praises, we should feel ashamed. But we are as hard as stone, and we pay no attention. We are rational people, and we have the scriptures in addition; but we do not have enough wisdom to imitate the birds. A little gold finch that can neither speak nor read is our teacher about our relationship to God.

"They neither sow nor reap nor gather into barns," Jesus says. To bring the farming methods of Jesus' day up to date: the birds know nothing about the various methods of cultivation, crop rotation, or land management, fertilizers or irrigation, the latest equipment or threats to a harvest, keeping track of the market or storing in barns.

What Jesus says does not mean that we should not sow,

harvest, and gather into barns. This may be the way God feeds us. But God does not depend on our sowing, reaping, and gathering. He can do it in other ways as He does with the birds. Sometimes to show us that, He does not let our work prosper. Yet, we are supplied with our needs.

Sometimes people cage up birds to hear them sing. They provide them with food in abundance, and the birds ought to be happier and more satisfied than when left to themselves. But they are not. When they fly free in the air, they are happier and fatter. Their singing of praise to God early in the morning before they eat is more excellent and more pleasant. They are happier in the woods than cooped up in a cage where they may be taken care of constantly. They prefer to be in the Lord's kitchen. Every day, God feeds and nourishes innumerable little birds.

Jesus not only opens our eyes to see worry as a temptation, He also gives us the way of escape. He bids us trust God who provides for the birds and makes the lilies grow their splendid garments. Besides what Jesus says, we believe what Jesus did. His death for us on a cross shows His love for us in an unmistakable way.

We should use the abilities God has given us to serve our fellowmen, and through this use God will provide for our physical needs. We should not worry. We are much higher, nobler, and better than the birds. The greatest evidence of how much God values us is Jesus' crucifixion. We are lords not only over the birds but over all living creatures. Everything was given to us for our use and created for our sake.

Jesus does not deal in this Lesson with the birds that starve or the human beings who suffer. His ministry illustrates that He is acquainted with such situations, too.

The translator struggles with v. 27, but its meaning is that through worry we do not add anything to our life. The Greek word helikia can mean "the period of time that one's life continues, age, time of life," or "the age which is sufficient or required for certain things," or "bodily stature."[149] The Greek word pechus means forearm or cubit. It refers to something insignificant having to do either with length of life, or bodily size, or a measure of time. Scholars choose various combinations. The expression in Matt. 6:27 has produced two major lines of interpretation, reflected in the text and the footnote of the NRSV, one referring to length of life and the other to bodily growth.[150]

The words of vs. 28-30 parallel those of v. 26. Jesus has been talking about food and drink; now He talks about clothes. The imagery shifts from birds and food to flowers and clothing, from men's work in the fields to women's work at the loom. The pattern is repeated pressing the point more urgently. Just as the God who feeds the birds feeds us, so He who clothes the flowers will clothe us, too. Lilies are witnesses to the providence of God.

"The lilies of the field" are not the cultivated flowers to which we give that name. They are wild flowers that grow on the mountainsides of Galilee. Travelers say that in spring when the rain has been plentiful, the hillsides of Palestine present a gorgeous spectacle, a riot of colors.

Numerous candidates have been suggested by Biblical scholars and botanists as the flower that Jesus calls "the lilies of the field." The first-century A.D. Greek botanist and pharmacologist Dioscorides suggested krinon agrion with the Hebrew name aviv lavan meaning "white spring flower." It is the flower that the Bedouin in the remote areas south of Gaza probably called "white flower" (hanun abiad in Arabic). Today it is called the daisy. It is not gaudy but has a modest and delicate beauty. It is pleasing at all hours of the day and exquisite at every period of its growth, even when it is old and drying up. When it has dried up, it is gathered with dried grass and cast into the stove as kindling. In addition, the daisy has a crown, appropriate to the allusion to King Solomon. The common field daisy grows like grass in Israel.[151]

King Solomon lived in great splendor. People came from many parts of the world to see the wonders of his kingdom, e.g., the Queen of Sheba in 1 Kings 10:4-7.

Jesus makes wild flowers our theologians. They may even embarrass us. He speaks satirically in v. 30 in order to describe how mistaken our thinking is and to show us how ridiculous worry is. He compares our life with the shortness of the existence of flowers. By comparison, we live a long time.

Jesus was often amazed at the little faith His disciples demonstrated. He uses the phrase "you of little faith" speaking to the disciples in the raging Sea of Galilee in Matt. 8:26, to Peter when he begins to sink as he is walking on the sea in Matt. 14:31, and to the disciples when they have no bread to eat in Matt. 16:8. They were not unbelievers, but their faith wavered in moments of crisis.

Instead of expending their efforts in the pursuit of food and clothing, Jesus encourages His disciples to strive for God's kingdom and God's righteousness. God wants us to have all good. Moreover, He defines good. His thoughts are not always our thoughts nor our ways His ways. Sometimes we become absorbed in all sorts of things that, if not in themselves harmful, distract us from God and the good He wants us to have.

What would we include in an inventory of good things? Health, certainly. But there have been times when sickness has given us a whole new understanding of our blessings. For most of us, money seems good. Again, there are instances when money, not being used for good purposes, becomes a tyrant and insists on being accumulated and hoarded. It may be a blessing from God to lose some of the things we count dear. Their loss may draw us nearer to Him. We may count on these questionable goods for happiness, only to discover when they are gone that happiness is in some other place. God waits in the wings to give us unexpected comfort and joy. For Him to draw us nearer to Himself is the greatest blessing of all.

We should not be concerned about food and clothing, because our Father knows we need them. Jesus' logic is simple and irrefutable. It is He who distributes food and clothing, and He loves us. Jesus Himself and His passion are the demonstration of the Father's love. Here the Second Article of the Apostles' Creed impinges on the First. The promise of the God who said that He will provide us with all that we need to support this body and life underscores the love of God for us. Jesus' death for us assures us that our trust in Him is well founded.

541

Jesus' promises do not make prayer unnecessary. Prayer does not cause God to give us what we need. He gives to the wicked as well as to His children. Prayer expresses our faith that all things come from God, that we trust Him, and that He will provide.

What do we imagine will make our lives perfect and fulfill them? Jesus points to what must be the chief object that we should desire. Rather than being concerned for food and clothing, He encourages us to seek God's kingdom and God's righteousness. This is the quintessence of the gospel that brings freedom and perfect joy. Similar to this is the word Jesus spoke to Martha in which He said that only a few things were necessary, maybe only one, namely, hearing the Word of God, cf. Luke 10:41-42.

The Jews thought that the coming of the kingdom of God was closely associated with food and drink. When Jesus fed the 5000, they wanted to make Him king. Paul speaks to this in Rom. 14:17.

Food, drink, and clothing are great and wonderful gifts from God. The point Jesus makes is that the kingdom and righteousness are of greater value. See Ps. 37:4 and 25.

When we let God rule us, His Spirit effects in us repentance that reorients us away from ourselves and our narrow concerns and points us toward the purposes of God.

Jesus does not ignore nor does He ask His disciples to despise creaturely existence and the need for food and clothes. Disciples still pray the Fourth Petition of the Lord's Prayer. They work for daily bread. But they have shed the delusion that by their anxious and agonized exertion they secure and guarantee their life. They lay their tomorrow into the hands of God. What is definitely prohibited is that a person give first place to material needs.

All that we really need is something to eat every day and shelter. More than this no one can have, even if they have all the goods and all the glory in the world. The poorest beggar may have as much of this as the mightiest emperor. He may even get more enjoyment and benefit out of his crumbs than the emperor gets out of a banquet. Our bread feeds us as well as an emperor's or a king's feasts. Our clothes cover and warm us as well as his gold and silver garments.

If the question is asked whether Jesus' promise, "all these things will be given to you as well," finds its fulfillment in the life of every Christian, we confidently answer yes. If there is a case where famine strikes Christian families so that they go hungry and in addition are without shelter, we may be sure that there are special circumstances which induce God to accord this treatment to His children. Maybe He is giving us the opportunity to help them.

The disciples who followed Jesus during His earthly ministry were always provided for. Storms of persecution came, and they had to suffer; but they did not brand Jesus' promises false. Whatever befell them always worked for their good.

We can depend on the heavenly Father each day. In such dependence is peace and happiness. Our Father takes responsibility for tomorrow. To try to see beyond the coming night or to forfeit sleep to worry and scheme is a sign not of prudence but of unbelief. It is playing God and acting as if the future were in our hands.

Scholars are divided over the precise meaning of the term "righteousness" in v. 33. Some ascribe to it a typical Pauline meaning, righteousness as God's gift. Others ascribe to it an ethical meaning, righteousness as the conduct of the faithful. Must it be either-or?

Righteousness comes from a faith that is busy and active in good works. It is continually progressing. Disciples are to keep on seeking it, since they have not yet obtained it, according to Phil. 3:12, learned it, or lived it perfectly.

Jesus is not unrealistically optimistic. He knows that every day will have its evils. He implies that tomorrow will be troublesome. Jesus does not idealize or gloss over the hard economic realities of life. They are there, and they are no fun. But our King and Father will help us deal with them.

Daily in this life, we must see and expect that something will be stolen from us, we will suffer some other damage, or we will get sick. But we should not become concerned about those things until we reach the day. "Do not cross your bridges until you come to them." It is absurd to add the worry of tomorrow to that of today.

Instead of worrying and constantly cataloging the possible evils the future may hold, we should give ourselves to the problems of today. Tomorrow's calamities may never come; and if they do, by worrying we will have weakened our strength, to deal with them. We should suffer sorrow, anguish, and trouble, and receive it with joy. We should be content. Worry only increases and aggravates our troubles. God tried to teach ancient Israel this in the way He gave them manna, cf. Deut. 8:2-3.

8th Sunday after the Epiphany

Year B

Hosea 2:14-20

"Go, marry a whore!" the Lord commanded His prophet Hosea, cf. Hosea 1:2-3. So he married Gomer. The relationship between them is a metaphor of the relationship between the people of Israel and Jahweh, their God. It is a love story with more twists and turns than a soap opera.

Hosea's marriage to Gomer depicts the unfaithfulness of Israel to the Lord and her guilt. The people forsook Jahweh like a faithless wife who runs after her lovers. They worshiped and participated in the cultic practices of the Canaanite fertility gods. Some scholars think, on the basis of ch. 2, that after they were married Gomer committed adultery, left Hosea, and became the legal wife of another man.

Many used to believe that the story of Hosea was only an allegory and did not deal with a real situation, because God would never order anyone to be involved with a prostitute the way Hosea was with Gomer. But now it is generally accepted that the story is about historical happenings.

We know very little about the life of Hosea. He seems to have lived and worked during the calamitous last years of the

Northern Kingdom up to about the time of the capture of Samaria by the Assyrians. He is the only literary prophet of the Northern Kingdom.

The literary form Hosea used in ch. 2 to carry his message is a legal process called rib. Ribu is the opening word in the Hebrew of Hosea 2:2 (v. 4 in the Hebrew text).[152] It is an imperative form of the verb. The matter being considered is the divorce of Hosea from Gomer.

Ch. 2 is not a reconstruction of the legal process. Rather it is a loose collection of prophetic sayings that seem to have the setting of a court procedure. The verses are woven together, but they remain discontinuous. Their sequence and their logic are impossible to work out, although the drift can be surmised.

Hosea 2 is a poem. It is not a narrative poem in the usual sense of that term, but it tells the story of the relationship between Jahweh and Israel as the relationship between Hosea and Gomer. In the beginning, Jahweh warns and threatens Israel. He does not want to terminate His relationship with His people; He wants them to change their ways and to return to Him.

One thing that unites the sayings is that God suffers under Israel's unfaithfulness. He refuses to accept as final the divorce His wife both desires and initiates. He laments that she has forgotten Him, cf. vs. 8 and 13.

An example of the problems in the narration is the personal pronouns in vs. 14-20. The text jumps from "her"/"she" in vs. 14-15 to "you" in v. 16 back to "her" in v. 17 and returns to "you" in vs. 18-20. The struggle translators have in making sense of this is indicated by the footnote with the first "you" in v. 18. The Hebrew original reads "them." All of these personal pronouns refer to Israel.

The confusion may be a part of the literary intention of the author. He may be trying to reflect the will of a God who is somewhat convoluted. He cannot abandon His faithless people. This does not mean that God is this way, but the prophet pictures Him this way to portray His great love for Israel. He struggles with Himself. He is like a person who is deeply in love, who has been jilted, and who is trying to convince his beloved to reestablish their warm relationship. Scholars try to reorganize the sayings to make them follow more naturally, but it is really impossible. All attempts destroy the character of the text.

The idea of marriage between a deity and an earthly partner was familiar to Hosea and his contemporaries through the mythology of the Canaanite nature religion. The Hebrew people lived in the cultural setting of Canaan. That culture had a deep influence on their way of life. At certain levels, the Old Testament religion assimilated characteristics of Baalism. The Old Testament prophets fought against this.

Our knowledge of the myth of Baal was greatly enlarged in 1929 through the discovery of an ancient library by a peasant plowing a field in northern Syria. His plow point struck a rock. When he cleared away the earth to remove the obstruction, he found it to be part of a stairway that led to a tomb. Excavation revealed the site to be the ancient city of Ugarit which was destroyed in the fourteenth century B.C.

Many artifacts of great importance were discovered, including Hittite and Egyptian materials. As far as the Old Testament is concerned, the most significant discovery was a library located between two temples, one dedicated to the Philistine god Dagon who is mentioned in Judges 16:23; 1 Sam. 5:1-7; and 1 Chron. 10:10, and the other to Baal, the Canaanite fertility god. Hundreds of clay tablets written in cuneiform, representing a language hitherto unknown to scholars, were found. When the language was deciphered, some texts revealed the myth of Baal.

Baal is sometimes presented as the king of the gods. He is a storm god and the provider of all fertility. The myth begins with a violent battle between Baal and Yam, the god of the sea, to determine who should be lord of the land. Baal's victory gives him lordship of the earth, while Yam is confined to the sea. The fertility powers of Baal are central in the Canaanite religion. He gives rain to sustain life and promote growth.

Later Baal encounters Mot, the god of aridity and death, and Baal is slain in the ensuing battle. With Baal dead, rain ceases to fall, the stream beds become dry, and Mot's power to destroy begins to encroach on the fertile lands. Rites of mourning and mortification performed by El, the benign father-god, include dust and sackcloth. In addition, El gashes (actually "plows") his face, arms, chest, and back until the blood runs. Baal is dead, and the loss of his life-sustaining powers endangers all life.

Meanwhile, Anath, Baal's sister and mistress, mourns his passing. Over hill and mountain (the high places), she conducts her rites of weeping and wailing. Ultimately, she discovers that Mot killed Baal. She meets the god of death in battle and defeats him. Baal is revived. Overcome by his embrace, Anath conceives and bears a calf. This is the mythical background for sacral prostitution. With Baal's return, the rains come and the wadies flow with water. Life power has been restored to the parched earth.

There were a number of individual Baal deities. They often gained dominion over large geographical areas and became identified with other Baals. The Old Testament mentions the Baal-Berith of Shechem in Judges 8:33 and 9:4, the Baal of Samaria in 1 Kings 16:32, the Baal of Carmel in 1 Kings 18:19-29, the Baal-zebub of Ekron in 2 Kings 1:2-6, the Baal-Hermon in Judges 3:3, and the Baal of Peor in Num. 25:3-5. There were numerous Baal sanctuaries. Baal is sometimes used as a collective term for the Canaanite deities.

The Baal myth was related to the cycle of the seasons in Palestine. During the rainy season, Baal was reigning. During the dry periods, he was dead. The cultic ritual reflected and dramatized the myth. Because Baal and Anath engaged in sexual relations in the myth, the worshippers of Baal promoted fertility by imitating the divine behavior.

There were no extension services sponsored by agricultural universities in those days. All agricultural practices and information were conserved by the various cultic centers. Most people lived by working the land. For information regarding seasons, the time to plant and harvest, and practices, they participated in the rituals of the fertility religions.

Hosea transferred to Jahweh and Israel what the Canaanite myth said of the god and the goddess, although the relationship between Jahweh and Israel was historical and the story of the relationship between the god and the goddess was mythological.

Into this myth, Hosea introduced the ideas of adultery and divorce. This changed the myth into a parable that was intended to terminate the introduction of Canaanite mythology into Israel.

The sins of Israel and the warnings, threats, and punishments of the Lord are described in Hosea 2:2-13. The warnings, threats, and punishments do not result in the restoration of the relationship between Jahweh and Israel. God's judgment is not retributive but redemptive in its purpose. His one aim is to bring Israel back to Himself. Harsh words do not accomplish this, so Jahweh acts to save the relationship with promises, gifts, and acts of salvation. His saving acts and the result are described in vs. 14-15. Jahweh takes Israel back to the wilderness where a new beginning is effected.

Jahweh is described as wooing Israel. He will take her back to the place where He began with her in the exodus, the wilderness. Israel's return to the wilderness will accomplish the purpose the Lord sought to achieve. Jahweh will allow Israel to have nothing more to do with her "lovers." She will be His alone. In a crudely anthropomorphic picture, Jahweh is represented as a seducer who allures a young woman who has other suitors. Israel as a nation will experience Jahweh's overwhelming persuasive power. The words, "speak tenderly to her," can be literally translated, "I will speak to her heart." This is the language of courtship. The new saving event is typologically prefigured in the old one. The things that marred the first saving event will be cancelled out.

As a part of the courtship, Jahweh will give Israel gifts. From the wilderness, He will return to her the land He once gave her but took away because of her infidelity. He will give her "her vineyards" which represent the arable lands in their totality. They are the pledge of a new beginning. They are the gifts of love given to a young woman by her suitor. What He does confirms His words. Jahweh is to be betrothed anew to Israel.

The words, "she shall respond as in the days of her youth," mean that Israel will accept the hand of her Benefactor. She will willingly follow, cf. Jer. 2:2. She is prepared to begin the marriage relationship anew. This is like the attitude of Israel during "her youth," during the period of the exodus from Egypt to Canaan.

The "day" of salvation, which is called "that day," is described in Hosea 2:16-17. The phrase "on that day" may echo the old, popular expectation of the Day of the Lord.

On "that day," Jahweh's punishment of the people of Israel who had turned away from Him, cf. vs. 2-13, will accomplish its intended aim of salvation. The sayings in vs. 16 and 17 elaborate especially vs. 7 and 14-15. Some details of God's courtship of Israel in the wilderness referred to in v. 15 are made known. V. 16 tells us what "she shall respond," according to v. 15. V. 17 makes clear that the new attitude is the result of what Jahweh does.

That Israel will call the Lord "My husband" should be understood against the background of the marriage metaphor Hosea uses. "My husband" is apparently an endearing expression of a deep personal relationship. In contrast, "my Baal" emphasizes the legal position of the husband as lord and owner of his wife. Israel will not just respect Jahweh somewhat reluctantly, since He is her legal Lord, but she knows herself to be in a completely new and loving relationship with Him.

That Israel will no longer call Jahweh "my Baal" implies that they called Jahweh Baal. Israel's life among the Canaanites led to the identification of one god with the other. It is sometimes difficult to determine whether Jahweh was worshiped as Baal, or they were worshiped together.

That Israel will no longer mention the name of Baal is a reference to the solemn occasion in the ritual when the god's name was spoken, cf. Joshua 23:7. By removing from the ritual the name of Baal, Jahweh will reform Israel's worship.

The "day" of salvation is further described in Hosea 2:18-20. After the restoration of Israel's worship of Him, Jahweh will restore the world.

The collection of prophetic sayings in vs. 18-20 is unified by the consistent use of "I" as the subject. God speaks and will act. Many difficulties are caused by the change in topics and the different personal pronouns that refer to Israel.[153]

On the day of salvation, Jahweh will make a new covenant

for Israel. This is not the restoration of the old covenant which Jahweh made with Israel. New wine will not be poured into old wineskins, cf. Mark 2:18-22. Israel's worship of Baal destroyed the old covenant. This is the first reference to the new covenant of the endtime which the prophet Jeremiah announces in Jer. 31:31-34.

The covenant has three parts. One is the restoration of the relationship between animals and humans. Two, Israel will be at peace with the hostile nations. Three, God will create rest and security for His beloved.

The new covenant will be effected not because of anything that Israel does. She will live in the peace and security Jahweh prepares for her. Her task is to respond faithfully with thanksgiving.

Jahweh will act on Israel's behalf and prove His covenant loyalty by mediating a covenant between opposing forces within creation, cf. Ezek. 34:25-30. The covenant includes peace "with the wild animals, the birds of the air, and the creeping things of the ground." These animals can harm people, their vineyards, and their crops. This peace will reestablish the harmony between humans and the animals of Paradise. Animals will no longer be harmful, and beasts will live peaceably among themselves. Ordinarily in those days after wars that cost many lives, wild animals multiplied and ravaged the countryside, cf. 2 Kings 17:25-28. The beasts were considered a scourge sent by Jahweh against sinful people. Hostility among humans, between humans and animals, or between animals is discord in God's creation. The Messianic era will be characterized by perfect love and peace.

The second part of the covenant is that Israel will be at peace with the hostile nations. "The land" in v. 18 means the land of Israel, the area in which Israel lives.[154]

The third part of the covenant is that Jahweh will create living conditions in which one can sleep in peace unafraid of attacks by animals or an enemy.

On that day, a new marriage will be constituted between Jahweh and Israel in love, cf. vs. 19-20 and Is. 62:5. The old marriage will not be reconstituted but a completely new one will be created that will establish a new, final communion between God and Israel. The new relationship is stated three times in vs. 19 and 20.

The piel form ("I will take you for my wife") marks the end of the premarital status in that it denotes the act of paying the bridal price. The last possible objection the bride's father might raise will be removed, cf. Gen. 34:12; 1 Sam. 18:25; 2 Sam. 3:14. Translating with the word "engaged," as that word is used today, does not carry the sense intended. Wolff freely translates: "I will eliminate your father's last objections to our marriage by paying the amount he demands; I will do everything to win your complete and lasting companionship."

The bridal price Jahweh will pay, which will guarantee the indissolubility of the relationship, is described by five nouns. Zedek ("righteousness") means the faithful performance of duties in the community that helps those in need. Mishpat ("justice") means a way of life that maintains and restores the community's existence through just legal decisions. Chesed ("steadfast love") means kindhearted actions that create and establish a sense of community by spontaneous love and the faithful meeting of responsibilities. Rachamim ("mercy") emphasizes a loving sensitivity founded on an indissoluble togetherness which is sympathetically moved to pity especially for those in need of help. Emunah ("faithfulness") is emphasized by being placed last in the series. It underlines the divine constancy and dependability of the intimate, living community that will be established.

Leolam ("forever") is legal terminology for a lifelong, final, unalterable commitment.[155]

The outcome of Jahweh's payment of the bridal price is that Israel will acknowledge Jahweh as Lord. She will call Jahweh "My husband," cf. v. 16, and "my God," cf. v. 23. The knowledge of the Lord has been absent from Israel, according to vs. 8 and 13. She will recognize the gifts of the new marriage covenant, cf. v. 20. There will be thankful response for them.

Hosea originates that proclamation which will reach its culmination in the New Testament's metaphor of Christ Jesus as the bridegroom of His bride, the church.

The imagery and allegory reach fulfillment in history when John the Baptist calls God's people out into the wilderness, and there God gives them the baptism of repentance for the forgiveness of sins, cf. Mark 1:2-5 and Is. 40:1-3. Jesus, too, begins in the wilderness, cf. Mark 1:12. The Jews of New Testament times expected the age of salvation to begin there, cf. Acts 21:38 and Matt. 24:26. Hosea's message of Jahweh's love for Israel points toward the great love God demonstrated in Jesus and His death on Calvary's cross, cf. Rom. 5:8 and Eph. 2:4-9.

The Valley of Achor is the place of sacrilege and of the stoning of Achan in Joshua 7. God will make it "a door of hope" for Israel.

2 Corinthians 3:1-6

Paul is defending his status as a "minister of a new covenant." That title is roughly equivalent to "apostle" which Paul uses to identify himself in the opening words of this letter. Diakonos ("minister") means, first of all, one who serves, but it can also refer to one who has been dispatched on some kind of an errand for another. Paul was made competent to be a minister of a new covenant when he was called by Jesus to be an apostle, cf. Acts 9:1-22.

The term "new covenant" appears first in Jer. 31:31-34. It is found nowhere else in the Old Testament. The covenant concept, however, is basic in Biblical theology.

A new covenant implies at least one previous covenant. The Old Testament describes several but two main ones between God and the human race. God covenanted with Israel at Mt. Sinai through the mediation of Moses, cf. Ex. 19:3-6; 24:3-8; and 34:1-28. He declared Israel to be His people and said that He would be her God. This covenant implied protection and blessing for Israel. It stipulated that Israel was to conform to the norms set forth in the Ten Commandments and other legal collections. This covenant set Israel apart from all other nations.

But the situation had changed by the time of Jeremiah. That prophet said the people of Israel turned their backs on God, and so God had declared holy war against them. The land and cities where Israel lived, including Jerusalem, would be devastated. Jeremiah said that the victories of the Babylonian king Nebuchadrezzar over Judah in 597 and 587 executed God's punishment. The covenant made at Sinai was dead.

But Jeremiah also said that God would make a new covenant with Israel that would be essentially different from the old one. The provisions of the Sinai covenant had been written on tablets of stone, but God would write the provisions of the new covenant on the people's hearts. The concept of heart in the Old Testament centers more on volition than on emotion. The heart is the center of planning and the carrying out of plans. The law written on tablets of stone had resulted in disobedience. Writing the stipulations of the new covenant on the hearts of the people would make them a part of the will of people, so that they would obey God not because they were supposed to but because they wanted to. The people would not need to teach each other to know God, because they all would be in close relationship to Him. Furthermore, God would forgive their sins.

Jesus uses the term "new covenant" in connection with the Last Supper in 1 Cor. 11:25. The new covenant was instituted in and with Jesus' death, cf. Luke 22:20 and Heb. 8:8-13. The demonstration of God's love in what Jesus did is so strong that it causes people to love God. God's love empowers people to do God's will.

The book of Hebrews quotes the entire Jeremiah passage and relates it to the sacrifice of Jesus. The writer says that the new covenant is better than the old in 7:22 and that it will last forever, cf. 13:20. The old covenant was temporary. The new covenant is founded on better promises, according to 8:6. The old covenant was not faultless, according to 8:7. The new covenant makes the old one weak, ineffectual, and obsolete, according to 8:13 and 7:18-19. The problem with the old one was the law.

The new covenant is "not of letter but of spirit." With the phrase "of letter," Paul refers to the covenant made at Mt. Sinai. It was inscribed in letters on tablets of stone, cf. 2 Cor. 3:7 and Ex. 34:28.

That the new covenant is "of spirit" means it has a qualitatively new character. Obedience to letter makes compliance primarily an external demand, but the word "spirit" describes a radical transformation that produces harmony between will and action. "The letter kills." Paul calls the old covenant a ministry of death in 2 Cor. 3:7. It pronounces a judicial decree on people and sentences the disobedient to death. In contrast to this "ministry of condemnation," the new covenant is "a ministry of justification," according to 2 Cor. 3:9. It "gives life."

This covenant language is another way to talk about the gospel of Jesus Christ. Paul uses it to counter the teaching of those who oppose him in Corinth. They are challenging his status as a minister of a new covenant. Reference is made to his opponents in 1 Cor. 1:11-13; 2 Cor. 2:17 ("many"); and 3:1 ("some").

Paul defends his status with great confidence in 2 Cor. 2:14-17. He says that he speaks God's Word sincerely in 2:17. He speaks as a person sent by God and as though he is standing in the presence of God. He defends this confident attitude in the opening words of ch. 3. Many commentators consider vs. 1-3 to be a kind of parenthesis, but what Paul says is not beside the point. He is emphasizing the validity of his claim to be a "minister of a new covenant."

He dismisses as ridiculous the idea that he is commending himself in vs. 1 and 2. In 2 Cor. 5:12, he states explicitly what he only points to in the first question of v. 1; he denies commending himself. But he frankly does commend himself in 6:4-10 not by boasting about his successes but by listing the things he has endured as a minister of the new covenant.

He takes a swipe at his detractors when he says that he does not need "letters of recommendation" to the Corinthians or from the Corinthians "as some do." The negative particle me indicates that he expects a negative answer to his question. He widens the distinction he makes in 2 Cor. 2:17 between himself and those who challenge his status. He calls them "peddlers of God's word."

Some think that they are members of the Cephas group

mentioned in 1 Cor. 1:12.[156] They are Jews and proud of it, Hebrews, Israelites, and descendants of Abraham, according to 2 Cor. 11:22. They also are new arrivals in Corinth. They may have come with letters of recommendation from one of the eastern churches. This does not imply that any of the eastern churches is responsible for the divisions they were causing.

"Letters of recommendation" is a technical term in a well-established custom of Paul's day. They are common among the papyri.[157] The letters were ordinarily carried by the person being recommended in order that he or she might be received hospitably by the people he or she wanted to contact and perhaps aided in some specified way. The letters played a large role in the ancient world, because communications were poor and hospitality in distant places was more important than today. Paul used such letters before his conversion, especially when he went to Damascus, according to Acts 9:1-2 and 22:5. He gives a good example of them in Rom. 16:1-2. The New Testament book Philemon is such a letter.

Paul is not criticizing the use of letters of recommendation. He is emphasizing that his relationship to the Corinthian congregation is quite different from that of his detractors. They used such letters when they came, because they needed them. But there was no church in Corinth when Paul arrived. The detractors' use of introductory letters shows that their ministry is not comparable to Paul's. This is Paul's point in the second question of v. 1.

Those who oppose Paul and carried letters of recommendation when they came to Corinth will want such letters from the Corinthians when they leave and go elsewhere. Paul refers to the second letters with the phrase "from you."

The Corinthians themselves are the only letter Paul needs. Their Christian faith testifies that Paul is a minister of the new covenant. They are the fruit of his ministry.

Paul brings together the prophecy of Jer. 31:33 regarding the new covenant the Lord "will write on their hearts," i. e. "the house of Israel," with the prophecy of Ezek. 36:26 regarding "a new spirit" the Lord God will give "the house of Israel," removing "the heart of stone" and giving them "a heart of flesh."

556

Bultmann says that the reading "your" should be used not "our" in the second occurrence of the word in v. 2.[158] But Furnish says that "our" is the best attested reading and has been adopted by many modern commentators and by virtually all the modern translations.[159] Some say it is a literary plural and refers to Paul alone, i.e., "my heart." If the pronoun "your" is accepted, the clause means that the Corinthians give testimony that they are people of the new covenant from their inner being. If the pronoun "our" is used, the integrity of Paul is not visible but comes from his "heart."

According to the Semitic understanding, the heart is that inward sphere which is the revealer of a person's most authentic being. It is contrasted in 1 Thess. 2:17 with what is merely present in an obvious way.

The mere existence of the Corinthian church testifies to the work Paul did and says that he is a minister of the new covenant. This testimony can "be known and read by all." He doesn't need a letter of recommendation as his opponents do.

The Corinthian Christians themselves are "a letter of Christ, prepared by us." The genitive, "a letter of Christ," is not objective, i.e., a letter about Christ, but subjective, i.e., a letter whose origin is Christ. The thought is less about what is in the letter than its existence as an attestation to Paul's ministry. Paul is the writer of the letter dictated by Christ. The aorist tense points back to the founding of the Corinthian congregation.

The Corinthian testimony is "written not with ink but with the Spirit of the living God." In Paul's day, ink was made of a sooty carbon and a thin solution of gum. It was applied to papyrus with a reed pen. The gospel took root in Corinth because of the powerful working of the Holy Spirit, cf. 1 Cor. 2; Gal. 3:2-5; and 1 Thess. 1:5-6.

As "a letter of Christ," the Corinthians are, "written . . . not on tablets of stone but on tablets of human hearts." "Tablets of stone" refers to "the tablets of stone, with the law and the commandment, which I (the Lord) have written for their (Israel's) instruction," described in Ex. 24:12. "When God finished speaking with Moses on Mount Sinai, he gave him the two tablets of the covenant, tablets of stone, written with the finger of God," cf. Ex. 31:18. Moses broke the tablets when he saw Israel worshipping the golden calf. The Lord told Moses to make two new tablets of stone like the first ones and bring them up the mountain. He did this, and the Lord reconstituted the covenant with Israel, cf. Ex. 34:10-26. Then Moses "wrote on the tablets the words of the covenant, the ten commandments," cf. Ex. 34:28. Moses retells the story of the first two tablets in Deut. 9:9-17.

Paul seems to have in mind not only the references in Exodus and Deuteronomy to the stone tablets God gave Moses but also the contrast between "the heart of stone" and "a heart of flesh" in Ezek. 11:19 and 36:26. Ezekiel uses the word "flesh" for that which is a living substance in contrast to that which is stone. The heart and the spirit are the instruments by which God's commands are established in His people for their obedience.

In 2 Cor. 2:16, Paul asks, "Who is sufficient (to proclaim the good news of Christ)?" In 3:1-3, he says that he fulfilled his responsibility in Corinth. He asserts in vs. 4-6 that he has such confidence before God through Christ. A comparable declaration of confidence occurs in Rom. 15:17. Both there and here, the declaration is followed immediately by an explanatory and, in a sense, qualifying statement. In Romans, it takes the form of a resolve to speak confidently only of "what Christ has accomplished through me," cf. Rom. 15:18. Here Paul says that he makes no claims to self-sufficiency; his sufficiency rests on God alone. He makes another statement of self-evaluation in 1 Cor. 15:9-10.

Mark 2:13-22

The account of Jesus' call of Levi follows the pattern set in the call of Simon, Andrew, James, and John in Mark 1:16-20. It emphasizes some of the same aspects of discipleship. The decision to follow Jesus is not initiated by those who follow Him. It is a response. Jesus calls, and a disciple responds.

Many Bible students feel that Jesus and Levi came to know each other earlier, and in this way they explain Levi's readiness to follow Jesus. Unfortunately, the text is silent on this matter, and this seems to suggest that the sequence of call and response is important. Mark shows no interest in a psychological explanation for Levi's decision. The cause behind his response was Jesus Himself. Jesus summoned people to follow Him not as a teacher but as the Christ. Not a word of praise was directed to Levi for his decision. Mark focuses attention on Him who called.

Jesus' call to discipleship typically was made with the words "Follow me," cf. John 1:43 and Mark 1:17. That verb in v. 15 does not seem to have the same intensity.

The rabbis of Jesus' day did not get their followers in the same way He did. His style is comparable only to God's call of the Old Testament prophets.

Jesus' imperious call of Levi triggered an immediate and apparently enthusiastic response. Although the word "immediately" (euthus) is not used, as it is in 1:18, the aorist form of the Greek verb describes an immediate response.

Jesus did not explain to Levi what He wanted him to do, as He did to Simon and Andrew in 1:17. He offered no program or way of life, no goal or ideal to strive after. Levi left his "tax booth" not because he thought he would be doing something more worthwhile but simply because of Him who called. The blunt command, "Follow me," without elaboration intensifies the confiscating character of Jesus' call.

Levi was called out of relative security into a life of insecurity. His old life was left behind and surrendered. Actually, he was given the only security and safety that counts which is the fellowship of Jesus.

Jesus' call takes precedence over everything: vocation, family, and even oneself, cf. Luke 14:26-27. Disciples of Jesus must look on themselves as people who have been condemned to death, cf. Mark 8:34. Jesus' contemporaries knew very well that people who took up a cross were on their way to the nearest place of execution.

Levi realized a considerable income through his tax job. Leaving it was a greater sacrifice for him than for the fishermen of 1:16-20. When Levi left the tax booth, it was final; but the fishermen could return on occasion to their fishing, and they did. But Jesus' call is first and foremost an expression of divine grace.

Positively identifying Levi is not possible with the knowledge available. Levi, son of Alphaeus and follower of Jesus, is named only here and in Luke 5:27 and 29. The name Levi is not included in the list of the apostles in Mark 3:16-19 or in Matt. 10:2-4. Matthew is the only apostle explicitly described as a tax collector. A "son of Alphaeus" is listed, but the name given him is James. Many think Levi is Matthew. It was common in Galilee to have two names, one Jewish and the other Galilean.

Levi's tax booth may have been a station on a trade route or a place where people who used the Sea of Galilee paid their port duties and fishing tolls.

Tax collectors were universally despised by the Jews of that day for a variety of reasons. One was their contact with gentiles. The Jews thought that they should not pay tribute to Caesar, because God was their ruler. In paying tribute, they acknowledged Rome's rule. Tax collectors were considered traitors or collaborators, because they provided support for the Roman legions. The Jews considered tax collectors an insult to their God. Tax collectors were sometimes unjust, cruel, and practiced extortion. Much hatred can also be credited to the inconvenience of being stopped frequently on the road to pay the various taxes, having to unload all one's goods, and being searched meticulously. Tax collectors were biased, showing favor to their friends and disfavor to those who were not.

The Talmud distinguishes two classes of tax collectors. One is the tax-gatherer in general and the other the custom-house official. Both fall under the rabbinic ban but especially officials like Levi.

The taxes of Judea were no longer farmed out. Tax officials were appointed by politicians, and the tax was paid directly to the government. Thus tax collectors were government officials. This alleviated some of the corruption and oppression, but it made the tax-gatherers more obnoxious to Jews.

The taxes collected were numerous and oppressive. There were head taxes, property taxes, sales taxes, shipping fees, transport tolls, and other customs and duties. The patronage heap was large and began with Caesar. Client rulers like Herod Antipas were a part of the system with various agents and functionaries taking their cut. Even the Jerusalem temple was allowed to collect taxes in exchange for keeping the peace.

Levi was a part of this corrupt system. His location by the Sea of Galilee suggests that Simon and his friends got their fishing license from him and gave him the first tax on a catch. Mark does not tell us what the fishermen thought of Levi being called to be a part of their group. The evangelist did not consider this important.

Becoming a part of the group associated with the immensely popular young rabbi, Jesus, gave religious status to the outcast Levi and to all his colleagues. Jews shunned tax collectors. For obvious reasons, Levi's friends flocked to Jesus. When Levi invited them to dinner at his house, they were happy to come and meet Jesus. "Many" came.

The NRSV says that the dinner was "in Levi's house." The footnote points out that the Greek actually uses the relative pronoun "in his house" which could mean that the dinner was in Jesus' house. Luke 5:29, however, says that Levi gave the banquet.

The Pharisees criticized Jesus for eating with "tax collectors and sinners." The term "sinners" could refer to people who were gross and open violators of the law, but not necessarily. They may have led an immoral life, but not necessarily. Sinners were people who did not observe the law according to the Pharisaic ideal. They lived outside the law's frame of reference. The designation was oriented to a person's relationship to the law. A person was called a "sinner" if he/she was not familiar with the law or was not earnest about it. In the synoptic gospels, especially tax collectors, cf. Luke 18:13; 19:7; 15:1, harlots, cf. Luke 7:37 and 39, and gentiles, cf. Mark 14:41, are referred to as sinners. In normal daily life at that time, it was not difficult to tell who was a "sinner." Actually, for the Pharisees, everyone who did not belong to their group was.

Jesus offended the scribes by consorting with tax collectors and sinners. The name "scribes" refers to the job of copying. It was always done by hand in those days. They copied holy writings. Because of their close attention to the words of the scriptures, they also became experts in interpreting them. Because Jesus' teaching and conduct ran counter to the dominant interpretation of the law, the scribes opposed Him. They interpreted the law as prescribed by tradition. Surprisingly, Jesus accepted the Jewish distinction between sinners and the righteous when He likened Himself to a physician. His fellowship with them was not that of a partner in crime but of a physician. They were sick.

Some scribes became Pharisees. Israel was split in Jesus' day into clearly distinguishable religious parties, including Pharisees, Sadduccees, Essenes, and Herodians. The Jewish community had a theocratic shape, and so these religious parties also assumed the character of political parties. They were small in number, but their influence on the political and religious life was immense.

The Pharisees who were virtually in control religiously were the most important opponents of Jesus. They preserved postexilic Judaism. They saw themselves as the true Israel and sought to enlist the whole nation for their causes.

For Jesus, too, the Pharisees represented Israel. They represented the highest standard of excellence in Israel. They represented life under the law.

The Pharisees were devoted to the traditions. They taught as law not only what was in the writings but also the traditions passed on by the rabbis. They drew up a list of 621 laws. Recognizing the impossibility of one person keeping all those laws, they divided them between several of them; and thus fulfilled the law. They offered themselves as examples of the life pleasing to God.

Their name is commonly derived from an Aramaic word that means separatists. It is explained as meaning that in fidelity to the law they separated themselves from all uncleanness and especially from the common people who were called "the people of the land."

Bible students are puzzled by the question the scribes of the Pharisees put to the disciples of Jesus.[160] They wonder when the scribes of the Pharisees arrived on the scene. Was it during the meal or after the meal? It is doubtful that they were a part of the group eating. That would have violated their principles and made the challenge implied by their question pretty hollow.

Seeing Jesus eating with tax collectors and sinners, they confronted Jesus' disciples. The scribes may have spoken to them rather than to Jesus, because the disciples' relationship with Jesus was new. They may have been trying to shake the disciples' confidence in their new rabbi.

The implication of their question is that Jesus should not be associating with tax collectors and sinners. In eating with them, He was practicing the closest fellowship. Not only the scribes and Pharisees criticized Jesus for doing this, but also the common people did in Luke 19:7. They felt that whoever associated with sinners showed little regard for the law.

Jesus may have heard the Pharisees speaking to the disciples, or what they said may have been reported to Him. In reply to the criticism, Jesus likens Himself to a physician. He said that His mission is "to call not the righteous but sinners." Other statements regarding Jesus' mission are in Mark 10:45; Luke 19:10; and John 3:17.

The "call" to which Jesus referred was the call to the kingdom stated in Mark 1:15.

"The righteous" Jesus did not come for were represented by the scribes. Jesus was using irony. The scribes of the Pharisees considered themselves God's favorite people. Jesus said that God wanted nothing to do with their piety.

Jesus' table fellowship with tax collectors and sinners marked a new era in the relationship between God and the human race. A new era is always difficult to accept, because there is much that is unknown; and we tend to fear the unknown. We compromise; we try to accommodate the new to the old. One reason Jesus was opposed was because He did not follow all of the old customs and traditions. One of the most popular forms of piety among the Jews was fasting. Sharp criticism was directed against Him because He did not fast when others did. Jesus replied to this criticism on one occasion by telling three parables.

In the parables, Jesus said that trying to accommodate the old to the new is folly. The day of salvation is not a time for the somber penance represented by fasting; it is a time for the joy of a wedding celebration. The old garment of Judaism could not be patched. The old forms could not contain the fermenting wine of God's new order. The grace of the gospel and the legalism of the law are not compatible.

One of the groups fasting at this time was the disciples of John the Baptist. It is not necessary to assume that John's disciples and the Pharisees were observing the same fast. The death of John is told in Mark 6:14-29, but he was arrested earlier, according to Mark 1:14. Jesus' public ministry began when John's ended. Some commentators think that the disciples of John may have been fasting as a sign of mourning for their leader.

The only fast commanded by the law was on the Day of Atonement, but the Pharisees observed additional fasts twice a week, on Mondays and Thursdays. Traditional fasts, commemorative of historical events were also observed. It is impossible to be certain what fast or fasts were being observed in v. 18.

The parable of the Wedding Guests is set against the background of the Old Testament metaphor of Jahweh as the Bridegroom and Israel as His bride, cf. Hos. 2:19; Is. 54:4-8; 62:4-5. The imagery is used also in the New Testament, cf. John 3:29; Rev. 19:7; and 21:2. Jesus is the Bridegroom, and His disciples are the wedding guests. When Jesus said that the Bridegroom was with the wedding guests, He was saying that the time of His ministry was marriage week, the time of the wedding celebration. By universal consent and according to rabbinic law, marriage week was a time of unmixed festivity. All mourning was suspended. It was regarded as a religious duty to gladden the bride and bridegroom. Jesus was saying that the kingdom of God was present, He was its Lord, and it was incompatible with a situation so joyous that there should be penitential mourning. Mourning was uppermost in fasting.

Jesus said there would be fasting "when the bridegroom is taken away from them." His death was not unexpected. He knew that His death was a part of what He had to do to carry out the divine plan of salvation. It belonged to His Messianic mission. From the beginning, Jesus anticipated that His life would end on a cross. He pursued that goal with set and steadfast purpose, cf. Mark 8:31; 9:31; 10:33-34; 10:45; 12:1-10; 14:24; Matt. 12:39-40; 26:28; Luke 13:31-33; 22:20; 1 Cor. 11:24-26.

The sayings regarding patches and wineskins emphasize the revolutionary character of Jesus' mission. In the sayings, Jesus declared that His new gospel must find fresh vehicles. He was effecting not merely a reformation. The old forms would not work. All things had to become new. A new patch of material that is not sanforized used to repair the hole in an old cloak will shrink. When it does, it will create a hole larger than the one it repaired. A wineskin bottle loses its pliability. If new wine is placed into an old bottle, it will create pressure as it ages that will destroy the old bottle.

Mark's gospel emphasizes the popularity of Jesus during His Galilean ministry, cf. 1:28, 33, 37, 45; 2:2, 4, 13, 15; 3:20; 6:31. But conflict with the religious leaders was almost immediate, too. The story of the calling of Levi is the second of five events that emphasize this conflict, cf. 2:1-11, 15-20, 23-28; 3:1-6. At the very beginning of his gospel, Mark directs his readers to the climax of the story and to the point of Jesus' life, His passion. The final story in this early conflict series concludes with the words, "The Pharisees went out and immediately conspired with the Herodians against him, how to destroy him," 3:6.

The gospel of Mark is the story of Jesus on His way to the cross. The opening words of the gospel are its title: "The beginning of the good news of Jesus Christ, the Son of God." The climax is reached in the words of the centurion under the cross: "Truly this man was the Son of God," cf. 15:39.

8th Sunday after the Epiphany

Year C

Isaiah 55:10-13

God promises Israel in exile that He will lead her back home, from Babylon to the promised land. He will save her. He appeals to Israel through the prophet Isaiah to trust Him. He says that His Word is powerful and accomplishes what He wants it to do in history as well as in nature.

As God's herald, the prophet talks about a new exodus that will be better than the first. Israel's forefathers left Egypt in fear and haste, but they will return home in joy and peace. The return will be a triumphant parade.

The prophet imagines all creation standing along the highway watching and rejoicing. Even the hills, the mountains, and the trees will consider the spectacle wonderful. They will celebrate and applaud. All of nature has a stake in the reign of God.

The thorns and briers the prophet talks about are symbols of life diminished by God's condemnation, cf. Is. 5:6; 7:23-25; 27:4; and 32:13. These prickly evidences of negativity will no longer thrive. In their place will be cypress and myrtle that are signs of growth, life, and beauty. They witness to the character of God's new reign.

Israel's experience of exile may have caused her to think that God had abandoned her. But God wants Israel to know that He is trustworthy, powerful, and He saves His people. See Is. 40:8.

His word is like rain and snow. They water the earth. They make the earth produce grain and bread and sustain the food chain. Rain and snow are strong images in dry Palestine.

The water cycle of nature is essential for life. To the ancients, it was not so much nature's law as God's law/word. They understood the water cycle much as we do, but they believed that it was God who, either actively or tacitly through His allowance, produces it. His hot breath withers the grass and evaporates the streams. His cold breath freezes the water. He causes it to rain on the just and the unjust alike. He makes the plants grow and produces the future.

The power of God's word is demonstrated especially in the creation story. Everything happens as the result of His word. When He speaks, nothing can keep what He says from happening.

Jahweh's promises are not idle chatter. They carry the full power of His majestic rule. His word will produce a new future for Israel in exile.

God's saving word to us today is Jesus Christ and the gospel. Like rain and snow, Jesus came down to a parched and dead earth. He came from the Father and assumed fleshly form. In the prologue of the gospel of John, Jesus is called the word. He became the Bread of Life whom we eat that we might live forever.

There is no scarcity of God's word. If the fruits of righteousness in our lives are not as abundant as they should be, the reason is that we are not receiving the word and soaking it up, as we should.

God's word appeals to us to seek Him and to call on Him, to forsake our evil thoughts and ways, and to return to Him, cf. Is. 55:6-7. As He delivered ancient Israel from exile in Babylon, so He wants to save all people, as 1 Tim. 2:4 says. In Jesus' death, He has done this.

God's word will work with us, through us, in us, without us, and despite us. It will consume us, roll over us, control us, create us, and liberate us. It will not fail to save us.

1 Corinthians 15:51-58

The future shines brightly with all the possibilities of life as Paul talks about the end. He stimulates our hope by emphasizing that we will become imperishable and immortal and that we have the victory over death through our Lord Jesus Christ. This hope enables us to "be steadfast, immovable, always excelling in the work of the Lord."

The end is a subject of great interest. One interesting thing is that all of us will not die before the end. Three things will happen "in the twinkling of an eye." The trumpet will sound, the dead will be raised, and we all will be changed from being perishable to being imperishable.

The events associated with the end are developed a little more in 1 Thess. 4:15-17. At the sound of God's trumpet and with the archangel's call, the Lord Himself will descend from heaven with a cry of command. We who are still alive will not precede those who have died, but we will be caught up together with them in the clouds when they are raised. Together, we will meet the Lord in the air.

The nearness of Jesus' return is asserted in Phil. 4:5 and James 5:8. This means that the end is near. This is stated also in 1 Pet. 4:7. Paul, as well as other apostles, seem to have had no idea that centuries would pass before Jesus would come again.

When Paul uses the word "all" in v. 51, he is referring to believers. He does not talk about what will happen to non-believers.

The end will come "at the last trumpet." According to Jewish speculation, God will sound the trumpet seven times at the end of the world to raise the dead. The trumpets will sound for the various stages of the resurrection. At the seventh, all believers will be made alive and stand on their feet. They will be raised no matter how they died, whether they lie ten feet under the water or the ground, whether they were burned to ashes which were scattered to the four winds, whether they were consumed by beasts, birds, or worms.

Resurrection means transformation to a new form of life. The change from perishable to imperishable and from mortal to immortality is necessary, because "flesh and blood cannot inherit the kingdom of God, nor does the perishable inherit the imperishable." The change will not involve a long process. It will happen "in a moment, in the twinkling of an eye." The change is described as being like changing clothes in vs. 53-54.

When "this perishable body puts on imperishability," death will be swallowed up in victory. The battle between God and the anti-God powers in the world is still going on. "The last enemy to be destroyed is death," cf. 1 Cor. 15:26. Until the end, death will continue to exercise its power.

Two Old Testament passages, Is. 25:8 and Hos. 13:14, are combined in vs. 54-55. The Lord will swallow up death in the Messianic age. The thought of victory over death causes Paul to burst into a song of triumph. The curse pronounced upon Adam in Gen. 3:19 will be removed. He who hears Jesus' word and believes Him "does not come under judgment," cf. John 5:24.

Athanasius said: "man is by nature afraid of death and of the dissolution of the body; but there is this most startling fact, that he who has put on the faith of the cross despises even what is naturally fearful, and for Christ's sake is not afraid of death." He likens it to a person putting on asbestos and being made less fearful of fire which has the natural property of burning.[161]

Paul explains this victory by using the metaphor of the sting of a scorpion. The word kentron ("sting") is used of the sting of the infernal locusts in Rev. 9:10. Death is like a scorpion that is made harmless when its sting is removed.

No species of living being is tormented by the fear of death as much as we humans are. Christians and God-fearing people know that their death, together with all the other miseries of life, is to be associated with the wrath of God. In this sense, death, to a Christian, is more terrible than it is for other people. Wicked people do not know sin and the wrath of God. Christians, however, know that God is incensed because of sin and that sin is the cause of all miseries. But in the cross of Jesus Christ, God has forgiven our sin. In this way, He removed death's sting and gives us hope.

Another way Paul explains our victory over death is, "the power of sin is the law." The Jews felt that the law could not be one of the causes of transgression. Judaism believed that torah produces life. But Paul says that the law makes sin a deadly force. In Rom. 4:15, he says, "the law brings wrath" and produces guilt. It leads to death. But Jesus Christ achieved a threefold redemption by His sacrifice: from the law, from sin, and from death. We are no longer bound by sin, because we are no longer bound to the law, cf. Rom. 6:14 and 8:1-2.

Some people think that the cosmic battle going on in the world between God and the anti-God powers is beyond the imagination of modern people. But the interest shown in the Harry Potter stories of J. K. Rowling suggests otherwise.

The battle against evil is fought not by reducing it to a laundry list of sins and trying really hard to avoid them. Nor is it fought by identifying evil in other people and restraining or eliminating the people. Evil is God's enemy, and God has not left us alone and powerless. Jesus destroyed sin and death and will finally crush Satan on our behalf. Confidence in this is the beginning of peace and joy and of the obedience of faith.

After talking at length about the end, Paul concludes with an injunction about the present. Our hope in Jesus Christ makes us durable. We do not look for glory and reward in this life, but we wait for what will happen in the resurrection. Life is our investment in the future.

The word translated "immovable" may be a synonym of the word edraioi which is translated "steadfast." What Paul means more specifically may be indicated in Col. 1:23: "without shifting from the hope promised by the gospel that you heard." Confidence in the resurrection can withstand opposition and will empower us so that we are not pushed around. It enables us to excel in the work of the Lord.

Believing that our labor is not in vain gives consolation to Christians who suffer. It enables them to persevere in good works. If we did not have such consolation, we could not stand the misery, persecution, trouble, ingratitude, and abuse we experience as we do good.

The money, property, popularity, reputation, and recognition we have gained for ourselves while we live on this earth will endure only so long as we live here. When we pass out of the world or the world passes away, all of those things will pass away, too. There are things, however, that will last forever. They are the things we do for the Lord. They will follow us into heaven, cf. Rev. 14:13. Jesus encourages us to lay up treasures in heaven, in Matt. 6:19-21. This motivates us to abound in the work of the Lord.

Luke 6:39-49

Five sayings conclude Jesus' Sermon on the Plain. Jesus uses some of the sayings in other connections, too. He uses the parable of the Blind Leading the Blind in Matt. 15:14 as He responds to an attack by the Pharisees and scribes. He uses in Matt. 10:24-25 the saying of v. 40 to warn His disciples that they will experience opposition just as He is. The words of vs. 44b-45 are used in Matt. 12:35 to condemn the Pharisees who accuse Him of blasphemy and of working with the power of demons. Other sayings are a part of the Sermon on the Mount in Matt. 5-7, cf. vs. 41-42, vs. 43-44a, vs. 44b-45, and vs. 46-49. The saying in v. 45 is used not only in the Sermon on the Mount but also in another context.

The parable of the Blind Leading the Blind is directed to people who teach Godly living. Jesus wants His disciples to teach, but they must not be false teachers. They themselves must follow the way of God.

Jesus' disciples should teach what He is teaching. They should not suppose that they know better than He does. They should not think that they are greater than He is.

To teach others, a person must first engage in honest self-evaluation and serious self-improvement. Only the person who overcomes his own faults is able to help others.

"The speck" to which Jesus refers is a splinter, anything

small and dry. "The log" is the main beam on which other beams rest in the roof or floor of a building.

Jesus calls the person a hypocrite who tries to teach another person without first cleaning up his own mess. The word "hypocrite" in Greek came to mean an actor on a stage. From that use, it developed the transferred meaning of pretender. In the LXX, it occurs in Job 34:30 and 36:13 as a translation of the Hebrew word meaning "godless." In the literature of the Jews of the diaspora, it came to be listed with terms for lying and deceit.

Jesus' tree and fruit figures in vs. 43-44 are applied to human beings in v. 45. What people say reveals what is going on inside of them.

The final words of the Sermon on the Plain examine the foundation on which we build our life. That foundation should be characterized by following Jesus, hearing His words of promise and instruction, and doing what He says.

The word "Lord" describes a relationship that has great influence. In the Old Testament, the word kurios is reserved for the true God. It is used to translate God's proper name, Jahweh.

To call Jesus our Lord without letting Him influence our behavior is phony. If Jesus is our Lord, He controls our life. Jesus rejects a relationship with a person that does not go very deep.

His instruction is not theory to be discussed and argued. Rather, it is to be done. To hear and do what Jesus says is to build on rock. To hear and not do what He says is to build on sand. A house built on that foundation will be destroyed when a time of stress comes. Jesus wants obedience.

The houses of Palestine in Jesus' day customarily did not have good foundations. Actually, the happening Jesus describes in v. 48 would have been unlikely there. Matthew's description in Matt. 7:25 is more likely.

Jesus died on a cross to save us from our sins. His death for us inspires and empowers us to obey Him.

The Transfiguration of Our Lord

Year A

Exodus 24:12-18

The ratification of the old covenant that made Israel the people of God is described in Ex. 24. "The tablets of stone with the law and the commandment" which God gave Moses represent the old covenant. The intention of that covenant was fulfilled in the new covenant that Jesus established by His death on a cross. Through it, we are the people of God.

·   The close relationship between the two covenants is signaled by some of the things that happened at Mt. Sinai and Mt. Calvary. One set of things is the role of blood in the covenant making. Another is the meal associated with both.

Heb. 9:11-22 brings the blood of the animals sacrificed at Sinai into a close relationship with the blood of Christ.

The meal briefly indicated in Ex. 24:11 corresponds to the Last Supper, the Eucharistic Meal (the Holy Communion), of the New Covenant. At the meal of the church, as the blood of Jesus is drunk by the worshippers in, with, and under the wine, the words Moses spoke as he splashed the blood of the animals on the people at Sinai is recalled: "See the blood of the covenant that the Lord has made with you," cf. Ex. 24:8. At the memorial meal of the new covenant, we remember Jesus' words by which He made it clear that the blood of the new covenant is not the blood of animals but His own blood shed on the cross. As people drink from the chalice, the words are spoken, "This is the blood of Jesus, the blood of the new covenant, shed for you for the forgiveness of sins."

In the scheme of fulfillment, the element of enhancement is often present. Two clear examples of enhancement are the sacrifice of the animals at Mt. Sinai which was fulfilled in Jesus' sacrifice of Himself and the blood of the oxen which was fulfilled in the blood of Jesus.

The Old Testament Lesson for the Transfiguration of Our Lord includes only a part of the ratification of the old covenant, but its context involves all of ch. 24.

Moses went up Mt. Sinai to receive the two tablets of stone on which were written the law of God and further instruction by which Moses was to guide the people. He broke those tablets in the incident involving the golden calf in Ex. 32:1-20. Two new tablets were written in Ex. 34.

Israel's covenant with God committed that people to a style of life and to behavior stipulated by God. This life-style and behavior marked that people and identified them with God. Although their performance was always inadequate, their life and behavior was understood as ordered by the God who created them and covenanted with them. What they expressed publicly by their behavior was not accidental or incidental. God chose them and called them to such a life. Whatever affront this produced in the nations among whom they lived is related to what is called the scandal of the cross.

A very conscious gradation on Mt. Sinai separated the elders from the people and Moses from the elders. Moses alone entered the cloud formed by "the glory of the Lord." The cloud marked the special presence of God. It is mentioned also in Ex. 19:16.

The appointment of the 70 elders who are mentioned in vs. 1, 9, and 14 takes place in Ex. 18:13-27 and Num. 11:16-30.

Moses' instructions to those who filled in for him while he was on the mountain in v. 14 suggest that much of his regular work involved dispute resolution.

2 Peter 1:16-21

Some scholars have argued that the event described in vs. 16-18 is not the transfiguration story of the synoptic gospels in Mark 9:2-9; Matt. 17:1-9; and Luke 9:28-36. Some have said that it is an appearance of the risen Christ to Peter. Although certain features of the synoptic accounts of the transfiguration are missing, those omissions do not necessarily mean that they were not a part of the writer's understanding. They may simply mean that those features were not needed to say what he wanted to say. We have in 2 Peter only a fragmentary reference to an event whose larger context is not given. The voice from heaven, the mountain, and the visible majesty of Jesus are enough to identify the event as the transfiguration story of the synoptics.

The verses cannot describe an appearance of the risen Christ to Peter, because it is clear from the use of the first person plural pronouns that Peter is not alone. The change from the first person singular in vs. 12-15 is deliberate. The pronouns are not epistolary plurals. It is easier to identify what is said in vs. 16-18 as the transfiguration than to postulate an event otherwise unknown.

Too much importance should not be given to the fact that the voice comes from a cloud in the synoptic accounts, cf. Matt. 17:5; Mark 9:7; and Luke 9:35, while in 2 Peter it comes "from heaven." The point is that it comes from God. Peter may have preferred an expression that is self-explanatory to one that would require an explanation.

The opponents charge that what the apostles are teaching are "cleverly devised myths." Peter uses the experience of the transfiguration to support the apostolic proclamation of "the power and coming of our Lord Jesus Christ." The phrase probably refers to both Jesus' earthly ministry and His coming again. In 2 Pet. 1:3, the writer speaks of Christ's "divine power" at work in His incarnate life, passion, and resurrection. The word parousia ("coming") is the usual New Testament term for Christ's coming again in glory, cf. Matt. 24:3, 27, 37, 39; 1 Cor. 15:23; 1 Thess. 3:13; 4:15; Jas. 5:7-8; 1 John 2:28; 2 Pet. 3:4 and 12.

Some scholars think that in the phrase, "we did not follow cleverly devised myths," the author is, by implication, charging his opponents with teaching myths. But the wording favors the idea that this is a charge brought against the apostles. It is a more straightforward reading of the text.

"Cleverly devised myths" seems to be parallel to the term "human will" used in v. 21. The opponents are rejecting the teaching of the apostles as the fabrication of human cleverness. The Epicureans held that the Greek stories of punishment in the afterlife were invented as instruments of moral control to keep people in fear, and the false teachers being countered in 2 Peter may be saying something similar about the apostolic teaching.

The connotations of the term muthos in the first century A.D. were almost as varied as those of the modern English word "myth." The old Greek myths, the stories about the gods, could be seen as stories which were not literally true but expressed religious, moral, or philosophical truths in metaphorical form. The Hellenistic age showed a preference for muthos over rational argument as a way to express the truth. On the other hand, there was a strong tradition of criticism and repudiation of myths as morally unedifying or as childish, nonsensical, and fabulous.

In v. 16, muthos means a story that is not true, a fable or fairy tale in a derogatory sense. Myth is opposed to history and to a true account and is associated with being an invention. Philo repudiated the notion that the Biblical stories are mythical. This seems to have been a charge made against Christians in the early years of the church. Such a charge is referred to in 2 Clem. 13:3: "the Gentiles, when they hear from our mouth the oracles of God, marvel at them for their beauty and greatness; then, when they discover that our works are not worthy of the words which we speak, they turn to blasphemy, saying that it is a myth and a delusion."

"We made known to you" refers to the apostles' preaching of the gospel. Peter does not say that he himself taught his readers, nor does the phrase necessarily imply that any of the twelve had done so personally. All that it says is that the teaching which the readers received had come to them from apostles.

The first person plural is probably best taken as a reference to the apostles in general. Some of them founded the churches the author is addressing. Peter is a prominent representative of the group of twelve. This interpretation is really a little awkward, because in the last part of v. 16 "we" means the three apostles who witnessed the transfiguration. None of them may have founded the churches addressed. But such a variation happens quite naturally.

The apostles were eyewitnesses of Jesus' "majesty." It is clear in v. 17 that this is an explicit reference to the transfiguration.

The author conceives of the event not as a disclosure of Jesus' hidden divine being but as a bestowal of glory and honor on Him by the Father. Caiaphas and the Jewish council heaped shame, mockery, and a death verdict for blasphemy on Jesus, but "he received honor and glory from God the Father."

The apostles were "eyewitnesses" of Jesus' ministry, passion, and resurrection. All the apostles witnessed Jesus' ministry from His baptism to His ascension, according to Acts 1:21-22, but not all of them witnessed His transfiguration. Only Peter, James, and John did, according to the synoptic record.

Danker[162] says that <u>epoptai</u> ("eyewitnesses") is a technical term of the mystery religions that designates those who have been initiated into the highest grade of the mysteries. They saw the vision of the divine mysteries.

The apostle John emphasizes that his testimony is based on his personal experience. In his gospel, he writes, "we have seen his glory," cf. 1:14. In his first letter, he writes, "what we have heard, what we have seen with our eyes, what we have looked at and touched with our hands . . . we have seen it and testify to it . . . we declare to you what we have seen and heard . . . ," cf. 1 John 1:1-3. Peter and John both responded to the sanhedrin when they were told not to preach anymore in the name of Jesus that they could not keep from speaking about what they had seen and heard, cf. Acts 4:20.

The transfiguration is an example of how the common apostolic message was in part based on the personal experience of only some of the apostles. The writer presupposes that all the apostles preached the same message.

The writer is not defending apostolic authority so much as he is defending what the apostles taught. His point is that it is soundly based on what they saw and heard.

"Honor and glory" were "conveyed" to Jesus by the voice. The voice is the climax of Peter's narrative of the transfiguration. Some commentators think that the words "honor and glory" refer to the change in Jesus' appearance. His radiance was a participation in the splendor which, according to Old Testament conceptions, belongs to the very being of God. But the text says that "honor and glory . . . was conveyed to him by" the voice which said, "This is my Son, etc."

The writer sees the transfiguration not just as the revelation of Jesus' kingship but also as a restatement of His commissioning. The same words were spoken at His baptism, cf. Mark 1:11.

Although the voice begins "This is" rather than "You are," the writer says that the words were directed to Jesus. They were "conveyed to him."

That the voice belongs to God the Father is clear from the words, "This is my Son." God the Father is called "the Majestic Glory." It was common for the Jews to use such expressions when referring to God.

The words "This is my Son, my Beloved" were first spoken to Pharaoh regarding Israel in Ex. 4:22. The only difference is that in Exodus the word "firstborn" is used instead of "Beloved." Actually, the LXX of Gen. 22 helps to resolve this difference. In vs. 2, 12, and 16, the LXX uses the word <u>agapetos</u> (translated "beloved" in 2 Pet. 1:17) to translate the Hebrew word <u>jechidh</u> which means "only one" and refers to Isaac.[163]

The phrase, "This is my Son, my Beloved," occurs seven times in the New Testament in slightly altered form, three times in the narratives of Jesus' baptism and four times in the records of the transfiguration. God gives to Jesus the precious names "my Son, my Beloved" which He first used for ancient Israel.

The double use of the relative pronoun "my" suggests that the author is thinking of two titles. "My Son" should be understood not as expressing the deity of Jesus but as asserting that He is Israel. He is fulfilling the terms of the old covenant that call for Israel to be obedient. St. Paul says that Jesus was obedient to the point of dying in Phil. 2:8. His obedience is credited to us. He is our representative. Through Him we are saved. We are the new Israel, the new people of God, cf. Gal. 6:16.

The phrase, "with whom I am well pleased," is from the Suffering Servant Song in Is. 42:1 and is not found in the transfiguration accounts of Mark and Luke. It emphasizes that the Father appointed Jesus. It points to the mission for which the Son was chosen and to His appointment to the kingly office of Messiah. The aorist form of the verb indicates that the election took place in eternity.[164]

Defending the apostolic proclamation against the charge that it is based on myths, Peter points to the testimony of the prophets as well as to the experience of the apostles. He gives the witness of the apostles greater status than the prophetic word. He says that the apostolic witness confirms the prophetic message or word.

The pronoun "we" in v. 19 is commonly considered to include all Christians.

"The prophetic message" refers to the Old Testament and perhaps to other sacred scriptures. The Old Testament canon may not have been firmly established at the time 2 Peter was written. It can but need not refer to specific passages. The entire Old Testament is probably understood as Messianic prophecy.

The Greek word bebaios means reliable and valid and was a legal, commercial term, like the word "guaranteed" today. The comparative form has superlative meaning in this passage, and no comparison is intended. The prophetic word is more reliable as the result of the transfiguration and is confirmed by that event.

Peter appeals to his readers to pay attention to the prophetic word. He calls it "a lamp shining in a dark place." The comparison of the Word of God to a lamp is common, cf. Ps. 119:105. The lamp of prophecy lights up the darkness of this present world's hopeless ignorance with a bright beam of hope.

The word auchmeros ("dark") does not seem to portray

absolute darkness but dingy and dusky obscurity. The word may also communicate the idea of dirty since that which is dirty lacks brightness, and the thought may be that light shows up the dirt and makes possible its removal. Another translation is "a murky place."

The "dark place" is the world as it at present exists. In the New Testament, the world is regularly characterized as in darkness. It is dark because it is ignorant of God's message through the prophets and therefore without hope. Into this darkness, the prophetic message casts a ray of light and awakens hope.

Peter appeals to his readers to pay attention to the prophetic word "until the day dawns." "The day" is a symbol for the eschatological age which will dawn at the parousia. It will be a time of light in contrast to the present darkness. Prophecy's function of illuminating the darkness of ignorance will be unnecessary when the full light of revelation floods God's people.

The word diaugazo ("dawns") is picturesque. It was used of the first streaks of dawn breaking through the darkness.

Peter's readers should pay attention to the prophetic word until "the morning star rises in (their) hearts." This cannot mean until they are converted, because Peter is addressing Christians. Some commentators think that the apostle is speaking of the day when faith is made perfect in love. But it is more probable that the day of the parousia, the day of Jesus' coming again, is meant. The prophetic word will guide us until the full revelation of Jesus Christ is given to us at His parousia.

"The morning star" is the planet Venus. It normally accompanies the first glimmerings of dawn and can therefore be thought of as introducing daylight into the world. The imagery was available, for the famous prophecy in Num. 24:17, "there shall come a star out of Jacob," was understood in Judaism as pointing to the Messiah. The coming of the Messiah is also compared to the dawn in Mal. 4:2. In Greek and Roman times, the term was applied not only to the morning star but also to royal and divine persons. Jesus is called "the bright morning star" in Rev. 22:16. The rising of the morning star is a symbol

582

for the parousia of Christ. His coming will be like the daylight that dispels the darkness of the night. The author writes in expectation that his readers will survive until the parousia, cf. 2 Pet. 3:14.

In support of his appeal to pay attention to the prophetic word, the writer asserts that the prophets "were moved by the Holy Spirit," and they "spoke from God." Because of its inclusive policy, the NRSV text reads "men and women," but the Greek text has only the word for men.

Embodied in vs. 20-21 may be two statements made by the false teachers: "the prophecies of scripture are a matter of one's own interpretation" and "prophecy came by human will." The Ebionites recognized no prophets after Moses and were accused of asserting that prophecy was of human origin. This is not to say the opponents of the author were Ebionites.

The phrase, "First of all you must understand this," marks the statement it introduces for special attention. Two main interpretations are possible for the clause, "no prophecy of scripture is a matter of one's own interpretation." One, the writer is talking about the interpretation of prophecy in the present. Most commentators and translations adopt this understanding. Two, no prophecy of scripture derives from the prophet's own interpretation. The writer is talking about the divine origin of the scripture. He is countering the idea that the prophecies of the Old Testament are only the prophets' interpretations of the visions God gave them. NIV translates following Calvin, "No prophecy of Scripture came about by the prophet's own interpretation."

The question is whether epilusis ("interpretation") refers to the interpretation of the contemporary exegete or that of the original author of the prophecy. The prophet is not mentioned, and so most modern commentators and translations prefer "one's own" to "the prophet's own."

The "scripture" refers mainly to the body of writings today called the Old Testament scriptures, because the New Testament scriptures were still being written.

Much debate has centered around the meaning of the statement that the prophets "moved by the Holy Spirit spoke from God." Pheromenoi ("moved") was used of a ship carried along by the wind. The metaphor pictures the Holy Spirit filling the sails of the prophets and carrying them along in the direction He wished. Some have interpreted "moved by the Holy Spirit" to mean that the writing of the scriptures was done in a mechanical way. Abraham Calov, Johann Quenstedt, David Hollaz, and most of the Reformed theologians of the later 17th century took the position that the Biblical writers took nothing from their memory or experience or from the memory of any other writer, but that everything was dictated by the Holy Spirit from scratch. But the discrepancies and contradictions evident in the Old Testament scriptures, including some historical statements in the books of Samuel, Kings, and Chronicles, as well as the frequency of passages like 2 Chron. 35:26-27 make that idea questionable.

Peter says that the prophets did not speak on their own initiative, cf. Amos 3:8 and Jer. 20:9. They did not proclaim a message that was the product of their own mind. They spoke the word of the Lord when it came to them, but it seems clear that this was not a mechanical process. Their unique personality and experiences are evident in their writing style. But the prophets were not the originating source of their messages. The Holy Spirit was. They spoke as God's spokesmen.

Matthew 17:1-9

Some scholars[165] classify the transfiguration as an Easter story. But this does not do justice to the placing of the event in the three synoptic gospels nor to its many details. The narrative in Matthew follows Peter's confession in 16:16. Then comes Jesus' first announcement of His passion in 16:21. When Peter rebukes Jesus for such talk, Jesus talks about the suffering of His disciples and the future glory of the Son of Man in 16:24-28. The story of the transfiguration is a part of the evangelists' development of the necessity of Jesus' passion.[166]

Jesus' response to Peter's great confession was a crushing disappointment to the disciples. They were looking forward to participation in the glory of the Messianic kingdom, but instead

Jesus announced what seemed to be defeat. Suffering was diametrically opposed to the common Jewish notion of Messiahship, and Jesus' talk of being killed was a dash of cold water on the disciples' hopes. They were left with such thoughts for six days. Then in the transfiguration, they were given an experience that revived their conviction that Jesus was the Messiah of God. Their faith in Jesus was strengthened, even if their understanding of His passion really was not helped.

Jesus was the long expected Messiah, but He was not the kind of Messiah the Jewish people expected. They looked for a king to lead them along a glory road. But in Jesus, God came as love that sacrifices, serves, suffers, and by this route arrives at glory. This can help Jesus' modern disciples who sometimes struggle with thoughts like those of the first disciples.

The transfiguration did not find its place in the church year and in the lectionaries of the church as readily as did the resurrection, the baptism, or the ascension. In fact, it is not yet securely anchored. It eventually found a place in the old Roman calendar on August 6 during the Trinity season. The post-Vatican II lectionary of the Roman Church calls for the transfiguration story as the Gospel for the Second Sunday in Lent. Eastern Orthodoxy celebrates the transfiguration on August 6. Anglican lectionaries celebrate it on the second day after the Epiphany. Lutherans place it on the last Sunday after the Epiphany, just before Lent.

Scholars have wrestled with the problem of what really happened in the transfiguration. Some aspects of the descriptions are difficult to work out. Many of them are full of theological implications. Discerning what is intended visually and what theologically is not easy. Maybe such a distinction ought not be attempted, and the descriptions ought to be allowed to speak on their own. The three disciples seem to have had an experience that went beyond the power of human language to express. They articulated what happened in a manner understood by Jews of the first century using exodus and new Moses signals.

Jesus' form (morphe) was altered. He did not appear as an ordinary, earthbound mortal but as one from the divine side of reality. The change was highlighted by the shining of His face and the luminous whiteness of His garments.

Eastern Orthodoxy has made much of the light in the story. They elevate the transfiguration to a degree of importance virtually equal to that of the other major events in Jesus' life. Among the light features are "his face shone like the sun," "his clothes became dazzling white," and "a bright cloud overshadowed them." The Orthodox wonder what the light was. They speculate that it was the <u>ousia</u> (the very being) of God, because, according to the Bible, no one had ever seen that. On the other hand, it could not have been an illusion. In the Order of Matins for the Feast of the Transfiguration, the Eastern Orthodox Church prays: "In thy light, which has appeared today on Tabor, we have seen the Father as light and the Spirit as light." They speculate that since the light did not belong to the human nature of Jesus, it must have belonged to His divine nature. It must have been an uncreated light. The light was not a symbol. Gregory of Nazianzus called it "deity."

The idea has sometimes been proposed that Moses represents the law and Elijah the prophets and that in their appearance they testify to Jesus. But this notion lacks substantial foundation.

That Jesus' "face shown like the sun" points to Him as the new Moses promised in Deut. 18:15-20. Ex. 34:29-35 says that when Moses came down from Mt. Sinai with "the two tablets of the covenant" after talking with God, the skin of his face shone.

The appearance of Moses and Elijah produces thoughts of the exodus. Early Christians believed Jesus was "the prophet" like Moses promised in Deut. 18:15, cf. Acts 3:22-26 and 7:37. He was God's agent to lead God's people out of bondage in a new exodus accomplished by His death. Elijah was the great prophet who called God's people back to the God of the exodus and to the covenant God made with them in the exodus. In rabbinic thought, Elijah was a second Moses.

The exodus motif is explicit in Luke's transfiguration account. Luke 9:31 says that Moses and Elijah discussed with Jesus His <u>exodon</u>. "Departure" is the translation of the Greek word "<u>exodos</u>." Jesus' death was a new exodus. It was the fulfillment of the exodus. Jesus accomplished God's saving purpose in the exodus and established a people of God on the earth.

A bright cloud overshadowed everyone in the transfiguration, and God spoke from the cloud. In Ex. 24 and 34, the presence of God is indicated by a cloud that covers Mt. Sinai. The cloud is associated with "the glory of the Lord" which in appearance was like "a devouring fire."

The cloud in the story of the transfiguration might be related to the one that led the children of Israel in their exodus wanderings. The Lord went before them by day in a pillar of cloud and by night in a pillar of fire, according to Ex. 13:21-22; Deut. 1:33; Ps. 78:14; 105:39. A cloud overshadowed the tent of meeting when the glory of Jahweh filled the tabernacle in Ex. 40:34-38. The same verb, episkiazein, used in Ex. 40:35 is used in Matt. 17:5.

The voice from the cloud is another aspect of the exodus and new Moses motifs, cf. Ex. 19:9; 24:16; 34:5; Num. 11:25; 12:5-6 What the voice said confirms the witness to Jesus given by the presence of Moses and Elijah. The voice combined what is said in Ps. 2:7; Is. 42:1, and Deut. 18:15, 19.

The words "my Son" are usually associated with Ps. 2:7 which is a royal psalm, a Messianic psalm. The words "with him I am well pleased" are usually associated with Is. 42:1 which is a part of a Suffering Servant song. They emphasize the Messianic role of Jesus.

The words "listen to him" are an echo of Deut. 18:15 and 19. The authority given to Moses is given to Jesus. Some take the words "listen to him" to mean that the disciples are to listen to all that Jesus commands. They are to realize that the way of the cross is the way of sonship and discipleship.

The location of the transfiguration is identified as "a high mountain." Some see the verb anaphero as meaning more than that Jesus "led . . . up a high mountain" Peter, James, and John. It may indicate that in some way Jesus carried them up. This would help in identifying the place of the transfiguration with Mt. Hermon.

That the mountain is called "a high mountain" implies that they went to the top. If we assume that they went to the very top of Mt. Hermon, we may have to assume also a miraculous transit. Mt. Hermon has three peaks, 9,400 feet high, 11,000 feet, and 10,900 feet. Climbing Mt. Hermon is an alpine ascent. It would take a whole day, six hours in the ascent and four in the descent. It would require provisions of food and water. The sharp air would make it impossible to spend the night at the top. But nothing of this appears in the text. Luke's account says that Jesus and the three disciples went up one day and came down the next, cf. Luke 9:37.

Tradition does not support Mt. Hermon as the site of the transfiguration, although it probably was if we assume that Jesus was still in the area of Caesarea-Philippi where Peter made his great confession. Mt. Hermon is relatively near there.

Another old tradition says that Jesus had left Caesarea-Philippi, and the scene of the transfiguration was Mt. Tabor. That is the site of the transfiguration shown today when tourists visit the Holy Land. In Eastern Orthodoxy's prayer in the Order of Matins for the Feast of the Transfiguration on August 6, Mt. Tabor is named as the place. But Tabor is not a high mountain in comparison to Mt. Hermon. Also Tabor does not offer the solitude Matthew indicates in v. 1 with the words "by themselves." Some have said that Mt. Tabor was crowned with a fortified city at the time which would render the site unsuitable for the scene of the transfiguration.

There are three other mountains over 4,000 feet high southeast of Caesarea Philippi, but they are not dignified with names. Whichever mountain it was, that fact was not important for the evangelists. None of them identified it. They had no interest in geography for its own sake.

If Jesus was revealed in the transfiguration as the new Moses, the mount of transfiguration was the new Sinai. It may be futile to try to identify it geographically.

How did the disciples know that the two men were Moses and Elijah? They had never seen them before. Francis Pieper explains by saying that "the blessed will also know one another, even though they did not meet in this life (Matt. 17:3-4)."[167] This may be an overstatement on the basis of this passage alone. We shall see!

Peter, James, and John constituted the inner circle of Jesus' disciples. Jesus occasionally gave them experiences the other disciples did not receive. They went with Him to the home of Jairus when Jesus raised his daughter in Mark 5:37 and Luke 8:51. Jesus told them and Andrew about the destruction of Jerusalem and the last days in Mark 13:3-5. He took them along when He entered His deep sorrow in Gethsemane in Matt. 26:37 and Mark 14:33. On the mount of transfiguration, they were given a glimpse of the fullness of His glory. In Gethsemane, they were given a glimpse of the fullness of His humanity.

Skenas ("dwellings" or "tents") can designate any shelter, all the way from the poor tent of a nomad or a soldier through the tabernacle or temple to the heavenly dwelling place of God.

The Jews had come to look forward to the tabernacling presence of the Messiah with His people, cf. Ezek. 37:27; 43:7 and 9; and Zech. 2:10-11. John picked this up in John 1:14. This may help to explain Peter's suggestion.

Most recent commentators think that the reference to pitching tents was occasioned by the proximity of the Feast of Tabernacles. Tabernacles served as a reminder of the days when Jahweh "made the people of Israel live in booths when I brought them out of the land of Egypt," cf. Lev. 23:33-43. Together with Passover and Pentecost, it was one of the three great pilgrimage festivals obligatory for adult Jews. It was the most popular of all Jewish feasts. At the time of this feast, people longed more fervently than usual for the Messiah to come and restore to God's people their independence.

Both Mark 9:6 and Luke 9:33 say that Peter did not know what he was saying. He did not understand what was happening. He did not realize that the Christ still had to suffer. It was not a time for the spirit of Tabernacles.

When the disciples heard the voice, "they fell to the ground and were overcome by fear." This is the classic human reaction to the numinous, cf. Lev. 9:24; Num. 22:31; Josh. 5:14; Judges 13:20; 1 Kings 18:39; Ezek. 1:28; 43:3, 44:4; Dan. 8:17; Rev. 1:17. Fear was the reaction of the disciples to the miraculous draft of fish in Luke 5:9-10, the storm on the lake in Matt. 14:26-27, the events of Easter in Matt. 28:5 and 10; Mark 16:6, and the appearance of the glorified Son of Man to the Seer of Patmos in Rev. 1:17. The incomprehensible nature of that which they were experiencing produced fear.

Jesus touched the disciples and dismissed their fear. He healed them with His touch. Danker[168] lists this passage under hapto with the comment, "Gener. of touching persons who are ill." This was an act of healing. The disciples rose to resume the downward way with Jesus; but they had seen who Jesus really was, and He had showed them that they did not need to be afraid.

The Transfiguration of Our Lord

Year B

2 Kings 2:1-12

When God canned Elijah for being afraid of Jezebel, He chose Elisha to succeed him, cf. 1 Kings 19. This Lesson tells of the transition of religious leadership in Israel from Elijah to Elisha. Elisha was working as a farmer when Elijah called him. He was "plowing."

Some time seems to have elapsed between when Elisha was called and when God took Elijah to heaven. During this time, Elijah may have given Elisha the training he needed for his assignment. Earlier, Elisha may have attended one of the schools of the prophets under Elijah's supervision.

Before God took him up, Elijah visited two seminaries of the prophets. Elisha felt very close to Elijah and insisted on going with him. Elisha sensed that Elijah was about to be taken from him, although we are not told how he became aware of this. Later, the event is confirmed by the "sons of the prophets," cf. NRSV footnote. Elisha wanted to avoid being separated from Elijah, if possible.

The majority of the Elisha stories show him in the company of these prophets. The men were a separate group within the framework of Israelite society. They lived at several different places in the South. Their settlements may have been closely associated with some of the local sanctuaries. The existence of such an association of prophets at Ramah is presupposed in 1 Sam. 19:18-24. According to 1 Kings 20:35-42, the members of such associations were recognizable by their tattoo marks, cf. Zech. 13:6. They seem to have lived in communities, cf. 2 Kings 4:38-44 and 6:1. Elisha is clearly their master and is honored by being called master or father in 2 Kings 6:5, 21. Elisha honored Elijah in the same way, cf. 2:12. The members of the group seem to have been drawn from a very low economic and social stratum, and they were most likely without any status at all. Their standards of eating and housing were extremely miserable. A case of debt is described in 2 Kings 4:1-7. The sanctuaries may have served as places of asylum. Insolvency may have been the reason they turned their backs on middle-class and peasant life. Or their association may have been due more to religious than to economic factors. They may have been the last representatives of pure, uncontaminated Jahwism. They may have maintained the radical Jahwism that is found in the later prophets. They may have laid the foundations for the social and economic detachment and disregard for the considerations of state policies that gave rise to the later prophetic movement. They established the pattern for what it meant to be a prophet and what it meant to speak to Israel in the name of Jahweh. The Essenes who are associated with the Dead Sea Scrolls may have been such a community, although these associations should not be called the forerunners of the Essenes. But they show that such groups of religious radicals occasionally existed in Israel.[169]

The first "company of prophets" Elijah visited was at Bethel. Elijah told Elisha to stay behind, but Elisha insisted on going along. When they arrived, the prophets came out to meet them. They warned Elisha that the Lord was going to take his master, Elijah, from him. Elisha told them that he knew this, and he told them to shut up. He may have ordered them to silence, because he could not believe that he was going to lose Elijah. Or perhaps he was afraid of what it would mean for him to become Israel's head prophet.

When Elijah was going to visit the school of the prophets at Jericho, he again told Elisha to stay behind; but again he would not. When they got to Jericho, the prophets again told Elisha that the Lord was going to take his master from him. Again he told them that he knew, and again he ordered them to shut up.

When Elijah went to the Jordan River, he instructed Elisha for the third time to stay behind; and for the third time Elisha refused. Elijah knew that God was about to take him. So he asked Elisha what more he could do for him before that happened. Elisha asked for "a double share of your spirit."

The meaning of this request is not clear. It seems that Elisha wished that two portions of the spirit that rested on Elijah would be transferred to himself. This was the first-born son's portion of his father's inheritance, according to Deut. 21:17. Elisha was not asking to be greater than Elijah, but that he might be his worthy successor. Elisha wanted to take up Elijah's role like an elder son following in the footsteps of his father. Jewish tradition regarded Elisha as having worked twice as many miracles as Elijah - sixteen to eight - because he received a double portion of the Spirit.

Elijah responded to the request of his successor by telling him that he was asking for a hard thing. The prophetic spirit is not inherited but is the gift of God. "Yet," he said, "if you see me as I am being taken from you, it will be granted you; if not, it will not."

As they walked and talked, "a chariot of fire and horses of fire separated the two of them, and Elijah ascended in a whirlwind into heaven." This seems to have happened abruptly and with no forewarning.

The text does not say – as some Sunday School lessons used to have it - that "a chariot of fire and horses of fire" took Elijah into heaven. "Elijah (went) up to heaven by a whirlwind."

The whirlwind blew away Elisha's safety and robbed him of the one who gave him identity. He became totally dependent on God. He was the Lord's instrument and had to deliver the divine word to kings and throughout Israel.

As Elijah ascended, Elisha cried out to him, "The chariots of Israel and its horsemen!" The exclamation is repeated in 2 Kings 13:14, but its meaning and significance is uncertain.

When Elisha could no longer see Elijah, he tore his own clothes in two pieces. This may have been the way he expressed his grief.

Malachi said that Elijah would come again before the Messianic age began, cf. Mal. 4:5. The people in New Testament times thought a great deal about this. The angel of the Lord indicated to Zechariah in Luke 1:17 that his son, John, would carry out his assignment "with the spirit and power of Elijah." John was questioned as to whether he was Elijah in John 1:21. Some thought Jesus was the fulfillment of Malachi's promise, according to Matt. 16:14. Jesus identified John the Baptist as the fulfillment in Matt. 17:10-13.

The day of the Lord has come. Jesus saved mankind from the terrible wrath of God through His passion. We who have turned to God through Jesus have been saved from the curse that we deserve.

There is a strong feeling for the return of Elijah among orthodox Jews to this day. At each Seder meal, a chair is left empty for him. Reform Jews place new stress on the "cup of Elijah" in a revised Seder rite. It is the fifth cup in the seder meal. It is placed on the table for the prophet Elijah who, it is believed, will usher in the Messianic age. The Jews still anticipate Elijah's coming and keep the hope of his coming alive in this way.

2 Corinthians 4:3-6

Paul is passionately defending his gospel. It is Christ crucified, cf. 1 Cor. 1:17 and 2:2. He calls it "the gospel of the glory of Christ."

Christ, he says, "is the image of God." The word "image" (eikon) does not point to a faint copy of an original. Rather, it indicates that by which and in which the original is truly represented. Christ Jesus shares in God's real being and is a perfect manifestation of Him. To know Christ is to know God. Christ Jesus to Paul is always Him who was crucified. God is truly represented in Christ crucified.

Paul's gospel is the story of Jesus' passion, His crucifixion and resurrection. The message of the cross is that Jesus effected the salvation of mankind by His death. Paul calls Jesus' death on a cross "the glory of God." "The glory of God" is known "in the face of Jesus Christ." The gospel of Jesus' crucifixion and resurrection is the fundamental re-presentative agency for proclaiming the glory of God.

Those who do not see the splendor of Christ in Paul's gospel do not see the glory of God. Those who do not see the glory of Christ in Christ crucified do not see the splendor of God. Those who do not see the splendor of Christ in His passion do not see the splendor of God.[170]

Paul's detractors do not agree with him. Defending his apostolic ministry is a customary posture for Paul. He was the object of much criticism. Some said Paul's claim to be an apostle was false, because he had not known Jesus during His earthly ministry. They said he had not been intimate with those who had known Jesus intimately, men like Peter, James, and John. The Judaizers insisted that their knowledge of Christianity was more authentic than Paul's. They said that by declaring the law obsolete, Paul was opening the door to license. Peter said that some things Paul taught in his letters are "hard to understand," cf. 2 Pet. 3:16. He said "the ignorant and unstable twist (what Paul wrote) to their own destruction."

Paul is responding to the accusation that he is too confident and too bold in the exercise of his apostolic ministry. Some Corinthian Christians seem to feel that he has been presumptuous and brazen in his dealings with them. He confesses that he does act "with great boldness" in 2 Cor. 3:12. He attributes this to the splendor of the ministry in which he serves. He rejects the idea that he is promoting himself.

Paul uses the story of the renewal of the old covenant in Ex. 34, cf. 2 Cor. 3:7-4:6. He says in 2 Cor. 3:13 that Moses "put a veil over his face to keep the people of Israel from gazing at the end of the glory that was being set aside." Ex. 34 describes what happened in vs. 30-35: "When Aaron and all the Israelites saw Moses, the skin of his face was shining, and they were afraid to come near him. . . . When Moses had finished speaking with (the Israelites), he put a veil on his face, but whenever

Moses went in before the Lord to speak with him, he would take the veil off, until he came out, and when he came out, and told the Israelites what he had been commanded, the Israelites would see the face of Moses, that the skin of his face was shining; and Moses would put the veil on his face again, until he went in to speak with (the Lord)."

Paul relates the veil to the hardening of Israel's mind "to this day" in 2 Cor. 3:14.

He describes his style of preaching as an "open statement of the truth," but all of his hearers do not recognize the good news. His gospel "is veiled" to some. He says in 2 Cor. 3:14-16 that "the same veil" hides the meaning of "the old covenant" or "Moses," from the Jews, and "a veil" also hides his gospel from some people. He concedes the truth of the criticism that his hearers do not always understand what he is saying to them in the conditional clause "if our gospel is veiled." The Greek construction allows for the reality of the condition.

Paul calls the message he proclaims "our gospel." He uses this kind of language again in 1 Thess. 1:5 and 2 Thess. 2:14. The term is not different from "my gospel" in Rom. 2:16 and 16:25 or "the gospel that was proclaimed by me" in Gal. 1:11. See also Gal. 1:8 and 1 Cor. 15:1.

Paul often says that his gospel is "the gospel of Christ," that is, the gospel about Christ, cf. Rom. 15:19; 1 Cor. 9:12; 2 Cor. 2:12; 9:13; 10:14; Gal. 1:7; Phil. 1:27; 1 Thess. 3:2; Rom. 1:9; 2 Thess. 1:8. It is the good news of Christ crucified.

He refuses to change his gospel in response to his critics. He rejects their criticism in v. 3. "Even if," he says. Ei kai is a construction that carries a tone of contempt; Paul belittles his critics.

He goes on the attack against those who do not understand his gospel in v. 4 by asserting that they are "blinded" by "the god of this world." The reason they do not understand him is not the fault of his gospel or of him who preaches it. The blame is placed on the hearers. He says in v. 7 that his weaknesses promote his gospel.

The expression "the god of this world" occurs nowhere else in the Bible, although the idea is expressed in a number of places, cf. John 12:31; 14:30; 16:11; 1 John 5:19; Eph. 2:2; 6:12; 1 Cor. 2:6, 8. The term has been interpreted to imply a dualistic understanding of the universe, that the universe is ruled by a good and a bad principle. This is one of the passages to which dualists refer to support their contention. According to such thinking, the god of evil is a real god.

When the issue has been joined in the history of the church, the orthodox have insisted that good and evil are not to be explained on the basis of a dual principle. Although Christ called the devil "the ruler of this world" in John 12:31; 14:30; and 16:11, the devil is a creature of the one true God and Creator. Paul says, "'there is no God but one.' Indeed, even though there may be so-called gods in heaven or on earth - as in fact there are many gods and many lords - yet for us there is one God, the Father, from whom are all things and for whom we exist . . . ," cf. 1 Cor. 8:4-6.

God has not abdicated or surrendered any portion of His dominion to the devil. But some people have given the devil power over themselves. The devil has "blinded the minds" of such people. Ultimately, we must say that God has "blinded (their) minds," stopped their ears, shut their eyes, or hardened their hearts, as Is. 6:9-10 says.

In the term "the god of this world," the Greek word for "world" is <u>aion</u>. <u>Aion</u> refers to all current thoughts, opinions, maxims, speculations, hopes, impulses, aims, and aspirations. Paul implies that the devil reigns wherever there is opposition to the will of God. This is an enormous sphere.

Paul draws a strong contrast between those inside the church and those outside. He attaches a negative twist to those outside. He calls them "unbelievers" and says that they are under the influence of "the god of this world." The term "unbelievers" seems to be coterminous with "those who are perishing." "The god of this world has blinded" them to keep them from seeing "the glory of Christ." They identify themselves as people who are blinded by the devil as "the unbelievers," when they do not perceive that the splendor of the gospel is disclosed in the sufferings of Christ and of its ministers.

Paul's point is not that the present age is evil or even that

Satan's rule is exercised over it. His point is that "the god of this age" is the one who is responsible for the blindness of the unbelievers. The cause of their unbelief is not his gospel. The gospel brings enlightenment, because it is the splendor of Christ who is the image of God.

The boldness of Paul's style brought upon him the charge that he was promoting himself. One reason for that charge may have been the way he offered himself as a pattern to be imitated, cf. 1 Cor. 4:16. But Paul says, "we do not proclaim ourselves."

Paul insists that the focus of his preaching is Jesus Christ. He proclaims "Jesus Christ as Lord." To preach Jesus Christ as Lord is to preach Him as crucified, risen, and glorified. The background of the statement is the early confession of the church, "Jesus is Lord," cf. Rom. 10:9; 1 Cor. 12:3; Phil. 2:10-11. The unbelievers who reject Paul's preaching reject not Paul but the Lord Jesus.

Paul's bold style is not a display of arrogance, because he is the slave of his hearers "for Jesus' sake." The idea of slaves is suggested by the previous word "Lord."

The surprising word is the personal pronoun "your." In many other places, Paul calls himself "slave," but he is the slave of Jesus Christ, cf. Rom. 1:1 and Phil. 1:1. This is the only place where Paul speaks of himself as being the slave of his converts.

The ideas are not contradictory. Because Christian ministers are the slaves of Christ, they are the slaves of those to whom Christ has sent them. They are the slaves of the people they serve only so far as service to them does not interfere with their service to Him. By affirming himself as their slaves, Paul diminishes himself.

The use of the name Jesus without Christ is rare in the Pauline epistles. It commonly denotes our Lord in the time of His humiliation, cf. 2 Cor. 4:10, 14; 1 Thess. 1:10; 4:14. Usually, Paul calls Him Christ or the name Christ is combined with Jesus. The name Jesus alone occurs 17 times in Paul's letters. Eight of these occurrences are in 2 Corinthians, seven in 2 Cor. 4, cf. vs. 10 (2 times), 11 (two times), 14 (two times), and 2 Cor. 4:5. The other occurrence in 2 Corinthians is in 11:4.

In v. 6, Paul explains why he must preach Christ and not himself. He refers back to his Damascus experience. He says, "God . . . has shown in our hearts." He identifies the God who had made Himself known on the road to Damascus as "the God who said, 'Let light shine out of darkness.'" Paul is loosely quoting Gen. 1:3: "Then God said, 'Let there be light.'" The Creator of the old creation is also the Creator of the new creation. The Creator gave Paul "the light of the knowledge of the glory of God in the face of Jesus Christ" on the road to Damascus.

Judaism called the torah of Moses the light created on the first day of creation. Paul gave to Christ the place occupied in Judaism by torah. As Moses' face once radiated the splendor of the old covenant, the splendor of the new covenant is now to be seen in Jesus Christ, His crucifixion and His resurrection.

Mark 9:2-9

How kind of Jesus not to rebuke Peter. He could have said, "Don't just say something! Stand there! Be amazed! Be speechless!" Peter "did not know what to say," but he spoke anyway. And we, too, don't know what to say about many things in this narrative.

Scholars have spent a lot of time arguing its historical character. Is it historical? To what extent? How did the disciples recognize Moses and Elijah? Was this a vision? Matt. 17:9 uses the word <u>horama</u> which may denote a supernatural vision, whether the person is awake or asleep. It can also denote, however, what is seen in an ordinary way, cf. Deut. 28:34 and 67; Eccl. 6:9. Or did Jesus Himself have a mystical experience or vision that He later related to His disciples? Some have compared this vision to that of Joan of Arc, Joseph Smith, Muhammad, and others. Could it have been a resurrection narrative projected back into Jesus' ministry? Or did the church create this story, drawing on Ex. 24 and 34, the baptism story, and later Christological beliefs? Is this a legendary story applied to Jesus to enhance His person? Was there an historical core to which the early church added certain features in order to enhance the person of Jesus?

Some insist that it is impossible to determine exactly what happened. Bultmann promoted the idea that this is a resurrection story that has been read back into the earthly life of Jesus. Against this theory, it has been pointed out that all the resurrection appearances reported in the gospels begin with Jesus being absent, whereas here He is present from the beginning. In the resurrection narratives, something said by Jesus has an important place, whereas here He is silent throughout. Moses and Elijah would be a surprising feature in a resurrection appearance story. In the Easter stories of the gospels, the only featured figures from beyond are angels; they are never seen at the same time as Jesus. Peter's curious suggestion in v. 5 is difficult to explain, and it is even more difficult if the setting is the resurrection.

The transfiguration was a supernatural event. The visionary aspects were created by God and were a real revelation to the disciples.

The event was directed toward the three disciples, not toward Jesus. This is brought out in the words "before them" in v. 2, "there appeared to them" in v. 4, and the command directed to the disciples in v. 7 "listen to him." The disciples saw "that the kingdom of God has come with power," cf. Mark 9:1, in Jesus. It was a revelation of the heavenly glory that always belonged to Jesus. It enabled the disciples after the resurrection to realize that even during the time that He emptied Himself He retained His deity.

Peter's confession in 8:29 notwithstanding, the disciples did not understand Jesus. They did not understand what Messiahship meant. They were unable to accept the announcement of Jesus' death in Mark 8:31-32. Their difficulty is understandable and natural. Mark uses their difficulty to provide clarification of Jesus' Messianic role.

The focal point of the pericope is the saying of the Voice from the cloud. This is the second time this saying is recorded by Mark. The first declaration by the Father of Jesus' sonship occurred at Jesus' baptism as He began His public ministry, cf. 1:11. This second pronouncement immediately followed the first prediction of Jesus' passion and the call to the disciples to take up their own crosses in 8:34. The third and final declaration of sonship came from the centurion who confessed Jesus as the Son of God when he saw how Jesus died in 15:39. Presenting Jesus as the Son of God was one of the ways in which Mark witnessed to Jesus as the Christ, the Messiah, cf. 1:1.

Jesus is the Son of God not in spite of His suffering and ignominious death but precisely in and through that service. The Christian readers of this gospel are reminded that their experience of suffering by no means proves that they are not God's children. Sonship, service, and suffering are intimately connected. As the Christian readers move towards martyrdom, they can have the full confidence of God's fatherly care.

The radiance of Jesus' garments highlighted His transfiguration from an earthly form into a supraterrestrial form. Before the eyes of the disciples, His human appearance was changed into that of a heavenly being. The verb stilbo ("dazzling") is used of the appearance of polished or bright surfaces. In the LXX, it is used of the appearance of burnished brass and gold.

The Greek literally says that Jesus' "clothes became dazzling white, such as no fuller on earth could bleach them." A fuller was a person who cleaned woolen cloth using nitrium.

The Voice that came from the cloud "overshadowed them." In the Bible, a cloud often is closely associated with the visible presence of God, cf. Ex. 13:21-22; 14:19-20; 16:10; 19:16; 24:16; 33:9; 34:5; 40:34-38; Lev. 16:2; Num. 9:15-23; Deut. 5:22; Ps. 78:14; 99:7; 105:39; 1 Kings 8:10-11; 2 Chron. 5:13-14; Is. 4:5; Ezek. 10:3-4; Dan. 7:13; Mark 13:26; 14:62; Acts 1:9; 1 Thess. 4:17. It is both a self-revelation and a veiling of God. Sometimes it has the appearance of fire; maybe all the time.

The word "overshadowed" is a bridge between the story of the transfiguration and the story of the establishment of God's covenant with Israel in Ex. 24, cf. v. 16. The same word is used in the LXX, episkiazein.

The word "them" in v. 7 could refer to the three disciples or to Jesus, Moses, and Elijah and not the disciples. It seems most likely that it refers to Jesus, Moses, and Elijah and not to the three disciples. On the other hand, Luke 9:34 says that the disciples were enveloped by the cloud. Yet, that the disciples were addressed from the cloud suggests that they were outside of it.

God's intervention is the ultimate legitimation of Jesus. The auditory experience is added to the sight of Jesus' physical transformation. Peter emphasizes the Voice in 2 Pet. 1:16-19.

The affirmation of the Voice is basically the same as that made at the baptism of Jesus in Mark 1:11. The difference is that the Voice addresses Jesus at His baptism. Here the disciples are addressed. The words "hear him" are added.

The testimony from heaven interprets the event. The disciples are given overwhelming testimony that Jesus is the Son of God. Peter testifies to this in 2 Pet. 1:17-19. What Peter confesses in Mark 8:29 is affirmed by the Father. Son of God is a Messianic title.

The experience was intended to support the disciples when they saw Jesus nailed to a cross and for their own cross bearing. It failed, because they did not understand about cross bearing and the mission of the Messiah until after Jesus was risen from the dead.

The title Son of God applied to Jesus expresses the uniqueness of His relationship to His Father. It affirms His complete oneness with the Father in the performance of His mission. It presents Him as radically distinguished from all other people. This distinction highlights not primarily miraculous power but the absolute obedience of a son in the execution of His divine commission. Oscar Cullmann says, "This is the Synoptic emphasis." He says, "the Son of God passages in the Synoptic Gospels . . . give a completely un-Greek picture of the Son of God."[171] The one exception is Matthew's version of Jesus walking on the water in Matt. 14:33. Jesus is the Son of God not as a miracle worker but in the obedient fulfillment of His task, His suffering and death. The title Son of God has a more Hellenistic slant in the Gospel of John, Hebrews, and the letters of Paul. Nevertheless, His suffering and death have a place in giving the title to Jesus in Rom. 5:10; 8:32; Gal. 4:4; etc.

"Listen to him!" is virtually a quotation from Deut. 18:15. Jesus is the prophet promised by Moses. As Jesus is greater than Moses and Elijah, so His teaching transcends theirs. Moses and Elijah are not named alongside of Jesus as people to be obeyed, but Jesus alone is to be heard and obeyed.

On another level, "listen to him!" may refer specifically to the teaching Jesus has been giving the disciples about Messianic suffering, His and theirs, cf. Mark 8:31-38. Instead of erecting buildings, they should obey Jesus.

The Greek akouein has the strong meaning here that the Hebrew sama often has in the Old Testament, namely, "hear and obey." The disciples' obedience is their memorial to Jesus. Jesus will live in them and continue to act in the world through them.

Mark tells us that the transfiguration took place "six days later," but he does not tell us what it was later than. As it stands, the reference point is the day of Peter's confession in 8:29. But there is nothing in the text that chronologically relates Peter's confession to Jesus' transfiguration.

Luke's chronological indicator is "about eight days after these sayings," cf. Luke 9:28. The sayings in Luke 9:21-27 are basically the same as those in Mark 8:31-9:1.

The discrepancy between six and eight calls into question the historical character of Mark's chronological statement. It causes some scholars to think that the statement may not be chronological so much as theological. It may be intended to call the readers' attention to the story of the ratification of the Jahweh's covenant with Israel in Ex. 24, especially vs. 16-18. Both stories deal with covenants God made with the human race. Mark may be consciously relating the two stories with the phrase "after six days." On Mt. Sinai, God revealed Himself through Moses to Israel on the seventh day. After six days, that is, on the seventh day, Mark says, God revealed Himself to representatives of the new Israel. At the least, the exodus story colors the narrative of the transfiguration.

"Peter and James and John" are witnesses of the transfiguration. Three men are specifically named as going up Mt. Sinai with Moses in Ex. 24:1.

The transfiguration took place on "a high mountain." Jesus led the disciples up there. The mountain is not named. It is futile to try to identify it geographically. The evangelists had little interest in geography for its own sake.

Traditionally, Mt. Tabor has been identified with the transfiguration. But Mt. Tabor is not more than 1000 feet high and was at that time crowned by a fortified city that would have rendered it unsuitable for the transfiguration. Most modern commentators identify the mountain with Mt. Hermon that rises to a height of 9200 feet. Great problems exist with this decision, too. To resolve one of the problems, some scholars understand anaphero ("led . . . up") in such a way that it allows for Jesus to miraculously transport the disciples to one of Hermon's heights.

Mark emphasizes the exclusiveness of the transfiguration event. "Peter and James and John" were "apart, by themselves." The Ex. 24 event also was exclusive, cf. vs. 12-15. Clear distinctions were established in Exodus by the levels of ascent made by the people, the elders, and Moses.

The introduction of Elijah is another part of the new Moses theme. In rabbinic thought, Elijah was a second Moses. He contended for the torah of Moses. He had an encounter with God on "the holy mountain," Horeb/Sinai, in 1 Kings 19:8-12. According to rabbinic teaching, neither Moses nor Elijah died; although Deut. 34:5 explicitly says that Moses died. The rabbis believed they both were translated into heaven.

The appearance of Elijah with Moses bears witness to the greatness of Jesus. It is an event of confirmation. The primary function of Moses and Elijah for the three disciples and the reader is to attest to Jesus' glory. One reason for the appearance of the two of them may be the Old Testament law about two witnesses, cf. Deut. 19:15; Matt. 18:16; Mark 15:47.

No figures stood higher in the Jewish tradition than Moses and Elijah. The New Testament contains more explicit references to Moses than to any other Old Testament figure - 80. There are other implicit references to him. Moses was a very prominent man in the Old Testament and in Judaism.

Mark tells us that "Elijah with Moses . . . were talking with Jesus." Luke tells us what they were talking about. He uses the

604

word exodon in Luke 9:31 which is translated "departure." The disciples did not yet understand that in His death Jesus would fulfill the exodus.

Peter often was the spokesman of the disciples. He called Jesus _rabbi_ which means "my teacher." It is strange that Jesus should be so addressed at a point in the narrative at which His deity is beginning to be revealed.

More than a few guesses have been made as to why it was good for the disciples to be there, as Peter says. Two good ones are that the experience was unique and that the disciples had the opportunity to serve Jesus and His heavenly visitors.

When Peter made his great confession in 8:29, his words were fine; but his understanding was very mistaken. He wanted to place Jesus alongside the giants of the old Israel. With this misunderstanding, he rebuked Jesus when He spoke of His death. Jesus was not the Christ Peter envisioned. When Jesus rebuked Peter in 8:33, He repudiated Peter's earlier confession. The validating appearance of Moses and Elijah and the Voice from the cloud including what the Voice said show how mistaken Peter was.

Mark's comment in v. 6 seems to be an apology. Peter's remark is incompetent, but it is in keeping with his impulsive character.

Mark gives fear as the reason for Peter's statement. The same phenomenon is described in Mark 16:8 of the women at the resurrection of Jesus. We can think of the consistent human response to the numinous.

According to some interpreters, the transfiguration was a prophetic event depicting what was to come. It was a sort of anticipation or preview of the resurrection of Jesus or a prophecy of His return in glory. The true meaning of the vision was discernible only after the resurrection. Thus the disciples were not to talk about it until then.

The inability of the disciples to understand Jesus may not have been a sign of weakness on their part. It may simply have been the way God meant it to be. This seems apparent from the conclusion of the story of Jesus' walking on the stormy sea in Mark 6:45-52. The astonishment of the disciples there is due not to their unwillingness to comprehend but to their sheer inability to do so. They do not understand because "their hearts were hardened." The very ability to understand what Jesus is about is withheld from them by God. Jesus' fate is determined not by the mental sharpness, or lack of it, of His followers. His fate is in God's hands, and hence His suffering is not an accident. His passion predictions emphasize that His passion is planned, cf. Mark 8:31; 9:31; 10:33-34.

The announcement by Jesus of His impending suffering met by the incomprehension of the disciples becomes a repeated pattern in the section on instruction to the disciples about discipleship. The pattern consists of a prediction, evidence of incomprehension, and then words of Jesus on the nature of true discipleship, cf. 8:31-38; 9:31-37; 10:33-45. Between the first and third repetitions of this pattern, cf. 9:1-30 and 9:38-10:32, Mark has included a variety of stories, all of which deal, in one way or another, with the theme of discipleship. Even the story of the boy possessed by a demon in 9:14-29 points to Jesus' disciples and their inability to do what others think the disciples should be able to do, cf. vs. 14, 18, 28-29. Mark uses this pattern to make the point that one can understand Jesus, be His disciple, and follow Him only in the light of His cross and resurrection. Until those events take place, no one can understand Him. Indeed, until a person accepts those events today, the person still cannot understand Him.

The same failure of the disciples is vividly portrayed in the account of Jesus' final hours. Perhaps the most striking feature of that portrayal is the stark contrast between what the disciples express as their intention, and what they do. The first element in that contrast occurs in the setting of the Last Supper, when Jesus solemnly announces that one of them will betray Him. The answer of the disciples is, "Surely, not I?" cf. 14:19. The question is so constructed in Greek that a negative answer is anticipated: "It's not I, is it Lord?" Each disciple clearly expects Jesus to answer, "No, of course, it will not be you." Each of them is fully convinced that such a deed would be impossible for him. The events that follow in Mark's narrative cast a painfully brilliant light on the gulf that yawns between what the disciples claim for themselves and what they do. When

Jesus returns from prayer in Gethsemane, He finds them sleeping. When Jesus is arrested, there is some small resistance; but, Mark says in 14:50, "All of them deserted him and fled." Peter follows from a distance. That leads to his three-fold denial of Jesus. In this way, Mark makes it clear that human resolve and intended loyalty come to grief in their supreme test. Mark is not portraying merely a psychological study of human values and actions under stress. Rather he is describing the sheer inability of those closest to Jesus to follow Him before the cross and His resurrection. That such following became possible after those events is clear enough. After His resurrection, the scales fall from their eyes.

The Transfiguration of Our Lord

Year C

Exodus 34:29-35

This Lesson helps the church remember the story of the renewal of the covenant Jahweh made with Israel. The story includes all of Ex. 34.

Israel's deliverance from captivity in Egypt reaches its climax in God's establishment of a covenant with that people at Mt. Sinai. The story of the announcement of the covenant is given in Ex. 19:1-9. The ritual establishment of the covenant is described in Ex. 24.

God wrote the covenant on two tablets of stone and gave them to Moses. When Moses came down from Mt. Sinai carrying the two tablets of stone, he saw the people worshipping a golden calf. The story is told in Ex. 32. Israel broke the covenant God made with them even before the covenant was ritually established. In reaction to the idolatry, Moses threw down the two tablets of stone and broke them.

In Ex. 34, God renews the covenant. At God's direction, Moses makes two new tablets of stone like the first ones and takes them to the top of Mt. Sinai where the covenant is rewritten. When Moses comes down from Mt. Sinai with the stone tablets, his face is shining because he has been talking to God. After Moses gives to Israel all the commandments from the Lord, he puts a veil on his face because his shining face frightens them. The veil is a continuing factor in Moses' relationship with God and with Israel. Whenever he talks to God, he removes the veil. When he reports to Israel what God has said, they see his shining face. When he completes his report, he puts the veil on again.

The Bible's affirmation of God's mercy, grace, and love is made most strongly in His covenants with the human race. A widely held belief is that the God of the Old Testament is a vengeful, wrathful God; but God's essential graciousness is revealed in His relationship to Israel. God Himself strongly asserts this in Ex. 34:6-7. In these verses, He proclaims the reason He renews the covenant with Israel after that people so flagrantly broke it.

The Bible is held together by a single plot: God creates the world, the world rebels against Him, and He seeks to restore the world to the glory for which He created it. God is essentially, characteristically, and fundamentally gracious. The New Testament tells the story of the new, last, and final covenant God made with the human race through the passion of Jesus of Nazareth.

The most curious thing in this Lesson is Moses' shining face and the veil/mask he uses to cover it. His shining face is a reflection of God's glory. Moses himself is unaware of his transformation when he comes down the mountain. When Aaron and the Israelites see his shining face, they are frightened by it. Moses has to call them to come to him. What function the mask performs is not fully clear.

Moses is the mediator between God and Israel. In his office, he bridges the enormous gap between the awesome, holy, and jealous God and the fearful, sinful, and repentant people of Israel.

After he comes down from Mt. Sinai, Moses continues speaking with God. Apparently, this no longer happens on the top of Mt. Sinai but in the tent of meeting as described in Ex. 33:10-11. Moses' face-to-face intimacy with God is continuously displayed in the afterglow of the divine majesty.

The verb qrn ("shone") is related to the noun qeren which means horn. The word is used in the sense of a ray as a symbol of divinity in the Ancient Near East. The Vulgate translated it literally. This led to the artistic depiction of Moses with horns on his head.[172]

Moses' veil is used in a metaphorical way in 2 Cor. 3:7-18 by the apostle Paul to assert the superiority of the new covenant over the old. He calls the old covenant that was chiseled on stone tablets "the ministry of death" and "the ministry of condemnation." He calls the brightness of Moses' face "glory." He says the people could not endure that glory, because "their minds were hardened." That glory is now set aside and has been surpassed by the new covenant which he calls "the ministry of the Spirit" and "the ministry of justification." The new covenant has "greater glory" than the old, because it is "permanent."

The veil Moses wore is still in place for Jews, "when they hear the reading of the old covenant." "Whenever Moses is read, a veil lies over their minds." "Only in Christ is it set aside." "When one turns to the Lord, the veil is removed." Believers have "unveiled faces." They see "the glory of the Lord as though reflected in a mirror." They "are being transformed into the same image from one degree of glory to another." This is the reason, Paul says, that he has great "confidence" and that he acts "with great boldness" in the performance of his ministry. This is a part of his defense against the charge made by some in the church in Corinth that his arrogance is not befitting an apostle.

In 2 Cor. 3:1-3, Paul calls the Christians in Corinth "a letter of Christ" written "not on tablets of stone but on tablets of human hearts." He says that he - and perhaps other apostles are meant, too - has "prepared" them as Moses prepared the two stone tablets he took up Mt. Sinai, and "the Spirit of the living God" has "written" on them. They are "letters of recommendation" testifying that Paul is an apostle of Jesus Christ.

2 Corinthians 3:12-4:2

"Cocky" may be a valid word to characterize the apostle Paul. He uses the word "bold." A cocky person irritates some people, and Paul seems always to have people who are out to get him. His attitude seems to be under attack by some members of the church in Corinth. His cockiness may be unseemly and wrong to them. But Paul does not back off. Rather he defends his behavior by asserting the character of the new covenant he proclaims. He says that his "great boldness" is founded on his hope in the permanence of the glory of the new covenant, cf. 2 Cor. 3:7-11. It is not like the old covenant Moses mediated that has been set aside.

As its ministers, the apostles made very great claims for the new covenant. Paul summarizes his proclamation in Rom. 1:16-17; 1 Cor. 2:1-8; 15:1-23 and 35-57; 2 Cor. 5:18-21; Gal. 1:3-4; Eph. 1:3-14; 2:4-10; etc. He is so confident of the new covenant that he proclaims these preposterous things boldly. His rivals in Corinth seem to feel that he is presumptuous and brazen. Paul attributes his attitude not to self promotion but to the splendor of the ministry in which he serves. He does not consider his apostolic status to be a personal accomplishment. In 2 Cor. 3:5-6, he says that apostles are inadequate of themselves. Their adequacy is from God.

Paul uses the word "boldness" to describe the open and public way he and the apostles proclaim the new covenant. They act with courage and without fear. They expect and hope that they will not be put to shame for what they say about what God did in Jesus' passion and for what they do, cf. Phil. 1:20.

The transparent character of Paul's ministry is described in 2 Cor. 4:2. When he uses the word "we," he is referring probably not only to himself but also to Timothy, cf. 1:1, and to all the apostles. However, his own call seems to be foremost in his mind.

When he says, "We have renounced the shameful things that one hides," he is not suggesting that he has done "the shameful things." A person skilled in rhetoric can hide the true meaning and intent of what he is saying. He can falsify what he is saying through cunning and deceit. Paul refuses to use rhetorical tricks but speaks plainly. He does not try to manipulate his hearers. Through rhetorical cunning, he does not promote himself or exaggerate his importance. He does not try to make the gospel say anything other than what it says.

Paul may be writing not only in self-defense but also criticizing his rivals for the tricks they employ in their rhetoric. He talks about the crafty ways they present themselves in 11:13-15.

Cunning (panourgia) is readiness to do anything. A cunning person is capable of every deceit.

"To falsify" (doloo) is to use deceit and bait to ensnare and to corrupt by using fallacious arguments and misinterpretations. Paul refers to his detractors in 2:17 as "peddlers of God's word." He draws a contrast between the true apostles and those who misrepresent both themselves and their message.

"God's word" is called "our gospel" in 2 Cor. 4:3. Paul uses the term "the word of God" with reference to the gospel also in 1 Thess. 1:8; 2:13; Rom. 9:6; and 1 Cor. 14:36.

Paul's response to those who bring charges against him is "the truth" he preaches. "The truth" is another reference to the gospel of Jesus Christ. Christian faith is called "obedience to the truth" in 1 Pet. 1:22 and Gal. 5:7. The gospel is called "the word of truth" in Col. 1:5 and Eph. 1:13. To accept the Christian gospel is to know the truth.

Paul assumes that the conscience of everyone will agree that his ministry is not flawed by deceitful and self-serving motives. The word "conscience" refers to an individual's capacity to experience guilt when considering his own past acts, and in v. 2 he includes assessing the actions of others. He uses the word in the same way in 5:11. In 1:12, he refers to his own conscience as a witness to his sincerity. He appeals to the conscience of others as they evaluate and pass judgment on his actions.

The judgment of God is another thing to which he appeals for the truthfulness of his ministry. He makes the double appeal to the judgment of God and to his hearers' conscience again in 5:11.

"Then" (oun) in v. 12 of an exceedingly complex passage ties closely what Paul said previously with what he is about to say. In vs. 12-18, he applies what he says in vs. 7-11. The apostles act with great boldness, because the apostolic ministry has a splendor greater than the ministry of Moses.

"Since . . . we have such hope" in v. 12 is equivalent to

"such is the confidence that we have" in v. 4. To the extent that faith is hope, faith is confidence. Confidence in or trust in God is complete surrender of one's own care and strength to God. Faith is not just trust in God in general, but it is trust that accepts the cross and has its foundation in God's saving work. Out of that trust grows the boldness that has no fear of being "put to shame." The "permanent" splendor of the new covenant fires this hope so that the apostles do not lose heart.

Paul uses the story of the establishment of the old covenant through Moses at Mt. Sinai in Ex. 34 to praise the glory of the new covenant. At God's direction, Moses presented himself to the Lord on the top of Mt. Sinai with two tablets of stone in his hand. Jahweh made a covenant with him and with Israel. Moses was with the Lord forty days and forty nights, writing the words of the covenant on the two tablets. As he came down from the mountain with the two tablets of stone, Moses did not know that the skin of his face shone because he had been talking with God. When Aaron and the Israelites saw Moses' shining face, they were afraid to come near him. But Moses called to them, and they came. He gave them what the Lord had said on the mountain. When he finished speaking, he covered his face with a veil. Whenever Moses went in before the Lord to speak with Him, he would take the veil off until he came out. When he came out, he told the Israelites what the Lord had said. The Israelites would see his shining face. He would put the veil on again, until he went in again to speak with the Lord.

As Paul uses this story to contrast Moses' ministry with his own ministry, he makes some adjustments. Moses' attitude is in sharp contrast to Paul's. The word the Old Testament uses for the attitude of Moses in Num. 12:3 is "very humble" (NRSV), "devout" (footnote), or "very meek" (RSV). Paul almost seems to say that that attitude fit Moses, because Moses knew that the old covenant he mediated "was being set aside." The midrashic tradition connects Ex. 34 with Num. 12:3 and interprets Moses' veil as a sign of his meekness.

Paul says that "the people of Israel could not gaze at Moses' face because of the glory of his face," cf. 2 Cor. 3:7. Again he says that Moses "put a veil over his face to keep the people of

Israel from gazing at the end of the glory that was being set aside." This is not a direct contradiction of what Ex. 34 says, but it is pretty close. V. 35 says, "the Israelites would see the face of Moses, that the skin of his face was shining." The exact timing of Moses' taking off and putting on the veil is not explicitly stated in Exodus; it is only implied.

Moses "put a veil over his face to keep the people of Israel from gazing at the end of the glory that was being set aside" seems to imply that Moses knew that the old covenant would be set aside. He did not act boldly, because he knew that the splendor of the old covenant was destined to pass away.

Paul's words "the end of the glory that was being set aside" are difficult to interpret. Greek grammar may help. The Greek literally says, "what was being set aside or annulled." A neuter participle is used. Not just the radiant splendor of Moses' face was being annulled. That would require a feminine participle. Not the covenant law specifically is meant. That would require a masculine form. Rather the entire ministry of the old covenant is meant.

Can this be understood as making Moses responsible for the fading glory of the old covenant? Paul does not want to blame Moses. He clarifies by saying in v. 14 that not Moses but the Israelites were responsible for the fading glory of the old covenant. "Their minds were hardened."

In Ex. 34, the veil is an object Moses uses to cover his shining face. Paul describes it in the same way: "that same veil is still there." With these words, he is expanding it historically. He also expands its function. He says, the "veil lies over their minds." It prevents the Jews of Paul's day from properly understanding "Moses." That the veil prevents understanding is not stated in Ex. 34.

Paul also relates the removal of the veil to Christian faith. He says that "only in Christ is (the veil) set aside." "When one turns to the Lord, the veil is removed."

Vs. 14 and 15 do not move forward Paul's defense of the character of his apostolic ministry, but they correct a false inference of what he says in v. 13. They clarify and, in a sense, correct the reference to Moses' veiling himself. The hard heartedness of Israel is the subject of vs. 14-15.

"Their hearts were hardened" is a numinous passive. The same thought is expressed in Deut. 29:4 and Is. 6:9-10. God is said to cause the eyes of His people to be darkened and their ears to be stopped from accepting His good news.

Using the idea of the veil, Paul describes the failure of the Jews of his day to accept his gospel. Moses' veil symbolizes the problem. The veil is not over the law, nor over the shining face of Moses and what it represents, but over the mind of the hearers. This is the deep tragedy of Judaism. The Jews hold the law high and read it in their services of worship, but they do not understand it.

When Paul talks about Moses being read, he is referring to the public reading of the law in the synagogues. "Moses" in v. 15 stands for the book of Moses or the Pentateuch as it does in 2 Chron. 25:4; Neh. 13:1; Mark 12:26; Rom. 10:5 and 19. The phrase "when they hear the reading of the old covenant" means the same as "whenever Moses is read."

The use of the term "the old covenant" is the first known use of that phrase. Paul may have originated it. Strictly speaking, the reference may be only to the stone tablets engraved on Mt. Sinai. Paul refers to them in 2 Cor. 3:3 and 7. The reference is not to all of the old covenant scriptures in general but only to the writings of Moses. Some scholars and even some translations think that "the old covenant" refers to all of the Old Testament writings, but the canon of the Old Testament had not yet been established when Paul wrote.

In the Vulgate (the Latin translation of the Bible), diatheke is always rendered testamentum even where the meaning is obviously "covenant." In classical Greek, diatheke usually means a will or testament, while suntheke is a covenant or agreement. However, suntheke implies an equality between the contracting parties, and so the LXX does not use it to translate the Hebrew berith (covenant) but uses diatheke. A covenant between God and people is not made between equal partners but represents a divine testament or bequeathing. But since in English we have no word meaning both covenant and testament, the word "covenant" is used as being nearer to the New Testament meaning of diatheke. The word "testament" is used

616

in the titles for the two parts of the Bible, Old Testament and New Testament, but it would be better if they were called the Old Covenant and the New Covenant.

"Only in Christ is (the veil) set aside." Only after Jesus' resurrection did the disciples come to understand what Jesus had taught them and done before their eyes. The Holy Spirit in every age gives an understanding of the things of Christ to believing hearts. Without the inward testimony of the Holy Spirit at the reading or preaching of the scriptures, human understanding remains locked up in the written and spoken word. Or to put it the way Paul does: the meaning of scripture remains veiled until the Spirit of Christ does away with the veil that lies over the hearts of people. The letter of torah or the written scriptures merely deadens. It is the Spirit who gives life to the words, cf. 2 Cor. 3:6. The Spirit of the crucified and risen Christ interprets in all the scriptures the things concerning Himself. Apart from His presence and inspiration, the scriptures are a mysterious enigma. They remain that to this day to the unbelieving Jews.

Paul says the old covenant is "set aside." Katargeo means to render inoperative, to do away with.

"When one turns to the Lord" can be regarded as a technical term for the act of conversion.[173] Shub (a turning from idols to the living Lord) is often used in the Old Testament to express conversion. New Testament ways of saying this other than epistrophe (conversion), the word used in v. 16, are metanoia (a change of orientation), anagennan paliggennesia (regeneration), and anakainosis (renewal). Making a distinction between these terms is only of academic value, because the same process is involved. Regeneration describes the process as a new creation. Repentance and conversion make the same process a total transformation, a break with the old and a beginning of the new. To turn to the Lord means to acknowledge and receive reconciliation with God through Christ. People know the comfort of regeneration when they daily experience repentance and conversion.

The word "conversion," seems to make the person the active agent. The word "regeneration," seems to make the person the

617

recipient. A human act can have a person as the subject and God as the author at the same time.[174]

When the NRSV translates "one turns to the Lord," it assumes the subject of the phrase. The subject is not stated in the original. Others identify the subject as the Israelites, their hearts, and Moses. Furnish says, "the fact that the subject is left unexpressed is probably a clue that Paul wishes to broaden the reference to include" everyone.[175]

Many take "Lord" as a reference to Christ, others to God.

The form of the verb translated "is removed" is generally considered passive, although it may be middle. If it is middle, the subject could be "the Lord." "The Lord removes the veil." The meaning is not changed.

The Lord by whom the veil of misunderstanding is or should have been removed is the Spirit. The Lord is not only Jahweh of the Sinai theophany to Moses to whom Moses spoke with his face uncovered but also the God who is Jesus Christ to whom Paul's Corinthian readers have been converted.

Paul, in 2 Cor. 3:6, has contrasted the life-giving Spirit with the death-dealing letter, identifying the life-giving Spirit with the ministry of the new covenant "inscribed . . . with the Spirit of the living God . . . on tablets that are human hearts," cf. 3:3, and the death-dealing letter with the ministry of the old covenant "chiseled in letters on stone tablets," cf. 3:7. The Lord to whom the Corinthians turned at their conversion is the God of the new covenant who operates through the Spirit and not through the letter. He gives life and righteousness rather than death and condemnation.

Attempts have been made to distinguish between the Lord Jesus and the Spirit,[176] but this is difficult to do.

Lordship is a relationship in which the Spirit controls our life and protects us from drifting. He has authority to command and does so. The servant of the Lord yields in obedience. But Jesus does not exercise dominion over those who belong to Him by the promulgation of laws and the pronouncement of judgment. Rather He does this by fellowship with sinners and by forgiveness. His lordship is not intended as a burden but as a help, cf. Matt. 11:28-30.

618

The concept Lord needs to be complemented by us accepting the category of servant. But it is not the kind of servanthood that a subject owes because of a law that is to be observed by everyone. It is personal service under our Lord and for Him. There is a major difference between the two. Life under law demands the accommodation of a person's will to the will of the lawgiver. Personal service presumes that our will is attuned to the will of the Lord. We are guided by the Spirit of the Lord who is not a Spirit of slavery. "Where the Spirit of the Lord is, there is freedom." See also Rom. 8:1-4.

Werner Elert says, "We are not servants of the Lord because it is demanded of us but because he has made us his servants; we are his servants not by compulsion but by grace. We serve him because he has redeemed us, and this relationship is correlative so that the cessation of service to Christ leads immediately to relapse into servitude (guilt, sin, death). Unity of will with Christ means that we want what he wants, i.e. redemption from guilt, sin, death. Service under Christ is life as redemption."[177]

Elert continues: "we live continuously under grace through the continuous presence of Christ. Like his first disciples we live in permanent dependence upon him. . . . This dependence is a relationship of one person to another. We can only live it in this manner if he is as concretely real to us as to his first disciples, if we see him and hear him as they saw him and heard him, if we know that the same questions are addressed to us as were to them, if we are humbled and uplifted by the same words which he spoke to them. In this manner he exercises his power over the actual events in our life. This continuous encounter constitutes him as our ethical authority as he was authority for his first disciples."[178]

On the last day, He will be the judge. This does not mean that in His relationship with us He will no longer be the helping, healing, redeeming Lord. He will not become a demanding sovereign who rules by the law of retribution. He does not now attract followers by His gentleness in order to judge them later by the severity of the law. The Jesus who dealt with people when He lived here on earth is the same Jesus who will be the

619

judge at the end. He will deal with us then just as He did with the people of the first century.

Elert says, "the exalted Christ is identical with the earthly Christ and we can believe, therefore, that he deals with us exactly as he dealt with those of his own generation who were sinners and became his disciples."[179] His recorded sayings in the Bible apply to us now even as they did to the people then. The obligations He laid on His first disciples do not have a different character from those He lays on us now.

The end of the dominance of the written law means freedom. Jesus' death atoned for our guilt. The guilty judgment God pronounced on us has been changed. We are free. We no longer live under the law but under grace. This is what reconciliation means. We have been pardoned and forgiven. We are justified before God. Such a life is realized in a continuous relationship to Christ. This is what it means that He is our Lord.

Three other passages in which Paul associates the Spirit with freedom are Rom. 7:6; Rom. 8; and Gal. 4:21-5:25. In Rom. 7:6, he argues that slavery to righteousness is true freedom. He describes freedom from the law in its positive aspect as the new life of the Spirit. The thought is repeated and elaborated in Rom. 8:2-27. He contrasts "walking according to the Spirit" with "walking according to the flesh" in vs. 3-8. He refers to the believers' ultimate hope of obtaining "the glorious freedom of the children of God" in v. 21. His discussion of freedom in Gal. 4:21-5:25 moves into an appeal to "walk by the Spirit," cf. 5:16-25. Under the Spirit's leading, one is freed from the law, cf. 5:18.

The idea of freedom is carried forward in 2 Cor. 3:18 as Paul describes its meaning. The subject is "all of us." "All of us" refers not just to all of us apostles but to all of us who believe, to all Christians, to all who have turned to the Lord. Two phrases describe "all of us." One is "with unveiled faces." The other is "seeing the glory of the Lord as though reflected in a mirror."

There is disagreement as to whether the description of Christian believers as having "unveiled faces" is intended to contrast us with Moses who, according to Paul, veiled his face when talking to the Israelites or to unbelieving Israel whose understanding has been veiled. The use of the word "face" suggests a contrast with Moses, but the context favors the veiled minds of Israel.

Paul gives his readers a picture of Christians with faces unveiled beholding the glory of the Lord and "being changed into his likeness, from one degree of glory to another." Believers are contrasted with those who have a veil lying over their understanding. The apostle associates the removal of the veil with Christ's annulment of the old covenant. He says that "in Christ is (the veil) set aside." Believers in Christ have been freed from the impediments of the law.

"Unveiled" (anakekalummeno) is a perfect form. It indicates the continual state resulting from a previous act. The veil, once lifted, remains lifted.

The Aramaic expression for confidence means literally "to uncover the face." This Aramaic expression must have been lurking in Paul's mind as he wrote of his boldness. This may explain why he uses the story in Ex. 34 to contrast Moses' conduct with that of the apostles in v. 13.[180]

The idea of boldness is closely related to Christian freedom. The Greek word parresia means the freedom to speak and act without fear, openly and straightforwardly. It means not having to shrink back out of cowardice or to act secretively and deceptively.

Katoptrizomenoi can mean either to see in a mirror or to reflect like a mirror. The present participle shows that the beholding is continuous and free from interruption. Christ Himself is the mirror in whose face the glory of God is revealed, cf. 2 Cor. 4:6. He is the image of God, cf. 4:4. This is not the ultimate beholding of 1 Cor. 13:12.

Paul may have had in mind the bronze mirrors for which Corinth was famous. Several ancient writers attest to the distinctive quality of Corinthian bronze. Pliny wrote that it was valued throughout the empire "before silver and almost before gold."[181] It had an unusually high tin content that gave it an unusual color. Corinthian mirrors were famous for their brilliance.[182]

There is no thought here, as in 1 Cor. 13:12, of the imperfect quality of a mirrored image. Philo thinks of a mirror as an instrument by which one "gains a lucid view of all that mind can perceive."[183]

Not only the seeing but also the transforming is going on in the present. There was a widespread idea in the Hellenistic age that the beholding of a god or goddess could have a transforming effect on the worshiper. Such a transformation can be found also in the literature of Judaism.[184]

"Are being transformed" is the predicate of v. 18. The transformation is described in three phrases: "into the same image," "from one degree of glory to another," and "this comes from the Lord, the Spirit."

Paul speaks of this change also in 1 Cor. 15:51-52; Rom. 8:29; and Phil. 3:21. For him, transformation means conformity to the image of Christ, cf. Rom. 8:29, "to be like his glorious body," cf. Phil. 3:21. He speaks of Christ's being "formed in" the believer in Gal. 4:19. He speaks of "a new creation" in 2 Cor. 5:17.

The believer's transformation into a new being has both a present and a future aspect. Here Paul is thinking of the present. Faith is being conformed to the image of God in Christ. This means, first of all, sharing Christ's sufferings, "becoming like him in his death," cf. Phil. 3:10, by being "crucified with him," cf. Rom. 6:6. Even now, believers "walk in newness of life," cf. Rom. 6:4; 7:6; etc. Although they remain in this age, they are not conformed to it. They are so far "transformed" by renewal of their lives, cf. Rom. 12:2, of their "inner nature," cf. 2 Cor. 4:16, that they may be said to be part of "a new creation," cf. Gal. 6:15; 2 Cor. 5:17.

This transformation does not take place through some ecstatic experience. It is a transformation in that the believer is conformed to the image of God in His Son. One dies to the old self and is raised up to new life through the renewing power of the Spirit. It is that daily inward renewal of one's being which occurs where one's life is put at God's disposal and which thereby becomes the hallmark of the believer's existence while he or she is still in this world. The transformation is dynamic, "from one degree of glory to another."

The image of God is visible in Christ, cf. 2 Cor. 4:4 and Col. 1:15. He is God's Son in whom God is seen, and the image into which believers are being transformed is the same one they see mirrored there.

If we ask whether our transformation is a physical or merely an ethical process, the answer is that it is both. Moral goodness has numinous manifestations.

We are being transformed "from one degree of glory to another." Literally, the Greek reads "from glory to glory." This is a Hebrew way of expressing the superlative. The increasing splendor of Christians is emphasized in contrast to the diminishing splendor of Moses. Christians, seeing in Jesus the image of God, are not deified but are transformed into the same image. The glory they share with Him ever increases from one stage of glory to a higher stage. This divine glory is imparted by Christ to His disciples through the Spirit. The last phrase in v. 18 repeats what v. 17 says.

Luke 9:28-43a

One of the significant differences between Luke's account of Jesus' transfiguration and the accounts in Mark 9:2-8 and Matthew 17:1-8 is Luke's description of the conversation between Jesus, Moses, and Elijah. They talk about Jesus' – the Greek word is – exodon, the accusative form of exodos. The word is important, because it can help us understand Jesus' mission. As Jesus' visit to the synagogue at Nazareth is a curtain-raiser to His public ministry, so His transfiguration is a prelude to the travel section in Luke's gospel in which Jesus "set His face to go to Jerusalem," cf. 9:51.

Luke is the only evangelist who uses the word exodos to describe the conversation between Moses, Elijah, and Jesus. RSV and NRSV translate with the word "departure." TEV paraphrases: "the way in which he would soon fulfill God's purpose by dying." Exodos can refer to a man's death or his departure, cf. 2 Pet. 1:15. But strangely Luke couples it with the word pleroun which means "to fulfill." The very word echoes the exodus of Israel from Egypt. It seems clear that

Luke intentionally is referring not only to Jesus' death but to His fulfillment of the exodus in His death. The plan for His saving work was the exodus. The pronoun "his" establishes that Jesus' exodos is the one intended. The gospels are shot through with events that point to Jesus' fulfillment of the exodus. Matt. 2:15 is an example.

The scope of the word exodos is debated.[185] Some limit it to Jesus' death. Others understand it as a reference to Jesus' resurrection, His coming out of the grave. Others have insisted that it encompasses the transit of Jesus to the Father ending in the ascension. Jesus' entire life is involved, because in His life He fulfilled the exodus.

God sought, in the exodus, to create and constitute a people for Himself through whom His universal redemptive purpose would be effected. His intention was that through Israel all people would be brought back into the relationship with Him that He planned in the creation. The exodus was a series of events that began with Israel's departure from Egypt, continued as that people wandered in the wilderness where they received God's law, and ended when they entered the land of Canaan. But Israel's disobedience prevented the implementation of the divine intention. The exodus, like an incompletely fulfilled prophecy, remained an imperfect expression of God's purpose awaiting fulfillment. Luke says, in his account of Jesus' transfiguration, that the exodus was fulfilled in Jesus' death. God's act of salvation which was the central event of the Old Testament was the type for the salvation accomplished in Jesus. His resurrection reveals that His death was not defeat but the triumph of the divine will. In His passion, He saved the human race from the mess we got ourselves into through sin.

The topic of the conversation between Jesus, Moses, and Elijah suggests that the transfiguration is for Jesus' sake. Moses and Elijah do not appear to console Jesus but to strengthen Him for His coming suffering and death. Their function is not to inform Jesus of the details of His passion but to remind Him of the role He is playing in God's plan of salvation.

Another significant difference between the transfiguration account of Luke and the accounts of the other evangelists is that Jesus "went up on the mountain to pray." Luke is the only evangelist to say that the transfiguration took place "while he was praying."

A third significant difference between Luke's transfiguration account and the other accounts is that the Voice from the cloud calls Jesus "my Chosen." At His baptism, cf. Luke 3:22, the Voice called Jesus "my Son, the Beloved," as He does in the other accounts of the transfiguration, cf. Matt. 17:5; Mark 9:7; and 2 Pet. 1:17. At the baptism, the Voice addressed Jesus Himself, but in the transfiguration He addresses the disciples and through them the Christian community. The heavenly Voice rejects Peter's suggestion in v. 33 and corrects his implied identification of the experience with that of the feast of Booths. God Himself declares what He intends in the transfiguration.

The heavenly identification of Jesus as the Son of God is variously understood. Some commentators interpret it in the sense of Ps. 2:7 which is usually understood as an enthronement psalm for some heir to the Davidic throne. Some have argued that if the words of the Voice are an allusion to the psalm, they are not a clear identification of Jesus as the Messiah. There is no evidence that Ps. 2:7 was understood in a Messianic sense in pre-Christian Judaism.

It is not necessary to load the title Son of God here with all that was given it at the Council of Nicea.[186] Israel is called the son of God in Ex. 4:22. The king of Israel is also called the son of God in Ps. 2:7, because he is the representative of the people of Israel. In this sense, Son of God is a Messianic title.

But in Luke's account, the Voice calls Jesus also "my Chosen." That title brings to mind Is. 42:1, the opening words of a Servant Song, and suggests that Jesus is the Servant of the Lord. That the term is accepted as being Messianic is clearly brought out in Luke 23:35. The title is found also in the Qumran texts.

Another significant addition to the words of the Voice from heaven spoken at Jesus' baptism is the command, "Listen to him!" The words are a virtual quotation of Deut. 18:15. The Voice testifies that Jesus is the promised prophet like Moses to whom God's people should listen. Instead of trying to hold on to Moses and Elijah, the heavenly Voice charges the disciples to listen to Jesus. The implication is that He now speaks with greater authority than Moses and Elijah, as Peter says in Acts 3:22-23.

The reappearance of Moses and Elijah in some way was expected in connection with the coming of the Messiah, according to Jewish beliefs. The promise that God would raise up a prophet like Moses in Deut. 18:15 and 18 came to be understood as pointing to the coming of a special prophet in the future. The disciples believed that Jesus was that prophet.

Elijah is called the first great prophet for a revived Mosaic religion. He was the predecessor of the 8th century prophets who appealed for reform. In rabbinic thought, he was himself a second Moses. Both he and Moses had an encounter with God on the holy mount.

Some have said that Moses represents the law and Elijah the prophets and that both bear testimony to Jesus. But this is not strictly correct. Moses is essentially "the prophet," and Elijah is another Moses. The two are assimilated in Mal. 4:4-6. In the transfiguration, Moses and Elijah represent the old order, the old covenant, as contrasted with Jesus who represents the new covenant. The old is fulfilled in the new.

Moses and Elijah "appeared in glory." The rabbis taught that neither Moses nor Elijah died; they were translated to heaven. In the Old Testament, however, only Enoch, cf. Gen. 5:24, and Elijah, cf. 2 Kings 2:11, were translated to heaven without dying. Nevertheless, Moses' death was unique, cf. Deut. 34:5-6. By the first century A.D., he, too, was accorded the honor of never having died.

The work known as "The Assumption of Moses" was written shortly after the death of Herod the Great. The appendix contains references to the dispute between Michael and Satan over the body of Moses. This is followed by the triumphant assumption of Moses into heaven. A reference to this dispute is found also in Jude 9.

The transfiguration took place "on the mountain." The translation "he went up into the mountains" is linguistically just as valid as "he went up on the mountain." The singular noun can refer either to an individual mountain or to a mountain range. It is called "the holy mountain" in 2 Pet. 1:18.

'A definite article is used with the noun. This indicates that Luke has in mind a specific mountain or mountain range. It is futile to try to identify "the mountain" geographically. The evangelists had no interest in geography for its own sake. It was probably one of the slopes of Mt. Hermon that is in the vicinity of Caesarea Philippi.

Mt. Tabor is the traditional site of the transfiguration. But this tradition can be traced back only to Origen.[187] Also at the time of the transfiguration, Mt. Tabor was crowned with a fortified city which would make it unsuitable for the transfiguration event.

"Peter and John and James" is not the traditional order for listing the names of the three men Jesus took "up on the mountain" with Him, but the same order is found in 8:51. So it is not strange in the context of the gospel of Luke.

No other account of the transfiguration mentions the disciples seeing Jesus' glory. Glory is the status of the risen Christ in Luke 24:26. Does Luke intend some connection between the transfiguration and the resurrection?

The disciples are given a glimpse of the glory Jesus will receive when He has fulfilled the exodus deliverance, cf. Phil 2:8-11. It is a momentary revelation of glory in the darkness, like a lamp shining in a dark place, which must suffice until the day dawns and the day-star of the unveiled parousia-glory arises, cf. 2 Pet. 1:16-19.

Peter proposes to "make three dwellings," one for Jesus, one for Moses, and one for Elijah. He places Jesus, Moses, and Elijah on the same level. This shows that in his confession of Jesus as "the Messiah of God" in 9:20, he does not understand who Jesus is.

Luke says that Peter does not know "what he said." What Peter says is inappropriate. He fails to reckon with the fact that heavenly beings need no earthly dwellings. Old Testament prophecies say that God will come to live among His people again, cf. Ezek. 37:27; 43:6-9; Zech. 2:10-11; 8:3. But the age of tabernacles as the place for the divine presence is over. God is present in the person of Jesus.

The cloud that overshadows "them" is an exodus

phenomenon, cf. Ex. 16:10; 19:9; 24:15-18; 40:34. It is an expression of God's presence and glory, cf. 1 Kings 8:10-11 and Ezek. 10:3-4.

"Them" is a reference to the disciples and Jesus. Moses and Elijah had left, according to v. 33. The only people with Jesus on the mountain are the disciples. "They entered the cloud."

The occasion for fear in the disciples is different in each transfiguration account. They are terrorized by the sound of the Voice in Matt. 17:6. They are overcome with fear at the appearance of Moses and Elijah in Mark 9:6. They are frightened when the cloud of glory envelopes them in Luke. These divergences are not the result of carelessness with respect to detail by the writers. They reflect the respective interest of each evangelist. Matthew's gospel depicts Jesus as the new Moses. The words echo the prediction of Deut. 18:15 and 18. The second gospel is that of the Son of God who is also the Suffering Servant. To Mark, Moses and Elijah are the prophets of the end time. Hence the mention of fear at the appearance of the two ancient prophets. Luke, on the other hand, wants to show how intimately the disciples are involved in both the suffering and the glory of their Lord. Luke, too, works out the theme of Jesus as the new Moses as well as the new Elijah.

The disciples had an experience beyond the power of human language to express. They struggled when they talked about it. They understood the experience as a divine ratification that Jesus was the Messiah. They articulated this in different ways.

That "Peter and his companions were weighed down with sleep" suggests that the transfiguration took place at night. The four men come down from the mountain the next day.

In the Lutheran Church, the observance of the transfiguration climaxes the Epiphany cycle and anticipates the season of Lent. This supports Luke's theme that Jesus' suffering is the pathway to glory. As He conducted His ministry, Jesus followed a plan. Matthew's gospel especially shows that the plan had an exodus outline.

The sequel to Jesus' transfiguration is the healing of the boy with an unclean spirit that takes place on the following day.

From the mountain of transfiguration, Jesus descends to the sinful world of human suffering. "A great crowd" is waiting for Him. They know He is coming, because His disciples are there.

The symptoms of the child's ailment are those of an epileptic. "Epilepsy" is derived from the Greek epilepsia which means attack seizure. Today, epilepsy is regarded as a chronic nervous disorder involving changes in consciousness and motion resulting from either an inborn defect that produces convulsions of greater or lesser severity or an organic lesion of the brain (by tumor, toxic agents, or injury). The attacks often begin in childhood or at puberty. Foam appears at the mouth in epileptic seizures. It was probably through this ailment that the spirit exerted its power over the child, and the spirit was reluctant to give up that control.

The "spirit" is called "the demon" and "the unclean spirit." The demons, unclean spirits, or evil spirits of the synoptic gospels are not associated with Satan, and their control of a person is normally not an indication of moral failure. Though the evangelists distinguish at times between possession and illness, e.g. Luke 7:21 and 13:32, and do not explain all illness in terms of demonic influence, they closely relate the two.

Luke stresses the disciples' inability to cast out the spirit in contrast to Jesus' mighty power. The apostles are given the power to cast out demons and to cure diseases in 9:1. The disciples who cannot cast out the spirit need not be the apostles. The seventy report in 10:17 that the demons submit to them. Two reasons the disciples cannot cure the boy are given in Mark 9:28-29 and Matt. 17:19-20.

It is not clear who Jesus calls a "faithless and perverse generation." Some think He is speaking to the disciples, some to the father and the crowd.[188] Jesus is Moses again. Moses complained to God in the desert about having to act as Israel's nursemaid, cf. in Num. 11:12.

The people recognize that what Jesus does is done as God's agent. God's majesty and power are manifested through Him.

ENDNOTES

1 This is attested to by the "Treatise of Shem" which dates back to the first century BC and some of the Dead Sea Scrolls, cf. The Old Testament Pseudepigrapha edited by James H. Charlesworth (Garden City: Doubleday and Company, Inc., 1983), pp. 476-486.

2 Francis Pieper, Christian Dogmatics, Vol. III (St. Louis: Concordia Publishing House, 1953), pp. 211-215.

3 Dale C. Allison, Jr., "The Baptism of Jesus and a New Dead Sea Scroll," in Biblical Archaeology Review, Vol. 18, No. 2, March/April 1992, pp. 59-60.

4 Luther's Works, Vol. 1, edited by Jaroslav Pelikan (St. Louis: Concordia Publishing House, 1958), p. 3.

5 Ibid., p. 4.

6 Ibid.

7 Genesis (Atlanta: John Knox Press, 1973), p. 11.

8 "Science Leans Nearer to Bible's Story of Creation," Des Moines Sunday Register, January 30, 1949 and "Bible Reliability," The Lutheran Outlook, July 1949, p. 206.

9 "Why I believe in God," Woman's Home Companion, July 1950, p. 103.

10 Luther's Works, Vol. 54, edited and translated by Theodore G. Tappert (Philadelphia: Fortress Press, 1967), p. 159.

11 LW, Vol. 1, pp. 21-22.

12 Rudolf Bultmann, The History of the Synoptic Tradition, translated by John Marsh (Oxford: Basil Blackwell, 1968), p. 250.

13 Vincent Taylor, The Gospel According to St.Mark (London: Macmillan and Co.Ltd., 1953), p. 162.

14 Oscar Cullmann, The Christology of the New Testament, Revised Edition (Philadelphia: The Westminster Press, 1963), p. 66.

15 Ibid., p 162.

16 Ibid., p. 276.

17 Ibid., pp. 55-60.

18 LW, Vol. 54, p. 70.

19 Time, March 22, 2010, p. 4.

20 Luther's Works, Vol. 22, edited by Jaroslav Pelikan (St. Louis: Concordia Publishing House, 1957), pp. 160-161.

21 Antiquities V. 10. 4.

22 Werner Foerster, "exestin," Theological Dictionary of the New Testament, Vol. II, edited by Gerhard Kittel (Grand Rapids: Wm. B. Eerdmans Publishing Company, 1964), pp. 560-561.

23 The Gospel according to John (i-xii), (Garden City: Doubleday and Company, Inc., 1966), p. 83.

24 Rami Arav, Richard A. Freund, and John F. Shroder, Jr., "Bethsaida Rediscovererd," Biblical Archaeology Review, Vol. 20, No. 1, January/February 2000, pp. 44-56.

25 Brown, p.88.

26 Wayne A. Meeks, The First Urban Christians (New Haven: Yale University Press, 1983), pp. 119-121.

27 Hans Conzelmann, 1 Corinthians (Philadelphia: Fortress Press, 1981), p. 209.

28 Brown, p. 103.

29 Meeks, p. 117.

30 Oscar Cullmann, Peter (London: SCM Press Ltd., 1953), pp. 53-54.

31 Luther's Works, Vol. 31, edited by Harold J. Grimm (Philadelphia: Muhlenberg Press, 1957), p. 84.

32 Ibid., p. 85.

33 "Studies in Discipleship," Concordia Theological Monthly, October 1960, pp. 608-609.

34 Pieper, pp. 542-543.

35 Archibald Robertson and Alfred Plummer, A Critical and Exegetical Commentary on the First Epistle of St.Paul to the Corinthians (Edinburgh: T. and T Clark, 1953), p. 152.

36 C. S. Lewis, Beyond Personality, p. 31.

37 "Epeita," A Greek-English Lexicon of the New Testament and other Early Christian Literature, Third Edition, revised and edited by Frederick William Danker (Chicago: The University of Chicago Press, 2000), p. 361.

38 James A. Sanders, "Isaiah in Luke," Interpretation, April 1982, p. 151.

39 Ibid., p. 144.

40 Ibid., p. 152.

41 Roland de Vaux, Ancient Israel, Vol. 2 (New York: McGraw-Hill Book Company, 1965), pp. 143-144.

42 John Reumann, "A History of Lectionaries: From the Synagogue at Nazareth to Post-Vatican II," Interpretation, April 1977, pp. 116-120.

43 James Luther Mays, "Justice: Perspectives from the Prophetic Tradition," Interpretation, January 1983, pp. 5-17.

44 Time, July 21, 2008, p. 20.

45 LW, Vol. 31, p. 53.

46 Works of Martin Luther, Vol. I, "A Treatise on Good Works" (Philadelphia: Muhlenberg Press, 1943), pp. 213-214.

47 Luther's Works, Vol. 21, edited by Jaroslav Pelikan (St. Louis: Concordia Publishing House, 1956), p. 45.

48 Ibid., p. 52.

49 Robert L. Wilken, "Religious Pluralism and Early Christian Theology," Interpretation, October 1986, p. 380.

50 Rudolf Bultmann, Theology of the New Testament, Vol. 1 (New York: Charles Scribner's Sons, 1951), p. 216.

51 C. K. Barrett, The New Testament Background: Selected Documents (New York: Harper and Row, Publishers, 1966), pp. 31-33.

52 Stuart D. Currie, "Speaking in Tongues," Interpretation, July 1965, p. 276.

53 Ibid., p. 277.

54 William Harris, "'Sounding Brass' and Hellenistic Technology," <u>Biblical Archaelogy Review</u>, Vol. VIII, No. 1, January/February 1982, pp. 38-41.

55 <u>The New Testament in Four Versions</u> (Washington, D.C.: Christianity Today, Inc.,1965), p. 533.

56 <u>Ibid</u>.

57 "<u>Phusioo</u>," Danker, p. 1069.

58 <u>Ibid.</u>

59 <u>Ibid</u>., p. 224.

60 <u>Ibid</u>.

61 <u>Ibid</u>.

62 Victor Paul Furnish, "Corinth in Paul's Time," <u>Biblical Archaeology Review</u>, Vol. XV, No. 3, May/June 1988, p. 18.

63 Joachim Jeremias, <u>Jesus' Promise to the Nations</u>, translation by S. H. Hooke (Naperville, Ill.: Alec R. Allenson, 1958), pp. 44ff.

64 C. Clifton Black, "Journeying through Scripture with the Lectionary's Map," <u>Interpretation</u>, January 2002, p. 70.

65 For a discussion on the history of marriage and the relationship between the sexes, see <u>Theological Dictionary of the New Testament</u>, Vol. I, edited by Gerhard Kittel (Grand Rapids: Wm. B. Eerdmans Publishing Company, 1964), pp. 776-785.

66 <u>Luther's Works</u>, Vol. 28, edited by Hilton C. Oswald (St. Louis: Concordia Publishing House, 1973), p. 10.

67 Jaroslav Pelikan, <u>The Emergence of the Catholic Tradition</u> (Chicago: The University of Chicago Press, 1971), p. 288.

68 <u>The Book of Concord</u>, edited by Robert Kolb and Timothy J. Wengert (Minneapolis: Fortress Press, 2000), p. 84.

69 LW, Vol. 28, p. 13

70 <u>Ibid</u>., p. 14.

71 <u>Ibid</u>.

72 <u>Ibid</u>., p. 21-22; LW, Vol. 54, p. 271.

73 <u>The Book of Concord</u>, p. 62.

74 LW, Vol. 28, p. 27.

75 <u>Ibid</u>., pp. 27-28.

76 <u>Ibid</u>., p. 27.

77 Ibid., p. 28.

78 Leonhard Goppelt, Theology of the New Testment, Vol. 1, translated by John E. Alsup, edited by Juergen Roloff (Grand Rapids: William B. Eerdmans Publishing Company, 1981), p. 17.

79 LW, Vol. 28, pp. 31-32.

80 Third Edition, Revised (St. Louis: Concordia Publishing House, 1946), p. 157.

81 LW, Vol. 28, p. 33.

82 Ibid., pp. 33-34.

83 Ibid., pp. 34-35.

84 Ibid., p. 36.

85 Baptism in the New Testament, translated by J. K. S. Reid (London: SCM Press Ltd., 1954) , pp. 43-45.

86 LW, Vol. 28, p. 36.

87 LW, Vol. 54, pp. 302-303.

88 LW, Vol. 28, p. 37.

89 Ibid., p. 38.

90 Ibid., pp. 38-39.

91 Time, May 17, 2010, p. 44.

92 W. Gutbrod, "Nomos," Theological Dictionary of the New Testament, Vol. IV, edited by Gerhard Kittel (Grand Rapids: Wm. B. Eerdmans Publishing Company, 1967), p. 1059.

93 LW, Vol. 31, p. 344.

94 Luther's Works, Vol. 26, edited by Jaroslav Pelikan (St. Louis: Concordia Publishing House, 1963), p. 76.

95 W. D. Davies, Paul and Rabbinic Judaism (London:SPCK, 1962), pp. 69-74.

96 Andrew F. Walls, "Old Athens and New Jerusalem," International Bulletin of Missionary Research, Vol. 21, No. 4, October 1997, pp. 146-153.

97 Gerhard Von Rad, Old Testament Theology, Vol. II, translated by D. M. G. Stalker (Edinburgh: Oliver and Boyd, 1966), pp. 152-153.

98 David C. Steinmetz, "John Calvin on Isaiah 6: A Problem in the History of Exegesis," Interpretation, April 1982, p. 164.

99 The Idea of the Holy, translated by John W. Harvey (New York: Oxford University Press, 1958).

100 Von Rad, Theology, Vol. 2, p. 363.

101 Ibid., p. 148.

102 H. J. Schoeps, Paul, translated by Harold Knight (Philadelphia: The Westminster Press, 1961), pp. 141-149.

103 LW, Vol. 28, pp. 90-91.

104 Rudolf Otto, The Idea of the Holy, Ibid., p. 50.

105 For the fish in the Sea of Galilee, see Mendel Nun, "Cast Your Net Upon the Waters," Biblical Archaeology Review, Vol. 19, No. 6, November/December 1993, pp. 48-51.

106 Mendul Nun, "Ports of Galilee," Biblical Archaeology Review, Vol. 25, No. 4, July/August 1999, p. 27.

107 Gerhard Von Rad, Old Testament Theology, Vol. 1, translated by D. M. G. Stalker (Edinburgh: Oliver and Boyd, 1968), pp. 193-196 and 229-231.

108 Conzelmann, p. 72.

109 Marianne H. Micks, The Future Present: The Phenomenon of Christian Worship, (New York: The Seabury Press, 1970), p. 143.

110 Luther has a considerable discussion on how "God . . . gives the growth" with many examples in Luther's Works, Vol. 13, edited by Jaroslav Pelikan (St. Louis: Concordia Publishing House, 1956), pp. 148-151.

111 A. N. Sherwin-White, Roman Society and Roman Law in the New Testament (Oxford: At the Clarendon Press, 1963), pp. 133-134.

112 LW, Vol. 1, p. 96.

113 LW, Vol. 21, pp. 86-89.

114 Flavius Josephus, The Works of Flavius Josephus, translated by William Whiston (London: T. Nelson and Sons, 1871), xv, vii, 10, 420.

115 LW, Vol. 54, p. 349.

116 LW, Vol. 21, pp. 93-98.

117 p. 123.

118 Frederick W. Danker, "Mark 1:45 and the Secrecy Motif," Concordia Theological Monthly, Vol. 37, No. 8, September 1966, pp. 496-497.

119 Helen Frenkley, "The Search for Roots," Biblical Archaeology Review, Vol. XII, No. 5, September/October 1986, p. 42. A picture of the fruit is on p. 43.

120 LW, Vol. 28, p. 94.

121 Hans-Joachim Schoeps, Jewish Christianity, translated by Douglas R. A. Hare (Philadelphia: Fortress Press, 1964), pp. 11 and 102.

122 Rodney S. Sadler, Jr., "Guest Editorial: Who is My Neighbor? – Introductory Explorations," Interpretation, April 2008, pp. 115-121.

123 Naim Ateek, "Who is My Neighbor?" Interpretation, April 2008, pp. 156-161.

124 These citations are taken from Paul G. Bretscher's After the Purifying, (River Forest: Lutheran Education Association, 1975), p. 75. They are also cited on p. 19 of "The Report on Dissent."

125 Lutheran Service Book (St. Louis: Concordia Publishing House, 2006), Hymn 644, Stanza 1.

126 Ibid., Hymn 575, Stanza 1.

127 Robert Preus in The Theology of Post-Reformation Lutheranism as quoted by Bretscher, pp. 74 and 93 n. 1.

128 Furnish, pp. 16-17.

129 1QSi.4, 10. See also 1QS 1:10; 2:4-9; 9:21-22; 1QM 4:1

130 Naim Ateek, p. 159.

131 Robert H. Pfeiffer, History of New Testament Times (New York: Harper and Brothers Publishers, 1949), p. 188.

132 "An Anonymous Sermon, Commonly Called Clement's Second Letter to the Corinthians," Early Christian Fathers, Vol. I, newly translated and edited by Cyril C. Richardson (Philadelphia: The Westminster Press, 1053), p. 198.

133 Heinrich Schlier, "Amen," Theological Dictionary of the New Testament, Vol. I, edited by Gerhard Kittel (Grand Rapids: Wm. B. Eerdmans Publishing Company, 1964), pp. 335-338.

134 Paul J. Achtemeier, "The Ministry of Jesus in the Synoptic Gospels," Interpretation, April 1981, p. 167.

135 In the text of the NRSV, "one like a son of man" is translated "one like a human being." The loss of the literal translation is one unfortunate result of the NRSV decision to use inclusive language.

136 Joseph A. Fitzmyer is one, cf. <u>Biblical Archaeology Review</u>, Vol. 19, No. 1, January/February 1993, p. 68.

137 Achtemeier, p. 340.

138 <u>Luther's Works</u>, Vol. 8, edited by Jaroslav Pelikan (St. Louis: Concordia Publishing House, 1966), pp. 6 and 9. There is much more in Luther on this.

139 <u>Ibid</u>., p. 34.

140 <u>Ibid</u>., p. 35.

141 <u>Ibid</u>., pp. 29-30.

142 <u>Ibid</u>., pp. 45-46.

143 Robertson and Plummer, p. 368.

144 Davies, pp. 183-185.

145 Mary Ann Beavis, "'Expecting Nothing in Return' – Luke's Picture of the Marginalized," <u>Interpretation</u>, October 1994, p. 363.

146 Joel B. Green, "The Death of Jesus and the Ways of God," <u>Interpretation</u>, January 1998, pp. 28-29.

147 Joachim Jeremias, <u>The Parables of Jesus</u>, Revised Edition (New York: Charles Scribner's Sons, 1962), p. 222.

148 <u>Luther's Works</u>, Vol. 40, edited by Conrad Bergendoff (Philadelphia: Muhlenberg Press, 1958), p. 35.

149 Danker, <u>Lexicon</u>, pp. 435-436.

150 <u>Ibid</u>., p. 815.

151 Frenkley, pp. 41-42.

152 The versification in the Hebrew and the English texts differs by two verses.

153 Hans Walter Wolff discusses the structure problems in much more detail, cf. <u>Joel and Amos</u> (Philadelphis: Fortress Press, 1977), pp. 47-49.

154 <u>Ibid</u>., p. 51, for a larger discussion of the word "earth" in Hosea.

155 <u>Ibid</u>., p. 52.

156 Martin H. Franzmann, <u>The Word of the Lord Grows</u> (St. Louis: Concordia Publishing House, 1961), pp. 81-87.

157 Barrett, p. 29.

158 Bultmann, <u>Theology</u>, Vol. 1, p. 222.

159 <u>Ibid</u>., p. 181.

160 Bultmann, <u>History</u>, p. 18.

161 Athanasius, "On the Incarnation of the Word," The Library of Christian Classics, Volume III, Christology of the Later Fathers, edited by Edward Rochie Hardy (London: SCM Press Ltd., 1954), p. 82.

162 Lexicon, p. 388.

163 For an extensive discussion of the phrase, see Richard J. Bauckham, Word Biblical Commentary, Volume 50, Jude, 2 Peter (Waco: Word Books, Publisher, 1983), pp. 206-209.

164 Gottlob Schrenk, "eudokeo, eudokia," Theological Dictionary of the New Testament, Vol. II, edited by Gerhard Kittel (Grand Rapids: Wm. B. Eerdmans Publishing Company,1964), p. 740 disagrees with this interpretation of the use of the aorist.

165 Bultmann, Wellhausen, Loisy, Bousset, Bertram, Goetz, Goguel, and others.

166 Dodd said that the pericope contrasts with the general type of post-resurrection narratives in almost every particular. The general theory that the transfiguration is a misplaced resurrection appearance narrative has been refuted by Boobyer (St. Mark, 11-16) and especially by Stein (JBL 95 [1976] 79-95; cf. also J. E. Alsup, The Post-Resurrection Appearance Stories of the Gospel Traditions [CTM 5, Stuttgart: Calwer/ London: S.P.C.K., 1975] 141-144).

167 Pieper, p. 551

168 Lexicon, p. 126.

169 von Rad, Vol. II, pp. 26-27.

170 Victor Paul Furnish, II Corinthians (New York: Doubleday and Company, Inc., 1985), p. 249.

171 Cullmann, Christology, pp. 276-277.

172 Brevard S. Childs, The Book of Exodus (Philadelphia: The Westminster Press, 1974), p. 604.

173 Furnish, II Corinthians, p. 211.

174 Werner Elert, The Christian Ethos, translated by Carl J. Schindler (Philadelphia: Muhlenberg Press, 1957), pp. 220-224.

175 Ibid., p. 211.

176 Davies, p. 196.

177 Elert, pp. 199-200.

178 Elert, p. 200.

179 <u>Ibid.</u>

180 Furnish, <u>II Corinthians</u>, p. 231.

181 <u>Ibid.</u>, p. 9.

182 Furnish, "Corinth," p. 18.

183 Furnish, <u>II Corinthians</u>, p. 239.

184 <u>Ibid.</u>, pp. 240-241.

185 Joseph A. Fitzmyer, <u>The Gospel According to Luke (I-IX)</u> (Garden City: Doubleday and Company, Inc., 1979), p. 800.

186 <u>Ibid.</u>, p. 794.

187 <u>Ibid.</u>, p. 798.

188 <u>Ibid.</u>, p. 809.